THE
Scholarship
BOOK
1998 - 1999

The Complete Guide to Private-Sector Scholarships, Grants, and Loans for Undergraduates

PRENTICE HALL

Daniel J. Cassidy

Library of Congress Cataloging-in-Publication Data

Cassidy, Daniel J.
   The scholarship book 1998-1999: the complete guide to private-sector
scholarships, grants, and loans for undergraduates / Daniel J.
Cassidy.
      p.   cm.
   Includes indexes.
   ISBN 0-13-955700-8 (ppc).—ISBN 0-7352-0007-6 (p)
   1. Scholarships—United States—Directories. 2. Student aid—
United States—Directories. 3. Associations, institutions, etc.—
Charitable contributions—United States—Directories. I. Title.
LB2337.2.C37 1998
378.3'4'0973—dc20
                                                    96-8138
                                                     CIP

LB2337.2
.C37

Warning!
Copy at your peril!

Printed in the United States of America   *Printed in the United States of America*
10 9 8 7 6 5 4 3 2 1   *10 9 8 7 6 5 4 3 2 1*

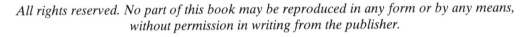

ISBN 0-13-955700-8 (pp case) ISBN 0-7352-0007-6 (p)

ATTENTION: CORPORATIONS AND SCHOOLS
Prentice Hall books are available at quantity discounts with bulk purchase for educational,
business, or sales promotional use. For information, please write to: Prentice Hall Special
Sales, 240 Frisch Court, Paramus, NJ 07652. Please supply: title of book, ISBN, quantity, how
the book will be used, date needed.

PRENTICE HALL
Paramus, NJ 07652

A Simon & Schuster Company

On the World Wide Web at http://www.phdirect.com

Prentice Hall International (UK) Limited, *London*
Prentice Hall of Australia Pty. Limited, *Sydney*
Prentice Hall Canada, Inc., *Toronto*
Prentice Hall Hispanoamericana, S.A., *Mexico*
Prentice Hall of India Private Limited, *New Delhi*
Prentice Hall of Japan, Inc., *Tokyo*
Simon & Schuster Asia Pte. Ltd., *Singapore*
Editora Prentice Hall do Brasil, Ltda., *Rio de Janeiro*

I want to thank all of those who have made this edition of *THE SCHOLARSHIP BOOK 1998-1999* a reality. My sincere thanks and gratitude to:

The staff at NSRS

especially:

Research & Computer Engineering
Administration & Public Relations

A very special thank you to
Jim Eason
ABC's, KGO & KSFO Radio, San Francisco
The man who made NSRS possible!

and Larry King for taking NSRS national!

And, Prentice Hall, et al.

Especially, as always . . .
Barbara Palumbo, Manager, Electronic Production

Preface

INTRODUCTION

The information in *THE SCHOLARSHIP BOOK* was compiled from the database of the largest private sector financial aid research service in the world. Located in Santa Rosa, California, NATIONAL SCHOLARSHIP RESEARCH SERVICE (NSRS) began tracking private sector scholarships in the late 1970s, using a specialized computer system. As awards increased and research uncovered new sources for today's students, the addition of the INTERNATIONAL SCHOLARSHIP RESEARCH SERVICE (ISRS) doubled the size of this independently developed database. Prospective college students and present undergraduates will find the information in this book valuable in directing their applications and broadening their prospects for scholarship selection.

THE FACTS

According to the Association of Fund Raising Counsel, more than 80 percent of the grant applications that went to the 28,000 foundations in the United States were either misdirected or filled out improperly. Many scholarships, fellowships, grants, loans, and internships go unclaimed each year—not because students do not qualify, but because they don't know that the money is available. In 1997, NSRS surveyed the private-sector scholarship sources and the results found that 3.5 percent of these private sector money's went undistributed. There is a great need to organize this "paper-chase" of information into a workable source for today's student. Utilizing the data collected in this book, students will have a broad base of information to convert to their advantage. The monies are there. Apply for them!

PRIVATE-SECTOR FUNDS

Philanthropy in the United States is alive and well. These funds, which totaled $58.67 billion in 1982, increased to a whopping $195.79 billion in 1994. Of that amount, 15 percent (or $29.36 billion) goes into the United States educational system, making the private sector the leader in funding at 53.65 percent of the available scholarships, fellowships, grants, and loans domestically. An additional $30-plus billion is dispersed by other countries worldwide.

And that amount increases daily. The interest alone on a properly invested $2 million is easily $100,000 annually. Private sector resources for higher education are as varied as the awards themselves.

Many scholarships are renewable. You simply sign for them year after year. Most allow you to 'piggy-back' several individual scholarships. The average undergraduate scholarship is $4,000 per year, ranging from a low of $100 to a high of $25,000. Graduate-level fellowships range from $10,000 to over $60,000. If you are a graduate student or planning to go on to graduate school, be sure to look at our "Graduate Scholarship Book" series and our "International Scholarship Book" series. Some graduate and post-graduate research projects can yield a quarter of a million dollars or more to fund your project. As inflation spirals, so does the cost of education and the need for financial assistance.

INVESTIGATE THE POSSIBILITIES

Don't think you can't apply because you earn too much money; 80 percent of the private sector does not require a financial statement or proof of need. Don't think that application deadlines occur only in the fall; private-sector deadlines are passing daily because often they are set to coincide with the tax year or organizational meeting dates. Don't believe that grades are the only consideration for an award; many application questions deal with personal, occupational, and educational background; organizational affiliation; talent, or ethnic origins; 90 percent are not concerned with grades. Don't be concerned with age; many organizations are interested in the re-entry student and the mid-career development student. The Business and Professional Women's Foundation awards hundreds of scholarships to applicants who must be older than 25 or even 35. There is a scholarship at the California state colleges for students over the age of 60.

PLAN TO COMPETE AND QUALIFY

The plan is simple—use this book and every other resource you can find. Inquire at your institution's financial aid office about government assistance and private endowments at the school. If you are a high school student in any year, begin by writing to ten or more schools. Select a range of institutions that interest you, both large and small, public and private. Request the application materials and school catalogs—many private endowments are available in the forms of scholarships and fellowships bequeathed by alumni and are listed in the school catalog under financial aid. A significant number of these go unclaimed because qualified students do not know they exist! The information is available, but the commitment and determination to find it belongs to the individual.

The private sector is easily accessed with this book. The student can use the tables provided to cross-reference the scholarships applicable to his or her personal background and educational goals. Choose twenty or more sources and request application forms and any pertinent materials. Some have specific requirements for applicants such as a personal interview, the submission of an essay or related work, or a promise to work for the company on completion of study and/or the earning of a degree. Others may have paid internships or work advancement programs. Still others may simply require that you fill out an application form.

The money is there. Many go unclaimed. Even the most common scholarship source, such as Rotary, Lions, Elks, Zonta, etc., are complaining that students are not requesting their scholarship application forms, nor applying. Students who do not take the time to inquire lose every advantage. The opportunity to advance to a graduate degree will widen many avenues for your future, and the rewards are incalculable. Information is merely a passage waiting to be used. The resources to achieve your goals are available to you; you need only pursue them.

A human mind, once stretched to a new idea,
never returns to its former dimension.
Oliver Wendell Holmes, Sr.

Good Luck! And remember:

There's nothing to it
but to do it!

Sincerely, Daniel J. Cassidy, President and Author

Just for Fun: A Potpourri of Scholarships

(Note: The following sources are identified by both our reference numbers, and some also have this book's record numbers. The numbers in parentheses identify the reference in our database. The record number refers to the numerical order of the listings in this book. In order to find out more about the sources not detailed in this book, call NSRS at 707/546-6777.

1. The Countess of Munster Musical Trust has scholarships in varying amounts to British and Commonwealth citizens studying music. (T74/R18)

2. Don't be bugged by a lack of funds. Money really does grow on trees. The **International Society of Arboriculture** invites horticulturists, plant pathologists, and entomologists to pluck a grant for the study of shade trees. (T14/R12)

3. Your tuition troubles could be gone with the wind! If you are a lineal descendant of a worthy Confederate soldier, contact the **United Daughters of the Confederacy** about their $400 to $1,500 scholarships. (T13/R790) Record 1544.

4. If you or your parents are actively involved in harness racing, you just might hitch yourself to one of the **Harness Tracks of America** scholarships worth $2,500 to $3,000. (T13/R423) Record 1291.

5. You could lace up a scholarship of up to $2,000 for undergraduate study if you are a dependent child of a worker in the footwear industry. It's a patent idea from **Two/Ten International Footwear Foundation**. (T13/R294) Record 1537.

6. Don't let financial woes cast a pall over your dreams. Bury those worries with a **Hilgenfeld Foundation for Mortuary Education** scholarship! It's available to qualified individuals interested in the funeral service or funeral education fields. (T99/R5) Record 1129.

7. *Jen unu mil pundo—nun EK!* (Here's a thousand pounds—now go!) If you understood that, you might be eligible for a **Norwich Jubilee Esperanto Foundation** scholarship paying $500 to study Esperanto in the United Kingdom. (K19/R10) Record 498.

8. For a left-handed freshman enrolled at Juniata College and who needs the money, **Beckley Scholarship Foundation** offers $700. (T13/R265) Record 1344.

9. For students whose ancestors put their John Hancocks on the Declaration of Independence, have scholarships worth $1,200 to $2,000 from **Descendants of the Signers of the Declaration of Independence**. (T19/R157) Record 1247.

10. Investigating scholarship possibilities? The **Association of Former Agents of the U.S. Secret Service** offers scholarships of $500 to $1,500 to undergraduate law enforcement and police administration students. You do have to give your real name, but fingerprints won't be necessary. (T95/R26) Record 1065.

THE TOP TEN CELEBRITY SCHOLARSHIPS

1. The proof is in the pudding! **Bill Cosby** and his wife Camille have been acclaimed 'The First Family of Philanthropy' for their generous donations to various colleges in excess of $28 million. Contact Spellman College.

2. The **Eddie Murphy/Paramount Pictures $25,000 Writing Fellowship**. Silver Screen? Let your talent shine with a postgraduate film & television writing internship at Paramount

Pictures presented to eligible bachelor degree grads of Hampton and Howard universities who are tuned into television and screen writing. Check with these colleges.

3. The cost of college doesn't go for the price of peanuts these days, so **The Scripps Howard Foundation** is offering the **Charles M. Schultz Award**. $2,500 for an outstanding college cartoonist, working at a college newspaper or magazine. Don't be a Blockhead! Apply! (T71/R17) Record 421.

4. "Average yet creative" is the punch line for junior telecommunications majors at Ball State University. **The David Letterman Telecommunications Scholarship Program** could pay your way to graduation if you are an average student with a very creative mind. (T93/R19) Record 981.

5. Don't make a big production out of the high cost of filmmaking! All it takes is "Forty Acres and a Mule"! **Spike Lee and Columbia Pictures** offer production fellowships to students in their second or third year of graduate study at the New York University Tisch School of Film. Two $5,000 fellowships are awarded per year to graduates rolling in action in production, filmmaking, and acting. (T71/R24)

6. This is certainly one house with high equity! Morehouse College received $1 million dollars from celebrity Oprah Winfrey to establish the **Oprah Winfrey Endowed Scholarship Fund**. (T14/R122)

7. Is the cost of college a dramatization? The right stage for you could be **Debbie Allen** and **Phylicia Rashad's** applause for their father in the **Dr. Andrew Allen Creative Arts Scholarship** of $15,000. A command performance is requested from undergraduate juniors and seniors at Howard University who portray excellence in drama, song, and dance. (T74/R33) Record 518.

8. Are you between the ages of 17 and 22, living in the Golden State? If you are a Mexican-American resident of California or Texas and in an undergraduate program, you may just strike gold with the **Vikki Carr Scholarship** of up to $3,000! (T13/R502) Record 1566.

9. College costs driving you up the wall? Go ahead and dance on the ceiling! **Lionel Richie** has made students of Tuskegee University lighter than air with his $500,000 donation for an endowment in the business school at Tuskegee. Contact Tuskegee University.

10. Well Hee-Haw, Y'all! Miniere's Network offers the **Minnie Pearl Scholarships** to financially-needy high school seniors who have a significant bilateral hearing loss, good grades, and who have been accepted for enrollment by an accredited university, college or technical school. (T13/R293) Record 1393.

TOP SCHOLARSHIPS FOR WOMEN

1. The **California Junior Miss Program** scholarship competition is open to girls in their junior year of high school who are U.S. citizens and California residents. Winner receives $15,000 for books, fees, and tuition at any college in the world. (T13/R763) Record 1209.

2. The **Women's Western Golf Foundation** has $2,000/year awaiting female high school seniors who are U.S. citizens and who have high academic standing, financial need, and an involvement with golf . . . skill is NOT a criterion! (T13/R347)

3. The **National Federation of the Blind** (Hermione Grant Calhoun Scholarship) offers $3,000 to legally blind women who are undergraduate or graduate students studying in any field. (T13/R786)

4. For women re-entry students, the **Jeanette Rankin Foundation** awards $1,000 to the winning woman aged 35 or older who is a U.S. citizen enrolled in a program of voc-tech training or in an undergraduate program. (T13/R18) Record 1332.

5. The **National Federation of Press Women, Inc.** (Helen M. Malloch Scholarship) offers $500-$1,000 to undergraduate women who are juniors or seniors or to grad students majoring in journalism at any college or university. (T93/R5) Record 1014.

6. The **Landscape Architecture Foundation** (Harriett Barnhart Wimmer Scholarship) offers $1,000 to women who have demonstrated excellent design ability in landscape architecture, have sensitivity to the environment, and who are going into their final year of undergraduate study. (T63/R2) Record 218.

7. **Society of Women Engineers** (General Electric Foundation Scholarship) offers $1,000 to women who are U.S. citizens studying engineering or computer science. For high school seniors entering an accredited school as freshmen. (T61/R7)

8. The **Astrae National Lesbian Action Foundation** (Margot Karle Scholarship) gives $500 to women students whose career path or extracurricular activities demonstrate political or social commitment to fighting for the civil rights of gays and lesbians. (T13/R1012) Record 1190.

9. **Mervyn's California/Women's Sports Foundation Scholarship Fund** offers $1,000 to college-bound high school senior girls involved in athletics. The program is not limited to California residents. Contact NSRS for particulars. (T13/R892)

10. The **International Society of Women Airline Pilots** (ISA International Career Scholarship/Fiorenze de Bernardi Merit Award) offers $500-$1,500 to women throughout the world who are pursuing careers as airline pilots and have at least 350 hours of flight experience. (T62/R5) Record 196.

TOP SCHOLARSHIPS FOR MEN

1. The **Fred A. Bryan Collegiate Students Fund** (Trust Fund Scholarships) offers scholarships for male graduates of South Bend High School in Indiana with preference to those who have been Boy Scouts. Recipients receive between $1,400 and $1,600 for undergraduate study at an accredited college or university. (T13/R47) Record 1276.

2. The **Phi Kappa Theta National Foundation** (Scholarship Program) offers undergraduate scholarships to members of the Phi Kappa Theta fraternity. Five scholarships are awarded based on financial need. (T13/R472) Record 1462.

3. The **ConRail-Consolidated Rail Corporation** (Frank Thomson Scholarships for Males) offers a $2,000 scholarship to high school seniors who are sons of ConRail or Predecessor Railroad company employees. Applicants must be studying in the engineering field. Twelve scholarships are awarded based on financial need and competitive exams. (T61/R10) Record 144.

4. The **NAACP National Office** offers the Willems Scholarship for male members of the NAACP studying engineering, chemistry, physics, or mathematics. Undergraduates receive $2,000, and the graduate award is $3,000. (T14/R200)

5. The **Maud Glover Folsom Foundation, Inc.** offers $2,500 to American males of Anglo-Saxon or German descent to age 35. For use in prep school, high school, college, and advanced education. Call NSRS for details. (T13/R1150)

6. The **Boys & Girls Clubs of San Diego** (Spence Reese Scholarship Fund) offer scholarships to male high school students planning a career in medicine, law, engineering, or

political science. Preference to students who live within a 250-mile radius of San Diego. Boys Club affiliation is not required. (T14/R286) Records 138, 760, 1066, and 1081.

7. The **Elmer O. & Ida Preston Educational Trust** (Grants and Loans) offers an award that is half-grant and half-loan to male residents of Iowa who are pursuing a collegiate or professional study at an Iowa college or university. Applicants must be planning on a career in Christian ministry and must provide a recommendation from a minister commenting on the student's potential. (T75/R22) Record 581.

8. The **Young American Bowling Alliance** offers the Chuck Hall Star of Tomorrow Scholarship of $4,000 to male students who are amateur bowlers and members of ABC or YABA up to age 21. Must be a high school senior or an undergraduate attending college. Call NSRS for details. (K13/R872)

9. The **Raymond J. Harris Education Trust** offers scholarships of various amounts to Christian males for use at nine Philadelphia area colleges. Students must be studying medicine, law, engineering, dentistry, or agriculture. Call NSRS for details. (T14/R586)

10. The **American Dental Hygienists Association** has several scholarships designated for under-represented groups in that field, specifically minorities and men. Call NSRS for details. (T89/R36, T89/R40, T89/43)

RECOMMENDATIONS

By using this book to track down all your potential sources of funding, you may need additional help. Following are some excellent sources that NSRS recommends. (Note: These are also listed in the "Helpful Publications" section.)

KIT: GUIDE TO WINNING SCHOLARSHIPS (booklet), SCHOLARSHIP RADIO SHOW (audio cassette), KIDS, COLLEGE, & CASH (VHS tape), $35

Write or phone:

National Scholarship Research Service
Box 6694
Santa Rosa, CA 95406-0694
707/546-6777

THE INSTITUTE OF INTERNATIONAL EDUCATION (IIE)

ACADEMIC YEAR ABROAD, $44.95 plus $5.00 handling. The most complete guide to planning study abroad describes over 1,900 post-secondary study programs outside the U.S. Concise descriptions provide the information you need on costs, academic programs and credits, dates and application, and more. (T11/R58)

VACATION STUDY ABROAD, $39.95. Describes over 1,800 summer or short-term study-abroad sponsored by United States colleges and universities and foreign institutions. (T11/R57)

All orders must be prepaid. IIE pays domestic postage. If you have questions, write or phone:

Institute of International Education (IIE)
Publications Service, IIE
809 United Nations Plaza, New York, NY 10017
212/984-5330

MAKING IT THROUGH COLLEGE, $1.00. Handy booklet describing how to make it through college. Includes information on how to cope with competition, getting organized, study techniques, solving work overloads, and much more. (T11/R16)

Recommendations

Write to:

Professional Staff Congress
25 West 43rd Street, 5th Floor
New York, NY 10036

10 STEPS IN WRITING THE RESEARCH PAPER, $9.95. Arranged to lead the student step-by-step through the writing of a research paper from finding a suitable subject to checking the final copy. Easy enough for the beginner, complete enough for the graduate student. 177 pages. (T11/R5)

Write to:

Barron's Educational Series Inc.
250 Wireless Blvd.
Hauppauge, NY 11788

NEED A LIFT? $3. Outstanding guide to education and employment opportunities. Contains complete information on the financial aid process (how, when, and where to start), scholarships, loans, and career information addresses. (T11/R24)

Write to:

American Legion National Emblem Sales
P.O. Box 1050
Indianapolis, IN 46206

COLLEGE FINANCIAL AID EMERGENCY KIT, $6.95 (prepaid). 40-page booklet filled with tips on how to meet the costs of tuition, room and board, and fees. Tells what is available, whom to ask, and how to ask! (T11/R62)

Write to:

Sun Features Inc.
Box 368 (Kit)
Cardiff, CA 92007

FISKE GUIDE TO COLLEGES, $18. Describes the 265 top-rated four-year colleges in the U.S. and rates for academics, social life, and quality of life. (T11/R28)

Write to:

Times Books
400 Hahn Road
Westminster, MD 21157

INDEX OF MAJORS AND GRADUATE DEGREES, $17. Add $3.95 postage. Describes over 580 major programs of study at 3,000 undergraduate and graduate schools. Also lists schools with religious affiliations, special academic programs, and special admissions procedures. (T11/R85)

Write to:

College Board Publications
P.O. Box 886
New York, NY 10101

PETERSON'S GUIDE TO FOUR-YEAR COLLEGES, $24.95. Detailed profiles of over 1,900 accredited four-year colleges in the U.S. and Canada. Also includes entrance difficulty directory, majors directory, and college cost directory. (T11/R87)

INTERNSHIPS, $29.95 plus $6.75 shipping and handling. Are you a college student? Looking for your first job? Re-entering the work force? Thinking about making a career change? Or just taking a break before higher education and would like to try a particular career field? This book lists numerous job training opportunities, arranged by career field and indexed geographically. (T11/R92)

If you are somewhat undecided on the question of a career, simply browsing
through the myriad possibilities may spark an unexpected interest.
—Business Week

Write to:

Peterson's Inc.
Dept. 7707, P.O. Box 2123
Princeton, NJ 08543

COLLEGE DEGREES BY MAIL, $12.95 plus $2.50 shipping and handling. John Bear, Ph.D, describes every approach known to earning a degree without ever taking a single traditional course! It lists 100 reputable colleges that offer bachelor's, master's, doctorate's., and law degrees through home study. The book also lists colleges reputed to be diploma mills and cautions against them. (T11/R90)

Write to:

Ten Speed Press
P.O. Box 7123
Berkeley, CA 94707

COLLEGE FINANCIAL AID FOR DUMMIES, $19.95. Dr. Herm Davis and Joyce Lain Kennedy suggest "great ways to pay without going broke." Find this at your bookseller or call 800/762-2974. For high school and college students and adults returning to school.

HOW TO WIN A SPORTS SCHOLARSHIP, $14.95 plus $2.95 shipping and handling. This is an easy-to-use workbook that teaches high school students and their families a step-by-step process for winning sports scholarships. You don't have to be a superstar! $100,000 scholarships offered in 35 sports each year! Over $500 million awarded annually! There is a special section for female athletes. 250 pages (T11/R8)

Write to:

Hastings Communications
P.O. Box 14927
Santa Rosa, CA 95402

WHERE THERE'S A WILL THERE'S AN "A" HOW TO GET BETTER GRADES IN COLLEGE (OR HIGH SCHOOL) Video tape seminars on how to get better grades, $49.95.

Available from:

Olney "A" Seminars
P.O. Box 686
Scottsdale, AZ 85252-0686
800/546-3883

SAMPLE FORM LETTER
REQUESTING APPLICATION INFORMATION

Use this sample letter as a guide to create a general letter requesting information. Photocopy your letter and address the envelopes for mailing. Include the name of the scholarship you are applying for with the address on the envelope. Remember to apply well in advance of the deadlines. You should keep a calendar to keep track of them.

Date

Scholarship Program Office

Dear Scholarship Director:

Please send me application forms for the scholarships or fellowships you might offer. I am enclosing a self-addressed stamped envelope for your convenience in replying.

Sincerely,

Bryan Schwab
2280 Airport Boulevard
Santa Rosa, California 95403
707/546-6777

THE PLAN

Once you have written to scholarship sources for complete information, you might consider starting three financial aid boxes to maintain your information. You might call them "Government Funding," "School Endowments," and "Private Sector."

The Government Funding Box

Put all information from state and federal programs in this box.

Remember:
Dept. of Educ. 800/433-3243.

The Coordinating Board for your state is in your phone book under "Government."

The School Endowments Box

The college catalogs will usually list the endowments from alumni and local businesses. Put the catalogs in this box.

The Private Sector Box

This box should contain material you have gleaned from this book and/or from your NSRS computer printout.

Call 800/432-3782.

THE SEARCH

Believe it or not, just about everything about you will come into play in your search for scholarships—your ancestry, religion, place of birth and residence, parent's union or corporate affiliation, or simply your interest in a particular field can all be eligibility factors.

Using the tables in this book, the average student will find at least 20 to over 100 different private-sector scholarship sources. Next, write to them and ask for their scholarship applications and requirements. The letter can be a general request for information "form" letter that can be photocopied, but you should be specific about the name of the scholarship you are inquiring about on the envelope.

Write to each source as far in advance of their scholarship deadline as possible, and don't forget to send a self-addressed stamped envelope—it not only expedites their reply, some organizations won't respond without one.

Remember, on the outside of the envelope, list the name of the specific scholarship you are inquiring about. That way the person opening the mail will know where to direct your inquiry. Replies to these letters should be sorted into the appropriate boxes.

THE GOVERNMENT BOX

On a quiet Saturday or when you have time, sit down and review the information. In the "Government" box, you will find that the state and federal forms are very similar, asking a multitude of questions regarding income, assets, and expenses. Don't automatically exclude yourself from state and federal funding thinking that you or your family make too much money. These programs vary tremendously from state to state and the federal programs have changed quite a bit. For example, there is no longer a $32,500 limit on the amount parents can earn in order to qualify for a student loan; but since that limit has been raised to $45,000, there will be less federal money to go around, so be sure to get in line quickly.

A bit of good news in the student loan arena is that the federal government no longer will consider the value of your house or farm in determining the amount of aid for which you qualify.

At the very least these state and federal forms are the beginning of your scholarship profile at the financial aid office at the school. Some of the schools are now using these forms for their private endowment-based scholarship. So, even if you do not receive government funding, you will be ready to apply for loans from various sources and the school-based endowments.

THE SCHOOL ENDOWMENTS BOX

You will usually find a list of endowments from alumni listed in the financial aid section of the college catalog. Often endowments to schools are not advertised and may go unclaimed. For example, at a small school like the University of San Francisco, the total endowments average $20 million to $30 million per year. At Ivy League schools, endowments range from $100 million to $200+ million each year. Of those endowments, 10 percent to 15 percent goes to the financial aid office in the form of scholarships, fellowships, grants, and loans.

You will discover that sources in the "School Endowments" box are really just other forms of private-sector scholarships. The difference is that endowment money is given directly to the school and is administered exclusively by the school's financial aid office, so you must deal directly with the college. You'll find that the myths I talked about earlier also apply to these private endowments—again, don't exclude yourself because of those old clichés regarding your grades, financial status, deadlines, or age.

THE PRIVATE SECTOR BOX

With your "Private Sector" box, you will find that once you have seen one or two forms, you have pretty much seen them all. Usually they are two pages asking where you are going to school, what you are going to major in and why you think you deserve the scholarship. Some scholarship sources require that you join their organization. If the organization relates to your field of study, you should strongly consider joining because it will keep you informed (via newsletters, etc.) about developments in that field.

Other scholarship organizations may want you to promise that you will work for them for a period of time. The Dow Jones Newspaper Fund offers up to $80,000 in scholarships annually for journalism and mass communications students. In addition, a two-week intensive course (equivalent to advanced editing courses at most journalism departments) is followed by summer employment at a newspaper—interns receive a minimum weekly salary of $225. This could even yield a permanent job for the student.

THE ESSAY

Most organizations awarding scholarships require an essay as part of the application process. The essay is the most important part of the private—sector scholarship search.

The following excerpt from the University of California at Los Angeles (UCLA) application material emphasizes the importance of the essay and contains good advice no matter where you are going to college:

> *The essay is an important part of your application for admission and for scholarships.*
>
> *For these purposes, the University seeks information that will distinguish you from other applicants. You may wish, therefore, to write about your experiences, achievements, and goals. You might, for example, discuss an important life experience and what you learned from it. You might also describe unusual circumstances, challenges, or hardships you have faced. School activities and experiences are also topics to discuss in your essay but they do not need to be the focus.*
>
> *Rather than listing activities, describe your level of achievement in areas you have pursued—including employment or volunteer activities—and the personal qualities revealed by the time and effort you have devoted to them.*
>
> *Also, discuss your interest in your intended field of study. If you have a disability, you may also include a description of its impact on your experiences, goals and aspirations.*
>
> *The University seeks information about any exceptional achievements such as activities, honors, awards, employment or volunteer work that demonstrate your motivation, achievement, leadership and commitment.*
>
> *Make sure your essay is neatly typed, is well written, and does not contain grammatical errors or misspelled words.*

THE APPLICATION

When filling out scholarship application forms, be complete, concise, and creative. People who read these applications want to know the real you, not just your name. Scholarship applications should clearly emphasize your ambitions, motivations, and what makes you different from everyone else. Be original!

Your application should be typewritten and neat. I had a complaint from one foundation about a student who had an excellent background and qualifications but used a crayon to fill out the application.

Once your essay is finished, make a master file of it and other supporting items. Photocopy your essay and attach it to each application. If requested, also include: a résumé or curriculum vitae, extracurricular activities sheet (usually one page), transcripts, SAT or ACT scores, letters of recommendation (usually one each from a teacher, employer and friend) outlining your moral character, and if there are any newspaper articles, etc., about you, it is a good idea to include them, as well.

Application Checklist

The following supporting documents may be requested with your application. I suggest you make a master file for these documents and photocopy them. You can then just pull a copy from your file and attach it to the application upon request.

❑ 1. Include your essay.
❑ 2. Include résumé or curriculum vitae.
❑ 3. Include extracurricular activities sheet.
❑ 4. Include transcripts.
❑ 5. Include SAT or ACT scores.
❑ 6. Include letters of recommendation.
❑ 7. Include any newspaper articles, etc., about yourself (if you have any).

You might also include your photograph, whether it's a high school picture or a snapshot of you working at your favorite hobby. This helps the selection committee feel a little closer to you. Instead of just seeing a name, they will have a face to match it.

Mail your applications in early—at least a month before the deadline.

THE CALENDAR

I also find it helpful to keep a calendar with deadlines circled so you can stay organized. You can hang it above your three scholarship boxes so it is easily visible. Each application should have its own file. On the outside of the file, you might rate your chances of getting the scholarship on a scale of 1 to 10.

			Calendar			
Sun	M	T	W	Th	F	Sat
1	2	3	4	5	6	7
8	9	10	11	12	13	14
15	16	17	18	19	20	21
22	23	24	25	26	27	28
29	30	31				

Government Box **Endowment Box** **Private Sector Box**

Box With Master Files 1–7.

If a scholarship application deadline has passed, save it for the next year. If you are turned down for a scholarship, don't worry. Some organizations want to see if you will apply a second time. The important point is to stay motivated and be persistent.

WHERE THE INFORMATION IN THIS BOOK CAME FROM

The information in this book was compiled from the database of the largest private-sector college financial aid research service in the world: National Scholarship Research Service (NSRS) located in Santa Rosa, California.

Since the late 1970s, NSRS had been using computers to research and update information on potential sources of financial assistance for college students. Many thousands of students have used NSRS's services to locate sources offering financial aid.

NATIONAL SCHOLARSHIP RESEARCH SERVICE (NSRS)

NSRS computers store information on thousands of private-sector aid programs for all levels of college study: from high school seniors just entering college to post-doctoral researchers.

Applicants for NSRS services first complete a biographical questionnaire, indicating their particular area(s) of interest. This information is entered into the computer which searches NSRS files for the scholarships for which the applicant may qualify. Since each applicant has a different background and each of the thousands of aid programs has different requirements, this computer search can save valuable time and often provides students with potential sources of aid that they might never have considered applying for.

If you consider that all the financial aid programs listed in this book are constantly changing, with new application dates, qualifying requirements, etc., you may want to utilize these services.

Since NSRS is a privately-owned company, there is a modest fee for the services provided. For a product list, write or call:

NATIONAL SCHOLARSHIP RESEARCH SERVICES
Box 6609
Santa Rosa, CA 95406-0609
24-Hour Phone: 707/546-6777
24-Hour Fax: 707/546-6785

THE WORLDWIDE WEB

National Scholarship Research Service (NSRS) travels on the worldwide web's super highway.

Computer operators throughout the world can communicate with "Mr. Scholarship," Daniel Cassidy, president of NSRS, by using the worldwide highway at the following NSRS addresses:

Internet
800HEADSTART.COM
and SCHOLARSHIPBOOK.COM

MicroSoft Network
NSRS.COM
Example: NSRS@MSN.COM

IMPORTANT NOTE

This book is an abridged version of the NSRS database. For a more comprehensive search for sources of educational financing, write to NSRS.

Every effort has been made to supply you with the most accurate and up-to-date information possible, but—even as this book goes to print—awards are being added and application requirements are being changed by sponsoring organizations. Such circumstances are beyond our control.

Since the information we have supplied may not reflect the current status of any particular award program you are interested in, you should use this book only as a guide. Contact the source of the award for current application information.

If questions arise during your search for educational funding, you are welcome to call a NSRS counselor at 707/546-67777.

SCHOLARSHIP SEARCH SCAMS

A disturbing number of scholarship-sponsoring organizations have reported in recent months that they are receiving a high volume of inquiries from students who are unqualified for the awards about which they are asking.

Because of the number of these types of reports, we are investigating the origins of the misguided inquiries. Most often we find that someone has taken *only* names and addresses from our scholarship books and is selling the information—a general listing of scholarships available in a particular field of study—to students without regard to the student's qualifications. Most of these "rip-off operations" make no effort to match the student's educational goals and personal background with the requirements of the scholarships.

The books that we publish contain 40 tables along with the source description, providing accurate cross-matching of the student's characteristics to the requirements at scholarship sources. National Scholarship Research Service (NSRS) and the publishers of our books are doing all we can to stop any abuse of our copyright which might result in an inconvenience to our scholarship-sponsoring organizations. We've assisted the Federal Trade Commission in closing down one "rip-off operation" and we are currently pursuing six others.

Last, if any scholarship service guarantees a scholarship, savings bond, or a fountain pen, "buyer beware!" If it sounds too good to be true, then it probably is. Since it is solely at the discretion of the scholarship-sponsoring organizations to choose their scholarship recipients each year, these scholarship search scams cannot guarantee that users of their service will get a scholarship. Use this book to accurately cross-match scholarship sources you are eligible for and avoid those scholarship search scams that merely copy information from our books.

How to Use This Book

Each award, book, and resource listed has a record number preceding it. All of our indexes are based on these record numbers. See "LEGEND" for the meaning of *Letters used in some of these record numbers.*

Here is a short guide to finding the information you need.

QUICK FIND INDEX

Most private-sector awards have certain eligibility qualifications. We have selected several of the most common requirements for this Quick Find index.

Here you can find awards targeted for people of a particular race, religion, or family ancestry, for people who will be studying in a particular state or community, for the physically handicapped, and much more. Simply go through each of the tables and write down the reference numbers that apply to you. Then proceed to those sources and read each one carefully to see if you qualify.

FIELD OF STUDY INDEX

Since the awards listed in this book are also based on your intended field of study, we have structured this index along the lines of a college catalog.

First, look under your particular field of study (e.g., "School of Business"). Then, look under your area of interest (e.g., "Accounting") and, finally, under your specific subject (e.g., "Banking"). In this section, you will find record numbers that reference both financial aid awards and other resources that can help you in your career. Again, since there might be several eligibility requirements you must meet in order to be able to qualify for any listed award, be sure you read each listing *carefully* and that you *meet the requirements of the award* before requesting an application.

SCHOLARSHIP AND AWARD LISTINGS

Each listing contains a very condensed description of the award, its eligibility requirements, deadline dates, and where to get more information or an application.

You will notice a large "General" section. These are awards that do not usually specify a particular field of study in their eligibility requirements. You need to use the indexes provided and read each listing carefully to see if you might qualify for one of these awards.

Use the information we have provided only as a guide. Write to the source for a complete description of qualifications.

HELPFUL PUBLICATIONS

This section contains a selection of books and pamphlets that we consider helpful to the student. These publications are excellent sources of information on a wide variety of college and financial aid subjects.

If you discover a publication you find particularly helpful, let us know so we can share the information with others.

CAREER INFORMATION

This is a list of organizations that can help you decide where to study, give you information on job opportunities available in your field of study, and much more. We encourage you to write to these organizations for information.

ALPHABETICAL INDEX

A to Z, this index lists the reference number of every award, book, and career organization that is included in this book.

LEGEND FOR "QUICK FIND INDEX" AND "FIELD OF STUDY INDEX":

D = Dependent
DIS = Disabled
DEC = Deceased

Examples:

Choose Fireman if you are a Fireman.
Choose **Fireman-D-DIS** if you are a **dependent** of a **disabled** Fireman.
Choose **Fireman-D-DEC** if you are a **dependent** of a **deceased** Fireman.

B = Booklet source in "HELPFUL PUBLICATIONS" section.
C = Career source in "CAREER INFORMATION" section.

Quick Find Index

ARMED FORCES

A Current Member, 1152, 1155, 1349, 1379, 1399, B1636

A Dependent-Current Member, 1148, 1152, 1155, 1187, 1216, 1217, 1230, 1241, 1246, 1251, 1270, 1349, 1395, 1399, 1419, 1432, 1499, 1561, B1627, B1636

A Dependent-Former Member, 1147, 1148, 1152, 1155, 1157, 1173, 1198, 1216, 1230, 1246, 1251, 1268, 1270, 1348, 1349, 1360, 1365, 1388, 1395, 1399, 1419, 1432, 1435, 1440, 1448, 1459, 1504, 1531, 1561, 1562, 1578, 1583, B1627, B1636

A Dependent-Retired Member, 1217

A Former Member, 1349, 1376, 1392, 1399, 1431, 1452, 1559, B1627, B1636

A Spouse-Current Member, 1152, 1158, 1246, 1270, 1349, 1399, B1636

A Spouse-Former Member, 1152, 1198, 1270, 1349, 1360, 1365, 1399, B1636

A Widow-Former Member, 1152, 1158, 1207, 1246, 1349, 1360, 1399, 1583, B1636

Officer, 1241, 1499

State National Guard, 1207, 1349, 1379, 1535

U.S. Air Force (any branch), 1152, 1155, 1241

U.S. Air Force-Reserve, 1155

U.S. Air Force-Air Natl Guard, 1155, 1379

U.S. Army (any branch), 1187, 1241

U.S. Army-1st Cavalry Div Assn, 1268

U.S. Army-37th Div, 1148

U.S. Coast Guard (any branch), 1241

U.S. Marines (any branch), 1241, 1561

U.S. Marines-1st Div, 1147

U.S. Marines-3rd Div, 1531

U.S. Navy (any branch), 1241, 1531

U.S. Navy-Fleet Reserve Assn, 1270

U.S. Navy-Submarine Force, 1251, 1562

U.S. Navy-Supply Corps, 1419

Vet Deceased in Retir-D, 1152, 1499

Vet-Blind, 1198

Vet-Deceased, 1147, 1187, 1246, 1268, 1349, 1360, 1365, 1448, 1583

Vet-Deceased in Service-D, 1152, 1207, 1246, 1251, 1318, 1348, 1353, 1373, 1375, 1391, 1399, 1504, 1507, 1531

Vet-Desert Shield/Desert Storm, 1173, 1268, 1399, 1452, 1459, 1531

Vet-Disabled, 1147, 1157, 1158, 1207, 1230, 1246, 1268, 1349, 1360, 1365, 1388, 1440, 1448, 1459, 1499, 1504, 1559

Vet-Disabled in Service-D, 1353, 1373

Vet-KIA, 1157, 1158, 1207, 1230, 1348, 1388, 1435, 1440, 1459, 1499, 1504, 1578

Vet-MIA, 1157, 1158, 1230, 1246, 1348, 1349, 1395, 1432, 1440, 1504

Vet-POW, 1157, 1158, 1230, 1246, 1348, 1349, 1395, 1432, 1440, 1504

Vet-Retired, 1152, 1155, 1187, 1499

Vet-Vietnam, 1173, 1268, 1348, 1395, 1452, 1459, 1531

Vet-WWII or Korea, 1148, 1173, 1452, 1459, 1562

CITY/COUNTY INTENDED STUDY

Atlanta, GA/USA, 11, 377, 378

Boston, MA/USA, 510, 1409

Houston, TX/USA, 14, 383, 972

Los Angeles Metro, CA/USA, 11, 377, 378, 1000, 1001, 1002, 1003

Muncie, IN/USA, 981

New York City, NY/USA, 54, 55, 211, 235, 236, 407, 552, 1019, 1089, 1090, 1110, 1111, 1190

Philadelphia Metro, PA/USA, 1235

San Francisco, CA/USA, 1520

COMPANIES

American Nat'l Can Co.-D, 1175

Conrail-D, 144, 1234

H & R Block-D, 1223

Johnson Controls-D, 1343

North American Philips-D, 1463

Penn Central-D, 1234

Penn Railroad Co.-D, 1234

RBS Corp.-D, 1557

Washington Post Carrier, 1574

Quick Find Index

CONTINENT OF INTENDED STUDY

COUNTRY OF INTENDED STUDY

COUNTRY OF RESIDENCE

CURRENT GRADE-POINT AVERAGE

DEGREES RECEIVED

ETHNIC BACKGROUND

EXTRACURRICULAR ACTIVITIES

FAMILY ANCESTRIES

FOREIGN LANGUAGES SPOKEN

HONORS/AWARDS/CONTESTS

LEGAL CITY OF RESIDENCE

Quick Find Index

LEGAL STATE/PROVIDING OF RESIDENCE

MARITAL STATUS

OCCUPATIONAL GOALS

Journalism, 973, 980, 986, 987, 988, 989, 990, 1005, 1007, 1008, 1206, B1621, B1658
Law Enforcement, 1079
Librarian/Archivist, 480, 702, 1061
Ministry, 574, 575, 576, 577, 578, 579, 581, 582, 583, 586, 589, 590, 592
Missionary, 589, 590
Music, 535, 543, B1621, B1625, B1665
Newspaper Industry, 974, 986, 987, 988, 989, 990, 991, 1206, B1658
Pilot, 196, 197, 198, 200, C1711, C1726, C1871
Rabbinate, 366, 367
Real Estate, 20
Research Scientist, 202, 671, 693, 741, 749, 781, 839, 1057, B1621
Sports Writer, 986, 987, 988, 989, 990, 991, 1042, 1206, B1658
Teacher, 95, 96, 97, 104, 105, 107, 113, 114, 116, 117, 120, 122, 123, 124, 126, 127, 464, 495, 824, 839, 854, 891, 1197, B1621, C1765, C1807, C1816, C1854
Transportation/Traffic Man., 66, 67, 68, 69, 70, 71

OCCUPATIONS

Adult Professional, 1479
Agriculture-D, 1518
Architect, 206, 210, 211, 212
Artist, 213, 385, 390, 391, 395, 396, 400, 403, 408, 412, 415, 420, 426, 433, 439, 442, 449, 450, 455, 457, 476, 506, 511, 518, 521, 526, 529, 539, 559
Author/Writer, 75, 202, 391, 395, 396, 403, 408, 426, 442, 449, 450, 452, 455, 457, 465, 466, 467, 468, 470, 472, 473, 476, 478, 479, 511, 518, 521, 529, 539, 559, 671, 741, 749, 992, 996, 1038, 1047, 1057, 1103, C1735
Calif Youth Authority-D-DIS, 1213
Calif Youth Authority-D-DEC, 1213
Cinematographer, 396, 403, 433, 450, 455, 521, 529
Composer, 391, 395, 396, 403, 426, 442, 449, 450, 455, 476, 500, 511, 518, 521, 529, 559
Conservatn of Natrl Resources, 639, 685
Dept Corrections-D-DEC, 1213, 1375, 1430
Dept Corrections-D-DIS, 1213
Engineer, 250
Fireman, 884, 1134

Fireman-D-DEC, 1213, 1353, 1373, 1375, 1394, 1430
Fireman-D-DIS, 1213, 1353, 1373, 1394
Foodservice/hospitality, 959, 1118
Footwear/Leather Industry, 1537
Footwear/Leather Industry-D, 1537
Harness Racing, 1291
Harness Racing-D, 1291
Health Care Administrator, 866
Journalist, 535, 992, 996, 1021, 1027, 1038, B1658, B1668
Landscape Architect, 206
Librarian, 447
MD/DO Family Medicine, 866
New Jersey St.Emp-D, 354
Nwspapr Carrier-WA Post, 1574
Performer, 395, 396, 403, 408, 426, 449, 450, 455, 457, 476, 518, 521, 529, 539, 550, 551, 556, 559
Photographer, 391, 395, 396, 403, 408, 420, 433, 442, 449, 450, 455, 457, 511, 518, 521, 529, 539
Pilot-Commerical, 196, 197, 200, 1146, C1711
Pilot-Helicopter, 1146, C1711
Police-D-DEC, 1213, 1353, 1373, 1375, 1394, 1430
Police-D-DIS, 1213, 1353, 1394
RN-Registered Nurse, 866, 901, 907, 925, 928, 932
Research Scholar or Scientist, 75, 251, 357, 640, 732, 732, 795, 844, 844, 866, B1618, B1624, B1696, B1698
Respiratory Care Practitioner, 866
Sculptor, 396, 450, 521
Seaman, 1492
Seaman-D, 1493
Teacher-College, 78, 102, 241, 363, 489, 719, 732, 732, 844, 844, 1197
Teacher-Non College, 77, 93, 94, 102, 105, 125, 1197
U.S. Federal Employee, 1266
U.S. Federal Employee-D, 1266

ORGANIZATIONS

Air Force Sgt's Assn.-D, 1153
Am Assn Critical Care Nurses, 901
Am Assn Nurse Anesthetists, 902
Am College Health Care Exec, 791

PHYSICAL HANDICAPS

PREVIOUS/CURRENT/FUTURE SCHOOLS

RELIGIOUS AFFILIATION

SEX

SORORITY/FRATERNITY

STATE/PROVINCE OF INTENDED STUDY

UNIONS

UNUSUAL CHARACTERISTICS

Field of Study Index

SCHOOL OF BUSINESS

General, 1, 2, 3, 4, B1611, B1621

BUSINESS ADMINISTRATION

General, 1, 2, 8, 11, 19, 21, 29, 40, 46, 48, 51, 60, 64, 65, 73, 76, 83, 130, 161, 187, 257, 262, 271, 277, 279, 296, 319, 345, 377, 611, 634, 643, 706, 727, 738, 748, 751, 797, 941, 1012, 1036, 1092, 1124, B1611, B1621, B1629

Accounting, 6, 9, 24, 25, 26, 27, 28, 32, 34, 42, 43, 52, 56, 57, 64, 158, 159, 237, 238, 266, 277, 292, 312, 751, 776, 777, 822, 823, 877, 889, 890, 935, 936, 1076, 1077, 1100, 1101, 1112, 1113, 1127, C1712, C1713, C1714

Actuarial Science, 23, 63, 64, 277, 751, C1715, C1798

Advertising, 14, 44, 383, 394, 972, 978, 993, C1719

Artistic Administration, 58

Aviation/Airport Management, 33, 195, 1126

Banking, 36, C1737

Club Management, 22

Economics, 30, 35, 36, 41, 45, 60, 64, 65, 161, 262, 271, 277, 296, 634, 698, 748, 751, 767, 837, 916, 986, 989, 1036, 1050, 1083, 1084, 1092, 1098, 1108

Finance, 36, 38, 45, 64, 277, 751, 986, 989, C1729

Garden Center Management, 18, 606

Golf Course Management, 22, 619, 620, 621, C1806

Hotel Administration, 7, 39, 43, 959, 960, C1796

Industrial & Labor Relations, 75

Insurance, 23, 64, 277, 751, C1798, C1799

Integrated Resource Mngmnt., 15

International Business, 49, 75, 370

Labor Studies/Human Resources, 59, 74, 75

Management, 12, 31, 36, C1709, C1806

Manufacturing, 45

Marketing, 5, 14, 17, 31, 44, 60, 64, 161, 262, 271, 277, 296, 383, 603, 634, 748, 751, 972, 993, 1010, 1011, C1806

Production/Operations Mngmnt., 15

Public Administration, 54, 55, 61, 235, 236, 1078, 1089, 1090, 1091, 1110, 1111, 1114

Public Relations, 10, 971, 978, 1010, 1011, 1044, B1610

Real Estate, 16, 20, 62, C1729

Real Estate Appraising, 16

Restaurant Management, 43

Retail Management, 5, 18, 22, 606, C1806

Sports Management, 110

Traffic Management, 66, 67, 68, 69, 70, 71

Transportation, 50, 66, 67, 68, 69, 70, 71, 228, C1726

Travel & Tourism, 13, 34, 53, 72, 877, 1127

SCHOOL OF EDUCATION

General, 79, 805

EDUCATION

General, 8, 83, 88, 90, 91, 93, 94, 95, 97, 98, 103, 105, 106, 108, 113, 114, 115, 117, 118, 120, 121, 127, 140, 142, 265, 326, 352, 464, 706, 708, 723, 736, 745, 761, 797, 803, 824, 891, 1067, 1122, B1621, B1630, B1685, C1765, C1854

Administration, B1648, C1853

Blind/Visually Impaired Education, 81, 82, 86, 99, B1659, C1763

Child Care, 968

Christian Leadership Education, 124, 589, 590

Deaf/Hearing Impaired Education, 84, 99, 109, 114, 464, 798, 824, 833, 873, 885, 891, B1659, C1763

Early Childhood Education, 89, 103, 114, 124, 464, 824, 891

Elementary Education, 80, 93, 94, 96, 97, 103, 104, 107, 111, 114, 116, 118, 122, 123, 124, 126, 131, 464, 824, 891, B1630

Learning Disabled Education, 96, 99, 109, 114, 464, 824, 885, 891, B1659, C1763

Music Education, 524

Physical Education, 110, 112, 114, 128, 129, 464, 821, 824, 888, 891

Post-Secondary Education, 96, 111, B1630

SCHOOL OF ENGINEERING

AERONAUTICS

ARCHITECTURE

CIVIL ENGINEERING

COMPUTER SCIENCE

ELECTRICAL ENGINEERING

General, 32, 60, 135, 137, 149, 161, 163, 174, 185, 262, 264, 266, 268, 271, 274, 280, 281, 282, 283, 284, 285, 286, 287, 288, 289, 290, 291, 292, 293, 294, 295, 296, 297, 298, 299, 311, 312, 313, 324, 342, 343, 347, 634, 665, 744, 747, 748, C1766, C1797, C1852
Communications, 280, 281, 283, 284, 285, 286, 287, 289, 290

ENGINEERING TECHNOLOGY

General, 32, 48, 121, 163, 168, 190, 203, 257, 263, 266, 292, 293, 298, 309, 312, 313, 319, 323, 324, 326, 330, 333, 343, 345, 347, 349, 675, 727, 738, 747, 753, 942, 1012, B1685, C1844
Arc Welding Technology, 310, 316, 1119, 1133, C1870
Automotive Technology, 165, 298, 314, 324, 347, C1736
Chemical Engineering, 137, 172, 185, 264, 291, 298, 301, 302, 303, 304, 311, 324, 325, 342, 347, 348, 744, C1745
Die Casting Technology, 321
Environmental Engineering, 165, 327, 332, 596, 674, 683, 687, 690, 716
Hting, Refrgeratn & Air-Cond, 307, 308, 318, 322, C1791
Industrial Engineering, 293, 298, 313, 315, 324, 343, 347, 747
Manufacturing Engineering, 165, 293, 298, 313, 324, 343, 347, 747
Nuclear Engineering, 305, 306, 317
Optical Engineering, 328
Plumbing, 318
Pulp & Paper Technology, 320, 329, 331
Remote Sensing, C1786
Satellites, C1786

MECHANICAL ENGINEERING

General, 48, 137, 163, 172, 185, 203, 257, 263, 264, 291, 293, 298, 309, 311, 313, 319, 324, 325, 330, 333, 334, 335, 336, 337, 338, 339, 340, 342, 343, 345, 347, 348, 349, 675, 727, 738, 744, 747, 753, 942, 1012, B1685, C1808
Mat'ls Science/Metallurgy, 298, 324, 341, 344, 347, 596, C1813
Mining Engineering, 346, 596, C1786

Naval Science, C1861, C1863
Naval/Marine Engineering, 135, 246, 350, 694, C1820
Petroleum Engineering, 172, 596, C1786, C1833

SCHOOL OF HUMANITIES

General, 90, 118, 142, 352, 354, 708, B1628

AREA STUDIES

General, 118
American Indian Studies, 372, 373, 423, 670, 682, 701, 731, 1056
Asian-American Studies, 143, 358, 614, 696, 724, 746, 1048, 1082, 1096
Asian Pacific Studies, 362
Chinese Studies, 357, 368
Creole Studies, 359, 448, 697
French Studies, 356, 485, 492
German Studies, 363, 486
International Studies, 365, 370, 1086
Irish Studies, 364
Italian-American Studies, 371
Jewish Studies, 366, 367
New York State Studies, 369
Norwegian Studies, 374
Scandinavian Studies, 374
United States Studies, 372, 423, 670, 682, 701, 731, 1056

ART

General, 118, 243, 244, 351, 353, 355, 372, 374, 376, 387, 392, 393, 395, 396, 398, 399, 400, 403, 404, 408, 409, 410, 411, 413, 419, 422, 423, 426, 427, 429, 430, 432, 433, 449, 450, 455, 457, 458, 459, 461, 471, 476, 507, 512, 518, 521, 523, 526, 529, 539, 540, 541, 544, 555, 559, 569, 670, 682, 700, 701, 704, 731, 958, 1056, B1595, B1621
Art Administration, 243, 422, 425, 700
Art History, 243, 372, 384, 388, 407, 422, 423, 425, 433, 435, 573, 670, 682, 700, 701, 731, 1056
Commercial Art, 11, 244, 377, 378, 384, 388, 394, 414, 432, 569, B1619, C1787, C1789
Crafts, 372, 384, 388, 401, 412, 423, 433, 670, 682, 701, 731, 1056, C1754

544, 546, 555, 557, 558, 563, 565, 570, 573, B1625, B1665, C1816

Opera & Music Management, 58, 524, 538, 552, 565, B1625, B1665

Orchestra, 505, 510, 519, 524, 535, 549, 565, 571, B1625, B1665

Organ, 560, 561, 562

Piano, 351, 510, 519, 524, 536, 547, 556, 565, 566, 571, B1625, B1665

Singing, 351, 499, 501, 502, 508, 509, 510, 513, 515, 520, 525, 528, 533, 534, 536, 538, 542, 546, 548, 550, 551, 552, 556, 565, B1625, B1665

String Instruments, 510, 524, 532, 535, 536, 556, 565, B1625, B1665

PHILOSOPHY

General, 118, B1621, B1683

Theology, 162, 239, 574, 575, 576, 577, 578, 579, 580, 581, 582, 583, 584, 585, 586, 587, 588, 589, 590, 591, 592, 740, 762, 770, 779, 827, 881, 920, 1398, 1411, 1464, 1569, 1570

SCHOOL OF NATURAL RESOURCES

General, 147, 593, 594, 615, 666, 677, 680, 692, 699, 709, 710, 726, B1655, C1854

AGRICULTURE

General, 21, 73, 143, 187, 279, 358, 593, 597, 598, 599, 610, 611, 612, 613, 614, 615, 616, 617, 623, 624, 626, 627, 629, 631, 632, 638, 641, 643, 644, 646, 648, 666, 677, 692, 699, 709, 724, 726, 746, 787, 941, 948, 1048, 1082, 1096, 1124, B1600, B1685, C1722, C1723

Agribusiness, 598, 622, 625

Agricultural Marketing, 622, 625, 645

Agronomy/Crop Sciences, 618, 620, C1707

Animal Science, 598, 636, C1727

Dairy Science, 630, 645

Farm Management, 622, 628

Floriculture, 152, 604, 608, 620, C1775

Golf Grounds Mngmnt, 618, 620, 621

Green Industry, 620

Herb Studies, 620, 640

Horticulture, 17, 18, 152, 601, 602, 603, 604, 605, 606, 607, 617, 620, 622, 633, 640, 642, 647, C1775, C1794

Pomology, 600, 620

Soil Science, 620, 622, 639, 685, C1707, C1858

Turf/Grounds/Range Management, 152, 620, 621, 635, 639, 647, 685

Turfgrass Science, 618, 620, 621

EARTH SCIENCE

General, 118, 136, 202, 203, 263, 327, 330, 349, 372, 423, 593, 596, 615, 657, 662, 666, 667, 669, 670, 671, 674, 675, 677, 682, 687, 691, 692, 699, 701, 709, 716, 722, 726, 731, 734, 735, 741, 749, 753, 759, 800, 942, 1056, 1057, B1621, B1685, C1786, C1854

Astronomy, 372, 423, 657, 660, 670, 682, 691, 701, 731, 734, 1056, C1733, C1786

Astrophysics, C1786

Cartography/Geodetic Surveying, 649, 650, 652, 653, 654, 655, 656, 657, 691, 734, C1786

Energy, 665, 669

Environmental Education, 327, 674, 687, 716

Forestry/Forest Science, 620, 663, B1655, C1781, C1782, C1849

Geography, 667, 669, C1784

Geology, 596, 657, 668, 672, 673, 691, 734, C1785, C1786

Geophysics, 657, 672, 673, 691, 734, C1786

Geoscience, 669

Hydrology, 657, 658, 659, 660, 691, 734, C1786

Materials Sci. & Engineering, 669

Meteorology, 657, 658, 659, 660, 661, 669, 691, 734

Mineral Economics, 669

Mineral Engineering, 669

Surveying Technology, 145, 146, 651, 664

ENVIRONMENTAL STUDIES

General, 327, 593, 595, 615, 639, 666, 674, 677, 678, 680, 683, 685, 687, 688, 689, 692, 699, 709, 716, 726, B1621, B1685, C1707, C1770, C1858

Conservation, 165, 327, 639, 674, 676, 680, 685, 687, 716

Ecology, 372, 423, 639, 670, 676, 678, 680, 682, 685, 701, 731, 1056

Environmental Economics, 669

MEDICAL-RELATED DISCIPLINES

MEDICAL RESEARCH

MEDICAL TECHNOLOGIES

NURSING

NUTRITION

SCHOOL OF SOCIAL SCIENCE

Scholarships and Award Listings

SCHOOL OF BUSINESS

1

NATIONAL ITALIAN AMERICAN FOUNDATION (George L. Graziano Fellowship for Business)
1860 19th Street NW
Washington, D.C. 20009
202/530-5315

AMOUNT: $2,500
DEADLINE(S): May 31
FIELD(S): Business and Management

Open to undergraduate American students of Italian ancestry studying at the George L. Graziano School of Business and Management at Pepperdine University, California.
2 awards given. Academic merit, financial need, and community service are considered.

2

NATIONAL ITALIAN AMERICAN FOUNDATION (Norman R. Peterson Scholarship)
1860 19th Street NW
Washington, D.C. 20009
202/530-5315

AMOUNT: $5,000 (1); $2,500 (1)
DEADLINE(S): May 31
FIELD(S): Business

For undergraduate American students from the mid-west (Michigan-based) of Italian ancestry for study at John Cabot University in Rome.
For info. contact: Francesca Gleason, Director of Admissions at 011-39-6-687-8881.

3

PRESIDENT'S COMMITTEE ON EMPLOYMENT OF PEOPLE WITH DISABILITIES (Scholarship Program)
1331 F Street NW
Washington, D.C. 20004
202/376-6200; TDD 202/376-6205

AMOUNT: $2,000
DEADLINE(S): Varies (Announced annually)
FIELD(S): Business

Open to high school seniors & 4-year college or university undergrads having a disability (a physical or mental impairment that substantially limits 1 or more major life activities). U.S. citizenship required.
Write for complete information.

4

THE GRAND RAPIDS FOUNDATION (Economic Club of Grand Rapids Scholarship)
209-C Waters Bldg.
161 Ottawa Ave. NW
Grand Rapids, MI 49503-2703
616/454-1751; 616/454-6455

AMOUNT: Varies
DEADLINE(S): Apr 3
FIELD(S): Business

Open to full-time undergraduate students pursuing a degree in business at an accredited college. Must have been a resident of Kent or Ottawa counties in Michigan for a minimum of 3 years and have at least a 3.0 GPA.
Send SASE to above address for complete information.

5

WOMEN GROCERS OF AMERICA (Mary Macey Scholarship Program)
1825 Samuel Morse Drive
Reston, VA 20190-5317
703/437-5300

AMOUNT: $1,000 (minimum)
DEADLINE(S): Jun 1
FIELD(S): Marketing/Management in grocery industry

Open to undergraduate & graduate students pursuing a course of study leading to a grocery industry-related career. Awards are tenable at recognized colleges & universities.
Write for complete information.

BUSINESS ADMINISTRATION

6

AMERICAN ACCOUNTING ASSOCIATION (Arthur H. Carter Scholarships)
5717 Bessie Drive
Sarasota, FL 34233-2399
941/921-7747; Fax 941/923-4093

AMOUNT: $2,500
DEADLINE(S): Apr 1
FIELD(S): Accounting

Applicants must be U.S. citizens who have completed at least two years of study at an accredited college and have at least one year left. During scholarship period student must have at least 12 hours of classroom work.
For undergraduate or graduate study. Students must also be enrolled in at least two accounting classes each semester. Awards are based on merit; financial need is not considered. Write for complete information.

7

AMERICAN HOTEL FOUNDATION (Ecolab Scholarship Program)
1201 New York Ave. NW, Suite 600
Washington, D.C. 20005-3931
202/289-3181; Fax 202/289-3199

AMOUNT: $1,000
DEADLINE(S): Jun 1
FIELD(S): Hospitality/Hotel Management

For students pursuing an A.A. or B.A. degree in hospitality or hotel management on a full-time basis (minimum 12 hours).
Twelve annual awards.

8

AMERICAN INDIAN SCIENCE & ENGINEERING SOCIETY (Burlington Northern Santa Fe Foundation Scholarship)
5661 Airport Blvd.
Boulder, CO 80301
303/939-0023
E-mail: ascholar@spot.colorado.edu;
Internet: www.colorado.edu/AISES

AMOUNT: $2,500 per year for up to 4 years
DEADLINE(S): Mar 31
FIELD(S): Business, Education, Science, Health Administration

Open to high school seniors who are 1/4 or more American Indian. Must reside in KS, OK, CO, AZ, NM, MN, OR, SD, ND, WA, or San Bernardino County, CA (Burlington Northern and Santa Fe Pacific service areas).
Must plan to attend a four-year post-secondary accredited educational institution. Write for complete information or apply online at above website.

9

AMERICAN INSTITUTE OF CERTIFIED PUBLIC ACCOUNTANTS (Minority Scholarship Program)
P.O. Box 2209
Jersey City, NJ 07303-2209

973/575-7641 (Request product #870110); Fax: 800/362-5066 (Request product #870110); Internet: www.aicpa.org

AMOUNT: Up to $5,000 per year

DEADLINE(S): Jul 1

FIELD(S): Accounting

Open to full-time students whose backgrounds are of African-American, Native American/Alaskan Native, Pacific Islander, or Hispanic origin. Undergrads must have a declared accounting major and an overall GPA of at least 3.0. Grad students must be in a 5-year accounting program or accepted in a master's-level accounting program.

288 awards given in 1996-1997. U.S. citizenship required. Awards based on academic achievement (financial need is evaluated as a secondary criteria).

10

AMERICAN INSTITUTE OF POLISH CULTURE (Scholarships)
1440 79th Street Causeway, Suite 117
Miami, FL 33141
305/864-2349; Fax 305/865-5150; E-mail: info@ampolinstitute.org; Internet: www.ampolinstitute.org

AMOUNT: $1,000

DEADLINE(S): Feb 15

FIELD(S): Journalism/Public Relations/Communications

Scholarships to encourage young Americans of Polish descent to pursue the above professions. Award can be used at any accredited American college. The ruling criteria for selection are achievement, talent, and involvement in public life.

$25 non-refundable application processing fee. For full-time study only. Renewable. Send self-addressed, stamped envelope to Harriet Irsay at address above for complete information.

11

AMERICAN INTERCONTINENTAL UNIVERSITY (Emilio Pucci Scholarships)
Admissions Committee
3330 Peachtree Road NE
Atlanta, GA 30326
404/812-8192; 888/248-7392

AMOUNT: $1,800 (deducted from tuition over 6 quarters)

DEADLINE(S): None

FIELD(S): Fashion Design; Fashion Marketing; Interior Design; Commercial Art; Business Administration; Video Production

Scholarships are for high school seniors who are interested in either a 2-year or 4-year program at one of the campuses of the American Intercontinental University: Atlanta, GA; Los Angeles, CA; London, UK; or Dubai, United Arab Emirates. Scholarship is applied toward tuition.

Write for applications and complete information.

12

AMERICAN MANAGEMENT ASSOCIATION INTERNATIONAL (Operation Enterprise - Business Leadership Training for Young Adults)
1601 Broadway
New York, NY 10019
315/824-2000; Fax 315/824-6710

AMOUNT: Varies

DEADLINE(S): Dec 1; Mar 1

FIELD(S): Management Seminars

Full and partial scholarships are available to high school and college students to attend 6-day Operation Enterprise business training seminars on practical leadership and management skills. Prominent executives serve as guest faculty. Must be over 16 years of age.

Write for complete information. Application procedures include writing an essay and providing transcripts and letters of recommendation.

13

**AMERICAN SOCIETY OF TRAVEL
AGENTS (ASTA Scholarship Foundation
Scholarship Funds)**
1101 King Street
Alexandria, VA 22314
703/739-2782

AMOUNT: $400-$3,000
DEADLINE(S): Jul 26
FIELD(S): Travel & Tourism

Foundation administers various scholarship
funds which are open to students enrolled
in accredited proprietary schools, 2-year or
4-year undergraduate schools, or graduate
schools. Minimum 2.5 GPA required.

Each fund has specific eligibility/residency
requirements; some awards are renewable.
U.S. or Canadian citizenship or legal residency required (unless stated otherwise in
the "Specific Requirements" section for
each fund). Some have December deadlines. Write for complete information.

14

**AMERICAN WOMEN IN RADIO &
TELEVISION (Houston Internship Program)**
Aprille Meek; AWRT—Houston
P.O. Box 980908
Houston, TX 77098
Written inquiry

AMOUNT: $500 per year
DEADLINE(S): Mar 1
FIELD(S): Radio; Television; Film & Video;
Advertising; Marketing

Internships open to students who are juniors;
seniors or graduate students at greater
Houston area colleges & universities.

Write for complete information.

15

**APICS EDUCATIONAL AND RESEARCH
FOUNDATION (Donald W. Fogarty
International Student Paper Competition)**
500 West Annandale Road
Falls Church, VA 22046-4274

800/444-APICS (2742); 703/237-8344

AMOUNT: $100-$1,700+
DEADLINE(S): May 15 (submit papers to a
local APICS chapter)
FIELD(S): Production and Operations
Management; Resource Management

Awards offered for winning papers on the subject of production and operations management or resource management, including
inventory issues. Open to full-time or part-
time undergraduate or graduate students.
Up to 180 awards per year.

For complete information, please call APICS
customer service at the above 800 number
to request a D.W.F. International Student
Paper Competition Manual (item #01002)
and the name of a local APICS chapter.

16

**APPRAISAL INSTITUTE EDUCATION
TRUST (Scholarships)**
875 N. Michigan Ave., Suite 2400
Chicago, IL 60611-1980
312/335-4136; Fax 312/335-4200

AMOUNT: $3,000 graduate; $2,000 undergrad
DEADLINE(S): Mar 15
FIELD(S): Real estate appraisal, land
economics, real estate, or allied fields

For graduate or undergraduate study in the
above fields. Awards are made on the basis
of academic excellence. Applications will be
distributed starting September 1. Must be
U.S. citizen.

Approximately 50 scholarships per year. Write
for complete information.

17

**BEDDING PLANTS FOUNDATION INC.
(Harold Bettinger Memorial Scholarship)**
P.O. Box 27241
Lansing, MI 48909
517/694-8537; Fax 517/694-8560;
E-mail: bpfi@grafix-net.com; Internet:
www.grafix-net.com/bpfi

AMOUNT: $1,000

DEADLINE(S): Apr 1

FIELD(S): Horticulture &
Business/Marketing

Open to undergraduate sophomores, juniors, and seniors as well as grad students enrolled in an accredited four-year college or university in the U.S. or Canada. Minimum 3.0 GPA required.

Must be horticulture major with a business marketing emphasis or business/marketing major with horticulture emphasis. Write for complete information.

18

BEDDING PLANTS FOUNDATION INC.
(Jerry Wilmot Scholarship)
P.O. Box 27241
Lansing, MI 48909
517/694-8537; Fax 517/694-8560; E-mail: bpfi@grafix-net.com; Internet: www.grafixnet.com/bpfi

AMOUNT: $2,000

DEADLINE(S): Apr 1

FIELD(S): Garden Center Management

For undergrads entering sophomore, junior, or senior year, who are majoring in horticulture or business/finance. Must be enrolled in an accredited four-year college/university in the U.S. or Canada and pursuing a career in garden center management.

Write for complete information.

19

BUSINESS & PROFESSIONAL WOMEN'S FOUNDATION EDUCATIONAL PROGRAMS (AVON Products Foundation Scholarship Program for Women in Business Studies)
2012 Massachusetts Ave. NW
Washington, D.C. 20036
202/293-1200 Ext. 169

AMOUNT: $1,000

DEADLINE(S): Apr 15

FIELD(S): Business Studies (management, business administration, marketing, sales, accounting, finance, and entrepreneurial education)

For women age 25+ (U.S. citizens) and accepted into an accredited program or course of study at a U.S. institution, including institutions in Puerto Rico and the Virgin Islands. Must graduate within 12 to 24 months from the date of grant and demonstrate critical need for assistance ($30,000 or less for a family of 4). Must have a plan to upgrade skills, train for a new career field, or to enter or re-enter the job market.

For full- or part-time study. For info. send a #10 self-addressed double-stamped (1st class) envelope. Write "scholarship" in upper left corner.

20

CALIFORNIA ASSOCIATION OF REALTORS (CAR Scholarship Foundation)
525 S. Virgil Ave.
Los Angeles, CA 90020
213/739-8200; Fax 213/480-7724; Internet: www.car.org

AMOUNT: $1,000 (2-year colleges); $2,000 (4-year colleges)

DEADLINE(S): Varies (three times per year)

FIELD(S): Real Estate

Open to students who have been legal residents of California for at least one year prior to date of application and have a valid CA drivers license or CA I.D. card. Must have completed at least 12 units prior to submitting applications and be currently enrolled in a minimum of 6 units. Minimum of 2.6 GPA required.

Renewable. Preference to students who show financial need. Write for complete information.

21

CDS INTERNATIONAL INC. (Congress-Bundestag Youth Exchange Program)
330 Seventh Ave., 19th Floor
New York, NY 10001
212/497-3500; Fax 212/497-3535; E-mail: cbyx@cdsintl.org; Internet: www.cdsintl.org

AMOUNT: Airfare, partial domestic travel, and host family payment

DEADLINE(S): Dec 15

FIELD(S): Business; Vocational/Technical Fields; Agricultural Fields

Year-long work/study programs in Germany for U.S. citizens aged 18-24. Program for Americans includes two-month language study, four-month tech or professional school study, and six-month internship. A cultural exchange designed to give participants an understanding and knowledge of everyday life in Germany.

60 awards per year. Contact Martin Black at above locations. Professional target and applicable work experience is required. Participants must provide their own spending money of $300-$350/month.

22

CLUB MANAGERS ASSOCIATION OF AMERICA (Grants)
1733 King Street
Alexandria, VA 22314
703/739-9500

AMOUNT: $1,000-$2,000

DEADLINE(S): May 1

FIELD(S): Management of clubs

Grants for sophomores, juniors, and seniors specializing in club management at an accredited college or university. Should have 2.5 or better GPA. Awards are not based solely on need.

Send SASE to above location for details.

23

COLLEGE OF INSURANCE (Scholarships)
101 Murray Street
Admissions Office
New York, NY 10007
212/962-4111

AMOUNT: $2,200 to $9,144 per semester

DEADLINE(S): May (for following Sep)

FIELD(S): Insurance Management; Actuarial Science

Awards tenable at the College of Insurance only. Open to applicants who are U.S. citizens; high school graduate.

50 scholarships per semester. Renewable. Write for complete information.

24

COLORADO SOCIETY OF CPAs EDUCATIONAL FOUNDATION (Scholarships for High School Seniors)
7979 E. Tufts Ave., #500
Denver, CO 80237-2843
303/773-2877; 800/523-9082

AMOUNT: $750

DEADLINE(S): Mar 1

FIELD(S): Accounting

Open to high school seniors in Colorado schools with at least a 3.75 GPA who intend to major in accounting at Colorado colleges and universities which offer an accredited accounting program. You must submit an official transcript from your school, including SAT or ACT scores and class rank at the end of 1st semester, senior year.

Write for complete information. If you have any questions or need additional applications, please contact Andrea Smith at the above location.

25

COLORADO SOCIETY OF CPAs EDUCATIONAL FOUNDATION (Gordon Scheer Scholarship)
7979 E. Tufts Ave., #500
Denver, CO 80237-2843
303/773-2877; 800/523-9082

AMOUNT: $1,000

DEADLINE(S): Jun 30

FIELD(S): Accounting

For undergraduates who have completed intermediate accounting, have 3.5 or better GPA, and are majoring in accounting at a Colorado college or university offering accredited accounting majors.

Scholarships are renewable with re-application. Write for complete information.

26

COLORADO SOCIETY OF CPAs EDUCATIONAL FOUNDATION (Scholarships for Ethnically Diverse H.S. Seniors)

    7979 E. Tufts Ave., #500
    Denver, CO 80237-2843
    303/773-2877; 800/523-9082

AMOUNT: $750
DEADLINE(S): Mar 1
FIELD(S): Accounting

Open to ethnically diverse high school seniors in Colorado schools with at least a 3.0 GPA who intend to major in accounting at Colorado colleges and universities which offer an accredited accounting program. Must be African-American, Hispanic, Asian-American, American Indian, or Pacific Islander.

Write for complete information. If you have any questions or need additional applications, please contact Andrea Smith at the above location.

27

COLORADO SOCIETY OF CPAs EDUCATIONAL FOUNDATION (Scholarships for Undergraduates and Graduates)

    7979 E. Tufts Ave., #500
    Denver, CO 80237-2843
    303/773-2877; 800/523-9082

AMOUNT: $750
DEADLINE(S): Jun 30; Nov 30
FIELD(S): Accounting

For undergraduates and graduates who have completed intermediate accounting, have 3.0 or better GPA, and are majoring in accounting at a Colorado college or university offering accredited accounting majors.

Scholarships are renewable with re-application. Write for complete information. Financial need considered.

28

COLORADO SOCIETY OF CPAs EDUCATIONAL FOUNDATION (Scholarships for Ethnically Diverse Undergraduates and Graduates)

    7979 E. Tufts Ave., #500
    Denver, CO 80237-2843
    303/773-2877; 800/523-9082

AMOUNT: $750
DEADLINE(S): Nov 30
FIELD(S): Accounting

For ethnically diverse undergraduates and graduates who have completed intermediate accounting, have 3.0 or better GPA, and are majoring in accounting at a Colorado college or university offering accredited accounting majors. Must be African-American, Hispanic, Asian-American, American Indian, or Pacific Islander.

Scholarships are renewable with re-application. Write for complete information. Financial need considered.

29

CONSORTIUM FOR GRADUATE STUDY IN MANAGEMENT (Fellowships for Talented Minorities)

    200 S. Hanley Road, Suite 1102
    St Louis, MO 63105-3415
    314/935-6364; Fax 314/935-5014; E-mail: cgsm@wuolin.wustl.edu; Internet: www.cgsm.wustl.edu:8010/

AMOUNT: Full tuition + fees
DEADLINE(S): Jan 15
FIELD(S): Business Administration

Fellowships for graduate study at any of 11 specified universities. For African-Americans, Native Americans, and Hispanic Americans who have received B.A. degrees in any field from accredited institution. U.S. citizenship.

Approx. 300 awards per year. Contact above address or website for complete information.

30

DAUGHTERS OF THE AMERICAN REVOLUTION (Enid Hall Griswold Memorial Scholarship Program)
Office of the Committee/Scholarships;
National Society DAR
1776 D Street NW
Washington, D.C. 20006-5392
202/879-3292

AMOUNT: $1,000 (one-time award)
DEADLINE(S): Feb 15
FIELD(S): History; Political Science; Government; Economics

Open to undergraduate juniors & seniors attending an accredited college or university in the U.S. Awards are judged on the basis of academic excellence; financial need & commitment to field of study. Must be U.S. citizen.

DAR affiliation is not required but applicants must be sponsored by a local DAR chapter. Not renewable. Write for complete information (include SASE).

31

DECA (Harry A. Applegate Scholarships)
1908 Association Drive
Reston, VA 22091
703/860-5000

AMOUNT: From $1,000
DEADLINE(S): Mar 1
FIELD(S): Marketing; Management; Entrepreneurship; Merchandising

Open to high school seniors or graduates who are members of DECA. Scholarships are for undergraduate study at accredited colleges or universities. U.S. citizens.

Scholarships are renewable. Write for complete information.

32

DEVRY INC. (Scholarship Program)
One Tower Lane
Oakbrook Terrace, IL 60181
708/571-7700; 800/323-4256

AMOUNT: Full tuition (40); 1/2 tuition (80)
DEADLINE(S): Mar 22
FIELD(S): Electronics Engineering Technology; Computer Information Systems; Business Operations; Telecommunications Management; Accounting

30 full-tuition & 90 1/2-tuition undergraduate scholarships. Open to U.S. high school graduates who wish to enroll in a fully-accredited bachelor of science degree program at one of the Devry Institutes located throughout North America.

Awards renewable provided 2.5 GPA is maintained. Must be a U.S. citizen. Contact your guidance counselor; nearest Devry Institutes located throughout North America.

33

EAA AVIATION FOUNDATION (Scholarship Program)
P.O. Box 3065
Oshkosh, WI 54903-3065
920/426-6815

AMOUNT: $200-$1,500
DEADLINE(S): May 1
FIELD(S): Aviation

Several different scholarship programs open to well-rounded individuals involved in school and community activities as well as aviation. Applicants' academic records should verify their ability to complete their educational program.

Financial need is a consideration.

34

EMPIRE COLLEGE (Dean's Scholarship)
3033 Cleveland Ave.
Santa Rosa, CA 95403
707/546-4000

AMOUNT: $250-$1,500
DEADLINE(S): Apr 15
FIELD(S): Accounting; Secretarial; Legal; Medical (Clinical & Administrative); Travel

& Tourism; General Business; Computer Assembly; Network Assembly

Open to high school seniors who meet admission requirements and want to attend Empire College in Santa Rosa, CA U.S. citizenship required.

10 scholarships per year. Contact Mary Farha at the above address for complete information.

35

EPILEPSY FOUNDATION OF AMERICA (Behavioral Sciences Student Fellowships)
4351 Garden City Drive
Landover, MD 20785
301/459-3700; 800/EFA-1000; Fax 301/577-2684; TDD: 800/332-2070; E-mail: postmaster@efa.org; Internet: www.efa.org

AMOUNT: $2,000
DEADLINE(S): Mar 3
FIELD(S): For the study of epilepsy in either research or practice settings in fields such as sociology, social work, psychology, anthropology, nursing, economics, vocational rehabilitation, counseling, political science, etc., relevant to epilepsy research.

Applicants may propose a 3-month project to be undertaken in a clinical or laboratory setting where there are ongoing programs of research, service, or training in the field of epilepsy.

Project may be conducted during any free period of the student's year at a U.S. institution of the student's choice. Write for complete information.

36

FIRST INTERSTATE BANK OF WASHINGTON (Scholarship Program)
P.O. Box 160, MS 803
Seattle, WA 98111
206/292-3482

AMOUNT: $1,000-$1,500
DEADLINE(S): Varies (Established by institutions making awards)

FIELD(S): Business; Finance; Economics

Open to Washington state residents who are entering specified colleges in Washington state as freshmen. Must exhibit need for financial aid and demonstrate academic or extracurricular achievement in business, finance or economics.

Apply directly to financial aid office of college or university.

37

FUKUNAGA SCHOLARSHIP FOUNDATION (Scholarships)
P.O. Box 2788
Honolulu, HI 96803
808/521-6511

AMOUNT: Varies
DEADLINE(S): Mar 15
FIELD(S): Business Administration

Scholarships to residents of Hawaii to study business administration at the University of Hawaii or other accredited universities. Must demonstrate academic ability, leadership qualities, interest in business in the Pacific Basin area, and financial need. Must plan to return to Hawaii or the Pacific Island region to work and live.

Awards for one year of study. Telephone above number for initial inquiry or write Scholarship Selection Committee at above address.

38

GEORGE HARDING SCHOLARSHIP FUND (Scholarship)
22344 Long Blvd.
Dearborn, MI 48124
313/225-2798

AMOUNT: $750
DEADLINE(S): Ongoing
FIELD(S): Business Administration/Finance

Scholarships for Michigan residents who are full-time students enrolled in four-year Michigan colleges or universities and pursuing finance-related degrees. To be used only for the senior year of college or first year of graduate school.

Write to Richard E. Gardner, Trustee, at above address for details.

39

**GOLDEN GATE RESTAURANT ASSN.
(David Rubenstein Memorial Scholarship
Foundation Awards)**
720 Market Street, Suite 200
San Francisco, CA 94102
415/781-5348

AMOUNT: $500-$2,500
DEADLINE(S): Mar 31
FIELD(S): Hotel & Restaurant
Management/Food Science

Open to students who have completed the first semester of college as a food-service major and have a 2.75 or better GPA (4.0 scale) in hotel and restaurant courses.

7 awards per year. Write for complete information.

40

**GOLDEN STATE MINORITY
FOUNDATION (College Scholarships)**
1055 Wilshire Blvd., Suite 1115
Los Angeles, CA 90017
213/482-6300

AMOUNT: $2,000
DEADLINE(S): Feb 1 (Application available then. Deadline is Apr 1.)
FIELD(S): Business Administration

Open to minority students attending school in California or California residents attending school elsewhere. Awards support study at the undergrad college junior/senior levels. Must maintain a 3.0 GPA or better.

May not work more than 25 hours a week. Income must be insufficient to cover expenses. Approx. 75 awards per year. Write for complete information.

41

**GRASS VALLEY GROUP, INC.
SCHOLARSHIP FOUNDATION**
P.O. Box 1114, MIS 8N
Grass Valley, CA 95945
916/478-3136

AMOUNT: Varies
DEADLINE(S): Apr 30
FIELD(S): Economics

Scholarships for students studying economics.

Write to Diane Masegan at above address for formal application information.

42

**INDEPENDENT ACCOUNTANTS
INTERNATIONAL EDUCATIONAL
FOUNDATION INC. (Robert Kaufman
Memorial Scholarship Award)**
9200 S. Dadeland Blvd., Suite 510
Miami, FL 33156
305/670-0580

AMOUNT: $250-$2,500
DEADLINE(S): Feb 28
FIELD(S): Accounting

Open to students who are pursuing or planning to pursue an education in accounting at recognized academic institutions throughout the world. Must demonstrate financial need for larger sums; not required for $250 honorary textbook award.

Up to 20 scholarships per year. Write for complete information.

43

**INTERNATIONAL ASSOCIATION OF
HOSPITALITY ACCOUNTANTS
(Scholarships)**
P.O. Box 203008
Austin, TX 78720-3008
512/346-5680

AMOUNT: $1,000-$1,500
DEADLINE(S): Jul 15

FIELD(S): Accounting or hospitality management

For students majoring in either accounting or hospitality management at an accredited college or university.

Applications must come through an IAHA local chapter president. Send SASE for details.

44

INTERNATIONAL RADIO & TELEVISION SOCIETY FOUNDATION (IRTS Summer Fellowship Program)
Ms. Maria De Leon
420 Lexington Ave., Suite 1714
New York, NY 10170
212/867-6650

AMOUNT: Housing, stipend, and travel
DEADLINE(S): Nov 21
FIELD(S): Broadcasting, Communications, Sales, or Marketing

Annual 9-week summer fellowship program in New York City open to outstanding full-time undergraduate juniors and seniors with a demonstrated interest in a career in communications.

Write for complete information.

45

KARLA SCHERER FOUNDATION (Scholarships)
737 N. Michigan Ave., Suite 2330
Chicago, IL 60611
312/943-9191

AMOUNT: Varies
DEADLINE(S): None
FIELD(S): Finance; Economics

Open to women who plan to pursue careers in finance and/or economics in the private manufacturing-based sector. Send letter stating what school you attend or plan to attend; the courses you plan to take and how you will use your education in your chosen career.

Scholarships are for undergraduate or graduate study at any accredited college and are renewable. Information described above should accompany request for application package.

46

MARYLAND ASSOCIATION OF CERTIFIED PUBLIC ACCOUNTANTS EDUCATIONAL FOUNDATION (Scholarship Program)
P.O. Box 4417
Lutherville, MD 21094-4417
410/296-6250; 800/782-2036; Fax 410/296-8713; Internet: www.macpa.org

AMOUNT: $1,000 per year (minimum)
DEADLINE(S): Apr 15
FIELD(S): Accounting

Open to Maryland residents who are in their junior or senior year at Maryland colleges or universities and are accounting majors. A cumulative GPA of 3.0 or better is required. Must demonstrate financial need.

Write or call for complete information.

47

MEXICAN AMERICAN GROCERS ASSOCIATION (Scholarships)
405 N. San Fernando Road
Los Angeles, CA 90031
213/227-1565; Fax 213/227-6935

AMOUNT: Varies
DEADLINE(S): Jul 31
FIELD(S): Business

Scholarships for Hispanic college students who are at least college sophomores. Must have 2.5 GPA or above, be U.S. citizen or permanent resident, and demonstrate financial need.

Send a self-addressed, stamped envelope to Jackie Solis at above address for further information.

48

NATIONAL ASSOCIATION OF WATER COMPANIES—NEW JERSEY CHAPTER (Scholarship)

Elizabethtown Water Co.
600 South Ave.
Westfield, NJ 07090
908/654-1234; Fax 908/232-2719

AMOUNT: $2,500
DEADLINE(S): Apr 1
FIELD(S): Business Administration; Biology; Chemistry; Engineering; Communications

For U.S. citizens who have lived in NJ at least 5 years and plan a career in the investor-owned water utility industry in disciplines such as those above. Must be undergrad or graduate student in a 2- or 4-year NJ college or university.

GPA of 3.0 or better required. Contact Gail P. Brady for complete information.

49

NATIONAL CUSTOMS BROKERS & FORWARDERS ASSN OF AMERICA INC (NCBFAA Scholarship)

One World Trade Center, Suite 1153
New York, NY 10048
212/432-0050

AMOUNT: $5,000
DEADLINE(S): Feb 1
FIELD(S): International Business - Customs Brokerage or Freight Forwarding

Open to family members and employees of regular NCBFAA members who are interested in a career in customs brokerage or freight forwarding. Applicants must have a 2.0 or better GPA and submit a 1,000- to 1,500-word essay.

Write for complete information.

50

NATIONAL DEFENSE TRANSPORTATION ASSOCIATION— SAN FRANCISCO BAY AREA CHAPTER (NDTA Scholarship)

P.O. Box 24676
Oakland, CA 94623
Written inquiry

AMOUNT: $2,000
DEADLINE(S): Mar 31
FIELD(S): Transportation-related Business; Engineering; Planning & Environmental fields

Open to U.S. citizens enrolled in a California accredited undergraduate degree or vocational program in the above fields who plan to pursue a career related to transportation. Financial need is considered.

Write for complete information.

51

NATIONAL ITALIAN AMERICAN FOUNDATION (F. D. Stella Scholarship)

1860 Nineteenth Street NW
Washington, D.C. 20009-5599
202/530-5315

AMOUNT: $1,000
DEADLINE(S): May 31
FIELD(S): For undergraduate and graduate business majors

Open to undergraduate or graduate business majors of Italian heritage. Write a typed essay on a family member or a personality you consider: "An Italian American Hero."

Also considered are academic merit, financial need, and financial need.

52

NATIONAL SOCIETY OF PUBLIC ACCOUNTANTS SCHOLARSHIP FOUNDATION (NSPA Annual Awards)

1010 North Fairfax Street
Alexandria, VA 22314-1574
703/549-6400; Fax 703/549-2984

AMOUNT: $500-$1,000

DEADLINE(S): Mar 10

FIELD(S): Accounting

Open to accounting students in an accredited two- or four-year college in the U.S. Must maintain an overall GPA of 3.0. Must be a U.S. or Canadian citizen.

Approx. 26 awards per year. Selection based on academic attainment, leadership ability and financial need. Write for complete information.

53

NATIONAL TOUR FOUNDATION
P.O. Box 3071
Lexington, KY 40596
606/253-1036

AMOUNT: $500

DEADLINE(S): Mar

FIELD(S): Travel & Tourism

For juniors and seniors majoring in travel and tourism at an accredited four-year college or university.

Send SASE to above address.

54

NEW YORK CITY DEPT. CITYWIDE ADMINISTRATIVE SERVICES (Urban Fellows Program)
1 Centre Street, 24th Floor
New York, NY 10007
212/487-5600; Fax 212/487-5720

AMOUNT: $18,000 stipend

DEADLINE(S): Jan 20

FIELD(S): Public Administration; Urban Planning; Government; Public Service; Urban Affairs

Fellowship program provides one academic year (9 months) of full-time work experience in urban government. Open to graduating college seniors and recent college graduates. U.S. citizenship required.

Write for complete information.

55

NEW YORK CITY DEPT. OF CITYWIDE ADMINISTRATIVE SERVICES (Government Scholars Internship Program)
1 Centre Street, 24th Floor
New York, NY 10007
212/487-5600; Fax 212/487-5720

AMOUNT: $3,000 stipend

DEADLINE(S): Jan 13

FIELD(S): Public Administration; Urban Planning; Government; Public Service; Urban Affairs

10-week summer intern program open to undergraduate sophomores, juniors, and seniors. Program provides students with unique opportunity to learn about NY City government. Internships available in virtually every city agency and mayoral office.

Write to New York City Fellowship Programs at above address for complete information.

56

NEW YORK STATE HIGHER EDUCATION SERVICES CORPORATION (N.Y. State Regents Professional/Health Care Opportunity Scholarships)
Cultural Education Center, Room 5C64
Albany, NY 12230
518/486-1319; Internet: www.hesc.com

AMOUNT: $1,000-$10,000/year

DEADLINE(S): Varies

FIELD(S): Medicine and Dentistry and related fields; Architecture; Nursing; Psychology; Audiology; Landscape Architecture; Social Work; Chiropractic; Law; Pharmacy; Accounting; Speech Language Pathology

For NY state residents who are economically disadvantaged and members of a minority group underrepresented in the chosen profession and attending school in NY state. Some programs carry a service obligation in New York for each year of support. For U.S. citizens or qualifying noncitizens.

Medical/dental scholarships require one year of professional work in NY.

57

NEW YORK STATE HIGHER EDUCATION SERVICES CORPORATION
Cultural Education Center, Room 5C64
Albany, NY 12230
518/486-1319; Internet: www.hesc.com

AMOUNT: Varies
DEADLINE(S): Varies
FIELD(S): Medicine and dentistry and related fields; Architecture; Nursing; Psychology; Audiology; Landscape architecture; Social Work; Chiropractic; Law; Pharmacy; Accounting; Speech Language Pathology

For NY state residents who are economically disadvantaged and members of a minority group underrepresented in the chosen profession and attending school in NY state. Some programs carry a service obligation in New York for each year of support. For U.S. citizens or qualifying noncitizens.

Medical/dental scholarships require one year of professional work in NY.

58

OPERA AMERICA (Fellowship Program)
1156 15th Street NW, Suite 810
Washington, D.C. 20005
202/293-4466

AMOUNT: $1,200/month + transportation & housing
DEADLINE(S): May 7
FIELD(S): General or Artistic Administration; Technical Direction or Production Management

Open to opera personnel; individuals entering opera administration from other disciplines and graduates of arts administration or technical/production training programs who are committed to a career in opera in North America.

Must be U.S. or Canadian citizen or legal resident lawfully eligible to receive stipend.

59

OREGON AFL-CIO (Scholarship Contest)
c/o AFSCME Labor Center
1174 Gateway Loop
Springfield, OR 97477
503/741-4770; E-mail: labor_ed@efn.org

AMOUNT: $3,000; $1,000; $750; $600
DEADLINE(S): Feb 15
FIELD(S): Labor Studies

Open to graduating seniors from any accredited high school in Oregon for undergraduate study at any accredited U.S. college or university or at an Oregon community college or trade school.

Candidates must take a written exam on labor history and labor issues. Finalists will be chosen on exam score, financial need and high school GPA. Write for complete information.

60

PACIFIC GAS & ELECTRIC CO. (Scholarships for High School Seniors)
77 Beale Street
Room 2837
San Francisco, CA 94106
415/973-1338

AMOUNT: $1,000-$4,000
DEADLINE(S): Nov 15
FIELD(S): Engineering; Computer Science; Mathematics; Marketing; Business; Economics

High school seniors in good academic standing who reside in or attend high school in areas served by PG&E are eligible to compete for scholarships awarded on a regional basis. Not open to children of PG&E employees.

36 awards per year. Applications & brochures are available in all high schools within PG&E's service area and at PG&E offices.

61

PRESIDENT'S COMMISSION ON WHITE HOUSE FELLOWSHIPS
712 Jackson Place NW
Washington, D.C. 20503
202/395-4522; Fax 202/395-6179; E-mail:
almanac@ace.esusda.gov

AMOUNT: Wage (up to GS-14 Step 3;
approximately $65,000 in 1995)
DEADLINE(S): Dec 1
FIELD(S): Public Service; Government;
Community Involvement; Leadership
Mid-career professionals spend one year as
special assistants to senior executive branch
officials in Washington. Highly competitive.
Non-partisan; no age or educational
requirements. Fellowship year runs
September 1 through August 31.
1,200 candidates applying for 11 to 19 fellowships each year. Write for complete information.

62

SACRAMENTO ASSOCIATION OF REALTORS (Eugene L. Williams Scholarship)
2003 Howe Ave.
Sacramento, CA 95825
916/922-7711; Fax 916/922-1221

AMOUNT: $500-$750
DEADLINE(S): Feb
FIELD(S): Real Estate and related fields
Open to students of not less than sophomore
standing at Sacramento City College, CSU
Sacramento, or American River College.
All applicants are interviewed and must
submit a statement of why they are plan-
ning a real estate career.
Write for complete information.

63

SOCIETY OF ACTUARIES (Actuarial Scholarships for Minority Students)
475 N. Martingale Road, Suite 800
Schaumburg, IL 60173-2226
708/706-3500

AMOUNT: Varies
DEADLINE(S): May 1
FIELD(S): Actuarial science
Open to students who are members of ethnic
minorities and are enrolled or accepted in
an actuarial science program at an accredited college or university. Must demonstrate
financial need and be a U.S. citizen or legal
resident.
Amount varies according to student's need
and credentials. Approximately 40 awards
per year. Write for complete information.

64

STATE FARM COMPANIES FOUNDATION (Exceptional Student Fellowship)
1 State Farm Plaza
Bloomington, IL 61710
309/766-2039

AMOUNT: $3,000
DEADLINE(S): Feb 15 (apps. available Nov 1)
FIELD(S): Accounting; Business
Administration; Actuarial Science;
Computer Science; Economics; Finance;
Insurance; Investments; Marketing;
Mathematics; Statistics; and Related Fields
Open to current full-time college juniors and
seniors majoring in any of the fields above.
Only students nominated by the college
dean or a department head qualify as candi-
dates. Applications without nominations
will NOT be considered.
U.S. citizen. 3.6 or better GPA (4.0 scale)
required. 50 fellowships per year. Write for
complete information.

65

THE FUND FOR AMERICAN STUDIES (Institutes on Political Journalism; Business & Government Affairs & Comparative Political & Economic Systems)
1526 18th Street NW
Washington, D.C. 20036
202/986-0384; 800/741-6964
Internet: www.dcinternships.com

AMOUNT: Up to $2,975

DEADLINE(S): Jan 31 (early decision); Mar 15 (general application deadline)

FIELD(S): Political Science; Economics; Journalism; Business Administration

The Fund for American Studies, in conjunction with Georgetown University, sponsors summer institutes that include internships, courses for credit, site briefings, and dialogues with policy leaders. Scholarships are available to sophomores and juniors to cover the cost of the program.

Approx. 100 awards per year. For Fund's programs only. Call, check website, or write for complete information.

66

TRANSPORTATION CLUBS INTERNATIONAL (Charlotte Woods Memorial Scholarship)
P.O. Box 1072
Glen Alpine, NC 28628
206/549-2251

AMOUNT: $1,000

DEADLINE(S): May 31

FIELD(S): Transportation Logistics; Traffic Management

Open to TCI members or their dependents enrolled at an accredited college or university in a program in transportation, traffic management, or related area and considering a career in transportation.

Type an essay of not more than 200 words on why you have chosen transportation or an allied field as a career path. Include your objectives. Financial need is also considered. Send SASE (business size) for complete information and application.

67

TRANSPORTATION CLUBS INTERNATIONAL (Denny Lydic Scholarship)
P.O. Box 1072
Glen Alpine, NC 28628
206/549-2251

AMOUNT: $500

DEADLINE(S): May 31

FIELD(S): Transportation Logistics; Traffic Management

For students enrolled in an accredited institution of higher learning in a degree or vocational program in the above areas.

Type an essay of not more than 200 words on why you have chosen transportation or an allied field as a career path. Include your objectives. Send an SASE for details.

68

TRANSPORTATION CLUBS INTERNATIONAL (Ginger & Fred Deines Canada Scholarships)
P.O. Box 1072
Glen Alpine, NC 28628
206/549-2251

AMOUNT: $500 and/or $1,000

DEADLINE(S): May 31

FIELD(S): Transportation Logistics; Traffic Management

For a student of Canadian nationality and enrolled in a school in Canada or U.S. in a degree or vocational program in the above or related areas.

Type an essay of not more than 200 words on why you have chosen transportation or an allied field as a career path. Include your objectives. Send an SASE for further details.

69

TRANSPORTATION CLUBS INTERNATIONAL (Ginger & Fred Deines Mexico Scholarships)
P.O. Box 1072
Glen Alpine, NC 28628
206/549-2251

AMOUNT: $500 and/or $1,000

DEADLINE(S): May 31

FIELD(S): Transportation Logistics; Traffic Management

Open to students of Mexican nationality who are enrolled in a Mexican or U.S. institution of higher learning in a degree or vocational program in the above or related areas.

Type an essay of not more than 200 words on why you have chosen transportation or an allied field as a career path. Include your objectives. Send SASE for complete information.

70

TRANSPORTATION CLUBS INTERNATIONAL (Hooper Memorial Scholarships)
P.O. Box 1072
Glen Alpine, NC 28628
206/549-2251

AMOUNT: $1,500
DEADLINE(S): May 31
FIELD(S): Transportation Logistics; Traffic Management

For students enrolled in an accredited college or university in a degree or vocational program in transportation logistics, traffic management, or related fields and preparing for a career in transportation.

Type an essay of not more than 200 words on why you have chosen transportation or an allied field as a career. Include your objectives. Financial need is considered. Send SASE (business size) for complete information.

71

TRANSPORTATION CLUBS INTERNATIONAL (Texas Transportation Scholarship)
1275 Kamus Drive, Suite 101
Fox Island, WA 98333
206/549-2251

AMOUNT: $1,000
DEADLINE(S): May 31
FIELD(S): Transportation Logistics; Traffic Management

Open to students who have been enrolled in a school in Texas during elementary, secondary or high school and enrolled in an accredited college or university in a degree or vocational program relating to transportation.

Type an essay of not more than 200 words on why you have chosen transportation or an allied field as a career path. Include your objectives. Financial need is considered. Send SASE (business size) for complete information.

72

TRAVEL AND TOURISM RESEARCH ASSOCIATION (Awards for Projects)
10200 West 44th Ave., Suite 304
Wheat Ridge, CO 80033
303/940-6557

AMOUNT: $500-$1,000
DEADLINE(S): Varies
FIELD(S): Travel & Tourism

3 awards for undergraduate, graduate, and doctoral students (Ph.D. and Doctor of Business Administration) in the area of travel and tourism research. Awards for outstanding papers and dissertations.

Send SASE to above location for details.

73

TYSON FOUNDATION INC. (Scholarship Program)
2210 W. Oaklawn
Springdale, AR 72762-6999
501/290-4955

AMOUNT: Varies according to need
DEADLINE(S): Apr 20
FIELD(S): Business; Agriculture; Engineering; Computer Science; Nursing

For Arkansas residents who are U.S. citizens. Must be enrolled full-time in an accredited institution and demonstrate financial need. Must be employed part-time and/or summers to help fund education. For undergrad study at schools in U.S.

Renewable up to 8 semesters or 12 trimesters as long as students meet criteria.

74

UNITED FOOD & COMMERCIAL WORKERS UNION—LOCAL 555 (L. Walter Derry Scholarship Fund)
P.O. Box 23555
Tigard, OR 97223
503/684-2822

AMOUNT: $1,200
DEADLINE(S): May 9
FIELD(S): Labor relations
Program open ONLY to Local 555 members (in good standing for at least 1 year) and their children and spouses. Scholarship for an outstanding student in the field of labor relations. Write a 500-word essay about your interest and future commitment in the field of labor relations. For use at any accredited university, college, technical-vocational school, junior college, or community college.
Write for complete information ONLY if you are a UFCW Local 555 member or relative of a member.

75

W. E. UPJOHN INSTITUTE FOR EMPLOYMENT RESEARCH (Grant)
300 South Westnedge Ave.
Kalamazoo, MI 49007-4686
616/343-5541; Fax 616/343-3308; Internet: www.upjohninst.org

AMOUNT: Up to $45,000 + $25,000 to conduct surveys or to assemble data
DEADLINE(S): Apr 1
FIELD(S): For research on employment-related issues which will be developed into a book
The grant program is to provide backing for a book on employment relationships, low wages and public policy, or decentralization

of government-sponsored employment programs.
Write for detailed information or find it on the website listed above.

76

Y'S MEN INTERNATIONAL; U.S. AREA (Alexander Scholarship Loan Fund)
7242 Natural Bridge Road
Normandy, MO 63121
Written inquiry only

AMOUNT: $1,000-$1,500 per year
DEADLINE(S): May 1; Oct 1
FIELD(S): Business Administration; Youth Leadership
Open to U.S. citizens or permanent residents with a strong desire to pursue professional YMCA service. For undergrads or grad students (YMCA staff only). Financial need must be demonstrated.
Repayment of loan is waived if recipient enters YMCA employment after graduation. Write for complete information.

SCHOOL OF EDUCATION

77

AMERICAN HISTORICAL ASSOCIATION (Beveridge Family Teaching Prize for K-12 Teaching)
400 A Street, SE
Washington, D.C. 20003
202/544-2422; Fax 202/544-8307; E-mail: ceaton@theaha.org

AMOUNT: Varies
DEADLINE(S): Mar 15
FIELD(S): History
To recognize excellence and innovation in elementary, middle school, and secondary history teaching. Awarded on a two-year cycle rotation: individual and group. In 1997, the prize was awarded to a group.
Letters of nomination deadline is March 15.

78

AMERICAN HISTORICAL ASSOCIATION (Eugene Asher Distinguished Teaching Award for Post-Secondary Teaching)
400 A Street SE
Washington, D.C. 20003
202/544-2422; Fax 202/544-8307; E-mail: ceaton@theaha.org

AMOUNT: Varies
DEADLINE(S): Apr 15
FIELD(S): History

This prize is awarded annually for excellence in teaching techniques and knowledge of the subject of history at the post-secondary level.
Letters of nomination deadline is April 15. Write for complete information.

79

CHARLES E SAAK TRUST (Educational Grants)
Wells Fargo Bank Trust Dept.
5262 N. Blackstone
Fresno, CA 93710
Written inquiry only

AMOUNT: Varies
DEADLINE(S): Mar 31
FIELD(S): Education; Dental

Undergraduate grants for residents of the Porterville-Poplar area of Tulare County CA. Must carry a minimum of 12 units; have at least a 2.0 GPA; be under age 21 and demonstrate financial need.
Approximately 100 awards per year; renewable with reapplication. Write for complete information.

EDUCATION

80

ALASKA COMMISSION ON POSTSECONDARY EDUCATION (Alaska Teacher Scholarship Loan Program)
3030 Vintage Blvd.
Juneau, AK 99801
907/465-6741; Fax 907/465-5316; E-mail: ftolbert@educ.state.ak.us

AMOUNT: Up to $7,500/year with $37,500 lifetime maximum
DEADLINE(S): May 1 (nominations from school superintendents)
FIELD(S): Education—elementary or secondary teaching

Loans for Alaska high school graduates from rural areas who intend to teach in rural areas. Students are nominated by their rural schools. Employment as a teacher in a rural area in Alaska can result in up to 100% forgiveness of the loan.
75-100 awards per year. Send to above location for details and the qualifications of a "rural" resident. For use both in Alaska and elsewhere.

81

AMERICAN FOUNDATION FOR THE BLIND (Delta Gamma Foundation Florence Harvey Memorial Scholarship)
11 Penn Plaza, Suite 300
New York, NY 10001
212/502-7661; TDD: 212/502-7662; Fax 212/502-7771; E-mail: juliet@afb.org; Internet: www.afb.org

AMOUNT: $1,000
DEADLINE(S): Apr 30
FIELD(S): Rehabilitation and/or education of the visually impaired or blind

Open to legally blind undergraduate and graduate college students of good character who have exhibited academic excellence and are studying in the field of education and/or rehabilitation of the visually impaired and blind.

Must be U.S. citizen. Write or access website for further information. E-mail and fax inquiries must include a complete U.S. postal service mailing address.

82

AMERICAN FOUNDATION FOR THE BLIND (Rudolph Dillman Memorial Scholarship)
11 Penn Plaza, Suite 300
New York, NY 10001
212/502-7661; TDD 212/502-7662; Fax 212/502-7771; E-mail: juliet@afb.org;
Internet: www.afb.org

AMOUNT: $2,500

DEADLINE(S): Apr 30

FIELD(S): Rehabilitation and/or education of the blind

Open to legally blind undergrad or graduate students accepted to or enrolled in an accredited program within the broad areas of rehabilitation and/or education of the blind and visually impaired. U.S. citizen.

3 awards per year. Write or visit website for further information. E-mail and fax inquiries must include a complete U.S. postal service mailing address.

83

AMERICAN INDIAN SCIENCE & ENGINEERING SOCIETY (Burlington Northern Santa Fe Foundation Scholarship)
5661 Airport Blvd.
Boulder, CO 80301
303/939-0023; E-mail: ascholar@spot.colorado.edu; Internet: www.colorado.edu/AISES

AMOUNT: $2,500 per year for up to 4 years

DEADLINE(S): Mar 31

FIELD(S): Business; Education; Science; Health Administration

Open to high school seniors who are 1/4 or more American Indian. Must reside in KS, OK, CO, AZ, NM, MN, OR, SD, ND, WA,

or San Bernardino County, CA (Burlington Northern and Santa Fe Pacific service areas).

Must plan to attend a four-year post-secondary accredited educational institution. Write for complete information or apply online at above website.

84

AMERICAN SPEECH-LANGUAGE-HEARING FOUNDATION (Graduate Student Scholarships)
10801 Rockville Pike
Rockville, MD 20852
301/897-5700; Fax 301/571-0457

AMOUNT: $4,000

DEADLINE(S): Jun 6

FIELD(S): Communication Sciences/Disorders; Speech Pathology; Speech Therapy

Open to full-time graduate students in communication sciences and disorders programs and demonstrating outstanding academic achievement.

Applications available in February.

85

ARKANSAS DEPARTMENT OF HIGHER EDUCATION (Emergency Secondary Education Loan)
114 East Capitol
Little Rock, AR 72201
501/371-2053; 800/547-8839; Fax 501/371-2001; E-mail: lillianw@adhe.arknet.edu

AMOUNT: $2,500

DEADLINE(S): Apr 1

FIELD(S): Secondary education teacher training

Open to full-time undergraduate/graduate students pursuing secondary education teaching certification in foreign language, math, science, or special education. Must attend an approved Arkansas 2- or 4-year public or private college or university. Must be an Arkansas resident.

Repayment of loan is forgiven at 20% for each year taught in approved subject shortage areas in Arkansas secondary schools after graduation.

86

ASSOCIATION FOR EDUCATION & REHABILITATION OF THE BLIND & VISUALLY IMPAIRED (Ferrell Scholarship Fund)
4600 Duke Street, #430
P.O. Box 22397
Alexandria, VA 22304
703/823-9690; Fax 703/823/9695; E-mail: aernet@laser.net

AMOUNT: Varies

DEADLINE(S): Apr 15 (of even-numbered years)

FIELD(S): Career field in services to the blind

Open to legally blind students enrolled in a college or university program related to blind services such as orientation and mobility, special education, rehabilitation teaching, and vision rehabilitation.

For undergraduate, graduate, or postgraduate study. Write for complete information.

87

ASSOCIATION FOR RETARDED CITIZENS (Brazoria County Scholarships)
Highway 2004 & 332
Lake Jackson, TX 77566
Internet:
www.window.state.tx.us/scholars/aid/scholarship/scarcbc.html

AMOUNT: $250

DEADLINE(S): None specified

FIELD(S): Special Education

For two graduating high school seniors from Brazoria County area. Scholarship to be used toward degree in special education.

Apply to above address, giving information concerning your schooling and plans for the future.

88

BUSINESS & PROFESSIONAL WOMEN'S FOUNDATION (Career Advancement Scholarships)
2012 Massachusetts Ave. NW
Washington, D.C. 20036
202/293-1200

AMOUNT: $500-$1,000

DEADLINE(S): Apr 15 (postmark)

FIELD(S): Computer Science; Education; Paralegal; Engineering; Science; Law; Dentistry; Medicine

Open to women (30 or older) within 12-24 months of completing undergrad or grad study in U.S. (including Puerto Rico & Virgin Islands). Studies should lead to entry/reentry in work force or improve career advancement chances.

Not for doctoral study. Must demonstrate financial need. Send self-addressed stamped ($.64) #10 envelope for complete info. Applications available Oct. 1 - April 1.

89

CALIFORNIA STUDENT AID COMMISSION (Child Development Teacher Loan Assumption Program)
Grant Services Division
P.O. Box 419027
Rancho Cordova, CA 95741-9027
916/526-7590

AMOUNT: Loan repayment up to $1,000 per year for 2 years for instructional permit holders; $2,000 per year for 2 years for holders of supervisory permits.

DEADLINE(S): None given

FIELD(S): Early Childhood Education

For repayment of certain student loans for students enrolled in a community college or four-year institution to obtain a Regular Children's Center Instructional Permit or for holders of this permit completing coursework for a B.A. degree and/or working to obtain a Regular Children's Center Supervisor's Permit.

Must agree to provide two consecutive years of full-time service in selected California licensed children's centers within three years of completing the coursework and maintain a 2.0 GPA. For full-time students (at least 12 semester units).

90

CIVIL AIR PATROL (CAP Undergraduate Scholarships)
National Headquarters
Maxwell AFB, AL 36112
334/953-5315

AMOUNT: $750
DEADLINE(S): Jan 31
FIELD(S): Humanities; Science; Engineering; Education

Open to CAP members who have received the Billy Mitchell Award or the senior rating in level II of the senior training program. For undergraduate study in the above areas.
Write for complete information.

91

DR. STANLEY SCHAINKER SCHOLARSHIP AWARD
203 Somerset Drive
Chapel Hill, NC 27514
919/929-1004

AMOUNT: $1,000
DEADLINE(S): Jun 1
FIELD(S): Education

Open to a graduating Salinas (CA) high school senior who plans to pursue a career in education. Must have 3.0 or better GPA and submit 300-word essay on why applicant wants to become a teacher.
Write for complete information.

92

EASTER SEAL SOCIETY OF IOWA, INC. (Scholarships & Awards)
P.O. Box 4002
Des Moines, IA 50333-4002
515/289-1933

AMOUNT: $400-$600
DEADLINE(S): Apr 15
FIELD(S): Physical Rehabilitation, Mental Rehabilitation, and related areas

Open ONLY to Iowa residents who are full-time undergraduate sophomores, juniors, seniors, or graduate students at accredited institutions planning a career in the broad field of rehabilitation. Must indicate financial need and be in top 40% of their class.
6 scholarships per year. Must re-apply each year.

93

FLORIDA DEPT. OF EDUCATION (Critical Teacher Shortage Tuition Reimbursement Program)
Office of Student Financial Assistance
255 Collins
Tallahassee, FL 32399-0400
904/487-0049; Internet:
www.firn.edu/doe/bin00065/home0065.htm

AMOUNT: Tuition reimbursement payments
DEADLINE(S): Varies (Specified on application)
FIELD(S): Education

Open to full-time Florida public school employees certified to teach in Florida and who are teaching or preparing to teach in critical teacher shortage subject areas approved by the State Board of Education. Minimum 3.0 GPA required.
1,800 awards. Will reimburse up to $78 per credit hour for up to 9 hours per academic year for up to a total of 36 credit hours. Applications at district offices and above location.

94

FLORIDA DEPT. OF EDUCATION (Critical Teacher Shortage Student Loan Forgiveness Program)
Office of Student Financial Assistance
255 Collins
Tallahassee, FL 32399-0400
904/487-0049

AMOUNT: $2,500-$5,000 per year
DEADLINE(S): Jul 15
FIELD(S): Teaching
Open to certified Florida public school teachers teaching full-time for the first time. Program provides repayment of education loans in return for teaching in Department of Education designated critical teacher shortage subject areas in Florida public schools. Teachers must apply during first 12 months they are certified and have taught full-time in a critical subject for at least 90 days.
900 awards. Applications are available from district offices or the above location.

95

**FLORIDA DEPT. OF EDUCATION
(Florida Teacher Scholarship & Forgivable Loan Program)**
Office of Student Financial Assistance
255 Collins
Tallahassee, FL 32399-0400
904/487-0049

AMOUNT: $1,500/year (freshmen/sophomore scholarship); $4,000/year (upper division loan); $8,000/year (graduate loan)
DEADLINE(S): Mar 15
FIELD(S): Teaching
Two-year scholarship program provides assistance to lower division undergrads; two-year loan program provides assistance to upper division undergrads & grads and may be repaid through teaching service in critical shortage areas in Florida or in cash.
1,100 annual awards. One student nominated from each public high school and a proportional number from Florida private high schools. Eligibility requirements vary with academic level. Contact Florida Dept. of Education at above location for details.

96

FLORIDA DEPT. OF EDUCATION/U.S. CONGRESS (Paul Douglas Teacher Scholarship Program)
Office of Student Financial Assistance
255 Collins
Tallahassee, FL 32399-0400
904/487-0049

AMOUNT: $5,000/year max
DEADLINE(S): Apr 15 (postmark)
FIELD(S): Teaching
Open to outstanding high school graduates & college students pursuing teaching careers at the preschool; elementary or secondary school levels. Must rank in top 10% of high school graduating class or in top 10% of GED graduates in Florida.
Must be U.S. citizen or eligible non-citizen. Teaching obligation or repayment requirements. Write for complete information.

97

**GENERAL FEDERATION OF WOMEN'S CLUBS OF MASSACHUSETTS
(Newtonville Women's Club Scholarship)**
Box 679
Sudbury, MA 01776-0679
Phone/Fax 508/443-4569

AMOUNT: $600
DEADLINE(S): Mar 1
FIELD(S): Education/Teaching
For a senior in a Massachusetts high school who will study to be a teacher. Send letter of endorsement from president of the sponsoring GFWC of MA club in the community of legal residence, a personal letter, a letter of recommendation from a high school department head or career counselor, and a transcript. A personal interview will be required.
Include SASE with all inquiries and applications.

98

ILLINOIS CONGRESS OF PARENTS AND TEACHERS (Lillian E. Glover Illinois PTA Scholarship Program)
901 S. Spring Street
Springfield, IL 62704
217/528-9617

AMOUNT: $500-$1,000
DEADLINE(S): Mar 1
FIELD(S): Education

Illinois residents. Open to graduating public high school seniors who plan to major in education at an accredited college or university in the U.S. and are in the upper 20% of their class.

2 awards per PTA district, of which there are 25. Applications are available after January 1 at public high schools. Write for complete information.

99

INTERNATIONAL ORDER OF THE ALHAMBRA (Undergraduate Scholarship Grant)
4200 Leeds Ave.
Baltimore, MD 21229-5496
410/242-0660; Fax 410/536-5729

AMOUNT: $400
DEADLINE(S): Jan 1; Jul 1
FIELD(S): Special Education

Open to undergraduate students who will be entering their junior or senior year in an accredited program for teaching the mentally challenged and the handicapped. Tenable in the United States and Canada.

U.S. or Canadian citizenship required. Write for complete information.

100

INTERNATIONAL READING ASSOCIATION (Jeanne S. Chall Research Fellowship)
800 Barksdale Road
P.O. Box 8139
Newark, DE 19714-8139

302/731-1600 Ext. 226; Fax 302/731-1057;
E-mail: research@reading.org

AMOUNT: Varies
DEADLINE(S): Oct 15
FIELD(S): Reading education for children/adults

To encourage and support reading research by promising scholars in these areas: beginning reading; readability; reading difficulties; stages of reading development; relation of vocabulary to reading diagnosing and teaching adults with limited ability.

Program is to honor and carry on the work to which Dr. Jeanne S. Chall has dedicated her academic life.

101

INTERNATIONAL READING ASSOCIATION (Nila Banton Smith Research Dissemination Support Grant)
P.O. Box 8139
Newark, DE 19714-8139
302/731-1600 Ext. 226; 302/731-1057;
E-mail: research@reading.org

AMOUNT: Up to $5,000
DEADLINE(S): Oct 15
FIELD(S): Reading research dissemination activity

To assist any IRA member to spend from 2 to 10 months working on a research dissemination activity.

Contact Gail Keating, Division of Research, at above address.

102

INTERNATIONAL READING ASSOCIATION (Teacher as Researcher Grant)
800 Barksdale Road
P.O. Box 8139
Newark, DE 19714-8139
302/731-1600 Ext. 226; Fax 302/731-1057;
E-mail: research@reading.org

AMOUNT: Up to $5,000

DEADLINE(S): Oct 15

FIELD(S): Reading and literacy instruction

To support teachers in their inquiries about literacy and instruction.

Priority will be given to smaller grants ($1,000-$2,000) to provide support for as many teacher researchers as possible.

103

JOHN A. BURNS FOUNDATION
P.O. Box 1149
Wahiawa, HI 96786
Written inquiry

AMOUNT: $1,000

DEADLINE(S): Ongoing

FIELD(S): Education—teacher training

Scholarships to public high school seniors from Hawaii for the study of education.

Send SASE to Robert C. Oshiro at above address for applications guidelines.

104

KANSAS BOARD OF REGENTS (Kansas Teacher Scholarship)
700 SW Harrison, Suite 1410
Topeka, KS 66603
913/296-3517

AMOUNT: $5,000/year

DEADLINE(S): Mar 15

FIELD(S): Elementary or Secondary Education

For Kansas residents committed to teaching in Kansas. Preference given to students who will teach in special education, secondary science, and vocational/practical arts.

Renewable for up to five years if in a five-year program. Graduate work can be funded if it is required for initial certification. If recipient does not teach in Kansas, the scholarship converts to a loan with 15% interest.

105

MARYLAND HIGHER EDUCATION COMMISSION (Sharon Christa McAuliffe Critical Shortage Teacher Program)
State Scholarship Administration
16 Francis Street
Annapolis, MD 21401-1781
410/974-5370; TTY: 800/735-2258

AMOUNT: Up to $9,600 for tuition, fees, and room & board

DEADLINE(S): Dec 31

FIELD(S): Education (critical shortages determined annually)

For Maryland residents who agree to teach in critical shortage area in Maryland for one year for each year of funding. Open to full- or part-time undergraduates or graduates studying at a Maryland degree-granting institution.

Minimum of 60 credits of undergraduate course work & GPA of 3.0 or better required. Renewable if 3.0 GPA is maintained. Write for complete information.

106

MINNESOTA FEDERATION OF TEACHERS (Flora Rogge College Scholarship)
168 Aurora Ave.
St. Paul, MN 55103
612/227-8583

AMOUNT: $1,000

DEADLINE(S): Mar

FIELD(S): Education

For prospective teachers who are high school seniors. Must be recommended by two senior high school teachers on the basis of financial need, academic achievement, leadership ability, and good character.

Write for complete information.

107

MISSISSIPPI OFFICE OF STATE STUDENT FINANCIAL AID (William Winter Teacher Education Program)
3825 Ridgewood Road
Jackson, MS 39211-6453
601/982-6570; 800-327-2980 (free in Miss.)

AMOUNT: Up to $3,000/year
DEADLINE(S): Jul 1
FIELD(S): Teaching (critical shortage subject areas)

For full-time undergraduate students in a Mississippi college or university who are in a teacher education program which will lead to "Class A" certification. Entering freshmen must have a cumulative high school GPA of 3.0; must maintain GPA of 2.5 or higher in college.

Recipients must agree to teach in a teacher shortage area in Mississippi upon completion of the program.

108

NAACP NATIONAL OFFICE (Sutton Education Scholarship)
4805 Mount Hope Drive
Baltimore, MD 21215-3297
410/486-9133

AMOUNT: $1,000 undergrads; $2,000 grads
DEADLINE(S): Apr 30
FIELD(S): Teacher education

Open to undergrads with a GPA of at least 2.5 and to grads with a GPA of at least 3.0 who are majoring in the field of education. Must be a full-time student and a member of the NAACP.

Renewable if GPA is maintained. Write for complete information; enclose self-addressed 9 x 12 envelope.

109

NATIONAL ASSOCIATION OF AMERICAN BUSINESS CLUBS (AMBUCS Scholarship)
P.O. Box 5127
High Point, NC 27262
910/869-2166; Fax 910/887-8451

AMOUNT: $500-$1,500
DEADLINE(S): Apr 15
FIELD(S): Physical Therapy, Music Therapy, Occupational Therapy, Speech-Language Pathology, Audiology, Rehabilitation, Recreation Therapy, and related areas

Open to undergraduate juniors and seniors or graduate students who have good scholastic standing and plan to enter the fields listed above. GPA of 3.0 or better (4.0 scale) and U.S. citizenship required. Must demonstrate financial need.

Renewable. Please include a self-addressed stamped envelope; applications are mailed in December; incomplete applications will not be considered.

110

NATIONAL COLLEGIATE ATHLETIC ASSOCIATION (NCAA Ethnic Minority and Women's Enhancement Program)
6201 College Blvd.
Overland Park, KS 66211
913/339-1906

AMOUNT: $6,000
DEADLINE(S): Feb 15
FIELD(S): Sports Administration; Coaching; Sports Medicine; Officiating

Scholarships for women and ethnic minorities entering the first semester of initial post-graduate studies in the above or related fields. Internships of approximately one year at the NCAA national office.

Write for complete information.

111

NATIONAL FEDERATION OF THE BLIND (Educator of Tomorrow Award)
805 Fifth Ave.
Grinnell, IA 50112
515/236-3366

AMOUNT: $3,000
DEADLINE(S): Mar 31
FIELD(S): Elementary, Secondary, or Post-Secondary Teaching

Open to legally blind student pursuing or planning to pursue a full time post-secondary course of study that leads to a career in elementary, secondary, or post-secondary teaching.

Award is based on academic excellence, service to the community, and financial need. Write for complete information.

112

NATIONAL STRENGTH & CONDITIONING ASSN. (Challenge Scholarships)
P.O. Box 38909
Colorado Springs, CO 80937-8909
719/632-6722; Fax 719/632-6722; E-mail: nsca@usa.net; Internet: www.colosoft.com/nsca

AMOUNT: $1,000
DEADLINE(S): Mar 1
FIELD(S): Fields related to body strength & conditioning

Open to National Strength & Conditioning Association members. Awards are for undergraduate or graduate study.

For membership information or an application, write to the above address.

113

NORTH CAROLINA ASSOCIATION OF EDUCATORS (Mary Morrow Scholarship)
P.O. Box 27347
700 S. Salisbury Street
Raleigh, NC 27611
919/832-3000

AMOUNT: $1,000
DEADLINE(S): Jan 13
FIELD(S): Education—Teaching

Awards given in junior year to students in an accredited North Carolina undergraduate institution for use in their senior year. Recipients must live in North Carolina & agree to teach in the state for at least 2 years after graduation.

Financial need is a consideration. 4-7 scholarships per year. Apply in junior year of college. Write for complete information.

114

NORTH CAROLINA DEPARTMENT OF PUBLIC INSTRUCTION (Scholarship Loan Program for Prospective Teachers)
301 N. Wilmington Street
Raleigh, NC 27601-2825
919/715-1120

AMOUNT: Up to $2,500/year
DEADLINE(S): Feb
FIELD(S): Education: Teaching, School Psychology and Counseling, Speech/Language Impaired, Audiology, Library/Media Services

For NC residents planning to teach in NC public schools. At least 3.0 high school GPA required; must maintain 2.5 GPA during freshman year and 3.0 cumulative thereafter. Recipients are obligated to teach one year in a NC public school for each year of assistance. Those who do not fulfill their teaching obligation are required to repay the loan plus interest.

200 awards per year. For full-time students. Applications available in Dec. from high school counselors and college and university departments of education.

115

OREGON PTA (Teacher Education Scholarships)
531 S.E. 14th
Portland, OR 97214
503/234-3928

27

AMOUNT: $250 (renewable 3 times)

DEADLINE(S): Mar 1

FIELD(S): Education

Open to outstanding students who are Oregon residents and are preparing to teach in Oregon at the elementary or secondary school level. The scholarships may be used for any Oregon public college where credits transfer for higher education.

Scholarships based on scholastic record, leadership, citizenship and need. Preference given to students with PTA connection. Send self-addressed stamped envelope for application.

116

PHI DELTA KAPPA (Scholarship Grants for Prospective Educators)
408 N. Union
P.O. Box 789
Bloomington, IN 47402-0789
812/339-1156; Fax 812/339-0018; E-mail: headquarters@PDKintl.org; Internet: www.PDKintl.org

AMOUNT: $1,000-$5,000

DEADLINE(S): Jan 31

FIELD(S): Education/Teaching Career

Undergraduate scholarships for high school seniors who plan to pursue a college major in education and to become teachers.

51 annual awards.

117

PHI DELTA KAPPA INC. (Scholarship Grants for Prospective Educators)
P.O. Box 789
8th & Union Ave.
Bloomington, IN 47402-0789
Written inquiry

AMOUNT: $1,000 (45); $2,000 (1); $5,000 (1); $4,000 (1)

DEADLINE(S): Jan 31

FIELD(S): Education—Teacher training

Open to high school seniors who plan to pursue careers as teachers or educators. Based on scholastic achievement, school/community activities, recommendations, and an essay. U.S. or Canadian citizen or legal resident.

Minimum of 47 scholarships per year. Send SASE to the attention of Scholarship Grants for complete information.

118

ROCKEFELLER BROTHERS FUND (Fellowships for Minority Students Entering the Teaching Profession)
Contact your participating school or the following web address:
E-mail: kskaggs@rbf.org; Internet: www.rbf.org/rbf/fellows.html

AMOUNT: $2,500 (summer project), $8,000-$9,000/yr (stipend after summer for graduate work); $1,200/yr (up to three years for loan repayment during teaching career)

DEADLINE(S): Dec 31

FIELD(S): Elementary/Secondary Education

For junior-year minority students in the arts and sciences to become teachers. Must be enrolled at a participating institution and have a mentor from there.

25 fellows/year. Applications, transcripts, and letters of recommendation must be filed with the school.

119

STATE STUDENT ASSISTANCE COMMISSION OF INDIANA (Scholarships for Special Education Teachers and Physical or Occupational Therapists)
150 W. Market Street, 5th Floor
Indianapolis, IN 46204
317/232-2350; Fax 317/232-3260; E-mail: grants@ssaci.in.us; Internet: www.ai.org/ssaci/

AMOUNT: $1,000

DEADLINE(S): Varies (with college)

FIELD(S): Education

For Indiana residents working toward degrees in special education or physical or occupational therapy. For full-time undergraduate or graduate study at an Indiana college. U.S.

citizenship and GPA of 2.0 or better (4.0 scale) is required.

Must demonstrate financial need (FAF). Indiana residency required.

120

STATE STUDENT ASSISTANCE COMMISSION OF INDIANA (Minority Teacher & Special Education Teacher Scholarship Program)
150 W. Market Street, 5th Floor
Indianapolis, IN 46204
317/232-2350; Fax 317/232-3260; E-mail: grants@ssaci.in.us; Internet: www.ai.org/ssaci/

AMOUNT: $1,000
DEADLINE(S): Varies (with college)
FIELD(S): Education
For black or Hispanic Indiana residents working toward a teaching certificate and who plan to enter the teaching field. For full-time undergraduate or graduate study at an Indiana college. GPA of 2.0 or better (4.0 scale) is required. U.S. citizenship.
Must demonstrate financial need (FAF). Indiana residency required. Must agree to teach 3 out of 5 years in the state of Indiana.

121

TECHNOLOGY STUDENT ASSOCIATION (Scholarships)
1914 Association Drive
Reston, VA 22091
703/860-9000

AMOUNT: $250 to $500
DEADLINE(S): May 1
FIELD(S): Technology Education
Open to student members of the Technology Student Association who can demonstrate financial need. Grade point average is NOT a consideration but applicants must be accepted to a 4-year college or university.

Funds are sent to and administered by the recipient's college or university. Write for complete information.

122

TENNESSEE STUDENT ASSISTANCE CORPORATION (Minority Teaching Fellows Program)
404 James Robertson Parkway
Nashville, TN 37243-0820
615/741-1346; 800/342-1663

AMOUNT: $5,000 per year; max. $20,000
DEADLINE(S): Apr 15
FIELD(S): Teacher education
For minority Tennessee residents who are entering freshmen attending a Tennessee institution studying to be teachers. Must agree to teach at a K-12 level Tennessee public school one year for each year the award is received.
Must be in top 25% of class or at least 18 on ACT or 850 on SAT. Apply at high school guidance office, financial aid office, or TSAC (above).

123

TENNESSEE STUDENT ASSISTANCE CORPORATION (Tennessee Teaching Scholars Program)
Suite 1950, Parkway Towers
404 James Robertson Parkway
Nashville, TN 37243-0820
615/741-1346; 800/342-1663

AMOUNT: $3,000 forgivable loan
DEADLINE(S): Apr 15
FIELD(S): Education
A $3,000 forgivable loan to college seniors, juniors, and post-baccalaureate students admitted to state-approved teacher education programs at a Tennessee institution of higher education. Applicants must pledge to teach at the public preschoool, elementary, or secondary level one year for each year the award is received.

Contact the school financial aid office, teacher education program or write to the above address for complete information.

124

THE ROOTHBERT FUND, INC.
(Scholarships and Grants)
475 Riverside Drive, Room 252
New York, NY 10015
212/870-3116

AMOUNT: $500-$2,000

DEADLINE(S): Feb 1

FIELD(S): Education—teacher training

Scholarships for undergraduates and graduate students pursuing teaching as a vocation, who are primarily motivated by spiritual values, and who need financial aid to further their education. Must be able to attend an interview in March in New York City, Washington, D.C., New Haven, or Philadelphia. Recipients are called Roothbert Fellows and may receive grants for projects after their education is completed. High scholastic achievement required. For study in the U.S.

20 awards yearly. Renewable. Send SASE (#10 envelope) to above address for application.

125

UNITED COMMERCIAL TRAVELERS OF AMERICA (Retarded Citizens Teacher Scholarships)
632 North Park Street
P.O. Box 159019
Columbus, OH 43215-8619
614/228-3276

AMOUNT: $750/year

DEADLINE(S): None

FIELD(S): Special Education

Open to undergraduate juniors and seniors, graduate students, teachers, and persons who plan to teach the mentally challenged in the U.S. or Canada. Awards tenable at accredited institutions. U.S. or Canadian citizenship required.

Approximately 500 awards per year. Preference (but not limited) to UCT members. Write for complete information.

126

UTAH STATE OFFICE OF EDUCATION
(T. H. Bell Teaching Incentive Loan Program)
Office of Certification
250 E. 500 So.
Salt Lake City, UT 84111
801/538-7741

AMOUNT: Full tuition

DEADLINE(S): Mar 30

FIELD(S): Education—teacher training

Student loans for outstanding seniors at a Utah high school who plan to attend a Utah college. Also for college-level juniors and seniors studying to become teachers.

Approx. 150 scholarships per year. High school seniors should get an application from their high school counselors after Jan. 15.

127

WISCONSIN CONGRESS OF PARENTS AND TEACHERS INC. (Brookmire-Hastings Scholarships)
4797 Hayes Road, Suite 2
Madison, WI 53704-3256
608/244-1455

AMOUNT: $1,000

DEADLINE(S): Feb 15

FIELD(S): Education; Teaching

Open to Wisconsin residents who are seniors in public high schools. Awarded to outstanding high school graduates who intend to pursue a career in the field of child care/education.

See your high school principal or counselor after Dec. 1 for application.

128

WOMEN'S SPORTS FOUNDATION (Jackie Joyner-Kersee/Ray Ban Minority Internship)
Eisenhower Park
East Meadow, NY 11554
800/227-3988; E-mail: wosport@aol.com;
Internet: www.lifetimetv.com/WoSport

AMOUNT: $4,000-$5,000
DEADLINE(S): Ongoing
FIELD(S): Sports/Physical Education/Sports-Related Careers

For women of color who are undergraduates, college graduates, graduate students, or women in career change to provide an opportunity to gain experience in a sports-related career and interact in the sports community.
The Foundation works to improve public understanding of the benefits of sports and fitness for females of all ages.

129

WOMEN'S SPORTS FOUNDATION (Zina Garrison/Visa Minority Internship)
Eisenhower Park
East Meadow, NY 11554
800/227-3988; E-mail: wosport@aol.com;
Internet: www.lifetimetv.com/WoSport

AMOUNT: $4,000-$5,000
DEADLINE(S): Ongoing
FIELD(S): Sports/Physical Education/Sports-Related Careers

For women of color who are undergraduates, college graduates, graduate students, or women in career change to provide an opportunity to gain experience in a sports-related career and interact in the sports community.
The Foundation works to improve public understanding of the benefits of sports and fitness for females of all ages.

130

Y'S MEN INTERNATIONAL; U.S. AREA (Alexander Scholarship Loan Fund)
7242 Natural Bridge Road
Normandy, MO 63121
Written inquiry only

AMOUNT: $1,000 to $1,500 per year
DEADLINE(S): May 1; Oct 1
FIELD(S): Business Administration; Youth Leadership

Open to U.S. citizens or permanent residents with a strong desire to pursue professional YMCA service. For undergrads or grad students (YMCA staff only). Financial need must be demonstrated.
Repayment of loan is waived if recipient enters YMCA employment after graduation. Write for complete information.

131

ZETA PHI BETA SORORITY, INC. NATIONAL EDUCATION FOUNDATION (Isabel M. Herson Scholarship in Education)
1734 New Hampshire Ave. NW
Washington, D.C. 20009
Written inquiry

AMOUNT: $500-$1,000
DEADLINE(S): Feb 1
FIELD(S): Elementary and Secondary Education

For graduate or undergraduate students enrolled in a degree program in either elementary or secondary education. For full-time study for one academic year.
Send for application with SASE. Apply between Sept. 1 and Feb. 1 preceding the academic year. Process includes acquiring letters of recommendation, providing transcripts, and writing an essay.

SCHOOL OF ENGINEERING

132

ALEXANDER GRAHAM BELL ASSOCIATION FOR THE DEAF (Robert H. Weitbrecht Scholarship Award)
3417 Volta Place
Washington, D.C. 20007
202/337-5220; E-mail: Agbell2@aol.com

AMOUNT: $750

DEADLINE(S): Apr 1

FIELD(S): Engineering/Science

Open to oral deaf students who were born with a profound hearing impairment or who suffered such a loss before acquiring language. Must be accepted into a full-time academic program for hearing students and studying science or engineering. North America citizenship preferred

Write for complete information.

133

AMERICAN CONSULTING ENGINEERS COUNCIL (Scholarships)
1015 15th Street NW, Suite 802
Washington, D.C. 20005
202/347-7474; Fax 202/898-0068; E-mail: acec@acec.org; Internet: www.acec.org

AMOUNT: $2,500-$5,000

DEADLINE(S): None given

FIELD(S): All engineering fields

For engineering students who are junior and senior undergraduates or graduates.

Contact Francis George at above address.

134

AMERICAN INSTITUTE OF CHEMICAL ENGINEERS (Washington Internships for Students in Engineering)
1300 I Street NW, Suite 1090E
Washington, D.C. 20005
202/962-8690; Fax 202/962-8699

AMOUNT: $1,400 stipend plus travel allowance and housing

DEADLINE(S): Dec

FIELD(S): Engineering—all fields

Many engineering societies sponsor this program. Third-year students are selected in a nationwide competition to spend 10 weeks in Washington, D.C. learning about the interaction between the engineering community and the government.

Write to: Internships for Students in Engineering (WISE) at above address.

135

AMERICAN SOCIETY OF NAVAL ENGINEERS (Scholarship)
1452 Duke Street
Alexandria, VA 22314-3458
703/836-6727

AMOUNT: $2,000

DEADLINE(S): Feb 15

FIELD(S): Naval Engineering

For U.S. citizens who are senior status full-time undergraduate, graduate, or post-graduate students. Selection is based on academic record, work history, professional promise, interest in naval engineering, extracurricular activities and recommendations of college faculty. Examples of programs of study which apply to naval engineering are naval architecture; marine, mechanical, civil, aeronautical, ocean, electrical and electronic engineering; and physical sciences.

Write to Dennis Pignotti at above address. 12-18 awards yearly.

136

ARTHUR & DOREEN PARRETT SCHOLARSHIP TRUST FUND (Scholarships)
c/o U.S. Bank of Washington
P.O. Box 720
Trust Dept. 8th Floor
Seattle, WA 98111-0720
206/344-4653

AMOUNT: Up to $3,500

DEADLINE(S): Jul 31

FIELD(S): Engineering; Science; Medicine; Dentistry

Washington state resident who has completed her/his first year of college by July 31. Open to students enrolled in above schools. Awards tenable at any accredited undergrad college or university.

Approximately 15 awards per year. Write for complete information.

137

AT&T BELL LABORATORIES (Summer Research Program for Minorities & Women)
101 Crawfords Corner Road
Holmdel, NJ 07733-3030
Written inquiry

AMOUNT: Salary + travel & living expenses for summer
DEADLINE(S): Dec 1
FIELD(S): Engineering; Math; Sciences; Computer Science

Program offers minority students & women students technical employment experience at Bell Laboratories. Students should have completed their third year of study at an accredited college or university. U.S. citizen or permanent resident.

Selection is based partially on academic achievement and personal motivation. Write special programs manager—SRP for complete information.

138

BOYS & GIRLS CLUBS OF SAN DIEGO (Spence Reese Scholarship Fund)
1761 Hotel Circle So., Suite 123
San Diego, CA 92108
619/298-3520

AMOUNT: $2,000 per year for 4 years
DEADLINE(S): May 15
FIELD(S): Medicine; Law; Engineering; Political Science

Open to male high school seniors planning a career in above fields. Girls and Boys Club affiliation is not required.

Applications are available in January. Must enclose a self-addressed stamped envelope to receive application. A $10 processing fee is required with completed application. Write for complete information.

139

BUSINESS & PROFESSIONAL WOMEN'S FOUNDATION (BPW Loans for Women in Engineering Studies)
2012 Massachusetts Ave. NW
Washington, D.C. 20036
202/293-1200

AMOUNT: Up to $5,000 per year
DEADLINE(S): Apr 15 (postmark)
FIELD(S): Engineering

Open to women accepted for undergraduate or graduate study in a program accredited by the Accrediting Board for Engineering and Technology. For last 2 years of study. U.S. citizenship required.

Must demonstrate financial need. Applications available between October 1 & April 1 ONLY. Send double-stamped self-addressed envelope for complete information.

140

BUSINESS & PROFESSIONAL WOMEN'S FOUNDATION (Career Advancement Scholarships)
2012 Massachusetts Ave. NW
Washington, D.C. 20036
202/293-1200

AMOUNT: $500-$1,000
DEADLINE(S): Apr 15 (postmark)
FIELD(S): Computer Science; Education; Paralegal; Engineering; Science; Law; Dentistry; Medicine

Open to women (30 or older) within 12-24 months of completing undergrad or grad study in U.S. (including Puerto Rico & Virgin Islands). Studies should lead to entry/reentry in work force or improve career advancement chances.

Not for doctoral study. Must demonstrate financial need. Send self-addressed stamped ($.64) #10 envelope for complete info. Applications available Oct. 1 - April 1.

141

BUSINESS & PROFESSIONAL WOMEN'S FOUNDATION EDUCATIONAL PROGRAMS (BPW Loan Fund for Women in Engineering Studies)

2012 Massachusetts Ave. NW
Washington, D.C. 20036
202/293-1200 Ext. 169

AMOUNT: Up to $5,000 per academic year
DEADLINE(S): Apr 15
FIELD(S): Engineering

For women 25+ (U.S. citizens) in their final 2 years of an engineering program accredited by the Accreditation Board of Engineering and Technology. Part- or full-time. Applicants must carry at least 6 semester hours each semester.

Interest of 7% per annum begins immediately after graduation. To be repaid in 20 equal quarterly installments commencing 12 months after graduation.

142

CIVIL AIR PATROL (CAP Undergraduate Scholarships)

National Headquarters
Maxwell AFB, AL 36112
334/953-5315

AMOUNT: $750
DEADLINE(S): Jan 31
FIELD(S): Humanities; Science; Engineering; Education

Open to CAP members who have received the Billy Mitchell Award or the senior rating in level II of the senior training program. For undergraduate study in the above areas.

Write for complete information.

143

COMMITTEE ON INSTITUTIONAL COOPERATION (CIC Pre-doctoral Fellowships)

Kirkwood Hall 111
Indiana University
Bloomington, IN 47405
812/855-0823

AMOUNT: $11,000 + tuition (4 years)
DEADLINE(S): Dec 1
FIELD(S): Humanities; Social Sciences; Natural Sciences; Mathematics; Engineering

Pre-doctoral fellowships for U.S. citizens of African-American, American Indian, Mexican-American, or Puerto Rican heritage. Must hold or expect to receive bachelor's degree by late summer from a regionally accredited college or university.

Awards for specified universities in IL; IN; IA; MI; MN; OH; WI; PA. Write for details.

144

CONRAIL-CONSOLIDATED RAIL CORPORATION (Frank Thomson Scholarships for Males)

Attn: Nancy Hoernig
2001 Market Street (18B)
P.O. Box 41418
Philadelphia, PA 19101-1418
215/209-1764

AMOUNT: $2,000
DEADLINE(S): Apr 1
FIELD(S): Engineering

Open ONLY to high school seniors who are sons of ConRail or predecessor railroad company employees. Must take SAT and certain achievement tests.

Approximately 12 scholarships awarded on basis of both financial need and competitive exams. Renewable up to 4 years. Write for complete information.

145

CONSULTING ENGINEERS AND LAND SURVEYORS OF CALIFORNIA (Undergraduate Scholarship)
1303 J Street, Suite 370
Sacramento, CA 95814
916/441-7991; Fax 916/441-6312; E-mail: staff@celsoc.org; Internet: www.celsoc.org

AMOUNT: $3,000-$5,000 and $7,500
DEADLINE(S): Feb 17
FIELD(S): Engineering; Land Surveying

For U.S. citizens working toward a B.A. degree in an accredited Board for Engineering and Technology-approved engineering program or in an accredited land surveying program in California. Must be entering their junior, senior, or fifth year in a five-year program. Must have a 3.5 GPA in engineering courses and 3.2 GPA overall.

Send for list of eligible colleges/universities and application information.

146

CONSULTING ENGINEERS COUNCIL OF NEW JERSEY (Louis Goldberg Scholarship Fund)
66 Morris Ave.
Springfield, NJ 07081
973/564-5848; Fax 973/564-7480

AMOUNT: $1,000
DEADLINE(S): Jan 1
FIELD(S): Engineering; Land Surveying

Open to undergraduate students who have completed at least two years of study (or fifth year in a five-year program) at an ABET-accredited college or university in New Jersey, are in top half of their class, and are considering a career as a consulting engineer or land surveyor. Must be U.S. citizen.

Recipients will be eligible for American Consulting Engineers Council national scholarships of $2,000 to $5,000. Write for complete information.

147

GENERAL LEARNING COMMUNICATIONS (Sponsored by Dupont, GLC, and the NSTA Science Essay Awards Programs)
900 Skokie Blvd., Suite 200
Northbrook, IL 60062
847/205-3000

AMOUNT: Up to $1,500
DEADLINE(S): Jan 31
FIELD(S): Sciences

Annual essay competition open to students in grades 7-12 in U.S. and Canada. Cash awards for 1st, 2nd, and honorable mention. 1st-place essayists, their science teacher, and a parent receive trip to space center in Houston, April 27-29.

Contact your science teacher or address above for complete information. Official entry blank must accompany essay entry.

148

H. FLETCHER BROWN FUND (Scholarships)
c/o PNC Bank
Trust Dept.
P.O. Box 791
Wilmington, DE 19899
302/429-2827

AMOUNT: Varies
DEADLINE(S): Apr 15
FIELD(S): Medicine; Dentistry; Law; Engineering; Chemistry

Open to U.S. citizens born and still residing in Delaware. For 4 years of study (undergrad or grad) leading to a degree that enables applicant to practice in chosen field.

Scholarships are based on need, scholastic achievement and good moral character. Applications available in February. Write for complete information.

149

ILLUMINATING ENGINEERING SOCIETY OF NORTH AMERICA (Robert W. Thunen Memorial Scholarships)
IES Golden Gate Section
460 Brannen Street
P.O. Box 77527
San Francisco, CA 94107-1527
Written inquiry

AMOUNT: $2,500
DEADLINE(S): Mar 1
FIELD(S): Illumination (Architectural; Commercial; Residential; Airport; Navigational; Theatrical or TV; Vision; etc.)

Open to junior and senior undergrads or grad students who are studying illumination full-time at an accredited 4-year college or university in Northern California or Nevada, Oregon, or Washington.
This scholarship is intended to cover any and all fields of lighting. Write for complete information.

150

JOSEPH BLAZEK FOUNDATION (Scholarships)
8 South Michigan Ave.
Chicago, IL 60603
312/372-3880

AMOUNT: $750 per year for 4 years
DEADLINE(S): Feb 1
FIELD(S): Science; Chemistry; Engineering; Mathematics; Physics

Open to residents of Cook County (Illinois) who are high school seniors planning to study in the above fields at a four-year college or university.
20 scholarships per year. Renewable. Write for complete information.

151

NATIONAL ACTION COUNCIL FOR MINORITIES IN ENGINEERING-NACME INC. (Incentive Grants Program)
3 West 35th Street, 3rd floor
New York, NY 10001
212/279-2626; Fax 212/629-5178

AMOUNT: $500-$3,000
DEADLINE(S): Varies (Set by colleges)
FIELD(S): Engineering

Open to American Indian; African-American; Mexican-American; or Puerto Rican. Demonstrate need or be designated to receive a merit award. For full-time enrollment in one of the participating colleges. U.S. citizen or permanent resident.
Must be an entering freshman or transfer student for the initial award. Write for complete information & list of participating colleges.

152

NATIONAL COUNCIL OF STATE GARDEN CLUBS, INC. (Scholarships)
4401 Magnolia Ave.
St. Louis, MO 63110-3492
314/776-7574; Fax 314/776-5108; E-mail: scsgc.franm@worldnet.att.net; Internet: www.gardenclub.org

AMOUNT: $3,500
DEADLINE(S): Mar 1
FIELD(S): Horticulture, Floriculture, Landscape Design, City Planning, Land Management, and allied subjects

Open to junior, seniors and graduate students who are U.S. citizens and are studying any of the above or related subjects. Student must have the endorsement of the state in which he/she resides permanently. Applications will be forwarded to the National State Chairman and judged on a national level.
32 scholarships are awarded. Write to the above address for complete information.

153

**NATIONAL FEDERATION OF THE
BLIND (Frank Walton Horn Memorial
Scholarship)**
805 Fifth Ave.
Grinnell, IA 50112
515/236-3366

AMOUNT: $3,000

DEADLINE(S): Mar 31

FIELD(S): All fields of study—preference to
architecture or engineering students

Scholarship for legally blind students studying
(or planning to study) at any post-secondary level. For all fields of study but preference will be given to architecture and
engineering majors.

Awards based on academic excellence, service
to the community, financial need. Write for
complete information.

154

**NATIONAL FEDERATION OF THE
BLIND**
805 Fifth Ave.
Grinnell, IA 50112
515/236-3366

AMOUNT: Varies

DEADLINE(S): Mar 31

FIELD(S): All fields of study-preference to
architecture or engineering students.

Scholarship for legally blind students studying
(or planning to study) at any post-secondary level. For all fields of study but preference will be given to architecture and
engineering majors.

Awards based on academic excellence, service
to the community, financial need. Write for
complete information.

155

**NATIONAL FEDERATION OF THE
BLIND (Howard Brown Rickard Scholarship)**
805 Fifth Ave.
Grinnell, IA 50112

515/236-3366

AMOUNT: $3,000

DEADLINE(S): Mar 31

FIELD(S): Natural Sciences; Architecture;
Engineering; Medicine; Law

Scholarships for undergraduate or graduate
study in the above areas. Open to legally
blind students enrolled full-time at accredited post-secondary institutions.

Awards based on academic excellence, service
to the community, and financial need. Write
for complete information.

156

**NATIONAL ITALIAN AMERICAN
FOUNDATION (Alexander Defilippis
Scholarship)**
1860 19th Street NW
Washington, D.C. 20009
202/530-5315

AMOUNT: $1,000

DEADLINE(S): May 31

FIELD(S): Engineering

For undergraduate engineering students of
Italian ancestry attending Virginia
Polytechnic Institute.

Scholastic merit, financial need, and community service are considered.

157

**NATIONAL ITALIAN AMERICAN
FOUNDATION (Raytheon Engineering
Scholarship)**
Dr. M. Lombardo, Education Director
1860 19th Street NW
Washington, D.C. 20009
202/387-0600

AMOUNT: $1,000

DEADLINE(S): May 31

FIELD(S): Engineering

Open to undergraduate and graduate students
of Italian heritage who are majoring in
engineering. Application requires evidence
of financial need and an essay (1 typed page

School of Engineering

maximum) describing student's Italian background.
Write for complete information.

158

NEW YORK STATE HIGHER EDUCATION SERVICES CORPORATION (N.Y. State Regents Professional/Health Care Opportunity Scholarships)
Cultural Education Center, Room 5C64
Albany, NY 12230
518/486-1319; Internet: www.hesc.com

AMOUNT: $1,000-$10,000/year

DEADLINE(S): Varies

FIELD(S): Medicine and Dentistry and related fields; Architecture; Nursing; Psychology; Audiology; Landscape Architecture; Social Work; Chiropractic; Law; Pharmacy; Accounting; Speech Language Pathology

For NY state residents who are economically disadvantaged and members of a minority group underrepresented in the chosen profession and attending school in NY state. Some programs carry a service obligation in New York for each year of support. For U.S. citizens or qualifying noncitizens.

Medical/dental scholarships require one year of professional work in NY.

159

NEW YORK STATE HIGHER EDUCATION SERVICES CORPORATION
Cultural Education Center, Room 5C64
Albany, NY 12230
518/486-1319; Internet: www.hesc.com

AMOUNT: Varies

DEADLINE(S): Varies

FIELD(S): Medicine and Dentistry and related fields; Architecture; Nursing; Psychology; Audiology; Landscape architecture; Social Work; Chiropractic; Law; Pharmacy; Accounting; Speech Language Pathology

For NY state residents who are economically disadvantaged and members of a minority group underrepresented in the chosen profession and attending school in NY state. Some programs carry a service obligation in New York for each year of support. For U.S. citizens or qualifying noncitizens.

Medical/dental scholarships require one year of professional work in NY.

160

NORTH CAROLINA STUDENT LOAN PROGRAM FOR HEALTH, SCIENCE, & MATHEMATICS (Loans)
3824 Barrett Drive, Suite 304
Raleigh, NC 27619
919/733-2164

AMOUNT: $2,500-$7,500 per year

DEADLINE(S): Jan 8 (Application available then. Deadline is May 5)

FIELD(S): Health Professions; Sciences; Engineering

Low-interest scholarship loans open to North Carolina residents of at least 1 year who are pursuing an associate, undergraduate or graduate degree in the above fields at an accredited institution in the U.S.

Loans may be retired after graduation by working (1 year for each year funded) at designated institutions. Write for complete details.

161

PACIFIC GAS & ELECTRIC CO. (Scholarships for High School Seniors)
77 Beale Street, Room 2837
San Francisco, CA 94106
415/973-1338

AMOUNT: $1,000-$4,000

DEADLINE(S): Nov 15

FIELD(S): Engineering; Computer Science; Mathematics; Marketing; Business; Economics

High school seniors in good academic standing who reside in or attend high school in areas served by PG&E are eligible to compete for scholarships awarded on a regional basis. Not open to children of PG&E employees. 36 awards per year. Applications & brochures are available in all high schools within PG&E's service area and at PG&E offices.

162

ROBERT SCHRECK MEMORIAL FUND (Grants)
c/o Texas Commerce Bank—Trust Dept
P.O. Drawer 140
El Paso, TX 79980
915/546-6515

AMOUNT: $500-$1,500
DEADLINE(S): Jul 15; Nov 15
FIELD(S): Medicine; Veterinary Medicine; Physics; Chemistry; Architecture; Engineering; Episcopal Clergy

Grants to undergraduate juniors or seniors or graduate students who have been residents of El Paso County for at least two years. Must be U.S. citizen or legal resident and have a high grade point average. Financial need is a consideration.
Write for complete information.

163

SOCIETY OF AUTOMOTIVE ENGINEERS (SAE Engineering Scholarships)
400 Commonwealth Drive
Warrendale, PA 15096-0001
412/772-8534; 412/776-2103; E-mail: lorile@sae.org

AMOUNT: $500-$6,000
DEADLINE(S): Dec 1
FIELD(S): Engineering and related sciences
For U.S. citizens who are undergraduates pursuing a degree in engineering or related sciences. 3.25 minimum GPA.
60 annual awards. Renewable.

164

SOCIETY OF AUTOMOTIVE ENGINEERS (SAE Scholarships)
400 Commonwealth Drive
Warrendale, PA 15096-0001
412/772-8534; 412/776-2103

AMOUNT: $500 to full tuition
DEADLINE(S): Dec 1
FIELD(S): Engineering and related sciences
For high school seniors who are U.S. citizens pursuing an engineering program accredited by ABET. Must have 3.25 GPA or better & rank in the 90th percentile for SAT and/or ACT scores.
50 awards yearly. Write to Lori Pail, Engineering Scholarships, at above location for details.

165

SOCIETY OF AUTOMOTIVE ENGINEERS (Yanmar/SAE Scholarship)
400 Commonwealth Drive
Warrendale, PA 15096-0001
412/772-8534

AMOUNT: $1,000 for each of two years
DEADLINE(S): Apr 1
FIELD(S): Engineering specialties related to conservation of energy in transportation, agriculture, and construction, and power generation

For citizens of North America entering their senior year of undergraduate engineering or enrolled in a graduate program of engineering or related science.
One annual award. Renewable for second year. Applications available in January. Contact Lori Pail, Yanmar/SAE Scholarship, at above location.

166

SOCIETY OF HISPANIC PROFESSIONAL ENGINEERS FOUNDATION (SHPE Scholarships)
5400 E. Olympic Blvd., Suite 210
Los Angeles, CA 90022

213/888-2080

AMOUNT: $500 to $3,000

DEADLINE(S): Apr 15

FIELD(S): Engineering & Science

Open to deserving students of Hispanic descent who are seeking careers in engineering and science. For full-time undergraduate or graduate study at a college or university. Academic achievement and financial need are considerations.

Send a self-addressed stamped envelope to request an application.

167

SOCIETY OF WOMEN ENGINEERS
(Admiral Grace Murray Hopper Scholarship)
120 Wall Street, 11th Floor
New York, NY 10005
212/509-9577; Fax 212/509-0224

AMOUNT: $1,000

DEADLINE(S): May 15 (postmark)

FIELD(S): Engineering; Computer Science

For women entering a four-year program for the study of engineering or computer science as freshmen. Applications available March-May.

5 awards. Send self-addressed stamped envelope for complete information.

168

SOCIETY OF WOMEN ENGINEERS (Ann Maureen Whitney Barrow Memorial Scholarship)
120 Wall Street, 11th Floor
New York, NY 10005
800/666-ISWE; 212/509-9577; Fax 212/509-0224

AMOUNT: $5,000 (approx.)

DEADLINE(S): May 15 (postmark)

FIELD(S): Engineering; Computer Science; Engineering Technology

Open to undergraduate women entering a program of study in engineering, computer science, or engineering technology. Award is renewable yearly until completion of the undergraduate degree.

Applications available March-May only with completed application and supporting materials to be postmarked by May 15. Send self-addressed stamped envelope for complete information.

169

SOCIETY OF WOMEN ENGINEERS
(Chrysler Corporation Re-entry Scholarship)
120 Wall Street, 11th Floor
New York, NY 10005-3902
212/509-9577; Fax 212/509-0224

AMOUNT: $2,000

DEADLINE(S): May 15

FIELD(S): Engineering; Computer Science

For women who have been out of the engineer job market and/or out of school for a minimum of two years.

Send SASE for applications between March and May. Completed applications MUST be postmarked by May 15.

170

SOCIETY OF WOMEN ENGINEERS
(Chrysler Corporation Scholarships)
120 Wall Street, 11th Floor
New York, NY 10005-3902
212/509-9577; Fax 212/509-0224

AMOUNT: $1,500

DEADLINE(S): May 15

FIELD(S): Engineering; Computer Science

Open to women entering an ABET-accredited school as freshmen majoring in engineering or computer science.

2 awards. Send self-addressed stamped envelope between March and May for info.

171

SOCIETY OF WOMEN ENGINEERS
(Chrysler Corporation Scholarship)
120 Wall Street, 11th Floor
New York, NY 10005-3902
212/509-9577; Fax 212/509-9577

AMOUNT: $1,750
DEADLINE(S): Feb 1
FIELD(S): Engineering; Computer Science
The Chrysler Corporation Scholarship is designated for a sophomore, junior or senior woman who is a minority or member of an under-represented group. Applicants must have a 3.5 GPA or higher and be studying engineering or computer science.
Send a self-addressed, stamped envelope to the above address between Oct.-Jan. for complete information.

172

SOCIETY OF WOMEN ENGINEERS (Chevron Scholarships)
120 Wall Street, 11th Floor
New York, NY 10005-3902
(212) 509-9577; Fax 212/509-0224

AMOUNT: $2,000
DEADLINE(S): Feb 1
FIELD(S): Chemical Engineering; Mechanical Engineering; Petroleum Engineering
The Chevron Scholarships are presented to female students, an entering sophomore and an entering junior year majoring in any of the three fields specified above. Students must hold a 3.5 GPA or above and be attending an ABET-accredited program or in a SWE-approved school.
Send a self-addressed, stamped envelope to the above address between the months of October and January for complete information.

173

SOCIETY OF WOMEN ENGINEERS (Dorothy Lemke Howarth Scholarships)
120 Wall Street, 11th Floor
New York, NY 10005
800/666-ISWE; 212/509-9577; Fax 212/509-0224

AMOUNT: $2,000
DEADLINE(S): Feb 1

FIELD(S): Engineering
Open to entering female sophomore students who are majoring in engineering and are U.S. citizens.
4 awards. Applications available Oct.-Jan. only. Send self-addressed stamped envelope for complete information.

174

SOCIETY OF WOMEN ENGINEERS (GTE Foundation Scholarships)
120 Wall Street, 11th Floor
New York, NY 10005-3902
212/ 509-9577; Fax 212/509-0224

AMOUNT: $1,000
DEADLINE(S): Feb 1
FIELD(S): Electrical Engineering; Computer Science
The GTE Foundation Scholarships are awarded to entering female sophomores and juniors majoring in the specified fields. Applicants must hold a 3.5 GPA or higher and be attending an ABET-accredited program or a SWE-approved school.
Send a self-addressed, stamped envelope to the above address between the months of October and January for complete information and application.

175

SOCIETY OF WOMEN ENGINEERS (General Electric Foundation Scholarships)
120 Wall Street, 11th Floor
New York NY 10005
212/509-9577; Fax: 212/509-0224

AMOUNT: $1,000
DEADLINE(S): May 15
FIELD(S): Engineering; Computer Science
Open to women who are U.S. citizens and are entering an ABET-accredited school as freshmen with an engineering/computer science major. Applications available March through May and are due by May 15 (postmark).

3 awards given. An additional $500 is awarded to recipients to attend the annual National Convention/Student Conference and/or to provide support to her local section. Renewable up to three years. Send self-addressed stamped envelope for complete information.

176

SOCIETY OF WOMEN ENGINEERS (Ivy Parker Memorial Scholarship)
120 Wall Street, 11th Floor
New York, NY 10005
800/666-ISWE; Fax 212/509-0224

AMOUNT: $2,000
DEADLINE(S): Feb 1
FIELD(S): Engineering

Open to a female engineering student who is entering her sophomore, junior or senior year. Applicants must demonstrate financial need.
Applications available Oct.-Jan. only. Send self-addressed stamped envelope for complete information.

177

SOCIETY OF WOMEN ENGINEERS (Judith Resnick Memorial Scholarship)
120 Wall Street, 11th Floor
New York, NY 10005-3902
212/509-9577; Fax 212/509-0224

AMOUNT: $2,000
DEADLINE(S): Feb 1
FIELD(S): Engineering field with a space-related major

For female college seniors pursuing a career in the space industry studying an engineering field with a space-related major.
Applications available Oct.-Jan. only. Send SASE for complete information.

178

SOCIETY OF WOMEN ENGINEERS (Lillian Moller Gilbreth Scholarship)
120 Wall Street; 11th Floor
New York, NY 10005
800/666-ISWE; 212/509-9577; Fax 212/509-0224

AMOUNT: $5,000
DEADLINE(S): Feb 1
FIELD(S): Engineering

For women of outstanding potential and achievement who are entering their sophomore, junior or senior year of college as an engineering student.
Applications available Oct.-Jan. only. Send self-addressed stamped envelope for complete information.

179

SOCIETY OF WOMEN ENGINEERS (MASWE Memorial Scholarships)
120 Wall Street, 11th Floor
New York, NY 10005
800/666-ISWE; 212/509-9577; Fax 212/509-0224

AMOUNT: $2,000
DEADLINE(S): Feb 1
FIELD(S): Engineering

For women of outstanding potential and achievement who are entering their sophomore, junior or senior year of college as an engineering student.
2 awards. Applications available Oct.-Jan. only. Send self-addressed stamped envelope for complete information.

180

SOCIETY OF WOMEN ENGINEERS (Northrop-Grumman Corporation Founders Scholarship)
120 Wall Street, 11th Floor
New York, NY 10005-3902
212/509-9577; Fax 212/509-0224

AMOUNT: $1,000
DEADLINE(S): Feb 1
FIELD(S): Engineering

For a woman engineering major entering her sophomore year. Must be SWE student member and a U.S. citizen.

Applications available Oct.-Jan. only. Send SASE for complete information.

181

SOCIETY OF WOMEN ENGINEERS
(Olive Lynn Salember Scholarship)
120 Wall Street, 11th Floor
New York, NY 10005-3902
212/509-9577; Fax 212/509-0224

AMOUNT: $2,000
DEADLINE(S): May 15
FIELD(S): Engineering; Computer Science

For women who have been out of the engineering job market and/or out of school for a minimum of two years. For any year undergraduate or graduate, including doctoral program.

1 award. Apply between March-May. Send SASE for application and information.

182

SOCIETY OF WOMEN ENGINEERS
(TRW Scholarships)
120 Wall Street, 11th Floor
New York, NY 10005-3902
212/509-9577; Fax 212/509-0224

AMOUNT: $2,500
DEADLINE(S): May 15
FIELD(S): Engineering; Computer Science

For women entering their freshman year of college majoring in engineering or computer science.

Winners are chosen by the Best National, Regional, and New Student Sections.

183

SOCIETY OF WOMEN ENGINEERS
(United Technologies Corporation Scholarship/Northrop Corp./Digital Equipment Corp. Scholarship)
120 Wall Street, 11th Floor
New York, NY 10005
212/705-7855

AMOUNT: $1,000-$5,000
DEADLINE(S): Feb 1
FIELD(S): Engineering

For women who are majoring in engineering at accredited colleges & pursuing an engineering degree. Must have 3.5 GPA if Soph/Jr/Sr. Northrop & Digital scholarships require recipients to be SWE members.

Digital requires attendance at a NY or New England college. United Technologies award is renewable for two years. Applications only available October through January. Send self-addressed stamped envelope for complete information.

184

SOCIETY OF WOMEN ENGINEERS
(Westinghouse-Bertha Lamme Scholarships)
120 Wall Street, 11th Floor
New York, NY 10005
212/509-9577; Fax 212/509-0224

AMOUNT: $1,000
DEADLINE(S): May 15 (postmark)
FIELD(S): Engineering; Computer Science

Open to women entering their freshman year of college. Award is to attract women to the field of engineering. Must be U.S. citizen.

3 awards. Applications available Mar.-May. Send self-addressed stamped envelope for complete information.

185

THE FLUOR FOUNDATION (Fluor Daniel Engineering Scholarship Program)
3333 Michelson Drive
Irvine, CA 92730
Written Inquiry

AMOUNT: Varies
DEADLINE(S): Mar
FIELD(S): Chemical, Civil, Electrical, Mechanical, and Environmental Engineering; Building Construction
Open to sophomores enrolled in a full-time undergraduate program in one of the above areas of study. Students must be selected by the dean of engineering or an appropriate selection committee to receive an application.
Contact the dean of engineering at the school you are enrolled to determine whether your school is designated as a participant in the Fluor Daniel Engineering Scholarship Program.

186

THE JOHNS HOPKINS UNIVERSITY APPLIED PHYSICS LAB (APL Summer Employment Program)
Johns Hopkins Road
Laurel, MD 20723
301/953-5000; Fax 301/953-5274; E-mail: jill.clevernger@juhapl.edu; Internet: www.jhuapl.edu

AMOUNT: Varies
DEADLINE(S): Mar 1
FIELD(S): Engineering; Computer Science
Paid internship for undergraduates who preferably have completed their sophomore year and graduate students studying engineering and/or computer science. Most positions require strong computer skills and U.S. citizenship.
50-100 awards per year. Program can be combined/alternated with programs in many other universities in the U.S.

187

TYSON FOUNDATION INC. (Scholarship Program)
2210 W. Oaklawn
Springdale, AR 72762-6999
501/290-4955

AMOUNT: Varies according to need
DEADLINE(S): Apr 20
FIELD(S): Business; Agriculture; Engineering; Computer Science; Nursing
For Arkansas residents who are U.S. citizens. Must be enrolled full-time in an accredited institution and demonstrate financial need. Must be employed part-time and/or summers to help fund education. For undergrad study at schools in U.S.
Renewable up to 8 semesters or 12 trimesters as long as students meet criteria.

188

U.S. DEPARTMENT OF DEFENSE (CO-OP Program-CECOM Research, Development, & Engineering Center-ADO)
U.S. Army CECOM
RD&E Center
ATTN: AMSEL-RD-ADO-MS-PD
Fort Monmouth, NJ 07703-5201
908/427-4889; DSN 987-4889;
Fax 908/427-3425; Internet:
www.acq.osd.mil/ddre/edugate/s-aindx.html

AMOUNT: Salary + college/university credit
DEADLINE(S): None specified
FIELD(S): Engineering
Students presently attending local colleges/universities work with engineers and scientists on specified projects for six-month periods. Open to all high-caliber college students majoring in engineering. Purpose is to stimulate interest in SME careers. Upon graduation, students often become candidates for recruitment and placement as engineer and scientist interns.
For more information, contact Connie Zimmerman at the above address.

189

WASHINGTON INTERNSHIPS FOR STUDENTS OF ENGINEERING

1899 L Street NW, #500
Washington, D.C. 20036
202/466-8744

AMOUNT: $2,700 stipend + travel allowance

DEADLINE(S): Dec 10

FIELD(S): Engineering-Public Policy

For top 3rd-year engineering students. 10-week summer internship in Washington, D.C. to learn how engineers contribute to public policy decisions on complex technological matters. Students receive 5 quarter credits from Univ. of Washington.

15 internships per summer. Write for complete information.

190

WESTINGHOUSE FOUNDATION (National Achievement Scholarships for Outstanding Negro Students)

One Rotary Center
1560 Sherman Ave., Suite 200
Evanston, IL 60201-4897
708/866-5100

AMOUNT: $2,000

DEADLINE(S): None specified

FIELD(S): Engineering or engineering technology

For any Negro student who is a U.S. citizen or is in the process of becoming a U.S. citizen and is enrolled full-time as a high school senior. Winners are selected on the basis of their PSAT/NMSQT scores taken in the fall of their junior year. Program is facilitated by the National Merit Scholarship Corporation at above address.

Student must enroll in an accredited U.S. college or university in the fall after completing high school as a full-time student working toward a BA degree.

AERONAUTICS

191

AIR TRAFFIC CONTROL ASSOCIATION INC (Scholarship Awards Program)

2300 Clarendon Blvd., #711
Arlington, VA 22201
540/364-3470

AMOUNT: $400-$2,500

DEADLINE(S): May 1

FIELD(S): Aeronautics, Aviation, and related areas

Open to undergraduate, postgraduate students enrolled in aviation-related course of study; aviation career employees doing part-time study to enhance job skills; and children of air traffic control specialists enrolled in a college program. Must demonstrate financial need.

Write for complete information.

192

AMERICAN INSTITUTE OF AERONAUTICS AND ASTRONAUTICS (Undergraduate Scholarship Program)

1801 Alexander Bell Drive, Suite 500
Reston, VA 20191-4344
800/639-AIAA; 703/264-7500; Fax 703/264-7551; Internet: www.aiaa.org

AMOUNT: $2,000

DEADLINE(S): Jan 31

FIELD(S): Science; Engineering; Aeronautics; Astronautics

Open to applicants who have completed at least one academic semester or quarter of full-time college work in the area of science or engineering encompassed by the technical activities of the AIAA. Must have GPA of at least 3.0, be currently enrolled in accredited college or university. Membership in AIAA not required to apply but must become one before receiving a scholarship award.

Sophomores and juniors who receive these awards are eligible for yearly continuation until completion of senior year upon submission of application, career essay, transcripts and 2 letters of recommendation from college professor.

193

**AOPA AIR SAFETY FOUNDATION
(Mcallister & Burnside Scholarships)**
421 Aviation Way
Frederick, MD 21701-4798
301/695-2170

AMOUNT: $1,000 (Mcallister); $1,000
(Burnside)
DEADLINE(S): Mar 31
FIELD(S): Aviation

Scholarships for undergraduate juniors and seniors who are enrolled in an accredited aviation degree program with an academic proficiency of 3.25 or better. U.S. citizen.
Send #10 SASE for complete information to above address.

194

**AVIATION DISTRIBUTORS AND
MANUFACTURERS ASSOCIATION
INTERNATIONAL (ADMA International
Scholarship Fund)**
1900 Arch Street
Philadelphia, PA 19103
215/564-3484

AMOUNT: Varies
DEADLINE(S): May 1
FIELD(S): Aviation Management;
Professional Pilot

Open to students seeking a career in aviation management or as a professional pilot. Emphasis may be in general aviation; airway science management; aviation maintenance; flight engineering or airway a/c systems management.
Applicants must be studying in the aviation field in a four-year school having an aviation program and must have completed at least two years of the program. Write for complete information.

195

**EAA AVIATION FOUNDATION
(Scholarship Program)**
P.O. Box 3065
Oshkosh, WI 54903-3065
920/426-6815

AMOUNT: $200-$1,500
DEADLINE(S): May 1
FIELD(S): Aviation

Several different scholarship programs open to well-rounded individuals involved in school and community activities as well as aviation. Applicants' academic records should verify their ability to complete their educational program.
Financial need is a consideration.

196

**INTERNATIONAL SOCIETY OF WOMEN
AIRLINE PILOTS (ISA International Career
Scholarship)**
2250 E. Tropicana Ave., Suite 19-395
Las Vegas, NV 89119-6594
Written inquiry

AMOUNT: Varies
DEADLINE(S): None specified
FIELD(S): Airline Pilot Advanced Ratings

Open to women whose goals are to fly the world's airlines. For advanced pilot ratings, such as the U.S. FAA ATP certificate or equivalent.
Applicants must have a U.S. FAA Commercial Pilot Certificate with an Instrument Rating and a First Class medical (or equivalent). Also must have a minimum of 750 flight hours. Personal interview is required. Write for complete information.

197

**INTERNATIONAL SOCIETY OF WOMEN
AIRLINE PILOTS (Fiorenze De Bernardi
Merit Award)**
2250 E. Tropicana Ave., Suite 19-395
Las Vegas, NV 89119-6594
Internet: www.aswap.org

AMOUNT: Varies

DEADLINE(S): Varies

FIELD(S): Airline Pilot Training

A merit scholarship for women throughout the world who are pursuing airline pilot careers. Selection based on need, demonstrated dedication to career goal, work history, experience, and recommendations.

To aid pilots with CFI, CFII, MEI, or any equivalents. Must have a U.S. FAA Commercial Pilot Certificate with an Instrument Rating and a First Class medical (or equivalent). Candidates must have a minimum of 350 flight hours. Personal interview required. Contact Gail Redden-Jones at above address.

198

INTERNATIONAL SOCIETY OF WOMEN AIRLINE PILOTS (Holly Mullins Memorial Scholarship)
2250 E. Tropicana Ave., Suite 19-395
Las Vegas, NV 89119-6594
Internet: www.aswap.org

AMOUNT: Varies

DEADLINE(S): Varies

FIELD(S): Airline Pilot Training

A merit scholarship for women who are single mothers and pursuing airline pilot careers. Selection is based on need, demonstrated dedication to career goal, work history experience, and recommendations.

To aid pilots with CFI, CRII, MEI, or any equivalents. Must have a U.S. FAA Commercial Pilot Certificate with an Instrument Rating and a First Class medical (or equivalent). Additionally, candidates must have a minimum of 750 flight hours.

199

INTERNATIONAL SOCIETY OF WOMEN AIRLINE PILOTS (The International Airline Scholarship)
2250 E. Tropicana Ave., Suite 19-395
Las Vegas, NV 89119-6594
Internet: www.aswap.org

AMOUNT: Varies

DEADLINE(S): None given

FIELD(S): Flight Engineering and Type Ratings

For women seeking careers in aviation and need Flight Engineer Certificates and Type Ratings on 727, 737, 747, 757, and DC-10 aircraft. For Flight Engineers, 1,000 hours flight time and a current FE written required. For Type Rating scholarship, an ATP Certificate and a current FE written.

Contact Gail Redden-Jones at above address.

200

INTERNATIONAL SOCIETY OF WOMEN AIRLINE PILOTS-ISA+21 (ISA Scholarship Fund)
2250 E. Tropicana Ave., Suite 19-395
Las Vegas, NV 89119-6594
847/599-9886; Internet: www.iswap.org

AMOUNT: $1,000-$3,000

DEADLINE(S): Apr 1

FIELD(S): Aviation

For women pilots needing advanced ratings and certificates.

Must have a minimum of 750 flight hours and a Commercial Pilot's License.

201

NATIONAL SPACE CLUB (Dr. Robert H. Goddard Space Science and Engineering Scholarship)
655 15th Street NW, #300
Washington, D.C. 20005
202/639-4210

AMOUNT: $10,000

DEADLINE(S): Jan 9

FIELD(S): Science and Engineering

Open to undergraduate juniors & seniors who have scholastic plans leading to future participation in the Aerospace sciences and technology. U.S. citizen.

Also offers Essay Award for $1,000 open to U.S. citizens. Send a self-addressed stamped envelope for more information.

202

SMITHSONIAN INSTITUTION (National Air & Space Museum Verville Fellowship)
National Air and Space Museum, MRC 312
Washington, D.C. 20560
Written inquiry

AMOUNT: $30,000 stipend for 12 months + travel and misc. expenses
DEADLINE(S): Jan 15
FIELD(S): Analysis of major trends, developments, and accomplishments in the history of aviation or space studies

A competitive nine- to twelve-month in-residence fellowship in the above field of study. Advanced degree is not a requirement. Contact Fellowship Coordinator at above location.

Open to all nationalities. Fluency in English required.

203

U.S. AIR FORCE ROTC (4-Year Scholarship Program)
AFROTC/RROO
Recruiting Operations Branch
551 E. Maxwell Blvd.
Maxwell AFB, AL 36112-6106
334/953-2091

AMOUNT: Tuition; fees & books + $150 per month stipend
DEADLINE(S): Dec 1
FIELD(S): Aeronautical Engineering; Civil Engineering; Mechanical Engineering; Mathematics; Physics; Nursing & some Liberal Arts

Open to U.S. citizens who are at least 17 and will graduate from college before age 25. Must complete application; furnish SAT/ACT scores; high school transcripts and record of extracurricular activities.

Must qualify on Air Force medical examination. About 1,600 scholarships awarded each year at campuses which offer Air Force ROTC.

204

VERTICAL FLIGHT FOUNDATION (Undergraduate/Graduate Scholarships)
217 N. Washington Street
Alexandria, VA 22314
703/684-6777; Fax 703/739-9279

AMOUNT: Up to $2,000
DEADLINE(S): Feb 1
FIELD(S): Vertical Flight Engineering

Annual scholarships open to undergraduate & graduate students in the above area. Academic excellence and proven interest in pursuing careers in some aspect of helicopter or vertical flight required. For full-time study at accredited school of engineering.

Write for complete information.

205

VIRGINIA AIRPORT OPERATORS COUNCIL (VAOC Aviation Scholarship Award)
c/o John Lillard
Box A-3
Richmond, VA 23231
804/236-2110

AMOUNT: $2,000
DEADLINE(S): Varies (Changes yearly/early spring)
FIELD(S): Aviation

Open to Virginia high school seniors who have been accepted into an accredited post-secondary aviation education program. Applicants need a 3.0 or better GPA and should be planning a career in aviation.

College students and non-Virginia residents are not eligible. Write for complete information.

ARCHITECTURE

206

AMERICAN ACADEMY IN ROME (Six-Month Fellowships)
7 East 60 Street
New York, NY 10022-1001
212/751-7200

AMOUNT: Up to $7,500
DEADLINE(S): Nov 15
FIELD(S): Architecture; Landscape Architecture; Design Arts; History, Preservation, & Conservation

Open to U.S. citizens who have 7 years of professional practice in above fields and be currently practicing in the field. Awards tenable at the American Academy in Rome, Italy.

2 AAR fellowships per year for 6-month term. Not renewable. Contact address above for complete information.

207

AMERICAN INSTITUTE OF ARCHITECTS (AIA/AIAF Scholarship Program)
1735 New York Ave. NW
Washington, D.C. 20006
202/626-7511; Fax 202/626-7420; E-mail: felberm@aiamail.aia.org

AMOUNT: $500-$2,500
DEADLINE(S): Jan 31
FIELD(S): Architecture

Open to undergraduate students in their final two years or graduate students pursuing their master's degree in architecture. Awards tenable at accredited institutions in the U.S. and Canada.

Applications available only through the office of the dean or department head at an NAAB or RAIC school of architecture.

208

AMERICAN INSTITUTE OF ARCHITECTS/AMERICAN ARCHITECTURAL FOUNDATION (Minority/Disadvantaged Scholarship Program)
1735 New York Ave. NW
Washington, D.C. 20006-5292
202/626-7511; Fax 202/626-7420; E-mail: felberm@aiamail.aia.org

AMOUNT: $500-$2,500
DEADLINE(S): Dec (nomination); Jan 15 (application)
FIELD(S): Architecture

Open to minority and/or disadvantaged students who are entering a program leading to a BA or MA of architecture. High school seniors, junior college students, and college freshmen may apply.

Renewable for three years. Nomination by an individual familiar with student's interest and potential to be an architect is required. 25 scholarships per year. Write for complete information.

209

AMERICAN INSTITUTE OF ARCHITECTS/AMERICAN ARCHITECTURAL FOUNDATION (RTKL Traveling Fellowship)
1735 New York Ave. NW
Washington, D.C. 20006
202/626-7511; Fax 202/626-7420; E-mail: felberm@aiamail.aia.org

AMOUNT: $2,500
DEADLINE(S): Feb 14
FIELD(S): Architecture

Fellowship to encourage and support foreign travel undertaken to further education toward a degree in architecture. Must be in second-to-last year of bachelor or master's program and planning to travel outside the U.S. or accepted in a professional degree program.

Forms are sent to all NAAB-accredited schools of architecture.

210

AMERICAN INSTITUTE OF ARCHITECTS/AMERICAN HOSPITAL ASSOCIATION (AIA/AHA Fellowships in Health Facilities Planning and Design)
1735 New York Ave. NW
Washington, D.C. 20006
202/626-7511; Fax 202/626-7420; E-mail: felberm@aiamail.aia.org

AMOUNT: $22,000
DEADLINE(S): Jan 15
FIELD(S): Architecture—Health Facilities

For architects, graduate students, and those in last year of undergraduate work in architecture who are U.S. or Canadian citizens for coursework or independent study. Funds provided by The American Sterilizer Company.
For one year. Write for complete information.

211

AMERICAN INSTITUTE OF ARCHITECTS, NEW YORK CHAPTER (Women's Architectural Auxiliary, Eleanor Allwork Scholarships)
200 Lexington Ave., 6th floor
New York, NY 10016
212/683-0023 Ext. 14; Fax 212/696-5022

AMOUNT: $5,000 (Honor Grants); $2,500 (Citation Grants)
DEADLINE(S): Mar 6
FIELD(S): Architecture

Scholarship grants for students seeking their first professional degree in architecture. Must be New York City resident or a NYC resident attending an upstate school. High level of academic achievement and legitimate financial need required as determined by the Financial Aid Officer at the school.
Write or call for complete information.

212

AMERICAN INSTITUTE OF ARCHITECTS, NEW YORK CHAPTER (Stewardson, Keefe, and LeBrun Travel Grants)
200 Lexington Ave., 6th floor
New York, NY 10016
212/683-0023 Ext. 14

AMOUNT: $3,000
DEADLINE(S): Feb 13
FIELD(S): Architecture Research

Travel grants for architectural education and professional development. Submit a statement of purpose regarding travel plans—a brief, 500-word description of where travel will take place, why it is important to professional development, etc. For professional architects who are U.S. citizens.
Write for complete information.

213

ARTS INTERNATIONAL; INSTITUTE OF INTERNATIONAL EDUCATION (Cintas Fellowship Program)
809 United Nations Plaza
New York, NY 10017
212/984-5370

AMOUNT: $10,000
DEADLINE(S): Mar 1
FIELD(S): Architecture; Painting; Photography; Sculpture; Printmaking; Music Composition; Creative Writing

Fellowships open to artists who are of Cuban ancestry or Cuban citizens living outside of Cuba. They are intended to foster & encourage the professional development & recognition of talented creative artists in the above areas.
Fellowships are not awarded for furtherance of academic study. 5-10 awards per year. Write for complete information.

214

DUMBARTON OAKS (Awards in Byzantine Studies, Pre-Columbian Studies, and the History of Landscape Architecture)
1703 32nd Street NW
Washington, D.C. 20007
202/339-6410

AMOUNT: Up to $37,700 per academic year

DEADLINE(S): Nov 1

FIELD(S): Byzantine Studies; Pre-Columbian Studies; History of Landscape Architecture

Residential doctoral and postdoctoral fellowships; junior fellowships & summer fellowships to support study and/or research in the above areas. All fellows are expected to be able to communicate satisfactorily in English.

Write for complete information.

215

LANDSCAPE ARCHITECTURE FOUNDATION (LAF/CLASS Fund Scholarships)
Use website below
202/216-2356; E-mail tpadian@asla.org;
Internet: www.asla.org

AMOUNT: $500 - $2,000

DEADLINE(S): Mar 31

FIELD(S): Landscape Architecture or Ornamental Horticulture

Scholarships and internships for students enrolled in certain California colleges: California Polytechnic Institute (Pomona or San Luis Obispo), UCLA, UC-Irvine & UC-Davis who show promise & a commitment to landscape architecture as a profession.

Access website for complete information.

216

LANDSCAPE ARCHITECTURE FOUNDATION (Edward D. Stone Jr. & Associates Minority Scholarship)
Use website below
202/216-2356; E-mail: tpadian@asla.org;
Internet: www.asla.org

AMOUNT: $1,000

DEADLINE(S): Mar 31

FIELD(S): Landscape Architecture

Open to African-American, Hispanic, Native American, and minority students of other cultural and ethnic backgrounds entering their final two years of undergrad study in landscape architecture.

Access website for details and for application.

217

LANDSCAPE ARCHITECTURE FOUNDATION (Edith H. Henderson Scholarship)
Use website below
202/216-2356; E-mail: tpadian@asla.org;
Internet: www.asla.org

AMOUNT: $1,000

DEADLINE(S): Mar 31

FIELD(S): Landscape Architecture

Scholarship available to any landscape architecture student who has in the past or is participating in a class in public speaking or creative writing. Must write a 200- to 400-word typed review of Edith H. Henderson's book "Edith Henderson's Home Landscape Companion."

Locate the book in a library or call 1-800-787-2665 or 1-800-241-0113 to order. Be sure and state that you are a landscape architect student applying for the Henderson scholarship.

218

LANDSCAPE ARCHITECTURE FOUNDATION (Harriett Barnhart Wimmer Scholarship)
Use website below
202/216-2356; E-mail: tpadian@asla.org;
Internet: www.asla.org

AMOUNT: $1,000

DEADLINE(S): Mar 31

FIELD(S): Landscape Architecture

Open to women going into their final year of undergraduate study at a U.S. university who have demonstrated excellence in their design ability and sensitivity to the environment.

Access website for details and application information.

219

**LANDSCAPE ARCHITECTURE
FOUNDATION (LANDCADD Inc.
Scholarship)**
    Use website below
    202/216-2356; E-mail: tpadian@asla.org;
    Internet: www.asla.org

AMOUNT: $500
DEADLINE(S): May 4
FIELD(S): Landscape Architecture

Scholarships open to undergraduate & gradu-
    ate students who wish to utilize technologi-
    cal advancements such as computer-aided
    design, video imaging and/or telecommuni-
    cations in their career.
Write for complete information.

220

**LANDSCAPE ARCHITECTURE
FOUNDATION (Lester Walls III
Scholarship)**
    Use website below
    202/216-2356; E-mail: tpadian@asla.org;
    Internet: www.asla.org

AMOUNT: $500
DEADLINE(S): May 4
FIELD(S): Landscape Architecture

Scholarship open to handicapped students
    pursuing a degree in landscape architecture
    or for research on barrier-free design for
    the disabled.
Write for complete information.

221

**LANDSCAPE ARCHITECTURE
FOUNDATION (Raymond E. Page
Scholarship)**
    Use website below
    202/216-2356; E-mail: tpadian@asla.org;
    Internet: www.asla.org

AMOUNT: $1,000
DEADLINE(S): Mar 31
FIELD(S): Landscape Architecture

Scholarships for undergraduate or graduate
    students pursuing studies in landscape
    architecture.
Access website for complete application
    information.

222

**LANDSCAPE ARCHITECTURE
FOUNDATION (Student Research Grants)**
    Use website below
    202/216-2356; E-mail: tpadian@asla.org;
    Internet: www.asla.org

AMOUNT: $1,000
DEADLINE(S): May 4
FIELD(S): Landscape Architecture

Research grants to encourage student efforts
    in practical research & expand the knowl-
    edge base of the profession. Open to under-
    graduate & graduate students.
Write for complete information.

223

**LANDSCAPE ARCHITECTURE FOUN-
DATION (Hawaii Chapter/The David T.
Woolsey Scholarship)**
    Use website below
    202/216-2356; E-mail: tpadian@asla.org;
    Internet: www.asla.org

AMOUNT: $1,000
DEADLINE(S): Mar 31
FIELD(S): Landscape Architecture

Scholarship open to third-, fourth-, and fifth-
    year or graduate student of landscape
    architecture who are residents of Hawaii.
Access website for application information.

224

**LANDSCAPE ARCHITECTURE
FOUNDATION (Thomas P. Papandrew
Scholarship)**
    Use website below
    202/216-2356; E-mail: tpadian@asla.org;
    Internet: www.asla.org

AMOUNT: $1,000
DEADLINE(S): Mar 31
FIELD(S): Landscape Architecture
Open to minority students enrolled full-time
   in the Landscape Architecture program at
   Arizona State University. Students must be
   legal residents of Arizona and U.S. citizens.
   Must demonstrate financial need.
Access website for complete application
   information.

225

**LANDSCAPE ARCHITECTURE
FOUNDATION (The Rain Bird Company
Scholarship)**
   Use website below
   202/216-2356; E-mail: tpadian@asla.org;
   Internet: www.asla.org

AMOUNT: $1,000
DEADLINE(S): Mar 31
FIELD(S): Landscape Architecture
For landscape architecture students in their
   final two years of undergraduate study who
   have demonstrated commitment to the
   profession through participation in
   extracurricular activities and exemplary
   scholastic with achievements.
Access website for complete information.

226

**LANDSCAPE ARCHITECTURE
FOUNDATION (William J. Locklin
Scholarship)**
   Use website below
   202/216-2356; E-mail: tpadian@asla.org;
   Internet: www.asla.org

AMOUNT: $1,000
DEADLINE(S): Mar 31
FIELD(S): Landscape Architecture
Scholarships open to undergraduate and
   graduate students pursuing a program in
   lighting design. Purpose is to stress the
   importance of 24-hour lighting in landscape
   design.
Access website for complete application
   information.

227

**NATIONAL ASSOCIATION OF WOMEN
IN CONSTRUCTION (El Camino Real
Chapter #158 Scholarship)**
   Marie Revere
   1737 1st Street, Suite 300
   San Jose, CA 95112
   408/452-4644

AMOUNT: $1,000
DEADLINE(S): May 1
FIELD(S): Civil Engineering; Construction;
   Architecture; Architectural Engineering
Open to men or women undergraduates who
   are going into their junior year at an
   accredited 4-year California college. U.S.
   citizen.
Write for complete information.

228

**NATIONAL DEFENSE
TRANSPORTATION ASSOCIATION—
SAN FRANCISCO BAY AREA CHAPTER
(NDTA Scholarship)**
   P.O. Box 24676
   Oakland, CA 94623
   Written inquiry

AMOUNT: $2,000
DEADLINE(S): Mar 31
FIELD(S): Transportation-related Business;
   Engineering; Planning & Environmental
   fields
Open to U.S. citizens enrolled in a California
   accredited undergraduate degree or
   vocational program in the above fields who
   plan to pursue a career related to
   transportation. Financial need is considered.
Write for complete information.

229

**NATIONAL FEDERATION OF THE
BLIND (Frank Walton Horn Memorial
Scholarship)**
   805 Fifth Ave.
   Grinnell, IA 50112
   515/236-3366

AMOUNT: $3,000

DEADLINE(S): Mar 31

FIELD(S): All fields of study—preference to architecture or engineering students

Scholarship for legally blind students studying (or planning to study) at any post-secondary level. For all fields of study but preference will be given to architecture and engineering majors.

Awards based on academic excellence, service to the community, financial need. Write for complete information.

230

NATIONAL FEDERATION OF THE BLIND
805 Fifth Ave.
Grinnell, IA 50112
515/236-3366

AMOUNT: Varies

DEADLINE(S): Mar 31

FIELD(S): All fields of study-preference to architecture or engineering students.

Scholarship for legally blind students studying (or planning to study) at any post-secondary level. For all fields of study but preference will be given to architecture and engineering majors.

Awards based on academic excellence, service to the community, financial need. Write for complete information.

231

NATIONAL FEDERATION OF THE BLIND (Howard Brown Rickard Scholarship)
805 Fifth Ave.
Grinnell, IA 50112
515/236-3366

AMOUNT: $3,000

DEADLINE(S): Mar 31

FIELD(S): Natural Sciences; Architecture; Engineering; Medicine; Law

Scholarships for undergraduate or graduate study in the above areas. Open to legally blind students enrolled full-time at accredited post-secondary institutions.

Awards based on academic excellence, service to the community, and financial need. Write for complete information.

232

NATIONAL ITALIAN AMERICAN FOUNDATION (Cesare Fera Memorial Scholarship)
1860 19th Street
Washington, D.C. 20009-5599
202/530-5315

AMOUNT: $1,000

DEADLINE(S): May 31

FIELD(S): Architecture

For graduate and undergraduate students of Italian ancestry majoring in architecture.

Financial need, academic merit, and community service are considered.

233

NATIONAL ROOFING FOUNDATION (NRF/North East Roofing Contractors Association Scholarship)
O'Hare International Center
10255 W. Higgins Road, Suite 600
Rosemont, IL 60018-5607
847/299-1183; Fax 847/299-1183; E-mail: NRCA@roofonline.org; Internet: www.roofonline.org

AMOUNT: $1,000/year

DEADLINE(S): Jan 9

FIELD(S): Architecture; Engineering; Construction

For undergraduate and graduate students in architecture, engineering, or another curriculum related to roofing. Applicants must reside in Connecticut, Maine, Massachusetts, New Hampshire, New York, Pennsylvania, Rhode Island, or Vermont.

Renewable up to four years. Send a self-addressed stamped envelope (#10) to receive an application ($.64 postage).

234

NATIONAL STONE ASSN./AMERICAN SOCIETY OF LANDSCAPE ARCHITECTS (Student Competition)
1415 Elliot Place NW
Washington, D.C. 20007
202/342-1100

AMOUNT: $1,000; $500; $300
DEADLINE(S): May 1
FIELD(S): Landscape Architecture
Contest in which undergraduate landscape architecture students work with a local rock quarry to produce a reclamation proposal.
Write for complete information.

235

NEW YORK CITY DEPT. CITYWIDE ADMINISTRATIVE SERVICES (Urban Fellows Program)
1 Centre Street, 24th Floor
New York, NY 10007
212/487-5600; Fax 212/487-5720

AMOUNT: $18,000 stipend
DEADLINE(S): Jan 20
FIELD(S): Public Administration; Urban Planning; Government; Public Service; Urban Affairs
Fellowship program provides one academic year (9 months) of full-time work experience in urban government. Open to graduating college seniors and recent college graduates. U.S. citizenship required.
Write for complete information.

236

NEW YORK CITY DEPT. OF CITYWIDE ADMINISTRATIVE SERVICES (Government Scholars Internship Program)
1 Centre Street, 24th Floor
New York, NY 10007
212/487-5600; Fax 212/487-5720

AMOUNT: $3,000 stipend
DEADLINE(S): Jan 13

FIELD(S): Public Administration; Urban Planning; Government; Public Service; Urban Affairs
10-week summer intern program open to undergraduate sophomores, juniors and seniors. Program provides students with unique opportunity to learn about NY City government. Internships available in virtually every city agency and mayoral office.
Write to New York City Fellowship Programs at above address for complete information.

237

NEW YORK STATE HIGHER EDUCATION SERVICES CORPORATION (N.Y. State Regents Professional/Health Care Opportunity Scholarships)
Cultural Education Center, Room 5C64
Albany, NY 12230
518/486-1319; Internet: www.hesc.com

AMOUNT: $1,000-$10,000/year
DEADLINE(S): Varies
FIELD(S): Medicine and Dentistry and related fields; Architecture; Nursing; Psychology; Audiology; Landscape Architecture; Social Work; Chiropractic; Law; Pharmacy, Accounting, Speech Language Pathology
For NY state residents who are economically disadvantaged and members of a minority group underrepresented in the chosen profession and attending school in NY state. Some programs carry a service obligation in New York for each year of support. For U.S. citizens or qualifying noncitizens.
Medical/dental scholarships require one year of professional work in NY.

238

NEW YORK STATE HIGHER EDUCATION SERVICES CORPORATION
Cultural Education Center, Room 5C64
Albany, NY 12230
518/486-1319; Internet: www.hesc.com

AMOUNT: Varies
DEADLINE(S): Varies

FIELD(S): Medicine and dentistry and related
fields, architecture, nursing, psychology,
audiology, landscape architecture, social
work, chiropractic, law, pharmacy,
accounting, speech language pathology

For NY state residents who are economically
disadvantaged and members of a minority
group underrepresented in the chosen profession and attending school in NY state.
Some programs carry a service obligation in
New York for each year of support. For U.S.
citizens or qualifying noncitizens.

Medical/dental scholarships require one year
of professional work in NY.

239

**ROBERT SCHRECK MEMORIAL FUND
(Grants)**
c/o Texas Commerce Bank-Trust Dept.
P.O. Drawer 140
El Paso, TX 79980
915/546-6515

AMOUNT: $500-$1500
DEADLINE(S): Jul 15; Nov 15
FIELD(S): Medicine; Veterinary Medicine;
Physics; Chemistry; Architecture;
Engineering; Episcopal Clergy

Grants to undergraduate juniors or seniors or
graduate students who have been residents
of El Paso County for at least two years.
Must be U.S. citizen or legal resident and
have a high grade point average. Financial
need is a consideration.
Write for complete information.

240

**SKIDMORE, OWINGS & MERRILL
FOUNDATION (Architecture Traveling
Fellowship Program)**
224 S. Michigan Ave., Suite 1000
Chicago, IL 60604
312/554-9090; Fax 312/360-4545

AMOUNT: $10,000
DEADLINE(S): None specified

FIELD(S): Architecture

For undergraduate and graduate architecture
students to help broaden their education
and take an enlightened view of society's
need to improve the built and natural envi-
ronments.

3 awards annually. Must submit portfolio and
a proposed travel itinerary. Write for complete information.

241

**SKIDMORE, OWINGS & MERRILL
FOUNDATION (Chicago Institute for
Architecture and Urbanism Award)**
224 S. Michigan Ave., Suite 1000
Chicago, IL 60604
312/554-9090; Fax 312/360-4545

AMOUNT: $5,000
DEADLINE(S): None specified
FIELD(S): Architecture; Urban Design;
Physical Planning

For a faculty or students in the fields listed
above. The award is to encourage writing
and research on the question of how architecture, urban design, and physical planning can contribute to improving the quality of life of the American city and is for
the best unpublished essay or research
paper addressing the question of how to
redirect the physical development of
American cities and their regions toward
sustainability.
Write for complete information.

242

**SKIDMORE, OWINGS & MERRILL
FOUNDATION (Urban Design Traveling
Fellowship Program)**
224 S. Michigan Ave., Suite 1000
Chicago, IL 60604
312/554-9090; Fax 312/360-4545

AMOUNT: $7,500
DEADLINE(S): None specified
FIELD(S): Architecture/Urban Design

For undergraduate or recent graduate in architecture with an interest in urban design to broaden his/her knowledge of the design of modern, high-density cities.

Must submit portfolio and a proposed travel itinerary, etc. Write for complete information.

243

SMITHSONIAN INSTITUTION (Cooper-Hewitt, National Design Museum—Peter Krueger Summer Internship Program)
Cooper-Hewitt National Design Museum
2 East 91st Street
New York, NY 10128
212/860-6868; Fax 212/860-6909

AMOUNT: $2,500

DEADLINE(S): Mar 31

FIELD(S): Art History, Design, Museum Studies, and Museum Education; Architectural History

Ten-week summer internships open to graduate and undergraduate students considering a career in the museum profession. Interns will assist on special research or exhibition projects and participate in daily museum activities.

6 awards each summer. Internship commences in June and ends in August. Housing is not provided. Write for complete information.

244

UNIVERSITY OF ILLINOIS AT URBANA-CHAMPAIGN (Lydia E. Parker Bates Scholarship)
Turner Student Services Bldg., MC-306
610 East John Street
Champaign, IL 61820
217/333-0100

AMOUNT: Varies

DEADLINE(S): Mar 15

FIELD(S): Art, Architecture, Landscape Architecture, Urban Planning, Dance, Theater, and all related subjects except Music

Open to undergraduate students in the College of Fine & Applied Arts who are attending the University of Illinois at Urbana-Champaign. Must demonstrate financial need and have 3.85 GPA. Complete the Free Application for Federal Student Aid.

175 awards per year. Recipients must carry at least 12 credit hours per semester. Contact Office of Student Financial Aid.

245

WAVERLY COMMUNITY HOUSE INC. (F. Lammot Belin Arts Scholarships)
Scholarships Selection Committee
P.O. Box 142
Waverly, PA 18471
717/586-8191

AMOUNT: $10,000

DEADLINE(S): Dec 15

FIELD(S): Painting; Sculpture; Music; Drama; Dance; Literature; Architecture; Photography

Applicants must have resided in the Abington or Pocono regions of Northeastern Pennsylvania. They must furnish proof of exceptional ability in their chosen field but no formal training in any academic or professional program.

U.S. citizenship required. Finalists must appear in person before the selection committee. Write for complete information.

246

WEBB INSTITUTE (Naval Architecture Scholarships)
Crescent Beach Road
Glen Cove, NY 11542
516/671-2213

AMOUNT: Full tuition for 4 years

DEADLINE(S): Feb 15

FIELD(S): Naval Architecture; Marine Engineering

Open to high school students aged 16-24 who are in the top 10% of their class & have at least a 3.2 GPA (4.0 scale). Selection based on college boards, SAT scores, demonstrated interest in above areas, & interview. U.S. citizenship required.

20 to 25 four-year full tuition undergrad scholarships per year to Webb Institute. Write for complete information.

247

WEST VIRGINIA SOCIETY OF ARCHITECTS/AIA (Scholarship)
P.O. Box 813
Charleston, WV 25323
304/344-9872

AMOUNT: $2,500
DEADLINE(S): May 30
FIELD(S): Architecture

Open to West Virginia residents enrolled in an accredited architectural program who have completed six semesters or its equivalent by May 30. Candidates must submit letter stating need, qualifications, and desire.

Request applications after January 30 each year. Write for complete information.

CIVIL ENGINEERING

248

AMERICAN SOCIETY OF CIVIL ENGINEERS (ASCE Construction Engineering Scholarship & Student Prizes)
1801 Alexander Bell Drive
Reston, VA 20191-4400
800/548-ASCE

AMOUNT: $1,000
DEADLINE(S): Feb 15
FIELD(S): Construction Engineering

Open to undergrad freshmen, sophomores or juniors of ASCE Student Chapter/Club. Must submit paper relating to specified con-

struction-related topics. Papers may not have been previously published or appeared in connection with course work.

A team of up to 4 students may submit a joint entry and share equally in the single stipend. Write for complete information.

249

AMERICAN SOCIETY OF CIVIL ENGINEERS (B. Charles Tiney Memorial ASCE Student Chapter Scholarship)
1801 Alexander Bell Drive
Reston, VA 20191-4400
800/548-ASCE

AMOUNT: $2,000
DEADLINE(S): Feb 20
FIELD(S): Civil Engineering

Open to undergrad freshmen, sophomores or juniors of an ASCE Student Chapter and also a National Student Member in good standing. Membership application may be submitted along with scholarship application. Financial need, educational plans, academic performance, potential for development, and are considered.

Award must be used to continue formal education at an accredited educational institution. Previous recipients may re-apply. Write for complete information.

250

AMERICAN SOCIETY OF CIVIL ENGINEERS (Freeman Fellowship)
1801 Alexander Bell Drive
Reston, VA 20191-4400
800/548-ASCE

AMOUNT: Varies
DEADLINE(S): Feb 20
FIELD(S): Civil Engineering

Fellowship to encourage research in civil engineering. Open to young engineers (under 45) who are ASCE members. Application may be submitted along with fellowship application. Grants are made toward expenses for experiments, observations, and compilations to discover new and accurate data useful in engineering.

May be used for assisting in the translation, or publication in English, of papers or books in foreign languages pertaining to hydraulics.

251

AMERICAN SOCIETY OF CIVIL ENGINEERS (O.H. Ammann Research Fellowship in Structural Engineering)

1801 Alexander Bell Drive
Reston, VA 20191-4400
800/548-ASCE

AMOUNT: $5,000
DEADLINE(S): Feb 20
FIELD(S): Structural Engineering

Fellowship to encourage the creation of new knowledge in the field of structural design and construction. Open to ASCE members. National membership applications may be submitted along with fellowship application. Write for complete information.

252

AMERICAN SOCIETY OF CIVIL ENGINEERS (Samuel Fletcher Tapman ASCE Student Chapter/Club Scholarships)

1801 Alexander Bell Drive
Reston, VA 20191-4400
800/548-ASCE

AMOUNT: $1,500
DEADLINE(S): Feb 20
FIELD(S): Civil Engineering

Open to undergrad freshmen, sophomores and juniors in an ASCE Student Chapter and also a National Student Member in good standing (NSM applications may be submitted along with scholarship applications). Only 1 application per Student Chapter.

Award must be used to continue formal education at an accredited educational institution. Previous recipients may re-apply. Write for complete information.

253

ASSOCIATED BUILDERS AND CONTRACTORS SCHOLARSHIP PROGRAM

1300 N. 17th Street
Rosslyn, VA 22209
703/812-2025; Fax 703/812-8235; E-mail: cmoore@abc.org

AMOUNT: $500-$2,000
DEADLINE(S): Jun 1
FIELD(S): Construction

Open to undergrads enrolled in an accredited 4-year degree program who have completed at least 1 year of study in construction (other than a design discipline). Must have at least 1 full year remaining subsequent to application deadline. If an ABC Student Chapter exists at the college or institution, student must be a member.

Approximately 20 scholarships per year. Applications available April 1 each year. Write for complete information.

254

ASSOCIATED GENERAL CONTRACTORS EDUCATION AND RESEARCH FOUNDATION (Undergraduate Scholarships)

1957 E Street NW
Washington, D.C. 20006
202/393-2040; Fax 202/347-4004

AMOUNT: $1,500 per year for up to 4 years
DEADLINE(S): Nov 1 (applications available Sep 1)
FIELD(S): Construction; Civil Engineering

Open to college freshmen, sophomores, and juniors enrolled in or planning to enroll in a 4- or 5-year degree program in construction and/or civil engineering.

Must be U.S. citizen or legal resident and desire a career in the construction industry. Write for complete information.

255

ASSOCIATED GENERAL CONTRACTOR'S EDUCATION AND RESEARCH FOUNDATION
(Horowitz/Heffner Scholarships for Graduate Students)
   1957 E. Street NW
   Washington, D.C. 20006
   202/393-2040; Fax 202/347-4004

AMOUNT: $7,500/year
DEADLINE(S): Nov 1
FIELD(S): Construction; Civil Engineering

Open to college seniors enrolled in a ABET- or ACCE-accredited construction or civil engineering program or students possessing an undergraduate construction or civil engineering degree from such a program. Applicants must have at least one full year of academic training remaining and be a U.S. citizen or a documented permanent resident of the U.S.

$7,500 will be used for the duration of the student's graduate degree and paid in two installments of $3,750. For complete information, write to the above address.

256

ASSOCIATED GENERAL CONTRACTOR'S EDUCATION AND RESEARCH FOUNDATION
(Undergraduate Scholarship Program)
   1957 E. Street NW
   Washington, D.C. 20006
   202/393-2040; Fax 202/347-4004

AMOUNT: $1,500
DEADLINE(S): Nov 1
FIELD(S): Construction; Civil Engineering

Open to college freshmen, sophomores, juniors or a beginning senior in a five-year program. Junior and senior applicants must have one full academic year of coursework. Must pursue a career in construction. Student must be a U.S. citizen or documented permanent resident of the U.S.

Award is renewable for up to four years of undergraduate study in construction, civil engineering or combination. Maximum award: $6,000.

257

NATIONAL ASSOCIATION OF WATER COMPANIES—NEW JERSEY CHAPTER
(Scholarship)
   Elizabethtown Water Co.
   600 South Ave.
   Westfield, NJ 07090
   908/654-1234; Fax 908/232-2719

AMOUNT: $2,500
DEADLINE(S): Apr 1
FIELD(S): Business administration; Biology; Chemistry; Engineering; Communications

For U.S. citizens who have lived in NJ at least 5 years and plan a career in the investor-owned water utility industry in disciplines such as those above. Must be undergrad or graduate student in a 2- or 4-year NJ college or university.

GPA of 3.0 or better required. Contact Gail P. Brady for complete information.

258

NATIONAL ASSOCIATION OF WOMEN IN CONSTRUCTION (El Camino Real Chapter #158 Scholarship)
   Marie Revere
   1737 1st Street, Suite 300
   San Jose, CA 95112
   408/452-4644

AMOUNT: $1,000
DEADLINE(S): May 1
FIELD(S): Civil Engineering; Construction; Architecture; Architectural Engineering

Open to men or women undergraduates who are going into their junior year at an accredited 4-year California college. U.S. citizen.
Write for complete information.

259

NATIONAL ASSOCIATION OF WOMEN IN CONSTRUCTION (Founders' Scholarship Foundation Awards)
327 S. Adams
Fort Worth, TX 76104
817/877-5551

AMOUNT: Not specified
DEADLINE(S): Feb 1
FIELD(S): Fields related to a career in construction

Open to full-time students (men or women) enrolled in a construction-related program leading to an associate's or bachelor's degree. Applicants should be in at least their 1st year of college and have at least 1 year remaining.

Awards committee considers grades; interest in construction; extracurricular activities; employment experience; financial need & evaluation by academic advisor. Write for complete information.

260

NATIONAL ROOFING FOUNDATION (NRF/North East Roofing Contractors Association Scholarship)
O'Hare International Center
10255 W. Higgins Road, Suite 600
Rosemont, IL 60018-5607
847/299-1183; Fax 847/299-1183; E-mail: NRCA@roofonline.org; Internet: www.roofonline.org

AMOUNT: $1,000/year
DEADLINE(S): Jan 9
FIELD(S): Architecture; Engineering; Construction

For undergraduate and graduate students in architecture, engineering, or another curriculum related to roofing. Applicants must reside in Connecticut, Maine, Massachusetts, New Hampshire, New York, Pennsylvania, Rhode Island, or Vermont.

Renewable up to four years. Send a self-addressed stamped envelope (#10) to receive an application ($.64 postage).

261

NORTH DAKOTA DEPARTMENT OF TRANSPORTATION (Grants)
Human Resources Division
608 East Blvd.
Bismarck, ND 58505
701/328-2574

AMOUNT: $1,000 per year
DEADLINE(S): Feb 15
FIELD(S): Civil Engineering; Civil Engineering & Survey Technology; Construction Engineering

Financial aid grants open to undergraduate students at recognized colleges & universities in North Dakota who have completed at least 1 year of study in the above fields.

2-4 grants per year. Renewable. Write for complete information.

262

PACIFIC GAS & ELECTRIC CO. (Scholarships for High School Seniors)
77 Beale Street, Room 2837
San Francisco, CA 94106
415/973-1338

AMOUNT: $1,000-$4,000
DEADLINE(S): Nov 15
FIELD(S): Engineering; Computer Science; Mathematics; Marketing; Business; Economics

High school seniors in good academic standing who reside in or attend high school in areas served by PG&E are eligible to compete for scholarships awarded on a regional basis. Not open to children of PG&E employees.

36 awards per year. Applications & brochures are available in all high schools within PG&E's service area and at PG&E offices.

263

U.S. AIR FORCE ROTC (4-Year Scholarship Program)
AFROTC/RROO
Recruiting Operations Branch
551 E. Maxwell Blvd.

Maxwell AFB, AL 36112-6106
334/953-2091

AMOUNT: Tuition; fees & books + $150 per month stipend
DEADLINE(S): Dec 1
FIELD(S): Aeronautical Engineering; Civil Engineering; Mechanical Engineering; Mathematics; Physics; Nursing & some Liberal Arts

Open to U.S. citizens who are at least 17 and will graduate from college before age 25. Must complete application, furnish SAT/ACT scores, high school transcripts and record of extracurricular activities.

Must qualify on Air Force medical examination. About 1,600 scholarships awarded each year at campuses which offer Air Force ROTC.

COMPUTER SCIENCE

264

AT&T BELL LABORATORIES (Summer Research Program for Minorities & Women)
101 Crawfords Corner Road
Holmdel, NJ 07733-3030
Written inquiry

AMOUNT: Salary + travel & living expenses for summer
DEADLINE(S): Dec 1
FIELD(S): Engineering; Math; Sciences; Computer Science

Program offers minority students & women students technical employment experience at Bell Laboratories. Students should have completed their third year of study at an accredited college or university. U.S. citizen or permanent resident.

Selection is based partially on academic achievement and personal motivation. Write special programs manager—SRP for complete information.

265

BUSINESS & PROFESSIONAL WOMEN'S FOUNDATION (Career Advancement Scholarships)
2012 Massachusetts Ave. NW
Washington, D.C. 20036
202/293-1200

AMOUNT: $500-$1,000
DEADLINE(S): Apr 15 (postmark)
FIELD(S): Computer Science; Education; Paralegal; Engineering; Science; Law; Dentistry; Medicine

Open to women (30 or older) within 12-24 months of completing undergrad or grad study in U.S. (including Puerto Rico & Virgin Islands). Studies should lead to entry/reentry in work force or improve career advancement chances.

Not for doctoral study. Must demonstrate financial need. Send self-addressed stamped ($.64) #10 envelope for complete info. Applications available Oct. 1-April 1.

266

DEVRY INC. (Scholarship Program)
One Tower Lane
Oakbrook Terrace, IL 60181
708/571-7700; 800/323-4256

AMOUNT: Full tuition (40); 1/2 tuition (80)
DEADLINE(S): Mar 22
FIELD(S): Electronics Engineering Technology; Computer Information Systems; Business Operations; Telecommunications Management; Accounting

30 full-tuition & 90 1/2-tuition undergraduate scholarships. Open to U.S. high school graduates who wish to enroll in a fully-accredited bachelor of science degree program at one of the Devry Institutes located throughout North America.

Awards renewable provided 2.5 GPA is maintained. Must be a U.S. citizen. Contact your guidance counselor; nearest Devry Institutes located throughout North America.

267

IEEE COMPUTER SOCIETY (Lance Stafford Larson Student Scholarship)
1730 Massachusetts Ave. NW
Washington, D.C. 20036-1992
202/371-1013; Fax 202/778-0884; Internet:
www.computer.org

AMOUNT: $500
DEADLINE(S): Oct 31
FIELD(S): Computer Science

Scholarships for undergraduate members of
the IEEE Computer Society who write a
winning essay on a computer-related subject. Minimum GPA of 3.0 required.
Contact organization for details.

268

IEEE COMPUTER SOCIETY (Richard Merwin Student Scholarship)
1730 Massachusetts Ave. NW
Washington, D.C. 20036-1992
202/371-1013; Fax 202/778-0884; Internet:
www.computer.org

AMOUNT: $3,000
DEADLINE(S): May 31
FIELD(S): Computer Science; Computer
Engineering; Electrical Engineering

Scholarships for active leaders in student
branch chapters of the IEEE Computer
Society who show promise in their academic and professional efforts.
4 awards. Contact above address or website
for details.

269

IEEE COMPUTER SOCIETY (Upsilon Pi Epsilon Student Award)
1730 Massachusetts Ave. NW
Washington, D.C. 20036-1992
202/371-1013; Fax 202/778-0884; Internet:
www.computer.org

AMOUNT: $500
DEADLINE(S): Oct 31

FIELD(S): Computer Science

Scholarships for undergraduate members of
the IEEE Computer Society who are full-
time students at an academic institution.
Minimum GPA of 3.0 required.
Contact organization for details.

270

NATIONAL FEDERATION OF THE BLIND (Computer Science Scholarship)
805 Fifth Ave.
Grinnel, IA 50112
515/236-3366

AMOUNT: $3,000
DEADLINE(S): Mar 31
FIELD(S): Computer Science

For a blind student pursuing a full-time, post-
secondary educational program specializing
in the field of computer science.
Awards based on academic excellence, service
to the community, and financial need.
Winners receive awards at the Federation's
annual convention.

271

**PACIFIC GAS & ELECTRIC CO.
(Scholarships for High School Seniors)**
77 Beale Street, Room 2837
San Francisco, CA 94106
415/973-1338

AMOUNT: $1,000-$4,000
DEADLINE(S): Nov 15
FIELD(S): Engineering; Computer Science;
Mathematics; Marketing; Business;
Economics

High school seniors in good academic standing
who reside in or attend high school in areas
served by PG&E are eligible to compete for
scholarships awarded on a regional basis.
Not open to children of PG&E employees.
36 awards per year. Applications & brochures
are available in all high schools within
PG&E's service area and at PG&E offices.

272

SOCIETY FOR SOFTWARE QUALITY
(Grant-In-Aid Essay Contest)
Scholarship Committee Chair
P.O. Box 86958
San Diego, CA 92138-6958
619/646-9214; E-mail: kozak@hctg.saic.com

AMOUNT: $500
DEADLINE(S): Varies
FIELD(S): Computer Software

Annual essay contest on a general computer
software subject. One contest is open to
high school seniors, college freshmen, and
college sophomores. Another is open to college juniors, college seniors, and graduate
students.

Contact the Society for Software Quality for
more information.

273

SOCIETY OF WOMEN ENGINEERS
(Admiral Grace Murray Hopper Scholarship)
120 Wall Street, 11th Floor
New York, NY 10005
212/509-9577; Fax 212/509-0224

AMOUNT: $1,000
DEADLINE(S): May 15 (postmark)
FIELD(S): Engineering; Computer Science

For women entering a four-year program for
the study of engineering or computer science as freshmen. Applications available
March-May.

5 awards. Send self-addressed stamped envelope for complete information.

274

SOCIETY OF WOMEN ENGINEERS
(Hewlett-Packard Scholarships)
120 Wall Street, 11th Floor
New York, NY 10005
800/666-ISWE; 212/509-0224; Fax 212/509-
0224

AMOUNT: $1,000

DEADLINE(S): Feb 1
FIELD(S): Electrical Engineering; Computer
Science

Open to women who are juniors or seniors
majoring in electrical engineering or computer science at an accredited school.
Applicants must be active supporters and
contributors to SWE.

Applications available Oct.-Jan. only. Send
self-addressed stamped envelope for complete information.

275

SOCIETY OF WOMEN ENGINEERS
(Microsoft Corporation Scholarships)
120 Wall Street, 11th Floor
New York, NY 10005
800/666-ISWE; 212/509-9577; Fax 212/509-
0224

AMOUNT: $1,000
DEADLINE(S): Feb 1 (postmark)
FIELD(S): Computer Science; Computer
Engineering

Open to women entering their sophomore,
junior or senior year and to first-year master's students at SWE approved schools.
Recipients must be pursuing a degree in
computer science or engineering and exhibit career interest in the field of microcom-
puter software.

10 awards. Applications available Oct.-Jan.
only. Send self-addressed stamped envelope
for complete information.

276

SOCIETY OF WOMEN ENGINEERS
(Olive Lynn Salember Scholarship)
120 Wall Street, 11th Floor
New York, NY 10005-3902
212/509-9577; Fax 212/509-0224

AMOUNT: $2,000
DEADLINE(S): May 15
FIELD(S): Engineering, Computer Science

For women who have been out of the engineering job market and/or out of school for

a minimum of two years. For any year undergraduate or graduate, including doctoral program.

1 award. Apply between March-May. Send SASE for application and information.

277

STATE FARM COMPANIES FOUNDATION (Exceptional Student Fellowship)

1 State Farm Plaza
Bloomington, IL 61710
309/766-2039

AMOUNT: $3,000

DEADLINE(S): Feb 15 (apps. available Nov 1)

FIELD(S): Accounting; Business Administration; Actuarial Science; Computer Science; Economics; Finance; Insurance; Investments; Marketing; Mathematics; Statistics; and related fields

Open to current full-time college juniors and seniors majoring in any of the fields above. Only students nominated by the college dean or a department head qualify as candidates. Applications without nominations will not be considered.

U.S. citizen. 3.6 or better GPA (4.0 scale) required. 50 fellowships per year. Write for complete information.

278

TANDY TECHNOLOGY SCHOLARS (Student Awards; Teacher Awards)

Texas Christian University
Box 298990
Fort Worth, TX 76129
817/924-4087

AMOUNT: $1,000 students; $2,500 teachers

DEADLINE(S): Oct 9

FIELD(S): Mathematics; Science; Computer Science

Program recognizes academic performance and outstanding achievements by Mathematics, Science, and Computer Science students and teachers. Students and teachers receive cash awards.

Must be a senior in an enrolled high school located in one of the 50 states. 100 of each awarded each year. Nomination packets sent to high schools.

279

TYSON FOUNDATION INC. (Scholarship Program)

2210 W. Oaklawn
Springdale, AR 72762-6999
501/290-4955

AMOUNT: Varies according to need

DEADLINE(S): Apr 20

FIELD(S): Business; Agriculture; Engineering; Computer Science; and Nursing

For Arkansas residents who are U.S. citizens. Must be enrolled full-time in an accredited institution and demonstrate financial need. Must be employed part-time and/or summers to help fund education. For undergrad study at schools in U.S.

Renewable up to 8 semesters or 12 trimesters as long as students meet criteria.

ELECTRICAL ENGINEERING

280

AMERICAN RADIO RELAY LEAGUE FOUNDATION (Charles N. Fisher Memorial Scholarship)

225 Main Street
Newington, CT 06111
860/594-0200; Fax 860/594-0259; Internet: www.arrl.org/arrlf

AMOUNT: $1,000

DEADLINE(S): Feb 15

FIELD(S): Electronics, communications, or related fields

Open to residents of the ARRL Southwestern Division (Arizona and the California counties of Los Angeles, Orange, San Diego, and

Santa Barbara) studying electronics, communications, or related fields and who hold any class radio amateur license. Must attend an accredited college or university in the region.

1 award per year.

281

AMERICAN RADIO RELAY LEAGUE FOUNDATION (Dr. James L. Lawson Memorial Scholarship)
225 Main Street
Newington, CT 06111
860/594-0200; Fax 860/594-0259; Internet: www.arrl.org/arrlf

AMOUNT: $500
DEADLINE(S): Feb 15
FIELD(S): Electronics; Communications
Open to radio amateurs holding at least a general license and residing in CT, MA, ME, NH, RI, VT, or NY and attending a school in one of those states.
1 award per year.

282

AMERICAN RADIO RELAY LEAGUE FOUNDATION (Edmund A. Metzger Scholarship Fund)
225 Main Street
Newington, CT 06111
860/594-0200; Fax 860/594-0259; Internet: www.arrl.org/arrlf

AMOUNT: $500
DEADLINE(S): Feb 15
FIELD(S): Electrical Engineering
Open to ARRL members who are residents of ARRL Central Div. (IL; IN; WI); attend school in the ARRL Central Division & are currently licensed radio amateurs at at-least "Novice" level.
1 award per year.

283

AMERICAN RADIO RELAY LEAGUE FOUNDATION (F. Charles Ruling, N6FR Memorial Scholarship)
225 Main Street
Newington, CT 06111
860/594-0200; Fax 860/594-0259; Internet: www.arrl.org/arrlf

AMOUNT: $1,000
DEADLINE(S): Feb 15
FIELD(S): Electronics, communications, or related fields
For undergraduate or graduate students who hold at least a "General" class of radio amateur license majoring in electronics, communications, or related fields.
1 award per year.

284

AMERICAN RADIO RELAY LEAGUE FOUNDATION (Fred R. McDaniel Memorial Scholarship)
225 Main Street
Newington, CT 06111
860/594-0200; Fax 860/594-0259; Internet: www.arrl.org/arrlf

AMOUNT: $500
DEADLINE(S): Feb 15
FIELD(S): Electronics; Communications
Open to radio amateurs holding at least a "General" license residing in either TX, OK, AK, LA, MI, or NM and attending school in one of those states. Preference to holders of GPA of 3.0 or higher.
1 award per year.

285

AMERICAN RADIO RELAY LEAGUE FOUNDATION (Irving W. Cook WA0CGS Scholarship)
225 Main Street
Newington, CT 06111
860/594-0200; Fax 860/594-0259; Internet: www.arrl.org/arrlf

AMOUNT: $1,000

DEADLINE(S): Feb 15

FIELD(S): Electronics, communications, or related fields

Open to residents of Kansas who hold any class of radio amateur license and are seeking a baccalaureate or higher degree. For study in any U.S. college or university.

1 award per year.

286

AMERICAN RADIO RELAY LEAGUE FOUNDATION (L. Phil Wicker Scholarship)
225 Main Street
Newington, CT 06111
860/594-0200; Fax 860/594-0259; Internet: www.arrl.org/arrlf

AMOUNT: $1,000

DEADLINE(S): Feb 15

FIELD(S): Electronics, communications, and related fields

Open to students who are residents of ARRL Roanoke Div. (NC; SC; VA; WV); attend a school in the Roanoke Div. as an undergraduate or graduate student & who are at least "General" class licensed radio amateurs.

1 award per year.

287

AMERICAN RADIO RELAY LEAGUE FOUNDATION (Paul & Helen L. Grauer Scholarship Fund)
225 Main Street
Newington, CT 06111
860/594-0200; 860/594-0259; Internet: www.arrl.org.arrlf

AMOUNT: $1,000

DEADLINE(S): Feb 15

FIELD(S): Electrical Engineering; Communications

Open to ARRL Midwest Div. residents (IA; KS; MO; NE) who are licensed radio amateurs at least at novice level & enrolled full-time as undergrad or grad students at an accredited institution in the ARRL Midwest Division.

1 award per year for ham radio enthusiast.

288

AMERICAN RADIO RELAY LEAGUE FOUNDATION (Perry F. Hadlock Memorial Scholarship Fund)
225 Main Street
Newington, CT 06111
860/594-0200; Fax 860/594-0259; Internet: www.arrl.org/arrlf

AMOUNT: $1,000

DEADLINE(S): Feb 15

FIELD(S): Electronic Engineering

Open to students who are "General" class licensed radio amateurs who are enrolled full-time as an undergraduate or graduate student at Clarkson University, Potsdam, NY.

1 award per year.

289

AMERICAN RADIO RELAY LEAGUE FOUNDATION (The Nemal Electronics Scholarship)
225 Main Street
Newington, CT 06111
860/594-0200; Fax 860/594-0259; Internet: www.arrl.org/arrlf

AMOUNT: $500

DEADLINE(S): Feb 15

FIELD(S): Electronics, communications, or related fields

For undergraduate or graduate students who hold at least a "General" level radio amateurs license majoring in electronics, communications, or related fields. Preference to students with GPA 3.0 or higher.

1 award given per year. Must write a brief letter explaining background and future plans.

290

AMERICAN RADIO RELAY LEAGUE FOUNDATION (The Mississippi Scholarship)

225 Main Street
Newington, CT 06111
860/594-0200; Fax 860/594-0259; Internet:
www.arrl.org/arrlf

AMOUNT: $500
DEADLINE(S): Feb 15
FIELD(S): Electronics; Communications

Open to radio amateurs under age 30 holding
any class of license, residing in Mississippi,
and attending a school in Mississippi.
1 award per year to a ham radio enthusiast.

291

AT&T BELL LABORATORIES (Summer Research Program for Minorities & Women)

101 Crawfords Corner Road
Holmdel, NJ 07733-3030
Written inquiry

AMOUNT: Salary + travel & living expenses
for summer
DEADLINE(S): Dec 1
FIELD(S): Engineering; Math; Sciences;
Computer Science

Program offers minority students & women
students technical employment experience
at Bell Laboratories. Students should have
completed their third year of study at an
accredited college or university. U.S. citizen
or permanent resident.
Selection is based partially on academic
achievement and personal motivation.
Write special programs manager—SRP for
complete information.

292

DEVRY INC. (Scholarship Program)

One Tower Lane
Oakbrook Terrace, IL 60181
708/571-7700; 800/323-4256

AMOUNT: Full tuition (40); 1/2 tuition (80)
DEADLINE(S): Mar 22

FIELD(S): Electronics Engineering
Technology; Computer Information
Systems; Business Operations;
Telecommunications Management;
Accounting

30 full-tuition & 90 1/2-tuition undergraduate
scholarships. Open to U.S. high school graduates who wish to enroll in a fully-accredited bachelor of science degree program at
one of the Devry Institutes located throughout North America.
Awards renewable provided 2.5 GPA is maintained. Must be a U.S. citizen. Contact your
guidance counselor; nearest Devry
Institutes located throughout North
America.

293

ELECTRONIC INDUSTRIES FOUNDATION (Scholarship Fund)

2500 Wilson Blvd., Suite 210
Arlington, VA 22201-3834
703/907-7408

AMOUNT: $5,000
DEADLINE(S): Feb 2
FIELD(S): Electrical Engineering; Industrial
Manufacturing; Industrial Engineering;
Physics; Electromechanical Technology;
Mechanical Applied Sciences

For students with disabilities who are pursuing
undergraduate or graduate studies directly
related to the electronics industry listed
above. Awards tenable at recognized undergraduate and graduate colleges and universities. Must be U.S. citizen. Financial need is
considered.
6 awards per year. Renewable. Send self-
addressed stamped envelope for complete
information.

294

IEEE COMPUTER SOCIETY (Richard Merwin Student Scholarship)

1730 Massachusetts Ave. NW
Washington, D.C. 20036-1992
202/371-1013; Fax 202/778-0884; Internet:
www.computer.org

AMOUNT: $3,000

DEADLINE(S): May 31

FIELD(S): Computer Science; Computer Engineering; Electrical Engineering

Scholarships for active leaders in student branch chapters of the IEEE Computer Society who show promise in their academic and professional efforts.

4 awards. Contact above address or website for details.

295

INSTITUTE OF ELECTRICAL & ELECTRONICS ENGINEERS (Charles Le Geyt Fortescue Fellowship)
445 Hoes Lane
Piscataway, NJ 08855-1331
908/562-3840

AMOUNT: $24,000

DEADLINE(S): Jan 15 (of odd-numbered years)

FIELD(S): Electrical Engineering

Fellowship is open to first-year graduate students at recognized engineering schools in the U.S. or Canada. Awards support full-time study for one academic year.

Awards granted every other year. Contact above location for details.

296

PACIFIC GAS & ELECTRIC CO. (Scholarships for High School Seniors)
77 Beale Street, Room 2837
San Francisco, CA 94106
415/973-1338

AMOUNT: $1,000-$4,000

DEADLINE(S): Nov 15

FIELD(S): Engineering; Computer Science; Mathematics; Marketing; Business; Economics

High school seniors in good academic standing who reside in or attend high school in areas served by PG&E are eligible to compete for

scholarships awarded on a regional basis. Not open to children of PG&E employees.

36 awards per year. Applications & brochures are available in all high schools within PG&E's service area and at PG&E offices.

297

RADIO FREE EUROPE/RADIO LIBERTY (Engineering Intern Program)
Personnel Division
1201 Connecticut Ave. NW
Washington, D.C. 20036
202/457-6936

AMOUNT: Daily stipend of 55 German marks + accommodations

DEADLINE(S): Feb 22

FIELD(S): Electrical Engineering

Internship in Germany open to graduate or exceptionally qualified undergrad electrical engineering students. Preference to those who have completed courses in subjects related to the technical aspects of international broadcasting.

At least basic ability to speak German is highly desirable. Write for complete information.

298

SOCIETY OF WOMEN ENGINEERS (General Motors Foundation Scholarships)
120 Wall Street, 11th Floor
New York, NY 10005
800/666-ISWE; 212/509-9577; Fax 212/509-0224

AMOUNT: $1,500

DEADLINE(S): Feb 1

FIELD(S): Engineering specialties: mechanical, electrical, chemical, industrial, materials, automotive, or manufacturing engineering or engineering technology

Open to women entering their junior year at selected universities having a declared major in one of the fields listed above. Recipients must demonstrate leadership characteristics and exhibit a career interest in the automotive industry and/or manufacturing environment.

4 awards. Renewable for senior year. Applications available October through January only. Send self-addressed stamped envelope for complete information.

299

SOCIETY OF WOMEN ENGINEERS (Hewlett-Packard Scholarships)
120 Wall Street, 11th Floor
New York, NY 10005
800/666-ISWE; 212/509-0224; Fax 212/509-0224

AMOUNT: $1,000
DEADLINE(S): Feb 1
FIELD(S): Electrical Engineering; Computer Science

Open to women who are juniors or seniors majoring in electrical engineering or computer science at an accredited school. Applicants must be active supporters and contributors to SWE.

Applications available Oct.-Jan. only. Send self-addressed stamped envelope for complete information.

ENGINEERING TECHNOLOGY

300

AMERICAN INSTITUTE OF CHEMICAL ENGINEERS (Donald F. Othmer Sophomore Academic Excellence Award)
345 E. 47th Street
New York, NY 10017
212/705-7478; Fax 212/752-3294; E-mail: awards@aiche.org

AMOUNT: One year's subscription to AIChE Journal or a copy of Perry's Chemical Engineers' Handbook
DEADLINE(S): Varies
FIELD(S): Chemical Engineering

Presented to an AIChE member in each student chapter who has attained the highest scholastic GPA during his/her freshman and sophomore years.

Based on recommendation of the Student Chapter Advisor.

301

AMERICAN INSTITUTE OF CHEMICAL ENGINEERS (Minority Scholarship Award for High School Students)
345 E. 47th Street
New York, NY 10017
212/705-7478; Fax 212/752-3294; E-mail: awards@aiche.org

AMOUNT: $1,000
DEADLINE(S): Apr 15
FIELD(S): Chemical Engineering

For minority high school students planning to study chemical engineering. Students must be nominated by a local section of AIChE. Call to find out the contact in your area.

Academic record and financial need considered.

302

AMERICAN INSTITUTE OF CHEMICAL ENGINEERS (Minority Scholarship Award for College Students)
345 E. 47th Street
New York, NY 10017
212/705-7478; Fax 212/752-3294; E-mail: awards@aiche.org

AMOUNT: $1,000
DEADLINE(S): Apr 15
FIELD(S): Chemical Engineering

Award for minority national student members of AIChE. Based on academic record, participation in AIChE activities, career objectives, and financial need.

6 awards.

303

AMERICAN INSTITUTE OF CHEMICAL ENGINEERS (National Scholarship Award)
345 E. 47th Street
New York, NY 10017
212/705-7478; Fax 212/752-3294; E-mail: awards@aiche.org

AMOUNT: $1,000
DEADLINE(S): Apr
FIELD(S): Chemical Engineering
Award for national student members of AIChE. Based on academic performance and activity in their AIChE Student Chapter.
15 awards.

304

AMERICAN INSTITUTE OF CHEMICAL ENGINEERS (National Student Design Competition)
345 E. 47th Street
New York, NY 10017
212/705-7478; Fax 212/752-3294; E-mail: awards@aiche.org

AMOUNT: $600; $300; $200; $100
DEADLINE(S): Jun 7
FIELD(S): Chemical Engineering
Chemical engineers from a designated company devise and judge a student contest problem that typifies a real, working, chemical engineering design situation. Students must be AIChE national members and have a faculty advisor's permission.
Runners-up receive Honorable Mention.

305

AMERICAN NUCLEAR SOCIETY (John & Muriel Landis Scholarships)
555 North Kensington Ave.
La Grange Park, IL 60526
312/352-6611

AMOUNT: $3,500
DEADLINE(S): Mar 1

FIELD(S): Nuclear Engineering
Open to any undergraduate or graduate student who has greater than average financial need & is planning a career in nuclear engineering or a nuclear-related field. Awards tenable at accredited institutions in the U.S.
Must be U.S. citizen or have a permanent resident visa. 8 awards per year. Write for complete information & include a SASE.

306

AMERICAN NUCLEAR SOCIETY (Undergraduate Scholarships)
555 North Kensington Ave.
La Grange Park, IL 60526
312/352-6611

AMOUNT: Varies
DEADLINE(S): Mar 1
FIELD(S): Nuclear Engineering
Scholarships open to undergraduate students who have completed at least 1 year of study in an accredited nuclear engineering (or nuclear-related area) program at a college or university in the U.S. Must be U.S. citizen or legal resident.
Write & include a SASE for complete information.

307

AMERICAN SOCIETY OF HEATING, REFRIGERATION, AND AIR-CONDITIONING ENGINEERS (ASHRAE Scholarship Program)
1791 Tullie Circle NE
Atlanta, GA 30329
404/636-8400; Fax 404/321-5478; Internet: www.ashrae.org

AMOUNT: $3,000
DEADLINE(S): Dec 1
FIELD(S): Heating, Refrigeration; Air-conditioning; Ventilation
Open to undergraduate students who plan a career in the above fields. Must have completed a full semester or quarter in an ABET-accredited college and have at least

one full year of undergraduate study remaining. Minimum 3.0 GPA (4.0 scale). Awards tenable at accredited institutions. 3 awards. Renewable. Financial need is considered. Write for complete information. Contact Lois Benedict at above location.

308

AMERICAN SOCIETY OF HEATING, REFRIGERATION, AND AIR-CONDITIONING ENGINEERS (ASHRAE Scholarship Program)

1791 Tullie Circle NE
Atlanta, GA 30329
404/636-8400; Fax 404/321-5478; Internet: www.ashrae.org

AMOUNT: $3,000
DEADLINE(S): May 1
FIELD(S): Engineering Technology

For full-time students in a two-year Associates program in an ABET-accredited program with one full year of study remaining.

Must demonstrate financial need and have GPA of 3.0 or higher. Contact Lois K. Benedict at above address.

309

AMERICAN SOCIETY OF MECHANICAL ENGINEERS (Auxiliary Student Loans)

345 E. 47th Street
New York, NY 10017
212/705-7375

AMOUNT: Up to $2,500
DEADLINE(S): Apr 1; Nov 1
FIELD(S): Mechanical Engineering; Engineering Technology

Loans to student members of ASME who are undergrad or grad students enrolled in schools with accredited mechanical engineering or engineering technology curricula. Minimum 2.2 GPA for undergrads; 3.2 GPA for grads. U.S. citizenship required.

First preference given to undergraduate juniors and seniors. Write for complete information.

310

AMERICAN WELDING SOCIETY (Scholarship Program)

550 NW Lejeune Road
Miami, FL 33126
305/443-9353; 800/443-9353

AMOUNT: Varies
DEADLINE(S): Apr 1
FIELD(S): Welding Technology

Open to students who reside in the U.S. and are enrolled in an accredited welding and joint material joining or similar program. Awards are tenable at junior colleges, colleges, universities, and institutions in the U.S.

Write for more information.

311

AT&T BELL LABORATORIES (Summer Research Program for Minorities & Women)

101 Crawfords Corner Road
Holmdel, NJ 07733-3030
Written inquiry

AMOUNT: Salary + travel & living expenses for summer
DEADLINE(S): Dec 1
FIELD(S): Engineering; Math; Sciences; Computer Science

Program offers minority students & women students technical employment experience at Bell Laboratories. Students should have completed their third year of study at an accredited college or university. U.S. citizen or permanent resident.

Selection is based partially on academic achievement and personal motivation. Write special programs manager—SRP for complete information.

312

DEVRY INC. (Scholarship Program)

One Tower Lane
Oakbrook Terrace, IL 60181
708/571-7700; 800/323-4256

AMOUNT: Full tuition (40); 1/2 tuition (80)

DEADLINE(S): Mar 22

FIELD(S): Electronics Engineering Technology; Computer Information Systems; Business Operations; Telecommunications Management; Accounting

30 full-tuition & 90 1/2-tuition undergraduate scholarships. Open to U.S. high school graduates who wish to enroll in a fully-accredited bachelor of science degree program at one of the Devry Institutes located throughout North America.

Awards renewable provided 2.5 GPA is maintained. Must be a U.S. citizen. Contact your guidance counselor; nearest Devry Institutes located throughout North America.

313

ELECTRONIC INDUSTRIES FOUNDATION (Scholarship Fund)
2500 Wilson Blvd., Suite 210
Arlington, VA 22201-3834
703/907-7408

AMOUNT: $5,000

DEADLINE(S): Feb 2

FIELD(S): Electrical Engineering; Industrial Manufacturing; Industrial Engineering; Physics; Electromechanical Technology; Mechanical Applied Sciences

For students with disabilities who are pursuing undergraduate or graduate studies directly related to the electronics industry listed above. Awards tenable at recognized undergraduate and graduate colleges and universities. Must be U.S. citizen. Financial need is considered.

6 awards per year. Renewable. Send self-addressed stamped envelope for complete information.

314

FEL-PRO/MECKLENBURGER FOUNDATION (Automotive Technicians Scholarship Program)
P.O. Box 297
St. Peter, MN 56082
507/931-1682

AMOUNT: $500

DEADLINE(S): May 1

FIELD(S): Automotive Technology—auto, diesel, heavy equipment, agricultural equipment, mechanics

For high school seniors, high school graduates (or equivalent), or post-secondary students currently enrolled or planning to enroll in a full-time course of study in automotive technology in the U.S. or Canada.

Renewable. 250 awards in the U.S. and 20 in Canada. Write to Scholarship Management Services, CSFA, at above location.

315

INSTITUTE OF INDUSTRIAL ENGINEERS (IIE Scholarships)
25 Technology Park/Atlanta
Norcross, GA 30092
404/449-0460

AMOUNT: $300-$2,500

DEADLINE(S): Nov 15 (nominations); Feb 15 (applications)

FIELD(S): Industrial Engineering

Undergraduate & graduate scholarships open to active IIE members with at least 1 full year of study remaining at an accredited college or university in North America. A GPA of 3.4 or better is required.

Applications will be mailed only to students nominated by their department head. Write for nomination forms & complete information.

316

JAMES F. LINCOLN ARC WELDING FOUNDATION (Awards Program)
P.O. Box 17035
Cleveland, OH 44117
216/481-4300

AMOUNT: Up to $2,000
DEADLINE(S): Jun 15
FIELD(S): Arc Welding Technology

Open to undergraduate & graduate engineering & technology students who solve design engineering or fabrication problems involving the knowledge or application of arc welding.

Total of 29 awards; 17 for undergraduate and 12 for graduate students. Write for complete information.

317

NATIONAL ACADEMY FOR NUCLEAR TRAINING (Scholarships)
Scott B. Law
700 Galleria Parkway
Atlanta, GA 30339
800/828-5489

AMOUNT: $2,500-$13,000
DEADLINE(S): Feb 1; Nov 1
FIELD(S): Nuclear Engineering

Open to full-time undergrads studying nuclear engineering who have at least one and at most three full academic years remaining before graduation. Must be U.S. citizen and have a 3.0 or better GPA

275 awards annually; renewable up to three years. Write for complete information.

318

NATIONAL ASSOCIATION OF PLUMBING-HEATING-COOLING CONTRACTORS (NAPHCC Educational Foundation Scholarship Program)
P.O. Box 6808
Falls Church, VA 22046
703/237-8100; 800/533-7694; Fax 703/237-7442

AMOUNT: $2,500
DEADLINE(S): Apr 1
FIELD(S): Plumbing; Heating; Cooling

For NAPHCC members in good standing or family members/friends/employees sponsored by NAPHCC member. Must be high school senior or college freshman planning to attend a four-year accredited college in the U.S. to study in the above fields.

Scholarships renewable for four years; maintaining a C average or better needed for renewal. Write for complete information.

319

NATIONAL ASSOCIATION OF WATER COMPANIES—NEW JERSEY CHAPTER (Scholarship)
Elizabethtown Water Co.
600 South Ave.
Westfield, NJ 07090
908/654-1234; Fax 908/232-2719

AMOUNT: $2,500
DEADLINE(S): Apr 1
FIELD(S): Business Administration; Biology; Chemistry; Engineering; Communications

For U.S. citizens who have lived in NJ at least 5 years and plan a career in the investor-owned water utility industry in disciplines such as those above. Must be undergrad or graduate student in a 2- or 4-year NJ college or university.

GPA of 3.0 or better required. Contact Gail P. Brady for complete information.

320

NCSU PULP & PAPER FOUNDATION (Scholarships)
Attn: J. Ben Chilton, Executive Director
P.O. Box 8005
Raleigh, NC 27695-8005
919/515-5661

AMOUNT: $1,200-$3,700
DEADLINE(S): Jan 15
FIELD(S): Pulp & Paper Science & Technology

Open to undergraduate students enrolled in North Carolina State University and majoring in pulp and paper science technology. U.S. citizen.

NC residents receive $1,200; out-of-state students receive $3,700. Awards renewable annually. Write for complete information.

321

NORTH AMERICAN DIE CASTING ASSOCIATION (David Laine Memorial Scholarships)
9701 W. Higgins Road, Suite 880
Rosemont, IL 60018
708/292-3600

AMOUNT: Varies
DEADLINE(S): May 1
FIELD(S): Die Casting Technology

Open to students enrolled at an engineering college affiliated with The Foundry Educational Foundation (FEF) & registered with FEF for the current year. U.S. citizen.

For undergraduate or graduate study. Write for complete information.

322

REFRIGERATION SERVICE ENGINEERS SOCIETY EDUCATIONAL FOUNDATION (J. W. Harris Company Scholarship)
Scholarship Committee
1666 Rand Road
Des Plaines, IL 60016-3552
847/297-6464; Fax 847/297-5038; E-mail: rses@starnetinc.com; Internet: www.rses.org

AMOUNT: Year's tuition
DEADLINE(S): Aug 1
FIELD(S): Heating; Ventilating; Air Conditioning; Refrigeration

A year's tuition for an RSES training course in refrigeration/air conditioning, heating, controls, heat pump, and electricity. Includes a one-year membership in RSES.

Contact Jane Hissong at above location.

323

SOCIETY OF MANUFACTURING ENGINEERING EDUCATION FOUNDATION (William E. Weisel Scholarship Fund)
One SME Drive
P.O. Box 930
Dearborn, MI 48121-0930
313/271-1500 Ext 512

AMOUNT: $500-$2,500
DEADLINE(S): Mar 1
FIELD(S): Engineering or Manufacturing Technology

Open to full-time undergraduate students at accredited schools who are seeking a career in manufacturing/robotics/automated systems; have completed 30 credit hours in this area & have at least 2.75 GPA (4.0 scale). U.S. or Canadian citizen.

5 different scholarships available ranging from $500-$2,500. Write for complete information.

324

SOCIETY OF WOMEN ENGINEERS (General Motors Foundation Scholarships)
120 Wall Street, 11th Floor
New York, NY 10005
800/666-ISWE; 212/509-9577; Fax 212/509-0224

AMOUNT: $1,500
DEADLINE(S): Feb 1
FIELD(S): Engineering specialties: mechanical, electrical, chemical, industrial, materials, automotive, or manufacturing engineering or engineering technology

Open to women entering their junior year at selected universities having a declared major in one of the fields listed above. Recipients must demonstrate leadership characteristics and exhibit a career interest in the automotive industry and/or manufacturing environment.

4 awards. Renewable for senior year. Applications available October through

January only. Send self-addressed stamped envelope for complete information.

325

SOCIETY OF WOMEN ENGINEERS (Texaco Foundation Scholarships)
120 Wall Street, 11th Floor
New York, NY 10005-3902
800/666-ISWE; 212/509-0224; Fax 212/509-0224

AMOUNT: $2,000
DEADLINE(S): Feb 1
FIELD(S): Chemical or Mechanical Engineering

Open to women in their junior year in mechanical or chemical engineering with at least a 3.5 GPA. Must be U.S. citizen or permanent resident and a student member of SWE.

Renewable for senior year with continued academic performance. Applications available Oct.-Jan. only. Send self-addressed stamped envelope for complete information.

326

TECHNOLOGY STUDENT ASSOCIATION (Scholarships)
1914 Association Drive
Reston, VA 22091
703/860-9000

AMOUNT: $250 to $500
DEADLINE(S): May 1
FIELD(S): Technology Education

Open to student members of the Technology Student Association who can demonstrate financial need. Grade point average is not a consideration but applicants must be accepted to a 4-year college or university.

Funds are sent to and administered by the recipient's college or university. Write for complete information.

327

THE EDWARD AND ANNA RANGE SCHMIDT CHARITABLE TRUST (Grants and Emergency Financial Assistance)
P.O. Box 770982
Eagle River, AK 99577
Written inquiry

AMOUNT: Varies
DEADLINE(S): None
FIELD(S): Sciences, especially earth and environmental sciences

Grants for both individual students and programs studying in the above fields. Alaska Natives and other minorities are urged to apply. Grants are awarded for a variety of expenses incurred by students, such as internship support, travel and/or expenses related to workshops and science fairs, support needed to secure employment in science-related fields, or emergency needs.

Requests are given immediate consideration. Application should be made by letter from a sponsor (teacher, advisor, or other adult familiar with the applicant's situation.) Both sponsor and applicant should send letters describing the applicant, the nature of the financial need, and amount requested.

328

THE INTERNATIONAL SOCIETY FOR OPTICAL ENGINEERING (Scholarships and Grants)
P.O. Box 10
Bellingham, WA 98225
360/676-3290; Fax 360/647-1445; E-mail: spie@spie.org; Internet: www.spie.org

AMOUNT: $500-$7,000
DEADLINE(S): Apr 6
FIELD(S): Optics and optical engineering

Open to college students at all levels for study of optical or optoelectronic applied science and engineering. May be awarded to students in community colleges or technical institutes and to undergraduate and graduate students at colleges and universities.

Write to the SPIE Scholarship Committee Chair or visit website (address above) for complete information.

329

UNIVERSITY OF MAINE PULP & PAPER FOUNDATION (Pulp & Paper Foundation Scholarships)
5737 Jenness Hall
Orono, ME 04469-5737
207/581-2297

AMOUNT: $1,000
DEADLINE(S): Feb 1
FIELD(S): Engineering

Open to undergraduate students accepted to or enrolled in the University of Maine at Orono who have demonstrated an interest in a paper-related career. U.S. citizenship.
25 $1,000 scholarships plus 100 tuition scholarships awarded.

330

U.S. AIR FORCE ROTC (4-Year Scholarship Program)
AFROTC/RROO
Recruiting Operations Branch
551 E. Maxwell Blvd.
Maxwell AFB, AL 36112-6106
334/953-2091

AMOUNT: Tuition; fees & books + $150 per month stipend
DEADLINE(S): Dec 1
FIELD(S): Aeronautical Engineering; Civil Engineering; Mechanical Engineering; Mathematics; Physics; Nursing & some Liberal Arts

Open to U.S. citizens who are at least 17 and will graduate from college before age 25. Must complete application, furnish SAT/ACT scores, high school transcripts and record of extracurricular activities.
Must qualify on Air Force medical examination. About 1,600 scholarships awarded each year at campuses which offer Air Force ROTC.

331

WASHINGTON PULP & PAPER FOUNDATION (Scholarship Program)
c/o Univ. of Washington
Box 352100
Seattle, WA 98195-2100
206/543-2763

AMOUNT: Varies—approx. 2/3 tuition
DEADLINE(S): Feb 1
FIELD(S): Paper Science & Engineering

Undergraduate tuition scholarships at the Univ. of Washington. Open to students who are accepted to or enrolled in the paper science & engineering curriculum at the university. For high school seniors or college transfer students ranking in the top 25% of class or otherwise recommended by principal. U.S. citizenship required.
Approximately 20 new awards per year (45 total). Renewable for up to 12 quarters. GPA 3.0 college or 3.5 high school. Write for complete information.

332

WATER ENVIRONMENT FEDERATION (Student Paper Competition)
Cheri Young
601 Wythe Street
Alexandria, VA 22314-1994
703/684-2407; Fax 703/684-2492

AMOUNT: $1,000 (1st prize); $500 (2nd); $250 (3rd) in each of 4 categories
DEADLINE(S): Feb 1
FIELD(S): Water pollution control and related fields

Awards for 500- to 1,000-word abstracts dealing with water pollution control, water quality problems, water-related concerns, or hazardous wastes. Open to undergrad (AA and BA) and grad students.
Also open to recently graduated students (within 1 calendar year of Feb. 1 deadline). Write for complete information.

MECHANICAL ENGINEERING

333

AMERICAN SOCIETY OF MECHANICAL ENGINEERS (Auxiliary Student Loans)
345 E. 47th Street
New York, NY 10017-2392
212/705-7733

AMOUNT: Up to $2,500
DEADLINE(S): Apr 1; Nov 1
FIELD(S): Mechanical Engineering;
Engineering Technology

Loans to student members of ASME who are undergrad or grad students enrolled in schools with accredited mechanical engineering or engineering technology curricula. Minimum 2.2 GPA for undergrads; 3.2 GPA for grads. U.S. citizenship required.

First preference given to undergraduate juniors and seniors. Write for complete information.

334

AMERICAN SOCIETY OF MECHANICAL ENGINEERS (Frank William and Dorothy Given Miller ASME Auxiliary Scholarship)
345 East 47th Street
New York, NY 10017-2392
212/705-7733

AMOUNT: $1,500
DEADLINE(S): Apr 15
FIELD(S): Mechanical Engineering

Open to ASME student members in their junior or senior year of study for an undergraduate degree in mechanical engineering. U.S. citizenship and residency required.

Write for complete information. Applications may be obtained from the mechanical engineering department head or ASME faculty advisor in January or February.

335

AMERICAN SOCIETY OF MECHANICAL ENGINEERS (Garland Duncan Scholarship)
345 East 47th Street
New York, NY 10017-2392
212/705-7733

AMOUNT: $2,500
DEADLINE(S): Apr 15
FIELD(S): Mechanical Engineering

Up to two annual scholarships open to undergraduate students who are ASME student members.

Write for complete information. Applications may be obtained from the mechanical engineering department head or ASME faculty advisor in January or February.

336

AMERICAN SOCIETY OF MECHANICAL ENGINEERS (John and Elsa Gracik Scholarship)
345 East 47th Street
New York, NY 10017-2392
212/705-7733

AMOUNT: $1,500
DEADLINE(S): Apr 15
FIELD(S): Mechanical Engineering

Open to ASME student members who are undergrads in a mechanical engineering or related program or to high school students accepted for enrollment in a mechanical engineering or related program. U.S. citizenship required.

Up to 4 scholarships per year. Write for complete information. Applications may be obtained from the mechanical engineering department head or ASME faculty advisor in January or February.

337

AMERICAN SOCIETY OF MECHANICAL ENGINEERS (Kenneth Andrew Roe Scholarship)
345 East 47th Street
New York, NY 10017-2392

212/705-7733

AMOUNT: $5,000
DEADLINE(S): Apr 15
FIELD(S): Mechanical Engineering
Open to ASME student members in their junior or senior year of study for an undergraduate degree in mechanical engineering. U.S. citizenship and residency required.
Write for complete information. Applications may be obtained from the mechanical engineering department head or ASME faculty advisor in January or February.

338

AMERICAN SOCIETY OF MECHANICAL ENGINEERS (William J. & Mary Jane E. Adams Jr. Scholarship)
345 East 47th Street
New York, NY 10017-2392
212/705-7733

AMOUNT: $1,000
DEADLINE(S): Apr 15
FIELD(S): Mechanical Engineering
Open to undergraduate students attending an accredited college or university in ASME Region IX (CA; HI; NV). ASME student membership required.
Write to the manager of engineering education at the above address for complete information.

339

AMERICAN SOCIETY OF MECHANICAL ENGINEERS AUXILIARY INC. (Sylvia W. Farny Scholarship)
345 E. 47th Street
New York, NY 10017-2392
212/705-7733

AMOUNT: $1,500
DEADLINE(S): Feb 15
FIELD(S): Mechanical Engineering
Open to U.S. citizens enrolled in junior year of undergraduate study in school with accredited mechanical engineering curricula in

U.S. Award is for senior year of study. Must be student member of ASME.
4-6 scholarships per year. Send inquiries to Mrs. Sue Flanders; 3556 Stevens Way; Martinez, GA 30907. Requests for applications must be received by chairman by February 1.

340

AMERICAN SOCIETY OF MECHANICAL ENGINEERS NATIONAL OFFICE (Student Assistance Loan Program)
345 East 47th Street
New York, NY 10017
212/705-7733

AMOUNT: $2,500 maximum
DEADLINE(S): Apr 15; Oct 7
FIELD(S): Mechanical Engineering
Open to citizens of the U.S., Canada & Mexico. Must be student member of ASME enrolled in an ABET-accredited program in the U.S. GPA of 2.2 or higher for undergrads; 3.2 or higher for grads (4.0 scale) is required. Must demonstrate need.
About 60 loans per year. Write for complete information.

341

ASM FOUNDATION FOR EDUCATION & RESEARCH
Scholarship Program
Materials Park, OH 44073-0002
440/338-5151; Fax 440/338-4643; E-mail: ASMFER@po.ASM~intl.org; Internet: www.asm~intl.org

AMOUNT: $500 to full tuition
DEADLINE(S): Jun 15
FIELD(S): Metallurgy; Materials Science
For undergraduate students majoring in metallurgy/materials. For citizens of U.S., Canada, or Mexico who are enrolled in a recognized college or university in one of those countries. Must be student member of ASM.
For some awards, applicant must be in junior or senior year and demonstrate financial need. Write for complete information.

342

AT&T BELL LABORATORIES (Summer Research Program for Minorities & Women)
101 Crawfords Corner Road
Holmdel, NJ 07733-3030
Written inquiry

AMOUNT: Salary + travel & living expenses for summer
DEADLINE(S): Dec 1
FIELD(S): Engineering; Math; Sciences; Computer Science

Program offers minority students & women students technical employment experience at Bell Laboratories. Students should have completed their third year of study at an accredited college or university. U.S. citizen or permanent resident.

Selection is based partially on academic achievement and personal motivation. Write special programs manager—SRP for complete information.

343

ELECTRONIC INDUSTRIES FOUNDATION (Scholarship Fund)
2500 Wilson Blvd., Suite 210
Arlington, VA 22201-3834
703/907-7408

AMOUNT: $5,000
DEADLINE(S): Feb 2
FIELD(S): Electrical Engineering; Industrial Manufacturing; Industrial Engineering; Physics; Electromechanical Technology; Mechanical Applied Sciences

For students with disabilities who are pursuing undergraduate or graduate studies directly related to the electronics industry listed above. Awards tenable at recognized undergraduate and graduate colleges and universities. Must be U.S. citizen. Financial need is considered.

6 awards per year. Renewable. Send self-addressed stamped envelope for complete information.

344

H. H. HARRIS FOUNDATION
One North Franklin Street, Suite 1200
Chicago, IL 60606-3401
Written inquiry

AMOUNT: Varies
DEADLINE(S): Jun 15
FIELD(S): Metallurgical and metal casting fields

Scholarships and other forms of educational aid to students and professionals who are U.S. citizens studying in the fields listed above.

Write to John Hough, Mgr., at above address for detailed information.

345

NATIONAL ASSOCIATION OF WATER COMPANIES—NEW JERSEY CHAPTER (Scholarship)
Elizabethtown Water Co.
600 South Ave.
Westfield, NJ 07090
908/654-1234; Fax 908/232-2719

AMOUNT: $2,500
DEADLINE(S): Apr 1
FIELD(S): Business Administration; Biology; Chemistry; Engineering; Communications

For U.S. citizens who have lived in NJ at least 5 years and plan a career in the investor-owned water utility industry in disciplines such as those above. Must be undergrad or graduate student in a 2- or 4-year NJ college or university.

GPA of 3.0 or better required. Contact Gail P. Brady for complete information.

346

NATIONAL STONE ASSOCIATION (NSA Quarry Engineering Scholarships)
1415 Elliot Place NW
Washington, D.C. 20007
Written inquiry only

AMOUNT: $2,500

DEADLINE(S): May 1

FIELD(S): Quarry Engineering

Open to students intending to pursue a career in the aggregate industry and who are enrolled in an undergraduate program working toward this objective.

Employment in industry a plus; write for complete information.

347

SOCIETY OF WOMEN ENGINEERS
(General Motors Foundation Scholarships)
120 Wall Street, 11th Floor
New York, NY 10005
800/666-ISWE; 212/509-9577; Fax 212/509-0224

AMOUNT: $1,500

DEADLINE(S): Feb 1

FIELD(S): Engineering specialties: mechanical, electrical, chemical, industrial, materials, automotive, or manufacturing engineering or engineering technology

Open to women entering their junior year at selected universities having a declared major in one of the fields listed above. Recipients must demonstrate leadership characteristics and exhibit a career interest in the automotive industry and/or manufacturing environment.

4 awards. Renewable for senior year. Applications available October through January only. Send self-addressed stamped envelope for complete information.

348

SOCIETY OF WOMEN ENGINEERS
(Texaco Foundation Scholarships)
120 Wall Street, 11th Floor
New York, NY 10005-3902
800/666-ISWE; 212/509-0224; Fax 212/509-0224

AMOUNT: $2,000

DEADLINE(S): Feb 1

FIELD(S): Chemical or Mechanical Engineering

Open to women in their junior year in mechanical or chemical engineering with at least a 3.5 GPA. Must be U.S. citizen or permanent resident and a student member of SWE.

Renewable for senior year with continued academic performance. Applications available Oct.-Jan. only. Send self-addressed stamped envelope for complete information.

349

U.S. AIR FORCE ROTC (4-Year Scholarship Program)
AFROTC/RROO
Recruiting Operations Branch
551 E. Maxwell Blvd.
Maxwell AFB, AL 36112-6106
334/953-2091

AMOUNT: Tuition; fees & books + $150 per month stipend

DEADLINE(S): Dec 1

FIELD(S): Aeronautical Engineering; Civil Engineering; Mechanical Engineering; Mathematics; Physics; Nursing & some Liberal Arts

Open to U.S. citizens who are at least 17 and will graduate from college before age 25. Must complete application, furnish SAT/ACT scores, high school transcripts and record of extracurricular activities

Must qualify on Air Force medical examination. About 1,600 scholarships awarded each year at campuses which offer Air Force ROTC.

350

WEBB INSTITUTE (Naval Architecture Scholarships)
Crescent Beach Road
Glen Cove, NY 11542
516/671-2213

AMOUNT: Full tuition for 4 years

DEADLINE(S): Feb 15

FIELD(S): Naval Architecture; Marine
Engineering

Open to high school students aged 16-24 who
are in the top 10% of their class & have at
least a 3.2 GPA (4.0 scale). Selection based
on college boards, SAT scores, demonstrated interest in above areas, & interview. U.S.
citizenship required.

20 to 25 four-year full tuition undergrad scholarships per year to Webb Institute. Write
for complete information.

SCHOOL OF HUMANITIES

351

CHAUTAUQUA INSTITUTION
(Scholarships)
Schools Office
Box 1098, Dept. 6
Chautauqua, NY 14722
716/357-6233

AMOUNT: Varies
DEADLINE(S): Apr 1
FIELD(S): Art; Music; Dance; Theater

Scholarships for summer school only. Awards
are based on auditions (portfolio in art)
indicating proficiency. Financial need is a
consideration.

Some auditions are required in person, but
taped auditions also are acceptable. 250
awards per year. Write or call for complete
information.

352

CIVIL AIR PATROL (CAP Undergraduate
Scholarships)
National Headquarters
Maxwell AFB, AL 36112
334/953-5315

AMOUNT: $750
DEADLINE(S): Jan 31
FIELD(S): Humanities; Science; Engineering;
Education

Open to CAP members who have received the
Billy Mitchell Award or the senior rating in
level II of the senior training program. For
undergraduate study in the above areas.
Write for complete information.

353

NATIONAL LEAGUE OF AMERICAN
PEN WOMEN, INC. (Scholarships for
Mature Women)
1300 Seventeenth Street NW
Washington, D.C. 20036
717/225-3023

AMOUNT: $1,000
DEADLINE(S): Jan 15 (even-numbered
years)
FIELD(S): Art; Music; Creative Writing

The National League of American Pen
Women gives three $1,000 grants in even-
numbered years to women aged 35 and
over. Should submit three 4" x 6" prints,
manuscripts, or musical compositions suited
to the criteria for the year.

Send for details at the above address.

354

SOPHIA SCHNITMAN EDUCATIONAL
FOUNDATION (Merit Scholarship)
41 Yorkshire Drive
East Windsor, NJ 08520
609/448-8729

AMOUNT: $1,000
DEADLINE(S): Jan 31
FIELD(S): Liberal Arts

Applicant must be the child of a current NJ
state employee with a high GPA, be in
junior year of college (or like transfer from
a junior college) enrolled in a liberal arts
discipline & demonstrate community service. NJ resident.

Renewable once upon written evidence of
recipient's maintenance of high academic
standards. Send SASE for more information.

355

UNITARIAN UNIVERSALIST ASSN.
(Stanfield Scholarship Program)
25 Beacon Street
Boston, MA 02108
617/742-2100

AMOUNT: $1,400-$12,000
DEADLINE(S): Feb 15
FIELD(S): Art; Law; Music

Art scholarships for undergraduate or graduate study. Law scholarships for graduates only. Applicants must be Unitarian Universalists.
Send a self-addressed stamped envelope to the above address for complete information. No phone calls please.

AREA STUDIES

356

AMERICAN ASSOCIATION OF TEACHERS OF FRENCH (National French Contest)
Sidney L. Teitelbaum
Box 32030
Sarasota, FL 34278
Fax 914/364-9820

AMOUNT: Varies
DEADLINE(S): Feb 4
FIELD(S): French Language; French Studies

National French contest is an examination taken throughout the country. Students are ranked regionally and nationally and are eligible for both local and national awards.
Not a scholarship. Winners receive trips, medals and books. Write for complete information or ask your French teacher.

357

CHINA TIMES CULTURAL FOUNDATION
43-27 36th Street
Long Island City, NY 11101
718/937-6110

AMOUNT: $1,000

DEADLINE(S): Aug 15
FIELD(S): Chinese studies, including language, culture, exchange programs, etc.

Undergraduate scholarships to individuals of Chinese ancestry, for Chinese language school students, for Sino-American cultural exchanges, and for scholarly discourses relating to Chinese studies.
Send SASE to James N. Tu at above address for application details.

358

COMMITTEE ON INSTITUTIONAL COOPERATION (CIC Pre-doctoral Fellowships)
Kirkwood Hall 111
Indiana University
Bloomington, IN 47405
812/855-0823

AMOUNT: $11,000 + tuition (4 years)
DEADLINE(S): Dec 1
FIELD(S): Humanities; Social Sciences; Natural Sciences; Mathematics; Engineering

Pre-doctoral fellowships for U.S. citizens of African-American, American Indian, Mexican-American, or Puerto Rican heritage. Must hold or expect to receive bachelor's degree by late summer from a regionally accredited college or university.
Awards for specified universities in IL; IN; IA; MI; MN; OH; WI; PA. Write for details.

359

CREOLE-AMERICAN GENEALOGICAL SOCIETY INC. (Creole Scholarships)
P.O. Box 3215
Church Street Station
New York, NY 10008
Written inquiry only

AMOUNT: $1,500
DEADLINE(S): None
FIELD(S): Genealogy or language or Creole culture

Awards in the above areas open to individuals of mixed racial ancestry who submit a four-generation genealogical chart attesting to

Creole ancestry and/or inter-racial parentage. For undergraduate or graduate study/research.

For scholarship/award information send $2.55 money order and self-addressed stamped envelope to address above. Cash and personal checks are not accepted. Letters without SASE and handling charge will not be answered.

360

DUMBARTON OAKS (Awards in Byzantine Studies, Pre-Columbian Studies, and the History of Landscape Architecture)
1703 32nd Street NW
Washington, D.C. 20007
202/339-6410

AMOUNT: Up to $37,700 per academic year
DEADLINE(S): Nov 1
FIELD(S): Byzantine Studies; Pre-Columbian Studies; History of Landscape Architecture

Residential doctoral and postdoctoral fellowships; junior fellowships & summer fellowships to support study and/or research in the above areas. All fellows are expected to be able to communicate satisfactorily in English.

Write for complete information.

361

DUMBARTON OAKS (The Bliss Prize Fellowship in Byzantine Studies)
1703 32nd Street NW
Washington, D.C. 20007
202/342-3232

AMOUNT: Varies—estimated by the graduate school in which successful candidate enrolls for two academic years
DEADLINE(S): Nov 1
FIELD(S): Byzantine Studies

Open to outstanding college seniors who plan to enter the field of Byzantine studies. Must be in last year of studies or already hold BA and have completed at least one year of Greek by the end of the senior year.

Students must be nominated by their advisors by October 15 and attend grad school in the U.S. or Canada. Write for complete information.

362

EAST-WEST CENTER (Undergraduate and Graduate Fellowships for Pacific Islanders)
1601 East-West Road, Room 2066
Honolulu, HI 96848-1601
808/944-7735; Fax 808/944-7730

AMOUNT: Varies
DEADLINE(S): None given
FIELD(S): Asian Pacific Studies

Open to Pacific Islanders who wish to pursue studies relevant to development needs in the Pacific Islands region. Applicants should have a strong academic record and a desire to broaden their knowledge of the Pacific, Asia, and the U.S.

Write for complete information.

363

GERMAN ACADEMIC EXCHANGE SERVICE (DAAD Programs)
950 Third Ave., 19th Floor
New York, NY 10022
212/758-3223; Fax 212/755-5780

AMOUNT: Varies (with program)
DEADLINE(S): Varies (with program)
FIELD(S): German Studies/Language

Open to U.S. or Canadian citizens who are either students or full-time faculty members at Canadian or U.S. colleges or universities. There are programs for study in the U.S. and in Germany.

Write for complete information.

364

IRISH AMERICAN CULTURAL INSTITUTE (Irish Way Scholarships)
1 Lackawanna Place
Morristown, NJ 07960
973/605-1991

AMOUNT: $250-$1,000

DEADLINE(S): Apr 1

FIELD(S): Irish Studies

A summer study & recreation program in Ireland. Open to 9th-12th grade high school students who have an interest in Irish culture & are U.S. citizens. This is not a scholarship.

30-40 awards per year. Write for complete information.

365

JUNIATA COLLEGE (The Baker Peace Scholarship)
Baker Institute, Peace and Conflict Studies
Huntingdon, PA 16652
814/641-3265

AMOUNT: $1,000-$2,000

DEADLINE(S): Feb 1

FIELD(S): Peace and Conflict Studies; International Affairs

Open to incoming freshmen who rank in the upper 20% of their high school class, have above-average SAT scores, and demonstrate an interest in peace-related issues. Applicants must submit 1,000 word essay on a designated topic and two letters of recommendation. Scholarship may be renewed for four years, provided 3.0 GPA is maintained and student participates in the Peace and Conflict Studies Program.

Write to the above address for complete information.

366

MEMORIAL FOUNDATION FOR JEWISH CULTURE (International Scholarship Program for Community Service)
15 East 26th Street, Room 1703
New York, NY 10010
212/679-4074

AMOUNT: Varies

DEADLINE(S): Nov 30

FIELD(S): Jewish Studies

Open to any individual regardless of country of origin for undergrad study that leads to careers in the Rabbinate, Jewish education, social work or as religious functionaries in Diaspora Jewish communities outside the U.S., Israel & Canada.

Must commit to serve in a community of need for 3 years. Those planning to serve in the U.S., Canada or Israel are excluded from this program. Write for complete information.

367

MEMORIAL FOUNDATION FOR JEWISH CULTURE (Soviet Jewry Community Service Scholarship Program)
15 East 26th Street, Room 1703
New York, NY 10010
212/679-4074

AMOUNT: Not specified

DEADLINE(S): Nov 30

FIELD(S): Jewish studies

Open to Jews from the former Soviet Union enrolled or planning to enroll in recognized institutions of higher Jewish learning. Must agree to serve a community of Soviet Jews anywhere in the world for a minimum of three years.

Grants are to help prepare well-qualified Soviet Jews to serve in the FSU. Write for complete information.

368

MINISTRY OF EDUCATION OF THE REPUBLIC OF CHINA (Scholarships for Foreign Students)
5 South Chung-Shan Road
Taipei, Taiwan REPUBLIC OF CHINA
356-5696; Fax 397-6778

AMOUNT: NT$10,000 (per month)

DEADLINE(S): Varies (inquire of school)

FIELD(S): Chinese studies or language

Undergraduate and graduate scholarships are available to foreign students wishing to study in Taiwan. Must have already studied in R.O.C. for at least one term. Must study full time.

Scholarships are renewable. 300 awards per year. Write for complete information or contact colleges directly.

369

NATIONAL ITALIAN AMERICAN FOUNDATION (Alex and Henry Recine Scholarships)
1860 19th Street NW
Washington, D.C. 20009-5599
202/530-5315

AMOUNT: $2,500
DEADLINE(S): May 31
FIELD(S): For a major of study of the New York state area

Open to undergraduates of Italian ancestry majoring in the study of the New York state area.

Financial need, academic merit, and community service are considered.

370

NATIONAL ITALIAN AMERICAN FOUNDATION (NIAF/Pepperdine University Scholarship)
1860 19th Street
Washington, D.C. 20009-5599
202/530-5315

AMOUNT: $2,000
DEADLINE(S): May 31
FIELD(S): International Program at Pepperdine University

For sophomore, junior and senior students of Italian ancestry at Pepperdine University accepted into the International Program. Academic merit, community service, and financial need are considered.

Call William B. Phillips at 310/456-4532.

371

NATIONAL ITALIAN AMERICAN FOUNDATION (Rose Basile Green Scholarship)
1860 Nineteenth Street NW
Washington, D.C. 20009-5599
202/530-5315

AMOUNT: $1,000
DEADLINE(S): May 31
FIELD(S): Italian-American Studies

Open to undergraduates of Italian heritage whose emphasis is on Italian-American studies. Write a 2- to 3-page typed essay on a family member or a personality you consider: "An Italian American Hero."

Write for complete information.

372

SMITHSONIAN INSTITUTION (Minority Undergraduate & Graduate Internship)
Office of Fellowships & Grants
955 L'Enfant Plaza, Suite 7000
Washington, D.C. 20560
202/287-3271; E-mail: www.si.edu/research+study; Internet: siofg@sivm.si.edu

AMOUNT: $250/wk. undergrads; $300/wk. grads
DEADLINE(S): Feb 15
FIELD(S): Animal Behavior; Ecology; Environmental Science (including an emphasis on the tropics, anthropology & archaeology); Astrophysics; Astronomy; Earth Sciences; Paleobiology; Evolutionary/Systematic Biology; History of Science and Technology; History of Art, esp. American, contemporary, African, and Asian; 20th-century American Crafts, Decorative Arts; Social/Cultural History of the U.S; Folklife

Internships in residence at the Smithsonian for U.S. minority students to participate in research or museum-related activities for 10 weeks.

Research is for above fields.

373

SMITHSONIAN INSTITUTION (Native American Internship Program)
955 L'Enfant Plaza, Suite 7000
Washington, D.C. 20560
202/287-3271; E-mail:
www.si.edu/research+study; Internet:
siofg@sivm.si.edu

AMOUNT: $250/wk. for undergrads; $300/wk. for grads.
DEADLINE(S): Mar 1; Jul 1; Nov 1
FIELD(S): Native American Studies
10-week internships for undergraduate and graduate Native American students to participate in research or museum activities related to Native American studies.
Travel allowance may be provided.

374

SONS OF NORWAY FOUNDATION (King Olav V Norwegian-American Heritage Fund)
1455 West Lake Street
Minneapolis, MN 55408
612/827-3611

AMOUNT: $250-$3,000
DEADLINE(S): Mar 1
FIELD(S): Norwegian Studies
For U.S. citizens 18 or older who have demonstrated a keen and sincere interest in the Norwegian heritage. Also for Norwegians with a demonstrated interest in American heritage. Must be enrolled in a recognized educational institution and be studying such topics as arts, crafts, literature, history, music, folklore, etc., of Norway/United States.
Financial need is a consideration but it is secondary to scholarship. 12 awards per year. Norwegian applicants write to: Sons of Norway Foundation, c/o Sons of Norway, Markensgt. 39, 4612 Kristiansand, NORWAY.

ART

375

ACADEMY OF MOTION PICTURE ARTS AND SCIENCES (Nicholl Fellowships in Screenwriting)
8949 Wilshire Blvd.
Beverly Hills, CA 90211
310/247-3059

AMOUNT: $25,000
DEADLINE(S): May 1
FIELD(S): Film/screenwriting
Student academy awards competition is open to student filmmakers who have no professional experience. No applicant may have earned money as a screenwriter for theatrical films or television, or for the sale of an option to, any original story treatment, screenplay or teleplay for more than $1,000. Awards are for completed film projects written in English.
Note: Award may not be used for educational purposes. Write for complete information.

376

ALEXANDER GRAHAM BELL ASSOCIATION FOR THE DEAF (Arts and Sciences Financial Aid Awards)
3417 Volta Place
Washington, D.C. 20007-2778
202/337-5220; E-mail: Agbcll2@aol.com

AMOUNT: Varies
DEADLINE(S): Apr 1 (request applications between Feb. 1 and Mar. 1)
FIELD(S): Art or Science
For aural/oral students between the ages of 5 and 19 who have moderate to profound hearing losses. Must use speech and residual hearing and/or speechreading as primary form of communication. May be used to help with participation in extracurricular activities in art or science during the summer, on weekends, or after school.
Write for complete information.

377

AMERICAN INTERCONTINENTAL UNIVERSITY (Emilio Pucci Scholarships)
Admissions Committee
3330 Peachtree Road NE
Atlanta, GA 30326
404/812-8192; 888/248-7392

AMOUNT: $1,800 (deducted from tuition over 6 quarters)
DEADLINE(S): None
FIELD(S): Fashion Design; Fashion Marketing; Interior Design; Commercial Art; Business Administration; Video Production
Scholarships are for high school seniors who are interested in either a 2-year or 4-year program at one of the campuses of the American Intercontinental University: Atlanta, GA; Los Angeles, CA; London, UK; or Dubai, United Arab Emirates. Scholarship is applied toward tuition.
Write for applications and complete information.

378

AMERICAN INTERCONTINENTAL UNIVERSITY (One Year Tuition Scholarship)
Admissions Committee
3330 Peachtree Road NE
Atlanta, GA 30326
404/812-8192; 888/248-7392

AMOUNT: Tuition for one academic year
DEADLINE(S): Mar 15
FIELD(S): Fashion Design; Fashion Marketing; Interior Design; Commercial Art; Video Production
Scholarships are for high school juniors or seniors who are interested in studying in the above fields at one of the campuses of the American Intercontinental University: Atlanta, GA; Los Angeles, CA; London, UK; or Dubai, United Arab Emirates.
Write or call for applications and complete information.

379

AMERICAN SOCIETY OF INTERIOR DESIGNERS (Joel Polsky-Fixtures Furniture Academic Achievement Award)
608 Massachusetts Ave. NE
Washington, D.C. 20002-6006
202/546-3480; 202/546-3240; E-mail: education@asid.noli.com

AMOUNT: $1,000
DEADLINE(S): Feb 4
FIELD(S): Interior Design
For an outstanding undergraduate or graduate student's interior design research or thesis project related to interior design topics.
1 award given.

380

AMERICAN SOCIETY OF INTERIOR DESIGNERS EDUCATIONAL FOUNDATION (Yale R. Burge Scholarship Competition)
608 Massachusetts Ave. NE
Washington, D.C. 20002-6006
202/546-3480; Fax 202/546-3240; E-mail: education@asid.noli.com

AMOUNT: $250-$500
DEADLINE(S): Jan 21 (Registration due then. Entries due Feb 7)
FIELD(S): Interior Design
Competition designed to encourage students to seriously plan their portfolios. Open to students in their final year of undergrad study who are enrolled in at least a 3-year program of interior design.
A $10 entry fee is required with registration. Send self-addressed stamped envelope for complete information.

381

AMERICAN SOCIETY OF INTERIOR DESIGNERS EDUCATIONAL FOUNDATION, INC. (ASID/Joel Polsky-Fixtures Furniture Prize)
608 Massachusetts Ave. NE
Washington, D.C. 20002-6006

202/546-3480; Fax 202/546-3240; E-mail:
education@asid.noli.com

AMOUNT: $1,000
DEADLINE(S): Feb 4
FIELD(S): Interior Design

This award is given by the ASID Educational
Foundation to recognize outstanding academic contribution to the discipline of interior
design through literature or visual communication. Material will be judged on innova-
tive subject matter, comprehensive cover-
age of topic, organization, graphic presenta-
tion, and bibliographic references.
Contact the above address for complete information.

382

**AMERICAN SOCIETY OF INTERIOR
DESIGNERS EDUCATIONAL
FOUNDATION, INC. (S. Harris Memorial
Scholarship)**
608 Massachusetts Ave. NE
Washington, D.C. 20002-6006
202/546-3480; Fax 202/546-3240; E-mail:
education@asid.noli.com

AMOUNT: $1,500
DEADLINE(S): Mar 4
FIELD(S): Interior Design

To assist talented undergraduate students of
interior design enrolled at a degree-granting
academic institution. A student must be in
at least his/her second year of studies to be
eligible. Awards based on financial need
and academic/creative standing.
2 awards yearly. Academic/creative accomplishment to be demonstrated by academic
transcripts and letters of recommendation
from faculty. Write to the above address for
complete information.

383

**AMERICAN WOMEN IN RADIO &
TELEVISION (Houston Internship Program)**
Aprille Meek
AWRT—Houston
P.O. Box 980908

Houston, TX 77098
Written inquiry

AMOUNT: $500 per year
DEADLINE(S): Mar 1
FIELD(S): Radio; Television; Film & Video;
Advertising; Marketing

Internships open to students who are juniors,
seniors or graduate students at greater
Houston area colleges & universities.
Write for complete information.

384

**ART INSTITUTE OF SOUTHERN
CALIFORNIA (Scholarships)**
2222 Laguna Canyon Road
Laguna Beach, CA 92651
714/376-6000; Fax 714/376-6009

AMOUNT: $500-$2,000
DEADLINE(S): May 1
FIELD(S): Art/Design

Merit scholarship is based on the strength of
the student's portfolio. Open to undergraduate art students at the Art Institute of
Southern California. Students must be U.S.
citizens and have a GPA of at least 2.5.
Some applicants may be asked to fill out a
FAFSA form. Write to the above address
for complete information.

385

**ARTS INTERNATIONAL; INSTITUTE OF
INTERNATIONAL EDUCATION (Cintas
Fellowship Program)**
809 United Nations Plaza
New York, NY 10017
212/984-5370

AMOUNT: $10,000
DEADLINE(S): Mar 1
FIELD(S): Architecture; Painting;
Photography; Sculpture; Printmaking;
Music Composition; Creative Writing

Fellowships open to artists who are of Cuban
ancestry or Cuban citizens living outside of
Cuba. They are intended to foster &
encourage the professional development &

recognition of talented creative artists in the above areas.

Fellowships are not awarded for furtherance of academic study. 5-10 awards per year. Write for complete information.

386

ASID EDUCATIONAL FOUNDATION (S. Harris Memorial Scholarship)
608 Massachusetts Ave., NE
Washington, D.C. 20002-6006
Written inquiries

AMOUNT: $1,500
DEADLINE(S): Varies (early Spring)
FIELD(S): Interior Design

Open to any undergraduate student of interior design enrolled at a degree-granting academic institution. Students must be in at least their second year study to be eligible.

Write to the above address for complete information.

387

AUSTRIAN CULTURAL INSTITUTE (Grants for Students in Music, Drama, and the Fine Arts)
950 Third Ave., 20th Floor
New York, NY 10022
212/759-5165; Fax 212/319-9636; E-mail: desk@aci.org; Internet: www.austriaculture.net

AMOUNT: ATS 7,400/month Oct.-June (U.S. $700)
DEADLINE(S): Jan 31
FIELD(S): Music; Drama; Fine Arts

Open to non-Austrian students between the ages of 19-34 for study in Austria in music, drama, or fine arts. Working knowledge of German language required.

Must pass artistic entrance exam. Students from abroad may send tapes, slides, pictures, etc., to evaluate their level of qualification.

388

BINNEY & SMITH INC.-LIQUITEX (Liquitex Student Paint Exchange)
1100 Church Lane
P.O. Box 431
Easton, PA 18044-0431
610/253-6272 Ext 4233

AMOUNT: Free paint & mediums awarded
DEADLINE(S): Varies (25th of each month)
FIELD(S): Art

Open to undergraduate or graduate students who are U.S. or Canadian citizens. Students must be enrolled in an accredited program.

Send an SASE to the above address for application.

389

BLACK AMERICAN CINEMA SOCIETY (Filmmakers Grants Program)
6922 Hollywood Blvd., Suite 923
Hollywood, CA 90028
213/737-3292; Fax 213/737-2842

AMOUNT: Up to $3,000
DEADLINE(S): Feb 27
FIELD(S): Filmmaking

Open to Black filmmakers. Applications accepted only from the individual(s) who have primary creative responsibility for the film. Project (1 per grant cycle) may be submitted in 16mm film or 3/4" video. U.S. citizenship or legal residency.

Projects must be made in the U.S. Write for complete information.

390

BOSTON SAFE DEPOSIT & TRUST CO. (Blanche E. Coleman Awards)
One Boston Place
Boston, MA 02108
617/722-7340

AMOUNT: $500-$5,000
DEADLINE(S): Mar 1

FIELD(S): Art (career support—NOT for students)

Open to mature artists age 21 & over who are perm. residents of New England (MA; NH; RI; VT; ME) & who have completed academic education. Recommendations from art professionals are required. Must provide copy of U.S. tax return to show need.

Award is for career support. It is NOT a scholarship. Students are ineligible. Write for complete information.

391

BUSH FOUNDATION (Bush Artist Fellowships)
E900 First National Bank Bldg.
322 Minnesota Street
St. Paul, MN 55101
612/227-5222; 800/605-7315

AMOUNT: $40,000
DEADLINE(S): Oct
FIELD(S): Literature; Music Composition; Choreography; Multimedia; Performance Art; Visual Arts; Scriptworks; Film/Video

For residents of MN, ND, SD, or western WI who are at least 25 years old. Awards are to help artists work full-time in their chosen fields—NOT for academic study. Each category offered every other year.

Students are NOT eligible to apply. 15 fellowships per year, 12-18 months in duration. Write for complete information.

392

CALIFORNIA COLLEGE OF ARTS & CRAFTS (Undergraduate and Graduate Scholarships)
450 Irwin Street
San Francisco, CA 94107
415/703-9500; 800/447-1278

AMOUNT: Varies
DEADLINE(S): Mar 1
FIELD(S): Art

Open to undergraduate and graduate students accepted to or enrolled in a degree program at the California College of Arts and Crafts. Must be a U.S. citizen or legal resident and demonstrate financial need.

Approximately 600 awards per year. Renewable. Contact Office of Enrollment Services for complete information.

393

CARMEN SCHOLARSHIP COMMITTEE (Nellie Martin Carmen Scholarship)
23825 15th Ave. SE, #128
Bothell, WA 98021
206/486-6575

AMOUNT: Up to $1,000
DEADLINE(S): Mar 15
FIELD(S): All fields of study except those noted below

Open to high school seniors in King, Pierce, and Snohomish counties in the state of Washington. For undergraduate study in a Washington institution in all fields EXCEPT music, sculpture, drawing, interior design, and home economics. U.S. citizenship required.

Applications available only through high schools; nomination by counselor is required. 25-30 awards per year. Awards are renewable. Write for complete information.

394

COMMUNITY FOUNDATION OF WESTERN MASSACHUSETTS (Joseph Bonfitto Scholarship)
P.O. Box 15769
1500 Main Street
Springfield, MA 01115
413/732-2858

AMOUNT: Varies
DEADLINE(S): Mar 15
FIELD(S): Creative Design; Advertising; Art

Open to graduating seniors of Agawam High School who are pursuing a career through higher education in one of the above areas of studies. 1 scholarship is awarded annually.

Write to the above address for complete information.

395

DISTRICT OF COLUMBIA COMMISSION ON THE ARTS & HUMANITIES (Grants)

410 Eighth Street NW, 5th Floor
Washington, D.C. 20004
202/724-5613; TDD 202/727-3148; Fax
202/727-4135

AMOUNT: $2,500

DEADLINE(S): Mar 1

FIELD(S): Performing Arts; Literature;
Visual Arts

Applicants for grants must be professional artists and residents of Washington, D.C. for at least one year prior to submitting application. Awards intended to generate art endeavors within the Washington, D.C. community.

Open also to art organizations that train, exhibit, or perform within D.C.. 150 grants per year. Write for complete information.

396

FLORIDA ARTS COUNCIL (Individual Artists' Fellowships)

FL Dept. of State
Div. of Cultural Affairs
State Capitol
Tallahassee, FL 32399-0250
850/487-2980; TDD 850/414-2214; Fax
850/922-5259

AMOUNT: $5,000

DEADLINE(S): Jan 16

FIELD(S): Visual Arts; Dance; Folk Arts;
Media; Music; Theater; Literary Arts;
Interdisciplinary

Fellowships awarded to individual artists in the above areas. Must be Florida residents, U.S. citizens, and over 18 years old. May not be a degree-seeking student—funding is for support of artistic endeavors only.

38 awards per year. Write for complete information.

397

FOUNDATION OF FLEXOGRAPHIC TECHNICAL ASSOCIATION (FFTA Scholarship Competition)

900 Marconi Ave.
Ronkonkoma, NY 11779
516/737-6020

AMOUNT: Varies

DEADLINE(S): Varies

FIELD(S): Flexography or Graphic Arts

Open to students who demonstrate interest in a career in flexography, are high school seniors or enrolled at a post-secondary school offering courses in flexography, exhibit exemplary performance in the study of Graphic Arts, and have a 3.0 GPA or higher.

Write to the above address for more information.

398

GENERAL FEDERATION OF WOMEN'S CLUBS OF MASS. (Undergraduate Scholarship Program)

P.O. Box 679
Sudbury, MA 01776-0679
508/443-4569

AMOUNT: Up to $600

DEADLINE(S): Feb 15; Mar 1; Mar 15

FIELD(S): Art & Music

Undergraduate scholarships available to MA residents only who have been accepted at either Mt. Ida College or Fisher College. A letter of endorsement from your local Federated Women's Club president must be submitted with transcript.

Write for a complete listing of scholarships at above address. Send a self-addressed stamped envelope. Information also available at your local Federated Women's Club.

399

GENERAL FEDERATION OF WOMEN'S CLUBS OF MASSACHUSETTS (Pennies for Art)
Box 679
Sudbury, MA 01776-0679
Phone/Fax 508/443-4569

AMOUNT: $500
DEADLINE(S): Feb 15
FIELD(S): Art

Scholarship for a senior in a Massachusetts high school who will major in art in a college or university. Send letter of endorsement from president of the sponsoring GFWC of MA in the community of legal residence, a personal letter stating goals, and a letter of recommendation from a high school art instruction, and a portfolio of 3 examples of original work.

Send SASE with all applications and materials.

400

GEORGIA COUNCIL FOR THE ARTS (Individual Artist Grants)
530 Means Street NW, Suite 115
Atlanta, GA 30318-5793
404/651-7920

AMOUNT: Up to $5,000
DEADLINE(S): Apr 1
FIELD(S): The Arts

Grants to support artistic projects by professional artists who have been Georgia residents at least one year prior to application. Selection is based on project's artistic merit and its potential for career development.

Grants do NOT support academic study. Write for complete information.

401

HAYSTACK MOUNTAIN SCHOOL OF CRAFTS (Scholarship Program)
Admissions Office
P.O. Box 518
Deer Isle, ME 04627
207/348-2306

AMOUNT: $500-$1,000
DEADLINE(S): Mar 25
FIELD(S): Crafts

Scholarships are for technical assistants and work-study students in graphics, ceramics, weaving, jewelry, glass, blacksmithing, fabric, and wood. Financial need necessary only for work study students.

Scholarships are tenable at the school of crafts for the six summer sessions. Each session is two or three weeks long. Write Candy Haskell for complete information.

402

HOME FASHION PRODUCTS ASSN. (Design Competition)
355 Lexington Ave.
New York, NY 10017
212/661-4261

AMOUNT: $1,000
DEADLINE(S): Jun 30
FIELD(S): Interior Design; Fashion Design

Annual textile or home furnishings design competition open to any undergraduate student who is enrolled in an accredited 2-year or 4-year school of art or design.

Application accepted from department chairman only—not individuals. Write for complete information.

403

ILLINOIS ARTS COUNCIL (Artists Fellowship Awards)
100 W. Randolph, Suite 10-500
Chicago, IL 60601-3298
312/814-6750

AMOUNT: $500; $5,000; $10,000
DEADLINE(S): Sep 1
FIELD(S): Choreography; Visual Arts; Poetry Prose; Film; Video; Playwriting; Music Composition; Crafts; Ethnic & Folk Arts; Performance Art; Photography; Audio Art

Open to professional artists who are Illinois residents. Awards are in recognition of work in the above areas; they are not for continuing study. Students are NOT eligible. Write to address above for application form.

404

JAPANESE AMERICAN CITIZENS LEAGUE (Henry and Chiyo Kuwahara Creative Arts Scholarship)
1765 Sutter Street
San Francisco, CA 94115
415/921-5225; E-mail: jacl@jacl.org

AMOUNT: Varies
DEADLINE(S): Apr 1
FIELD(S): Creative Arts

Open to JACL members or their children only. For students attending any institution of higher education. This award was established to encourage creative projects that reflect the Japanese-American experience and culture. All technical work of the applicant should be of the college level. Professional artists are not eligible to apply.

For membership information or an application, send a self-addressed stamped envelope to the above address.

405

LADIES AUXILIARY TO THE VETERANS OF FOREIGN WARS OF THE UNITED STATES (Young American Creative Patriotic Art Awards)
Attn. Judy Millick, Admin. of Programs
406 W. 34th Street
Kansas City, MO 64111
816/561-8655

AMOUNT: 1st-$3,000; 2nd-$2,000; 3rd-$1,500; 4th-$1,000; 5th-$500
DEADLINE(S): Jun 1
FIELD(S): Art competition

An opportunity for high school students to display their artistic talents and to demonstrate their American patriotism and at the same time be eligible to compete for educational funds. Art must be on paper or canvas. Watercolor, pencil, pastel, charcoal, tempera, crayon, acrylic, pen-and-ink, or oil may be used.

Contact local VFW auxiliary office or address above for complete information.

406

MEMPHIS COLLEGE OF ART (Portfolio Awards)
Overton Park
1930 Poplar Ave.
Memphis, TN 38104
Written inquiry

AMOUNT: $500-$4,925 (half tuition) per year
DEADLINE(S): Varies (Nov 15 through Jul 31)
FIELD(S): Visual Arts

Awards are given to excellent visual art portfolios submitted by either high school students or transfer students. Awards to be used for full-time enrollment at Memphis College of Art. International students are welcome.

Awards are renewable for four years. Write for complete information.

407

METROPOLITAN MUSEUM OF ART (Internships)
1000 Fifth Avenue
New York, NY 10028-0198
212/570-3710

AMOUNT: $2,750 (grads); $2,500 (college juniors & seniors)
DEADLINE(S): Jan; Feb
FIELD(S): Art History & related fields

Internships open to undergraduates & graduates who intend to pursue careers in art museums. Programs vary in length & requirements. Interns work in curatorial, education, conservation, administration or library department of museum.

Write for complete information.

408

MINNESOTA STATE ARTS BOARD
(Grants Program)
Park Square Court
400 Sibley Street, Suite 200
St. Paul, MN 55101-1928
612/215-1600

AMOUNT: Fellowships-$8,000; Career
Opportunity Grants-$100 to $1,500
DEADLINE(S): Aug (Visual Arts); Sep
(Music & Dance); Oct (Literature &
Theater)
FIELD(S): Literature; Music; Theater; Dance;
Visual Arts

Fellowship grants open to professional artists
who are residents of Minnesota. Grants
may not be used for support of tuition or
work toward any degree.
Career opportunity grants and fellowships are
available.

409

NATIONAL ART MATERIALS TRADE
ASSOCIATION (NAMTA Scholarships)
10115 Kincey Ave., Suite 260
Huntersville, NC 28078
704/948-5554

AMOUNT: $1,000
DEADLINE(S): Mar 1
FIELD(S): Creative disciplines: visual arts,
writing, drama, music, etc.

For NAMTA members, employees, and their
relatives or to individuals in an organization
related to art or the art materials industry.
For undergraduate or graduate study.
Selection based on financial need, grades,
activities, interests, and career choice. Write
for complete information.

410

NATIONAL ART MATERIALS TRADE
ASSOCIATION
10115 Kincey Ave., Suite 260
Huntersville, NC 28078

704/948-5554

AMOUNT: Varies
DEADLINE(S): Mar 1
FIELD(S): Creative disciplines: visual arts,
writing, drama, music, etc.

For NAMTA members, employees, and their
relatives. For undergraduate or graduate
study.
Selection based on financial need, grades,
activities, interests, and career choice. Write
for complete information.

411

NATIONAL COUNTRY HALL OF FAME
(Stacey Scholarship Foundation)
1700 N.E. 63rd
Oklahoma City, OK 73111
405/478-2250

AMOUNT: $2,000-3,000
DEADLINE(S): Feb 1
FIELD(S): Art

Open to art students who are between the
ages of 18 and 35. Applicants must be high
school graduates and U.S. citizens.
Contact Ed Muno at the above address for
complete information.

412

NATIONAL ENDOWMENT FOR THE
ARTS (Visual Artists Fellowships)
1100 Pennsylvania Ave. NW
Washington, D.C. 20506
202/682-5448

AMOUNT: $15,000-$20,000
DEADLINE(S): Jan; Feb; Mar
FIELD(S): Visual Arts

Fellowships open to practicing professional
artists of exceptional talent in all areas of
the visual arts. Awards are to assist creative
development. They will not support academic study. U.S. citizen or legal resident.
Students are NOT eligible to apply. Write for
complete information.

413

NATIONAL FOUNDATION FOR ADVANCEMENT IN THE ARTS (Arts Recognition and Talent Search)
800 Brickell Ave., Suite #500
Miami, FL 33131
305/377-1148

AMOUNT: $100-$3,000
DEADLINE(S): Jun 1; Oct 1
FIELD(S): Creative Arts; Performing Arts

Open to high school seniors with talent in such arts as dance; music; music/jazz; theater; visual arts; film; video; and writing. Awards can be used anywhere for any purpose. For U.S. citizens or residents. Entry fee is required.

Approximately 400 awards per year. Write for complete information.

414

NATIONAL SCHOLARSHIP TRUST FUND OF THE GRAPHIC ARTS
200 Deer Run Road
Sewickley, PA 15143-2600
412/741-6860 (ask for "Scholarship Request Line"); Fax: 412/741-2311; Internet: nstf@gatf.lm.com

AMOUNT: $500-$1,500/year
DEADLINE(S): Mar 1 (High School Students); Apr 1 (College Students); Jan 10 (Fellowships)
FIELD(S): Graphic Communications

Open to students enrolled full-time in a two- or four-year program in graphic communications and related fields. Fellowships also are available for post-graduate studies. Scholarships are renewed if student maintains a 3.0 yearly GPA.

Approximately 300 awards per year. Allow up to 12 weeks for receipt of application, so inquire well before above deadlines.

415

NATIONAL SCULPTURE SOCIETY (Alex J. Ettl Grant)
1177 Avenue of the Americas, 15th Floor
New York, NY 10036
212/764-5645

AMOUNT: $5,000
DEADLINE(S): Oct 31
FIELD(S): Sculpture

Open to U.S. citizens or residents who are realist or figurative sculptors & have demonstrated a commitment to sculpting & outstanding ability. Applicants submit at least ten 8 x 10 photos of work and a brief biography.

Applicants may NOT be sculptor members of the National Sculpture Society. Send SASE for complete information.

416

NATIONAL SCULPTURE SOCIETY (Young Sculptor Awards Competition)
1177 Avenue of the Americas
New York, NY 10036
212/764-5645

AMOUNT: $1,000; $750; $500; $250
DEADLINE(S): May 31
FIELD(S): Sculpture

Competition is open to sculptors under age 36 who are residents of the U.S. A jury of professional sculptors will make their selections based upon 5-10 black & white 8 x 10 photos of each entrant's works.

In addition to cash awards & prizes, photos of winners' works will be published in *Sculpture Review* magazine. Please send SASE for complete information.

417

PASTEL SOCIETY OF AMERICA (PSA Scholarships)
15 Gramercy Park South
New York, NY 10003
212/533-6931

AMOUNT: Tuition only for PSA-sponsored classes (no cash awards)

DEADLINE(S): May 30 (for submission of slides)

FIELD(S): Painting (pastels only)

Open to talented pastel artists at all levels of study. Awards are for the study of pastel arts at the Art Students League, PSA studio or with a private PSA teacher. Duration ranges from 1 week to 1 class per week for 1 year.

30-40 awards per year. Write for complete information.

418

PRINCESS GRACE FOUNDATION-U.S. (Scholarships for Undergraduate and Graduate Thesis Film Productions)
150 East 58th Street, 21st Floor
New York, NY 10155
212/317-1470; Fax 212-317-1473

AMOUNT: $3,500 undergrad seniors; $7,500 graduate thesis

DEADLINE(S): Jun 1

FIELD(S): Film

Scholarships for undergrad seniors and graduate students for thesis film productions. Must be nominated by deans or department chairman of established U.S. colleges & universities that have been invited to apply.

Nominees must have completed one film. U.S. citizenship or permanent residency required. Contact the dean or chair of your department or call the Foundation to see if your school is eligible.

419

RIPON COLLEGE (Music, Forensics, Art, and Theatre Scholarships)
P.O. Box 248
300 Seward Street
Admissions office
Ripon, WI 54971
414/748-8102; 800/94RIPON

AMOUNT: $1,000-$8,000

DEADLINE(S): Mar 1

FIELD(S): Music; Forensics; Art; Theatre

Scholarships to recognize and encourage academic potential and accomplishment in above fields. Renewable each year provided recipient maintains a good academic standing and participates in the program.

Must apply and be accepted for admission to Ripon College. Interview or audition required. Write for complete information.

420

SAN FRANCISCO FOUNDATION (James D. Phelan Art Awards)
685 Market Street, Suite 910
San Francisco, CA 94105
415/495-3100; 510/436-3100

AMOUNT: $2,500

DEADLINE(S): Varies (early fall)

FIELD(S): Printmaking; Photography; Film & Video

Open to California-born artists in the above areas. Printmaking & photography awards in odd-numbered years and film & video awards in even-numbered years. U.S. citizenship required.

Awards will be presented at a public reception and screening of winners' works. Write for complete information.

421

SCRIPPS HOWARD FOUNDATION (Charles M. Schulz Award)
312 Walnut Street, 28th Floor
P.O. Box 5380
Cincinnati, OH 45201-5380
513/977-3035; Internet: www.scripps.com/foundation

AMOUNT: $2,500

DEADLINE(S): Jan 31

FIELD(S): College Cartoonist

Award to honor an outstanding college cartoonist. Open to any student cartoonist at a college newspaper or magazine in the U.S. or its territories.

Applications available during the fall months. Write for complete information or visit website listed above.

422

SMITHSONIAN INSTITUTION (Cooper-Hewitt, National Design Museum—Peter Krueger Summer Internship Program)
Cooper-Hewitt National Design Museum
2 East 91st Street
New York, NY 10128
212/860-6868; Fax 212/860-6909

AMOUNT: $2,500

DEADLINE(S): Mar 31

FIELD(S): Art History, Design, Museum Studies, and Museum Education; Architectural History

Ten-week summer internships open to graduate and undergraduate students considering a career in the museum profession. Interns will assist on special research or exhibition projects and participate in daily museum activities.

6 awards each summer. Internship commences in June and ends in August. Housing is not provided. Write for complete information.

423

SMITHSONIAN INSTITUTION (Minority Undergraduate & Graduate Internship)
Office of Fellowships & Grants
955 L'Enfant Plaza, Suite 7000
Washington, D.C. 20560
202/287-3271; E-mail:
www.si.edu/research+study; Internet:
siofg@sivm.si.edu

AMOUNT: $250/wk. undergrads; $300/wk. grads

DEADLINE(S): Feb 15

FIELD(S): Animal Behavior; Ecology; Environmental Science (including an emphasis on the tropics, anthropology & archaeology); Astrophysics; Astronomy; Earth Sciences; Paleobiology; Evolutionary/Systematic Biology; History of Science and Technology; History of Art, esp. American, Contemporary, African, and Asian; 20th-century American Crafts; Decorative Arts; Social/Cultural History of the U.S.; Folklife

Internships in residence at the Smithsonian for U.S. minority students to participate in research or museum-related activities for 10 weeks.

Research is for above fields.

424

SOCIETY FOR IMAGING SCIENCE AND TECHNOLOGY (Raymond Davis Scholarship)
7003 Kilworth Lane
Springfield, VA 22151
703/642-9090; Fax 703/642-9094

AMOUNT: $1,000

DEADLINE(S): Dec 15

FIELD(S): Photographic Science or Engineering

Scholarships for undergraduate juniors or seniors or graduate students for full-time continuing studies in the theory or practice of photographic science including any kind of image formation initiated by radiant energy.

Write for complete information.

425

SOLOMON R. GUGGENHEIM MUSEUM (Fellowship and Voluntary Internship Programs)
1071 Fifth Ave.
New York, NY 10128
212/423-3600

AMOUNT: Stipends vary (some positions non-paid)

DEADLINE(S): Aug 1; Dec 1; Mar 1

FIELD(S): Arts Administration; Art History

Nine-week internship open to students in the above fields who have completed at least two years of undergraduate study; fellowships open to graduate students holding BA or MA in Art History.

Direct inquiries to address above—Attn: Internship program.

426

TENNESSEE ARTS COMMISSION
(Individual Artists' Fellowships)
401 Charlotte Ave.
Nashville, TN 37243-0780
615/741-1701

AMOUNT: $2,000
DEADLINE(S): Jan 11
FIELD(S): Visual Arts; Performing Arts; Creative Arts

Open to artists who are residents of Tennessee. Duration of award is one year. Applicants must be professional artists. FULL-TIME STUDENTS ARE NOT ELIGIBLE.

Write for complete information.

427

THE E.D. FOUNDATION
953 Fifth Ave.
New York, NY 10021
212/628-5632

AMOUNT: Varies
DEADLINE(S): Varies
FIELD(S): Art

Scholarships to art students.

Write to Enrico Donati, Trustee, at above location for application deadline and procedures.

428

THE GRAND RAPIDS FOUNDATION
(Mathilda Gallmeyer Scholarship)
209-C Waters Bldg.
161 Ottawa Ave. NW
Grand Rapids, MI 49503-2703

616/454-1751; 616/454-6455

AMOUNT: Varies
DEADLINE(S): Apr 3
FIELD(S): Painting; Fine Arts

Open to full-time undergrads studying painting or fine arts at an accredited institution. Must be a Kent County resident (for a minimum of 5 years), have a minimum 2.75 GPA, and demonstrate artistic talent.

Send SASE to above address for complete information.

429

THE GRAND RAPIDS FOUNDATION
(Paul Collins Scholarship)
209-C Waters Bldg.
161 Ottawa Ave. NW
Grand Rapids, MI 49503-2703
616/454-1751; Fax 616/454-6455

AMOUNT: Varies
DEADLINE(S): Apr 3
FIELD(S): Fine Arts; Applied Arts

Open to Kent County residents who are full-time undergrads at Aquinas or Calvin Colleges, Grand Valley State Univ., Grand Rapids Community College, or Kendall College of Art & Design. GPA of 2.5 or better. Must demonstrate artistic talent.

Awards based on academic achievement, extracurricular activities, personal aspirations/educational goals, and financial need. Write for complete information.

430

THE SCHOLASTIC ART & WRITING AWARDS
555 Broadway
New York, NY 10012
212/343-6493

AMOUNT: Varies
DEADLINE(S): Varies
  (Sep 15 through Jan 1)
FIELD(S): Art; Photography; Writing

Open to students in grades 7-12. Finalists in regional competitions go on to the national level.

More than 100 undergraduate scholarships are offered per year. Send requests for information between September 15 & January 1.

431

UNIVERSITY FILM AND VIDEO ASSN. (Grants)

Professor Julie Simon
University of Baltimore
1420 N. Charles Street
Baltimore, MD 21201
410/837-6061 (written inquiry only, please)

AMOUNT: $4,000-Production; $1,000-Research

DEADLINE(S): Jan 1

FIELD(S): Film; Video; Multimedia

Open to undergraduate & graduate students who are sponsored by a faculty member who is active in the film and video association. $4,000 grants for student film or video productions. $1,000 for research projects.

Research projects may be in historical, critical, theoretical or experimental studies of film or video. Write for complete information.

432

UNIVERSITY OF ILLINOIS AT URBANA-CHAMPAIGN (Lydia E. Parker Bates Scholarship)

Turner Student Services Bldg. MC-306
610 East John Street
Champaign, IL 61820
217/333-0100

AMOUNT: Varies

DEADLINE(S): Mar 15

FIELD(S): Art, Architecture, Landscape Architecture, Urban Planning, Dance, Theater, and all related subjects except Music

Open to undergraduate students in the College of Fine & Applied Arts who are attending the University of Illinois at

Urbana-Champaign. Must demonstrate financial need and have 3.85 GPA. Complete the Free Application for Federal Student Aid.

175 awards per year. Recipients must carry at least 12 credit hours per semester. Contact office of student financial aid.

433

VIRGINIA MUSEUM OF FINE ARTS (Undergrad/Graduate & Professional Fellowships)

2800 Grove Ave.
Richmond, VA 23221-2466
804/367-0824

AMOUNT: Up to $4,000 (undergrads); $5,000 (grads); $8,000 (professionals)

DEADLINE(S): Mar 1

FIELD(S): Art; Fine Arts; Art History (graduate only); Crafts; Drawing; Filmmaking; Painting; Photography; Printmaking; Sculpture; Video

Open to Virginia residents (minimum 1-year residency prior to deadline) who are U.S. citizens or legal residents. Professional artist fellowships are also available. Financial need is considered.

Write for complete information.

434

WAVERLY COMMUNITY HOUSE INC. (F. Lammot Belin Arts Scholarships)

Scholarships Selection Committee
P.O. Box 142
Waverly, PA 18471
717/586-8191

AMOUNT: $10,000

DEADLINE(S): Dec 15

FIELD(S): Painting; Sculpture; Music; Drama; Dance; Literature; Architecture; Photography

Applicants must have resided in the Abington or Pocono regions of Northeastern Pennsylvania. They must furnish proof of exceptional ability in their chosen field but no formal training in any academic or professional program.

U.S. citizenship required. Finalists must appear in person before the selection committee. Write for complete information.

435

WELLESLEY COLLEGE (Harriet A. Shaw Fellowships)
Career Center
Secretary Graduate Fellowships
Wellesley, MA 02181-8200
617/283-3525

AMOUNT: Up to $3,000 stipend per year
DEADLINE(S): Dec
FIELD(S): Music; Allied Arts

Open to women who hold a BA degree from Wellesley College for research in music and allied arts in the U.S. or abroad. Preference given to music candidates; undergrad work in art history is required for other candidates.
Write for complete information.

ENGLISH LANGUAGE/ LITERATURE

436

AMELIA MAGAZINE (Creative Writing Contest)
329 E Street
Bakersfield, CA 93304
805/323-4064

AMOUNT: $200
DEADLINE(S): May 15
FIELD(S): Literature

This creative writing contest is for U.S. high school students only. Winner is selected of best entries. There is no entry fee; however, if complete guideline and sample of past winners is desired, a $3 handling fee is required with request.
Write to Frederick A. Raborg, Jr., at the above address for complete information.

Always include a self-addressed stamped envelope.

437

AMERICAN FOUNDATION FOR THE BLIND (R.L. Gillette Scholarship Fund)
11 Penn Plaza, #300
New York, NY 10001
212/502-7661; TDD 212/502-7662; Fax 212/502-7771; E-mail: juliry@afb.org;
Internet: www.afb.org

AMOUNT: $1,000
DEADLINE(S): Apr 30
FIELD(S): Literature or music

Open to legally blind women who are enrolled in or can provide proof of acceptance to a four-year bachelor program at a recognized school or university. Writing sample or music performance tape will be required. Must be U.S. citizen.
2 awards. Write or visit website for further information. E-mail and fax inquiries must include a complete U.S. postal service mailing address.

438

AMERICAN LEGION (National High School Oratorical Contest)
P.O. Box 1055
Indianapolis, IN 46206
317/635-8411

AMOUNT: $14,000 to $18,000 (national); $1,500 (quarter finalist); $1,500 additional to semi-finalists who do not advance to the National Finals contest
DEADLINE(S): Dec 1
FIELD(S): Oratory

Competition open to high school students. Undergraduate scholarship awards go to the contestants. U.S. citizenship or lawful permanent resident.
Write to the American Legion headquarters in your state of residence for contest procedures.

439

ARTS INTERNATIONAL; INSTITUTE OF INTERNATIONAL EDUCATION (Cintas Fellowship Program)
809 United Nations Plaza
New York, NY 10017
212/984-5370

AMOUNT: $10,000
DEADLINE(S): Mar 1
FIELD(S): Architecture; Painting; Photography; Sculpture; Printmaking; Music Composition; Creative Writing

Fellowships open to artists who are of Cuban ancestry or Cuban citizens living outside of Cuba. They are intended to foster & encourage the professional development & recognition of talented creative artists in the above areas.

Fellowships are not awarded for furtherance of academic study. 5-10 awards per year. Write for complete information.

440

ASSOCIATION FOR LIBRARY & INFORMATION SCIENCE EDUCATION (ALISE Research Grants Program)
P.O. Box 7640
Arlington, VA 22207
703/243-8040

AMOUNT: $2,500
DEADLINE(S): Oct 1
FIELD(S): Library Science

Grants to help support research costs. Open to members of the Association for Library & Information Science.

For membership information or an application, write to the above address.

441

BEVERLY HILLS THEATRE GUILD (Julie Harris Playwright Award Competition)
2815 N. Beachwood Drive
Los Angeles, CA 90068-1923
213/465-2703

AMOUNT: $5,000 (first prize); $2,000 (second prize); $1,000 (third prize)
DEADLINE(S): Nov 1 (entries accepted Aug 1 to Nov 1)
FIELD(S): Playwriting competition

Annual competition of full-length (90 minutes) unproduced, unpublished plays. Musicals, short one-act plays, adaptations, translations, and plays having won other competitions or entered in previous BHTG competitions not eligible.

Must be U.S. citizen to enter. Co-authorship is allowed. Send SASE for complete information and applications which must be submitted with entry.

442

BUSH FOUNDATION (Bush Artist Fellowships)
E900 First National Bank Bldg.
322 Minnesota Street
St. Paul, MN 55101
612/227-5222; 800/605-7315

AMOUNT: $40,000
DEADLINE(S): Oct
FIELD(S): Literature; Music Composition; Choreography; Multimedia; Performance Art; Visual Arts; Scriptworks; Film/Video

For residents of MN, ND, SD, or western WI who are at least 25 years old. Awards are to help artists work full-time in their chosen fields—NOT for academic study. Each category offered every other year.

Students are NOT eligible to apply. 15 fellowships per year, 12-18 months in duration. Write for complete information.

443

CALIFORNIA LIBRARY ASSOCIATION (Reference Service Press Fellowship)
717 K Street, Suite 300
Sacramento, CA 95814-3477
916/447-8541

AMOUNT: $2,000
DEADLINE(S): May 31

FIELD(S): Reference/information service
librarianship
Open to college seniors or graduates who
have been accepted in an accredited MLS
program. For residents of any state pursuing
an MLS at a school in California.
Students pursuing an MLS on a part-time or
full-time basis are equally eligible. Write for
complete information.

444

CALIFORNIA LIBRARY ASSOCIATION
717 K Street, Suite 300
Sacramento, CA 95814-3477
916/447-8541

AMOUNT: Varies
DEADLINE(S): May 31
FIELD(S): Reference/information service
librarianship
Open to college seniors or graduates who
have been accepted in an accredited MLS
program. For California residents attending
library school in any state OR resident of
any state attending a library school in
California.
Students pursuing an MLS on a part-time or
full-time basis are equally eligible. Write for
complete information.

445

**CATHOLIC LIBRARY ASSOCIATION
(Bouwhuis Scholarship in Library Science)**
St. Joseph Central High School Library
22 Maplewood Ave.
Pittsfield, MA 01201-4780
413/443-2CLA

AMOUNT: $1,500
DEADLINE(S): Feb 1
FIELD(S): Library Science
Open to college seniors with GPA of 3.0 or
better. Must be accepted as a master's can-
didate by an accredited graduate library
school. Financial need is a consideration.
Write for complete information.

446

**CATHOLIC LIBRARY ASSOCIATION
(World Book, Inc., Award)**
100 North Street, Suite 224
Pittsfield, MA 01201-5109
413/443-2CLA; Fax 413/442-2CLA

AMOUNT: $1,500
DEADLINE(S): Mar 15
FIELD(S): Library Science
Open to members of national Catholic Library
Association. Purpose of award is continuing
education in school or children's librarian-
ship; may not be used for library science
degree.
Write for complete information. Include
SASE.

447

**CONNECTICUT LIBRARY
ASSOCIATION (Program for Education
Grants)**
P.O. Box 1046
Norwich, CT 06360
860/885-2758

AMOUNT: Varies
DEADLINE(S): None
FIELD(S): Librarianship
Continuing education grants for library
employees, volunteer trustees, or friends of
the library in the state of Connecticut. Must
join CLA to be eligible. Tuition cost is not
covered.
4-5 grants per year. Write for complete information.

448

**CREOLE-AMERICAN GENEALOGICAL
SOCIETY INC. (Creole Scholarships)**
P.O. Box 3215
Church Street Station
New York, NY 10008
Written inquiry only

AMOUNT: $1,500
DEADLINE(S): None

FIELD(S): Genealogy or language or Creole culture

Awards in the above areas open to individuals of mixed racial ancestry who submit a four-generation genealogical chart attesting to Creole ancestry and/or inter-racial parentage. For undergraduate or graduate study/research.

For scholarship/award information send $2.55 money order and self-addressed stamped envelope to address above. Cash and personal checks are not accepted. Letters without SASE and handling charge will not be answered.

449

DISTRICT OF COLUMBIA COMMISSION ON THE ARTS & HUMANITIES (Grants)
410 Eighth Street NW, 5th Floor
Washington, D.C. 20004
202/724-5613; TDD 202/727-3148; Fax 202/727-4135

AMOUNT: $2,500
DEADLINE(S): Mar 1
FIELD(S): Performing Arts; Literature; Visual Arts

Applicants for grants must be professional artists and residents of Washington, D.C. for at least one year prior to submitting application. Awards intended to generate art endeavors within the Washington, D.C. community.

Open also to art organizations that train, exhibit, or perform within D.C. 150 grants per year. Write for complete information.

450

FLORIDA ARTS COUNCIL (Individual Artists' Fellowships)
Florida Dept. of State
Div. of Cultural Affairs
State Capitol
Tallahassee, FL 32399-0250
850/487-2980; TDD 850/414-2214; Fax 850/922-5259

AMOUNT: $5,000
DEADLINE(S): Jan 16
FIELD(S): Visual Arts; Dance; Folk Arts; Media; Music; Theater; Literary Arts; Interdisciplinary

Fellowships awarded to individual artists in the above areas. Must be Florida residents, U.S. citizens, and over 18 years old. May NOT be a degree-seeking student—funding is for support of artistic endeavors only.

38 awards per year. Write for complete information.

451

GEORGE MASON UNIVERSITY (Associated Writing Programs Award Series; St. Martin's Press Award)
Tallwood House, Mail Stop 1E3
Fairfax, VA 22030
703/934-6920; Fax 703/352-7535; E-mail: awp@gmu.edu; Internet: web.gmu.edu/departments/awp/

AMOUNT: $2,000 honorarium; (AWP); $10,000 advance against royalties (St. Martin's Press)
DEADLINE(S): Jan 1 (through Feb 28—postmark)
FIELD(S): Writing: poetry, short fiction, creative nonfiction and novels

AWP competition is for book-length manuscripts in poetry, short fiction, and creative nonfiction; St. Martin's Press Young Writers Award is for a novel whose author is 32 years of age or younger. Open to authors writing in English, regardless of their nationality or residence.

Novel manuscripts will be judged and published by St. Martin's Press. All genres require a handling fee of $10 for a WP members and $15 for nonmembers. Contact above address or website for details.

452

GEORGE MASON UNIVERSITY (Mary Roberts Rinehart Fund)
Mail Stop 3E4
English Dept.
George Mason University
4400 University Drive
Fairfax, VA 22030
703/993-1180

AMOUNT: $10,000 (approx.)
DEADLINE(S): Nov 30
FIELD(S): Creative Writing

Contest awards prizes to unpublished creative writers who need financial aid to complete works of fiction, poetry, drama, biography, autobiography, or history. Only works written in English will be considered, but U.S. citizenship not required.

2 annual awards. Candidate must be nominated by writing program faculty member or a sponsoring writer, agent, or editor. Write to William Miller at address above for complete information.

453

GEORGE WASHINGTON UNIVERSITY (Maud E. McPherson Scholarship in English)
GWU Office of Student Financial Aid
Washington, D.C. 20052
202/994-6180

AMOUNT: Up to full tuition
DEADLINE(S): Jun 1
FIELD(S): English

Need-based scholarships up to full tuition at George Washington University for continuing or transfer students majoring in English. GPA of 3.0 or better (4.0 scale) is required. Must be U.S. citizen.

Write for complete information.

454

GLA ADMINISTRATIVE SERVICES (Hubbard Scholarship Fund)
1438 W. Peachtree Street, Suite 200
Atlanta, GA 30309-2955

Written inquiry only

AMOUNT: $3,000
DEADLINE(S): May 1
FIELD(S): Library Science

Offered by the Georgia Library Association to graduating seniors and graduates of accredited colleges who have been accepted into an ALA-accredited degree program. Must be ready to begin study in fall term of award year and intend to complete degree requirements within two years.

Recipients agree to work (following graduation) for one year in a library or library-related capacity in Georgia *or* to pay back a prorated amount of the award within 2 years (with interest). Write for complete information.

455

ILLINOIS ARTS COUNCIL (Artists Fellowship Awards)
100 W. Randolph, Suite 10-500
Chicago, IL 60601-3298
312/814-6750

AMOUNT: $500; $5,000; $10,000
DEADLINE(S): Sep 1
FIELD(S): Choreography; Visual Arts; Poetry; Prose; Film; Video; Playwriting; Music Composition; Crafts; Ethnic & Folk Arts; Performance Art; Photography; Audio Art

Open to professional artists who are Illinois residents. Awards are in recognition of work in the above areas; they are NOT for continuing study. Students are not eligible.

Write to address above for application form.

456

IOWA SCHOOL OF LETTERS (The John Simmons Short Fiction Award)
Department of English
University of Iowa
308 English Philosophy Bldg.
Iowa City, IA 52242
Written inquiry

AMOUNT: Winners' manuscripts will be published by University of Iowa under standard press contract

DEADLINE(S): Varies (Aug 1 through Sep 30)

FIELD(S): Creative Writing (fiction)

Any writer who has not previously published a volume of prose fiction is eligible to enter the competition. Revised manuscripts which have been previously entered may be resubmitted.

The manuscript must be a collection of short stories of at least 150 typewritten pages. Writers who have published a volume of poetry are eligible. Include SASE.

457

MINNESOTA STATE ARTS BOARD (Grants Program)
Park Square Court
400 Sibley Street, Suite 200
St. Paul, MN 55101-1928
612/215-1600

AMOUNT: Fellowships-$8,000; Career Opportunity Grants-$100 to $1,500

DEADLINE(S): Aug (Visual Arts); Sep (Music & Dance); Oct (Literature & Theater)

FIELD(S): Literature; Music; Theater; Dance; Visual Arts

Fellowship grants open to professional artists who are residents of Minnesota. Grants may not be used for support of tuition or work toward any degree.

Career opportunity grants and fellowships are available.

458

NATIONAL ART MATERIALS TRADE ASSOCIATION (NAMTA Scholarships)
10115 Kincey Ave., Suite 260
Huntersville, NC 28078
704/948-5554

AMOUNT: $1,000

DEADLINE(S): Mar 1

FIELD(S): Creative disciplines: visual arts, writing, drama, music, etc.

For NAMTA members, employees, and their relatives or to individuals in an organization related to art or the art materials industry. For undergraduate or graduate study.

Selection based on financial need, grades, activities, interests, and career choice. Write for complete information.

459

NATIONAL ART MATERIALS TRADE ASSOCIATION
10115 Kincey Ave., Suite 260
Huntersville, NC 28078
704/948-5554

AMOUNT: Varies

DEADLINE(S): Mar 1

FIELD(S): Creative disciplines: visual arts, writing, drama, music, etc.

For NAMTA members, employees, and their relatives. For undergraduate or graduate study.

Selection based on financial need, grades, activities, interests, and career choice. Write for complete information.

460

NATIONAL FEDERATION OF STATE POETRY SOCIETIES INC. (Scholarship Fund for Poets)
Ms. P. J. Doyle
4242 Stevens
Minneapolis, MN 55409-2004
Written inquiry

AMOUNT: $500

DEADLINE(S): Feb 15

FIELD(S): Poetry

Scholarships for undergraduate juniors and seniors at accredited colleges and universities in the U.S. 10 original poems to be submitted with completed application form and a bio of the applicant.

Send SASE (#10 envelope) for application form and complete information. Inquiries without SASE will not be acknowledged.

461

NATIONAL FOUNDATION FOR ADVANCEMENT IN THE ARTS (Arts Recognition and Talent Search)
800 Brickell Ave., Suite #500
Miami, FL 33131
305/377-1148

AMOUNT: $100-$3,000
DEADLINE(S): Jun 1; Oct 1
FIELD(S): Creative Arts; Performing Arts

Open to high school seniors with talent in such arts as dance; music; music/jazz; theater; visual arts; film; video; and writing. Awards can be used anywhere for any purpose. For U.S. citizens or residents. Entry fee is required.

Approximately 400 awards per year. Write for complete information.

462

NATIONAL JUNIOR CLASSICAL LEAGUE (Scholarships)
Miami University
Oxford, OH 45056
513/529-7741

AMOUNT: $500-$1,000
DEADLINE(S): May 1
FIELD(S): Classics

Open to NJCL members who are high school seniors and plan to study Classics (though Classics major is not required). Preference will be given to a student who plans to pursue a teaching career in the Classics (also not a requirement).

Must be a member of a National Junior Classical League club. Write for complete information.

463

NATIONAL SPEAKERS ASSOCIATION (NSA Scholarship)
1500 S. Priest Drive
Tempe, AZ 85281
602/968-2552; Fax 602/968-0911; E-mail: nsamain@aol.com; Internet: www.nsaspeaker.org

AMOUNT: $2,500
DEADLINE(S): Jun 2
FIELD(S): Speech

Open to college juniors, seniors, or graduate students who are majoring or minoring in speech. Must be full-time student in an accredited college or university. Need at least 3.5 GPA.

4 awards per year to well-rounded students capable of leadership and having potential to make an impact by using oral communications. Write to the above address for complete details.

464

NORTH CAROLINA DEPARTMENT OF PUBLIC INSTRUCTION (Scholarship Loan Program for Prospective Teachers)
301 N. Wilmington Street
Raleigh, NC 27601-2825
919/715-1120

AMOUNT: Up to $2,500/year
DEADLINE(S): Feb
FIELD(S): Education: teaching, school psychology and counseling, speech/language impaired, audiology, library/media services

For NC residents planning to teach in NC public schools. At least 3.0 high school GPA required; must maintain 2.5 GPA during freshman year and 3.0 cumulative thereafter. Recipients are obligated to teach one year in a NC public school for each year of assistance. Those who do not fulfill their teaching obligation are required to repay the loan plus interest.

200 awards per year. For full-time students. Applications available in Dec. from high school counselors and college and university departments of education.

465

PLAYWRIGHTS' CENTER (Jerome Fellowships)

2301 Franklin Ave. East
Minneapolis, MN 55406-1099
612/332-7481; Fax: 612/332-6037; E-mail:
pwcenter@mtn.org; Internet:
www.pwcenter.org

AMOUNT: $7,000
DEADLINE(S): Sep 15
FIELD(S): Playwriting

For emerging playwrights who are U.S. citizens
or permanent residents who have not had
more than 2 productions of their work fully
staged by professional theaters. Fellows
spend 12 months as core members of the
Playwrights' Center.

Fellowships are to provide playwrights with
funds and services to aid them in the development of their craft. Applications available after July 1. Send SASE for complete
information.

466

PLAYWRIGHTS' CENTER (PlayLabs)

2301 Franklin Ave. East
Minneapolis, MN 55406-1099
612/332-7481; Fax 612/332-6037; E-mail:
pwcenter@mtn.org; Internet:
www.pwcenter.org

AMOUNT: Honoraria; travel expenses; room
and board
DEADLINE(S): Dec 15
FIELD(S): Playwriting

Two-week workshop open to U.S. citizens who
are authors of unproduced, unpublished
full-length plays (no one-acts). Each play
receives a public reading followed by audi-
ence discussion of the work. Must live within a 110-mile radius of the Twin Cities.

4 to 6 playwrights chosen by open script competition. Conference is intended to allow
playwrights to take risks free of artistic
restraint. Applications available by Oct 1.
Send SASE for complete information.

467

POETRY SOCIETY OF AMERICA (Contests for PSA members)

15 Gramercy Park
New York, NY 10003
212/254-9628; Fax 212/673-2352; Internet:
www.poetrysociety.org

AMOUNT: $100-$1,000
DEADLINE(S): Dec 20
FIELD(S): Poetry

Various contests open to PSA members. Only
one submission allowed per contest. All
submissions must be unpublished on the
date of entry and not scheduled for publication by the date of the PSA awards ceremony held in the spring.

This is a contest, NOT a scholarship; write for
complete details.

468

POETRY SOCIETY OF AMERICA (George Bogin Memorial Award)

15 Gramercy Park
New York, NY 10003
212/254-9628; Fax 212/673-2352; Internet:
www.poetrysociety.org

AMOUNT: $500
DEADLINE(S): Dec 20
FIELD(S): Poetry

Prizes for the best selections of four or five
poems that reflect the encounter of the
ordinary and the extraordinary, use language in an original way, and take a stand
against oppression in any of its forms. $5
entry fee for non-members.

Write to above location for complete details.

469

POETRY SOCIETY OF AMERICA (Louise Louis/Emily F. Bourne Student Poetry Award)

15 Gramercy Park
New York, NY 10003
212/254-9628; Fax 212/673-2352; Internet:
www.poetrysociety.org

AMOUNT: $100
DEADLINE(S): Dec 20
FIELD(S): Poetry

Prizes for the best unpublished poems by high or preparatory school students (grades 9-12). High schools may submit an unlimited number of their students' poems for $10 in one submission; individual entry fee is $100. Write to above location for complete details.

470

POETRY SOCIETY OF AMERICA (Robert H. Winner Memorial Award)
15 Gramercy Park
New York, NY 10003
212/254-9628; Fax 212/673-2352; Internet: www.poetrysociety.org

AMOUNT: $2,500
DEADLINE(S): Dec 20
FIELD(S): Poetry

For poets over 40 years of age who have not published or who have no more than one book. This award acknowledges original work done in midlife by someone who has not had substantial recognition. Send a brief but cohesive manuscript of up to 10 poems or 20 pages. Poems entered here may be submitted to other contests as well. Please include date of birth on cover page.

$5 entry fee. Write to above location for complete details.

471

RIPON COLLEGE (Music, Forensics, Art, and Theatre Scholarships)
P.O. Box 248
300 Seward Street
Admissions office
Ripon, WI 54971
414/748-8102; 800/94RIPON

AMOUNT: $1,000-$8,000
DEADLINE(S): Mar 1
FIELD(S): Music; Forensics; Art; Theatre

Scholarships to recognize and encourage academic potential and accomplishment in above fields. Renewable each year provided recipient maintains a good academic standing and participates in the program.

Must apply and be accepted for admission to Ripon College. Interview or audition required. Write for complete information.

472

SAN FRANCISCO FOUNDATION (James D. Phelan Literary Award)
446 Valencia Street
San Francisco, CA 94103
415/626-2787

AMOUNT: $2,000
DEADLINE(S): Jan 31
FIELD(S): Literature, fiction, nonfiction

Open to California-born authors of unpublished works-in-progress (fiction; nonfiction or poetry) who are between the ages of 20 & 35 and are U.S. citizens.

Writers of nonfiction are also eligible for the $1,000 "Special Award in Non-Fictional Prose." Write to the above address for complete information.

473

SAN FRANCISCO FOUNDATION (Joseph Henry Jackson Literary Award)
446 Valencia Street
San Francisco, CA 94103
415/626-2787

AMOUNT: $2,000
DEADLINE(S): Jan 31
FIELD(S): Literature

Open to N. California or Nevada residents (for 3 consecutive years immediately prior to closing date of the competition) who are authors of unpublished work-in-progress (fiction; nonfiction; poetry) & between 20-35 years of age.

Writers of nonfiction are also eligible for the $1,000 "Special Award in Non-Fictional Prose." Write for complete information.

474

**SANTA BARBARA FOUNDATION
(Pillsbury Creative Writing Scholarship
Program)**
  15 E. Carrillo Street
  Santa Barbara, CA 93101-2780
  805/963-1873; Fax 805/966-2345; E-mail:
  dano@SBFoundation.org

AMOUNT: Varies
DEADLINE(S): Oct 31
FIELD(S): Creative writing

For students of creative writing who have
  resided in Santa Barbara County for two
  years prior to application deadline or who
  have resided long-term in the county. Must
  be planning to attend an accredited college
  or university or the Music and Arts
  Conservatory of Santa Barbara.
Applications at high school counselor's office
  and from English and writing teachers at
  UCSB, Santa Barbara City College, and
  Westmont.

475

**STANLEY DRAMA AWARD
(Playwriting/Musical Awards Competition)**
  Department of Humanities
  Wagner College
  631 Howard Ave. & Campus Road
  Staten Island, NY 10301
  718/390-3256

AMOUNT: $2,000
DEADLINE(S): Sep 1
FIELD(S): Playwriting; Music Composition

Annual award for an original full-length play
  or musical which has not been professional-
  ly produced or received tradebook publication.
Submit musical works on cassette tape w/
  book & lyrics. A series of 2-3 thematically
  related one-act plays will also be considered. Send script with SASE large enough
  to accommodate script. Write for complete
  information.

476

**TENNESSEE ARTS COMMISSION
(Individual Artists' Fellowships)**
  401 Charlotte Ave.
  Nashville, TN 37243-0780
  615/741-1701

AMOUNT: $2,000
DEADLINE(S): Jan 11
FIELD(S): Visual Arts; Performing Arts;
  Creative Arts

Open to artists who are residents of
  Tennessee. Duration of award is one year.
  Applicants must be professional artists.
  Full-time students are NOT eligible.
Write for complete information.

477

**THE PLAYWRIGHTS' CENTER (Many
Voices Residency and Collaboration Grants
Programs)**
  2301 Franklin Ave. East
  Minneapolis, MN 55406-1099
  612/332-7481; Fax 612/332-6037; E-mail:
  pwcenter@mtn.org; Internet:
  www.pwcenter.org

AMOUNT: $750 stipend + tuition to a Center
  class
DEADLINE(S): Jul 1
FIELD(S): Playwriting

Residencies are for minority individuals interested in becoming playwrights who live in
  Minnesota or within a 110-mile radius of
  the Twin Cities at the time of application
  whose work demonstrates exceptional artistic merit and potential. Award recipients
  will spend an 8- to 9-month residency at the
  Center, have a one-on-one mentorship with
  a playwright, and other opportunities to
  develop their craft.
Collaboration grants are for culturally diverse
  teams of 2 or more writers to create new
  theater pieces. Awards range from $200 to
  $2,000. Send SASE to above address for
  complete information.

478

THE PLAYWRIGHTS' CENTER (McKnight Advancement Grant)
2301 Franklin Ave. East
Minneapolis, MN 55406-1099
612/332-7481; Fax 612/332-6037; E-mail:
pwcenter@mtn.org; Internet:
www.pwcenter.org

AMOUNT: $8,500
DEADLINE(S): Feb 1
FIELD(S): Playwriting

Open to playwrights whose primary residence is Minnesota and whose work demonstrates exceptional artistic merit and potential. Two works by applicant must have been fully produced by professional theatres.

Recipients must designate two months of the grant year for active participation in center programs. Applications available December 1. Write for complete information.

479

THE PLAYWRIGHTS' CENTER (McKnight Fellowships)
2301 Franklin Ave. East
Minneapolis, MN 55406-1099
612/332-7481; Fax 612/332-6037; E-mail:
pwcenter@mtn.org; Internet:
www.pwcenter.org

AMOUNT: $10,000
DEADLINE(S): Jan 15
FIELD(S): Playwriting

Open to playwrights whose work demonstrates exceptional artistic merit and potential. Two works by applicant must have been fully produced by professional theatres.

2 annual awards. Recipients must spend one month or more in residence at the Playwrights' Center during the fellowship year. Applications available October 15. Send SASE to above address for complete information.

480

U.S. MARINE CORPS HISTORICAL CENTER (College Internships)
Building 58
Washington Navy Yard
Washington, D.C. 20374
202/433-3839

AMOUNT: Stipend to cover daily expenses
DEADLINE(S): None specified
FIELD(S): U.S. Military History; Library Science; History; Museum Studies

Open to undergraduate students at a college or university which will grant academic credit for work experience as interns at the address above or at the Marine Corps Air-Ground Museum in Quantico, Virginia.

All internships are regarded as beginning professional-level historian, curator, librarian, or archivist positions. Write for complete information.

481

VETERANS OF FOREIGN WARS OF THE UNITED STATES (Voice of Democracy Audio-Essay Competition)
VFW Bldg.
406 W. 34th Street
Kansas City, MO 64111
816/968-1117

AMOUNT: $1,000-$20,000
DEADLINE(S): Nov 1
FIELD(S): Creative writing/speech

Open to undergraduates in public, private & parochial high schools. Contestants will be judged on their treatment of an annual theme. They may not refer to their race, national origin, etc., as a means of identification.

55 national awards per year. Must be U.S. citizen. Contact local VFW post or high school for details.

482

WAVERLY COMMUNITY HOUSE INC. (F. Lammot Belin Arts Scholarships)

Scholarships Selection Committee
P.O. Box 142
Waverly, PA 18471
717/586-8191

AMOUNT: $10,000

DEADLINE(S): Dec 15

FIELD(S): Painting; Sculpture; Music; Drama; Dance; Literature; Architecture; Photography

Applicants must have resided in the Abington or Pocono regions of Northeastern Pennsylvania. They must furnish proof of exceptional ability in their chosen field but no formal training in any academic or professional program.

U.S. citizenship required. Finalists must appear in person before the selection committee. Write for complete information.

FOREIGN LANGUAGE

483

ACL/NJCL NATIONAL LATIN EXAM (Scholarships)

P.O. Box 95
Mount Vernon, VA 22121
703/360-4354

AMOUNT: $1,000

DEADLINE(S): Jan 10

FIELD(S): Latin Language

Open to gold medal winners of the National Latin Exam. Students must take the Latin exam in their high schools and be among the top scorers in order to qualify for this scholarship. Recipients of this scholarship must agree to take at least one year of Latin or Classical Greek in college. The deadline of January 10 is the last day that teachers can send for the exams, which are to be administered during the second full week in March.

Write to Jane Hall at the above address for application and information.

484

ALPHA MU GAMMA NATIONAL OFFICE (Goddard; Indovina; and Krakowski Scholarships)

c/o Los Angeles City College
855 N. Vermont Ave.
Los Angeles, CA 90029
213/664-8742

AMOUNT: $500 (3-ea.); $400 & $200 (1-ea.)

DEADLINE(S): Jan 4

FIELD(S): Language

Scholarships open to college or university students who are members of Alpha Mu Gamma Chapters. Students must have completed at least 1-1/2 semesters of college work and have two 'A' grades in a foreign language.

Applications available only from local AMG chapter advisors in mid-October. Applicants must participate in a national scholarship competition.

485

AMERICAN ASSOCIATION OF TEACHERS OF FRENCH (National French Contest)

Sidney L. Teitelbaum
Box 32030
Sarasota, FL 34278
Fax 941/364-9820

AMOUNT: Varies

DEADLINE(S): Feb 4

FIELD(S): French Language; French Studies

National French contest is an examination taken throughout the country. Students are ranked regionally and nationally and are eligible for both local and national awards.

Not a scholarship. Winners receive trips, medals and books. Write for complete information or ask your French teacher.

486

AMERICAN ASSOCIATION OF TEACHERS OF GERMAN (National AATG/PAD Awards)
112 Haddontowne Ct., #104
Cherry Hill, NJ 08034
609/795-5553

AMOUNT: Costs of study trip
DEADLINE(S): Dec 1 (deadline for teachers to order test)
FIELD(S): German Language

This summer-study trip award to Germany is open to high school students aged 16 or older who score at or above the 90 percentile on the AATG National German Test. U.S. citizenship or permanent residency is required.

Up to 47 travel-study awards per year. Tests are administered by high school German teachers—write to address above for complete information or inquire with your German teacher. Financial aid for post-secondary education is NOT available.

487

AMERICAN COUNCIL OF LEARNED SOCIETIES (East European Summer Language Training Grants)
Office of Fellowships & Grants
228 E. 45th Street
New York, NY 10017
Written inquiry

AMOUNT: $2,500
DEADLINE(S): Jan 30
FIELD(S): East European Languages

Grants of $2,500 each offered for intensive summer study of an East European language (except Russian) at the intermediate or advanced level in Eastern Europe.

U.S. citizen or legal resident. For grad or post-grad study; BA is required. Write for complete information.

488

AMERICAN INSTITUTE OF INDIAN STUDIES (AIIS 9-month Language Program)
c/o University of Chicago
Foster Hall
1130 E. 59th Street
Chicago, IL 60637
773/702-8638; E-mail: aiis@midway.uchicago.edu; Internet: ccat.sas.upenn.edu.80/aiis/

AMOUNT: $3,000 plus travel
DEADLINE(S): Jan 31
FIELD(S): Languages of India

Fellowships for classes held in India for U.S. citizens who have a minimum of 2 years, or 240 hours, of classroom instruction in a language of India—Hindi, Bengali, Tamil, or Telugu.

10 fellowships per year. Write for complete information.

489

AMERICAN RESEARCH INSTITUTE IN TURKEY (Summer Fellowship of Intensive Advanced Turkish Language Study)
33rd and Spruce Streets
Philadelphia, PA 19104-6324
215/898-3474; Fax 215/898-0657; E-mail: leinwand@sas.upenn.edu

AMOUNT: $2,500 stipend
DEADLINE(S): Feb 15
FIELD(S): Advanced Turkish Language

An eight-week summer program at Bosphorus University in Istanbul in advanced Turkish. Covers round-trip airfare, application and tuition fees, room and board, and stipend. For U.S. citizens or permanent residents who are upper-level undergraduates, graduates, or instructors of Turkish or related language and area studies. Must have minimum of B average.

10 fellowships. Contact ARIT, c/o University of Pennsylvania Museum, at the above location for applications.

490

**AUSTRIAN CULTURAL INSTITUTE
(Grants for Foreign Students to Study
German in Austria)**

950 Third Ave., 20th Floor
New York, NY 10022
212/759-5165; Fax 212/319-9636; E-mail:
desk@aci.org; Internet:
www.austriaculture.net

AMOUNT: ATS 10,000 (approx. U.S. $900)
for four weeks; ATS 8,000 (approx. U.S.
$750) for three weeks. Additionally, the
costs for the language course are refunded
up to ATS 7,000 (approx. U.S. $650).

DEADLINE(S): Jan 31

FIELD(S): German Language

For students foreign to Austria between 20
and 35 who have completed at least 2 years
of college. A working knowledge of
German is required. To be used during July
and August.

A highly competitive scholarship program is
offered to applicants from around the
world. Classes are held at several language
Institutes throughout Austria.

491

**CENTER FOR ARABIC STUDY ABROAD
(CASA Fellowships)**

c/o Johns-Hopkins University
1619 Massachusetts Ave. NW
Washington, D.C. 20036-1983
202/663-5750; E-mail:
casa@mail.jhuwash.jhu.edu; Internet:
www.sais-jhu.edu/languages/CASA

AMOUNT: Tuition, allowance, and airfare

DEADLINE(S): Dec 31

FIELD(S): Advanced Arabic Language
Training

Fellowships for summer and full-year intensive
Arabic training at the American University
in Cairo, Egypt. Open to U.S. graduate students and a limited number of undergrads.
Minimum 2 years of Arabic study. U.S. citizen or permanent resident.

Approximately 20 fellowships per year. Write
for complete information.

492

**CENTRE D'ETUDES FRANCO-
AMERICAIN (Scholarship)**

10.12.14 Boulevard Carnot; B.P.176
14104 Lisieux Cedex France
31.31.22.01

AMOUNT: U.S. $500-$600

DEADLINE(S): None specified

FIELD(S): French

An immersion study program in France open
to students of the French language from
beginning to advanced. Awards are made
on the basis of academic achievement,
financial need and planned use of the language.

Write for complete information.

493

**INSTITUTE OF INTERNATIONAL
EDUCATION (National Security Education
Program Undergraduate Scholarship)**

1400 K Street NW
Washington, D.C. 20005-2403
202/326-7697; 800/618-NSEP; Fax 202/326-
7698; E-mail: nsep@iie.org; Internet:
www.iie.org/nsep/

AMOUNT: Varies: up to $8,000

DEADLINE(S): Varies

FIELD(S): Foreign Language

Scholarships are available to enable recipients
to pursue serious study abroad in critical
world areas that do NOT include Western
Europe, Canada, Australia, or New Zealand

A foreign language component must be
included in every applicant's study-abroad
proposal. Check with NSEP representative
at your local campus or write or call above
location for complete information.

494

LUSO-AMERICAN EDUCATION FOUNDATION (General Scholarships)
P.O. Box 2967
Dublin, CA 94568
510/828-3883

AMOUNT: Varies
DEADLINE(S): Mar 1
FIELD(S): Portuguese Language or Portuguese Descent-related fields

Open to Calif. high school seniors (under 21) of Portuguese descent who will enroll full-time in a 4-year program that includes Portuguese language classes. Also open to members of Luso-American Fraternal Federation.
Write for complete information.

495

NATIONAL ITALIAN AMERICAN FOUNDATION (Frances M. Rello Scholarship)
Dr. M. Lombardo, Education Director
1860 19th Street N.W.
Washington, D.C. 20009-5599
202/387-0600

AMOUNT: $1,000
DEADLINE(S): May 31
FIELD(S): Italian Language (Teacher)

Open to undergraduate and graduate Italian-American women with an Italian language major who are planning to teach Italian in the secondary schools. Evidence of financial need and essay on applicant's Italian heritage are required.
Write for complete information.

496

NATIONAL ITALIAN AMERICAN FOUNDATION (Mola Foundation of Chicago Scholarships)
1860 19th Street NW
Washington, D.C. 20009-5599
202/530-5315

AMOUNT: $1,000
DEADLINE(S): May 31
FIELD(S): Italian major

Open to undergraduates majoring in Italian and who are of Italian ancestry. Must be from Illinois, Indiana, Michigan, Wisconsin, Ohio, Iowa, Minnesota, Kentucky, South Dakota, or North Dakota.

497

NATIONAL ITALIAN AMERICAN FOUNDATION (Paragano Scholarship)
1860 19th Street NW
Washington, D.C. 20009-5599
202/530-5315

AMOUNT: $2,000
DEADLINE(S): May 31
FIELD(S): Italian majors

For undergraduate Italian majors of Italian ancestry who reside in New Jersey.
Financial need, community service, and academic merit are considered.

498

NORWICH JUBILEE ESPERANTO FOUNDATION (Travel Grants)
37 Granville Court
Oxford 0X3 0HS England
01865-245509

AMOUNT: 1,000 pounds sterling (maximum award)
DEADLINE(S): None
FIELD(S): Esperanto

Travel grants open to those who speak Esperanto and wish to improve their use of the language through travel in the U.K. Candidates must be under the age of 26 and be able to lecture in Esperanto.
Inquiries without indication of fluency and interest in Esperanto will not be acknowledged. Up to 25 awards per year. Renewable. Write for complete information.

PERFORMING ARTS

499

ACADEMY OF VOCAL ARTS
(Scholarships)
  1920 Spruce Street
  Philadelphia, PA 19103
  215/735-1685

AMOUNT: Full tuition
DEADLINE(S): Varies (2 weeks prior to
  auditions in Spring)
FIELD(S): Vocal Music; Operatic Acting
Tenable only at the Academy of Vocal Arts.
  Open to unusually gifted singers with 2
  years college vocal training or equivalent.
  College degree recommended. Full tuition
  scholarships & complete training in voice,
  operatic acting, & repertoire.
Winners selected in Spring competitive auditions. Total student enrollment limited to
  30. Write for complete information.

500

AMERICAN ACCORDION
MUSICOLOGICAL SOCIETY (Contest)
  334 South Broadway
  Pitman, NJ 08071
  609/854-6628

AMOUNT: $100-$250
DEADLINE(S): Sep 10
FIELD(S): Music Composition for Accordion
Annual competition open to amateur or pro-
  fessional music composers who write a seri-
  ous piece music (of six minutes or more) for
  the accordion.
Write for complete information.

501

AMERICAN FOUNDATION FOR THE
BLIND (Gladys C. Anderson Memorial
Scholarship)
  11 Penn Plaza, Suite 300
  New York, NY 10001
  212/502-7600; TDD 212/502-7662

AMOUNT: $1,000
DEADLINE(S): Apr 1
FIELD(S): Music performance or singing
Undergrad scholarships open to legally blind
  women studying religious or classical music
  at the college level. Sample performance
  tape of voice or instrumental selection will
  be required. U.S. citizen.
Write for complete information.

502

AMERICAN FOUNDATION FOR THE
BLIND (Gladys C. Anderson Memorial
Scholarship)
  11 Penn Plaza, Suite 300
  New York, NY 10001
  212/502-7661; TDD 212/502-7662; Fax
  212/502-7771; E-mail: juliet@afb.org;
  Internet: www.afb.org

AMOUNT: $1,000
DEADLINE(S): Apr 30
FIELD(S): Religious or classical music
Open to legally blind female college students
  studying religious or classical music.
Must be U.S. citizen. Write or access website
  for further information. E-mail and fax
  inquiries must include a complete U.S.
  postal service mailing address.

503

AMERICAN FOUNDATION FOR THE
BLIND (R. L. Gillette Scholarship Fund)
  11 Penn Plaza, Suite #300
  New York, NY 10001
  212/502-7661; TDD 212/502-7662; Fax
  212/502-7771; E-mail: juliry@afb.org;
  Internet: www.afb.org

AMOUNT: $1,000
DEADLINE(S): Apr 30
FIELD(S): Literature or music
Open to legally blind women who are enrolled
  in or can provide proof of acceptance to a
  four-year bachelor program at a recognized
  school or university. Writing sample or

music performance tape will be required. Must be U.S. citizen.

2 awards. Write or visit website for further information. E-mail and fax inquiries must include a complete U.S. postal service mailing address.

504

AMERICAN SOCIETY OF COMPOSERS, AUTHORS, AND PUBLISHERS (The ASCAP Foundation Morton Gould Young Composer Awards)
ASCAP Building
1 Lincoln Plaza
New York, NY 10023
212/621-6219; E-mail: www.ascap.org

AMOUNT: Not given

DEADLINE(S): Mar 15

FIELD(S): Music Composition Competition

Competition is for composers who are under 30 years of age as of March 15 of the year of application. Original music of any style will be considered. Winning compositions selected by panel of music authorities.

Contact Frances Richard, ASCAP/Morton Gould Young Composer Awards, at above location for details.

505

AMERICAN SYMPHONY ORCHESTRA LEAGUE (Music Assistance Fund)
1156 15th Street NW, Suite 800
Washington, D.C. 20005-1704
202/776-0212; Fax 202/776-0223

AMOUNT: $500; $3,500

DEADLINE(S): Dec 15

FIELD(S): Music Assistance Fund

Open to U.S. citizens of African descent studying and performing an orchestra instrument, and intending to pursue a career in symphony orchestras. Voice, piano, composition, and conducting not included.

Scholarships to be applied toward summer music program, academic tuition, or any performance-related study. Must apply each year.

506

ARTS INTERNATIONAL; INSTITUTE OF INTERNATIONAL EDUCATION (Cintas Fellowship Program)
809 United Nations Plaza
New York, NY 10017
212/984-5370

AMOUNT: $10,000

DEADLINE(S): Mar 1

FIELD(S): Architecture; Painting; Photography; Sculpture; Printmaking; Music Composition; Creative Writing

Fellowships open to artists who are of Cuban ancestry or Cuban citizens living outside of Cuba. They are intended to foster & encourage the professional development & recognition of talented creative artists in the above areas.

Fellowships are not awarded for furtherance of academic study. 5-10 awards per year. Write for complete information.

507

AUSTRIAN CULTURAL INSTITUTE (Grants for Students in Music, Drama, and the Fine Arts)
950 Third Ave., 20th Floor
New York, NY 10022
212/759-5165; Fax 212/319-9636; E-mail: desk@aci.org; Internet: www.austriaculture.net

AMOUNT: ATS 7,400/month Oct.-June (U.S. $700)

DEADLINE(S): Jan 31

FIELD(S): Music; Drama; Fine Arts

Open to non-Austrian students between the ages of 19-34 for study in Austria in music, drama, or fine arts. Working knowledge of German language required.

Must pass artistic entrance exam. Students from abroad may send tapes, slides, pictures, etc., to evaluate their level of qualification.

508

BALTIMORE OPERA COMPANY (Vocal Competition for North American Operatic Artists)
1202 Maryland Ave.
Baltimore, MD 21201
410/625-1600

AMOUNT: $1,000-$12,000
DEADLINE(S): Mar 1
FIELD(S): Singing
Biannual contest for operatic singers between the ages of 20 and 35 who are U.S., Canadian, or Mexican citizens and who can present two letters of recommendation from recognized musical authorities.
8 awards biannually renewable by competition. There is a $45 application fee. Write for complete information.

509

BARNUM FESTIVAL (Jenny Lind Competition for Sopranos)
1070 Main Street
Bridgeport, CT 06604
Written inquiry

AMOUNT: $2,000 scholarship & ticket to Sweden
DEADLINE(S): Varies (Before competition held May 30)
FIELD(S): Singing
Open to women between 18 and 25 who have had formal training in operatic or concert singing but have not reached professional status. Only residents or students from the state of Connecticut may apply.
Application forms, copies of the information memo and other materials on the Jenny Lind contest may be obtained from the Barnum Festival office.

510

BOSTON SAFE DEPOSIT & TRUST COMPANY (Madeline H. Soren Trust; Susan Glover Hitchcock Music Scholarship)
One Boston Place
Boston, MA 02108
617/722-7340

AMOUNT: $500-$2,000
DEADLINE(S): May 1
FIELD(S): Music
Open to women who are Massachusetts residents and are graduates of Massachusetts high schools for undergraduate study at Massachusetts colleges or universities.
Recommendation of music department and financial aid office of a Boston area university or college is required. Write for complete information.

511

BUSH FOUNDATION (Bush Artist Fellowships)
E900 First National Bank Bldg.
322 Minnesota Street
St. Paul, MN 55101
612/227-5222; 800/605-7315

AMOUNT: $40,000
DEADLINE(S): Oct
FIELD(S): Literature; Music Composition; Choreography; Multimedia; Performance Art; Visual Arts; Scriptworks; Film/Video
For residents of MI, ND, SD, or western WI who are at least 25 years old. Awards are to help artists work full-time in their chosen fields—NOT for academic study. Each category offered every other year.
Students are NOT eligible to apply. 15 fellowships per year, 12-18 months in duration. Write for complete information.

512

CARMEN SCHOLARSHIP COMMITTEE (Nellie Martin Carmen Scholarship)
23825 15th Ave. SE, #128
Bothell, WA 98021
206/486-6575

AMOUNT: Up to $1,000
DEADLINE(S): Mar 15
FIELD(S): All fields of study except those noted below

Open to high school seniors in King, Pierce, and Snohomish counties in the state of Washington. For undergraduate study in a Washington institution in all fields EXCEPT music, sculpture, drawing, interior design, and home economics. U.S. citizenship required.

Applications available only through high schools; nomination by counselor is required. 25-30 awards per year. Awards are renewable. Write for complete information.

513

CHATHAM COLLEGE (Minna Kaufmann Ruud Fund)
Woodland Road
Office of Admissions
Pittsburgh, PA 15232
412/365-1290

AMOUNT: $3,500/year (average) + fees & private accompanist
DEADLINE(S): Jan 31
FIELD(S): Vocal Music

Women only. Awards for full-time undergraduate study at Chatham College. Scholarships open to promising young female vocalists who are accepted for admission, pass an audition, and plan to major in music.

Awards renewable. Contact Office of Admissions for details.

514

COLUMBIA UNIVERSITY (Joseph H. Bearns Prize in Music)
Dept. of Music
621 Dodge Hall—MC 1813
New York, NY 10027
212/854-3825; Fax 212/854-8191

AMOUNT: $3,000; $2,000
DEADLINE(S): Mar 15 (of year given)
FIELD(S): Musical Composition

Competition open to young composers aged 18-25. There are two categories for music composition. One award of $3,000 for larger forms & one award of $2,000 for smaller forms. No more than one entry should be sent. U.S. citizenship required.

Write to Attn: Bearns Prize Committee at address above for complete details.

515

CURTIS INSTITUTE OF MUSIC (Tuition Scholarships)
Admissions Office
1726 Locust Street
Philadelphia, PA 19103
215/893-5252

AMOUNT: Full tuition
DEADLINE(S): Jan 15
FIELD(S): Music; Voice; Opera

Full-tuition scholarships open to students in the above areas who are accepted for full-time study at the Curtis Institute of Music. (Opera is for master of music only.)

Approx. 50 awards per year. Scholarships are renewable. Write for complete information.

516

DELTA OMICRON (Triennial Composition Competition for Solo Piano)
12297 W. Tennessee Place
Lakewood, CO 80228-3325
606/266-1215

AMOUNT: $500 + premiere performance at Conference

DEADLINE(S): Mar 18

FIELD(S): Music composition competition

Award for solo piano composition with a time length from seven to ten minutes. No music fraternity affiliation required.

Prior publication or performance not allowed. Entry fee of $10 is required. Contact Judith Eidson at above address for details.

517

DELTA OMICRON INTERNATIONAL MUSIC FRATERNITY (Triennial Composition Competition for Sacred Choral Anthem for Three- or Four-Part Voices)
12297 W. Tennessee Place
Lakewood, CO 80228-3325
606/266-1215

AMOUNT: $500 and premiere

DEADLINE(S): Mar 20

FIELD(S): Music Composition

Sacred choral anthem for 3- or 4-part voices; SSA, SAB, or SATB with keyboard accompaniment or a capella with optional obligato. Competition open to composers of college age or over. No music fraternity affiliation required.

Prior publication or public performance of entry is NOT allowed. Entry fee of $10 is required. Contact Judith Eidson at above address for complete information.

518

DISTRICT OF COLUMBIA COMMISSION ON THE ARTS & HUMANITIES (Grants)
410 Eighth Street NW, 5th Floor
Washington, D.C. 20004
202/724-5613; TDD 202/727-3148; Fax 202/727-4135

AMOUNT: $2,500

DEADLINE(S): Mar 1

FIELD(S): Performing Arts; Literature; Visual Arts

Applicants for grants must be professional artists and residents of Washington, D.C. for at least one year prior to submitting application. Awards intended to generate art endeavors within the Washington, D.C. community.

Open also to art organizations that train, exhibit, or perform within D.C. 150 grants per year. Write for complete information.

519

ETUDE MUSIC CLUB OF SANTA ROSA (Music Competition for Instrumentalists)
P.O. Box 823
Santa Rosa, CA 95402
707/538-1370

AMOUNT: Varies

DEADLINE(S): Mar 1

FIELD(S): Classical Instrumental Music

Competition is open to any high school student (grades 9-12) who is a resident of Sonoma, Napa or Mendocino counties & is studying music with a private teacher of music or is recommended by his/her school's music department.

Write for complete information.

520

ETUDE MUSIC CLUB OF SANTA ROSA (Music Competition for Vocalists)
P.O. Box 823
Santa Rosa, CA 95402
707/538-1370

AMOUNT: Varies

DEADLINE(S): Mar 2 (competition is Mar 16)

FIELD(S): Classical Vocalists

Competition is open to high school vocalists in grades 9-12 who are residents of Sonoma, Napa or Mendocino counties & are studying music with a private teacher of music or are recommended by their school's music department.

Write for complete information.

521

FLORIDA ARTS COUNCIL (Individual Artists' Fellowships)
Florida Dept. of State
Div. of Cultural Affairs
State Capitol
Tallahassee, FL 32399-0250
850/487-2980; TDD 850/414-2214; Fax 850/922-5259

AMOUNT: $5,000
DEADLINE(S): Jan 16
FIELD(S): Visual Arts; Dance; Folk Arts; Media; Music; Theater; Literary Arts; Interdisciplinary

Fellowships awarded to individual artists in the above areas. Must be Florida residents, U.S. citizens, and over 18 years old. May NOT be a degree-seeking student—funding is for support of artistic endeavors only.
38 awards per year. Write for complete information.

522

FORT COLLINS SYMPHONY ASSOCIATION (National Young Artist Competition)
P.O. Box 1963
Fort Collins, CO 80522-1963
970/482-4823; 970/482-4858; E-mail: Leehill@fcsymphony.org; Internet: www.fcsymphony.org

AMOUNT: 2 Divisions: Sr.-up to $3,000; Jr.- up to $250
DEADLINE(S): Jan 20
FIELD(S): Music

A competition for musical performance. Applicants must be ages 12 to 18 for the junior division and between 18 and 25 for the senior division.
Senior program: even years, piano; odd years, instrument; 1998 is a concerto competition for piano only. Junior program: both divisions every year. 1998's competition is one movement from a standard, readily available concerto or similar work from memory.

Write to the above address for complete information.

523

GENERAL FEDERATION OF WOMEN'S CLUBS OF MASS. (Undergraduate Scholarship Program)
P.O. Box 679
Sudbury, MA 01776-0679
Phone/Fax 508/443-4569

AMOUNT: Up to $600
DEADLINE(S): Feb 15; Mar 1; Mar 15
FIELD(S): Art & Music

Undergraduate scholarships available to MA residents only who have been accepted at either Mt. Ida College or Fisher College. A letter of endorsement from your local Federated Women's Club president must be submitted with transcript.
Write for a complete listing of scholarships at above address. Send a self-addressed stamped envelope. Information also available at your local Federated Women's Club.

524

GENERAL FEDERATION OF WOMEN'S CLUBS OF MASSACHUSETTS (Music Scholarship)
Box 679
Sudbury, MA 01776-0679
Phone/Fax 508/443-4569

AMOUNT: $500
DEADLINE(S): Feb 15
FIELD(S): Music Therapy; Piano, Instrument, or Music Education

For a senior in a Massachusetts high school who will study music or a related field in a college or university. Send letter of endorsement from the president of the sponsoring GFWC of MA in the community of legal residence, a personal letter, a letter of recommendation from either a high school principal or music teacher, a transcript, and audition tape.

Include SASE with inquiries. Contact Music
Coordinator at above address.

525

GENERAL FEDERATION OF WOMEN'S CLUBS OF MASSACHUSETTS (Dorchester Women's Club Scholarship)
Box 679
Sudbury, MA 01776-0679
Phone/Fax: 508/443-4569

AMOUNT: $500
DEADLINE(S): Feb 15
FIELD(S): Voice

For a senior in a Massachusetts high school
who will study voice in a college or university. Send letter of endorsement from the
president of the sponsoring GFWC of MA
club in the community of legal residence, a
personal letter stating your need for this
scholarship and other pertinent information, a letter of recommendation from a
high school music department head or
career counselor, and a transcript.
Contact Music Coordinator at above address.
Include SASE. An audition will be
required. Not renewable.

526

GEORGIA COUNCIL FOR THE ARTS (Individual Artist Grants)
530 Means Street NW, Suite 115
Atlanta, GA 30318-5793
404/651-7920

AMOUNT: Up to $5,000
DEADLINE(S): Apr 1
FIELD(S): The Arts

Grants to support artistic projects by professional artists who have been Georgia residents at least one year prior to application.
Selection is based on project's artistic merit
and its potential for career development.
Grants do NOT support academic study. Write
for complete information.

527

GLENN MILLER BIRTHPLACE SOCIETY (Instrumental and Vocal Competition)
711 N. 14th Street
Clarinda, IA 51632
712/542-4439

AMOUNT: $500-$1,500
DEADLINE(S): Mar 15
FIELD(S): Music Performance/Education

Instrumental and vocal music competitions
open to high school seniors and undergraduate freshmen who intend to make music a
central part of their future life. Audition
tape and $25 appearance fee required with
application. Finalists perform at Clarinda's
Glenn Miller Festival in June.
College music major is not required. All facets
of competition are reviewed after each
competition. Early inquiry is recommended.
Send SASE for complete information.

528

HOWARD UNIVERSITY (Debbie Allen & Phylicia Rashad's Dr. Andrew Allen Creative Arts Scholarship)
College of Fine Arts
Dept. of Theatre Arts
6th & Fairmont NW
Washington, D.C. 20059
202/806-7050

AMOUNT: $5,000
DEADLINE(S): Apr 1
FIELD(S): Drama; Singing; Dancing

Scholarship open only to students of senior
status who are in the Department of Theatre
Arts at Howard University in Washington,
D.C. For singing, dancing, and acting.
Write for complete information.

529

ILLINOIS ARTS COUNCIL (Artists Fellowship Awards)
100 W. Randolph, Suite 10-500
Chicago, IL 60601-3298

312/814-6750

AMOUNT: $500; $5,000; $10,000

DEADLINE(S): Sep 1

FIELD(S): Choreography; Visual Arts; Poetry; Prose; Film; Video; Playwriting; Music Composition; Crafts; Ethnic & Folk Arts; Performance Art; Photography; Audio Art

Open to professional artists who are Illinois residents. Awards are in recognition of work in the above areas; they are not for continuing study. Students are NOT eligible.

Write to address above for application form.

530

INTERNATIONAL COMPETITION FOR SYMPHONIC COMPOSITION (Premio Citta Di Trieste)

Piazza Dell'unita D'Italia 4
Palazzo municipale
34121 Trieste, Italy
040-366030

AMOUNT: 10 mil. lira (1st)

DEADLINE(S): Apr 30

FIELD(S): Music Composition

Open to anyone who submits an original composition for full orchestra (normal symphonic instrumentation). Composition must never have been performed and be unpublished.

Previous first-prize winners are excluded from competition. Write to secretariat of the music award at address above for complete information.

531

JAPANESE AMERICAN CITIZENS LEAGUE (Aiko Susanna Tashiro Hiratsuka Memorial Scholarship)

1765 Sutter Street
San Francisco, CA 94115
415/921-5225; E-mail: jacl@jacl.org

AMOUNT: Varies

DEADLINE(S): Apr 1

FIELD(S): Performing Arts

Open to JACL members or their children only. For students attending any institution of higher education who are studying in the performing arts. Professional artists are not eligible to apply.

For membership information or an application, send a self-addressed stamped envelope to the above address.

532

JULIUS AND ESTHER STULBERG COMPETITION, INC. (International String Competition)

P.O. Box 50107
Kalamazoo, MI 49005
616/372-6237; Fax 616/372-7513

AMOUNT: $3,000 (1st prize); $2,000 (2nd); $1,000 (3rd)

DEADLINE(S): Jan 10

FIELD(S): Stringed Instruments (Violin, Viola, Cello, Double Bass)

Contest is open to talented musicians aged 19 or younger who perform on violin, viola, cello, or double bass.

Application fee of $30. Send self-addressed stamped envelope to above location for complete information.

533

LIEDERKRANZ FOUNDATION (Scholarship Awards)

6 East 87th Street
New York, NY 10128
212/534-0880

AMOUNT: $1,000-$5,000

DEADLINE(S): Dec 1

FIELD(S): Vocal Music

20 scholarships awarded by competition each year. Awards can be used anywhere. There is a $30 application fee and a lower age limit of 20.

Contact competition director John Balme at address above for application regulations, audition schedules, and other details.

534

LOREN L. ZACHARY SOCIETY FOR THE PERFORMING ARTS (Annual National Vocal Competition for Young Opera Singers)
2250 Gloaming Way
Beverly Hills, CA 90210
310/276-2731

AMOUNT: First Prize $10,000; Finalist
DEADLINE(S): Feb (NY); Apr (LA); May (final competition)
FIELD(S): Opera Singing

Annual vocal competition open to young (aged 21-33, females; 21-35, males) Opera singers. The competition is geared toward finding employment for them in European Opera houses.

Approx. 10 awards per year. Applications available in November. Send self addressed stamped envelope to address above for application & complete information.

535

MARTIN MUSICAL SCHOLARSHIP FUND (Scholarships)
Lawn Cottage, 23a Brackley Road
Beckenham, Kent BR3 1RB England
Phone/Fax: 0181-658-9432

AMOUNT: Up to 2,000 pounds sterling
DEADLINE(S): Dec 1
FIELD(S): Instrumental Music

Scholarships are administered by the London Philharmonic Orchestra. For applicants of exceptional talent under age 25. Awards are for study at any approved institution in England for non-U.K. citizens; citizens of the U.K. may study anywhere. Candidates must be studying for a career as either soloist, chamber musician, or orchestral player. Additional programs are for viola players, violinists, and woodwind performers.

Not open to organists, singers, composers, or for academic studies. Awards are valid for two years. Auditions are held in London the January following the December deadline date. Write for complete information.

536

MERCYHURST COLLEGE D'ANGELO SCHOOL OF MUSIC (Young Artists Competition)
501 E. 38th Street
Erie, PA 16546
814/824-2394; Fax 814/824-2438; E-mail: KWOK@paradise.mercy.edu

AMOUNT: $10,000; $5,000; $3,000
DEADLINE(S): Jan 31
FIELD(S): Voice; Strings; Piano

For musicians aged 18-30 (voice—age 35). Rotating cycle of areas (piano 1998). Dollar awards & performance contracts. Write for application & repertoire requirements in the fall of the year preceding year of competition.
Write for complete information.

537

MERCYHURST COLLEGE D'ANGELO SCHOOL OF MUSIC (Scholarship)
501 E. 38th Street
Erie, PA 16546
814/824-2394; Fax 814/824-2438; E-mail: KWOK@paradise.mercy.edu

AMOUNT: Up to $10,000
DEADLINE(S): None
FIELD(S): Music

For music students who wish to attend the D'Angelo School of Music at Mercyhurst College in Erie, Pennsylvania. Audition required.

20 annual awards. Renewable for four years. Write to Glen Kwok for complete information.

538

METROPOLITAN OPERA NATIONAL COUNCIL AUDITIONS

Lincoln Center
New York, NY 10023
212/799-3100

AMOUNT: $800 (1st); $600 (2nd); $400 (3rd)
DEADLINE(S): Varies (early Fall)
FIELD(S): Operatic Singing

The National Opera Council Auditions is for serious musician with talent in the operatic style of singing. Student must be prepared to sing five operatic arias. Once a person has become a National Finalist or Winner, they are eligible for additional educational funding.

Write to the above address for complete information.

539

MINNESOTA STATE ARTS BOARD
(Grants Program)

Park Square Court
400 Sibley Street, Suite 200
St. Paul, MN 55101-1928
612/215-1600

AMOUNT: Fellowships-$8,000; Career Opportunity Grants-$100 to $1,500
DEADLINE(S): Aug (Visual Arts); Sep (Music & Dance); Oct (Literature & Theater)
FIELD(S): Literature; Music; Theater; Dance; Visual Arts

Fellowship grants open to professional artists who are residents of Minnesota. Grants may not be used for support of tuition or work toward any degree.

Career opportunity grants and fellowships are available.

540

NATIONAL ART MATERIALS TRADE ASSOCIATION (NAMTA Scholarships)

10115 Kincey Ave., Suite 260
Huntersville, NC 28078
704/948-5554

AMOUNT: $1,000
DEADLINE(S): Mar 1
FIELD(S): Creative disciplines: visual arts, writing, drama, music, etc.

For NAMTA members, employees, and their relatives or to individuals in an organization related to art or the art materials industry. For undergraduate or graduate study.

Selection based on financial need, grades, activities, interests, and career choice. Write for complete information.

541

NATIONAL ART MATERIALS TRADE ASSOCIATION

10115 Kincey Ave., Suite 260
Huntersville, NC 28078
704/948-5554

AMOUNT: Varies
DEADLINE(S): Mar 1
FIELD(S): Creative disciplines: visual arts, writing, drama, music, etc.

For NAMTA members, employees, and their relatives. For undergraduate or graduate study.

Selection based on financial need, grades, activities, interests, and career choice. Write for complete information.

542

NATIONAL ASSOCIATION OF TEACHERS OF SINGING (Artist Awards Competition)

2800 University Blvd. North
Jacksonville, FL 32211
904/744-9022

AMOUNT: Varies
DEADLINE(S): Varies
FIELD(S): Singing

Purpose of the program is to select young singers who are ready for professional careers and to encourage them to carry on the tradition of fine singing. Selection based on present accomplishments rather than future potential.

Applicants should be between 21 and 35 years old and have studied with a NATS teacher or a member of NATS. Write for complete information.

543

NATIONAL FEDERATION OF MUSIC CLUBS COMPETITIVE AWARDS PROGRAM (Student Awards)

1336 N Delaware Street
Indianapolis, IN 46202
317/638-4003; Fax 317/638-0503

AMOUNT: $100-$5,000
DEADLINE(S): Varies
FIELD(S): Music Performance; Music Composition

Numerous award programs open to young musicians aged 16-35 who are either group or individual members of the Nat'l. Fed. of Music Clubs. The programs provide opportunities for students interested in professional music careers.

Request awards chart from the address above. Include check for $1 to cover costs.

544

NATIONAL FOUNDATION FOR ADVANCEMENT IN THE ARTS (Arts Recognition and Talent Search)

800 Brickell Ave., Suite 500
Miami, FL 33131
305/377-1148

AMOUNT: $100-$3,000
DEADLINE(S): Jun 1; Oct 1
FIELD(S): Creative Arts; Performing Arts

Open to high school seniors with talent in such arts as dance; music; music/jazz; theater; visual arts; film; video; and writing. Awards can be used anywhere for any purpose. For U.S. citizens or residents. Entry fee is required.

Approximately 400 awards per year. Write for complete information.

545

NATIONAL GUILD OF COMMUNITY SCHOOLS OF THE ARTS (Young Composers Awards)

40 North Van Brunt Street, Suite 32
Englewood, NJ 07631
201/871-3337

AMOUNT: $1,000; $750; $500; $250
DEADLINE(S): May 1
FIELD(S): Music Composition

Competition open to students aged 13-18 (as of June 30 of award year) who are enrolled in a public or private secondary school, recognized musical school, or engaged in private study of music with an established teacher in the U.S. or Canada.

U.S. or Canadian citizenship or legal residency required. Write to Kate Brackett, Program Associate, NGCSA, at the above address for complete information.

546

NATIONAL ITALIAN AMERICAN FOUNDATION (NIAF-Pavarotti Scholarship)

1860 Nineteenth Street NW
Washington, D.C. 20009-5599
202/530-5315

AMOUNT: $1,000
DEADLINE(S): May 31
FIELD(S): Music

Open to undergraduate or graduate music students of Italian heritage from Southern California. Must send a cassette tape of your voice in performance and write an essay on a family member or personality you consider: "An Italian American Hero."

Academic merit, financial need, and community service also considered.

547

NATIONAL ITALIAN AMERICAN FOUNDATION (Nina Santavicca Scholarship)
1860 19th Street NW
Washington, D.C. 20009-5599
202/530-5315

AMOUNT: $1,000
DEADLINE(S): May 31
FIELD(S): Music major—piano

Open to undergraduate or graduate piano students of Italian heritage.

Academic merit, financial need, and community service considered.

548

NATIONAL ITALIAN AMERICAN FOUNDATION (Sergio Franchi Music Scholarship in Voice Performance)
1860 19th Street NW
Washington, D.C. 20009-5599
202/530-5315

AMOUNT: $1,000
DEADLINE(S): May 31
FIELD(S): Vocal Music (tenors)

Open to undergraduate or graduate vocal music students (tenors) of Italian heritage. Send cassette tape of your voice in performance.

Academic merit, financial need, and community service are considered.

549

NATIONAL ORCHESTRAL INSTITUTE (University of Maryland/Rossborough Festival)
Donald Reinhold
4321 Hartwick Road, Suite 208
College Park, MD 20740
301/403-8370

AMOUNT: Tuition
DEADLINE(S): Prior to audition
FIELD(S): Orchestra

This full scholarship institute offers intensive professional-level orchestral training to only the most advanced music students ages 18-28. Program is offered at the University of Maryland, College Park, for three weeks each June. Students must submit an application, application fee, résumé, and letter of recommendation.

Applicants must audition at one of the audition centers in 20 cities across the U.S. during February and March. Write to the above address for complete information.

550

NEW JERSEY STATE OPERA (Cash Awards)
50 Park Place, Robert Treat Center
Newark, NJ 07102
973/623-5757

AMOUNT: Awards total $10,000
DEADLINE(S): Varies
FIELD(S): Opera

Professional singers between the ages of 22 and 34 can apply for this competition. Singers competing should have been represented by an artist's management firm for no more than one year. Management representation not required for entry.

Contact address above for complete information.

551

NEW JERSEY STATE OPERA (International Vocal Competition)
Robert Treat Center, 10th Floor
Newark, NJ 07102
973/623-5757; Fax 973/623-5761

AMOUNT: $10,000 total
DEADLINE(S): Varies
FIELD(S): Opera singing

Professional opera singers between the ages of 22 and 34 can apply for this international competition.

Renewable yearly. Contact Mrs. Wanda Anderton at above address for information.

552

NEW YORK CITY OPERA (Julius Rudel Award)
New York State Theater
20 Lincoln Center
New York, NY 10023
212/870-5600

AMOUNT: $12,000
DEADLINE(S): None
FIELD(S): Opera & Music Management
(career support)

Applicants should present evidence of artistic accomplishments along with a résumé and letters of recommendation; also a statement outlining how affiliation with the NYC Opera will further applicant's artistic and career goals.

Award recipient performs administrative tasks for NYC Opera but recipient is encouraged to continue outside artistic work. Write for complete information.

553

PITTSBURGH NEW MUSIC ENSEMBLE (Harvey Gaul Composition Contest)
Duquesne University School of Music
Pittsburgh, PA 15282
412/261-0554

AMOUNT: $3,000
DEADLINE(S): Apr 15
FIELD(S): Music Composition

A contest for compositions for chamber ensembles of five players and up or orchestra. For U.S. citizens. An entry fee of $20 must accompany each composition submitted. Composers may enter more than one composition.

Send a score, cassette, and current biography. Write or call for complete information. The winning composition will be performed by the Pittsburgh New Music Ensemble.

554

PRINCESS GRACE FOUNDATION—U.S. (Theatre Scholarships)
150 East 58th Street, 21st Floor
New York, NY 10155
212/317-1470; Fax 212/317-1473

AMOUNT: $3,500-$15,000
DEADLINE(S): Mar 31
FIELD(S): Theater; Dance; Film

Open to undergraduate seniors or graduate students in their last year of professional training at a nonprofit school in the U.S. Must be nominated by the dean or department chairman of a professional school in theater.

U.S. citizenship or legal residency required. Write for complete information.

555

RIPON COLLEGE (Music, Forensics, Art, and Theatre Scholarships)
P.O. Box 248
300 Seward Street
Admissions office
Ripon, WI 54971
414/748-8102; 800/94RIPON

AMOUNT: $1,000-$8,000
DEADLINE(S): Mar 1
FIELD(S): Music; Forensics; Art; Theatre

Scholarships to recognize and encourage academic potential and accomplishment in above fields. Renewable each year provided recipient maintains a good academic standing and participates in the program.

Must apply and be accepted for admission to Ripon College. Interview or audition required. Write for complete information.

556

SAN ANGELO SYMPHONY SOCIETY (Sorantin Young Artist Award)
P.O. Box 5922
San Angelo, TX 76902
915/658-5877; Fax 915/653-1045

AMOUNT: $3,000 to winner; $1,000 to 3 others; $400 to runners-up

DEADLINE(S): Oct 15

FIELD(S): Music—Vocal, Instrumental, or Piano

A competition open to instrumentalists who have not reached their 28th birthdays by November 22 and to vocalists who have not reached their 31st birthdays by November 22. Provides opportunity for a cash award with the symphony orchestra.

Write to the above address for complete information.

557

SANTA BARBARA FOUNDATION (Mary & Edith Pillsbury Foundation Scholarships)
15 E. Carrillo Street
Santa Barbara, CA 93101-2780
805/963-1873

AMOUNT: Varies

DEADLINE(S): May 15

FIELD(S): Music Performance; Music Composition

Open to talented music students who are Santa Barbara county residents or have strong Santa Barbara ties. Awards may be used for music lessons, camps or college tuition. U.S. citizen. Financial need is a consideration.

Approximately 30 scholarships per year; renewable. Write for complete information.

558

SANTA BARBARA FOUNDATION (Pillsbury Music Scholarship Program)
15 E. Carrillo Street
Santa Barbara, CA 93101-2780
805/963-1873; Fax 805/966-2345; E-mail: dano@SBFoundation.org

AMOUNT: Varies

DEADLINE(S): May 15

FIELD(S): Music

For students of music who have resided in Santa Barbara County for two years prior to application deadline or who have resided long-term in the county. Must be planning to attend an U.S. accredited college or university.

Applications are available from April 1 to May 15 at the Foundation office.

559

TENNESSEE ARTS COMMISSION (Individual Artists' Fellowships)
401 Charlotte Ave.
Nashville, TN 37243-0780
615/741-1701

AMOUNT: $2,000

DEADLINE(S): Jan 11

FIELD(S): Visual Arts; Performing Arts; Creative Arts

Open to artists who are residents of Tennessee. Duration of award is one year. Applicants must be professional artists. Full-time students are NOT eligible.

Write for complete information.

560

THE AMERICAN GUILD OF ORGANISTS (National Competition in Organ Improvisation)
475 Riverside Drive, Suite 1260
New York, NY 10115
212/870-2310; Fax 212/870-2163

AMOUNT: $2,000; $1,000; $500

DEADLINE(S): Jan 1

FIELD(S): Organ performance

Competition seeks to further the art of improvisation in organ performance by recognizing and rewarding superior performers in the field. Membership in American Guild of Organists required. Open to all members, including student members. $35 registration fee.

Write for details.

129

561

THE AMERICAN GUILD OF ORGANISTS (Regional Competitions for Young Organists)

475 Riverside Drive, Suite 1260
New York, NY 10115
212/870-2310; Fax 212/870-2163

AMOUNT: $1,000; $500
DEADLINE(S): Jan 31
FIELD(S): Organ performance

Competition for young people up to age 23 in nine different regions of the U.S. Membership in AGO not required. $25 registration fee.

Contact above location for details.

562

THE AMERICAN GUILD OF ORGANISTS (Regional Competitions for Young Organists)

475 Riverside Drive, Suite 1260
New York, NY 10115
212/870-2310; Fax 212/870-2163

AMOUNT: $2,000; $1,500; $750
DEADLINE(S): None specified
FIELD(S): Organ performance

Competition for organists between the ages of 22 and 32. Must be members of AGO.

Contact above location for details.

563

THE BAGBY FOUNDATION FOR THE MUSICAL ARTS, INC. (Musical Study Grants)

501 Fifth Ave., Suite 1401
New York, NY 10017
212/986-6094

AMOUNT: $2,000-$6,000
DEADLINE(S): Ongoing
FIELD(S): Music

Musical study grants based on talent and need.

Send a letter to above location outlining financial need.

564

THE GRAND RAPIDS FOUNDATION (Grand Rapids Combined Theatre Scholarship Fund)

209-C Waters Bldg.
161 Ottawa Ave. NW
Grand Rapids, MI 49503-2703
616/454-1751; 616/454-6455

AMOUNT: Varies
DEADLINE(S): Apr 3
FIELD(S): Theatre Arts

Must be enrolled full-time in an accredited college or training program. Preference given to theatre arts majors. Must have worked in Grand Rapids, Michigan area community theatre. Must demonstrate talent, ability, dedication to the theatre arts.

Contact the Foundation, Actor's Theatre, Community Circle Theatre, Grand Rapids Civic Theatre, or Broadway Theatre Guild for more information.

565

THE GRAND RAPIDS FOUNDATION (Mildred E. Troske Music Scholarship)

209-C Waters Bldg.
161 Ottawa Ave. NW
Grand Rapids, MI 49503-2703
616/454-1751; 616/454-6455

AMOUNT: Varies
DEADLINE(S): Apr 3
FIELD(S): Music

Open to full-time undergrads attending an accredited institution with an educational emphasis on music. Must have been a Kent County, Michigan, resident at least 5 years, have 3.0 or better GPA, and demonstrate financial need.

Send SASE to above address for complete information.

566

THE QUEEN SONJA INTERNATIONAL MUSIC COMPETITION (Piano/Voice Competition)
P.O. Box 5190 Majorstua
N-0302 Oslo Norway
+47/22464055 ext. 430; Fax +47/22463630

AMOUNT: $40,000 approximate total prize money
DEADLINE(S): Mar 15
FIELD(S): Piano; Voice

In addition to cash awards for the 4 finalists (places 1-4) the Board of Directors will endeavor to provide them with solo engagements in Norway.

Write to the above address for complete information and conditions for applications.

567

UNIVERSITY FILM & VIDEO ASSOCIATION (Carole Fielding Student Grants)
University of Baltimore
School of Communication
1420 N. Charles Street
Baltimore, MD 21201
410/837-6061

AMOUNT: $1,000-$4,000
DEADLINE(S): Mar 31
FIELD(S): Film; Video; Multi-media Production

Open to undergraduate/graduate students. Categories are narrative, experimental, animation, documentary, multi-media/installation and research. Applicant must be sponsored by a faculty member who is an active member of the University Film and Video Association.

Write to the above address for application and complete details.

568

UNIVERSITY OF ALABAMA AT BIRMINGHAM (Theatre Scholarships)
UAB Station
School of Arts & Humanities
Dept. of Theatre
Birmingham, AL 35294-3340
205/934-3236

AMOUNT: $1,000
DEADLINE(S): Varies (spring)
FIELD(S): Theatre

Scholarships for high school seniors with above-average GPAs and theatre talent. For undergraduate study at the University of Alabama/Birmingham. Winners will appear in various shows and touring groups. Must be enrolled in UAB.

Approximately 20 awards per year. Renewable. Write to the department chairman for complete information.

569

UNIVERSITY OF ILLINOIS AT URBANA-CHAMPAIGN (Lydia E. Parker Bates Scholarship)
Turner Student Services Bldg., MC-306
610 East John Street
Champaign, IL 61820
217/333-0100

AMOUNT: Varies
DEADLINE(S): Mar 15
FIELD(S): Art, Architecture, Landscape Architecture, Urban Planning, Dance, Theater, and all related subjects except Music

Open to undergraduate students in the College of Fine & Applied Arts who are attending the University of Illinois at Urbana-Champaign. Must demonstrate financial need and have 3.85 GPA. Complete the Free Application for Federal Student Aid.

175 awards per year. Recipients must carry at least 12 credit hours per semester. Contact Office of Student Financial Aid.

570

**VIRGIN ISLANDS BOARD OF
EDUCATION (Music Scholarships)**
P.O. Box 11900
St. Thomas, VI 00801
809/774-4546

AMOUNT: $2,000
DEADLINE(S): Mar 31
FIELD(S): Music

Open to bona fide residents of the Virgin
Islands who are enrolled in an accredited
music program at an institution of higher
learning.

This scholarship is granted for the duration of
the course provided the recipients maintain
at least a 'C' average. Write for complete
information.

571

WAMSO (Young Artist Competition)
1111 Nicollet Mall
Minneapolis, MN 55403
612/371-5654

AMOUNT: $2,750 1st prize plus performance
with MN Orchestra
DEADLINE(S): Oct 15 (competition usually
held in Jan)
FIELD(S): Piano & Orchestral Instruments

Competition offers 4 prizes & possible scholarships to high school & college students in
schools in IA, MN, MO, NE, ND, SD, WI,
& the Canadian provinces of Manitoba &
Ontario. Entrants may not have passed
their 26th birthday on date of competition.

For list of repertoires & complete information,
specify your instrument & write to address
above.

572

**WAVERLY COMMUNITY HOUSE INC. (F.
Lammot Belin Arts Scholarships)**
Scholarships Selection Committee
P.O. Box 142
Waverly, PA 18471

717/586-8191

AMOUNT: $10,000
DEADLINE(S): Dec 15
FIELD(S): Painting; Sculpture; Music; Drama;
Dance; Literature; Architecture;
Photography

Applicants must have resided in the Abington
or Pocono regions of Northeastern
Pennsylvania. They must furnish proof of
exceptional ability in their chosen field but
no formal training in any academic or professional program.

U.S. citizenship required. Finalists must appear
in person before the selection committee.
Write for complete information.

573

**WELLESLEY COLLEGE (Harriet A. Shaw
Fellowships)**
Career Center
Secretary Graduate Fellowships
Wellesley, MA 02181-8200
617/283-3525

AMOUNT: Up to $3,000 stipend per year
DEADLINE(S): Dec
FIELD(S): Music; Allied Arts

Open to women who hold a BA degree from
Wellesley College for research in music and
allied arts in the U.S. or abroad. Preference
given to music candidates; undergrad work
in art history is required for other candidates.

Write for complete information.

PHILOSOPHY

574

**CHRISTIAN CHURCH—Disciples of Christ
(Associate for Black Ministry Scholarship)**
130 E. Washington Street
Indianapolis, IN 46206-1986
317/353-3113 Ext. 393; Fax 317/635-4426; E-
mail: cwebb@dhm.disciples.org

AMOUNT: $1,500-$2,000

DEADLINE(S): Mar 15

FIELD(S): Theology

Open to Christian Church (Disciples of Christ) members who are African-Americans enrolled in an accredited graduate school or seminary in preparation for the ministry. U.S. citizenship. Above-average GPA; financial need.

40-50 awards yearly. Renewable. Write for complete information.

575

CHRISTIAN CHURCH—Disciples of Christ (Black Star Supporter Scholarship/Loan)
P.O. Box 1986
Indianapolis, IN 46206-1986
317/635-3100; Fax 317/635-4426; E-mail: cwebb@dhm.disciples.org

AMOUNT: $1,000-$1,500

DEADLINE(S): Mar 15

FIELD(S): Theology

Open to Christian Church (Disciples of Christ) members who are African-American and are enrolled in an accredited bachelor's degree or graduate program in preparation for the ministry. Above-average GPA & financial need considered.

Renewable. Write for complete information.

576

CHRISTIAN CHURCH—Disciples of Christ (David Tamotsu Kagiwada Memorial Scholarship for Asian-American Ministerial Students)
P.O. Box 1986
Indianapolis, IN 46206-1986
317/353-3100; Fax 317/635-4425; E-mail: cwebb@dhm.disciples.org

AMOUNT: Varies

DEADLINE(S): Mar 15

FIELD(S): Theology

Open to Christian Church (Disciples of Christ) members of Asian descent who are enrolled in an accredited graduate school or seminary in preparation for the ministry. U.S. citizenship. Above-average GPA; financial need.

Renewable. Write for complete information.

577

CHRISTIAN CHURCH—Disciples of Christ (Katherine J. Schutze/Edwin G. & Lauretta M. Michael Scholarships)
P.O. Box 1986
Indianapolis, IN 46206-1986
317/635-3100; Fax 317/635-4426; E-mail: cwebb@dhm.disciples.org

AMOUNT: Varies

DEADLINE(S): Mar 15

FIELD(S): Theology

The Schutze program is for female Christian Church (Disciples of Christ) members enrolled in an accredited bachelor's degree or graduate program in preparation for the ministry. The Michael scholarship is for ministers' wives. Above-average GPA & financial need considered.

Renewable. Write for complete information.

578

CHRISTIAN CHURCH—Disciples of Christ (Rowley/Ministerial Education Scholarship)
P.O. Box 1986
Indianapolis, IN 46206-1986
317/635-3100; Fax 317/635-4426; E-mail: cwebb@dhm.disciples.org

AMOUNT: Varies

DEADLINE(S): Mar 15

FIELD(S): Theology

Open to Christian Church (Disciples of Christ) members who are enrolled in an accredited graduate school or seminary in preparation for the ministry. Above-average academic standing & financial need are considerations.

Renewable. Write for complete information.

579

CIVIL AIR PATROL (Cassaday-Elmore Ministerial Scholarship)
National Headquarters/ETTC
Maxwell AFB, AL 36112
334/293-5315

AMOUNT: $750
DEADLINE(S): Jan 31
FIELD(S): Ministry

Open to a CAP cadet who plans to enter the ministry and has been accepted into an accredited college. One-year scholarship for undergraduate study.
Write for complete information.

580

CLEM JAUNICH EDUCATION TRUST (Scholarships)
5353 Gamble Drive, Suite 110
Minneapolis, MN 55416
612/546-1555

AMOUNT: $750-$3,000
DEADLINE(S): Jul 1
FIELD(S): Theology; Medicine

For students who have attended public or parochial school in the Delano (MN) school district or currently reside within 7 miles of the city of Delano, MN. Awards support undergraduate or graduate study in theology or medicine.
4-6 scholarships per year. Write for complete information.

581

ELMER O. & IDA PRESTON EDUCATIONAL TRUST (Grants & Loans)
801 Grand Ave., Suite 3700
Des Moines, IA 50309
515/243-4191

AMOUNT: Varies
DEADLINE(S): Jun 30
FIELD(S): Christian Ministry

Open to male residents of Iowa who are pursuing collegiate or professional studies at an Iowa college or university. Applicants must provide recommendation from a minister commenting on student's potential in his chosen church vocation.
Awards are one-half grant and one-half loan. The loan is repayable at 6% per annum. Write for complete information.

582

ENGEN SEMINARY STUDENT SCHOLARSHIP ASSISTANCE TRUST
c/o Evangelical Lutheran Church
in America
Presho, SD 57568
Written inquiry

AMOUNT: Varies
DEADLINE(S): Ongoing
FIELD(S): Lutheran ministry

Scholarships for students who are members of the Evangelical Lutheran Church in America and attend an accredited ELCA seminary in preparation for the parish ministry.
Awards are based on financial need and promise for the pastoral ministry.

583

FITZGERALD TRUST FUND (Scholarships)
First of America Trust Company
301 S.W. Adams Street
Peoria, IL 61652
309/655-5000

AMOUNT: Varies
DEADLINE(S): None specified
FIELD(S): Theology

Undergraduate scholarships available for students preparing for priesthood at a Catholic university or college. Seminarians preparing for the Priesthood for the Diocese of Peoria only.
Write for complete information.

584

**J. HUGH & EARLE W. FELLOWS
MEMORIAL FUND (Scholarship Loans)**
Pensacola Junior College
Exec VP
1000 College Blvd.
Pensacola, FL 32504
904/484-1706

AMOUNT: Each is negotiated individually
DEADLINE(S): None
FIELD(S): Medicine; Nursing; Medical
Technology; Theology (Episcopal)
Open to bona fide residents of the Florida
counties of Escambia, Santa Rosa,
Okaloosa or Walton. For undergraduate
study in the fields listed above. U.S. citizen-
ship required.
Loans are interest-free until graduation. Write
for complete information.

585

**JIMMIE ULLERY CHARITABLE TRUST
(Scholarship Grant)**
Scholarship Committee
P.O. Box One
Tulsa, OK 74102
918/586-5594

AMOUNT: Varies
DEADLINE(S): Jun 1
FIELD(S): Theology
Open to presbyterian students in full-time
Christian service. Scholarships are usually
(but not always) awarded for study at
Presbyterian theological seminaries. U.S. cit-
izen or legal resident.
5-6 scholarships per year. Write for complete
information.

586

**MARY GONTER AND SARA O'BRIEN
SCHOLARSHIP FOUNDATION**
P.O. Box 232
Dover, OH 44622
Written inquiry

AMOUNT: Approx. $2,000
DEADLINE(S): Ongoing
FIELD(S): Protestant Christian ministry
Scholarships for young Ohio residents study-
ing to become ordained Protestant
Christian ministers.
Contact Larry Markworth, V.P., Huntington
Trust Co., at above location.

587

**OPAL DANCEY MEMORIAL
FOUNDATION**
45 South Croswell
Croswell, MI 48422
Written inquiry

AMOUNT: Varies
DEADLINE(S): Jun 15
FIELD(S): Theology
Scholarships to students pursuing theological
education.
Write to Rev. Gary Imms, Chair, at above
address for details.

588

**ROBERT SCHRECK MEMORIAL FUND
(Grants)**
c/o Texas Commerce Bank—Trust Dept.
P.O. Drawer 140
El Paso, TX 79980
915/546-6515

AMOUNT: $500-$1,500
DEADLINE(S): Jul 15; Nov 15
FIELD(S): Medicine; Veterinary Medicine;
Physics; Chemistry; Architecture;
Engineering; Episcopal Clergy
Grants to undergraduate juniors or seniors or
graduate students who have been residents
of El Paso County for at least two years.
Must be U.S. citizen or legal resident and
have a high grade-point-average. Financial
need is a consideration.
Write for complete information.

589

UNITED METHODIST CHURCH (Youth Ministry—Richard S. Smith Scholarship)
P.O. Box 480
Nashville, TN 37202-0840
615/340-7184; Fax 615/340-1702; E-mail: nymo@aol.com; Internet: www.umc.org/nymo/nymohome

AMOUNT: Up to $1,000
DEADLINE(S): Jun 1
FIELD(S): Church-Related Vocation
Open to United Methodist church youth from ethnic minority backgrounds who have at least a 2.0 high school GPA, been active in a local church at least 1 year, and are entering college as freshmen in pursuit of a church-related career.
Must be able to establish need. Obtain application between Nov. 1 and May 15.

590

UNITED METHODIST CHURCH (Youth Ministry—David W. Self Scholarship)
P.O. Box 840
Nashville, TN 37202-0840
615/340-7184; Fax 615/340-1702; E-mail: nymo@aol.com; Internet: www.umc.org/nymo/nymohome

AMOUNT: Up to $1,000
DEADLINE(S): Jun 1
FIELD(S): Church-Related Vocation
Open to United Methodist church youth who have at least a 2.0 high school GPA, been active in a local church at least 1 year, and are entering college as freshmen in pursuit of a church-related career.
Must be able to establish need. Obtain application between November 1 and May 15. Write for complete information.

591

VIOLET R. AND NADA V. BOHNETT MEMORIAL FOUNDATION
15600 Redmond Way, #200
Redmond, WA 98052

Fax 206/869-8195; E-mail: here4dads@aol.com

AMOUNT: $475-$1,000
DEADLINE(S): Ongoing
FIELD(S): Christian ministry
Scholarships for individuals in western Washington, California, Arizona, Colorado, and Hawaii for the study of Christian ministry. Students from western Washington have priority.
Apply by sending a letter of no more than one page to Mr. Jamie Bohnett, Administrator, at above address.

592

VIRGINIA BAPTIST MISSION BOARD (Virginia Baptist Ministerial Undergraduate Student Loans)
P.O. Box 8568
Richmond, VA 23226-0568
Written inquiry

AMOUNT: Varies
DEADLINE(S): Aug 1
FIELD(S): Theology
Open to residents of Virginia who are enrolled full-time as an undergrad college student and are studying to become a Southern Baptist minister. Must be a member of a church associated with the Baptist General Association of Virginia.
50 awards per year. Loans are non-repayable if recipient works for a Christian-related service for 2 years. Write for complete information.

SCHOOL OF NATURAL RESOURCES

593

EXPLORERS CLUB (Youth Activity Fund)
46 East 70th Street
New York, NY 10021
212/628-8383; Fax 212/288-4449

AMOUNT: $200-$1,000

136

DEADLINE(S): Apr 15

FIELD(S): Natural Sciences; Biological Sciences; Physical Sciences

Open to high school and undergraduate college students to help them participate in field research in the natural sciences anywhere in the world. Grants are to help with travel costs and expenses. Joint funding is strongly recommended.

U.S. citizen or legal resident. Applications available in February before April deadline. Write for complete information.

594

GENERAL LEARNING COMMUNICATIONS (Sponsored by Dupont, GLC, and the NSTA Science Essay Awards Programs)
900 Skokie Blvd., Suite 200
Northbrook, IL 60062
847/205-3000

AMOUNT: Up to $1,500

DEADLINE(S): Jan 31

FIELD(S): Sciences

Annual essay competition open to students in grades 7-12 in U.S. and Canada. Cash awards for 1st, 2nd, and honorable mention. 1st-place essayists, their science teacher, and a parent receive trip to space center in Houston, April 27-29.

Contact your science teacher or address above for complete information. Official entry blank must accompany essay entry.

595

SLOCUM-LUNZ FOUNDATION (Scholarships & Grants)
P.O. Box 12559
205 Fort Johnson
Charleston, SC 29422
803/762-5052

AMOUNT: Up to $2,000

DEADLINE(S): Apr 1

FIELD(S): Natural Sciences; Marine Sciences

Open to beginning graduate students & PhD candidates enrolled at institutions located in South Carolina. Awards support research studies in the above areas.

Academic work must be performed in South Carolina. Write for complete information.

596

WOMEN'S AUXILIARY TO THE AMERICAN INSTITUTE OF MINING METALLURGICAL & PETROLEUM ENGINEERS (WAAIME Scholarship Loan Fund)
345 E. 47th Street, 14th Floor
New York, NY 10017
212/705-7692

AMOUNT: Varies

DEADLINE(S): Mar 15

FIELD(S): Earth Sciences, as related to the Minerals Industry

Open to undergraduate juniors & seniors and grad students, whose majors relate to an interest in the minerals industry. Eligible applicants receive a scholarship loan for all or part of their education. Recipients repay only 50% with no interest charges.

Repayment to begin by 6 months after graduation and be completed within 6 years. Write to WAAIME Scholarship Loan Fund (address above) for complete information.

AGRICULTURE

597

ABBIE SARGENT MEMORIAL SCHOLARSHIP INC. (Scholarships)
295 Sheep Davis Road
Concord, NH 03301
603/224-1934

AMOUNT: $200

DEADLINE(S): Mar 15

FIELD(S): Agriculture; Veterinary Medicine; Home Economics

Open to New Hampshire residents who are high school graduates with good grades and character. For undergraduate or graduate study. Must be legal resident of U.S. and demonstrate financial need.

Renewable with reapplication. Write for complete information.

598

AMERICAN FEED INDUSTRY ASSOCIATION (Scholarship Program)
1501 Wilson Blvd., Suite 1100
Arlington, VA 22209
703/524-0810

AMOUNT: $1,000
DEADLINE(S): Mar 15
FIELD(S): Animal Science; Agriculture; Agri-Business

Open to undergraduate and graduate agriculture and animal science students. Academic excellence and participation in student activities are considered.

Various sponsors establish individual criteria. Contact Dorann Towery at above address for complete information.

599

AMERICAN JUNIOR BRAHMAN ASSOCIATION (Ladies of the ABBA Scholarship)
1313 La Concha Lane
Houston, TX 77054-1890
Written inquiry

AMOUNT: $500-$1,000
DEADLINE(S): Apr 30
FIELD(S): Agriculture

Open to graduating high school seniors who are members of the Junior Brahman Association. For full-time undergraduate study. U.S. citizenship required.

Up to 4 awards per year. Write for complete information.

600

AMERICAN POMOPLOGICAL SOCIETY (U. P. Hedrick Awards)
103 Tyson Bldg., Penn State University
University Park, PA 16802
814/863-6163

AMOUNT: $100, second place; $300, first place
DEADLINE(S): Jun 1
FIELD(S): Pomology

Open to students who have written a paper in topics related to fruit/fruit cultivation. Paper content should relate to cultivars of deciduous, tropical, or subtropical fruit as related to climate, soil, rootstocks, a specific experiment, a breeding project, history and performance of new or old cultivars.

Write to the above address for complete information.

601

BEDDING PLANTS FOUNDATION INC. (Carl Dietz Memorial Scholarship)
P.O. Box 27241
Lansing, MI 48909
517/694-8537; Fax 517/694-8560; E-mail: bpfi@grafix-net.com; Internet: www.grafix-net.com/bpfi

AMOUNT: $1,000
DEADLINE(S): Apr 1
FIELD(S): Horticulture

Open to undergrads entering sophomore, junior or senior year who are enrolled in accredited four-year college/university in the U.S. or Canada. Must be a horticulture major with a specific interest in bedding plants. Minimum 3.0 GPA required.

Write for complete information.

602

BEDDING PLANTS FOUNDATION INC. (Earl J. Small Growers, Inc. Scholarships)
P.O. Box 27241
Lansing, MI 48909

517/694-8537; Fax 517/694-8560; E-mail:
bpfi@grafix-net.com; Internet:
www.grafix-net.com/bpfi

AMOUNT: $2,000
DEADLINE(S): Apr 1
FIELD(S): Horticulture

Open to U.S. and Canadian citizens who are
undergrads entering sophomor, junior or
senior year. Must be enrolled in accredited
four-year college or university program in
the U.S. or Canada and intend to pursue a
career in greenhouse production.
Write for complete information.

603

BEDDING PLANTS FOUNDATION INC.
(Harold Bettinger Memorial Scholarship)
P.O. Box 27241
Lansing, MI 48909
517/694-8537; Fax 517/694-8560; E-mail:
bpfi@grafix-net.com; Internet:
www.grafix-net.com/bpfi

AMOUNT: $1,000
DEADLINE(S): Apr 1
FIELD(S): Horticulture &
Business/Marketing

Open to undergraduate sophomores, juniors
and seniors as well as grad students
enrolled in an accredited four-year college
or university in the U.S. or Canada.
Minimum 3.0 GPA required.
Must be horticulture major with a business/
marketing emphasis or business/marketing
major with horticulture emphasis. Write for
complete information.

604

BEDDING PLANTS FOUNDATION INC.
(James K. Rathmell Jr. Memorial Scholarship)
P.O. Box 27241
Lansing, MI 48909
517/694-8537; Fax 517/694-8560; E-mail:
bpfi@grafix-net.com; Internet: www.bpfi.org

AMOUNT: Up to $2,000

DEADLINE(S): Apr 1
FIELD(S): Horticulture or Floriculture

Open to upper-level undergrad or grad students for work/study programs outside of
the U.S. in the fields of floriculture or horticulture. Preference to those planning programs of six months or more.
Write for complete information.

605

BEDDING PLANTS FOUNDATION INC.
(Jerry Baker/America's Master Gardener
College Freshman Scholarship)
P.O. Box 27241
Lansing, MI 48909
517/694-8537; Fax 517/694-8560; E-mail:
bpfi@grafix-net.com/bpfi; Internet:
www.grafix-net.com/bpfi

AMOUNT: $1,000
DEADLINE(S): Apr 1
FIELD(S): Horticulture; Landscaping;
Gardening

Open to undergraduates entering their freshman year who are interested in careers in
horticulture, landscaping, or gardening.
2 awards per year. Write for complete information.

606

BEDDING PLANTS FOUNDATION INC.
(Jerry Wilmot Scholarship)
P.O. Box 27241
Lansing, MI 48909
517/694-8537; Fax 517/694-8560; E-mail:
bpfi@grafix-net.com; Internet:
www.grafix-net.com/bpfi

AMOUNT: $2,000
DEADLINE(S): Apr 1
FIELD(S): Garden Center Management

For undergrads entering sophomore, junior or
senior year, who are majoring in horticulture or business/finance. Must be enrolled
in an accredited four-year college/university

in the U.S. or Canada and pursuing a career in garden center management.

Write for complete information.

607

BEDDING PLANTS FOUNDATION INC. (Vocational Scholarships)
P.O. Box 27241
Lansing, MI 48909
517/694-8537; Fax 517/694-8560; E-mail: bpfi@grafix-net.com; Internet: www.grafix-net.com/bpfi

AMOUNT: $500-$1,000
DEADLINE(S): Apr 1
FIELD(S): Horticulture

Open to undergrads accepted in a one- or two-year vocational program. Must be U.S. or Canadian citizen enrolled for the entire academic year and intend to become a floriculture plant producer and/or operations manager. Minimum 3.0 GPA required.

2-4 awards per year. Write for complete information.

608

BEDDING PLANTS FOUNDATION, INC. (Fran Johnson Scholarship for Non-traditional Students)
P.O. Box 27241
Lansing, MI 48909
517/694-8537; Fax 517/694-8560; E-mail: bpfi@grafix-net.com; Internet: www.grafix-net.com/bpfi

AMOUNT: $500-$1,000
DEADLINE(S): Apr 1
FIELD(S): Floriculture

Open to students who are re-entering the academic setting after an absence of at least five years. Specific interest should be in bedding plants or other floral crops. Scholarship is for undergraduate or graduate study in Canada or the United States at an accredited institution.

U.S. or Canadian citizenship or residency is required. Write to the above address for complete information.

609

BURLINGTON NORTHERN SANTE FE FOUNDATION (Future Farmers of America Scholarship)
5632 Mt. Vernon Memorial Hwy
P.O. Box 15160
Alexandria, VA 22309-0160
703/360-3600

AMOUNT: $1,000
DEADLINE(S): Varies
FIELD(S): Agriculture

Open to students during their senior year in high school who are FFA members. Applicants must live in one of the following states: Arizona, California, Colorado, Illinois, Iowa, Kansas, Minnesota, Missouri, Montana, Nebraska, New Mexico, North Dakota, Oklahoma, Oregon, South Dakota, Texas, or Washington.

To be used at a land-grant college within the applicant's home state and for study of agriculture. Write to the above address for complete information.

610

CALIFORNIA FARM BUREAU SCHOLARSHIP FOUNDATION (Scholarships)
2300 River Plaza Drive
Sacramento, CA 95833
800/698-3276

AMOUNT: Varies ($1,250 average)
DEADLINE(S): Mar 1
FIELD(S): Agriculture

Open to U.S. citizens who are students entering or attending an accredited 4-year college or university in California. Must be majoring in a field related to agriculture; however, membership in a county farm bureau is NOT required.

Renewable. Write for complete information.

611

CDS INTERNATIONAL INC. (Congress-Bundestag Youth Exchange Program)

330 Seventh Ave., 19th Floor
New York, NY 10001
212/497-3500; Fax 212/497-3535; E-mail:
cbyx@cdsintl.org; Internet: www.cdsintl.org

AMOUNT: Airfare, partial domestic travel, and host family payment

DEADLINE(S): Dec 15

FIELD(S): Business; Vocational/Technical Fields; Agricultural Fields

Year-long work/study programs in Germany for U.S. citizens aged 18-24. Program for Americans includes two-month language study, four-month tech or professional school study, and six-month internship. A cultural exchange designed to give participants an understanding and knowledge of everyday life in Germany.

60 awards per year. Contact Martin Black at above location. Professional target and applicable work experience is required. Participants must provide their own spending money of $300-$350/month.

612

CENEX FOUNDATION SCHOLARSHIP PROGRAM (Agricultural Studies)

5500 Cenex Drive
Inver Grove Heights, MN 55077
612/451-5129

AMOUNT: $600

DEADLINE(S): Feb 15

FIELD(S): Agriculture

Open to students attending a participating vocational, technical or community college enrolled in agricultural programs. Must be attending school in one of the following states: Colorado, Idaho, Iowa, Kansas, Minnesota, Montana, Nebraska, North Dakota, Oregon, South Dakota, Utah, Washington, Wisconsin, or Wyoming.

Write to the above address for complete information. Scholarships are handled through the participating schools.

613

CENEX FOUNDATION SCHOLARSHIP PROGRAM (Cooperative Studies)

5500 Cenex Drive
Inver Grove Heights, MN 55077
612/451-5129

AMOUNT: $750

DEADLINE(S): Varies (Spring)

FIELD(S): Agriculture

Open to students attending the agriculture college of a participating university enrolled in courses on cooperative principles and cooperative business practices. Students must be in their junior or senior year of studies.

79 scholarships are awarded at selected universities within the Cenex market area. Write to the above address for complete information and a list of participating schools. Scholarships are handled through the participating schools.

614

COMMITTEE ON INSTITUTIONAL COOPERATION (CIC Pre-doctoral Fellowships)

Kirkwood Hall 111, Indiana University
Bloomington, IN 47405
812/855-0823

AMOUNT: $11,000 + tuition (4 years)

DEADLINE(S): Dec 1

FIELD(S): Humanities; Social Sciences; Natural Sciences; Mathematics; Engineering

Pre-doctoral fellowships for U.S. citizens of African-American, American Indian, Mexican-American, or Puerto Rican heritage. Must hold or expect to receive bachelor's degree by late summer from a regionally accredited college or unviersity.

Awards for specified universities in IL; IN; IA; MI; MN; OH; WI; PA. Write for details.

615

EXPLORERS CLUB (Youth Activity Fund)

46 East 70th Street
New York, NY 10021
212/628-8383; Fax 212/288-4449

AMOUNT: $200-$1,000
DEADLINE(S): Apr 15
FIELD(S): Natural Sciences; Biological Sciences; Physical Sciences

Open to high school and undergraduate college students to help them participate in field research in the natural sciences anywhere in the world. Grants are to help with travel costs and expenses. Joint funding is strongly recommended.

U.S. citizen or legal resident. Applications available in February before April deadline. Write for complete information.

616

FLORIDA RURAL REHABILITATION SCHOLARSHIP

P.O. Box 110270
Gainesville, FL 32611
Written inquiry

AMOUNT: Up to $1,000
DEADLINE(S): Jan 15
FIELD(S): Agriculture

Scholarships for Florida students from rural areas who plan to study agriculture at the Institute of Food and Agricultural Sciences at the University of Florida. Financial need, leadership ability, and merit are considered.

Write to Institute of Food and Ag Sciences, University of Florida, at above address.

617

GARDEN CLUB OF AMERICA (Katharine M. Grosscup Scholarships)

Mrs. Nancy Stevenson
Grosscup Scholarship Com.
Cleveland Botanical Gardens
11030 East Boulevard
Cleveland, OH 44106

Fax 216/721-2056 (no phone calls)

AMOUNT: $2,000
DEADLINE(S): Feb 15
FIELD(S): Horticulture; Agriculture

For college juniors, seniors, or graduate students to encourage the study of horticulture, agriculture, or related subjects in the field of gardening.

Preference given to students from Ohio, Pennsylvania, West Virginia, Michigan, and Indiana. Write for complete information.

618

GOLF COURSE SUPERINTENDENTS ASSOCIATION OF AMERICA (GCSAA Essay Contest)

1421 Research Park Drive
Lawrence, KS 66049-3859
913/841-2240; 800/472-7878 Ext. 445

AMOUNT: $2,000 (total prizes)
DEADLINE(S): Mar 31
FIELD(S): Turfgrass science, agronomy, or any field related to golf course management

Contest open to undergraduate and graduate students pursuing degrees in one of the above fields.

Essays should be 7-12 pages long and should focus on the relationship between golf courses and the environment.

619

GOLF COURSE SUPERINTENDENTS ASSOCIATION OF AMERICA (GCSAA Scholars Program)

1421 Research Park Drive
Lawrence, KS 66049-3859
913/841-2240; 800/472-7878 Ext. 445

AMOUNT: $1,500-$3,500
DEADLINE(S): Jun 1
FIELD(S): Golf/turf management

Awards available to outstanding undergraduate students planning careers as golf course superintendents. Applicants must be enrolled in a recognized major field related to golf/turf management.

Must successfully have completed at least 24 credit hours or the equivalent of one year of full-time study in an appropriate major.

620

GOLF COURSE SUPERINTENDENTS ASSOCIATION OF AMERICA (The Scotts Company Scholars Program)
1421 Research Park Drive
Lawrence, KS 66049-3859
913/841-2240; 800/472-7878 Ext. 445

AMOUNT: $500 award; $2,500 scholarship
DEADLINE(S): Mar 1
FIELD(S): Green Industry

Applicants must be pursuing a career in the "green industry" and be a graduating high school senior, or collegiate freshman, sophomore, or junior who has been accepted at an accredited university, college, or junior college for the next academic year.

Although all qualified students are urged to apply, candidates from diverse ethnic, cultural, and socio-economic backgrounds may receive preferential consideration in judging.

621

GOLF COURSE SUPERINTENDENTS ASSOCIATION OF AMERICA (Valderrama Award)
1421 Research Park Drive
Lawrence, KS 66049-3859
913/841-2240; 800/472-7878 Ext. 445

AMOUNT: $7,000
DEADLINE(S): None
FIELD(S): Golf/turfgrass Management

Awarded to a citizen of Spain who wishes to study golf/turfgrass management in the United States.

The selection is based on academic achievement, interest in the profession, and leadership potential.

622

HORTICULTURAL RESEARCH INSTITUTE (Timothy Bigelow Scholarship)
1250 I Street NW, Suite 500
Washington, D.C. 20005
202/789-2900; Fax 202/789-1893

AMOUNT: Varies
DEADLINE(S): May 20
FIELD(S): Horticulture

Open to New England residents enrolled in a two- or four-year institution. Students must be seniors in a two-year program, juniors in a four-year program, or graduate students. Applicants must have at least a 2.25 GPA and be interested in horticulture.

Write to the above address for complete information.

623

JAPANESE AMERICAN CITIZENS LEAGUE (Sam S. Kuwahara Memorial Scholarship)
1765 Sutter Street
San Francisco, CA 94115
415/921-5225; E-mail: jacl@jacl.org

AMOUNT: Varies
DEADLINE(S): Apr 1
FIELD(S): Agriculture

Open to JACL members or their children only. For undergraduate students with an interest in agriculture or a related field, and who are enrolled in, or planning to enroll in, a college, university, trade school, business school, or any institution of higher learning.

For membership information or an application, send a self-addressed stamped envelope to the above address.

624

JONATHAN BALDWIN TURNER AGRICULTURAL MERIT SCHOLARSHIP PROGRAM
101 Mumford Hall
1301 West Gregory Drive
Urbana, IL 61801
Written inquiries

AMOUNT: $4,000

DEADLINE(S): Varies (Junior year in high school)

FIELD(S): Agriculture

Scholarships in agriculture study for outstanding incoming freshmen at the University of Illinois. Interviews conducted in late summer before the student's senior year in high school.

Approximately 60 awards each year. Based on class rank, ACT or SAT score, leadership and communications ability. Contact Charles Olson, Assistant Dean, College of Agriculture, Office of the Dean, at above address for details.

625

MICHIGAN AGRI-BUSINESS ASSOCIATION EDUCATIONAL TRUST FUND
Ag. Hall, Room 120
East Lansing, MI 48824
517/355-0190

AMOUNT: Varies

DEADLINE(S): Ongoing

FIELD(S): Agri-business or related field, such as grain elevator management

Scholarships for students in Michigan studying in the fields listed above. Selections based on grades, acceptance at an accredited college or university in an agri-business-related program, financial need, references, participation in student affairs, and personal character.

Send SASE to Dr. Clifford Jump, Michigan State University, at above address for details.

626

MINNESOTA HIGHER EDUCATION SERVICES OFFICE (Assistance for Farm Families)
Capitol Square Bldg., Suite 400
550 Cedar Street
St. Paul, MN 55101
612/296-3974; Fax 612/297-8880; E-mail: info@heso.state.mn.us; Internet: www.heso.state.mn.us/

AMOUNT: Up to $4,000

DEADLINE(S): Jan 15

FIELD(S): Agriculture

For Minnesota agricultural students who are current students, new freshmen, and students transferring to the College of Agriculture. Must have graduated in the upper 10 percent of their high school class or have a GPA of 3.25 at a previous college.

Contact: Scholarships, College of Agricultureal, Food, and Environmental Sciences, University of Minnesota, 120 Biosystems & Agricultural Engineering, 1390 Eckles Ave., St. Paul, MN 55108. Also availabe at certain private colleges for farm families in rural areas. Financial need and academic merit considered.

627

NATIONAL ASSOCIATION OF COUNTY AGRICULTURE AGENTS (Scholarship Fund)
P.O. Box 367
Conway, NH 03818
Written inquiry

AMOUNT: $1,000

DEADLINE(S): None

FIELD(S): Agriculture

Undergraduate scholarships open ONLY to members of the National Assn. of County Agricultural Agents. Scholarships are awarded based upon a written application. U.S. citizen or legal resident.

Approx. 180 awards per year. Write for complete information.

628

NATIONAL COUNCIL OF FARMER COOPERATIVES (Undergraduate Awards)

50 F Street NW, Suite 900
Washington, D.C. 20001
202/626-8700

AMOUNT: $200

DEADLINE(S): Jun 1 (postmark)

FIELD(S): U.S. Farming Cooperatives

Award is for an outstanding term paper on topics related to the operations of American cooperatives. Open to undergrads in their junior or senior year or 2nd-year students at a junior/community college or voc-tech school.

Five awards per year. Write or call for complete information.

629

NATIONAL COUNCIL OF FARMER COOPERATIVES (W. Malcolm Harding Award & NCFC Education Foundation Awards)

50 F Street NW, Suite 900
Washington, D.C. 20001
202/626-8700

AMOUNT: $1,000

DEADLINE(S): Jun 15

FIELD(S): Agriculture (Farming Cooperatives)

Applicants must be enrolled in an accredited four-year college or university in the U.S., have completed at least one full year of course work, and have at least 1/2 of an academic year remaining for completion of degree program.

Upper 1/4 rank of class or minimum 3.0 GPA required. 4 awards per year. Nonrenewable. Write for complete information.

630

NATIONAL DAIRY SHRINE (Dairy Student Recognition Program Scholarship Awards)

Maurice E. Core, Exec. Dir.
1224 Alton Darby Creek Road
Columbus, OH 43228-9792
614/878-5333; Fax 614/870-2622

AMOUNT: $500-$1,500

DEADLINE(S): Mar 15

FIELD(S): Dairy Science

Scholarships for college juniors and seniors majoring in dairy science and related fields who plan to work with dairy cattle and/or within the dairy industry after graduation. Must be nominated by college dairy science department.

5 or more awards per year. Contact your dairy science department or write for complete information.

631

NATIONAL FFA FOUNDATION (College & Voc-Tech School Scholarship Program)

P.O. Box 15160
Alexandria, VA 22309
Written inquiry

AMOUNT: Varies

DEADLINE(S): None

FIELD(S): Agriculture

Agriculture scholarships offered to FFA and non-FFA members.

Write for scholarship guide which contains application form and details of the awards.

632

NATIONAL ITALIAN AMERICAN FOUNDATION (Piancone Family Agricultural Scholarship)

1860 19th Street NW
Washington, D.C. 20009-5599
202/530-5315

AMOUNT: $2,000

DEADLINE(S): May 31

FIELD(S): Study of agriculture

Open to undergraduate or graduate student of Italian ancestry from New Jersey, New York, Pennsylvania, Delaware, Virginia, Maryland, Washington, D.C., and Massachusetts.

Evidence of financial need, academic merit, and community service also considered.

633

NATIONAL JUNIOR HORTICULTURAL ASSOCIATION (Scottish Gardening Scholarship)
1424 N. 8th
Durant, OK 74701
Written inquiry

AMOUNT: Transportation; stipend; food and lodging

DEADLINE(S): Oct 1

FIELD(S): Horticulture

Program provides a 1-year horticultural study & work experience program in Scotland at the Threave School of Practical Gardening. Previous work in horticulture is essential. Must be 18 or older and a U.S. citizen.

Write for program outline and complete information.

634

PACIFIC GAS & ELECTRIC CO. (Scholarships for High School Seniors)
77 Beale Street, Room 2837
San Francisco, CA 94106
415/973-1338

AMOUNT: $1,000-$4,000

DEADLINE(S): Nov 15

FIELD(S): Engineering; Computer Science; Mathematics; Marketing; Business; Economics

High school seniors in good academic standing who reside in or attend high school in areas served by PG&E are eligible to compete for scholarships awarded on a regional basis. Not open to children of PG&E employees.

36 awards per year. Applications & brochures are available in all high schools within PG&E's service area and at PG&E offices.

635

PROFESSIONAL GROUNDS MANAGEMENT SOCIETY (PGMS Anne Seaman Memorial Scholarship)
120 Cockeysville Road, Suite 104
Hunt Valley, MD 21031
Written inquiries only

AMOUNT: $1,000

DEADLINE(S): Jul 5

FIELD(S): Grounds Management

The Professional Grounds Management Society offers 1 to 4 scholarships in the Grounds Management or other closely related fields. This scholarship can be used toward a 2- or 4-year degree or graduate study. Applicants must be U.S. or Canadian citizens.

Write to the above address for complete information.

636

SAN DIEGO COUNTY COW-BELLES (Memorial Scholarship)
P.O. Box 570
Campo, CA 91906
619/478-2364

AMOUNT: $700

DEADLINE(S): Jul 31

FIELD(S): Animal Science

Open to students with a beef industry-related career goal who have completed 1 year of a 4-year college or have been accepted by a 4-year college after 2 years in a community college. Must live in San Diego County and show financial need.

Need a 3.0 or better GPA. Write for complete details.

637

**SAN MATEO COUNTY FARM BUREAU
(Scholarship)**
765 Main Street
Half Moon Bay, CA 94019
415/726-4485

AMOUNT: Varies
DEADLINE(S): Apr 1
FIELD(S): All areas of study

Open to entering college freshmen and continuing students who are members of the San Mateo County Farm Bureau or the dependent child of a member.
Write for complete information.

638

**SCHOLARSHIPS FOR EXCELLENCE IN
AGRICULTURE**
Iowa State University
Ames, IA 50011
Written inquiry

AMOUNT: Full in-state tuition
DEADLINE(S): Dec 2
FIELD(S): Agriculture

Scholarships for Iowa State University freshmen studying agriculture.
15 annual awards. Renewable if recipients remain academically eligible. Based on scholarship, ACT, or SAT scores. Write to Associate Dean for Academic Programs, 124 Curtis Hall, at above location.

639

**SOIL AND WATER CONSERVATION
SOCIETY (Donald A. Williams Soil
Conservation Scholarship)**
7515 Northeast Ankeny Road
Ankeny, IA 50021-9764
515/289-2331; 800-THE-SOIL; Fax 515/289-1227

AMOUNT: $1,500
DEADLINE(S): Apr 1
FIELD(S): Conservation-related (technical or administrative course work)

Open to SWCS members who are currently employed in a related field & have completed at least 1 year of natural resource conservation work with a governmental agency, organization or business firm. Must show reasonable financial need.
Applicants who have not received a bachelor's degree will be given preference. Attainment of degree not required. Write for complete information.

640

**THE HERB SOCIETY OF AMERICA, INC.
(Research Grant)**
9019 Kirtland Chardon Road
Kirtland, OH 44094
Written inquiries

AMOUNT: Up to $5,000
DEADLINE(S): Jan 31
FIELD(S): Herb Studies

Open to persons with a proposed program of scientific, academic, or artistic investigation of herbal plants. This grant is for research only and can be terminated at any time.
Write to the above address for complete information.

641

**THERESA CORTI FAMILY
AGRICULTURAL TRUST (Scholarship
Program)**
Wells Fargo Bank Trust Dept.
5262 N. Blackstone
Fresno, CA 93710
209/442-6232

AMOUNT: Varies
DEADLINE(S): Feb
FIELD(S): Agriculture

Open to students who are agriculture majors and graduates of Kern County high schools. For undergraduate study at accredited colleges and universities. Must carry at least 12 units and have a 2.0 or better GPA.
Financial need is a consideration. Write for complete information.

642

TOWER HILL BOTANIC GARDEN
(Procter-Chanin Scholarship)
Worcester County Horticultural Society
P.O. Box 598
Boylston, MA 01505-0598
508/869-6111

AMOUNT: $500-$2,000
DEADLINE(S): May 1
FIELD(S): Horticulture

Open to undergraduates in their junior or senior year and to graduate students who reside in New England or attend a New England college or university and are majoring in horticulture or a horticure-related field.

Selections based on interest in horticulture; sincerity of purpose; academic performance; financial need. Write for complete information.

643

TYSON FOUNDATION INC. (Scholarship Program)
2210 W. Oaklawn
Springdale, AR 72762-6999
501/290-4955

AMOUNT: Varies according to need
DEADLINE(S): Apr 20
FIELD(S): Business; Agriculture; Engineering; Computer Science; Nursing

For Arkansas residents who are U.S. citizens. Must be enrolled full-time in an accredited institution and demonstrate financial need. Must be employed part-time and/or summers to help fund education. For undergrad study at schools in U.S.

Renewable up to 8 semesters or 12 trimesters as long as students meet criteria.

644

UNITED AGRIBUSINESS LEAGUE (UAL Scholarship Program)
54 Corporate Park
Irvine, CA 92714
714/975-1424; E-mail: ual@earthlink.net

AMOUNT: $1,000-$4,000
DEADLINE(S): Apr 1
FIELD(S): Agriculture; Agribusiness

Open to undergraduate students enrolled or planning to enroll during the next academic year in an institution in which the study of agribusiness leads to a degree. Must submit essay that reflects vision of career path and résumé of community and/or educational activities.

10-12 awards per year. Must re-apply each year to renew. Write to above address for complete information.

645

UNITED DAIRY INDUSTRY ASSOCIATION (Dairy Shrine—UDIA Milk Marketing Scholarships)
10255 W. Higgins Road, #900
Rosemont, IL 60018
708/803-2000

AMOUNT: Varies
DEADLINE(S): Apr 1
FIELD(S): Dairy Marketing

Open to undergraduate sophomores, juniors & seniors enrolled in an accredited agricultural program in the U.S. At least 2.5 GPA on 4.0 scale. Purpose is to encourage qualified applicants to pursue a career in dairy marketing.

Write for complete information.

646

UNIVERSITY OF MINNESOTA COLLEGE OF AGRICULTURE (Scholarship Program)
277 Coffey Hall
1420 Eckles Ave.
St. Paul, MN 55108

612/624-3009; 800/866-2474

AMOUNT: Varies

DEADLINE(S): Feb 1

FIELD(S): Agriculture

Extensive scholarship program through the College of Agriculture for freshmen, transfer, and continuing students.

Write or call Annette Day, COA Scholarship Program, University of Minnesota, at above location.

647

WORCESTER COUNTY HORTICULTURE SOCIETY (Proctor-Chanin Scholarship)
11 French Drive
P.O. Box 598
Boylston, MA 01505-0598
508/869-6111

AMOUNT: $500-$2,000

DEADLINE(S): May 1

FIELD(S): Horticulture or Horticulture-related fields

Open to residents of the New England states or students who are attending a college in New England. Students must be junior, senior or graduate status. Students must demonstrate financial need.

Write to the above address for complete information.

648

YOUNKERS FARM AID AGRICULTURAL SCHOLARSHIP FUND
P.O. Box 1495
Des Moines, IA 50397
Written inquiry

AMOUNT: Varies

DEADLINE(S): Dec 1

FIELD(S): Agriculture

For agricultural students in Iowa, Nebraska, Minnesota, Illinois, and South Dakota who plan to attend Iowa State University, South Dakota University, or the University of

Nebraska. Family income must come from farming. Must rank in upper half of class and national test scores, demonstrate leadership, and show financial need.

Approximately 49 annual awards totaling $30,000. Write to Younkers Farm Aid Agricultural Scholarships at above address.

EARTH SCIENCE

649

AMERICAN CONGRESS ON SURVEYING AND MAPPING (American Association for Geodetic Surveying Joseph F. Dracup Scholarship Award)
5410 Grosvenor Lane, Suite 100
Bethesda, MD 20814-2122
301/493-0200; Fax 301/493-8245

AMOUNT: $2,000

DEADLINE(S): Dec

FIELD(S): Geodetic Surveying

For undergraduate students in a four-year program studying geodetic surveying.

Must join ACSM. Contact Membership Director at above location for complete information.

650

AMERICAN CONGRESS ON SURVEYING AND MAPPING (Berntsen International Scholarship in Surveying)
5410 Grosvenor Lane, Suite 100
Bethesda, MD 20814-2122
301/493-0200; Fax 301/493-8245

AMOUNT: $1,500

DEADLINE(S): Dec

FIELD(S): Surveying

For undergraduate students in a four-year surveying program.

Must join ACSM. Contact Membership Director at above location for complete information.

651

AMERICAN CONGRESS ON SURVEYING AND MAPPING (Berntsen International Scholarship in Surveying Technology)
5410 Grosvenor Lane, Suite 100
Bethesda, MD 20814-2122
301/492-0200; Fax 301/493-8245

AMOUNT: $500
DEADLINE(S): DEC
FIELD(S): Surveying Technology

For two-year surveying technology students. Must join ACSM. Contact Membership Director at above location for complete information.

652

AMERICAN CONGRESS ON SURVEYING AND MAPPING (Leica Surveying Scholarship)
5410 Grosvenor Lane, Suite 100
Bethesda, MD 20814-2122
301/493-0200; Fax 301/493-8245

AMOUNT: $1,000
DEADLINE(S): Dec 18
FIELD(S): Surveying

For undergraduate students in an accredited four-year surveying program. In addition to the $1,000 award, each recipient's school receives a $2,000 credit toward the purchase of Leica surveying instruments and systems. Additionally, every student majoring in surveying or a related field in the graduating class during the year of the award will receive a certificate for $500 for Leica surveying instruments.

Must join ACSM. Contact Membership Director at above location for complete information.

653

AMERICAN CONGRESS ON SURVEYING AND MAPPING (National Society of Professional Surveyors Scholarship)
5410 Grosvenor Lane, Suite 100
Bethesda, MD 20814-2122
301/493-0200; Fax 301/493-8245

AMOUNT: $1,000
DEADLINE(S): Dec 18
FIELD(S): Surveying

For undergraduate students enrolled in a full-time degree program in surveying.
Must join ACSM. Contact Membership Director at above location for complete information.

654

AMERICAN CONGRESS ON SURVEYING AND MAPPING (Porter McDonnell Memorial Award)
5410 Grosvenor Lane, Suite 100
Bethesda, MD 20814-2122
301/493-0200; Fax 301/493-8245

AMOUNT: $1,000
DEADLINE(S): Dec 18
FIELD(S): Surveying/Mapping

For women enrolled in an accredited four-year surveying and mapping degree program.
Must join ACSM. Contact Membership Director at above location for complete information.

655

AMERICAN CONGRESS ON SURVEYING AND MAPPING (Schonstedt Scholarship in Surveying)
5410 Grosvenor Lane, Suite 100
Bethesda, MD 20814-2122
301/493-0200; Fax 301/493-8245

AMOUNT: $1,500
DEADLINE(S): Dec 18
FIELD(S): Surveying

For junior or senior students studying in the field of surveying and attending four-year institutions. Schonstedt donates a magnetic locator to the surveying program at the school of each recipient.

2 awards. Must join ACSM. Contact Membership Director at above location for complete information.

656

AMERICAN CONGRESS ON SURVEYING AND MAPPPING
(Cartography and Geographic Information Society Scholarship)
5410 Grosvenor Lane, Suite 100
Bethesda, MD 20814-2122
301/493-0200; Fax 301/493-8245

AMOUNT: $1,000
DEADLINE(S): Dec 18
FIELD(S): Cartography or other mapping sciences curriculum

For full-time students of junior or senior standing enrolled in a cartography or other mapping sciences curriculum in a four-year degree granting institution.

Must join ACSM. Contact Membership Director at above location for complete information.

657

AMERICAN GEOLOGICAL INSTITUTE
(AGI Minority Geoscience Scholarships)
4220 King Street
Alexandria, VA 22302-1502
703/379-2480; Fax 703/379-7563; E-mail: ehr@agiweb.org; Internet: www.agiweb.org

AMOUNT: Amounts vary
DEADLINE(S): Feb 1
FIELD(S): Geoscience

Open to full-time undergrads or grads majoring in geology; geophysics; geochemistry; hydrology; meteorology; physical oceanography; planetary geology or earth-science education (NOT for engineering; mathematics or natural science majors).

Must be ethnic minority & U.S. citizen. Financial need must be demonstrated. Must reapply for renewal. Contact Veronika Litvale at above location for details.

658

AMERICAN METEOROLOGICAL SOCIETY (AMS/Industry Minority Scholarships)
45 Beacon Street
Boston, MA 02108-3693
617/227-2426 Ext. 235; E-mail: sarmstrg@ametsoc.org; Internet: www.ametsoc.org

AMOUNT: $3,000
DEADLINE(S): Feb 2
FIELD(S): Atmospheric, Oceanic, and Hydrological sciences

Open to minority students who will be entering their freshman year of college. Students must plan to pursue careers in the above areas of study.

Send SASE or access website for complete information.

659

AMERICAN METEOROLOGICAL SOCIETY (AMS Undergraduate Scholarships)
45 Beacon Street
Boston, MA 02108-3693
617/227-2426 Ext. 235; E-mail: sarmstrg@ametsoc.org; Internet: ametsoc.org

AMOUNT: $700-$5,000
DEADLINE(S): Jun 15
FIELD(S): Atmospheric or Related Oceanic & Hydrologic Sciences

Seven different scholarships for the final year of undergrad study in the field of atmospheric or related oceanic & hydrologic sciences at an accredited U.S. institution. GPA of 3.0 or better; U.S. citizenship or permanent residency required.

Financial need must be demonstrated for some awards. All scholarships are for full-time students only. Write for complete information (send SASE to receive application or check website).

660

AMERICAN METEOROLOGICAL SOCIETY (AMS/Industry Undergraduate Scholarships)
45 Beacon Street
Boston, MA 02108-3693
617/227-2426, Ext. 235; E-mail: sarmstrg@ametsoc.org; Internet: ametsoc.org

AMOUNT: $2,000
DEADLINE(S): Feb 23
FIELD(S): Atmospheric, Hydrological, Oceanic sciences
Open to students who will be juniors in a bachelor's program. Students must show promise of pursuing a career in the above areas of study.
Send SASE to above address or access website for complete information.

661

AMERICAN METEOROLOGICAL SOCIETY (Father James B. Macelwane Annual Awards)
45 Beacon Street
Boston, MA 02108-3693
617/227-2426 Ext. 235; E-mail: sarmstrg@ametsoc.org; Internet: www.ametsoc.org

AMOUNT: $300 (1st); $200 (2nd); $100 (3rd)
DEADLINE(S): Jun 15
FIELD(S): Meteorology/Atmosphere Chemistry
Awards are for original papers on meteorology. Open to all undergraduate students enrolled in colleges & universities in the Americas at the time paper is written. Purpose is to stimulate interest in meteorology among college students. No more than

two students from any one institution may enter papers in any one contest.
Send SASE or check website for complete information.

662

ARTHUR & DOREEN PARRETT SCHOLARSHIP TRUST FUND (Scholarships)
c/o U.S. Bank of Washington
P.O. Box 720
Trust Dept., 8th Floor
Seattle, WA 98111-0720
206/344-4653

AMOUNT: Up to $3,500
DEADLINE(S): Jul 31
FIELD(S): Engineering; Science; Medicine; Dentistry
Washington state resident who has completed her/his first year of college by July 31. Open to students enrolled in above schools. Awards tenable at any accredited undergrad college or university.
Approximately 15 awards per year. Write for complete information.

663

AUBURN UNIVERSITY SCHOOL OF FORESTRY (Various Scholarships)
Chairman, Scholarship Committee
Auburn University
100 M. White Smith Hall
Auburn, AL 36849-5418

AMOUNT: Varies
DEADLINE(S): Varies
FIELD(S): Forestry
Various scholarships for students attending Auburn University School of Forestry. Many give preference to Alabama or Georgia residents.
Write for a complete listing of scholarships.

664

CONSULTING ENGINEERS COUNCIL OF NEW JERSEY (Louis Goldberg Scholarship Fund)
66 Morris Ave.
Springfield, NJ 07081
973/564-5848; Fax 973/564-7480

AMOUNT: $1,000
DEADLINE(S): Jan 1
FIELD(S): Engineering or Land Surveying

Open to undergraduate students who have completed at least two years of study (or fifth year in a five-year program) at an ABET-accredited college or university in New Jersey, are in top half of their class, and are considering a career as a consulting engineer or land surveyor. Must be U.S. citizen.

Recipients will be eligible for American Consulting Engineers Council national scholarships of $2,000 to $5,000. Write for complete information.

665

DEMONSTRATION OF ENERGY-EFFICIENT DEVELOPMENTS (DEED Scholarship Program)
2301 M Street
Washington, D.C. 20037
202/467-2960

AMOUNT: $3,000
DEADLINE(S): Varies
FIELD(S): Energy or related fields

Open for undergraduate and graduate students who are interested in energy. Students must have a specific project that can benefit public power electric utilities.

Write to the above address for complete information.

666

EXPLORERS CLUB (Youth Activity Fund)
46 East 70th Street
New York, NY 10021
212/628-8383; Fax 212/288-4449

AMOUNT: $200-$1,000
DEADLINE(S): Apr 15
FIELD(S): Natural Sciences; Biological Sciences; Physical Sciences

Open to high school and undergraduate college students to help them participate in field research in the natural sciences anywhere in the world. Grants are to help with travel costs and expenses. Joint funding is strongly recommended.

U.S. citizen or legal resident. Applications available in February before April deadline. Write for complete information.

667

GAMMA THETA UPSILON—INTERNATIONAL GEOGRAPHIC HONOR SOCIETY (Buzzard, Richason, Maxfield, Presidents Scholarships)
1725 State Street
La Crosse, WI 54601
608/785-8355; Fax 608/785-8332; E-mail: holdevh@mail.uwlax.edu

AMOUNT: $500
DEADLINE(S): Aug 1
FIELD(S): Geography

Undergraduate and graduate scholarships open to Gamma Theta Upsilon members who maintain at least a 'B' grade point average in any accredited geography program.

Contact Dr. Virgil Holder, Dept. of Geography, University of Wisconsin, at above address.

668

GEOLOGICAL SOCIETY OF AMERICA (Research Grants Program)
Research Grants Administrator
P.O. Box 9140
Boulder, CO 80301-9140
303/447-2020 Ext. 137; Fax 303/447-1133; E-mail: jforstro@geosociety.org

AMOUNT: Varies
DEADLINE(S): Feb 1

FIELD(S): Geology

Open to undergraduates and graduates studying in the field of geology at colleges and universities in the U.S., Canada, Mexico, and Central America. GSA Membership is NOT required.

Approx. 175 awards per year. Contact above location for details of various programs and specialties.

669

PENN STATE UNIVERSITY—COLLEGE OF EARTH & MINERAL SCIENCES (Scholarships)

Committee on Scholarships & Awards
116 Deike Bldg.
University Park, PA 16802
814/865-6546

AMOUNT: $500-$2,500

DEADLINE(S): None

FIELD(S): Geosciences; Meteorology; Energy, Environmental, and Mineral Economics; Materials Science and Engineering; Mineral Engineering; Geography

Scholarship program open to outstanding undergraduate students accepted to or enrolled in Penn State's College of Earth & Mineral Sciences. Minimum GPA of 3.15 on 4.0 scale.

Approximately 275 awards per year. Renewable. Contact Dean's office for complete information.

670

SMITHSONIAN INSTITUTION (Minority Undergraduate & Graduate Internship)

Office of Fellowships & Grants
955 L'Enfant Plaza, Suite 7000
Washington, D.C. 20560
202/287-3271; E-mail:
www.si.edu/research+study; Internet:
siofg@sivm.si.edu

AMOUNT: $250/wk. undergrads; $300/wk. grads

DEADLINE(S): Feb 15

FIELD(S): Animal Behavior; Ecology; Environmental Science (including an emphasis on the tropics); Anthropology (& Archaeology); Astrophysics; Astronomy; Earth Sciences; Paleobiology; Evolutionary/Systematic Biology; History of Science and Technology; History of Art, esp. American, Contemporary, African, and Asian; 20th-century American Crafts; Decorative Arts; Social/Cultural History of the U.S.; Folklife

Internships in residence at the Smithsonian for U.S. minority students to participate in research or museum-related activities for 10 weeks.

Research is for above fields.

671

SMITHSONIAN INSTITUTION (National Air & Space Museum Verville Fellowship)

National Air and Space Museum, MRC 312
Washington, D.C. 20560
Written inquiry

AMOUNT: $30,000 stipend for 12 months + travel and misc. expenses

DEADLINE(S): Jan 15

FIELD(S): Analysis of major trends, developments, and accomplishments in the history of aviation or space studies

A competitive nine- to twelve-month in-residence fellowship in the above field of study. Advanced degree is NOT a requirement. Contact Fellowship Coordinator at above location.

Open to all nationalities. Fluency in English required.

672

SOCIETY OF EXPLORATION GEOPHYSICISTS (SEG) FOUNDATION

P.O. Box 702740
Tulsa, OK 74170-2740
918/497-5530

AMOUNT: $500-$3,000

DEADLINE(S): Mar 1

FIELD(S): Physics; Mathematics; Geology

Open to a high school student with above-average grades planning to enter college the next fall term, or an undergraduate college student whose grades are above average, or a graduate college student whose studies are directed toward a career in exploration geophysics in operations, teaching, or research.

Write to the above address for complete information.

673

SOCIETY OF EXPLORATION GEOPHYSICISTS FOUNDATION (Scholarship Program)
P.O. Box 702740
Tulsa, OK 74170
918/493-3516

AMOUNT: $500-$3,000

DEADLINE(S): Mar 1

FIELD(S): Geophysics & Related Earth Sciences

Undergraduate & graduate scholarships open to students who are accepted to or enrolled in an accredited program in the U.S. or its possessions & intend to pursue a career in exploration geophysics.

60-100 awards per year. Renewable. Interest and an aptitude for physics, mathematics and geology required. Write for complete information.

674

THE EDWARD AND ANNA RANGE SCHMIDT CHARITABLE TRUST (Grants and Emergency Financial Assistance)
P.O. Box 770982
Eagle River, AK 99577
Written inquiry

AMOUNT: Varies

DEADLINE(S): None

FIELD(S): Sciences, especially earth and environmental sciences

Grants for both individual students and programs studying in the above fields. Alaska Natives and other minorities are urged to apply. Grants are awarded for a variety of expenses incurred by students, such as internship support, travel and/or expenses related to workshops and science fairs, support needed to secure employment in science-related fields, or emergency needs.

Requests are given immediate consideration. Application should be made by letter from a sponsor (teacher, advisor, or other adult familiar with the applicant's situation). Both sponsor and applicant should send letters describing the applicant, the nature of the financial need, and amount requested.

675

U.S. AIR FORCE ROTC (4-Year Scholarship Program)
AFROTC/RROO
Recruiting Operations Branch
551 E. Maxwell Blvd.
Maxwell AFB, AL 36112-6106
334/953-2091

AMOUNT: Tuition; fees & books + $150 per month stipend

DEADLINE(S): Dec 1

FIELD(S): Aeronautical Engineering; Civil Engineering; Mechanical Engineering; Mathematics; Physics; Nursing & some Liberal Arts

Open to U.S. citizens who are at least 17 and will graduate from college before age 25. Must complete application; furnish SAT/ACT scores, high school transcripts and record of extracurricular activities.

Must qualify on Air Force medical examination. About 1,600 scholarships awarded each year at campuses which offer Air Force ROTC.

ENVIRONMENTAL STUDIES

676

CHAUTAUQUA LAKE FISHING ASSOCIATION (Scholarship)
P.O. Box 473
Celeron, NY 14720
Written inquiry

AMOUNT: $500
DEADLINE(S): May 31
FIELD(S): Conservation or Environmental Studies

Open to graduating high school seniors from Chautauqua County, NY, who have been accepted at an accredited college and who are interested in conservation or other environment-related fields.

Write to the above address for complete information.

677

EXPLORERS CLUB (Youth Activity Fund)
46 East 70th Street
New York, NY 10021
212/628-8383; Fax 212/288-4449

AMOUNT: $200-$1,000
DEADLINE(S): Apr 15
FIELD(S): Natural Sciences; Biological Sciences; Physical Sciences

Open to high school and undergraduate college students to help them participate in field research in the natural sciences anywhere in the world. Grants are to help with travel costs and expenses. Joint funding is strongly recommended.

U.S. citizen or legal resident. Applications available in February before April deadline. Write for complete information.

678

GARDEN CLUB OF AMERICA (GCA Awards for Summer Environmental Studies)
Mrs. Monica Freeman, GCA
598 Madison Ave.

New York, NY 10022-1614
212/753-8287; Fax 212/753-0134; Internet: www.interport.net/~gca

AMOUNT: $1,500
DEADLINE(S): Feb 15
FIELD(S): Ecology and related fields

For college sophomores, juniors, and seniors, and graduate students, who wish to pursue summer courses in environmental studies. Encourage those interested in furthering their studies and careers in the field of ecology and offer an opportunity to gain knowledge and experience beyond the regular course of study.

Send self-addressed stamped envelope for more information.

679

GARDEN CLUB OF AMERICA (Frances M. Peacock Scholarship for Native Bird Habitat)
Scott Sutcliffe, Cornell Lab of Ornithology
159 Sapsucker Woods Road
Ithica, NY 14850
Fax 607/254-2415; E-mail:
mec15@cornell.edu (no phone calls)

AMOUNT: Varies
DEADLINE(S): Jan 15
FIELD(S): Habitats of Threatened/Endangered Native Birds

For college seniors and graduate students to study habitat-related issues that will benefit threatened or endangered bird species and lend useful information for land management decisions.

Study in areas of the U.S. that provide winter or summer habitat for threatened and endangered birds. Write for complete information.

680

LAND IMPROVEMENT FOUNDATION FOR EDUCATION (Scholarship)
3060 Ogden Ave., Suite 304
Lisle, IL 60532-1690

630/548-1984

AMOUNT: Varies
DEADLINE(S): Mar 15
FIELD(S): Natural Resources/Conservation

Open to students who are interested in land improvement. Applicants must send three letters of recommendation along with a photo when applying.

Send SASE to above address for complete information.

681

NATIONAL ENVIRONMENTAL HEALTH ASSOC. (NEHA/AAS Scholarship)
720 South Colorado Blvd., Suite 970
South Tower
Denver, CO 80222
303/756-9090

AMOUNT: $1,000-$2,000
DEADLINE(S): Feb 1
FIELD(S): Environmental Health

Open to undergraduate juniors & seniors as well as grad students enrolled in an environmental health curriculum at an approved U.S. college or university.

Financial need is not a consideration. 3 awards. Write for complete information.

682

SMITHSONIAN INSTITUTION (Minority Undergraduate & Graduate Internship)
Office of Fellowships & Grants
955 L'Enfant Plaza, Suite 7000
Washington, D.C. 20560
202/287-3271; E-mail:
www.si.edu/research+study; Internet:
siofg@sivm.si.edu

AMOUNT: $250/wk. undergrads; $300/wk. grads
DEADLINE(S): Feb 15
FIELD(S): Animal Behavior; Ecology; Environmental Science (including an emphasis on the tropics); Anthropology (& Archaeology); Astrophysics; Astronomy;

Earth Sciences; Paleobiology; Evolutionary/Systematic Biology; History of Science and Technology; History of Art, esp. American, Contemporary, African, and Asian; 20th-century American Crafts; Decorative Arts; Social/Cultural History of the U.S.; Folklife

Internships in residence at the Smithsonian for U.S. minority students to participate in research or museum-related activities for 10 weeks.

Research is for above fields.

683

SMITHSONIAN INSTITUTION ENVIRONMENTAL RESEARCH CENTER (Work/Learn Program in Environmental Studies)
P.O. Box 28
Edgewater, MD 21037
301/261-4084; E-mail: education@serc.si.edu

AMOUNT: $190/week + dorm housing; minority graduate students receive $240/wk.
DEADLINE(S): Mar 1; Nov 1
FIELD(S): Environmental Studies; Ecology; Ornithology; Marine Life; Computer Science.

Work/learn internships at the center open to undergraduate & graduate students. Competitive program which offers unique opportunity to gain exposure to & experience in environmental research. Selected students paid $180 per week when they live at the center in Edgewater. No academic credit.

Projects generally coincide with academic semesters & summer sessions and are normally 12-15 weeks in duration. Write for complete information. Can E-mail for application.

684

SOCIETY FOR RANGE MANAGEMENT (Masonic-Range Science Scholarship)
1839 York Street
Denver, CO 80206
303/355-7070

AMOUNT: Not specified

DEADLINE(S): Jan 15

FIELD(S): Range Management

Open to high school seniors planning to major in range science or college freshmen majoring in range science. Must be sponsored by Society for Range Mgmt., Nat'l. Ass'n. of Conservation Districts, or the Soil & Water Conservation Society. Must attend a college or university with a range science program. Write for complete information.

685

SOIL AND WATER CONSERVATION SOCIETY (Donald A. Williams Soil Conservation Scholarship)
7515 Northeast Ankeny Road
Ankeny, IA 50021-9764
515/289-2331; 800-THE-SOIL; Fax 515/289-1227

AMOUNT: $1,500

DEADLINE(S): Apr 1

FIELD(S): Conservation-related (technical or administrative course work)

Open to SWCS members who are currently employed in a related field & have completed at least 1 year of natural resource conservation work with a governmental agency, organization or business firm. Must show reasonable financial need.

Applicants who have not received a bachelor's degree will be given preference. Attainment of degree not required. Write for complete information.

686

STANFORD YOUTH ENVIRONMENTAL SCIENCE PROGRAM (SYESP Summer Residence Program)
P.O. Box 8453
Stanford, CA 94305
415/854-5220 Ext. 2; Internet: www.leland.stanford.edu/group/syesp/program/program.html

AMOUNT: Internship

DEADLINE(S): None specified

FIELD(S): Environmental Concerns

A summer residence program for exceptionally gifted, low-income, underserved, predominantly minority high school juniors and seniors who are concerned with the environment. SYESP hopes to foster future environmental leaders from this traditionally non-environmentally career-oriented group, who could impact their neighborhoods and other disenfranchised communities.

300-600 applicants for 22 positions. California resident, preferably Northern California. Interest in professional/graduate school; demonstration of aptitude in math and science; and demonstration of maturity, initiative, and curiosity, as well as a concern for the environment.

687

THE EDWARD AND ANNA RANGE SCHMIDT CHARITABLE TRUST (Grants and Emergency Financial Assistance)
P.O. Box 770982
Eagle River, AK 99577
Written inquiry

AMOUNT: Varies

DEADLINE(S): None

FIELD(S): Sciences, especially earth and environmental sciences

Grants for both individual students and programs studying in the above fields. Alaska Natives and other minorities are urged to apply. Grants are awarded for a variety of expenses incurred by students, such as internship support, travel and/or expenses related to workshops and science fairs, support needed to secure employment in science-related fields, or emergency needs.

Requests are given immediate consideration. Application should be made by letter from a sponsor (teacher, advisor, or other adult familiar with the applicant's situation). Both sponsor and applicant should send letters describing the applicant, the nature of the financial need, and amount requested.

688

U.S. ENVIRONMENTAL PROTECTION AGENCY—NATIONAL NETWORK FOR ENVIRONMENTAL MANAGEMENT STUDIES PROGRAM (Undergraduate and Graduate Fellowships)
401 M Street SW (1707)
Washington, D.C. 20460
202/260-5283

AMOUNT: Varies
DEADLINE(S): Dec 20
FIELD(S): Pollution abatement and control
Fellowships for undergrads and grads working on research projects in the above field either full-time during the summer or part-time during the school year. Must be U.S. citizens or legal residents.
Applications and other information can be obtained in the Career Service Center of participating universities. No application materials will be sent directly to students.

689

V. M. EHLERS MEMORIAL FUND, INC.
6813 Comanche Trail
Austin, TX 78732
512/266-2573

AMOUNT: Varies
DEADLINE(S): Jul 1
FIELD(S): Environmental health fields
Scholarships to Texas residents studying in environmental health fields.
Write to above address for application guidelines.

690

WATER ENVIRONMENT FEDERATION (Student Paper Competition)
Cheri Young
601 Wythe Street
Alexandria, VA 22314-1994
703/684-2407; Fax 703/684-2492

AMOUNT: $1,000 (1st prize); $500 (2nd); $250 (3rd) in each of 4 categories
DEADLINE(S): Feb 1
FIELD(S): Water pollution control and related fields
Awards for 500- to 1,000-word abstracts dealing with water pollution control, water quality problems, water-related concerns, or hazardous wastes. Open to undergrad (AA and BA) and grad students.
Also open to recently graduated students (within 1 calendar year of Feb. 1 deadline). Write for complete information.

MARINE SCIENCE

691

AMERICAN GEOLOGICAL INSTITUTE (AGI Minority Geoscience Scholarships)
4220 King Street
Alexandria, VA 22302-1502
703/379-2480; Fax 703/379-7563; E-mail: ehr@agiweb.org; Internet: www.agiweb.org

AMOUNT: Varies
DEADLINE(S): Feb 1
FIELD(S): Geoscience
Open to full-time undergrads or grads majoring in geology; geophysics; geochemistry; hydrology; meteorology; physical oceanography; planetary geology or earth-science education (NOT for engineering; mathematics; or natural science majors).
Must be ethnic minority & U.S. citizen. Financial need must be demonstrated. Must reapply for renewal. Contact Veronika Litvale at above location for details.

692

EXPLORERS CLUB (Youth Activity Fund)
46 East 70th Street
New York, NY 10021
212/628-8383; Fax 212/288-4449

AMOUNT: $200-$1,000
DEADLINE(S): Apr 15

FIELD(S): Natural Sciences; Biological Sciences; Physical Sciences

Open to high school and undergraduate college students to help them participate in field research in the natural sciences anywhere in the world. Grants are to help with travel costs and expenses. Joint funding is strongly recommended.

U.S. citizen or legal resident. Applications available in February before April deadline. Write for complete information.

693

OUR WORLD—UNDERWATER SCHOLARSHIP SOCIETY (Scholarship and Mini-Grants)
P.O. Box 4428
Chicago, IL 60680
312/666-6525; Fax 312/666-6846; E-mail: owu@ycg.com

AMOUNT: $13,000 (experience-based scholarship); Mini-Grants
DEADLINE(S): None specified
FIELD(S): Marine- and Aquatics-related disciplines

Candidates must be certified SCUBA divers, be no younger than 21 and no older than 24 on March 1 of the scholarship year, and have not yet been awarded a post-graduate degree. Experiences include active participation in field studies, underwater research, scientific expeditions, laboratory assignments, equipment testing and design, and photographic instruction.

1 scholarship and several mini-grants per year. Scholarship funds are used for transportation and minimal living expenses, if necessary.

694

SEASPACE SCHOLARSHIPS
P.O. Box 3753
Houston, TX 77253-3753
Written inquiry

AMOUNT: $2,000 (average)

DEADLINE(S): Mar 1
FIELD(S): Marine Sciences; Marine Biology or Geology; Nautical Archaeology; Biological Oceanography; Ocean & Fishery Sciences; Naval/Marine Engineering

Open to college juniors, seniors, and graduate students who aspire to a career in the marine sciences and attend a U.S. school. Undergrads should have at least a 3.5 GPA; graduates at least 3.0. Must demonstrate financial need.

Average of 15 awards per year. Applications must be received by March 1 deadline to be considered. Write for complete information by November 30.

695

WOODS HOLE OCEANOGRAPHIC INSTITUTION (Summer Student Fellowship)
Fellowships Committee
Woods Hole, MA 02543
508/457-2000 Ext 2709

AMOUNT: $3,900 stipend for 12-week program & possible travel allowance
DEADLINE(S): Mar 1
FIELD(S): Oceanography

Summer fellowships to study oceanography at the Woods Hole Oceanographic Institution. Open to undergraduates who have completed their junior year and beginning graduate students.

Applicants must be studying in any fields of science or engineering and have at least a tentative interest in oceanography. Write for complete information.

NATURAL HISTORY

696

COMMITTEE ON INSTITUTIONAL COOPERATION (CIC Pre-doctoral Fellowships)
Kirkwood Hall 111, Indiana University
Bloomington, IN 47405
812/855-0823

AMOUNT: $11,000 + tuition (4 years)

DEADLINE(S): Dec 1

FIELD(S): Humanities; Social Sciences; Natural Sciences; Mathematics; Engineering

Pre-doctoral fellowships for U.S. citizens of African-American, American Indian, Mexican-American, or Puerto Rican heritage. Must hold or expect to receive bachelor's degree by late summer from a regionally accredited college or university.

Awards for specified universities in IL; IN; IA; MI; MN; OH; WI; PA. Write for details.

697

CREOLE-AMERICAN GENEALOGICAL SOCIETY INC. (Creole Scholarships)
P.O. Box 3215
Church Street Station
New York, NY 10008
Written inquiry only

AMOUNT: $1,500

DEADLINE(S): None

FIELD(S): Genealogy or language or Creole culture

Awards in the above areas open to individuals of mixed racial ancestry who submit a four-generation genealogical chart attesting to Creole ancestry and/or inter-racial parentage. For undergraduate or graduate study/research.

For scholarship/award information send $2.55 money order and self-addressed stamped envelope to address above. Cash and personal checks are not accepted. Letters without SASE and handling charge will not be answered.

698

EPILEPSY FOUNDATION OF AMERICA (Behavioral Sciences Student Fellowships)
4351 Garden City Drive
Landover, MD 20785
301/459-3700; 800/EFA-1000; Fax 301/577-2684; TDD 800/332-2070; E-mail: postmaster@efa.org; Internet: www.efa.org

AMOUNT: $2,000

DEADLINE(S): Mar 3

FIELD(S): For the study of epilepsy in either research or practice settings in fields such as sociology, social work, psychology, anthropology, nursing, economics, vocational rehabilitation, counseling, political science, etc., relevant to epilepsy research

Applicants may propose a 3-month project to be undertaken in a clinical or laboratory setting where there are ongoing programs of research, service, or training in the field of epilepsy.

Project may be conducted during any free period of the student's year at a U.S. institution of the student's choice. Write for complete information.

699

EXPLORERS CLUB (Youth Activity Fund)
46 East 70th Street
New York, NY 10021
212/628-8383; Fax 212/288-4449

AMOUNT: $200-$1,000

DEADLINE(S): Apr 15

FIELD(S): Natural Sciences; Biological Sciences; Physical Sciences

Open to high school and undergraduate college students to help them participate in field research in the natural sciences anywhere in the world. Grants are to help with travel costs and expenses. Joint funding is strongly recommended.

U.S. citizen or legal resident. Applications available in February before April deadline. Write for complete information.

700

SMITHSONIAN INSTITUTION (Cooper-Hewitt, National Design Museum-Peter Krueger Summer Internship Program)
Cooper-Hewitt National Design Museum
2 East 91st Street
New York, NY 10128
212/860-6868; Fax 212/860-6909

AMOUNT: $2,500

DEADLINE(S): Mar 31

FIELD(S): Art History; Design; Museum Studies; Museum Education; Architectural History

Ten-week summer internships open to graduate and undergraduate students considering a career in the museum profession. Interns will assist on special research or exhibition projects and participate in daily museum activities.

6 awards each summer. Internship commences in June and ends in August. Housing is not provided. Write for complete information.

701

SMITHSONIAN INSTITUTION (Minority Undergraduate & Graduate Internship)
Office of Fellowships & Grants
955 L'Enfant Plaza, Suite 7000
Washington, D.C. 20560
202/287-3271; E-mail:
www.si.edu/research+study; Internet:
siofg@sivm.si.edu

AMOUNT: $250/wk. undergrads; $300/wk. grads

DEADLINE(S): Feb 15

FIELD(S): Animal Behavior; Ecology; Environmental Science (including an emphasis on the tropics); Anthropology (& Archaeology); Astrophysics; Astronomy; Earth Sciences; Paleobiology; Evolutionary/ Systematic Biology; History of Science and Technology; History of Art, esp. American, Contemporary, African, and Asian; 20th-century American Crafts; Decorative Arts; Social/Cultural History of the U.S.; Folklife

Internships in residence at the Smithsonian for U.S. minority students to participate in research or museum-related activities for 10 weeks.

Research is for above fields.

702

U.S. MARINE CORPS HISTORICAL CENTER (College Internships)
Building 58
Washington Navy Yard
Washington, D.C. 20374
202/433-3839

AMOUNT: Stipend to cover daily expenses

DEADLINE(S): None specified

FIELD(S): U.S. Military History, Library Science; History; Museum Studies

Open to undergraduate students at a college or university which will grant academic credit for work experience as interns at the address above or at the Marine Corps Air-Ground Museum in Quantico, Virginia.

All internships are regarded as beginning professional-level historian, curator, librarian, or archivist positions. Write for complete information.

SCHOOL OF SCIENCE

703

ALEXANDER GRAHAM BELL ASSOCIATION FOR THE DEAF (Robert H. Weitbrecht Scholarship Award)
3417 Volta Place
Washington, D.C. 20007-2778
202/337-5220; E-mail: Agbell2@aol.com

AMOUNT: $750

DEADLINE(S): Apr 1

FIELD(S): Engineering/Science

Open to oral deaf students who were born with a profound hearing impairment or who suffered such a loss before acquiring language. Must be accepted into a full-time academic program for hearing students and studying science or engineering. North America citizenship preferred.

Write for complete information.

704

ALEXANDER GRAHAM BELL ASSOCIATION FOR THE DEAF (Arts and Sciences Financial Aid Awards)
3417 Volta Place
Washington, D.C. 20007-2778
202/337-5220; E-mail: Agbell2@aol.com

AMOUNT: Varies
DEADLINE(S): Apr 1 (request applications between Feb. 1 and Mar. 1)
FIELD(S): Art or Science

For aural/oral students between the ages of 5 and 19 who have moderate to profound hearing losses. Must use speech and residual hearing and/or speechreading as primary form of communication. May be used to help with participation in extracurricular activities in art or science during the summer, on weekends, or after school.

Write for complete information.

705

ALPHA KAPPA ALPHA SORORITY INC. (AKA/PIMS Summer Youth Mathematics & Science Camp)
5656 S. Stony Island Ave.
Chicago, IL 60637
312/684-1282

AMOUNT: $1,000 value (for room, board & travel)
DEADLINE(S): May 1
FIELD(S): Mathematics; Science

Open to high school students grades 9-11 who have at least a 'B' average. Essay required for entry. This 2-week camp includes A.M. classes; P.M. activities & a minimum of 4 field trips.

30 awards. Write for complete information.

706

AMERICAN INDIAN SCIENCE & ENGINEERING SOCIETY (Burlington Northern Santa Fe Foundation Scholarship)
5661 Airport Blvd.
Boulder, CO 80301
303/939-0023; E-mail: ascholar@spot.colorado.edu; Internet: www.colorado.edu/AISES

AMOUNT: $2,500 per year for up to 4 years
DEADLINE(S): Mar 31
FIELD(S): Business; Education; Science; Health Administration

Open to high school seniors who are 1/4 or more American Indian. Must reside in KS, OK, CO, AZ, NM, MN, ND, OR, SD, WA, or San Bernardino County, CA (Burlington Northern and Santa Fe Pacific service areas).

Must plan to attend a four-year post-secondary accredited educational institution. Write for complete information or apply online at above website.

707

BFGOODRICH (Collegiate Inventors Program) (BFG-CIP)
c/o Inventure Place
221 S. Broadway Street
Akron, OH 44308-1505
330/849-6887; E-mail: pkunce@invent.org

AMOUNT: Varies
DEADLINE(S): Jun 3
FIELD(S): Invention, Idea, or Process

National competition for college and university students across the country whose innovations, discoveries, and research are deemed the year's most outstanding. Must be an original idea and the work of a student or team with his/her university advisor. Should be reproducible; may not have been 1) available to public or 2) patented/published more than one year prior to submission.

Up to 3 entries All-Collegiate category will receive $7,500 prize; their advisors $2,500 each. In addition, up to 3 undergrad entries receive $3,000; their advisors $1,000 each. Students may enter as teams. Contact Paul Kunce, Program Coordinator, for more information.

708

CIVIL AIR PATROL (CAP Undergraduate Scholarships)
National Headquarters
Maxwell AFB, AL 36112
334/953-5315

AMOUNT: $750
DEADLINE(S): Jan 31
FIELD(S): Humanities; Science; Engineering; Education

Open to CAP members who have received the Billy Mitchell Award or the senior rating in level II of the senior training program. For undergraduate study in the above areas.
Write for complete information.

709

EXPLORERS CLUB (Youth Activity Fund)
46 East 70th Street
New York, NY 10021
212/628-8383; Fax 212/288-4449

AMOUNT: $200-$1,000
DEADLINE(S): Apr 15
FIELD(S): Natural Sciences; Biological Sciences; Physical Sciences

Open to high school and undergraduate college students to help them participate in field research in the natural sciences anywhere in the world. Grants are to help with travel costs and expenses. Joint funding is strongly recommended.
U.S. citizen or legal resident. Applications available in February before April deadline. Write for complete information.

710

GENERAL LEARNING COMMUNICATIONS (Sponsored by Dupont, GLC, and the NSTA Science Essay Awards Programs)
900 Skokie Blvd., Suite 200
Northbrook, IL 60062
847/205-3000

AMOUNT: Up to $1,500
DEADLINE(S): Jan 31
FIELD(S): Sciences

Annual essay competition open to students in grades 7-12 in U.S. and Canada. Cash awards for 1st, 2nd, and honorable mention. 1st-place essayists, their science teacher, and a parent receive trip to space center in Houston, April 27-29.
Contact your science teacher or address above for complete information. Official entry blank must accompany essay entry.

711

JOSEPH BLAZEK FOUNDATION (Scholarships)
8 South Michigan Ave.
Chicago, IL 60603
312/372-3880

AMOUNT: $750 per year for 4 years
DEADLINE(S): Feb 1
FIELD(S): Science; Chemistry; Engineering; Mathematics; Physics

Open to residents of Cook County (Illinois) who are high school seniors planning to study in the above fields at a four-year college or university.
20 scholarships per year. Renewable. Write for complete information.

712

NATIONAL FEDERATION OF THE BLIND (Howard Brown Rickard Scholarship)
805 Fifth Ave.
Grinnell, IA 50112
515/236-3366

AMOUNT: $3,000
DEADLINE(S): Mar 31
FIELD(S): Natural Sciences; Architecture; Engineering; Medicine; Law

Scholarships for undergraduate or graduate study in the above areas. Open to legally blind students enrolled full-time at accredited post-secondary institutions.

Awards based on academic excellence, service to the community, and financial need. Write for complete information.

713

NORTH CAROLINA STUDENT LOAN PROGRAM FOR HEALTH, SCIENCE,& MATHEMATICS (Loans)
3824 Barrett Drive, Suite 304
Raleigh, NC 27619
919/733-2164

AMOUNT: $2,500 to $7,500 per year
DEADLINE(S): Jan 8 (Application available then. Deadline is May 5)
FIELD(S): Health Professions; Sciences; Engineering
Low-interest scholarship loans open to North Carolina residents of at least 1 year who are pursuing an associate's, undergraduate or graduate degree in the above fields at an accredited institution in the U.S.
Loans may be retired after graduation by working (1 year for each year funded) at designated institutions. Write for complete details.

714

SOCIETY OF HISPANIC PROFESSIONAL ENGINEERS FOUNDATION (SHPE Scholarships)
5400 E. Olympic Blvd., Suite 210
Los Angeles, CA 90022
213/888-2080

AMOUNT: $500-$3,000
DEADLINE(S): Apr 15
FIELD(S): Engineering; Science
Open to deserving students of Hispanic descent who are seeking careers in engineering and science. For full-time undergraduate or graduate study at a college or university. Academic achievement and financial need are considerations.
Send a self-addressed stamped envelope to request an application.

715

TANDY TECHNOLOGY SCHOLARS (Student Awards; Teacher Awards)
Texas Christian University
Box 298990
Fort Worth, TX 76129
817/924-4087

AMOUNT: $1,000 students; $2,500 teachers
DEADLINE(S): Oct 9
FIELD(S): Mathematics; Science; Computer Science
Program recognizes academic performance and outstanding achievements by Mathematics, Science, and Computer Science students and teachers. Students and teachers receive cash awards.
Must be a senior in an enrolled high school located in one of the 50 states. 100 of each awarded each year. Nomination packets sent to high schools.

716

THE EDWARD AND ANNA RANGE SCHMIDT CHARITABLE TRUST (Grants and Emergency Financial Assistance)
P.O. Box 770982
Eagle River, AK 99577
Written inquiry

AMOUNT: Varies
DEADLINE(S): None
FIELD(S): Sciences, especially earth and environmental sciences
Grants for both individual students and programs studying in the above fields. Alaska Natives and other minorities are urged to apply. Grants are awarded for a variety of expenses incurred by students, such as internship support, travel and/or expenses related to workshops and science fairs, support needed to secure employment in science-related fields, or emergency needs.
Requests are given immediate consideration. Application should be made by letter from a sponsor (teacher, advisor, or other adult familiar with the applicant's situation). Both

sponsor and applicant should send letters describing the applicant, the nature of the financial need, and amount requested.

717

WILLIAM M. GRUPE FOUNDATION INC. (Scholarships)
P.O. Box 775
Livingston, NJ 07039
973/428-1190

AMOUNT: $2,000-$3,000
DEADLINE(S): Mar 1
FIELD(S): Medicine; Nursing

For residents of Bergen, Essex, or Hudson counties, NJ. Annual scholarship aid to good students in need of financial support in the above fields. Must be U.S. citizen.

20-30 awards per year. Students may apply every year. Write for complete information.

BIOLOGY

718

AMERICAN SOCIETY FOR ENOLOGY AND VITICULTURE (Scholarship)
P.O. Box 1855
Davis, CA 95617
916/753-3142

AMOUNT: No predetermined amounts
DEADLINE(S): Mar 1
FIELD(S): Enology (Wine Making); Viticulture (Grape Growing)

For college juniors, seniors or grad students enrolled in an accredited North American college or university in a science curriculum basic to the wine and grape industry. Must be resident of North America.

GPA requirements of 3.0 or better for undergrads; 3.2 or better for grads. Scholarships are renewable. Financial need is considered. Write for complete information.

719

AMERICAN SOCIETY FOR MICROBIOLOGY (ASM Faculty Fellowship Program)
1325 Massachusetts Ave. NW
Washington, D.C. 20005
Written inquiry or E-mail: Fellowships-Careerinformation@asmusa.org; Internet: www.asmusa.org/edusrc/edu23f.htm

AMOUNT: Up to $4,000 stipend
DEADLINE(S): Feb 1
FIELD(S): Microbiological Sciences

For minority full-time undergraduate faculty or full-time undergraduate faculty at underserved institutions. Must be an ASM member.

Fellowship is for 1-2 months.

720

AMERICAN SOCIETY FOR MICROBIOLOGY (Minority Undergraduate Research Fellowship [MURF])
1325 Massachusetts Ave. NW
Washington, D.C. 20005
Written inquiry or E-mail: Fellowships-Careerinformation@asmusa.org; Internet: www.asmusa.org/edusrc/edu23b.htm

AMOUNT: $2,500 stipend; up to $1,000 for travel; up to $500 for housing
DEADLINE(S): Jun 1
FIELD(S): Biological Sciences with emphasis in Microbiological Sciences

Fellowships for under-represented minority undergraduates in microbiological sciences. Must be planning to attend grad school.

Fellowship is for 2-3 months.

721

AMERICAN SOCIETY FOR MICROBIOLOGY (Undergraduate Research Fellowship)
1325 Massachusetts Ave. NW
Washington, D.C. 20005

Written inquiry or E-mail: Fellowships-Careerinformation@asmusa.org; Internet: www.asmusa.org/edusrc/edu23a.htm

AMOUNT: Up to $2,500 stipend; $800 for equipment; $700 for travel
DEADLINE(S): Feb 1
FIELD(S): Microbiological Sciences
Fellowship awarded to 2nd- or 3rd-year undergraduates planning to attend grad school. Must be U.S. citizen or legal resident.
Fellowship is for 3-6 months. Send for complete information and application.

722

ARTHUR & DOREEN PARRETT SCHOLARSHIP TRUST FUND (Scholarships)

c/o U.S. Bank of Washington
P.O. Box 720
Trust Dept., 8th Floor
Seattle, WA 98111-0720
206/344-4653

AMOUNT: Up to $3,500
DEADLINE(S): Jul 31
FIELD(S): Engineering; Science; Medicine; Dentistry
Washington state resident who has completed her/his first year of college by July 31. Open to students enrolled in above schools. Awards tenable at any accredited undergrad college or university.
Approximately 15 awards per year. Write for complete information.

723

BUSINESS & PROFESSIONAL WOMEN'S FOUNDATION (Career Advancement Scholarships)

2012 Massachusetts Ave. NW
Washington, D.C. 20036
202/293-1200

AMOUNT: $500-$1,000
DEADLINE(S): Apr 15 (postmark)

FIELD(S): Computer Science; Education; Paralegal; Engineering; Science; Law; Dentistry; Medicine
Open to women (30 or older) within 12-24 months of completing undergrad or grad study in U.S. (including Puerto Rico & Virgin Islands). Studies should lead to entry/reentry in work force or improve career advancement chances.
Not for doctoral study. Must demonstrate financial need. Send self-addressed stamped ($.64) #10 envelope for complete info. Applications available Oct. 1 - April 1.

724

COMMITTEE ON INSTITUTIONAL COOPERATION (CIC Pre-doctoral Fellowships)

Kirkwood Hall 111, Indiana University
Bloomington, IN 47405
812/855-0823

AMOUNT: $11,000 + tuition (4 years)
DEADLINE(S): Dec 1
FIELD(S): Humanities; Social Sciences; Natural Sciences; Mathematics; Engineering
Pre-doctoral fellowships for U.S. citizens of African-American, American Indian, Mexican-American, or Puerto Rican heritage. Must hold or expect to receive bachelor's degree by late summer from a regionally accredited college or unviersity.
Awards for specified universities in IL; IN; IA; MI; MN; OH; WI; PA. Write for details.

725

ENTOMOLOGICAL SOCIETY OF AMERICA (Undergraduate Scholarships)

9301 Annapolis Road, Suite 300
Lanham, MD 20706
301/731-4535; Fax 301/731-4538; E-mail: esa@entsoc.org; Internet: www.entsoc.org

AMOUNT: $1,500
DEADLINE(S): May 31
FIELD(S): Entomology; Biology; Zoology, or related science

For undergraduate study in the above fields. Must be enrolled in a recognized college or university in the U.S., Canada, or Mexico. Applicants must have accumulated at least 30 semester hours by the time award is presented and have completed at least one class or project on entomology.

Send SASE for complete information.

726

EXPLORERS CLUB (Youth Activity Fund)
46 East 70th Street
New York, NY 10021
212/628-8383; Fax 212/288-4449

AMOUNT: $200-$1,000

DEADLINE(S): Apr 15

FIELD(S): Natural Sciences; Biological Sciences; Physical Sciences

Open to high school and undergraduate college students to help them participate in field research in the natural sciences anywhere in the world. Grants are to help with travel costs and expenses. Joint funding is strongly recommended.

U.S. citizen or legal resident. Applications available in February before April deadline. Write for complete information.

727

NATIONAL ASSOCIATION OF WATER COMPANIES—NEW JERSEY CHAPTER (Scholarship)
Elizabethtown Water Co.
600 South Ave.
Westfield, NJ 07090
908/654-1234; Fax 908/232-2719

AMOUNT: $2,500

DEADLINE(S): Apr 1

FIELD(S): Business Administration; Biology; Chemistry; Engineering; Communications

For U.S. citizens who have lived in NJ at least 5 years and plan a career in the investor-owned water utility industry in disciplines such as those above. Must be undergrad or graduate student in a 2- or 4-year NJ college or university.

GPA of 3.0 or better required. Contact Gail P. Brady for complete information.

728

NATIONAL FEDERATION OF THE BLIND (Howard Brown Rickard Scholarship)
805 Fifth Ave.
Grinnell, IA 50112
515/236-3366

AMOUNT: $3,000

DEADLINE(S): Mar 31

FIELD(S): Natural Sciences; Architecture; Engineering; Medicine; Law

Scholarships for undergraduate or graduate study in the above areas. Open to legally blind students enrolled full-time at accredited post-secondary institutions.

Awards based on academic excellence, service to the community, and financial need. Write for complete information.

729

NATIONAL RESEARCH COUNCIL (Howard Hughes Medical Institute Predoctoral Fellowships in Biological Sciences)
Fellowship Office
2101 Constitution Ave. NW
Washington, D.C. 20418
202/334-2872

AMOUNT: $14,500 annual stipend + $14,000 cost of education allowance

DEADLINE(S): Nov 3

FIELD(S): Biological Sciences

Open to college seniors or graduates at or near the beginning of their study toward a Ph.D or Sc.D in Biological Sciences. U.S. citizens may study in the U.S. or abroad; foreign nationals may study only in the U.S.

Write for complete information.

730

NATIONAL RESEARCH COUNCIL (Howard Hughes Medical Institute Pre-doctoral Fellowships in Biological Sciences)
Fellowship Office
2101 Constitution Ave. NW
Washington, D.C. 20418
202/334-2872; E-mail: infofell@nas.edu

AMOUNT: $15,000 annual stipend + $15,000 cost of education allowance
DEADLINE(S): Nov 12
FIELD(S): Biological Sciences

For college seniors or graduates at or near the beginning of their study toward a Ph.D or Sc.D in Biological Sciences. For full-time study 12 months a year. U.S. citizens may study in the U.S. or abroad; foreign nationals may study only in the U.S.

Renewable for a maximum of 5 years. 80 awards. Application can be generated online at above location or write for complete information.

731

SMITHSONIAN INSTITUTION (Minority Undergraduate & Graduate Internship)
Office of Fellowships & Grants
955 L'Enfant Plaza, Suite 7000
Washington, D.C. 20560
202/287-3271; E-mail:
www.si.edu/research+study; Internet:
siofg@sivm.si.edu

AMOUNT: $250/wk. undergrads; $300/wk. grads
DEADLINE(S): Feb 15
FIELD(S): Animal Behavior; Ecology; Environmental Science (including an emphasis on the tropics); Anthropology (& Archaeology); Astrophysics; Astronomy; Earth Sciences; Paleobiology; Evolutionary/Systematic Biology; History of Science and Technology; History of Art, esp. American, Contemporary, African, and Asian; 20th-century American Crafts; Decorative Arts; Social/Cultural History of the U.S.; Folklife

Internships in residence at the Smithsonian for U.S. minority students to participate in research or museum-related activities for 10 weeks.

Research is for above fields.

732

WHITEHALL FOUNDATION INC. (Research Grants-in-Aid)
251 Royal Palm Way, Suite 211
Palm Beach, FL 33480
561/655-4474; Fax 561/659-4978; Internet:
www.whitehall.org

AMOUNT: $30,000 maximum
DEADLINE(S): Jun 1; Sep 1; Feb 15
FIELD(S): Basic research in invertebrate and vertebrate neurobiology

Grants-in-aid for assistant professors and senior scientists for investigations of neural mechanisms involved in sensory, motor, and other complex functions of the whole organism as they relate to behavior.

Initial approach should be a one-page letter summarizing the project. Write for complete information.

733

WILSON ORNITHOLOGICAL SOCIETY (Fuertes; Nice & Stewart Grants)
c/o Museum of Zoology
University of Michigan
Ann Arbor, MI 48109
Written inquiry only

AMOUNT: $600 (Fuertes); $200 (Nice & Stewart)
DEADLINE(S): Jan 15
FIELD(S): Ornithology

Grants to support research on birds only—NOT for general college funding. Open to anyone presenting a suitable research problem in ornithology. Research proposal required.

5-6 grants per year. NOT renewable. Write for complete information.

CHEMISTRY

734

AMERICAN GEOLOGICAL INSTITUTE (AGI Minority Geoscience Scholarships)
4220 King Street
Alexandria, VA 22302-1502
703/379-2480; Fax 703/379-7563; E-mail: ehr@agiweb.org; Internet: www.agiweb.org

AMOUNT: Amounts vary

DEADLINE(S): Feb 1

FIELD(S): Geoscience

Open to full-time undergrads or grads majoring in geology; geophysics; geochemistry; hydrology; meteorology; physical oceanography; planetary geology or earth-science education (NOT for engineering; mathematics or natural science majors).

Must be ethnic minority & U.S. citizen. Financial need must be demonstrated. Must reapply for renewal. Contact Veronika Litvale at above location for details.

735

ARTHUR & DOREEN PARRETT SCHOLARSHIP TRUST FUND (Scholarships)
c/o U.S. Bank of Washington
P.O. Box 720
Trust Dept., 8th Floor
Seattle, WA 98111-0720
206/344-4653

AMOUNT: Up to $3,500

DEADLINE(S): Jul 31

FIELD(S): Engineering; Science; Medicine; Dentistry

Washington state resident who has completed her/his first year of college by July 31. Open to students enrolled in above schools. Awards tenable at any accredited undergrad college or university.

Approximately 15 awards per year. Write for complete information.

736

BUSINESS & PROFESSIONAL WOMEN'S FOUNDATION (Career Advancement Scholarships)
2012 Massachusetts Ave. NW
Washington, D.C. 20036
202/293-1200

AMOUNT: $500-$1,000

DEADLINE(S): Apr 15 (postmark)

FIELD(S): Computer Science; Education; Paralegal; Engineering; Science; Law; Dentistry; Medicine

Open to women (30 or older) within 12-24 months of completing undergrad or grad study in U.S. (including Puerto Rico & Virgin Islands). Studies should lead to entry/reentry in work force or improve career advancement chances.

Not for doctoral study. Must demonstrate financial need. Send self-addressed stamped ($.64) #10 envelope for complete info. Applications available Oct. 1 - April 1.

737

H. FLETCHER BROWN FUND (Scholarships)
c/o PNC Bank
Trust Dept.
P.O. Box 791
Wilmington, DE 19899
302/429-2827

AMOUNT: Varies

DEADLINE(S): Apr 15

FIELD(S): Medicine; Dentistry; Law; Engineering; Chemistry

Open to U.S. citizens born and still residing in Delaware. For 4 years of study (undergrad or grad) leading to a degree that enables applicant to practice in chosen field.

Scholarships are based on need, scholastic achievement and good moral character. Applications available in February. Write for complete information.

738

NATIONAL ASSOCIATION OF WATER COMPANIES—NEW JERSEY CHAPTER (Scholarship)
Elizabethtown Water Co.
600 South Ave.
Westfield, NJ 07090
908/654-1234; Fax 908/232-2719

AMOUNT: $2,500
DEADLINE(S): Apr 1
FIELD(S): Business Administration; Biology; Chemistry; Engineering; Communications

For U.S. citizens who have lived in NJ at least 5 years and plan a career in the investor-owned water utility industry in disciplines such as those above. Must be undergrad or graduate student in a 2- or 4-year NJ college or university.

GPA of 3.0 or better required. Contact Gail P. Brady for complete information.

739

NATIONAL RESEARCH COUNCIL (Howard Hughes Medical Institute Pre-doctoral Fellowships in Biological Sciences)
Fellowship Office
2101 Constitution Ave. NW
Washington, D.C. 20418
202/334-2872; E-mail: infofell@nas.edu

AMOUNT: $15,000 annual stipend + $15,000 cost of education allowance
DEADLINE(S): Nov 12
FIELD(S): Biological Sciences

For college seniors or graduates at or near the beginning of their study toward a Ph.D or Sc.D in Biological Sciences. For full-time study 12 months a year. U.S. citizens may study in the U.S. or abroad; foreign nationals may study only in the U.S.

Renewable for a maximum of 5 years. 80 awards. Application can be generated online at above location or write for complete information.

740

ROBERT SCHRECK MEMORIAL FUND (Grants)
c/o Texas Commerce Bank—Trust Dept.
P.O. Drawer 140
El Paso, TX 79980
915/546-6515

AMOUNT: $500-$1,500
DEADLINE(S): Jul 15; Nov 15
FIELD(S): Medicine; Veterinary Medicine; Physics; Chemistry; Architecture; Engineering; Episcopal Clergy

Grants to undergraduate juniors or seniors or graduate students who have been residents of El Paso County for at least two years. Must be U.S. citizen or legal resident and have a high grade-point average. Financial need is a consideration.

Write for complete information.

741

SMITHSONIAN INSTITUTION (National Air & Space Museum Verville Fellowship)
National Air and Space Museum, MRC 312
Washington, D.C. 20560
Written inquiry

AMOUNT: $30,000 stipend for 12 months + travel and misc. expenses
DEADLINE(S): Jan 15
FIELD(S): Analysis of major trends, developments, and accomplishments in the history of aviation or space studies

A competitive nine- to twelve-month in-residence fellowship in the above field of study. Advanced degree is NOT a requirement. Contact Fellowship Coordinator at above location.

Open to all nationalities. Fluency in English required.

MATHEMATICS

742

**ALPHA KAPPA ALPHA SORORITY INC.
(AKA/PIMS Summer Youth Mathematics &
Science Camp)**
   5656 S. Stony Island Ave.
   Chicago, IL 60637
   312/684-1282

AMOUNT: $1,000 value (for room, board &
   travel)
DEADLINE(S): May 1
FIELD(S): Mathematics; Science
Open to high school students grades 9-11 who
   have at least a 'B' average. Essay required
   for entry. This 2-week camp includes A.M.
   classes; P.M. activities & a minimum of 4
   field trips.
30 awards. Write for complete information.

743

**AMERICAN PHYSICAL SOCIETY
(Scholarships for Minority Undergraduate
Students in Physics)**
   One Physics Ellipse
   College Park, MD 20740
   301/209-3232

AMOUNT: $2,000
DEADLINE(S): Feb (early)
FIELD(S): Physics
Open to any Black, Hispanic, or American
   Indian U.S. citizen who is majoring or plans
   to major in physics and is a high school
   senior, college freshman, or sophomore.
Write for complete information.

744

**AT&T BELL LABORATORIES (Summer
Research Program for Minorities & Women)**
   101 Crawfords Corner Road
   Holmdel, NJ 07733-3030
   Written inquiry

AMOUNT: Salary + travel & living expenses
   for summer
DEADLINE(S): Dec 1
FIELD(S): Engineering; Math; Sciences;
   Computer Science
Program offers minority students & women
   students technical employment experience
   at Bell Laboratories. Students should have
   completed their third year of study at an
   accredited college or university. U.S. citizen
   or permanent resident.
Selection is based partially on academic
   achievement and personal motivation.
   Write special programs manager—SRP for
   complete information.

745

**BUSINESS & PROFESSIONAL WOMEN'S
FOUNDATION (Career Advancement
Scholarships)**
   2012 Massachusetts Ave. NW
   Washington, D.C. 20036
   202/293-1200

AMOUNT: $500-$1,000
DEADLINE(S): Apr 15 (postmark)
FIELD(S): Computer Science; Education;
   Paralegal; Engineering; Science; Law;
   Dentistry; Medicine
Open to women (30 or older) within 12-24
   months of completing undergrad or grad
   study in U.S. (including Puerto Rico &
   Virgin Islands). Studies should lead to
   entry/reentry in work force or improve
   career advancement chances.
Not for doctoral study. Must demonstrate
   financial need. Send self-addressed stamped
   ($.64) #10 envelope for complete info.
   Applications available Oct. 1 - April 1.

746

**COMMITTEE ON INSTITUTIONAL
COOPERATION (CIC Pre-doctoral
Fellowships)**
   Kirkwood Hall 111, Indiana University
   Bloomington, IN 47405
   812/855-0823

AMOUNT: $11,000 + tuition (4 years)

DEADLINE(S): Dec 1

FIELD(S): Humanities; Social Sciences; Natural Sciences; Mathematics; Engineering

Pre-doctoral fellowships for U.S. citizens of African-American, American Indian, Mexican-American, or Puerto Rican heritage. Must hold or expect to receive bachelor's degree by late summer from a regionally accredited college or unviersity.

Awards for specified universities in IL; IN; IA; MI; MN; OH; WI; PA. Write for details.

747

ELECTRONIC INDUSTRIES FOUNDATION (Scholarship Fund)

2500 Wilson Blvd., Suite 210
Arlington, VA 22201-3834
703/907-7408

AMOUNT: $5,000

DEADLINE(S): Feb 2

FIELD(S): Electrical Engineering; Industrial Manufacturing; Industrial Engineering; Physics, Electromechanical Technology; Mechanical Applied Sciences

For students with disabilities who are pursuing udergraduate or graduate studies directly related to the electronics industry listed above. Awards tenable at recognized undergraduate and graduate colleges and universities. Must be U.S. citizen. Financial need is considered.

6 awards per year. Renewable. Send self-addressed stamped envelope for complete information.

748

PACIFIC GAS & ELECTRIC CO. (Scholarships for High School Seniors)

77 Beale Street, Room 2837
San Francisco, CA 94106
415/973-1338

AMOUNT: $1,000-$4,000

DEADLINE(S): Nov 15

FIELD(S): Engineering; Computer Science; Mathematics; Marketing; Business; Economics

High school seniors in good academic standing who reside in or attend high school in areas served by PG&E are eligible to compete for scholarships awarded on a regional basis. Not open to children of PG&E employees.

36 awards per year. Applications & brochures are available in all high schools within PG&E's service area and at PG&E offices.

749

SMITHSONIAN INSTITUTION (National Air & Space Museum Verville Fellowship)

National Air and Space Museum, MRC 312
Washington, D.C. 20560
Written inquiry

AMOUNT: $30,000 stipend for 12 months + travel and misc. expenses

DEADLINE(S): Jan 15

FIELD(S): Analysis of major trends, developments, and accomplishments in the history of aviation or space studies

A competitive nine- to twelve-month in-residence fellowship in the above field of study. Advanced degree is NOT a requirement. Contact Fellowship Coordinator at above location.

Open to all nationalities. Fluency in English required.

750

SOCIETY OF PHYSICS STUDENTS (SPS Scholarships)

National Office
One Physics Ellipse
College Park, MD 20740
301/209-3007

AMOUNT: $4,000, 1st place; $2,000, second; $1,000, all others

DEADLINE(S): Jan 31

FIELD(S): Physics

SPS members. For final year of full-time study leading to a BS degree in physics.

Consideration given to high scholastic performance; potential for continued scholastic development in physics; and active SPS participation.

Nonrenewable. 14 scholarships per year. Write for complete information.

751

STATE FARM COMPANIES FOUNDATION (Exceptional Student Fellowship)
1 State Farm Plaza
Bloomington, IL 61710
309/766-2039

AMOUNT: $3,000
DEADLINE(S): Feb 15 (apps. available Nov 1)
FIELD(S): Accounting; Business Administration; Actuarial Science; Computer Science; Economics; Finance; Insurance; Investments; Marketing; Mathematics; Statistics; and related fields

Open to current full-time college juniors and seniors majoring in any of the fields above. Only students nominated by the college dean or a department head qualify as candidates. Applications without nominations will NOT be considered.

U.S. citizen. 3.6 or better GPA (4.0 scale) required. 50 fellowships per year. Write for complete information.

752

TANDY TECHNOLOGY SCHOLARS (Student Awards; Teacher Awards)
Texas Christian University
Box 298990
Fort Worth, TX 76129
817/924-4087

AMOUNT: $1,000 students; $2,500 teachers
DEADLINE(S): Oct 9
FIELD(S): Mathematics; Science; Computer Science

Program recognizes academic performance and outstanding achievements by Mathematics, Science, and Computer Science students and teachers. Students and teachers receive cash awards.

Must be a senior in an enrolled high school located in one of the 50 states. 100 of each awarded each year. Nomination packets sent to high schools.

753

U.S. AIR FORCE ROTC (4-Year Scholarship Program)
AFROTC/RROO
Recruiting Operations Branch
551 E. Maxwell Blvd.
Maxwell AFB, AL 36112-6106
334/953-2091

AMOUNT: Tuition; fees & books + $150 per month stipend
DEADLINE(S): Dec 1
FIELD(S): Aeronautical Engineering; Civil Engineering; Mechanical Engineering; Mathematics; Physics; Nursing & some Liberal Arts

Open to U.S. citizens who are at least 17 and will graduate from college before age 25. Must complete application, furnish SAT/ACT scores, high school transcripts and record of extracurricular activities.

Must qualify on Air Force medical examination. About 1,600 scholarships awarded each year at campuses which offer Air Force ROTC.

MEDICAL DOCTOR

754

AEI SCHOLARSHIP FUND
c/o Society Bank
100 So. Main Street
Ann Arbor, MI 48104
Written inquiry

AMOUNT: $4,000/year
DEADLINE(S): May 31
FIELD(S): Medicine

For financially needy female students accepted to, or attending, accredited medical schools in the U.S.

2 awards/year. Contact B. Todd Jones at above location for details. Must demonstrate financial need.

755

AMA EDUCATION AND RESEARCH FOUNDATION (Jerry L. Pettis Memorial Scholarship for 1998)
515 North State Street
Chicago, IL 60610
312/464-4543; Fax 312/464-5678; E-mail: amaerf@ama-assn.org

AMOUNT: $2,500

DEADLINE(S): Jan 1

FIELD(S): Medicine—Communication of science

Open to junior or senior medical students with a demonstrated interest and involvement in the communication of science. Recipient will be selected from among nominees proposed by the deans of AMA-approved medical schools. Financial need is not a consideration. Each school may propose one student.

Send inquiries to Rita M. Palulonis at above address.

756

AMA EDUCATION AND RESEARCH FOUNDATION (Rock Sleyster Memorial Scholarship)
515 North State Street
Chicago, IL 60610
312/464-4657; Fax 312/464-5678; E-mail: amaerf@ama-assn.org

AMOUNT: $2,500

DEADLINE(S): May 1

FIELD(S): Psychiatry

Open to U.S. citizens enrolled in accredited U.S. or Canadian medical schools that grant the M.D. degree. Candidates must aspire to specialize in psychiatry and demonstrate financial need. Nominees must be rising seniors, submit letter from Office of Dean outlining basis of nomination, letter from student outlining career goals in psychiatry, and letter from Dept. of Psychiatry of medical school supporting the nomination.

Submit AMA-ERF Student's Financial Statement to be completed by Medical School Financial Aid Office. Official Medical School Transcript. Awards made for one year. Write to: Harry S. Jonas, M.D., Director, Division of Undergraduate Medical Education, at the above address for complete information.

757

AMA-ERF (Jerry L. Pettis Memorial Scholarship)
515 North State Street
Chicago, IL 60610
312/464-4543

AMOUNT: $2,500

DEADLINE(S): Jan 31

FIELD(S): Medicine, Science

Open to junior or senior medical students with demonstrated interest in the communication of science. Requires: letter of nomination from Office of Dean, Letter and CV from student, Letter from Director of Library, Audio-visual unit or appropriate professional interested in communications; reprints or other materials prepared by student to support nomination. For complete information write to: President - AMA-ERF at above address.

Individuals who will be considered for scholarship will be selected from nominees proposed by the Deans of AMA approved medical schools.

758

ARMENIAN GENERAL BENEVOLENT UNION (Educational Loan Program)
Education Dept.
31 W. 52nd Street
New York, NY 10019-6118
212/765-8260; Fax 212/765-8209/8209

AMOUNT: $5,000 to $7,500/year

DEADLINE(S): May 15

FIELD(S): Law (J.D.); Medicine (M.D.)

Loans for full-time students of Armenian heritage pursuing their first professional degrees in law or medicine. Must be attending highly competitive institutions in the U.S.

Loan repayments begin within 12 months of completion of full-time study and extends 5 to 10 years, depending on the size of the loan. Interest is 3% Write for complete information.

759

ARTHUR & DOREEN PARRETT SCHOLARSHIP TRUST FUND
(Scholarships)

c/o U.S. Bank of Washington
P.O. Box 720
Trust Dept., 8th Floor
Seattle, WA 98111-0720
206/344-4653

AMOUNT: Up to $3,500

DEADLINE(S): Jul 31

FIELD(S): Engineering; Science; Medicine; Dentistry

Washington state resident who has completed her/his first year of college by July 31. Open to students enrolled in above schools. Awards tenable at any accredited undergrad college or university.

Approximately 15 awards per year. Write for complete information.

760

BOYS & GIRLS CLUBS OF SAN DIEGO
(Spence Reese Scholarship Fund)

1761 Hotel Circle So., Suite 123
San Diego, CA 92108
619/298-3520

AMOUNT: $2,000 per year for 4 years

DEADLINE(S): May 15

FIELD(S): Medicine; Law; Engineering; Political Science

Open to male high school seniors planning a career in above fields. Girls and Boys Club affiliation is not required.

Applications are available in January. Must enclose a self-addressed stamped envelope to receive application. A $10 processing fee is required with completed application. Write for complete information.

761

BUSINESS & PROFESSIONAL WOMEN'S FOUNDATION (Career Advancement Scholarships)

2012 Massachusetts Ave. NW
Washington, D.C. 20036
202/293-1200

AMOUNT: $500-$1,000

DEADLINE(S): Apr 15 (postmark)

FIELD(S): Computer Science; Education; Paralegal; Engineering; Science; Law; Dentistry; Medicine

Open to women (30 or older) within 12-24 months of completing undergrad or grad study in U.S. (including Puerto Rico & Virgin Islands). Studies should lead to entry/reentry in work force or improve career advancement chances.

Not for doctoral study. Must demonstrate financial need. Send self-addressed stamped ($.64) #10 envelope for complete info. Applications available Oct. 1 - April 1.

762

CLEM JAUNICH EDUCATION TRUST
(Scholarships)

5353 Gamble Drive, Suite 110
Minneapolis, MN 55416
612/546-1555

AMOUNT: $750-$3,000

DEADLINE(S): Jul 1

FIELD(S): Theology; Medicine

For students who have attended public or parochial school in the Delano (MN) school district or currently reside within 7 miles of the city of Delano, MN. Awards support undergraduate or graduate study in theology or medicine.

4-6 scholarships per year. Write for complete information.

763

CUYAHOGA COUNTY MEDICAL FOUNDATION (Scholarship Grant Program)
6000 Rockside Woods Blvd., Suite 150
Cleveland, OH 44131-2352
216/520-1000

AMOUNT: $500-$1,500
DEADLINE(S): Jun 1
FIELD(S): Medicine; Dentistry; Pharmacy; Nursing; Osteopathy

Grants open to residents of Cuyahoga County who are accepted to or enrolled in an accredited professional school in one of the above areas.

Approx. 40 awards per year. Write for complete information.

764

DEKALB COUNTY PRODUCERS SUPPLY & FARM BUREAU (Medical Scholarship)
1350 W. Prairie Drive
Sycamore, IL 60178
815/756-6361

AMOUNT: Varies
DEADLINE(S): Jun
FIELD(S): Medical Doctor; Nursing

Applicants (or their parents) must have been voting or associate members of Dekalb County Farm Bureau for at least 2 years prior to application; agree to practice in rural Illinois for 3 years upon completion of training. U.S. citizen.

Must have been accepted to or be attending medical school or a nursing program. Write to Virginia Fleetwood at above address for complete information.

765

DEPT. OF THE ARMY (Armed Forces Health Professions Scholarships)
Attn: SGPS-PDE
5109 Leesburg Pike
Falls Church, VA 22041
Written Inquriy

AMOUNT: Varies
DEADLINE(S): None specified
FIELD(S): Physicians: Anesthesiology, surgical specialties; Nursing: Anesthesia, operating room, or medical surgical nursing

For health professionals and students participating in a Reserve Service of the U.S. Armed Forces training in the specialties listed above and for undergraduate nursing students. A monthly stipend is paid and varying lengths of service are required to pay back the stipend.

Army: above address; *or* Commander, Naval Reserve Recruiting Command, ATTN: Code 132, 4400 Dauphine Street, New Orleans, LA 70146-50001; *or* U.S. Air Force Reserve Personnel Center, ATTN: ARPC/SGI, Denver, CO 80280-5000.

766

EDWARD BANGS KELLEY AND ELZA KELLEY FOUNDATION, INC. (Scholarship Program)
P.O. Drawer M
Hyannis, MA 02601-1412
508/775-3117

AMOUNT: Up to $4,000
DEADLINE(S): Apr 30
FIELD(S): Medicine; Nursing; Health Sciences, and related fields

Open to residents of Barnstable County, Massachusetts. Scholarships are intended to benefit health and welfare of Barnstable County residents. Awards support study at recognized undergraduate, graduate, and professional institutions.

Financial need is a consideration. Write for complete information.

767

EPILEPSY FOUNDATION OF AMERICA
(Behavioral Sciences Student Fellowships)
4351 Garden City Drive
Landover, MD 20785
301/459-3700; 800/EFA-1000; Fax 301/577-2684; TDD 800/332-2070; E-mail: postmaster@efa.org; Internet: www.efa.org

AMOUNT: $2,000
DEADLINE(S): Mar 3
FIELD(S): For the study of epilepsy in either research or practice settings in fields such as sociology, social work, psychology, anthropology, nursing, economics, vocational rehabilitation, counseling, political science, etc., relevant to epilepsy research

Applicants may propose a 3-month project to be undertaken in a clinical or laboratory setting where there are ongoing programs of research, service, or training in the field of epilepsy.

Project may be conducted during any free period of the student's year at a U.S. institution of the student's choice. Write for complete information.

768

H. FLETCHER BROWN FUND
(Scholarships)
c/o PNC Bank
Trust Dept.
P.O. Box 791
Wilmington, DE 19899
302/429-2827

AMOUNT: Varies
DEADLINE(S): Apr 15
FIELD(S): Medicine; Dentistry; Law; Engineering; Chemistry

Open to U.S. citizens born and still residing in Delaware. For 4 years of study (undergrad or grad) leading to a degree that enables applicant to practice in chosen field.

Scholarships are based on need, scholastic achievement and good moral character.

Applications available in February. Write for complete information.

769

INTERNATIONAL ORDER OF THE KING'S DAUGHTERS AND SONS (Health Careers Scholarships)
c/o Mrs. Fred Cannon, Box 1310
Brookhaven, MS 39601
Written Inquiry

AMOUNT: Up to $1,000
DEADLINE(S): Apr 1
FIELD(S): Medicine; Dentistry; Nursing; Physical Therapy; Occupational Therapy; Medical Technologies; Pharmacy

Open to students accepted to/enrolled in an accredited U.S. or Canadian 4-yr or graduate school. RN candidates must have completed 1st year; M.D. or D.D.S. application must be for at least the second year of medical or dental school; all other candidates must be in at least 3rd year. Pre-Med students NOT eligible. U.S. or Canadian citizen.

Send a stamped, self-addressed envelope, along with a letter stating the field of study and present level, to the Director at the above address for complete information.

770

J. HUGH & EARLE W. FELLOWS MEMORIAL FUND (Scholarship Loans)
Pensacola Junior College
Exec VP
1000 College Blvd.
Pensacola, FL 32504
904/484-1706

AMOUNT: Each is negotiated individually
DEADLINE(S): None
FIELD(S): Medicine; Nursing; Medical Technology; Theology (Episcopal)

Open to bona fide residents of the Florida counties of Escambia, Santa Rosa, Okaloosa or Walton. For undergraduate study in the fields listed above. U.S. citizenship required.

Loans are interest-free until graduation. Write for complete information.

771

JEWISH VOCATIONAL SERVICE (Marcus & Theresa Levie Educational Fund Scholarships)
1 S. Franklin Street
Chicago, IL 60606
312/357-4500 or 4521

AMOUNT: To $5,000
DEADLINE(S): Mar 1
FIELD(S): Social Work; Medicine; Dentistry; Nursing & other related professions & vocations

Open to Cook County residents of the Jewish faith who plan careers in the helping professions. For undergraduate juniors and seniors and for graduate and vocational students. Applications available Dec 1 from Scholarship Secretary.

Must show financial need. 85-100 awards per year. Renewal possible with reapplication. Write for complete information.

772

MARYLAND HIGHER EDUCATION COMMISSION (Professional School Scholarships)
State Scholarship Administration
16 Francis Street
Annapolis, MD 21401
410/974-5370; TTY 800/735-2258

AMOUNT: $200-$1,000
DEADLINE(S): Mar 1 (for both FAFSA and separate SSA application)
FIELD(S): Dentistry; Pharmacy; Medicine; Law; Nursing

Open to Maryland residents who have been admitted as full-time students at a participating graduate institution of higher learning in Maryland or an undergraduate/graduate nursing program.

Renewable up to 4 years. Write for complete information.

773

MINNESOTA HEART ASSOCIATION (Helen N. and Harold B. Shapira Scholarship)
4701 West 77th Street
Minneapolis, MN 55435
612/835-3300

AMOUNT: $1,000
DEADLINE(S): May 1
FIELD(S): Medicine

Open to pre-med undergraduate students & medical students who are accepted to or enrolled in an accredited Minnesota college or university. Medical students should be in a curriculum that is related to the heart and circulatory system.

May be renewed once. U.S. citizenship or legal residency required. Write for complete information.

774

NATIONAL FEDERATION OF THE BLIND (Howard Brown Rickard Scholarship)
805 Fifth Ave.
Grinnell, IA 50112
515/236-3366

AMOUNT: $3,000
DEADLINE(S): Mar 31
FIELD(S): Natural Sciences; Architecture; Engineering; Medicine; Law

Scholarships for undergraduate or graduate study in the above areas. Open to legally blind students enrolled full-time at accredited post-secondary institutions.

Awards based on academic excellence, service to the community, and financial need. Write for complete information.

775

NATIONS BANK TRUST DEPT (Minne L. Maffett Scholarship Trust)
P.O. Box 831515
Dallas, TX 75283
214/559-6476

AMOUNT: $50-$1,000

DEADLINE(S): Apr 1

FIELD(S): All fields of study

Open to U.S. citizens who graduated from Limestone County, Texas high schools. Scholarships for full-time study at an accredited Texas institution.

30 scholarships per year. Write to Debra Hitzelberger, vice president and trust officer, address above, for complete information.

776

NEW YORK STATE HIGHER EDUCATION SERVICES CORPORATION (N.Y. State Regents Professional/Health Care Opportunity Scholarships)
Cultural Education Center, Room 5C64
Albany, NY 12230
518/486-1319; Internet: www.hesc.com

AMOUNT: $1,000-$10,000/year

DEADLINE(S): Varies

FIELD(S): Medicine and Dentistry and related fields; Architecture; Nursing; Psychology; Audiology; Landscape Architecture; Social Work; Chiropractic; Law; Pharmacy; Accounting; Speech Language Pathology

For NY state residents who are economically disadvantaged and members of a minority group underrepresented in the chosen profession and attending school in NY state. Some programs carry a service obligation in New York for each year of support. For U.S. citizens or qualifying noncitizens.

Medical/dental scholarships require one year of professional work in NY.

777

NEW YORK STATE HIGHER EDUCATION SERVICES CORPORATION
Cultural Education Center, Room 5C64
Albany, NY 12230
518/486-1319; Internet: www.hesc.com

AMOUNT: Varies

DEADLINE(S): Varies

FIELD(S): Medicine and Dentistry and related fields; Architecture; Nursing; Psychology; Audiology; Landscape Architecture; Social Work; Chiropractic; Law; Pharmacy; Accounting; Speech Language Pathology

For NY state residents who are economically disadvantaged and members of a minority group underrepresented in the chosen profession and attending school in NY state. Some programs carry a service obligation in New York for each year of support. For U.S. citizens or qualifying noncitizens.

Medical/dental scholarships require one year of professional work in NY.

778

NORTH CAROLINA STUDENT LOAN PROGRAM FOR HEALTH, SCIENCE, & MATHEMATICS (Loans)
3824 Barrett Drive, Suite 304
Raleigh, NC 27619
919/733-2164

AMOUNT: $2,500 to $7,500 per year

DEADLINE(S): Jan 8 (Application available then. Deadline is May 5)

FIELD(S): Health Professions; Sciences; Engineering

Low-interest scholarship loans open to North Carolina residents of at least 1 year who are pursuing an associate's, undergraduate or graduate degree in the above fields at an accredited institution in the U.S.

Loans may be retired after graduation by working (1 year for each year funded) at designated institutions. Write for complete details.

779

ROBERT SCHRECK MEMORIAL FUND (Grants)
c/o Texas Commerce Bank—Trust Dept.
P.O. Drawer 140
El Paso, TX 79980
915/546-6515

AMOUNT: $500-$1,500

DEADLINE(S): Jul 15; Nov 15

FIELD(S): Medicine; Veterinary Medicine; Physics; Chemistry; Architecture; Engineering; Episcopal Clergy

Grants to undergraduate juniors or seniors or graduate students who have been residents of El Paso County for at least two years. Must be U.S. citizen or legal resident and have a high grade point average. Financial need is a consideration.

Write for complete information.

780

SANTA BARBARA FOUNDATION (Schwalenberg Medical School Loan/Rollo P. Bourbon, MD Scholarship)
15 E. Carrillo Street
Santa Barbara, CA 93101-2780
805/963-1873; Fax 805/966-2345; E-mail: dano@SBFoundation.org

AMOUNT: Varies

DEADLINE(S): Jan 31

FIELD(S): Medicine

For medical students who graduated from high school in Santa Barbara County and who have attended schools in the county since 7th grade. Loans are interest-free; repayment begin 18 months after receipt of MD or if student leaves school. For students who enter family practice or internal medicine, only 50% of the loan needs to be repaid. Based on financial need.

For up to 14 quarters of medical school plus a maximum of 3 years of undergraduate loans. 1 Bourbon, MD Scholarship will be awarded to a Schwalenberg Loan applicant. Applications available October 1 to January 24.

781

SOCIETY OF BIOLOGICAL PSYCHIATRY (Ziskind-Somerfield Research Award)
Elliot Richelson, MD
Mayo Clinic—Jacksonville
Jacksonville, FL 32224
904/953-2842

AMOUNT: $2,500

DEADLINE(S): Jan 31

FIELD(S): Biological Psychiatry

Open to senior investigators who are members of the Society of Biological Psychiatry. Award is for basic or clinical research by senior investigators 35 or older.

Candidates must be members in good standing of the Society of Biological Psychiatry. Write for complete information.

782

THE EDUCATIONAL AND SCIENTIFIC TRUST OF THE PENNSYLVANIA MEDICAL SOCIETY (Loan Program for Pennsylvania Medical School Students)
777 East Park Drive
P.O. Box 8820
Harrisburg, PA 17105-8820
717/558-7750 Ext. 1257; Fax 717/558-7818; E-mail: studentloans-trust@pamedsoc.org; Internet: www.pitt.edu/HOME/GHNet/PA_Trust

AMOUNT: Up to $3,000 for bona fide Pennsylvania residents

DEADLINE(S): Jun 1

FIELD(S): Medicine

Open to Pennsylvania residents with demonstrated financial need who are seeking a medical degree.

Approx. 200 loans per year. Must be U.S. citizen. Contact above location for complete information.

783

THE EDUCATIONAL AND SCIENTIFIC TRUST OF THE PENNSYLVANIA MEDICAL SOCIETY (Loan Program for Out-of-State Pennsylvania Medical School Students)
777 East Park Drive
P.O. Box 8820
Harrisburg, PA 17105-8820

717/558-7750 Ext. 1257; Fax 717/558-7818;
E-mail: studentloans-trust@pamedsoc.org;
Internet:
www.pitt.edu/HOME/GHNet/PA_Trust

AMOUNT: Up to $3,000 for bona fide
Pennsylvania residents
DEADLINE(S): Jun 1
FIELD(S): Medicine
Open to Pennsylvania residents with demonstrated financial need who are seeking a
medical degree and are attending an out-of-
state school.
Approx. 200 loans per year. Must be U.S. citizen. Contact above location for complete
information.

784

**UNIVERSITY SYSTEM OF WEST
VIRGINIA (Health Sciences Scholarship
Program)**
1018 Kanawha Blvd. East, Suite 1101
Charleston, WV 25301-2827
304/558-0530

AMOUNT: $10,000
DEADLINE(S): Oct 31
FIELD(S): Osteopathic Medicine; Family
Medicine; Pediatric Medicine; Internal
Medicine; Obstetrical/Gynecological
Medicine; General Psychiatry; Nurse
Practitioner; Physician Assistants; Nurse-
Midwifery
Open to West Virginia undergraduate and
graduate students. Students must make a
commitment to practice primary care for
two years in an underserved rural area of
West Virginia upon completion of training.
Write to the above address for complete infor-
mation.

785

**U.S. DEPT. OF HEALTH & HUMAN
SERVICES (Indian Health Service's Health
Scholarship Program; Public Law 94-437)**
Twinbrook Metro Plaza, Suite 100
12300 Twinbrook Pkwy.
Rockville, MD 20852

301/443-6197

AMOUNT: Tuition + fees & monthly stipend
DEADLINE(S): Apr 1
FIELD(S): Health professions
Open to American Indians or Alaska natives
who enroll in courses leading to a baccalau-
reate degree (preparing them for accep-
tance into health professions schools). U.S.
citizenship required. Renewable annually
with reapplication.
Scholarship recipients must intend to serve the
Indian people as a health care provider.
They incur a 1-year service obligation to the
IHS for each year of support. Write for
complete information.

786

**VIRGIN ISLANDS BOARD OF
EDUCATION (Nursing & Other Health
Scholarships)**
P.O. Box 11900
St. Thomas, VI 00801
809/774-4546

AMOUNT: Up to $1,800
DEADLINE(S): Mar 31
FIELD(S): Nursing; Medicine; Health-related
Areas
Open to bona fide residents of the Virgin
Islands who are accepted by an accredited
school of nursing or an accredited institu-
tion offering courses in one of the health-
related fields.
This scholarship is granted for one academic
year. Recipients may reapply with at least a
'C' average. Write for complete information.

MEDICAL-RELATED DISCIPLINES

787

**ABBIE SARGENT MEMORIAL
SCHOLARSHIP INC. (Scholarships)**
295 Sheep Davis Road
Concord, NH 03301

603/224-1934

AMOUNT: $200

DEADLINE(S): Mar 15

FIELD(S): Agriculture; Veterinary Medicine; Home Economics

Open to New Hampshire residents who are high school graduates with good grades and character. For undergraduate or graduate study. Must be legal resident of U.S. and demonstrate financial need.

Renewable with reapplication. Write for complete information.

788

ALUMNI ASSOCIATION, COLLEGE OF PHARMACEUTICAL SCIENCES, COLUMBIA UNIVERSITY (Scholarship Fund)

P.O. Box 5078
New York, NY 10022
Written inquiry

AMOUNT: $1,000; $500

DEADLINE(S): Jul 31

FIELD(S): Pharmacy

For undergraduates studying pharmacy in any accredited college or university.

3 $1,000 grants and 2 $500 grants. Write to Sandro A. Rogers at above address.

789

ALUMNI ASSOCIATION OF THE COLLEGE OF PHARMACEUTICAL SCIENCES IN THE CITY OF NY (Tuition Grants)

P.O. Box 5078
FDR Post Office
New York, NY 10022
Written inquiry

AMOUNT: $500-$1,000

DEADLINE(S): Jul 30

FIELD(S): Pharmaceutical Sciences

Open to students of any accredited college of pharmacy in the United States. Awards

based on financial need; scholastic aptitude and community service.

3 $1,000 grants and 2 $500 grants per year. Write for complete information.

790

AMERICAN ASSOCIATION OF WOMEN DENTISTS (Gillette Hayden Memorial Foundation)

401 N. Michigan Ave.
Chicago, IL 60611
800/920-2293; E-mail: aawd@sba.com

AMOUNT: $2,000

DEADLINE(S): Aug 1

FIELD(S): Dentistry

Loans available to women who are 3rd- and 4th-year pre-dental students or are graduate degree candidates. Academic achievement, need for assistance, and amount of debt currently accumulated are main points considered.

10 awards yearly. Write for complete information.

791

AMERICAN COLLEGE OF HEALTH CARE EXECUTIVES (Albert W. Dent Scholarship)

One N. Franklin Street, Suite 1700
Chicago, IL 60606-3491
312/424-2800; Internet: www.ache.org

AMOUNT: $3,000

DEADLINE(S): Mar 31

FIELD(S): Health Care Administration

Open to ACHE student associates who are handicapped or are members of a minority group and have been accepted to or are enrolled full-time in an accredited graduate program. U.S. or Canadian citizen. Previous recipients are not eligible.

Must demonstrate financial need. Apply between Jan. 1 and Mar. 31. Write for complete information.

792

AMERICAN COLLEGE OF MEDICAL PRACTICE EXECUTIVES (ACMPE Scholarships)
104 Inverness Terrace East
Englewood, CO 80112-5306
303/643-9573 Ext. 206

AMOUNT: $500-$2,000
DEADLINE(S): Jun 1
FIELD(S): Health Care Administration/Medical Practice Management

Open to undergraduate or graduate students who are pursuing a degree relevant to medical practice management at an accredited university or college.
Send #10 SASE to receive application.

793

AMERICAN FOUNDATION FOR PHARMACEUTICAL EDUCATION (First-Year Graduate Scholarship Program)
One Church Street, Suite 202
Rockville, MD 20850
301/738-2160; Fax 301/738-2161

AMOUNT: $5,000-$7,000
DEADLINE(S): Jan 1; May 1
FIELD(S): Pharmacy

Several scholarships for pharmacy students beginning their first graduate year and are seeking doctorates in pharmacy. Must be U.S. citizens or legal residents. Some require membership in professional organizations, and deadline dates vary.
Students may apply during last year of BA/BS program. Write for complete information.

794

AMERICAN FOUNDATION FOR PHARMACEUTICAL EDUCATION (Gateway Scholarship Program)
One Church Street, Suite 202
Rockville, MD 20850
301/738-2160; Fax 301/738-2161

AMOUNT: $9,250
DEADLINE(S): Dec 1
FIELD(S): Pharmacy

Open to undergraduates in the last three years of a bachelor's program in a college of pharmacy or Pharm.D graduate students. U.S. citizen or permanent resident.
Purpose is to encourage undergraduates to pursue the Ph.D in a pharmacy college graduate program. Multiple scholarships available. Write for complete information.

795

AMERICAN FOUNDATION FOR VISION AWARENESS (Education/Research Grants)
243 North Lindbergh Blvd.
St. Louis, MO 63141
314/991-1949

AMOUNT: $5,000-$10,000 (research grants); $1,000 (scholarships)
DEADLINE(S): Feb 1
FIELD(S): Optometry

Scholarships open to U.S. optometry students who have finished at least one semester and participated in vision-related public service. Research grants open to scientists doing research in the field of vision.
Write for complete information.

796

AMERICAN FOUNDATION FOR VISION AWARENESS OF WASHINGTON (Scholarships)
c/o Mrs. Chris Cash
28923 15th Place South
Federal Way, WA 98003
206/941-7554

AMOUNT: $700-$1,000
DEADLINE(S): Dec 15
FIELD(S): Optometry

Competitive awards open to Washington state residents accepted and enrolled in an accredited school of optometry. Winners cannot be related to a Washington state optometrist as an immediate family member.

Can win the award each year the student is enrolled in optometry school (on a competitive basis). Write for complete information.

797

AMERICAN INDIAN SCIENCE & ENGINEERING SOCIETY (Burlington Northern Santa Fe Foundation Scholarship)
5661 Airport Blvd.
Boulder, CO 80301
303/939-0023; E-mail:
ascholar@spot.colorado.edu; Internet:
www.colorado.edu/AISES

AMOUNT: $2,500 per year for up to 4 years
DEADLINE(S): Mar 31
FIELD(S): Business; Education; Science; Health Administration

Open to high school seniors who are 1/4 or more American Indian. Must reside in KS, OK, CO, AZ, NM, MN, ND, OR, SD, WA, or San Bernardino County, CA (Burlington Northern and Santa Fe Pacific service areas).

Must plan to attend a four-year post-secondary accredited educational institution. Write for complete information or apply online at above website.

798

AMERICAN SPEECH-LANGUAGE-HEARING FOUNDATION (Graduate Student Scholarships)
10801 Rockville Pike
Rockville, MD 20852
301/897-5700; Fax 301/571-0457

AMOUNT: $4,000
DEADLINE(S): Jun 6
FIELD(S): Communication Sciences/ Disorders; Speech Pathology; Speech Therapy

Open to full-time graduate students in communication sciences and disorders programs and demonstrating outstanding academic achievement.

Applications available in February.

799

AMERICAN VETERINARY MEDICAL FOUNDATION (AVMA Auxiliary Student Loan Fund)
1931 N. Meacham Road, Suite 100
Schaumburg, IL 60173
847/925-8070 Ext. 208; E-mail:
74234.1722@compuserve.com

AMOUNT: Up to $4,000 for seniors; up to $8,000 for sophomores and juniors
DEADLINE(S): Mar 31 (for seniors)
FIELD(S): Veterinary Medicine

Loans available to worthy students in AVMA-accredited colleges of veterinary medicine who need financial aid to complete their schooling. Preference to seniors but sophomores and juniors may be considered. U.S. citizenship required.

Applicants must be members of AVMA student chapter. Write for membership information or an application.

800

ARTHUR & DOREEN PARRETT SCHOLARSHIP TRUST FUND (Scholarships)
c/o U.S. Bank of Washington
P.O. Box 720
Trust Dept., 8th Floor
Seattle, WA 98111-0720
206/344-4653

AMOUNT: Up to $3,500
DEADLINE(S): Jul 31
FIELD(S): Engineering; Science; Medicine; Dentistry

Washington state resident who has completed her/his first year of college by July 31. Open to students enrolled in above schools. Awards tenable at any accredited undergrad college or university.

Approximately 15 awards per year. Write for complete information.

801

ASSOCIATION FOR WOMEN VETERINARIANS (Student Scholarship)
3201 Henderson Mill Road, Apt. 27C
Atlanta, GA 30341
Written inquiries only

AMOUNT: $1,500
DEADLINE(S): Feb 18
FIELD(S): Veterinary Medicine

Open to second- or third-year veterinary medicine students in the U.S. or Canada who are U.S. or Canadian citizens. Both women and men are eligible. Essay is required.

Write for complete information or contact the Dean of your veterinary school.

802

AUXILIARY TO THE MICHIGAN OPTOMETRIC ASSOCIATION (Scholarship Program)
Linda Moleski
3440 Williamson NE
Grand Rapids, MI 49505
906/635-0861

AMOUNT: $400-$1,000
DEADLINE(S): Mar 1
FIELD(S): Optometry

Michigan resident & student member of Michigan Optometric Assn. Apply in 3rd year of study at a recognized school of optometry. Maintain 'B' average. U.S. citizen.

2-5 scholarships per year. Applications available in November at all optometric colleges. Write for complete information.

803

BUSINESS & PROFESSIONAL WOMEN'S FOUNDATION (Career Advancement Scholarships)
2012 Massachusetts Ave. NW
Washington, D.C. 20036
202/293-1200

AMOUNT: $500-$1,000
DEADLINE(S): Apr 15 (postmark)

FIELD(S): Computer Science; Education; Paralegal; Engineering; Science; Law; Dentistry; Medicine

Open to women (30 or older) within 12-24 months of completing undergrad or grad study in U.S. (including Puerto Rico & Virgin Islands). Studies should lead to entry/reentry in work force or improve career advancement chances.

Not for doctoral study. Must demonstrate financial need. Send self-addressed stamped ($.64) #10 envelope for complete info. Applications available Oct. 1 - April 1.

804

BUSINESS & PROFESSIONAL WOMEN'S FOUNDATION EDUCATIONAL PROGRAMS (New York Life Foundation Scholarship Program for Women in the Health Professions)
2012 Massachusetts Ave. NW
Washington, D.C. 20036
202/293-1200 Ext. 169

AMOUNT: $500-$1,000
DEADLINE(S): Apr 15
FIELD(S): Health-care professions.

For women ages 25+ (U.S. citizens) accepted into an accredited program or course of study at a U.S. institution, including institutions in Puerto Rico and the Virgin Islands. Must graduate within 12 to 24 months from the date of grant and demonstrate critical need for assistance ($30,000 or less for a family of 4). Must have a plan to upgrade skills, train for a new career field, or to enter or re-enter the job market.

For part- or full-time study. For info. send a #10 SASE. Write "scholarship" in upper left corner.

805

CHARLES E. SAAK TRUST (Educational Grants)
Wells Fargo Bank Trust Dept.
5262 N. Blackstone
Fresno, CA 93710
Written inquiry only

AMOUNT: Varies

DEADLINE(S): Mar 31

FIELD(S): Education; Dental

Undergraduate grants for residents of the Porterville-Poplar area of Tulare County CA. Must carry a minimum of 12 units; have at least a 2.0 GPA; be under age 21; and demonstrate financial need.

Approximately 100 awards per year; renewable with reapplication. Write for complete information.

806

CUYAHOGA COUNTY MEDICAL FOUNDATION (Scholarship Grant Program)
6000 Rockside Woods Blvd., Suite 150
Cleveland, OH 44131-2352
216/520-1000

AMOUNT: $500-$1,500

DEADLINE(S): Jun 1

FIELD(S): Medicine; Dentistry; Pharmacy; Nursing; Osteopathy

Grants open to residents of Cuyahoga County who are accepted to or enrolled in an accredited professional school in one of the above areas.

Approx. 40 awards per year. Write for complete information.

807

DR. GUILLERMO R. RECINO & HISPANIC DENTAL ASSOCIATION FOUNDATION (Undergraduate/Graduate Scholarship)
One South Wacker Drive, Suite 1800
Chicago, IL 60606
800/852-7921; Fax 312/634-0228; E-mail: hdassoc@ao.com; Internet: members.aol.com/hdassoc/index.html

AMOUNT: $5,000

DEADLINE(S): Jul 1

FIELD(S): Dentistry

Scholarship for Hispanic dental student enrolled in or accepted by a school in Massachusetts. Academic standing, financial need, and community involvement are considered.

Contact above location for details.

808

EDWARD BANGS KELLEY AND ELZA KELLEY FOUNDATION, INC. (Scholarship Program)
P.O. Drawer M
Hyannis, MA 02601-1412
508/775-3117

AMOUNT: Up to $4,000

DEADLINE(S): Apr 30

FIELD(S): Medicine; Nursing; Health Sciences; and related fields

Open to residents of Barnstable County, Massachusetts. Scholarships are intended to benefit health and welfare of Barnstable County residents. Awards support study at recognized undergraduate, graduate, and professional institutions.

Financial need is a consideration. Write for complete information.

809

G. WILSON GRIER SCHOLARSHIP
c/o Peter K. Schaeffer, D.D.S.
1071 S. Governors Ave.
Dover, DE 19904-6933
302/674-1080; Fax 302/674-1046

AMOUNT: $1,000

DEADLINE(S): Varies

FIELD(S): Dentistry

For residents of Delaware who are attending a certified dental school. Applicants must be at least sophomore status.

Write to the above address for complete information.

810

GONSTEAD CHIROPRACTIC EDUCATIONAL TRUST
One West Main Street
Madison, WI 53705
608/252-5958

AMOUNT: Varies
DEADLINE(S): Ongoing
FIELD(S): Chiropractic medicine
Scholarships for students who have maintained at least a 3.0 GPA for two years at a member college of the Council of Chiropractic Education.
Write to Oscar Seibel, Marshall & Illsley Trust Co., at above address, or obtain application forms from a member college.

811

H. FLETCHER BROWN FUND (Scholarships)
c/o PNC Bank
Trust Dept.
P.O. Box 791
Wilmington, DE 19899
302/429-2827

AMOUNT: Varies
DEADLINE(S): Apr 15
FIELD(S): Medicine; Dentistry; Law; Engineering; Chemistry
Open to U.S. citizens born and still residing in Delaware. For 4 years of study (undergrad or grad) leading to a degree that enables applicant to practice in chosen field.
Scholarships are based on need, scholastic achievement and good moral character. Applications available in February. Write for complete information.

812

INTERNATIONAL CHIROPRACTORS ASSOCIATION (ICA/King Koil Scholarship Programs)
1110 N. Glebe Road, Suite 1000
Arlington, VA 22201

800/423-4690; Fax 703/528-5023

AMOUNT: $400-$3,000
DEADLINE(S): Varies (spring—check with organization)
FIELD(S): Chiropractic
For student members of ICA who have a minimum 2.5 GPA & who are enrolled in a chiropractic college. Awards are based on academic achievement and do not cover the total cost of tuition. Must be within 1- 1/2 to 2 years of graduation from chiropractic college.
Additional requirements are determined by the individual SICA chapter scholarship committee. Contact ICA chapter officer or representative at your chiropractic college or write to address above for complete information & application.

813

INTERNATIONAL ORDER OF THE KING'S DAUGHTERS AND SONS (Health Careers Scholarships)
c/o Mrs. Fred Cannon
Box 1310
Brookhaven, MS 39601
Written inquiry

AMOUNT: Up to $1,000
DEADLINE(S): Apr 1
FIELD(S): Medicine; Dentistry; Nursing; Physical Therapy; Occupational Therapy; Medical Technologies; Pharmacy
Open to students accepted to/enrolled in an accredited U.S. or Canadian 4-year or graduate school. RN candidates must have completed 1st year; M.D. or D.D.S. application must be for at least the second year of medical or dental school; all other candidates must be in at least 3rd year. Pre-Med students NOT eligible.
U.S. or Canadian citizen. Send a stamped self-addressed envelope, along with a letter stating the field of study and present level, to the Director at the above address for complete information.

814

IOWA PHARMACY FOUNDATION
8515 Douglas Ave., Suite 16
Des Moines, IA 50322
Written inquiry

AMOUNT: Varies
DEADLINE(S): Ongoing
FIELD(S): Pharmacology
Scholarships and research grants in pharmacology to residents of Iowa.
Write to Thomas R. Temple, Secretary-Treasurer, at above address for details.

815

JEWISH VOCATIONAL SERVICE (Marcus & Theresa Levie Educational Fund Scholarships)
1 S. Franklin Street
Chicago, IL 60606
312/357-4500 or 4521

AMOUNT: Up to $5,000
DEADLINE(S): Mar 1
FIELD(S): Social Work; Medicine; Dentistry; Nursing & other related professions & vocations
Open to Cook County residents of the Jewish faith who plan careers in the helping professions. For undergraduate juniors and seniors and for graduate and vocational students. Applications available Dec. 1 from Scholarship Secretary.
Must show financial need. 85-100 awards per year. Renewal possible with reapplication. Write for complete information.

816

MARYLAND HIGHER EDUCATION COMMISSION (Professional School Scholarships)
State Scholarship Administration
16 Francis Street
Annapolis, MD 21401
410/974-5370; TTY 800/735-2258

AMOUNT: $200-$1,000
DEADLINE(S): Mar 1 (for both FAFSA and separate SSA application)
FIELD(S): Dentistry; Pharmacy; Medicine; Law; Nursing
Open to Maryland residents who have been admitted as full-time students at a participating graduate institution of higher learning in Maryland or an undergraduate/graduate nursing program.
Renewable up to 4 years. Write for complete information.

817

MISSISSIPPI OFFICE OF STATE STUDENT FINANCIAL AID (Dental Education Loan/Scholarship Program)
3825 Ridgewood Road
Jackson, MS 39211-6453
601/982-6663; 800-327-2980

AMOUNT: $4,000/year up to 4 years
DEADLINE(S): Jul 1
FIELD(S): Dentistry
For Mississippi residents who have been accepted for admission to the University of Mississippi School of Dentistry. Post-graduate training must be taken at an accredited hospital in family medicine dentistry and shall not exceed one year.
In acceptance of this loan/scholarship, the student is obligated to practice full-time in a geographical area of critical need in Mississippi or enter full-time public health work at a state health institution or community health center. Obligation can be discharged on the basis of one year's service for one year's loan/scholarship.

818

MISSISSIPPI OFFICE OF STATE STUDENT FINANCIAL AID (Veterinary Medicine Minority Loan/Scholarship Program)
3825 Ridgewood Road
Jackson, MS 39211-6453
601/982-6663; 800-327-2980

AMOUNT: $6,000/year up to 4 years

DEADLINE(S): May 16

FIELD(S): Veterinary Medicine

For full-time minority veterinary students who are Mississippi residents accepted to Mississippi State University College of Veterinary Medicine. The applicant must be classified as a minority student by the Registrar's Office at MSU.

The student is obligated to serve in the profession in Mississippi one year for each year's scholarship.

819

NATIONAL FEDERATION OF THE BLIND (Howard Brown Rickard Scholarship)
805 Fifth Ave.
Grinnell, IA 50112
515/236-3366

AMOUNT: $3,000

DEADLINE(S): Mar 31

FIELD(S): Natural Sciences; Architecture; Engineering; Medicine; Law

Scholarships for undergraduate or graduate study in the above areas. Open to legally blind students enrolled full-time at accredited post-secondary institutions.

Awards based on academic excellence, service to the community, and financial need. Write for complete information.

820

NATIONAL RESEARCH COUNCIL (Howard Hughes Medical Institute Predoctoral Fellowships in Biological Sciences)
Fellowship Office
2101 Constitution Ave. NW
Washington, D.C. 20418
202/334-2872; E-mail: infofell@nas.edu

AMOUNT: $15,000 annual stipend + $15,000 cost of education allowance

DEADLINE(S): Nov 12

FIELD(S): Biological Sciences

For college seniors or graduates at or near the beginning of their study toward a Ph.D or Sc.D in Biological Sciences. For full-time study 12 months a year. U.S. citizens may study in the U.S. or abroad; foreign nationals may study only in the U.S.

Renewable for a maximum of 5 years. 80 awards. Application can be generated online at above location or write for complete information.

821

NATIONAL STRENGTH & CONDITIONING ASSN. (Challenge Scholarships)
P.O. Box 38909
Colorado Springs, CO 80937-8909
719/632-6722; Fax 719/632-6722; E-mail: nsca@usa.net; Internet: www.colosoft.com/nsca

AMOUNT: $1,000

DEADLINE(S): Mar 1

FIELD(S): Fields related to body strength & conditioning

Open to National Strength & Conditioning Association members. Awards are for undergraduate or graduate study.

For membership information or an application, write to the above address.

822

NEW YORK STATE HIGHER EDUCATION SERVICES CORPORATION (N.Y. State Regents Professional/Health Care Opportunity Scholarships)
Cultural Education Center, Room 5C64
Albany, NY 12230
518/486-1319; Internet: www.hesc.com

AMOUNT: $1,000-$10,000/year

DEADLINE(S): Varies

FIELD(S): Medicine and dentistry and related fields; Architecture; Nursing; Psychology; Audiology; Landscape Architecture; Social Work; Chiropractic; Law; Pharmacy; Accounting; Speech Language Pathology

For NY state residents who are economically disadvantaged and members of a minority group underrepresented in the chosen profession and attending school in NY state. Some programs carry a service obligation in New York for each year of support. For U.S. citizens or qualifying noncitizens.

Medical/dental scholarships require one year of professional work in NY.

823

NEW YORK STATE HIGHER EDUCATION SERVICES CORPORATION
Cultural Education Center, Room 5C64
Albany, NY 12230
518/486-1319; Internet: www.hesc.com

AMOUNT: Varies

DEADLINE(S): Varies

FIELD(S): Medicine and dentistry and related fields; Architecture; Nursing; Psychology; Audiology; Landscape Architecture; Social Work; Chiropractic; Law; Pharmacy; Accounting; Speech Language Pathology

For NY state residents who are economically disadvantaged and members of a minority group underrepresented in the chosen profession and attending school in NY state. Some programs carry a service obligation in New York for each year of support. For U.S. citizens or qualifying noncitizens.

Medical/dental scholarships require one year of professional work in NY.

824

NORTH CAROLINA DEPARTMENT OF PUBLIC INSTRUCTION (Scholarship Loan Program for Prospective Teachers)
301 N. Wilmington Street
Raleigh, NC 27601-2825
919/715-1120

AMOUNT: Up to $2,500/year

DEADLINE(S): Feb

FIELD(S): Education: teaching, school psychology and counseling, speech/language impaired, audiology, library/media services

For NC residents planning to teach in NC public schools. At least 3.0 high school GPA required; must maintain 2.5 GPA during freshman year and 3.0 cumulative thereafter. Recipients are obligated to teach one year in a NC public school for each year of assistance. Those who do not fulfill their teaching obligation are required to repay the loan plus interest.

200 awards per year. For full-time students. Applications available in Dec. from high school counselors and college and university departments of education.

825

NORTH CAROLINA STUDENT LOAN PROGRAM FOR HEALTH, SCIENCE, & MATHEMATICS (Loans)
3824 Barrett Drive, Suite 304
Raleigh, NC 27619
919/733-2164

AMOUNT: $2,500 to $7,500 per year

DEADLINE(S): Jan 8 (Application available then. Deadline is May 5)

FIELD(S): Health Professions; Sciences; Engineering

Low-interest scholarship loans open to North Carolina residents of at least 1 year who are pursuing an associate's, undergraduate or graduate degree in the above fields at an accredited institution in the U.S.

Loans may be retired after graduation by working (1 year for each year funded) at designated institutions. Write for complete details.

826

PHYSICIAN ASSISTANT FOUNDATION (Scholarships, Traineeships, Grants)
950 North Washington Street
Alexandria, VA 22314
703/836-2272

AMOUNT: $2,000-$5,000

DEADLINE(S): Feb 1

FIELD(S): Physician Assistant

Must be attending an accredited physician assistant program in order to qualify. Judging is based on financial need, academic standing, community involvement, and knowledge of physician assistant profession.

Multiple sources of financial aid for physician assistant training are available through this organization. Write for complete information.

827

ROBERT SCHRECK MEMORIAL FUND (Grants)

c/o Texas Commerce Bank—Trust Dept.
P.O. Drawer 140
El Paso, TX 79980
915/546-6515

AMOUNT: $500-$1,500

DEADLINE(S): Jul 15; Nov 15

FIELD(S): Medicine; Veterinary Medicine; Physics; Chemistry; Architecture; Engineering; Episcopal Clergy

Grants to undergraduate juniors or seniors or graduate students who have been residents of El Paso County for at least two years. Must be U.S. citizen or legal resident and have a high grade-point average. Financial need is a consideration.

Write for complete information.

828

THE ADA ENDOWMENT AND ASSISTANCE FUND, INC. (Minority Dental Student Scholarship)

211 East Chicago Ave.
Chicago, IL 60611
312/440-2567

AMOUNT: Up to $2,000

DEADLINE(S): Jul 1

FIELD(S): Dentistry

Applicants must be U.S. citizens and a member of one of the following groups: Black/African American, Native American Indian, Hispanic. For students entering second year at a dental school accredited by the Commission on Dental Accreditation. GPA 2.5 or higher. Must demonstrate financial need.

Application forms are available at the dental schools or write to the above address for complete information.

829

THE ADA ENDOWMENT AND ASSISTANCE FUND INC. (Dental Student Scholarship)

211 East Chicago Ave.
Chicago, IL 60611
312/440-2567

AMOUNT: Varies

DEADLINE(S): Jun 15

FIELD(S): Dentistry

Open to second-year students who are currently attending a dental school accredited by the Commission on Dental Accreditation. Applicants must have an accumulative grade-point average of 3.0.

Write to above address for complete information or check with your school's financial aid office.

830

U.S. DEPT. OF HEALTH & HUMAN SERVICES (Indian Health Service's Health Scholarship Program; Public Law 94-437)

Twinbrook Metro Plaza, Suite 100
12300 Twinbrook Pkwy.
Rockville, MD 20852
301/443-6197

AMOUNT: Tuition + fees & monthly stipend

DEADLINE(S): Apr 1

FIELD(S): Health professions

Open to American Indians or Alaska natives who enroll in courses leading to a baccalaureate degree (preparing them for acceptance into health professions schools). U.S. citizenship required. Renewable annually with reapplication.

Scholarship recipients must intend to serve the Indian people as a health care provider. They incur a 1-year service obligation to the IHS for each year of support. Write for complete information.

831

WOMEN OF THE EVANGELICAL LUTHERAN CHURCH IN AMERICA (The Kahler Fund; Vickers/Raup Memorial Fund/Emma Wettstein Fund)
8765 Higgins Road
Chicago, IL 60631-4189
800/638-3522 Ext. 2736

AMOUNT: $2,000 maximum

DEADLINE(S): Nov 1; Apr 1; Jun 1

FIELD(S): To prepare for service in health professions associated with ELCA projects abroad

For ELCA laywomen age 21 or older who have experienced an interruption in schooling of at least 2 years since high school. Must provide academic record of course work completed in the last 5 years. Must demonstrate scholastic ability, financial need, and Christian commitment.

May apply again. Assistance available to maximum of 2 years.

MEDICAL RESEARCH

832

AMERICAN FOUNDATION FOR AGING RESEARCH (Scholarship Program)
c/o NC State Univ.
Biochem Dept., Box 7622
Raleigh, NC 27695
919/515-5679

AMOUNT: $500-$1,000
DEADLINE(S): None
FIELD(S): Gerontology; Aging; Cancer

Scholarships for research on age-related diseases or the biology of aging. Open to undergraduate and graduate students at accredited institutions in the U.S. U.S. citizen only.

6 to 10 scholarships per year. Write for complete information.

833

AMERICAN SPEECH-LANGUAGE-HEARING FOUNDATION (Graduate Student Scholarships)
10801 Rockville Pike
Rockville, MD 20852
301/897-5700; Fax 301/571-0457

AMOUNT: $4,000

DEADLINE(S): Jun 6

FIELD(S): Communication Sciences/Disorders; Speech Pathology; Speech Therapy

Open to full-time graduate students in communication sciences and disorders programs who demonstrate outstanding academic achievement.

Applications available in February.

834

CROHN'S AND COLITIS FOUNDATION (Student Research Fellowship Awards)
386 Park Ave. South
New York, NY 10016
212/685-3440; 800/932-2423; Fax 212/779-4098

AMOUNT: $2,500

DEADLINE(S): Feb 1

FIELD(S): Inflammatory Bowel Disease

For students not yet engaged in thesis research in accredited North American institutions to conduct full-time research with a mentor investigating a subject relevant to IBD. Project duration is a minimum of 10 weeks.

Up to 16 awards per year. Contact Rose Buttigieg at above address.

835

CYSTIC FIBROSIS FOUNDATION
(Research and Training Programs)
6931 Arlington Road
Bethesda, MD 20814
301/951-4422; 800/FIGHT CF

AMOUNT: Up to $55,000/year
DEADLINE(S): Varies
FIELD(S): Cystic Fibrosis Research

Several doctoral/postdoctoral (MD/or Ph.D) grants for research and training related to cystic fibrosis. Senior-level undergrads planning to pursue graduate training also may apply.

Summer programs also available. Contact the foundation for further information on programs and application procedures.

836

CYSTIC FIBROSIS FOUNDATION
(Student Traineeship Research Grants)
6931 Arlington Road
Bethesda, MD 20814
301/951-4422; 800/FIGHT CF

AMOUNT: $1,500
DEADLINE(S): None
FIELD(S): Cystic Fibrosis Research

Doctoral (MD/or Ph.D) research grants to introduce students to research related to cystic fibrosis and to maintain an interest in this area of biomedicine. Must be in or about to enter a doctoral program. Senior-level undergrads planning to pursue graduate training also may apply. The project's duration should be 10 weeks or more.

Contact the foundation for further information on application procedures.

837

EPILEPSY FOUNDATION OF AMERICA
(Behavioral Sciences Student Fellowships)
4351 Garden City Drive
Landover, MD 20785

301/459-3700; 800/EFA-1000; Fax 301/577-2684; TDD: 800/332-2070; E-mail: postmaster@efa.org; Internet: www.efa.org

AMOUNT: $2,000
DEADLINE(S): Mar 3
FIELD(S): For the study of epilepsy in either research or practice settings in fields such as sociology, social work, psychology, anthropology, nursing, economics, vocational rehabilitation, counseling, political science, etc., relevant to epilepsy research

Applicants may propose a 3-month project to be undertaken in a clinical or laboratory setting where there are ongoing programs of research, service, or training in the field of epilepsy.

Project may be conducted during any free period of the student's year at a U.S. institution of the student's choice. Write for complete information.

838

FIGHT FOR SIGHT RESEARCH DIVISION (Student Research Fellowship)
500 East Remington Road
Schaumburg, IL 60173
847/843-2020

AMOUNT: $1,500 maximum ($500/month)
DEADLINE(S): Mar 1
FIELD(S): Ophthalmology and Visual Sciences

Stipend open to undergraduates, medical students, or graduate students for full-time eye-related research, usually during the summer months.

Write for brochure and application. Awards may be renewed.

839

INTERMURAL RESEARCH TRAINING AWARD (Summer Intern Program)
Office of Education
Bldg. 10, Room 1C-129
Bethesda, MD 20892

301/496-2427

AMOUNT: Stipend

DEADLINE(S): Feb 1

FIELD(S): Research Training (Biomedical Research)

Summer intern program is designed to provide 'academically talented' undergraduate, graduate or medical students a unique opportunity to acquire valuable hands-on research training and experience in the neurosciences.

Write for complete information.

840

LUPUS FOUNDATION OF AMERICA (Student Summer Fellowship Program)
  1300 Pickard Drive, Suite 200
  Rockville, MD 20850
  800/558-0121; 310/670-9292; Fax 301/670-9486; Internet: www.lupus.org/lupus

AMOUNT: $2,000

DEADLINE(S): Feb 1

FIELD(S): Lupus Erythematosus Research

Summer fellowships open to undergrads, grads, and post-grads, but applicants already having college degree are preferred. Applications are evaluated NIH-style. Purpose is to encourage students to pursue research careers in above areas.

Research may be conducted at any recognized institution in the U.S. Application materials available in November. 10 awards per year. Write for complete information.

841

NATIONAL FEDERATION OF THE BLIND (Howard Brown Rickard Scholarship)
  805 Fifth Ave.
  Grinnell, IA 50112
  515/236-3366

AMOUNT: $3,000

DEADLINE(S): Mar 31

FIELD(S): Natural Sciences; Architecture; Engineering; Medicine; Law

Scholarships for undergraduate or graduate study in the above areas. Open to legally blind students enrolled full-time at accredited post-secondary institutions.

Awards based on academic excellence, service to the community, and financial need. Write for complete information.

842

NATIONAL INSTITUTES OF HEALTH— NATIONAL CENTER FOR RESEARCH RESOURCES (Minority High School Research Apprentice Program)
  Westwood Bldg.
  Room 10A11
  5333 Westbard Ave.
  Bethesda, MD 20892
  301/496-6743

AMOUNT: $2,000

DEADLINE(S): Jan 31

FIELD(S): Health Sciences Research

Summer program designed to offer minority high school students a meaningful experience in various aspects of health-related research. Its aim is to stimulate students' interest in science. U.S. citizen or permanent resident.

NIH supports this program at over 350 research institutions. Students must apply through program director at the institution. NOT a scholarship.

843

NATIONAL RESEARCH COUNCIL (Howard Hughes Medical Institute Predoctoral Fellowships in Biological Sciences)
  Fellowship Office
  2101 Constitution Ave. NW
  Washington, D.C. 20418
  202/334-2872; E-mail: infofell@nas.edu

AMOUNT: $15,000 annual stipend + $15,000 cost of education allowance

DEADLINE(S): Nov 12

FIELD(S): Biological Sciences

For college seniors or graduates at or near the beginning of their study toward a Ph.D or Sc.D in Biological Sciences. For full-time study 12 months a year. U.S. citizens may study in the U.S. or abroad; foreign nationals may study only in the U.S.

Renewable for a maximum of 5 years. 80 awards. Application can be generated on-line at above location or write for complete information.

844

WHITEHALL FOUNDATION INC. (Research Grants-in-Aid)
251 Royal Palm Way, Suite 211
Palm Beach, FL 33480
561/655-4474; Fax 561/659-4978; Internet: www.whitehall.org

AMOUNT: $30,000 maximum
DEADLINE(S): Jun 1; Sep 1; Feb 15
FIELD(S): Basic research in invertebrate and vertebrate neurobiology

Grants-in-aid for assistant professors and senior scientists for investigations of neural mechanisms involved in sensory, motor, and other complex functions of the whole organism as they relate to behavior.

Initial approach should be a one-page letter summarizing the project. Write for complete information.

MEDICAL TECHNOLOGIES

845

AMERICAN ART THERAPY ASSOCIATION (Cay Drachnik Minorities Fund)
1202 Allanson Road
Mundelein, IL 60060
708/949-6064; Fax 708/566-4580

AMOUNT: For purchase of books
DEADLINE(S): Jun 15
FIELD(S): Art Therapy

For ethnic minority group members enrolled in an AATA-approved program. Fund is specifically for the purchase of books. Must demonstrate financial need through letters of reference, copies of financial aid forms, etc.

Write for application.

846

AMERICAN ART THERAPY ASSOCIATION (Gladys Agell Award for Excellence in Research)
1202 Allanson Road
Mundelein, IL 60060
708/949-6064; Fax 708/566-4580

AMOUNT: Not specified
DEADLINE(S): Jun 15
FIELD(S): Art Therapy

For AATA student members. Award is designed to encourage student research and goes to the most outstanding project completed within the past year in the area of applied art therapy. Verify student status in an AATA-approved program.

Research project must follow APA guidelines.

847

AMERICAN ASSOCIATION OF MEDICAL ASSISTANTS ENDOWMENT (Maxine Williams Scholarship Fund)
20 N. Wacker Drive, #1575
Chicago, IL 60606
312/899-1500

AMOUNT: $500
DEADLINE(S): Feb 1; Jun 1
FIELD(S): Medical Assistant

Undergraduate scholarships open to high school graduates who submit a written statement expressing interest in a career as a medical assistant and will attend a program accredited by the CAAHEP.

3-6 scholarships per year. Renewable. Write for complete information.

848

AMERICAN DENTAL HYGIENISTS ASSN. (ADHA Institute Minority Scholarship)
444 North Michigan Ave., Suite 3400
Chicago, IL 60611
312/440-8900

AMOUNT: Varies
DEADLINE(S): Jun 1
FIELD(S): Dental Hygiene

For dental hygiene students who have completed at least one year of study and who belong to an under-represented minority group in the field: African-Americans, Hispanics, Asians, Native Americans, and males.
2 awards. Minimum 3.0 GPA required.

849

AMERICAN DENTAL HYGIENISTS ASSN. (Baccalaureate Scholarship Program)
444 North Michigan Ave., Suite 3400
Chicago, IL 60611
312/440-8900

AMOUNT: $1,500
DEADLINE(S): Jun 1
FIELD(S): Dental Hygiene

For full-time students pursuing a BA degree in dental hygiene at a 4-year institution in the U.S. Must be eligible for licensure in the academic year the award is being made. Must have completed one year of program.
Minimum GPA of 3.0 is required. Write for complete information.

850

AMERICAN DENTAL HYGIENISTS ASSN. (Certificate/Associate Degree Scholarship Program)
444 North Michigan Ave., Suite 3400
Chicago, IL 60611
312/440-8900

AMOUNT: $1,500
DEADLINE(S): Jun 1
FIELD(S): Dental Hygiene

For students entering their second and final year in an associate's/certificate program for dental hygienists. Must be eligible for licensure the year the award is being made.
Minimum GPA of 3.0 (4.0 scale) is required. Write for complete information.

851

AMERICAN DENTAL HYGIENISTS ASSN. (Colgate "Bright Smiles, Bright Futures" Minority Scholarships)
444 North Michigan Ave., Suite 3400
Chicago, IL 60611
312/440-8900

AMOUNT: Varies
DEADLINE(S): Jun 1
FIELD(S): Dental Hygiene

For students in dental hygiene who have completed at least one year of study and who belong to an under-represented minority in the field: African-Americans, Hispanics, Asians, Native Americans, and males.
2 awards. Minimum 3.0 GPA required.

852

AMERICAN DENTAL HYGIENISTS ASSN. (Colgate Minority Scholarships)
444 North Michigan Ave., Suite 3400
Chicago, IL 60611
312/440-8900

AMOUNT: Varies
DEADLINE(S): Jun 1
FIELD(S): Dental Hygiene

For dental hygiene students who have completed at least one year of study and who belong to an under-represented minority group in the field: African-Americans, Hispanics, Asians, Native Americans, and males.
6 awards. Minimum 3.0 GPA required. Sponsored by Colgate Oral Pharmaceuticals.

853

AMERICAN DENTAL HYGIENISTS ASSN. (Colgate Scholarships for Academic Excellence)
444 North Michigan Ave., Suite 3400
Chicago, IL 60611
312/440-8900

AMOUNT: Varies

DEADLINE(S): Jun 1

FIELD(S): Dental Hygiene

For students in either a certificate/associate's or baccalaureate Degree program in dental hygiene with at least a 3.5 GPA on a 4.0 scale.
6 awards. Sponsored by Colgate Oral Pharmaceuticals.

854

AMERICAN DENTAL HYGIENISTS ASSN. (Dr. Alfred C. Fones Scholarship)
444 North Michigan Ave., Suite 3400
Chicago, IL 60611
312/440-8900

AMOUNT: Varies

DEADLINE(S): Jun 1

FIELD(S): Dental Hygiene Education

For dental hygiene students in the baccalaureate or graduate degree categories who intend to become dental hygiene teachers/educators.
GPA minimum of 3.0 required.

855

AMERICAN DENTAL HYGIENISTS ASSN. (Dr. Harold Hillenbrand Scholarship)
444 North Michigan Ave., Suite 3400
Chicago, IL 60611
312/440-8900

AMOUNT: Varies

DEADLINE(S): Jun 1

FIELD(S): Dental Hygiene

For a dental hygiene student who demonstrates specific academic excellence and outstanding clinical performance and has a min. GPA of 3.5
Must have completed at least one year of dental hygiene training.

856

AMERICAN DENTAL HYGIENISTS ASSN. (Irene E. Newman Scholarship)
444 North Michigan Ave., Suite 3400
Chicago, IL 60611
312/440-8900

AMOUNT: Varies

DEADLINE(S): Jun 1

FIELD(S): Dental Hygiene

For a dental hygiene student in the baccalaureate or graduate degree categories who demonstrates strong potential in public health or community dental health.
Minimum 3.0 GPA required. 1 award.

857

AMERICAN DENTAL HYGIENISTS ASSN. (Margaret E. Swanson Scholarship)
444 North Michigan Ave., Suite 3400
Chicago, IL 60611
312/440-8900

AMOUNT: Varies

DEADLINE(S): Jun 1

FIELD(S): Dental Hygiene

For a dental hygiene student who demonstrates exceptional organization leadership potential.
Minimum GPA 3.0.

858

AMERICAN DENTAL HYGIENISTS ASSN. (Part-Time Scholarship)
444 North Michigan Ave., Suite 3400
Chicago, IL 60611
312/440-8900

AMOUNT: Varies

DEADLINE(S): Jun 1

FIELD(S): Dental Hygiene

For an eligible dental hygiene student pursuing an associate'/certificate, baccalaureate, or graduate degree on a part-time basis. Minimum 3.0 GPA required.

859

AMERICAN DENTAL HYGIENISTS ASSN. (Procter & Gamble Oral Health Scholarship Program)
444 N. Michigan Ave., Suite 3400
Chicago, IL 60611
312/440-8900

AMOUNT: $1,000
DEADLINE(S): Jun 15
FIELD(S): Dental Hygiene

For full-time, first-year dental hygiene students accepted into an entry-level dental hygiene program in the U.S. Must show evidence of community service and leadership and have a minimum high school cumulative GPA of 3.3.

25 awards for students accepted into programs located throughout Procter & Gamble's sales areas in the U.S.

860

AMERICAN DENTAL HYGIENISTS ASSN. (Sigma Phi Alpha Undergraduate Scholarship)
444 North Michigan Ave., Suite 3400
Chicago, IL 60611
312/440-8900

AMOUNT: Varies
DEADLINE(S): Jun 1
FIELD(S): Dental Hygiene

For an outstanding dental hygiene student pursuing an associate'/certificate or baccalaureate degree at an accredited dental hygiene school with an active chapter of the Sigma Phi Alpha Dental Hygiene Honor Society.

Minimum 3.0 required.

861

AMERICAN HEALTH INFORMATION MANAGEMENT ASSOCIATION (Barbara Thomas Enterprises Scholarship)
919 N. Michigan Ave., Suite 1400
Chicago, IL 60611-1683
312/787-2672 Ext. 302; Fax 312/787-5926; E-mail: juanita@ahima.mhs.compuserve.com;
Internet: www.ahima.org

AMOUNT: $5,000
DEADLINE(S): May 30
FIELD(S): Health Information Management; Medical Records; Health Information Technology

For undergraduates and graduates studying one of the above fields. Must be a single parent accepted to a HIM or technology (HIT) program accredited by the Commission on Accreditation of Allied Health Education programs or to AHIMA's Independent Study Program.

Contact the above address for complete information.

862

AMERICAN HEALTH INFORMATION MANAGEMENT ASSOCIATION (Foundation of Research and Education in Health Information Management)
919 N. Michigan Ave., Suite 1400
Chicago, IL 60611-1683
312/787-2672 Ext. 302; Fax 312/787-5926; E-mail: juanita@ahima.mhs.compuserve.com;
Internet: www.ahima.org

AMOUNT: $1,000-$5,000
DEADLINE(S): May 30; Oct 20
FIELD(S): Health Information Management; Medical Records; Health Information Technology

Loans for undergraduates and graduates studying one of the above fields. U.S. citizenship required.

Contact the above address for complete information.

863

AMERICAN HEALTH INFORMATION MANAGEMENT ASSOCIATION (Undergraduate Scholarships)
919 N. Michigan Ave., Suite 1400
Chicago, IL 60611-1683
312/787-2672 Ext. 302; Fax 312/787-5926; E-mail: juanita@ahima.mhs.compuserve.com;
Internet: www.ahima.org

AMOUNT: $1,000-$5,000
DEADLINE(S): May 30
FIELD(S): Health Information Management

Open to undergraduates who have been accepted for admission to a HIM or technology program (HIT) accredited by the Commission on Accreditation of Allied Health Education Programs or accepted to AHIMA's Independent Study Program and successfully completed three individual modules.

Several awards. Write for complete information.

864

AMERICAN MEDICAL TECHNOLOGISTS (AMT Scholarships)
710 Higgins Road
Park Ridge, IL 60068
847/823-5169

AMOUNT: $250
DEADLINE(S): Apr 1
FIELD(S): Medical Laboratory Technician; Medical Technology; Dental Assistant; Medical Assistant; Phlebotomy

Open to high school graduates or high school seniors residing in the U.S. and plan to enroll or are enrolled in an accredited program in the above fields in the U.S. Financial need is a consideration.

Write for complete information. Include a legal-sized SASE and a listing of your educational and career goals with your request.

865

AMERICAN RESPIRATORY CARE FOUNDATION (Fellowships, Awards & Grants)
11030 Ables Lane
Dallas, TX 75229-4593
972/243-2272

AMOUNT: $500-$3,500
DEADLINE(S): Jun 30
FIELD(S): Respiratory Care & Research

Various fellowships, awards, and grants for projects, papers & research relating to respiratory care. Most awards include airfare & lodging to attend the AARC Annual Convention Awards Ceremony.

Write for complete information and requirements.

866

AMERICAN RESPIRATORY CARE FOUNDATION (International Fellowship Program)
11030 Ables Lane
Dallas, TX 75229-4593
972/243-2272

AMOUNT: Not specified
DEADLINE(S): None specified
FIELD(S): Respiratory Therapy

For health care professionals from other countries to observe respiratory care practice and education in the United States. The three-week itinerary provides for visits to two U.S. cities before attending the AARC annual convention. Fellows will observe the practice of respiratory care in tours of hospitals, schools, and home care programs, etc.

Write to above location for details.

867

AMERICAN RESPIRATORY CARE FOUNDATION (Jimmy A. Young Memorial Scholarship)
11030 Ables Lane
Dallas, TX 75229

972/243-2272

AMOUNT: $1,000
DEADLINE(S): Jun 30
FIELD(S): Respiratory Therapy

For a minority candidate enrolled in an accredited respiratory therapy program. Must have letters of recommendation from program director or other senior faculty member and provide six copies of an original referenced paper on some aspect of respiratory care.

Must have GPA of 3.0 or better and be U.S. citizen or permanent resident. Contact above location for details.

868

AMERICAN RESPIRATORY CARE FOUNDATION (Morton B. Duggan, Jr. Memorial Scholarship)
11030 Ables Lane
Dallas, TX 75229
972/243-2272

AMOUNT: $500
DEADLINE(S): Jun 30
FIELD(S): Respiratory Therapy

Candidate must be enrolled in an accredited respiratory therapy program. Must have medical or technical director's recommendation, maintain a 3.0 or better GPA, and be a citizen or permanent resident of the U.S.

Must provide six copies of an original referenced paper on some aspect of respiratory care. Contact above location for details.

869

AMERICAN RESPIRATORY CARE FOUNDATION (Robert M. Lawrence, MD, Scholarship)
11030 Ables Lane
Dallas, TX 75229
972/243-2272

AMOUNT: $2,500
DEADLINE(S): Jun 30

FIELD(S): Respiratory Therapy

For third- or fourth-year students enrolled in an accredited respiratory therapy program. The award also includes registration, travel and one night's lodging to the AARC annual convention. Must have a GPA of 3.0 or better and be a U.S. citizen or permanent resident. Letters of recommendation and two essays are required.

For details on essays and other application information, contact above location.

870

AMERICAN RESPIRATORY CARE FOUNDATION (Scholarship)
11030 Ables Lane
Dallas, TX 75229
972/243-2272

AMOUNT: $1,250
DEADLINE(S): Jun 30
FIELD(S): Respiratory Therapy

Candidate must be enrolled in an accredited respiratory therapy program. Must have medical or technical director's sponsorship, maintain a 3.0 or better GPA, and be a citizen or permanent resident of the U.S.

Must provide six copies of an original, referenced paper on some aspect of respiratory care. Contact above location for details on this and other programs.

871

AMERICAN RESPIRATORY CARE FOUNDATION (William W. Burgin, Jr., MD Scholarship)
11030 Ables Lane
Dallas, TX 75229
972/243-2272

AMOUNT: $2,500
DEADLINE(S): Jun 30
FIELD(S): Respiratory Therapy

For second-year students enrolled in an accredited respiratory therapy program leading to a BA degree. The award also includes registration, travel, and one night's lodging to the AARC annual convention. Must maintain 3.0 or better GPA and be U.S. citizen or permanent resident. Letters of recommendation and two essays required.

For details on essays and other application information, contact above location.

872

AMERICAN SOCIETY OF CLINICAL PATHOLOGISTS (Scholarship Program)

2100 W. Harrison Street
Chicago, IL 60612-3798
312/738-1336 Ext. 159; E-mail:
info@ascp.org

AMOUNT: $1,000

DEADLINE(S): Oct 31

FIELD(S): Cytotechnology; Histologic Technician; Medical Laboratory Technician; Medical Technology

Open to undergraduates in their final clinical year of training in a CAHEA-accredited program in the above fields. Official transcripts and three letters of recommendation are required.

Contact Jennifer Jones at above address.

873

AMERICAN SPEECH-LANGUAGE-HEARING FOUNDATION (Graduate Student Scholarships)

10801 Rockville Pike
Rockville, MD 20852
301/897-5700; Fax 301/571-0457

AMOUNT: $4,000

DEADLINE(S): Jun 6

FIELD(S): Communication Sciences/Disorders; Speech Pathology; Speech Therapy

Open to full-time graduate students in communication sciences and disorders programs who demonstrate outstanding academic achievement.

Applications available in February.

874

DAUGHTERS OF THE AMERICAN REVOLUTION (NSDAR Occupational Therapy Scholarships)

Office of the Committee/Scholarships
National Society DAR
1776 D Street NW
Washington, D.C. 20006-5392
202/879-3292

AMOUNT: $500 to $1,000 (one-time award)

DEADLINE(S): Feb 15; Aug 15

FIELD(S): Occupational Therapy; Physical Therapy

Open to graduate and undergrad students enrolled in an accredited therapy program in the U.S. Must be sponsored by a local DAR chapter. Biannual award is based on academic excellence, recommendation, need, and commitment to field of study.

U.S. citizenship required. Send SASE for complete information.

875

EASTER SEAL SOCIETY OF IOWA, INC. (Scholarships & Awards)

P.O. Box 4002
Des Moines, IA 50333-4002
515/289-1933

AMOUNT: $400-$600

DEADLINE(S): Apr 15

FIELD(S): Physical Rehabilitation; Mental Rehabilitation; and related areas

Open only to Iowa residents who are full-time undergraduate sophomores, juniors, seniors, or graduate students at accredited institutions planning a career in the broad field of rehabilitation. Must indicate financial need and be in top 40% of their class.

6 scholarships per year. Must re-apply each year.

876

EDWARD BANGS KELLEY AND ELZA KELLEY FOUNDATION, INC. (Scholarship Program)
P.O. Drawer M
Hyannis, MA 02601-1412
508/775-3117

AMOUNT: Up to $4,000
DEADLINE(S): Apr 30
FIELD(S): Medicine; Nursing; Health Sciences; and related fields

Open to residents of Barnstable County, Massachusetts. Scholarships are intended to benefit health and welfare of Barnstable County residents. Awards support study at recognized undergraduate, graduate, and professional institutions.

Financial need is a consideration. Write for complete information.

877

EMPIRE COLLEGE (Dean's Scholarship)
3033 Cleveland Ave.
Santa Rosa, CA 95403
707/546-4000

AMOUNT: $250-$1,500
DEADLINE(S): Apr 15
FIELD(S): Accounting; Secretarial; Legal; Medical (Clinical & Administrative); Travel & Tourism; General Business; Computer Assembly; Network Assembly

Open to high school seniors who meet admission requirements and want to attend Empire College in Santa Rosa, California. U.S. citizenship required.

10 scholarships per year. Contact Ms. Mary Farha at the above address for complete information.

878

FLORIDA DENTAL ASSOCIATION (Dental Hygiene Scholarship Program)
1111 E. Tennessee Street, Suite 102
Tallahassee, FL 32308

904/681-3620

AMOUNT: Varies
DEADLINE(S): May 1; Nov 1
FIELD(S): Dental Hygiene

Open to Florida residents who have been accepted for enrollment in an accredited dental hygiene school in Florida. Preference to applicants from areas in Florida with dental hygienist shortages.

Write for complete information.

879

FLORIDA DEPT. OF EDUCATION (Occupational Therapist & Physical Therapist Scholarship Loan Program)
601 Florida Education Center
Tallahassee, FL 32399-0400
904/488-4246

AMOUNT: Up to $4,000—cost of education minus other student financial aid
DEADLINE(S): Apr 15 (postmark)
FIELD(S): Occupational Therapy; Physical Therapy

Open to students enrolled full-time in therapist assistant programs or upper division or grad-level therapist programs at eligible Florida institution. Requires a three-year commitment to work full-time in Florida public schools or loan must be repaid in full.

15 annual awards. Write to Bureau of Student Services and Exceptional Education at above location for complete information.

880

INTERNATIONAL ORDER OF THE KING'S DAUGHTERS AND SONS (Health Careers Scholarships)
c/o Mrs. Fred Cannon
Box 1310
Brookhaven, MS 39601
Written inquiry

AMOUNT: Up to $1,000
DEADLINE(S): Apr 1

FIELD(S): Medicine; Dentistry; Nursing; Physical Therapy; Occupational Therapy; Medical Technologies; Pharmacy

Open to students accepted to/enrolled in an accredited U.S. or Canadian 4-year or graduate school. RN candidates must have completed 1st year; M.D. or D.D.S. application must be for at least the second year of medical or dental school; all other candidates must be in at least 3rd year. Pre-Med students NOT eligible.

U.S. or Canadian citizen. Send a stamped self-addressed envelope, along with a letter stating the field of study and present level, to the Director at the above address for complete information.

881

J. HUGH & EARLE W. FELLOWS MEMORIAL FUND (Scholarship Loans)
Pensacola Junior College
Exec. VP
1000 College Blvd.
Pensacola, FL 32504
904/484-1706

AMOUNT: Each is negotiated individually
DEADLINE(S): None
FIELD(S): Medicine; Nursing; Medical Technology; Theology (Episcopal)

Open to bona fide residents of the Florida counties of Escambia, Santa Rosa, Okaloosa or Walton. For undergraduate study in the fields listed above. U.S. citizenship required.

Loans are interest-free until graduation. Write for complete information.

882

JEWISH VOCATIONAL SERVICE (Marcus & Theresa Levie Educational Fund Scholarships)
1 S. Franklin Street
Chicago, IL 60606
312/357-4500/4521

AMOUNT: Up to $5,000

DEADLINE(S): Mar 1
FIELD(S): Social Work; Medicine; Dentistry; Nursing & other related professions & vocations

Open to Cook County residents of the Jewish faith who plan careers in the helping professions. For undergraduate juniors and seniors and for graduate and vocational students. Applications available Dec. 1 from Scholarship Secretary.

Must show financial need. 85-100 awards per year. Renewal possible with reapplication. Write for complete information.

883

MARYLAND HIGHER EDUCATION COMMISSION (Physical & Occupational Therapists & Assistants Scholarships)
State Scholarship Administration
16 Francis Street
Annapolis, MD 21401
410/974-5370

AMOUNT: $2,000
DEADLINE(S): Jul 1
FIELD(S): Occupational Therapy; Physical Therapy

Open to Maryland residents who enroll full-time in post-secondary institutions having approved occupational or physical therapy programs that lead to Maryland licensing as a therapist or assistant.

Recipients agree to one year of service at a public school, state hospital, or other approved site for each year of award. Write for complete information.

884

MARYLAND HIGHER EDUCATION COMMISSION (Reimbursement of Firefighter & Rescue Squad Members)
State Scholarship Administration
16 Francis Street
Annapolis, MD 21401
410/974-5370; TTY 800/735-2258; Internet: www.ubalt.edu/www.mhec

AMOUNT: $3,480

DEADLINE(S): Jul 1

FIELD(S): Firefighting or Emergency Medical Technology

For Maryland residents who are firefighters or rescue squad members. Reimbursement made one year after successful completion of course(s) in fire or EMT program.

Write for complete information.

885

NATIONAL ASSOCIATION OF AMERICAN BUSINESS CLUBS (AMBUCS Scholarship)
P.O. Box 5127
High Point, NC 27262
910/869-2166; Fax: 910/887-8451

AMOUNT: $500-$1,500

DEADLINE(S): Apr 15

FIELD(S): Physical Therapy; Music Therapy; Occupational Therapy; Speech-Language Pathology; Audiology; Rehabilitation; Recreation Therapy; and related areas

Open to undergraduate juniors and seniors or graduate students who have good scholastic standing and plan to enter the fields listed above. GPA of 3.0 or better (4.0 scale) and U.S. citizenship required. Must demonstrate financial need.

Renewable. Include a self-addressed stamped envelope; applications are mailed in December; incomplete applications will not be considered.

886

NATIONAL ATHLETIC TRAINERS ASSOCIATION (NATA Undergraduate & Graduate Scholarship Program)
2952 Stemmons Freeway
Dallas, TX 75247
214/637-6282

AMOUNT: $2,000

DEADLINE(S): Feb 1

FIELD(S): Athletic Trainer

Scholarship program for student members of NATA who have excellent academic records, have excelled as student athletic trainers. Undergraduates may apply after completion of sophomore year, and graduates may apply after completion of fall semester of their senior year.

Send SASE to address above for complete information.

887

NATIONAL FEDERATION OF THE BLIND (Howard Brown Rickard Scholarship)
805 Fifth Ave.
Grinnell, IA 50112
515/236-3366

AMOUNT: $3,000

DEADLINE(S): Mar 31

FIELD(S): Natural Sciences; Architecture; Engineering; Medicine; Law

Scholarships for undergraduate or graduate study in the above areas. Open to legally blind students enrolled full-time at accredited post-secondary institutions.

Awards based on academic excellence, service to the community, and financial need. Write for complete information.

888

NATIONAL STRENGTH & CONDITIONING ASSN. (Challenge Scholarships)
P.O. Box 38909
Colorado Springs, CO 80937-8909
719/632-6722; Fax 719/632-6722; E-mail: nsca@usa.net; Internet: www.colosoft.com/nsca

AMOUNT: $1,000

DEADLINE(S): Mar 1

FIELD(S): Fields related to body strength & conditioning

Open to National Strength & Conditioning Association members. Awards are for undergraduate or graduate study.

For membership information or an application, write to the above address.

889

NEW YORK STATE HIGHER EDUCATION SERVICES CORPORATION (N.Y. State Regents Professional/Health Care Opportunity Scholarships)

Cultural Education Center, Room 5C64
Albany, NY 12230
518/486-1319; Internet: www.hesc.com

AMOUNT: $1,000-$10,000/year

DEADLINE(S): Varies

FIELD(S): Medicine and Dentistry and related fields; Architecture; Nursing; Psychology; Audiology; Landscape Architecture; Social Work; Chiropractic; Law; Pharmacy; Accounting; Speech Language Pathology

For NY state residents who are economically disadvantaged and members of a minority group underrepresented in the chosen profession and attending school in NY state. Some programs carry a service obligation in New York for each year of support. For U.S. citizens or qualifying noncitizens.

Medical/dental scholarships require one year of professional work in NY.

890

NEW YORK STATE HIGHER EDUCATION SERVICES CORPORATION

Cultural Education Center, Room 5C64
Albany, NY 12230
518/486-1319; Internet: www.hesc.com

AMOUNT: Varies

DEADLINE(S): Varies

FIELD(S): Medicine and dentistry and related fields; Architecture; Nursing; Psychology; Audiology; Landscape Architecture; Social Work; Chiropractic; Law; Pharmacy; Accounting; Speech Language Pathology

For NY state residents who are economically disadvantaged and members of a minority group underrepresented in the chosen profession and attending school in NY state. Some programs carry a service obligation in New York for each year of support. For U.S. citizens or qualifying noncitizens.

Medical/dental scholarships require one year of professional work in NY.

891

NORTH CAROLINA DEPARTMENT OF PUBLIC INSTRUCTION (Scholarship Loan Program for Prospective Teachers)

301 N. Wilmington Street
Raleigh, NC 27601-2825
919/715-1120

AMOUNT: Up to $2,500/year

DEADLINE(S): Feb

FIELD(S): Education: teaching, school psychology and counseling, speech/language impaired, audiology, library/media services

For NC residents planning to teach in NC public schools. At least 3.0 high school GPA required; must maintain 2.5 GPA during freshman year and 3.0 cumulative thereafter. Recipients are obligated to teach one year in a NC public school for each year of assistance. Those who do not fulfill their teaching obligation are required to repay the loan plus interest.

200 awards per year. For full-time students. Applications available in Dec. from high school counselors and college and university departments of education.

892

NORTH CAROLINA SOCIETY FOR CLINICAL LABORATORY SCIENCE (Scholarship Award)

The University of NC at Chapel Hill
Medical School Wing E, CB #7145
Chapel Hill, NC 27599-7145
Written inquiry only

AMOUNT: Approximately $300 to $700 (amounts approved annually)

DEADLINE(S): Jun 1

FIELD(S): Medical Technology/Medical Laboratory Technician

Open to North Carolina residents who have been accepted in an approved clinical laboratory science program. Must meet North Carolina residency requirements.

Renewable. Write to NCSCLS Scholarship Chair Rebecca J. Laudicina, Ph.D., CLS (NCA), for complete information.

893

NORTH CAROLINA STUDENT LOAN PROGRAM FOR HEALTH, SCIENCE, & MATHEMATICS (Loans)

3824 Barrett Drive, Suite 304
Raleigh, NC 27619
919/733-2164

AMOUNT: $2,500 to $7,500 per year

DEADLINE(S): Jan 8 (Application available then. Deadline is May 5)

FIELD(S): Health Professions; Sciences; Engineering

Low-interest scholarship loans open to North Carolina residents of at least 1 year who are pursuing an associate's, undergraduate or graduate degree in the above fields at an accredited institution in the U.S.

Loans may be retired after graduation by working (1 year for each year funded) at designated institutions. Write for complete details.

894

PRO THERAPY OF AMERICA INC.
("Learn While You Earn" Student Advance)

P.O. Box 1600
Birmingham, MI 48012-1600
800/438-4788

AMOUNT: $5,000; $10,000

DEADLINE(S): Varies

FIELD(S): Physical Therapy; Occupational Therapy

Loan is open to students in their last 6-15 months of a physical or occupational therapy program at an accredited U.S. school. Must have at least a 2.7 GPA. Must be a U.S. citizen or legal resident.

$5,000 loan forgiven after 1-year work commitment. $10,000 loan forgiven after 18-month work commitment. Applicants do not have to demonstrate financial need. Write above address for complete information.

895

ROY AND ROXIE CAMPANELLA PHYSICAL THERAPY SCHOLARSHIP FOUNDATION

2995 Gateway Oaks Drive, Suite 200
Sacramento, CA 95833
916/989-2782; Fax 916/646-5960;
Internet: www.dennis
mc.com/baseball/dtw/dtwcampy.html-ssi

AMOUNT: Varies

DEADLINE(S): Mar 1

FIELD(S): Physical Therapy

Scholarships for senior physical therapy students who successfully exhibit awareness of cultural and ethical considerations that contribute to optimum patient care and recovery.

Request application packets only between Jan. 15 and Feb. 15 at address above.

896

STATE STUDENT ASSISTANCE COMMISSION OF INDIANA (Scholarships for Special Education Teachers and Physical or Occupational Therapists)

150 W. Market Street, 5th Floor
Indianapolis, IN 46204
317/232-2350; Fax 317/232-3260; E-mail:
grants@ssaci.in.us; Internet:
www.ai.org/ssaci/

AMOUNT: $1,000

DEADLINE(S): Varies (with college)

FIELD(S): Education

For Indiana residents working toward degrees in special education or physical or occupational therapy. For full-time undergraduate or graduate study at an Indiana college. U.S.

citizenship and GPA of 2.0 or better (4.0 scale) is required.

Must demonstrate financial need (FAF). Indiana residency required.

897

THE ADA ENDOWMENT AND ASSISTANCE FUND, INC. (Allied Dental Health Scholarship—Dental Hygiene)
211 East Chicago Ave.
Chicago, IL 60611
312/440-2567

AMOUNT: $1,000
DEADLINE(S): Aug 15
FIELD(S): Dental Hygiene

For students entering second year and currently enrolled in a dental hygiene program accredited by the Commission on Dental Accreditation. Applicants must have an accumulative grade-point average of 3.0.

Write to the above address for complete information.

898

THE ADA ENDOWMENT AND ASSISTANCE FUND, INC. (Allied Dental Health Scholarship—Dental Assisting)
211 East Chicago Ave.
Chicago, IL 60611
312/440-2567

AMOUNT: $1,000
DEADLINE(S): Sep 15
FIELD(S): Dental Assisting

Applicants must be entering students enrolled in a dental assisting program accredited by the Commission on Dental Accreditation.

Apply at your school or write to above address for complete information.

899

THE ADA ENDOWMENTS AND ASSISTANCE FUND, INC. (Allied Dental Health Scholarship—Dental Laboratory Technician)
211 East Chicago Ave.
Chicago, IL 60611
312/440-2567

AMOUNT: $1,000
DEADLINE(S): Aug 15
FIELD(S): Dental Laboratory Technician

Applicants must be entering first-year or entering second-year students currently attending or enrolled in a dental laboratory technology program accredited by the Commission on Dental Accreditation. Applicants must have an accumulated grade-point average of 2.8 and demonstrate a minimum financial need of $1,000.

Write to the above address for complete information.

900

UNITED CEREBRAL PALSY ASSOCIATIONS OF NEW YORK STATE (Physical Therapy Scholarship)
330 W. 34th Street
New York, NY 10001
212/947-5770; Fax 212/594-4538

AMOUNT: $5,000
DEADLINE(S): Dec 1
FIELD(S): Physical Therapy; Occupational Therapy; Speech Therapy

Open to qualifying senior clinical therapy students. Recipients must agree to accept employment by UCP of NY full time for 18 consecutive months. Applicants are judged on academic record, references, and personal interview.

Applicants must be eligible to sit for New York State clinical therapy licensing exam upon graduation. Write for complete information.

NURSING

901

AMERICAN ASSOCIATION OF CRITICAL CARE NURSES (Educational Advancement Scholarship Program)
101 Columbia
Aliso Viejo, CA 92656-1491
800/899-2226; 714/362-2020 (outside U.S.)

AMOUNT: $1,500
DEADLINE(S): May 15 (postmark)
FIELD(S): Critical Care Nursing

Open to AACN members who are RNs and are working or have worked in a critical care unit. For undergraduate (junior or senior status) or graduate study. Should have worked in critical care for 1 year of the last 3 & have 3.0 or better GPA.

37 awards for baccalaureate study and 17 for graduate study per year. At least 20% of the awards will go to ethnic minorities. Write for complete information.

902

AMERICAN ASSOCIATION OF NURSE ANESTHETISTS (Educational Loans)
222 S. Prospect Ave.
Park Ridge, IL 60068
708/692-7050

AMOUNT: $500-$2,500
DEADLINE(S): None
FIELD(S): Nurse Anesthetist

Loans available to AANA members & associate members enrolled in a school of anesthesia approved by the Council on Accreditation of Nurse Anesthesia Educational Programs. Loans are intended to cover unexpected events of an emergency nature.

Contact the finance director, address above, for complete information.

903

AMERICAN COLLEGE OF NURSE-MIDWIVES FOUNDATION (Scholarships Program)
818 Connecticut Ave. NW, Suite 900
Washington, D.C. 20006
202/728-9865

AMOUNT: Varies
DEADLINE(S): Feb 15
FIELD(S): Nurse-Midwifery

Scholarships open to students currently enrolled in ACNM accredited certificate or graduate nurse-midwifery programs. Student membership in ACNM and completion of one clinical module or semester also required.

Number of awards per year varies. Applications and information available from directors of nurse-midwifery programs at accredited schools. Or contact the address above for membership information.

904

AMERICAN LEGION—KANSAS (John and Geraldine Hobbie Licensed Practical Nursing Scholarship)
1314 SW Topeka Blvd.
Topeka, KS 66612-1886
913/232-9315

AMOUNT: $250
DEADLINE(S): Feb 15
FIELD(S): Licensed Practical Nursing

This scholarship is open to Kansas residents who have reached the age of 18 before taking the Kansas State Board Examination, and attend an accredited Kansas school which awards diplomas for LPN.

Write to the above address for complete information.

905

AMERICAN LEGION AUXILIARY (Past Presidents Parley Nursing Scholarship)
State Veterans Service Building
St. Paul, MN 55155

612/224-7634

AMOUNT: $500
DEADLINE(S): Mar 15
FIELD(S): Nursing

Minnesota resident who is a member of the Dept. of Minnesota American Legion Auxiliary and has a 2.0 or better GPA. To help needy & deserving students or adults commence or further their education in nursing at a Minnesota school.
Write for complete information.

906

AMERICAN RED CROSS, SONOMA COUNTY CHAPTER (Nurse Assistant Program Scholarships)
465 Tesconi Circle
Santa Rosa, CA 95401-4619
707/577-7600; Fax 707/577-7621

AMOUNT: Varies
DEADLINE(S): None
FIELD(S): Nurse Assistant Training

Scholarships for a four-week course leading to a certificate as a Nurse Assistant. Based on eligibility and need.
Write or call for details.

907

ARCHBOLD MEDICAL CENTER (Archbold Scholarship, Service Cancelable Loan)
P.O. Box 1018
Thomasville, GA 31799-1018
912/228-2795

AMOUNT: $1,000-$6,000
DEADLINE(S): Varies
FIELD(S): Nursing; Occupational Therapy; Physical Therapy; Laboratory

Open to S.W. Georgia residents within two years of completion of a degree in nursing. Must be pursuing a degree utilized by the hospital. Commit to full-time employment at the Medical Center for 1-3 years upon completion.
50 awards. Write to Donna McMillan at the above address for complete information.

908

ASSOCIATION OF OPERATING ROOM NURSES (AORN Scholarship Program)
Scholarship Board
2170 S. Parker Road, Suite 300
Denver, CO 80231
303/755-6300

AMOUNT: Tuition & fees
DEADLINE(S): May 1; Oct 1
FIELD(S): Nursing or complementary fields

Open to active & associate AORN members for at least 12 consecutive months prior to deadline date. Awards support bachelor's, master's & doctoral degree programs accredited by the NLN or other acceptable accrediting body.
For full- or part-time study in the U.S. Minimum 3.0 GPA on 4.0 scale. Renewable. For membership information or an application, write to the above address.

909

CONNECTICUT LEAGUE FOR NURSING (CLN Scholarships)
P.O. Box 365
Wallingford, CT 06492
203/265-4248

AMOUNT: $1,500
DEADLINE(S): Oct 15
FIELD(S): Nursing

2 undergrad scholarships open to Connecticut residents in their final year of study at a Connecticut school of nursing. 1 graduate award for student having completed 20 credits in nursing school. School must be agency member of CLN.
Awards are based on merit & need. Write for complete information.

910

CONNECTICUT LEAGUE FOR NURSING (Nursing Scholarship)
P.O. Box 365
Wallingford, CT 06492-0365
Written inquiry

AMOUNT: Varies
DEADLINE(S): Oct 1
FIELD(S): Nursing

Open to residents of Connecticut who are enrolled in an NLN-accredited Connecticut School of Nursing which is a CLN agency member. Bachelor's applicants must be seniors, diploma and associate applicants must have completed 1st year, RN applicants must be entering senior year, graduate students must have completed 20 units.

Write to the above address for complete information.

911

CUYAHOGA COUNTY MEDICAL FOUNDATION (Scholarship Grant Program)
6000 Rockside Woods Blvd., Suite 150
Cleveland, OH 44131-2352
216/520-1000

AMOUNT: $500-$1,500
DEADLINE(S): Jun 1
FIELD(S): Medicine; Dentistry; Pharmacy; Nursing; Osteopathy

Grants open to residents of Cuyahoga County who are accepted to or enrolled in an accredited professional school in one of the above areas.

Approx. 40 awards per year. Write for complete information.

912

DAUGHTERS OF THE AMERICAN REVOLUTION (Caroline Holt Nursing Scholarships)
Office of the Committee/Scholarships
National Society DAR
1776 D Street NW
Washington, D.C. 20006-5392
202/879-3292

AMOUNT: $500 (one-time award)
DEADLINE(S): Feb 15; Aug 15
FIELD(S): Nursing

Open to undergrad students enrolled in an accredited nursing program in the U.S. No affiliation or relation to DAR is required but applicants must be sponsored by a local DAR chapter. U.S. citizenship required.

Awards are based on academic excellence, financial need and recommendations. Send SASE for complete information.

913

DEKALB COUNTY PRODUCERS SUPPLY & FARM BUREAU (Medical Scholarship)
1350 W. Prairie Drive
Sycamore, IL 60178
815/756-6361

AMOUNT: Varies
DEADLINE(S): Jun
FIELD(S): Medical Doctor; Nursing

Applicants (or their parents) must have been voting or associate members of Dekalb County Farm Bureau for at least 2 years prior to application; agree to practice in rural Illinois for 3 years upon completion of training. U.S. citizen.

Must have been accepted to or be attending medical school or a nursing program. Write to Virginia Fleetwood at above address for complete information.

914

DEPT. OF THE ARMY (Armed Forces Health Professions Scholarships)
Attn: SGPS-PDE
5109 Leesburg Pike
Falls Church, VA 22041
Written inquiry

AMOUNT: Varies

DEADLINE(S): None specified

FIELD(S): Physicians: Anesthesiology, surgical specialties; Nursing: Anesthesia, operating room, or medical surgical nursing

For health professionals and students participating in a Reserve Service of the U.S. Armed Forces training in the specialties listed above and for undergraduate nursing students. A monthly stipend is paid and varying lengths of service are required to pay back the stipend.

Army: above address; *or* Commander, Naval Reserve Recruiting Command, ATTN: Code 132, 4400 Dauphine Street, New Orleans, LA 70146-50001; *or* U.S. Air Force Reserve Personnel Center, ATTN: ARPC/SGI, Denver, CO 80280-5000.

915

EDWARD BANGS KELLEY AND ELZA KELLEY FOUNDATION, INC. (Scholarship Program)
P.O. Drawer M
Hyannis, MA 02601-1412
508/775-3117

AMOUNT: Up to $4,000

DEADLINE(S): Apr 30

FIELD(S): Medicine; Nursing; Health Sciences; and related fields

Open to residents of Barnstable County, Massachusetts. Scholarships are intended to benefit health and welfare of Barnstable County residents. Awards support study at recognized undergraduate, graduate, and professional institutions.

Financial need is a consideration. Write for complete information.

916

EPILEPSY FOUNDATION OF AMERICA (Behavioral Sciences Student Fellowships)
4351 Garden City Drive
Landover, MD 20785
301/459-3700; 800/EFA-1000; Fax 301/577-2684; TDD 800/332-2070; E-mail: postmaster@efa.org; Internet: www.efa.org

AMOUNT: $2,000

DEADLINE(S): Mar 3

FIELD(S): For the study of epilepsy in either research or practice settings in fields such as sociology, social work, psychology, anthropology, nursing, economics, vocational rehabilitation, counseling, political science, etc., relevant to epilepsy research

Applicants may propose a 3-month project to be undertaken in a clinical or laboratory setting where there are ongoing programs of research, service, or training in the field of epilepsy.

Project may be conducted during any free period of the student's year at a U.S. institution of the student's choice. Write for complete information.

917

GOOD SAMARITAN FOUNDATION (Nursing Scholarships)
P.O. Box 271108
Houston, TX 77277-1108
713/529-4647

AMOUNT: Varies

DEADLINE(S): None specified

FIELD(S): Nursing

Open to nursing students at Texas schools who have attained the clinical level of their nursing education. Awards support full-time study in all accredited nursing programs (LVN; Diploma; ADN; RN; BSN). U.S. citizen or legal resident.

Students should apply at least 6 months before the start of clinical courses. Approximately 600 awards per year. Renewable. Write for complete information.

918

HARVEY AND BERNICE JONES FOUNDATION (Scholarships)
P.O. Box 233
Springdale, AR 72765
501/756-0611

AMOUNT: Varies
DEADLINE(S): None specified
FIELD(S): Nursing

Scholarships available to residents of Springdale, AR who want to pursue a career in nursing. Must be U.S. citizen and demonstrate financial need.

Number of awards per year varies. Contact address above for complete information.

919

INTERNATIONAL ORDER OF THE KING'S DAUGHTERS AND SONS (Health Careers Scholarships)
c/o Mrs. Fred Cannon
Box 1310
Brookhaven, MS 39601
Written inquiry

AMOUNT: Up to $1,000
DEADLINE(S): Apr 1
FIELD(S): Medicine; Dentistry; Nursing; Physical Therapy; Occupational Therapy; Medical Technologies; Pharmacy

Open to students accepted to/enrolled in an accredited U.S. or Canadian 4-year or graduate school. RN candidates must have completed 1st year; M.D. or D.D.S. application must be for at least the second year of medical or dental school; all other candidates must be in at least 3rd year. Pre-Med students NOT eligible.

U.S. or Canadian citizen. Send a stamped self-addressed envelope, along with a letter stating the field of study and present level, to the Director at the above address for complete information.

920

J. HUGH & EARLE W. FELLOWS MEMORIAL FUND (Scholarship Loans)
Pensacola Junior College
Exec VP
1000 College Blvd.
Pensacola, FL 32504
904/484-1706

AMOUNT: Each is negotiated individually
DEADLINE(S): None
FIELD(S): Medicine; Nursing; Medical Technology; Theology (Episcopal)

Open to bona fide residents of the Florida counties of Escambia, Santa Rosa, Okaloosa or Walton. For undergraduate study in the fields listed above. U.S. citizenship required.

Loans are interest-free until graduation. Write for complete information.

921

JEWISH VOCATIONAL SERVICE (Marcus & Theresa Levie Educational Fund Scholarships)
1 S. Franklin Street
Chicago, IL 60606
312/357-4500 or 4521

AMOUNT: Up to $5,000
DEADLINE(S): Mar 1
FIELD(S): Social Work; Medicine; Dentistry; Nursing & other related professions & vocations

Open to Cook County residents of the Jewish faith who plan careers in the helping professions. For undergraduate juniors and seniors and for graduate and vocational students. Applications available Dec. 1 from Scholarship Secretary.

Must show financial need. 85-100 awards per year. Renewal possible with reapplication. Write for complete information.

922

KANSAS BOARD OF REGENTS (Nursing Scholarship)

> 700 SW Harrison, Suite 1410
> Topeka, KS 66603
> 913/296-3517

AMOUNT: $2,500/year—Licensed Practical Nurse students; $3,500/year—Registered Nurse students

DEADLINE(S): May 1

FIELD(S): Nursing (RN or LPN)

For RN or LPN students accepted to nursing programs in Kansas and who will commit to nursing in Kansas one year for each year of the scholarship. Must also demonstrate commitment by an eligible sponsor to fund up to half the scholarship and who will provide full-time employment to the recipient after licensure.

Renewable. If recipient changes majors or decides not to work for the sponsor as a nurse, the scholarship becomes a loan with 15% interest.

923

MARYLAND HIGHER EDUCATION COMMISSION (Professional School Scholarships)

> State Scholarship Administration
> 16 Francis Street
> Annapolis, MD 21401
> 410/974-5370; TTY 800/735-2258

AMOUNT: $200-$1,000

DEADLINE(S): Mar 1 (for both FAFSA and separate SSA application)

FIELD(S): Dentistry; Pharmacy; Medicine; Law; Nursing

Open to Maryland residents who have been admitted as full-time students at a participating graduate institution of higher learning in Maryland or an undergraduate/graduate nursing program.

Renewable up to 4 years. Write for complete information.

924

MARYLAND HIGHER EDUCATION COMMISSION (State Nursing Scholarship and Grant)

> State Scholarship Administration
> 16 Francis Street
> Annapolis, MD 21401-1781
> 410/974-5370; TTY 800/735-2258; Internet: www.ubalt.edu/www.mhec

AMOUNT: $2,400/year (scholarship); $2,400/year (grant)

DEADLINE(S): Mar 1 (FAFSA); Jun 30 (SSA)

FIELD(S): Nursing

For full- or part-time grad or undergrad study in nursing for Maryland residents. Must have 3.0 or better GPA.

Grant portion requires demonstration of financial need. Renewable. Write for complete information.

925

MATERNITY CENTER ASSOCIATION (Hazel Corbin Assistance Fund/Stipend Awards)

> 281 Park Ave. South, 5th Floor
> New York, NY 10010
> 212/777-5000; Fax 212/777-9320; E-mail: mcabirth@aol.com

AMOUNT: $5,000/year

DEADLINE(S): Aug 1

FIELD(S): Nurse-Midwifery

For nurses enrolled in an ACNM-accredited midwifery program. Grantees are expected to submit annual reports of their accomplishments toward the advancement of midwifery for five years. Must demonstrate academic excellence, financial need, and a commitment to family-centered maternity care.

Write for complete information and application.

926

MCFARLAND CHARITABLE FOUNDATION TRUST (Nursing Scholarships)

Linda Butler
Havana National Bank
P.O. Box 200
Havana, IL 62644
309/543-3361

AMOUNT: $3,000-$20,000
DEADLINE(S): May 1
FIELD(S): Registered Nursing

Open to IL residents nursing students. Recipients must agree to return to Havana, IL area to work as RN for one year for each year of funding. Written contracts with co-signers are required, and an employment commitment is required prior to award of scholarship. A breach of contract requires repayment with interest from date of each disbursement plus recruitment and replacement costs.

Up to 3 awards per year.

927

MINNESOTA HIGHER EDUCATION SERVICES OFFICE (Nursing Grants for Persons of Color)

Capitol Square Bldg., Suite 400
550 Cedar Street
St. Paul, MN 55101
612/296-3974; Fax 612/297-8880; E-mail: info@heso.state.mn.us; Internet: www.heso.state.mn.us/

AMOUNT: Up to $4,000/year
DEADLINE(S): None given
FIELD(S): Nursing

For persons of color entering or enrolled in an educational program leading to licensure as a registered nurse or advanced nursing education. Ethnic background must be Asian-Pacific, African-American, American Indian, Hispanic/Latino, or Puerto Rican and U.S. citizen or permanent resident and Minnesota resident.

Contact Minnesota schools, colleges, or nursing programs or the above location for complete details.

928

MISSISSIPPI OFFICE OF STATE STUDENT FINANCIAL AID (Nursing Education Loan/Scholarship Program)

3825 Ridgewood Road
Jackson, MS 39211-6453
601/982-6663; 800-327-2980 (toll free in Miss.); Fax 601/982-6527

AMOUNT: Up to $5,000/year
DEADLINE(S): Jul 1
FIELD(S): Nursing

For registered nurses who have lived in Mississippi at least one year and are enrolled in a nursing program at an accredited Mississippi institution in pursuit of a BS degree (RN to BSN program). May be juniors, seniors, or graduate students. Also for nurses pursuing master's and doctorate degrees.

Scholarships are renewable. Write for complete information.

929

MISSOURI LEAGUE FOR NURSING (Scholarships)

P.O. Box 104476
Jefferson City, MO 65110
314/635-5355

AMOUNT: $100-$5,000
DEADLINE(S): Sep 30
FIELD(S): Nursing

Open to nursing students who reside in Missouri and are attending a NLN-accredited school in Missouri. For course work leading to licensing as a LPN or RN or to a BSN or MSN degree. Financial need must be demonstrated.

Application must be made through the director of nursing at the student's school.

930

**NATIONAL BLACK NURSES'
ASSOCIATION INC. (Dr. Lauranne Sams
Scholarship)**
P.O. Box 1823
Washington, D.C. 20013
202/393-6870

AMOUNT: $1,000
DEADLINE(S): Apr 15
FIELD(S): Nursing
Scholarships for students enrolled in a nursing
program (A.D.; diploma; BSN; LPN/LVN)
who are in good scholastic standing and are
members of the association.
Write for complete information.

931

**NATIONAL FOUNDATION FOR LONG-
TERM HEALTH CARE (James D. Durante
Nurse Scholarship Program)**
1201 L Street NW
Washington, D.C. 20005
202/842-4444; Hotline Info. 202/898-9352

AMOUNT: $500
DEADLINE(S): May 30
FIELD(S): Nursing
Open to LPN and RN students who seek to
continue or further their education and are
interested in long-term care.
20 $500 scholarships per year. Send a self-
addressed stamped legal-size envelope with
request for application in late winter.

932

**NATIONAL HEMOPHILIA
FOUNDATION (Nursing Excellence
Fellowship)**
110 Greene Street, Suite 203
New York, NY 10012
212/219-8180; 212/966-9247

AMOUNT: $5,000
DEADLINE(S): Jun 1

FIELD(S): Nursing
The National Hemophilia Foundation offers
fellowships to 2 registered nurses who are
dedicated to the care of persons with hemophilia. They must be recommended by three
professionals. Not renewable.
Write to the above address for complete information.

933

**NATIONAL STUDENT NURSES' ASSN.
FOUNDATION (Scholarship Program)**
555 West 57th Street, Suite 1327
New York, NY 10019
212/581-2215; Fax: 212/581-2368; E-mail:
nsna@nsna.org; Internet: www.nsna.org

AMOUNT: Varies
DEADLINE(S): Jan 30
FIELD(S): Nursing
Open to students enrolled in state-approved
schools of nursing or pre-nursing in associate degree or baccalaureate programs.
Financial need, grades, and community
activities are considerations.
Graduating seniors not eligible. Applications
available August through January 15. Write
for complete information. Include self-
addressed stamped ($.55) business-size
envelope for application.

934

**NEW HAMPSHIRE POST-SECONDARY
EDUCATION COMMISSION (Nursing
Education Assistance Grants)**
Two Industrial Park Drive
Concord, NH 03301-8512
603/271-2555

AMOUNT: $600-$2,000
DEADLINE(S): Jun 1; Dec 15
FIELD(S): Nursing
Open to New Hampshire residents who are
accepted to or enrolled in an approved
nursing program in the state of New
Hampshire. U.S. citizenship or legal residen-

cy required. Financial need must be demonstrated.

Approximately 110 grants per year. Write for complete information.

935

NEW YORK STATE HIGHER EDUCATION SERVICES CORPORATION (N.Y. State Regents Professional/Health Care Opportunity Scholarships)
Cultural Education Center, Room 5C64
Albany, NY 12230
518/486-1319; Internet: www.hesc.com

AMOUNT: $1,000-$10,000/year
DEADLINE(S): Varies
FIELD(S): Medicine and Dentistry and related fields; Architecture; Nursing; Psychology; Audiology; Landscape Architecture; Social Work; Chiropractic; Law; Pharmacy; Accounting; Speech Language Pathology

For NY state residents who are economically disadvantaged and members of a minority group underrepresented in the chosen profession and attending school in NY state. Some programs carry a service obligation in New York for each year of support. For U.S. citizens or qualifying noncitizens.

Medical/dental scholarships require one year of professional work in NY.

936

NEW YORK STATE HIGHER EDUCATION SERVICES CORPORATION
Cultural Education Center, Room 5C64
Albany, NY 12230
518/486-1319; Internet: www.hesc.com

AMOUNT: Varies
DEADLINE(S): Varies
FIELD(S): Medicine and dentistry and related fields; Architecture; Nursing; Psychology; Audiology; Landscape Architecture; Social Work; Chiropractic; Law; Pharmacy; Accounting; Speech Language Pathology

For NY state residents who are economically disadvantaged and members of a minority group underrepresented in the chosen profession and attending school in NY state. Some programs carry a service obligation in New York for each year of support. For U.S. citizens or qualifying noncitizens.

Medical/dental scholarships require one year of professional work in NY.

937

OHIO BOARD OF REGENTS (Nurse Education Assistance Loan Program)
State Grants & Scholarships Dept.
P.O. Box 182452
Columbus, OH 43218-2452
888/833-1133; 614/644-7420; Fax 614/752-5903

AMOUNT: $3,000/year for up to 4 years
DEADLINE(S): None specified
FIELD(S): Nursing

For Ohio students enrolled for at least half-time study (or accepted for enrollment) in an approved Ohio nurse education program. Awards are based on the basis of financial need.

Contact a college financial aid administrator, your high school counselor, or the above location for details.

938

OHIO LEAGUE FOR NURSING (Grants and Loans)
Student Aid Committee
2800 Euclid Ave., Suite 235
Cleveland, OH 44115
216/781-7222

AMOUNT: Varies
DEADLINE(S): Apr 15
FIELD(S): Nursing

Open to nursing students who are residents of Greater Cleveland area (Cuyahoga; Grauga; Lake; Lorain counties) & will agree to work in a health care facility in that area for at least a year after graduation. U.S. citizen or legal resident.

20-25 awards per year. Write for complete information.

939

ONCOLOGY NURSING FOUNDATION (Scholarships, Grants, Awards, and Honors)
501 Holiday Drive
Pittsburgh, PA 15220-2749
412/921-7373 Ext. 231 or 242; Fax 412/921-6565; E-mail: onsmain@nauticom.net

AMOUNT: Varies (with program)

DEADLINE(S): Varies (with program)

FIELD(S): Oncology Nursing

For registered nurses seeking further training in the field of oncology nursing. Various programs range from bachelor's degree level through post-doctorate. Also honors and awards for oncology nurses who have contributed to professional literature and excellence in their field.

Awards include "Oncology Certified Nurse of the Year Award." Write for detailed information.

940

STATE STUDENT ASSISTANCE COMMISSION OF INDIANA (Nursing Scholarship Fund)
150 W. Market Street, 5th Floor
Indianapolis, IN 46204
317/232-2350; Fax 232-3260; E-mail: grants@ssaci.in.us; Internet: www.ai.org/ssaci

AMOUNT: Up to $5,000

DEADLINE(S): Varies (with college)

FIELD(S): Nursing

Open to Indiana residents enrolled at least half-time in an undergraduate nursing program at an Indiana college or university. Applicants must have a GPA of 2.0 or better (4.0 scale). U.S. citizenship.

275-700 awards. Must demonstrate financial need. Write for complete information.

941

TYSON FOUNDATION INC. (Scholarship Program)
2210 W. Oaklawn
Springdale, AR 72762-6999
501/290-4955

AMOUNT: Varies according to need

DEADLINE(S): Apr 20

FIELD(S): Business; Agriculture; Engineering; Computer Science; Nursing

For Arkansas residents who are U.S. citizens. Must be enrolled full-time in an accredited institution and demonstrate financial need. Must be employed part-time and/or summers to help fund education. For undergrad study at schools in U.S.

Renewable up to 8 semesters or 12 trimesters as long as students meet criteria.

942

U.S. AIR FORCE ROTC (4-Year Scholarship Program)
AFROTC/RROO
Recruiting Operations Branch
551 E. Maxwell Blvd.
Maxwell AFB, AL 36112-6106
334/953-2091

AMOUNT: Tuition; fees & books + $150 per month stipend

DEADLINE(S): Dec 1

FIELD(S): Aeronautical Engineering; Civil Engineering; Mechanical Engineering; Mathematics; Physics; Nursing & some Liberal Arts

Open to U.S. citizens who are at least 17 and will graduate from college before age 25. Must complete application, furnish SAT/ACT scores, high school transcripts and record of extracurricular activities.

Must qualify on Air Force medical examination. About 1,600 scholarships awarded each year at campuses which offer Air Force ROTC.

943

U.S. DEPT. OF HEALTH & HUMAN SERVICES (Indian Health Service's Health Scholarship Program; Public Law 94-437)
Twinbrook Metro Plaza, Suite 100
12300 Twinbrook Pkwy.
Rockville, MD 20852
301/443-6197

AMOUNT: Tuition + fees & monthly stipend
DEADLINE(S): Apr 1
FIELD(S): Health professions

Open to American Indians or Alaska natives who enroll in courses leading to a baccalaureate degree (preparing them for acceptance into health professions schools). U.S. citizenship required. Renewable annually with reapplication.

Scholarship recipients must intend to serve the Indian people as a health care provider. They incur a 1-year service obligation to the IHS for each year of support. Write for complete information.

944

VIRGIN ISLANDS BOARD OF EDUCATION (Nursing & Other Health Scholarships)
P.O. Box 11900
St. Thomas, VI 00801
809/774-4546

AMOUNT: Up to $1,800
DEADLINE(S): Mar 31
FIELD(S): Nursing; Medicine; Health-related areas

Open to bona fide residents of the Virgin Islands who are accepted by an accredited school of nursing or an accredited institution offering courses in one of the health-related fields.

This scholarship is granted for one academic year. Recipients may reapply with at least a 'C' average. Write for complete information.

945

VIRGINIA DEPT. OF HEALTH—OFFICE OF PUBLIC HEALTH NURSING (Mary Marshall Nursing Scholarships)
P.O. Box 2448
Richmond, VA 23218
804/371-4090

AMOUNT: Varies
DEADLINE(S): Jun 30 (Nurse Practitioner/Midwife Programs); Jul 30 (Reg. Nurse/Practical Nurse Programs)
FIELD(S): Nursing: RNs, Practical Nursing, Nurse Practitioner, or Midwifery

Nursing scholarships program for the above fields for Virginia residents enrolled or accepted in a VA school of nursing. For full-time study leading to undergrad or grad nursing degree. GPA of 3.0 or better in required courses.

Must agree to engage in full-time nursing practice in VA upon graduation (1 month for every $100 received). Financial need must be demonstrated. Applications accepted after April 30. Write or call for complete information.

946

WISCONSIN LEAGUE FOR NURSING, INC. (Scholarship)
2121 East Newport Ave.
Milwaukee, WI 53211
414/332-6271

AMOUNT: $500
DEADLINE(S): Feb 28
FIELD(S): Nursing

Open to Wisconsin residents enrolled in a National League for Nursing (NLN)-accredited program in WI. Must be halfway through academic program.

Must have 3.0 or better GPA and demonstrate financial need. Applications are mailed ONLY to NLN-accredited schools in January of each year for distribution to students. Contact your school for application. Specify that you are already in nursing school.

947

WISCONSIN LEAGUE FOR NURSING, INC. (Scholarships for High School Seniors)
2121 East Newport Ave.
Milwaukee, WI 53211
414/332-6271

AMOUNT: $500
DEADLINE(S): Feb
FIELD(S): Nursing

For high school seniors who are Wisconsin residents accepted to a National League for Nursing (NLN)-accredited program in WI. Must demonstrate financial need, scholastic excellence, and leadership potential.

Obtain application from Wisconsin League for Nursing, Inc., c/o Mary Ann Tanner, P.O. Box 107, Long Lake, WI 54542-0107. Specify that you are a high school senior.

NUTRITION

948

ABBIE SARGENT MEMORIAL SCHOLARSHIP INC. (Scholarships)
295 Sheep Davis Road
Concord, NH 03301
603/224-1934

AMOUNT: $200
DEADLINE(S): Mar 15
FIELD(S): Agriculture; Veterinary Medicine; Home Economics

Open to New Hampshire residents who are high school graduates with good grades and character. For undergraduate or graduate study. Must be legal resident of U.S. and demonstrate financial need.

Renewable with reapplication. Write for complete information.

949

ADELLE DAVIS FOUNDATION (Scholarships; Grants)
231 North Grand Ave.
Monrovia, CA 91016
818/445-8406

AMOUNT: Varies
DEADLINE(S): Ongoing
FIELD(S): Food Science; Nutrition

Graduate and undergraduate scholarships and research grants for the study of food science and nutrition.

Write to Stephen E. Thurman, Treasurer, at above address for application information.

950

AMERICAN ASSOCIATION OF CEREAL CHEMISTS (Undergraduate Scholarships and Graduate Fellowships)
Scholarship Dept.
3340 Pilot Knob Road
St. Paul, MN 55121
612/454-7250

AMOUNT: $1,000-$2,000 undergrad; $1,000-$3,000 grad
DEADLINE(S): Apr 1
FIELD(S): Food Science

Open to undergrads & grads majoring or interested in a career in cereal science or technology (incl. baking or related area) as evidenced by coursework or employment. Undergrads must have completed at least 1 quarter or semester of college/university work at time of application. Dept. head endorsement required. Fields such as culinary arts or dietetics not eligible.

AACC membership is helpful but not necessary. Strong academic record & career interest are important criteria. Write for complete information.

951

AMERICAN CULINARY FEDERATION, INC. (Ray and Gertrude Marshall Scholarship Fund)
10 San Bartola Drive
St. Augustine, FL 32086
904/824-4468; 904/824-4460; 800/624-9458; Fax 904/825-4758; E-mail: acf@aug.com; Internet: www.acfchefs.org/acf.html

AMOUNT: $500; $1,000

DEADLINE(S): Feb 15; Jun 15; Oct 15

FIELD(S): Culinary Arts

For junior members of the American Culinary Federation enrolled in post-secondary culinary arts programs and ACFEI apprenticeship programs. Must have been in a program for one complete grading period. The fee for a junior/apprentice membership is $40/year.

50 $500 awards and 1 $1,000 awards. For application send a #10 SASE to Debbie Moore at the above location.

952

AMERICAN DIETETIC ASSOCIATION (Dietetic Technician)
216 W. Jackson Blvd., Suite 800
Chicago, IL 60606
800/877-1600 Ext 4876

AMOUNT: $250-$1,000

DEADLINE(S): Jan 15 (Request application by then. Deadline is Feb 15)

FIELD(S): Dietetic Technician

Open to students in their first year of study in an ADA-approved dietetic technician program. If selected, student may use the scholarship for study during second year. Must be U.S. citizen and show evidence of leadership & academic ability.

Financial need, professional potential & scholarship are considerations. Write for complete information.

953

AMERICAN DIETETIC ASSOCIATION FOUNDATION (Baccalaureate or Coordinated Program)
216 W. Jackson Blvd., Suite 800
Chicago, IL 60606
800/877-1600 Ext 4876

AMOUNT: $250-$1,000

DEADLINE(S): Jan 15 (Request application by then. Deadline is Feb 13)

FIELD(S): Dietetics

Open to students who have completed the academic requirements in an ADA-accredited or approved college or university program for minimum standing as a junior. Must be U.S. citizen and show promise of value to the profession.

Financial need, professional potential & scholarship are considerations. Write for complete information.

954

AMERICAN DIETETIC ASSOCIATION FOUNDATION (Dietetic Internships)
216 West Jackson Blvd., Suite 800
Chicago, IL 60606
800/877-1600 Ext 4876

AMOUNT: $250-$2,500

DEADLINE(S): Jan 15 (Must request application by then. Deadline is Feb 15)

FIELD(S): Dietetics

Open to students who have applied to an ADA-accredited dietetic internship and who show promise of being a valuable contributing member to the profession. U.S. citizenship required

Financial need, professional potential & scholarship are considerations. Write for complete information.

955

AMERICAN DIETETIC ASSOCIATION FOUNDATION (Kraft General Foods Fellowship Program)
216 West Jackson, Suite 800
Chicago, IL 60606
312/899-0040

AMOUNT: $10,000 per year

DEADLINE(S): Jun 1

FIELD(S): Nutrition

Open to senior undergraduate & graduate students who propose to pursue graduate work related to nutrition research or nutrition education & consumer awareness at recognized institutions in the U.S. For citizens of U.S., Mexico & Canada.

Fellowships renewable for up to 3 years. Write for complete information.

956

AMERICAN DIETETIC ASSOCIATION FOUNDATION (Pre-professional Practice Program—AP4)
216 W. Jackson Blvd., Suite 800
Chicago, IL 60606
800/877-1600 Ext 4876

AMOUNT: $250-$2,500
DEADLINE(S): Jan 15 (Request application by then. Deadline is Feb 13)
FIELD(S): Dietetics

Open to students who are enrolled or have applied to an ADA-approved pre-professional practice program and who show promise of being a valuable contributing member of the profession. U.S. citizenship required.

Financial need, professional potential & scholarship are considerations. Write for complete information.

957

AMERICAN SOCIETY FOR HEALTHCARE FOOD SERVICE ADMINISTRATORS (Dorothy Killian Scholarship for Undergraduates)
One North Franklin, 31st Floor
Chicago, IL 60606
312/422-3870

AMOUNT: Part-time, $500; Full-time, $1,000
DEADLINE(S): Mar 1
FIELD(S): Healthcare Food Service Management

Open to undergraduate students at 2- or 4-year colleges.

Write to LeNora Rodriguez at the above address for complete information.

958

CARMEN'S SCHOLARSHIP COMMITTEE (Nellie Martin Carmen Scholarship)
23825 15th Ave. SE, #128
Bothell, WA 98021
206/486-6575

AMOUNT: Up to $1,000
DEADLINE(S): Mar 15
FIELD(S): All fields of study except those noted below

Open to high school seniors in King, Pierce, and Snohomish counties in the state of Washington. For undergraduate study in a Washington institution in all fields EXCEPT music, sculpture, drawing, interior design, and home economics. U.S. citizenship required.

Applications available only through high schools; nomination by counselor is required. 25-30 awards per year. Awards are renewable. Write for complete information.

959

EDUCATIONAL FOUNDATION OF NATIONAL RESTAURANT ASSOC. (Undergraduate Scholarship Program)
250 S. Wacker Drive, Suite 1400
Chicago, IL 60606
800-765-2122 Ext. 760; Fax 312/715-0807

AMOUNT: $1,000-$5,000
DEADLINE(S): Mar 1
FIELD(S): Food Service; Hospitality

Open to full-time undergrads in a food service/hospitality degree-granting program. Must have completed the first semester toward degree and worked in food service/hospitality industry for 1,000 hours.

Applications available starting Dec. 31.

960

GOLDEN GATE RESTAURANT ASSN. (David Rubenstein Memorial Scholarship Foundation Awards)
720 Market Street, Suite 200
San Francisco, CA 94102

415/781-5348

AMOUNT: $500-$2,500
DEADLINE(S): Mar 31
FIELD(S): Hotel & Restaurant
Management/Food Science

Open to students who have completed the
first semester of college as a food service
major and have a 2.75 or better GPA (4.0
scale) in hotel and restaurant courses.

7 awards per year. Write for complete information.

961

**HOTEL EMPLOYEES & RESTAURANT
EMPLOYEES INTERNATIONAL UNION
(Edward T. Hanley Scholarship)**
1219 28th Street NW
Washington, D.C. 20007
202/393-4373

AMOUNT: Tuition, fees, room & board; value
over $6,500 per year
DEADLINE(S): Apr 1
FIELD(S): Culinary Arts

Two-year scholarship to Culinary Institute of
America in NY. Open to HERE union
members (minimum 1 year) and candidates
recommended by union members.
Applications are by the vice presidential
district in which the member lives.

Residents of odd-numbered districts apply in
odd-numbered years; even-numbered districts in even years. Applications are published in Jan.; Feb. & March editions of
Catering Industry Employee. Write for complete information.

962

**ILLINOIS RESTAURANT ASSN.
(Scholarship Fund)**
200 N. LaSalle, Suite 880
Chicago, IL 60610-1014
312/787-4000

AMOUNT: Varies
DEADLINE(S): Jun 15

FIELD(S): Food Management; Food Science;
Culinary Arts; School-to-Work

Open to Illinois residents for undergraduate
study of food service management, culinary
arts, food processing and related subjects at
accredited institutions in the U.S.

Write for complete information.

963

**INSTITUTE OF FOOD TECHNOLOGISTS
(Freshman Scholarships)**
221 N. LaSalle Street
Chicago, IL 60601
312/782-8424; Fax 313/782-8348

AMOUNT: $750; $1,000
DEADLINE(S): Feb 15
FIELD(S): Food Science; Food Technology

Open to scholastically outstanding high school
graduates or seniors entering college for the
first time in an approved food science or
food technology program.

15 scholarships per year (1 at $1,000; 14 at
$750). Write for complete information.

964

**INSTITUTE OF FOOD TECHNOLOGISTS
(Junior/Senior Scholarships)**
221 N. LaSalle Street
Chicago, IL 60601
312/782-8424; Fax 312/782-8348

AMOUNT: $750-$2,000
DEADLINE(S): Feb 1
FIELD(S): Food Science; Food Technology

Open to undergraduate sophomores and
juniors pursuing an approved program in
food science/technology in a U.S. or
Canadian institution. Applicants should be
scholastically outstanding & have a well-
rounded personality.

For junior or senior year of study. 65
junior/senior awards per year (8 at $2,000; 3
at $1,500; 44 at $1,000 & 10 at $750). Write
for complete information.

965

INSTITUTE OF FOOD TECHNOLOGISTS (Sophomore Scholarships)
221 N. LaSalle Street
Chicago, IL 60601
312/782-8424; Fax 312/782-8348

AMOUNT: $750; $1,000
DEADLINE(S): Mar 1
FIELD(S): Food Science; Food Technology

Open to scholastically outstanding college freshmen who have a 2.5 or better grade-point average and are either pursuing or transferring to an approved program in food science/technology.

15 awards per year (1 at $1,000; 14 at $750). Write for complete information.

966

INTERNATIONAL ASSOCIATION OF CULINARY PROFESSIONALS FOUNDATION (Scholarships)
304 W. Liberty Street, Suite 201
Louisville, KY 40202-3068
502/587-7953; Fax 502/589-3602; E-mail: iacp@hqtrs.com

AMOUNT: Varies
DEADLINE(S): Dec 1
FIELD(S): Culinary Arts

Open to individuals 18 and older desiring an education to establish or further a career in the food industry. Awards are made on the basis of merit; ability and need. A non-refundable processing fee of $25 is required with application.

Write for complete information.

967

KAPPA OMICRON NU (Research/Project Grants)
4990 Northwind Drive, Suite 140
East Lansing, MI 48823
517/351-8335

AMOUNT: $500; $3,500

DEADLINE(S): Feb 15
FIELD(S): Home Economics and related fields

Open to Kappa Omicron Nu members who have demonstrated scholarship, research, and leadership potential. Awards are for home economics research at institutions having strong research programs.

2 grants. Write for complete information.

968

MONTGOMERY COUNTY ASSOCIATION FOR FAMILY + COMMUNITY EDUCATION (Mary Irene Waters Scholarship Fund)
13011 Margot Drive
Rockville, MD 20853
301/942-6086

AMOUNT: 2 at $1,000
DEADLINE(S): Mar 31
FIELD(S): Child Care

Open to graduates of Montgomery County, MD high schools or permanent Montgomery County residents.

Write for complete information.

969

SCHOOL FOOD SERVICE FOUNDATION (Scholarships)
1600 Duke Street, 7th Floor
Alexandria, VA 22314
703/739-3900; 800-877-8822

AMOUNT: Up to $1,000
DEADLINE(S): Apr 15
FIELD(S): Food Science & Nutrition; Food Service Management

Must be an ASFSA member and/or the child of an ASFSA member who plans to study in the above field(s). Must express a desire to make school food service a career & be pursuing an AA degree or higher for this undergraduate scholarship.

Must have satisfactory academic record. Write for complete information.

SCHOOL OF SOCIAL SCIENCE

970

ASSOCIATION OF FORMER INTELLIGENCE OFFICERS/AFIO (Lt. Gen. Eugene F. Tighe, Jr. Memorial Scholarship)
1142 Miramonte Glen
Escondido, CA 92026-1724
760/432-8844

AMOUNT: $1,000
DEADLINE(S): Jan 10
FIELD(S): Government; Political Science; Criminal Justice; Law

Open to undergraduate and graduate students. Students must have a 3.0 GPA and be full-time students. For use at all four-year and grad schools in the U.S. and affiliated institutions overseas.
Send SASE to the above address for complete information.

COMMUNICATIONS

971

AMERICAN INSTITUTE OF POLISH CULTURE (Scholarships)
1440 79th Street Causeway, Suite 117
Miami, FL 33141
305/864-2349; Fax 305/865-5150; E-mail: info@ampolinstitute.org; Internet: www.ampolinstitute.org

AMOUNT: $1,000
DEADLINE(S): Feb 15
FIELD(S): Journalism; Public Relations; Communications

Scholarships to encourage young Americans of Polish descent to pursue the above professions. Award can be used at any accredited American college. The ruling criteria for selection are achievement, talent, and involvement in public life.
$25 non-refundable application processing fee. For full-time study only. Renewable. Send self-addressed stamped envelope to Mrs.

Harriet Irsay at address above for complete information.

972

AMERICAN WOMEN IN RADIO & TELEVISION (Houston Internship Program)
Aprille Meek
AWRT—Houston
P.O. Box 980908
Houston, TX 77098
Written inquiry

AMOUNT: $500 per year
DEADLINE(S): Mar 1
FIELD(S): Radio; Television; Film & Video; Advertising; Marketing

Internships open to students who are juniors, seniors or graduate students at greater Houston area colleges & universities.
Write for complete information.

973

ASBURY PARK PRESS (Scholarship Program in the Media for Minority Students Who Are College Sophomores)
3601 Highway 66, Box 1550
Neptune, NJ 07754-1551
732/922-6000

AMOUNT: $2,000
DEADLINE(S): Mar 1
FIELD(S): Newspaper Career

Open to students entering their junior year of college with a demonstrated commitment to a newspaper career. Open only to African-Americans, Hispanic Americans, Asian-Americans, and Native Americans.
Write to the above address for complete information.

974

ASBURY PARK PRESS (Scholarship in the Media for Minority High School Graduating Seniors)
3601 Highway 66, Box 1550
Neptune, NJ 07754-1551
732/922-6000

AMOUNT: $2,000

DEADLINE(S): Apr (last Friday)

FIELD(S): Newspaper Career

Open to students living in either Monmouth or Ocean counties, New Jersey. Students must be high school seniors with demonstrated interest in a newspaper career. Applicants must be African-American, Hispanic American, Asian-American or Native American.

2 awards. Renewable for one year.

975

ASIAN AMERICAN JOURNALISTS ASSOCIATION (Scholarships/Grants)

1765 Sutter Street, Suite 1000
San Francisco, CA 94115-3125
415/346-2051 Ext. 300; Fax 415/346-6343; E-mail: aaja1@aol.com; Internet: www.aaja.org

AMOUNT: Up to $2,000

DEADLINE(S): Apr 15

FIELD(S): Photo, print, or broadcast journalism

Open to Asian-American students with a demonstrated ability and serious career interest in print, photo, or broadcast journalism. Awards based on scholastic achievement, commitment to journalism, demonstrated community involvement in the Asian-American community, and financial need. Internships grants are also available.

For undergraduate or graduate study. High school seniors may apply. Many local chapters operate their own scholarship or internship programs. Send SASE to above address for application. Visit website for more information.

976

ASSOCIATED PRESS TELEVISION-RADIO ASSOCIATION OF CALIFORNIA/NEVADA (APTRA—Clete Roberts Memorial Journalism Scholarship Awards)

Rachel Ambrose, Associated Press
221 S. Figueroa Street, #300
Los Angeles, CA 90012
213/626-1200

AMOUNT: $1,500

DEADLINE(S): Dec 12

FIELD(S): Broadcast Journalism

Open to students with a broadcast journalism career objective who are studying in California or Nevada. For undergraduate or graduate study.

3 awards. Must complete entry form and may submit examples of broadcast-related work. Write for complete information.

977

ASSOCIATION FOR EDUCATION IN JOURNALISM & MASS COMMUNICATION (Mary A. Gardner Scholarship)

LeConte College, Room 121
Columbia, SC 29208-0251
803/777-2005

AMOUNT: Up to $500

DEADLINE(S): Apr 15

FIELD(S): Journalism; Mass Communication

Open to full-time incoming juniors or seniors in a college journalism and mass communication program and have at least a 3.0 GPA (4.0 scale).

Send a self-addressed stamped envelope for complete information.

978

ASSOCIATION FOR EDUCATION IN JOURNALISM AND MASS COMMUNICATIONS (Summer Journalism Internship for Minorities)
NYU Institute of Afro-American Affairs
269 Mercer, Suite 601
New York, NY 10003
212/998-2130

AMOUNT: Salary of at least $200 per week
DEADLINE(S): Nov 3 (Application request due then. Application deadline is Dec 15)
FIELD(S): Journalism; Mass Communications; Advertising; Public Relations; Photojournalism; Broadcasting

Open to members of ethnic minorities whose credentials reflect an interest in and commitment to journalism. Interns will be placed for 10 weeks in an entry-level position with participating companies, primarily in the NY/NJ area.
Write for complete information.

979

ATLANTA ASSOCIATION OF MEDIA WOMEN (Scholarship)
Chair Scholarship Committee
P.O. Box 4132
Atlanta, GA 30302
Written inquiry

AMOUNT: $500-$1,000
DEADLINE(S): Mar 15
FIELD(S): Journalism; Communications

Open to African-American women residing in Georgia who are pursuing an undergraduate degree in journalism or communications in a Georgia institution. Must have the desire and intention to pursue a career in journalism or communications.
Financial need considered but not a determining factor. Write for complete information.

980

ATLANTA JOURNAL AND CONSTITUTION (Cox Minority Scholarship Program)
72 Marrietta Street
Atlanta, GA 30303
404/526-5120

AMOUNT: Full four-year tuition
DEADLINE(S): Apr 1
FIELD(S): Newspaper Business; Journalism

Open to undergraduate students who live in the Metro Atlanta, GA area and plan to attend a Georgia university. Students must be U.S. citizens, have a 3.0 GPA, and be a member of a minority group. Students must be interested in the newspaper business.
Write to the above address for complete information.

981

BALL STATE UNIVERSITY (David Letterman Telecommunications Scholarship Program)
Dept. of Telecommunications
Muncie, IN 47306
317/285-1480

AMOUNT: Full tuition (1st); 1/2 tuition (2nd); 1/3 tuition (3rd)
DEADLINE(S): Apr 1
FIELD(S): Telecommunications

Open to undergraduate juniors at Ball State who have demonstrated reasonable expectations of becoming professionals in the telecommunications industry. Scholarships are based on creativity; grades are NOT considered.
Any creative effort connected with the telecommunications field will be considered. Write for complete information.

982

BROADCAST EDUCATION ASSOCIATION (Scholarships in Broadcasting)
1771 N Street NW
Washington, D.C. 20036-2891
202/429-5354; Internet: www.beaweb.org

AMOUNT: $1,250-$5,000
DEADLINE(S): Jan 15
FIELD(S): Broadcasting

Scholarships are awarded for one scholastic year of degree work at the junior, senior, or graduate level. Applicants must show evidence of superior academic performance and potential. Applications will not be sent out after December 16.

Scholarship winners must study at a campus where at least one department is a BEA institutional member. Write for complete information.

983

CENTRAL NEWSPAPERS INC. (Pulliam Journalism Fellowships)
Russell B. Pulliam, Editor
The Indianapolis News
P.O. Box 145
Indianapolis, IN 46206-0145
317/633-9121

AMOUNT: $5,000 stipend
DEADLINE(S): Mar 1 (postmark)
FIELD(S): Journalism

Open to recent graduates & to undergraduate seniors who will receive their bachelor's degree between August and June preceding fellowship. Award is for a 10-week work and study internship at one of CNI's newspapers in Indianapolis or Phoenix.

Includes sessions with a writing coach and seminars with local & national journalists. 20 awards per year. Contact Mr. Russ Pulliam, editor, for complete information.

984

COX NEWSPAPERS, INC. (Cox Minority Journalism Scholarship)
P.O. Box 105720
Atlanta, GA 30348
404/843-7904; Fax 404/843-5000

AMOUNT: Varies
DEADLINE(S): Apr 30
FIELD(S): Journalism and related fields

Each year a Cox-owned newspaper is chosen to administer the program; applicant must plan to attend college within that newspaper's circulation area. For high school seniors who are African-American, Native American, Asian, or Latino and a U.S. citizen. Must be pursuing a career in the newspaper industry.

Contact your senior guidance office in February for information and application for the upcoming school year. The 1998 scholarship has been award to the Atlanta Journal-Constitution, 72 Marietta Street N.W., Atlanta, GA 30303. Contact: Mr. Booker Izell.

985

DAYTON FOUNDATION (Larry Fullerton Photojournalism Scholarship)
2100 Kettering Tower
Dayton, OH 45423
513/222-0410

AMOUNT: Varies
DEADLINE(S): Jan 31
FIELD(S): Photojournalism

Open to Ohio residents who are full-time undergrad students at an Ohio college, junior college, or school with a structured curriculum & who plan to pursue a photojournalism career. Financial need & personal circumstances are considered.

Portfolio must be submitted following guidelines established by Ohio News Photographers Association. Contact the journalism/photojournalism department at your college for an application.

986

DOW JONES NEWSPAPER FUND INC.
(Business Reporting Intern Program for
Minority Sophomores and Juniors)
P.O. Box 300
Princeton, NJ 08543
609/452-2820; 800/DOWFUND; E-mail:
dowfund@wsj.dowjones.com; Internet:
www.dowjones.com/dowfund

AMOUNT: $1,000 + paid summer internship
DEADLINE(S): Nov 15
FIELD(S): Journalism; Business Reporting;
Editing.

Summer internships for college sophomores
and juniors whose ethnic backgrounds are
African-American, Hispanic, Asian, Native
American/Eskimo, or Pacific Islanders who
will work at daily newspapers as business
reporters. Must demonstrate interest in a
similar career. Interns are paid and will
attend a two-week training program.
Students returning to full-time studies will
receive $1,000 scholarships.

Journalism major not required. Up to 12
awards per year. Applications available
from Aug. 15 to Nov. 1. Contact above location for complete information.

987

DOW JONES NEWSPAPER FUND INC.
(Newspaper Editing Intern/Scholarship
Program for College Juniors, Seniors, and
Graduate Students)
P.O. Box 300
Princeton, NJ 08543
609/452-2820; 800/DOWFUND; E-mail:
dowfund@wsj.dowjones.com; Internet:
www.dowjones.com/dowfund

AMOUNT: $1,000 + paid summer internship
DEADLINE(S): Nov 15
FIELD(S): Journalism; Editing

Summer internships for college juniors,
seniors, and graduate students to work as
copy editors at daily newspapers. Must
demonstrate a commitment to a career in
journalism. Interns are paid by the newspa-

pers for which they work and attend a two-
week training program paid for by the
Newspaper Fund. Those returning to full-
time studies will receive a $1,000 scholar-
ship.

Journalism major not required. Up to 80
awards per year. Applications available
from Aug. 15 to Nov. 1. Contact above location for complete information.

988

DOW JONES NEWSPAPER FUND INC.
(On-line Newspaper Editing
Intern/Scholarship Program)
P.O. Box 300
Princeton, NJ 08543
609/452-2820; 800/DOWFUND; E-mail:
dowfund@wsj.dowjones.com; Internet:
www.dowjones.com/dowfund

AMOUNT: $1,000 + summer internship
DEADLINE(S): Nov 15
FIELD(S): Journalism; Online Editing

Summer internships for college juniors,
seniors, and graduate students to work as
editors for on-line newspapers. Must
demonstrate a commitment to a career in
journalism. Interns are paid by the newspapers for which they work and attend a two-
week training program paid for by the
Newspaper Fund. Those returning to full-
time studies will receive a $1,000 scholar-
ship.

Journalism major not required. Up to 12
awards per year. Applications available
from Aug. 15 to Nov. 1. Contact above location for complete information.

989

DOW JONES NEWSPAPER FUND INC.
(Real-Time Financial News Service
Intern/Scholarship Program)
P.O. Box 300
Princeton, NJ 08543
609/452-2820; 800/DOWFUND; E-mail:
dowfund@wsj.dowjones.com; Internet:
www.dowjones.com/dowfund

AMOUNT: $1,000 + paid summer internship

DEADLINE(S): Nov 15

FIELD(S): Journalism; Financial Journalism; Editing

Summer internship for college juniors, seniors, and graduate students to work as editors and reporters for real-time financial news services. Must demonstrate a commitment to a similar career. Interns are paid by the news service for which they work and will attend a two-week training program paid for by the Newspaper Fund. Students returning to full-time studies will receive a $1,000 scholarship.

Journalism major not required. Up to 12 awards per year. Applications available from Aug. 15 to Nov. 1. Contact above location for complete information.

990

DOW JONES NEWSPAPER FUND INC. (Summer Workshops in Journalism for Minority High School Students)
P.O. Box 300
Princeton, NJ 08543-0300
609/452-2820; 800/DOWFUND; E-mail: dowfund@wsj.dowjones.com; Internet: www.dowjones.com/dowfund

AMOUNT: $1,000 + paid summer internship

DEADLINE(S): Nov 15

FIELD(S): Journalism

Offered at 35+ colleges around the U.S. for high school students interested in journalism and whose ethnic backgrounds are African-American, Pacific Islander, American Indian/Eskimo, Asian, or Hispanic. Ten days of learning to write, report, design, and lay out a newspaper (free). The eight best writers throughout the U.S. of an article relevant to youth will receive a $1,000 scholarship.

Contact the address above for details on which colleges/states are participating.

991

GEORGIA PRESS EDUCATIONAL FOUNDATION, INC. (Scholarship)
3066 Mercer University Drive, Suite 200
Atlanta, GA 30341-4137
770/454-6778; Fax 770/454-6778

AMOUNT: Varies

DEADLINE(S): Feb 1

FIELD(S): Print Journalism

Open to Georgia residents who are undergraduate and graduate students attending or plan to attend a school in Georgia. This scholarship is renewable by re-application.

Contact Scholarship Coordinator at above address for complete information.

992

INSTITUTE FOR HUMANE STUDIES (Felix Morley Journalism Competition)
George Mason University
4084 University Drive, Suite 101
Fairfax, VA 22030-6812
Internet: mason.gmu.edu/~ihs/morley.html

AMOUNT: $2,500 (first prize)

DEADLINE(S): Dec

FIELD(S): Journalism; Writing

This competition awards cash prizes to outstanding young writers whose work demonstrates an appreciation of classical liberal principles (i.e., individual rights; their protection through private property, contract, and laws; voluntarism; and the self-ordering market, free trade, free migration, and peace). Must be full-time students or be 25 or younger.

Three to five published items (in English) must be submitted with entry form, i.e., editorials, op-eds, articles, essays, and reviews. Last year's 1st, 2nd, & 3rd place winners not eligible this year. IHS reserves the right not to award a prize.

993

**INTERNATIONAL RADIO &
TELEVISION SOCIETY FOUNDATION
(IRTS Summer Fellowship Program)**
Ms. Maria De Leon
420 Lexington Ave., Suite 1714
New York, NY 10170
212/867-6650

AMOUNT: Housing, stipend, and travel
DEADLINE(S): Nov 21
FIELD(S): Broadcasting; Communications;
Sales; Marketing

Annual 9-week summer fellowship program in
New York City open to outstanding full-
time undergraduate juniors and seniors with
a demonstrated interest in a career in communications.
Write for complete information.

994

**IOWA BROADCASTERS ASSOCIATION
(Broadcast Scholarship)**
P.O. Box 71186
Des Moines, IA 50325
515/224-7237

AMOUNT: $2,500
DEADLINE(S): Apr 15
FIELD(S): Broadcasting

Open to Iowa high school seniors planning to
attend an Iowa college or university in the
fall after graduation. Applicant must be
Iowa resident and interested in studying
broadcasting. This scholarship is renewable.
Write to the above address for complete information.

995

**JOHN BAYLISS BROADCAST
FOUNDATION (Scholarship)**
P.O. Box 221070
Carmel, CA 93922
408/624-1536

AMOUNT: $2,500

DEADLINE(S): Apr 30
FIELD(S): Radio Broadcasting

Open to undergrads in their junior or senior
year and to graduate students who aspire to
a career in radio. Applicants should have a
3.0 or better GPA. Financial need is a consideration. U.S. citizen or legal resident.
Enclose a self-addressed stamped envelope for
more information. Transcript must be sent
with completed application.

996

**JOHN M. WILL JOURNALISM
SCHOLARSHIP FOUNDATION
(Scholarship)**
P.O. Box 290
Mobile, AL 36601
334/405-1300

AMOUNT: $2,000-$3,500 (varies)
DEADLINE(S): Mar; Apr
FIELD(S): Journalism

Open to full-time students majoring in journalism who are residents of the Alabama
counties of Mobile, Baldwin, Escambia,
Clarke, Conecuhu, Washington, or Monroe;
the Florida counties of Santa Rosa or
Escambia; or the Mississippi counties of
Jackson or George.
Also open to persons currently employed in
journalism who want to take journalism-
related training as a full-time student at an
accredited college. Write for complete
information.

997

JUST FOUNDATION
5844 Heather Ridge
Gurnee, IL 60031
847/680-7002

AMOUNT: Up to $4,000/year
DEADLINE(S): Mar 1
FIELD(S): Newspaper Business; Broadcasting
Scholarships to high school graduates interest-
ed in a career in the newspaper field or
broadcasting.

Communications

Candidates must rank in the upper half of the classes, establish clear financial need, and be outstanding in character and promise. Write to Richard F. Kennedy at above address for details.

998

KCPQ TELEVISION (KCPQ/Ewing C. Kelly Scholarship)
1813 Westlake Ave. No.
Seattle, WA 98109-2706
206/674-1777; Fax 206/674-1777; Internet: www.kcpq.com

AMOUNT: $2,000
DEADLINE(S): Feb 14
FIELD(S): All fields of study

Open to high school seniors who reside in Western Washington, specifically the KCPQ-TV viewing area (Seattle-Tacoma generally). Must have earned a composite score of at least 20 on the ACT or 840 on the SAT.

For application, see your high school counselor or principal.

999

KNTV TELEVISION (Minority Scholarship)
645 Park Ave.
San Jose, CA 95110
408/286-1111

AMOUNT: 2 at $1,000 each
DEADLINE(S): Apr 1
FIELD(S): Television Broadcasting

Open to Black, Hispanic, Asian/Pacific Islander, or American Indian students who are residents of Santa Clara, Santa Cruz, Monterey, or San Benito counties (Calif.) and attend or plan to attend an accredited four-year institution in California.

Must enroll in at least 12 semester units each semester. Considerations include interest in TV, financial need, community involvement, academics, and career aspirations. Write for complete information.

1000

LOS ANGELES CHAPTER OF SOCIETY OF PROFESSIONAL JOURNALISTS (Bill Farr Scholarship)
Linda Seebach
LA Daily News
P.O. Box 4200
Woodland Hills, CA 91365
818/713-3645; Fax 818/713-3723

AMOUNT: $1,000
DEADLINE(S): Nov 30 (postmark)
FIELD(S): Journalism (overall excellence)

Open to college juniors, seniors or graduate students who are residents of the area covered by the chapter (Los Angeles; Orange; Ventura counties) and who are preparing for a career in journalism.

Applications available after Sep 1. Write for complete information.

1001

LOS ANGELES CHAPTER OF SOCIETY OF PROFESSIONAL JOURNALISTS (Helen Johnson Scholarship)
Linda Seebach
LA Daily News
P.O. Box 4200
Woodland Hills, CA 91365
818/713-3645; Fax 818/713-3723

AMOUNT: $1,000
DEADLINE(S): Nov 30 (postmark)
FIELD(S): News Broadcasting—Radio or Television

Open to college juniors, seniors or graduate students who attend schools in the area covered by the chapter (Los Angeles; Ventura; Orange counties) and are preparing for a career in news broadcasting.

Applications available after Sep 1. Write for complete information.

1002

LOS ANGELES CHAPTER OF SOCIETY OF PROFESSIONAL JOURNALISTS (Ken Inouye Scholarship)
Linda Seebach
LA Daily News
P.O. Box 4200
Woodland Hills, CA 91365
818/713-3645; Fax 818/713-3723

AMOUNT: $1,000
DEADLINE(S): Nov 30 (postmark)
FIELD(S): Journalism (overall excellence)

Open to ethnic minority students who will be a junior, senior or graduate student the following year. Must reside or attend school in Los Angeles, Orange or Ventura county and be preparing for a career in journalism.
Applications available after Sep 1. Write for complete information.

1003

LOS ANGELES CHAPTER OF SOCIETY OF PROFESSIONAL JOURNALISTS (Carl Greenburg Prize)
Linda Seebach
LA Daily News
P.O. Box 4200
Woodland Hills, CA 91365
818/713-3645; Fax 818/713-3723

AMOUNT: $1,000
DEADLINE(S): Nov 30 (postmark)
FIELD(S): Journalism—Political or Investigative Reporting

Open to college juniors; seniors or graduate students who attend school in the area covered by the chapter (Los Angeles, Orange, Ventura counties) and are preparing for a career in journalism.
Applications available after Sep 1. Write for complete information.

1004

MARIO MACHADO (American Honda/Mario J. Machado Scholarship)
5750 Briarcliff Road
Los Angeles, CA 90068
213/460-4336; Fax 213/460-4685

AMOUNT: $1,000
DEADLINE(S): Varies
FIELD(S): Communications; Journalism

For high school seniors who attend schools in Los Angeles or Orange county and who plan to pursue a career in communications and/or journalism. For students who would not be able to attend college without it.
12 awards per year. Must demonstrate financial need. Write to the above address for complete information.

1005

MEXICAN AMERICAN WOMEN'S NATIONAL ASSOCIATION (MANA) (Rita DiMartino Scholarship in Communication)
1725 K Street NW, Suite 105
Washington, D.C. 20006
202/833-0060; Fax 202/496-0588; E-mail: HerMANA2@aol.com

AMOUNT: Varies
DEADLINE(S): Apr 1
FIELD(S): Communications

For Hispanic female students enrolled in undergraduate or graduate programs in communication at accredited colleges or universities. Must demonstrate financial need and academic achievement. Must be MANA member. There is a $10 application fee.
Send self-addressed stamped envelope for application for membership and scholarship.

1006

MIAMI INTERNATIONAL PRESS CLUB (Scholarship Program)
c/o Laura Englebright
625 Candia Ave.
Florida Gables, FL 33134
305/444-0345

AMOUNT: $500
DEADLINE(S): Jun 15
FIELD(S): Journalism; Broadcasting

South Florida residents who are deserving high school seniors are eligible for scholarships for undergraduate study at any accredited college or university in the above fields.

Scholarships are renewable. Write for complete information or call the club's scholarship chair at the number above.

1007

NATIONAL ASSN. OF HISPANIC JOURNALISTS (NAHJ Scholarship Program)
National Press Building, Suite 1193
Washington, D.C. 20045
202/622-7145

AMOUNT: $1,000-$2,000
DEADLINE(S): Jan 31
FIELD(S): Print or Broadcast Journalism; Photojournalism

Open to high school seniors, undergraduate & graduate students who are committed to a career in print or broadcast journalism or photojournalism. It is NOT required to be of Hispanic ancestry.

Awards tenable at accredited 2-year or 4-year schools in the U.S. & its territories. Send a self-addressed stamped envelope and a letter of request for information.

1008

NATIONAL ASSN. OF HISPANIC JOURNALISTS (Newhouse Scholarship Program)
National Press Building, Suite 1193
Washington, D.C. 20045
202/622-7145

AMOUNT: $5,000
DEADLINE(S): Jan 31
FIELD(S): Print or Broadcast Journalism; photojournalism

Open to undergrad juniors & seniors and grad students who are committed to pursuing a career in print or broadcast journalism or photojournalism. It is not necessary to be a journalism or broadcast major, nor is Hispanic ancestry required.

Awards tenable at accredited institutions in the U.S. & its territories. Write for complete information.

1009

NATIONAL ASSOCIATION OF BLACK JOURNALISTS (NABJ Scholarship Program)
11600 Sunrise Valley Drive
Reston, VA 22091
703/648-1270

AMOUNT: $2,500
DEADLINE(S): Mar 31
FIELD(S): Journalism

Open to African-American undergraduate or graduate students who are accepted to or enrolled in an accredited journalism program majoring in print, photo, radio or television. GPA of 2.5 or better (4.0 scale) is required.

12 awards per year. Write for complete information.

1010

NATIONAL ASSOCIATION OF GOVERNMENT COMMUNICATORS (Thomas Jefferson Scholarship)
669 S. Washington Street
Alexandria, VA 22314
703/519-3902; Fax 703/519-7732

AMOUNT: $1,000
DEADLINE(S): May 31
FIELD(S): Government Communications; Public Sector Communications

Open to members of NAGC who are continuing their education full- or part-time and have an income of less than $35,000 and who plan careers in public sector communications. Money is to pay for tuition and will be sent to the school. GPA of 3.0 or better (4.0 scale) is required.

Write a 500-word essay on "How to Improve Government Communications with the Public for the 21st Century." Submit by May 31.

1011

NATIONAL ASSOCIATION OF GOVERNMENT COMMUNICATORS (The Thomas Paine Scholarship)

669 South Washington Street
Alexandria, VA 22314
703/519-3902; Fax 703/519-7732

AMOUNT: $1,000
DEADLINE(S): May 31
FIELD(S): Government Communications; Public Sector Communications

For college sophomores or above majoring in communications (public relations, marketing, graphic arts, journalism, public affairs, etc.). Some preference will be given to children or families of NAGC members. GPA must be 3.0 or above.

Write a 500-word essay on "How to Improve Government Communications with the Public for the 21st Century."

1012

NATIONAL ASSOCIATION OF WATER COMPANIES—NEW JERSEY CHAPTER (Scholarship)

Elizabethtown Water Co.
600 South Ave.
Westfield, NJ 07090
908/654-1234; Fax 908/232-2719

AMOUNT: $2,500
DEADLINE(S): Apr 1
FIELD(S): Business Administration; Biology; Chemistry; Engineering; Communications

For U.S. citizens who have lived in NJ at least 5 years and plan a career in the investor-owned water utility industry in disciplines such as those above. Must be undergrad or graduate student in a 2- or 4-year NJ college or university.

GPA of 3.0 or better required. Contact Gail P. Brady for complete information.

1013

NATIONAL BROADCASTING SOCIETY (Alpha Epsilon Rho Scholarships)

P.O. Box 1058
St. Charles, MO 63302-1058
888/NBS-1-COM Ext. 2000

AMOUNT: $500-$1,000
DEADLINE(S): Jan 1
FIELD(S): Broadcasting

Open only to active student members of NBS-AERho as nominated by local chapters.

Awards are renewable. Contact local NBS-AERho chapter for complete information.

1014

NATIONAL FEDERATION OF PRESS WOMEN INC. (Helen M. Malloch Scholarship)

4510 W. 89th Street, Suite 110
Prairie Village, KS 66207-2282
913/341-0165

AMOUNT: $1,000
DEADLINE(S): May 1
FIELD(S): Journalism

Open to women who are undergraduate juniors/seniors or grad students majoring in journalism at a college or university of the student's choice.

Send SASE for complete information.

1015

NATIONAL FEDERATION OF PRESS WOMEN INC. (Professional Education Scholarship)

4510 W. 89th Street, Suite 110
Prairie Village, KS 66207-2282
913/341-0165

AMOUNT: $1,000
DEADLINE(S): May 1
FIELD(S): Journalism

For members of the National Federation of Press Women who want to continue or return to college as a journalism major. Financial need is a consideration but is not paramount.
Send SASE for complete information.

1016

NATIONAL ITALIAN AMERICAN FOUNDATION (Communications Scholarship)
Dr. M. Lombardo
Education Director
1860 19th Street NW
Washington, D.C. 20009-5599
202/387-0600

AMOUNT: $5,000
DEADLINE(S): May 30
FIELD(S): Communications; Journalism

Open to students of Italian heritage enrolled in or entering college as journalism and communication majors. Must submit an essay (not to exceed 1,000 words) describing how to 'Preserve the Italian Language and Culture in the U.S.'
Write for complete information.

1017

NATIONAL ITALIAN AMERICAN FOUNDATION (Ingoglia Family Scholarships)
1860 19th Street NW
Washington, D.C. 20009-5599
202/530-5315

AMOUNT: $1,000
DEADLINE(S): May 31
FIELD(S): Journalism; Media

For graduate and undergraduate students of Italian ancestry majoring in journalism and/or media.
Financial need, academic merit, and community service are considered.

1018

NATIONAL RIGHT TO WORK COMMITTEE (William B. Ruggles Journalism Scholarship)
8001 Braddock Road, Suite 500
Springfield, VA 22160
703/321-9820

AMOUNT: $2,000
DEADLINE(S): Mar 31
FIELD(S): Journalism

Scholarships are open to undergraduate and graduate students majoring in journalism at accredited U.S. institutions of higher learning who exemplify the dedication to principle & high journalistic standards of the late William B. Ruggles.
Write for complete information.

1019

NEW YORK FINANCIAL WRITERS' ASSOCIATION (Scholarship Program)
P.O. Box 20281, Greeley Square Station
New York, NY 10001-0003
800/533-7551

AMOUNT: $3,000
DEADLINE(S): Mar
FIELD(S): Financial Journalism

Open to undergraduate and graduate students enrolled in an accredited college or university in metropolitan New York City and are pursuing a course of study leading to a financial or business journalism career.
Write for complete information.

1020

NEW YORK UNIVERSITY (Gallatin Division Special Awards & Scholarships)
715 Broadway, 6th Floor
New York, NY 10003
212/598-7077

AMOUNT: Varies with award
DEADLINE(S): None specified
FIELD(S): Publishing

Various special awards and scholarships are available to undergraduate and graduate students enrolled in the Gallatin Division of New York University.

104 special awards and scholarships per year. Contact address above for complete information.

1021

ORGANIZATION OF CHINESE AMERICANS (Journalist Award)
 1001 Connecticut Ave. NW, Suite 707
 Washington, D.C. 20036
 202/223-5500; Fax 202/296-0540; E-mail: oca@ari.net; Internet: www2.ari.net/oca/html/awards.html

AMOUNT: $500 (1st prize); $300 (2nd); $200 (3rd)
DEADLINE(S): May 1
FIELD(S): Journalism

Given to the journalist with the most enlightening article or series of articles concerning Chinese-Americans and/or Asian-Americans in English or Chinese. Judged on flow of article, completeness/coverage, accuracy, thoroughness, sensitivity, and depth of understanding of issues concerning Asian-Americans.

Five copies of a résumé and copies of one or two articles should be sent to the above address.

1022

OUTDOOR WRITERS ASSOCIATION OF AMERICA (Bodie McDowell Scholarship Program)
 2017 Cato Ave., Suite 101
 State College, PA 16801-2768
 814/234-1011

AMOUNT: $2,000-$3,000
DEADLINE(S): Varies (Fall)
FIELD(S): Outdoor Communications/ Journalism

This scholarship is open to students interested in writing about outdoor activities, not including organized sports (i.e., hiking, backpacking, climbing, etc.). Availability varies with school participation.

Write to the above address for complete information.

1023

PENNSYLVANIA WOMEN'S PRESS ASSOCIATION (Scholarship)
 P.O. Box 152
 Sharpsville, PA 16150
 Written inquiry; Internet: www.regiononline.com/~pwpa/

AMOUNT: At least $750
DEADLINE(S): Apr 20
FIELD(S): Print Journalism

Scholarship for Pennsylvania residents majoring in print journalism in a four-year or graduate-level program in a Pennsylvania college or university. Must be a junior, senior, or graduate. Selection based on proven journalistic ability, dedication to journalism, and general merit.

Write a 500-word essay summarizing your interest in journalism, your career plans, and any other information on why you should receive this scholarship. You may include a statement of financial need. Send transcript copy, clippings of published work (photocopies ok), and list of your brothers and sisters, their ages and educational status. Send to Teresa Spatara at above address.

1024

PEORIA JOURNAL STAR (Scholarship Program)
 1 News Plaza
 Peoria, IL 61643
 309/686-3027

AMOUNT: $1,000 per year for 4 years
DEADLINE(S): May 1
FIELD(S): Newspaper Journalism

Open to high school seniors who reside in Bureau, Fulton, Henderson, Knox, LaSalle,

Marshall-Putnam, Mason, McDonough, Peoria, Schuyler, Stark, Tazewell, Warren or Woodford counties in Illinois.

Scholarship renewable annually for four years. Write for complete information.

1025

QUILL & SCROLL (Edward J. Nell Memorial Scholarship)

University of Iowa School of Journalism & Mass Communication
Iowa City, IA 52242-1528
319/335-5795

AMOUNT: $500
DEADLINE(S): May 10
FIELD(S): Journalism

Open to high school seniors who are winners in the national writing/photo or yearbook excellence contest sponsored by Quill & Scroll and who plan to enroll in an accredited journalism program. Must be U.S. citizen or legal resident.

Candidates should ask journalism teacher to write to address above for information on administration of the contest.

1026

RADIO AND TELEVISION NEWS DIRECTORS FOUNDATION (Electronic Journalism Scholarship Awards)

1000 Connecticut Ave. NW, Suite 615
Washington, D.C. 20036-5302
202/659-6510 Ext. 206; Fax 202/223-4007; E-mail: michellet@rtndf.org; Internet: www.rtndf.org

AMOUNT: $1,000; $2,000; $5,000
DEADLINE(S): Mar 2
FIELD(S): Radio/Television Journalism

Open to undergraduate sophomores and above and master's degree candidates whose career objective is electronic journalism. Awards are for one year of undergraduate or graduate study.

14 scholarships and 6 fellowships per year. Not renewable. Write for complete information.

1027

RADIO AND TELEVISION NEWS DIRECTORS FOUNDATION (Fellowships)

1000 Connecticut Ave. NW, Suite 615
Washington, D.C. 20036-5302
202/659-6510 Ext. 206; Fax 202/223-4007; E-mail: michellet@rtndf.org; Internet: www.rtndf.org

AMOUNT: $1,000; $2,000
DEADLINE(S): Mar 2
FIELD(S): Broadcast Journalism

Awards for young journalists in radio or television with 10 years or less experience.

6 awards. Send to above address for details.

1028

RADIO AND TELEVISION NEWS DIRECTORS FOUNDATION (Journalism and Communications Awards)

100 Connecticut Ave. NW, Suite 615
Washington, D.C. 20036-5302
202/467-5212; Fax 202/223-4007; E-mail: gwen@RTNDF.org; Internet: www.RTNDF.org/RTNDF/

AMOUNT: $1,000-$5,000
DEADLINE(S): Mar 1
FIELD(S): Journalism; Communications

For sophomores, juniors, and seniors studying journalism and/or communications.

21 annual awards.

1029

RADIO AND TELEVISION NEWS DIRECTORS FOUNDATION (Minority News Management Internships)

1000 Connecticut Ave. NW, Suite 615
Washington, D.C. 20036-5302
202/659-6510 Ext. 206; Fax 202/223-4007; E-mail: michellet@rtndf.org; Internet: www.rtndf.org

AMOUNT: $1,000/mo. for three months *or* $1,300/mo. for six months
DEADLINE(S): Mar 2

FIELD(S): Radio/Television Journalism—
News Management

For college juniors or more advance undergraduates or graduate minority students
whose career objective is news management
in radio/television. Three three-month, full-
time internships and three six-month internships (recent graduates only) for minorities
(African-American, Asian-American,
Hispanic, or Native American).

Applicants must be willing to relocate. Send
for application information.

1030

SCRIPPS HOWARD FOUNDATION
(Lighthouse Scholarship)
312 Walnut Street, 28th Floor
Cincinnati, OH 45201-5380
513/977-3035; E-mail:
cottingham@scripps.com; Internet:
www.scripps.com/foundation

AMOUNT: $15,000 for 2 years
DEADLINE(S): Feb 25
FIELD(S): Journalism

Scholarships are available to full-time students
who are college juniors attending 4-year
colleges to prepare for careers in journalism. U.S. citizenship required.

Apply to above location for complete information.

1031

SOCIETY FOR TECHNICAL
COMMUNICATION (Undergraduate
Scholarships)
901 N. Stuart Street, Suite 904
Arlington, VA 22203
703/522-4114

AMOUNT: $2,000
DEADLINE(S): Feb 15
FIELD(S): Technical Communication

Open to full-time undergraduate students who
have completed at least 1 year of study &
are enrolled in an accredited 2-year or 4-
year degree program for career in any area
of technical communication.

Awards tenable at recognized colleges & universities in U.S. & Canada. 7 awards per
year. Write for complete information.

1032

SOCIETY OF BROADCAST ENGINEERS
(Harold Ennes Scholarship Fund)
8445 Keystone Crossing, Suite 140
Indianapolis, IN 46240-2454
317/253-1640

AMOUNT: $1,000
DEADLINE(S): Jul 1
FIELD(S): Broadcasting

Open to undergraduate students interested in
a career in broadcasting. Two references
from SBE members are needed to confirm
eligibility. Submit a statement of purpose
and a brief biography.

Send self-addressed stamped envelope for
application and complete information.

1033

SONOMA COUNTY PRESS CLUB
(Scholarship)
P.O. Box 4692
Santa Rosa, CA 95402
Written inquiry

AMOUNT: $1,000
DEADLINE(S): Apr 10
FIELD(S): Journalism

Open to Sonoma County (CA) high school
seniors or graduates or students attending
either Santa Rosa Junior College or
Sonoma State University.

Write for complete information.

1034

SPORTS JOURNALISM INSTITUTE
(Scholarships/Internships)
Sports Illustrated
1271 Avenue of the Americas
New York, NY 10020-1393
212/522-6407; Fax 212/522-4543; E-mail:
sandrite@aol.com

AMOUNT: $500 for 6-week internship

DEADLINE(S): Jan (date varies yearly)

FIELD(S): Print Journalism with sports emphasis

Ten six-week scholarships for college juniors to support internships in sports journalism. Women and minorities are especially encouraged to apply.

Contact Sandy Baily at above location for details.

1035

THE ATLANTA PRESS CLUB, INC. (Atlanta Press Club Journalism)
260 14th Street NW, Suite 300
Atlanta, GA 30318
404/577-7377

AMOUNT: $1,000

DEADLINE(S): Varies

FIELD(S): Journalism: print, broadcast, radio

Applicants must be enrolled in an accredited journalism or communications degree program at a Georgia college or university and be interested in pursuing careers in journalism.

4 awards given per year. Write to the above address for complete information.

1036

THE FUND FOR AMERICAN STUDIES (Institutes on Political Journalism, Business & Government Affairs, & Comparative Political & Economic Systems)
1526 18th Street NW
Washington, D.C. 20036
202/986-0384; 800/741-6964; Internet: www.dcinternships.com

AMOUNT: Up to $2,975

DEADLINE(S): Jan 31 (early decision); Mar 15 (general application deadline)

FIELD(S): Political Science; Economics; Journalism; Business Administration

The Fund for American Studies, in conjunction with Georgetown University, sponsors summer institutes that include internships, courses for credit, site briefings, and dialogues with policy leaders. Scholarships are available to sophomores and juniors to cover the cost of the program.

Approx. 100 awards per year. For Fund's programs only. Call, check website, or write for complete information.

1037

THE MODESTO BEE (Scholarship Program for Minority Journalism Students)
P.O. Box 5256
Modesto, CA 95352
Written inquiries

AMOUNT: $500

DEADLINE(S): Apr 1

FIELD(S): Journalism

Open to seniors graduating from a high school in the Modesto Bee's home delivery circulation area. Applicants must have at least a 2.5 GPA and a minority affiliation.

Write to the above address for complete information.

1038

THE PHILLIPS FOUNDATION (Journalism Fellowship Program)
7811 Montrose Road, Suite 100
Potomac, MD 20854
301/340-2100

AMOUNT: $50,000 (1 full-time); $25,000 (2 part-time)

DEADLINE(S): Mar 1

FIELD(S): Journalism

For working print journalists with less than five years of professional experience. One full-time and two part-time awards to complete a one-year writing project supportive of American culture and a free society. Subject matter changes each year.

Contact above location for details.

1039

THE PUBLIC RELATIONS SOCIETY OF AMERICA (Multicultural Affairs Scholarship)
33 Irving Place
New York, NY 10003-2376
212/995-2230; Fax 212/995-0757; TDD 212/254-3464

AMOUNT: $1,500
DEADLINE(S): Apr 11
FIELD(S): Communications studies; Public relations

For students whose ethnic backgrounds are African-American, Hispanic, Asian, Native American, Alaskan Native, or Pacific Islander interested in practicing in the career of public relations. Must be a full-time undergraduate student at an accredited four-year college or university, at least a junior, and have a GPA of 3.0 or better.
2 awards given.

1040

UNITED METHODIST COMMUNICATIONS (Leonard M. Perryman Communications Scholarship for Ethnic Minority Students)
P.O. Box 320
Nashville, TN 37202
615/742-5140; Fax 615/742-5404; Internet: scholarships@umcom.umc.org

AMOUNT: $2,500
DEADLINE(S): Feb 15
FIELD(S): Religious Journalism; Communications

Christian faith. Scholarship for ethnic minority undergraduate juniors and seniors who are enrolled in accredited schools of communication or journalism (print, electronic, or audiovisual) in the U.S. U.S. citizen or legal resident.
Candidates should be pursuing a career in religious communication. Write for complete information.

1041

UNIVERSITY OF MARYLAND (College of Journalism Scholarships)
Journalism Building, Room 1118
College Park, MD 20742
301/405-2380

AMOUNT: $250-$1,500
DEADLINE(S): Feb 15
FIELD(S): Journalism

Variety of journalism scholarships, prizes and awards tenable at the University of Maryland. Application forms for all scholarships are available at the address above.
Write for complete information.

1042

VANDERBILT UNIVERSITY (Fred Russell-Grantland Rice Scholarship)
2305 West End Ave.
Nashville, TN 37203-1700
615/322-2561

AMOUNT: $10,000/year ($40,000 total award)
DEADLINE(S): Jan 1
FIELD(S): Journalism

Four-year scholarship to Vanderbilt University open to high school seniors who want to become a sports writer, have demonstrated outstanding potential in the field, and can meet entrance requirements of Vanderbilt's College of Arts & Science.
Write to Scholarship Coordinator at above address for complete information.

1043

WILLIAM RANDOLPH HEARST FOUNDATION (Journalism Awards Program)
90 New Montgomery Street, #1212
San Francisco, CA 94105
415/543-6033

AMOUNT: $500-$3,000
DEADLINE(S): Varies (Monthly contests at 95 accredited schools)

FIELD(S): 6 Print Journalism; 3 Photo Journalism; 2 Broadcast News competitions each academic year (Oct.-April)

Journalism awards program offers monthly competitions open to undergraduate college journalism majors who are currently enrolled in one of the 95 participating journalism schools.

Entry forms and details on monthly contests are only available through the Journalism department of participating schools.

1044

WOMEN IN COMMUNICATIONS (Seattle Professional Chapter Scholarships for Washington State Residents)
217 Ninth Ave. N.
Seattle, WA 98109
206/298-4966

AMOUNT: $600-$1,000
DEADLINE(S): Mar 1
FIELD(S): Communications

Open to Washington state residents who are graduate students or undergraduates in their junior or senior year at a Washington state 4-year college or university. Must be a communications major.

Awards are based on demonstrated excellence in communications, scholastic achievement and financial need. Write for complete information.

HISTORY

1045

AMERICAN HISTORICAL ASSOCIATION (J. Franklin Jameson Fellowship)
400 A Street SE
Washington, D.C. 20003
202/544-2422; Fax 202/544-8307; E-mail: ceaton@theaha.org

AMOUNT: $10,000
DEADLINE(S): Jan 15

FIELD(S): American History

To support significant scholarly research in the collections of the Library of Congress by young historians.

Write for complete information.

1046

AMERICAN HISTORICAL ASSOCIATION (Michael Kraus Research Award Grant)
400 A Street SE
Washington, D.C. 20003
202/544-2422

AMOUNT: $800
DEADLINE(S): Feb 1
FIELD(S): American Colonial History

For research in American colonial history with particular reference to intercultural aspects of American and European relations.

Should join AHA prior to applying since only members are eligible. Write for complete information.

1047

AMERICAN HISTORICAL ASSOCIATION (Published Book Awards)
400 A Street SE
Washington, DC 20003
202/544-2422; Fax 202/544-8307; E-mail: ceaton@theaha.org

AMOUNT: Varies
DEADLINE(S): May 15
FIELD(S): Historical Writing (already-published books only)

Awards offered for already-published books on historical subjects, ranging from 17th Century European history to the history of the feminist movement.

Not a contest and NOT for high school. FOR ALREADY-PUBLISHED WORKS ONLY. Write for details.

1048

**COMMITTEE ON INSTITUTIONAL
COOPERATION (CIC Pre-doctoral
Fellowships)**
Kirkwood Hall 111, Indiana University
Bloomington, IN 47405
812/855-0823

AMOUNT: $11,000 + tuition (4 years)
DEADLINE(S): Dec 1
FIELD(S): Humanities; Social Sciences;
Natural Sciences; Mathematics; Engineering

Pre-doctoral fellowships for U.S. citizens of
African-American, American Indian,
Mexican-American, or Puerto Rican heritage. Must hold or expect to receive bachelor's degree by late summer from a regionally accredited college or university.

Awards for specified universities in IL; IN; IA;
MI; MN; OH; WI; PA. Write for details.

1049

**DAUGHTERS OF THE AMERICAN
REVOLUTION (American History
Scholarships)**
Office of the Committee/Scholarships
National Society DAR
1776 D Street NW
Washington, D.C. 20006-5392
202/879-3292

AMOUNT: $2,000 per year for up to 4 years
DEADLINE(S): Feb 1
FIELD(S): American History

Open to graduating high school seniors planning to major in American History. Must be
U.S. citizen and attend an accredited U.S.
college or university. Awards based on academic excellence, financial need, & commitment to American history.

DAR affiliation not required but must be
sponsored by a local DAR chapter. Write
for complete information (include a self-
addressed stamped envelope).

1050

**DAUGHTERS OF THE AMERICAN
REVOLUTION (Enid Hall Griswold
Memorial Scholarship Program)**
Office of the Committee/Scholarships
National Society DAR
1776 D Street NW
Washington, D.C. 20006-5392
202/879-3292

AMOUNT: $1,000 (one-time award)
DEADLINE(S): Feb 15
FIELD(S): History; Political Science;
Government; Economics

Open to undergraduate juniors & seniors
attending an accredited college or university in the U.S. Awards are judged on the
basis of academic excellence, financial need
& commitment to field of study. Must be
U.S. citizen.

DAR affiliation is not required but applicants
must be sponsored by a local DAR chapter.
Not renewable. Write for complete information (include SASE).

1051

**EAST TEXAS HISTORICAL
ASSOCIATION (The Ottis Lock Endowment
Awards)**
P.O. Box 6223, SFA Station
Nacaogdoches, TX 75962
409/468-2407

AMOUNT: Varies
DEADLINE(S): May 1
FIELD(S): History; Social Science

This award is open to residents of East Texas
who will be attending an East Texas college
or university.

Write to the above address for complete information.

1052

INSTITUT FUR EUROPAISCHE GESCHICHTE (Fellowship Program)
Alte Universitatsstrasse 19
D-55116 Mainz Germany
06131/39 93 60; Fax 23 79 88

AMOUNT: DM 1.485 to DM 1.795
DEADLINE(S): None specified
FIELD(S): European History (16th-20th centuries); European Church History (History & Theology of Reformation)
Fellowships awarded for 6 to 12 months. Candidates must have a thorough command of German & should be either at an advanced stage of their dissertation or already in possession of their doctorate.
Various fellowships are scaled according to level of education, family and travel allowance, etc. Write for complete information.

1053

NATIONAL ITALIAN AMERICAN FOUNDATION (Rabbi Robert Feinberg Scholarship)
1860 19th Street
Washington, D.C. 20009-5599
202/530-5315

AMOUNT: $1,000
DEADLINE(S): May 31
FIELD(S): World War II studies
Open to undergraduate or graduate student of Italian heritage interested in WWII studies. Prepare a 5-page paper on the Italian assistance to Jewish brothers in Italy and its occupied territories.
Academic merit, financial need, and community service considered.

1054

NATIONAL SPACE CLUB (Dr. Robert H. Goddard Historical Essay Award)
2000 L Street NW, Suite 710
Washington, D.C. 20036
202/973-8661

AMOUNT: $1,000
DEADLINE(S): Dec 5
FIELD(S): Aerospace History
Essay competition open to any U.S. citizen on a topic dealing with any significant aspect of the historical development of rocketry and astronautics. Essays should not exceed 5,000 words and should be fully documented.
Write for complete information.

1055

PHI ALPHA THETA—INTERNATIONAL HONOR SOCIETY IN HISTORY (PAT Scholarship Grants)
50 College Drive
Allentown, PA 18104-6100
800/394-8195; Fax 610/433-4661

AMOUNT: $1,000
DEADLINE(S): Jun 1
FIELD(S): History
Scholarships for members of Phi Alpha Theta, history society.
Write for details.

1056

SMITHSONIAN INSTITUTION (Minority Undergraduate & Graduate Internship)
Office of Fellowships & Grants
955 L'Enfant Plaza, Suite 7000
Washington, D.C. 20560
202/287-3271; E-mail: www.si.edu/research+study; Internet: siofg@sivm.si.edu

AMOUNT: $250/wk. undergrads; $300/wk. grads
DEADLINE(S): Feb 15
FIELD(S): Animal Behavior; Ecology; Environmental Science (including an emphasis on the tropics) Anthropology (& Archaeology); Astrophysics; Astronomy; Earth Sciences; Paleobiology; Evolutionary/Systematic Biology; History of Science and Technology; History of Art, esp. American, contemporary, African, and Asian; 20th-century American crafts; Decorative Arts; Social/Cultural History of the U.S.; Folklife.

Internships in residence at the Smithsonian for U.S. minority students to participate in research or museum-related activities for 10 weeks.

Research is for above fields.

1057

SMITHSONIAN INSTITUTION (National Air & Space Museum Verville Fellowship)
National Air and Space Museum, MRC 312
Washington, D.C. 20560
Written inquiry

AMOUNT: $30,000 stipend for 12 months + travel and misc. expenses

DEADLINE(S): Jan 15

FIELD(S): Analysis of major trends, developments, and accomplishments in the history of aviation or space studies

A competitive nine- to twelve-month in-residence fellowship in the above field of study. Advanced degree is NOT a requirement. Contact Fellowship Coordinator at above location.

Open to all nationalities. Fluency in English required.

1058

SONS OF THE REPUBLIC OF TEXAS (Presidio La Bahia Award)
1717 8th Street
Bay City, TX 77414
409/245-6644

AMOUNT: $1,200 and up

DEADLINE(S): Sep 30

FIELD(S): Texas History—Spanish Colonial Period

A competition to promote suitable preservation of relics, appropriate dissemination of data, and research into Texas heritage with particular attention to the Spanish Colonial period. For the best book and paper on the subject mentioned above. Entries accepted between June 1 and September 30.

Contact Melinda Williams, SRT Executive Secretary, at above location for complete information.

1059

SOURISSEAU ACADEMY FOR STATE AND LOCAL HISTORY (Research Grant)
c/o San Jose State University
San Jose, CA 95192
408/924-6510; 408/227-2657

AMOUNT: $500

DEADLINE(S): Nov 1

FIELD(S): California History

Grants are available to support undergraduate and graduate research on California history. Preference to research on Santa Clara County history.

5-10 awards per year are granted for project expenses. Write for complete information.

1060

U.S. INSTITUTE OF PEACE (National Peace Essay Contest)
1550 M Street NW, Suite 700
Washington, D.C. 20005
202/429-3834; Fax 202/429-6063; Internet: essay_contest@usip.org

AMOUNT: $750-$5,000

DEADLINE(S): Varies (by year)

FIELD(S): American History; American Foreign Policy

1,500-word essay contest for college scholarships open to students in the 9th through 12th grades. U.S. citizenship required for students attending school overseas.

First-place state winners will receive an all-expense-paid trip to Washington for the 5-day awards program. 53 state winners; 3 national winners. Write for guidelines. Topic changes yearly.

1061

U.S. MARINE CORPS HISTORICAL CENTER (College Internships)
Building 58
Washington Navy Yard
Washington, D.C. 20374
202/433-3839

AMOUNT: Stipend to cover daily expenses
DEADLINE(S): None specified
FIELD(S): U.S. Military History; Library Science; History; Museum Studies

Open to undergraduate students at a college or university which will grant academic credit for work experience as interns at the address above or at the Marine Corps Air-Ground Museum in Quantico, Virginia.

All internships are regarded as beginning professional-level historian, curator, librarian, or archivist positions. Write for complete information.

LAW

1062

AMERICAN HISTORICAL ASSN. (Littleton-Griswold Grants)
400 A Street SE
Washington, D.C. 20003
202/544-2422

AMOUNT: $1,000
DEADLINE(S): Feb 1
FIELD(S): American Legal History

For support for a research project on American legal history in the fields of law and society. Should join the AHA prior to applying since only AHA members are eligible.

For membership information or an application, write to the above address.

1063

AMERICAN SOCIETY OF CRIMINOLOGY (Gene Carte Student Paper Competition)
1314 Kinnear Road, Suite 212
Columbus, OH 43212
614/292-9207

AMOUNT: $300; $150; $100
DEADLINE(S): Apr 15
FIELD(S): Criminology; Criminal Justice

Essay competition open to any student currently enrolled full time in an academic program at either the undergraduate or graduate level. Papers must be directly related to criminology and may be conceptual and/or empirical.

Write for complete information.

1064

ARMENIAN GENERAL BENEVOLENT UNION (Educational Loan Program)
Education Dept., 31 W. 52nd Street
New York, NY 10019-6118
212/765-8260; Fax 212/765-8209 or 8209

AMOUNT: $5,000 to $7,500/year
DEADLINE(S): May 15
FIELD(S): Law (J.D.); Medicine (M.D.)

Loans for full-time students of Armenian heritage pursuing their first professional degrees in law or medicine. Must be attending highly competitive institutions in the U.S.

Loan repayments begin within 12 months of completion of full-time study and extends 5 to 10 years, depending on the size of the loan. Interest is 3%. Write for complete information.

1065

ASSOCIATION OF FORMER AGENTS OF THE U.S. SECRET SERVICE (AFAUSS— Law Enforcement Career Scholarship Program)
P.O. Box 848
Annandale, VA 22003
Written inquiry

AMOUNT: $500-$1,500

DEADLINE(S): May 1

FIELD(S): Law Enforcement; Police Administration

Open to undergraduate students who have completed at least one year of study and graduate students working toward an advanced degree in the above areas. U.S. citizenship required.

Send SASE (#10 envelope) for complete information.

1066

BOYS & GIRLS CLUBS OF SAN DIEGO (Spence Reese Scholarship Fund)
1761 Hotel Circle So., Suite 123
San Diego, CA 92108
619/298-3520

AMOUNT: $2,000 per year for 4 years

DEADLINE(S): May 15

FIELD(S): Medicine; Law; Engineering; Political Science

Open to male high school seniors planning a career in above fields. Girls and Boys Club affiliation is not required.

Applications are available in January. Must enclose a self-addressed stamped envelope to receive application. A $10 processing fee is required with completed application. Write for complete information.

1067

BUSINESS & PROFESSIONAL WOMEN'S FOUNDATION (Career Advancement Scholarships)
2012 Massachusetts Ave. NW
Washington, D.C. 20036
202/293-1200

AMOUNT: $500-$1,000

DEADLINE(S): Apr 15 (postmark)

FIELD(S): Computer Science; Education; Paralegal; Engineering; Science; Law; Dentistry; Medicine

Open to women (30 or older) within 12-24 months of completing undergrad or grad study in U.S. (including Puerto Rico & Virgin Islands). Studies should lead to entry/re-entry in work force or improve career advancement chances.

Not for doctoral study. Must demonstrate financial need. Send self-addressed stamped ($.64) #10 envelope for complete info. Applications available Oct. 1 - April 1.

1068

COMMUNITY FOUNDATION OF WESTERN MASSACHUSETTS (Richard W. and Florence B. Irwin Law Scholarship)
P.O. Box 15769
1500 Main Street
Springfield, MA 01115
413/732-2858

AMOUNT: Varies

DEADLINE(S): Aug 31

FIELD(S): Law

Open to Northampton, MA residents of at least five years who attend or have been accepted to law school. Fleet Bank is the trustee for this award.

With application, include proof of Northampton residency for at least five years and a copy of LSAT scores. Write to the above address for complete information.

1069

EARL WARREN LEGAL TRAINING PROGRAM (Scholarships)
99 Hudson Street, 16th Floor
New York, NY 10013
212/219-1900

AMOUNT: Varies

DEADLINE(S): Mar 15

FIELD(S): Law

Scholarships for entering Black law students. Emphasis on applicants who wish to enter law schools in the south. Must submit proof of acceptance to an accredited law school. U.S. citizenship or legal residency required.

U.S. citizens under 35 years of age preferred. Write for complete information.

1070

**H. FLETCHER BROWN FUND
(Scholarships)**
c/o PNC Bank
Trust Dept.
P.O. Box 791
Wilmington DE 19899
302/429-2827

AMOUNT: Varies
DEADLINE(S): Apr 15
FIELD(S): Medicine; Dentistry; Law;
Engineering; Chemistry
Open to U.S. citizens born and still residing in
Delaware. For 4 years of study (undergrad
or grad) leading to a degree that enables
applicant to practice in chosen field.
Scholarships are based on need, scholastic
achievement and good moral character.
Applications available in February. Write
for complete information.

1071

**INTERNATIONAL ASSN. OF ARSON
INVESTIGATORS (John Charles Wilson
Scholarship Fund)**
300 S. Broadway, Suite #100
St. Louis, MO 63102
314/621-1966

AMOUNT: $1,000
DEADLINE(S): Feb 15
FIELD(S): Police Science; Fire Science; and
affiliated fields
Open to IAAI members, their immediate family & non-members who are recommended
& sponsored by members in good standing.
Awards are for undergraduate study in
above areas at accredited 2-year & 4-year
institutions.
Write for complete information.

1072

**JAPANESE AMERICAN CITIZENS
LEAGUE (Law Scholarships)**
1765 Sutter Street
San Francisco, CA 94115

415/921-5225; E-mail: jacl@jacl.org

AMOUNT: Varies
DEADLINE(S): Apr 1
FIELD(S): Law
Open to JACL members or their children
only. For students planning a career in law
and who are enrolled in, or planning to
enroll in, an accredited institution of higher
learning.
For membership information or an application, send a self-addressed, stamped envelope to the above address, stating your level
of study.

1073

**MARYLAND HIGHER EDUCATION
COMMISSION (Professional School
Scholarships)**
State Scholarship Administration
16 Francis Street
Annapolis, MD 21401
410/974-5370; TTY: 800/735-2258

AMOUNT: $200-$1,000
DEADLINE(S): Mar 1 (for both FAFSA and
separate SSA application)
FIELD(S): Dentistry; Pharmacy; Medicine;
Law; Nursing
Open to Maryland residents who have been
admitted as full-time students at a participating graduate institution of higher learning in Maryland or an undergraduate/gradu-
ate nursing program.
Renewable up to 4 years. Write for complete
information.

1074

**NATIONAL BLACK POLICE
ASSOCIATION (Alphonso Deal Scholarship
Award)**
3251 Mt. Pleasant Street NW, 2nd Floor
Washington, D.C. 20010
202/986-2070

AMOUNT: $500
DEADLINE(S): Jun 1

FIELD(S): Law Enforcement; Criminal Justice

Open to minority high school graduates who have been accepted for enrollment in a two- or four-year college. Must have a GPA of 2.5 or better and demonstrate financial need. U.S. citizenship required.
Write for complete information.

1075

NATIONAL FEDERATION OF THE BLIND (Howard Brown Rickard Scholarship)
805 Fifth Ave.
Grinnell, IA 50112
515/236-3366

AMOUNT: $3,000
DEADLINE(S): Mar 31
FIELD(S): Natural Sciences; Architecture; Engineering; Medicine; Law

Scholarships for undergraduate or graduate study in the above areas. Open to legally blind students enrolled full-time at accredited post-secondary institutions.
Awards based on academic excellence, service to the community, and financial need. Write for complete information.

1076

NEW YORK STATE HIGHER EDUCATION SERVICES CORPORATION (N.Y. State Regents Professional/Health Care Opportunity Scholarships)
Cultural Education Center, Room 5C64
Albany, NY 12230
518/486-1319; Internet: www.hesc.com

AMOUNT: $1,000-$10,000/year
DEADLINE(S): Varies
FIELD(S): Medicine and Dentistry and related fields; Architecture; Nursing; Psychology; Audiology; Landscape Architecture; Social Work; Chiropractic; Law; Pharmacy; Accounting; Speech Language Pathology

For NY state residents who are economically disadvantaged and members of a minority group underrepresented in the chosen profession and attending school in NY state. Some programs carry a service obligation in New York for each year of support. For U.S. citizens or qualifying non-citizens.
Medical/dental scholarships require one year of professional work in NY.

1077

NEW YORK STATE HIGHER EDUCATION SERVICES CORPORATION
Cultural Education Center, Room 5C64
Albany, NY 12230
518/486-1319; Internet: www.hesc.com

AMOUNT: Varies
DEADLINE(S): Varies
FIELD(S): Medicine and Dentistry and related fields; Architecture; Nursing; Psychology; Audiology; Landscape Architecture; Social Work; Chiropractic; Law; Pharmacy; Accounting; Speech Language Pathology

For NY state residents who are economically disadvantaged and members of a minority group underrepresented in the chosen profession and attending school in NY state. Some programs carry a service obligation in New York for each year of support. For U.S. citizens or qualifying noncitizens.
Medical/dental scholarships require one year of professional work in NY.

1078

PRESIDENT'S COMMISSION ON WHITE HOUSE FELLOWSHIPS
712 Jackson Place NW
Washington, D.C. 20503
202/395-4522; Fax 202/395-6179; E-mail: almanac@ace.esusda.gov

AMOUNT: Wage (up to GS-14 Step 3; approximately $65,000 in 1995)
DEADLINE(S): Dec 1
FIELD(S): Public Service; Government; Community Involvement; Leadership

Mid-career professionals spend one year as special assistants to senior executive branch officials in Washington. Highly competitive. Non-partisan; no age or educational requirements. Fellowship year runs September 1 through August 31.

1,200 candidates applying for 11 to 19 fellowships each year. Write for complete information.

1079

U.S. CUSTOMS SERVICE (Law Enforcement Explorer Scholarships)
1301 Constitution Ave., Room 3422
Washington, D.C. 20229
Written inquiries

AMOUNT: $1,000
DEADLINE(S): Mar 15 (local council); Mar 31 (U.S. Customs Service)
FIELD(S): Law Enforcement

For high school seniors who are active in a Law Enforcement Post of the Exploring division of Boy Scouts of America. Must plan to study law enforcement in an accredited college or university.

Send for application through local council or at above address.

POLITICAL SCIENCE

1080

AMERICAN JEWISH COMMITTEE (Harold W. Rosenthal Fellowship)
1156 15th Street NW, Suite 1201
Washington, D.C. 20005
202/785-4200

AMOUNT: $1,800 stipend
DEADLINE(S): Apr
FIELD(S): Political Science; Government Service; Foreign Affairs

Open to college seniors & grad students. Fellowship provides opportunity for a student to spend a summer working in the office of a member of Congress or Executive Branch on Foreign Affairs and government service issues. U.S. citizen.

Applications are available from the address above; however, they must be submitted with a recommendation from your dean. Selected fellows will also receive preferential treatment for a European community 3- to 5-week travel study.

1081

BOYS & GIRLS CLUBS OF SAN DIEGO (Spence Reese Scholarship Fund)
1761 Hotel Circle So., Suite 123
San Diego, CA 92108
619/298-3520

AMOUNT: $2,000 per year for 4 years
DEADLINE(S): May 15
FIELD(S): Medicine; Law; Engineering; Political Science

Open to male high school seniors planning a career in above fields. Girls and Boys Club affiliation is not required.

Applications are available in January. Must enclose a self-addressed stamped envelope to receive application. A $10 processing fee is required with completed application. Write for complete information.

1082

COMMITTEE ON INSTITUTIONAL COOPERATION (CIC Pre-doctoral Fellowships)
Kirkwood Hall 111, Indiana University
Bloomington, IN 47405
812/855-0823

AMOUNT: $11,000 + tuition (4 years)
DEADLINE(S): Dec 1
FIELD(S): Humanities; Social Sciences; Natural Sciences; Mathematics; Engineering

Pre-doctoral fellowships for U.S. citizens of African-American, American Indian, Mexican-American, or Puerto Rican heritage. Must hold or expect to receive bachelor's degree by late summer from a regionally accredited college or university.

Awards for specified universities in IL; IN; IA; MI; MN; OH; WI; PA. Write for details.

1083

DAUGHTERS OF THE AMERICAN REVOLUTION (Enid Hall Griswold Memorial Scholarship Program)
Office of the Committee/Scholarships
National Society DAR
1776 D Street NW
Washington, D.C. 20006-5392
202/879-3292

AMOUNT: $1,000 (one-time award)
DEADLINE(S): Feb 15
FIELD(S): History; Political Science; Government; Economics

Open to undergraduate juniors & seniors attending an accredited college or university in the U.S. Awards are judged on the basis of academic excellence, financial need & commitment to field of study. Must be U.S. citizen.

DAR affiliation is not required but applicants must be sponsored by a local DAR chapter. Not renewable. Write for complete information (include SASE).

1084

EPILEPSY FOUNDATION OF AMERICA (Behavioral Sciences Student Fellowships)
4351 Garden City Drive
Landover, MD 20785
301/459-3700; 800/EFA-1000; Fax 301/577-2684; TDD: 800/332-2070; E-mail: postmaster@efa.org; Internet: www.efa.org

AMOUNT: $2,000
DEADLINE(S): Mar 3
FIELD(S): For the study of epilepsy in either research or practice settings in fields such as sociology, social work, psychology, anthropology, nursing, economics, vocational rehabilitation, counseling, political science, etc., relevant to epilepsy research

Applicants may propose a 3-month project to be undertaken in a clinical or laboratory setting where there are ongoing programs of research, service, or training in the field of epilepsy.

Project may be conducted during any free period of the student's year at a U.S. institution of the student's choice. Write for complete information.

1085

HARRY S. TRUMAN SCHOLARSHIP FOUNDATION (Scholarships)
712 Jackson Place NW
Washington, D.C. 20006
202/395-4831; Internet: www.truman.gov

AMOUNT: Up to $3,000 for senior year; $13,500 for each year of graduate study, up to 2 years; $9,000 each year for 3 years' graduate study
DEADLINE(S): Dec 1
FIELD(S): Public Service; Government

Open to full-time students who are juniors in a 4-year college and committed to a career in government public service. Must have outstanding leadership potential and communication skills. Scholars may attend graduate or professional schools in the U.S. or in foreign countries. One award to a resident of each of the 50 states, the District of Columbia, Puerto Rico, and, considered as a single entity: Guam, Virgin Islands, American Samoa, and Northern Mariana Islands.

Candidates must be U.S. citizens nominated by their schools. Up to 80 scholarships per year. Send SASE for complete information.

1086

JUNIATA COLLEGE (The Baker Peace Scholarship)
Baker Institute, Peace and Conflict Studies
Huntingdon, PA 16652
814/641-3265

AMOUNT: $1,000-$2,000

DEADLINE(S): Feb 1

FIELD(S): Peace and Conflict Studies;
International Affairs

Open to incoming freshman who rank in the upper 20% of their high school class, have above-average SAT scores, and demonstrate an interest in peace-related issues. Applicants must submit 1,000-word essay on a designated topic and two letters of recommendation. Scholarship may be renewed for four years, provided 3.0 GPA is maintained and student participates in the Peace and Conflict Studies Program.

Write to the above address for complete information.

1087

LAVINIA ENGLE SCHOLARSHIP
(Undergraduate Women Scholarships)
c/o Judith Heimann
6900 Marbury Road
Bethesda, MD 20817
301/229-4647

AMOUNT: Varies

DEADLINE(S): Apr 15

FIELD(S): Political Science; Government;
Public Administration

Open to women residing in Montgomery County, Maryland. For undergraduate study at a college or university in Maryland.

Send self-addressed stamped envelope for application and complete information.

1088

NATIONAL ITALIAN AMERICAN
FOUNDATION (Caligueri Scholarship)
Dr. M. Lombardo
Education Director
1860 19th Street NW
Washington, D.C. 20009
202/387-0600

AMOUNT: $1,000

DEADLINE(S): May 31

FIELD(S): Political Science

Open to undergraduate and graduate students of Italian heritage majoring in political science. Applicants must provide evidence of financial need and write an essay (1 typed page maximum) on their Italian background.

Write for complete information.

1089

NEW YORK CITY DEPT. CITYWIDE
ADMINISTRATIVE SERVICES (Urban
Fellows Program)
1 Centre Street, 24th Floor
New York, NY 10007
212/487-5600; Fax 212/487-5720

AMOUNT: $18,000 stipend

DEADLINE(S): Jan 20

FIELD(S): Public Administration; Urban
Planning; Government; Public Service;
Urban Affairs

Fellowship program provides one academic year (9 months) of full-time work experience in urban government. Open to graduating college seniors and recent college graduates. U.S. citizenship required.

Write for complete information.

1090

NEW YORK CITY DEPT. OF CITYWIDE
ADMINISTRATIVE SERVICES
(Government Scholars Internship Program)
1 Centre Street, 24th Floor
New York, NY 10007
212/487-5600; Fax 212/487-5720

AMOUNT: $3,000 stipend

DEADLINE(S): Jan 13

FIELD(S): Public Administration; Urban
Planning; Government; Public Service;
Urban Affairs

10-week summer intern program open to undergraduate sophomores, juniors, and seniors. Program provides students with unique opportunity to learn about NY City government. Internships available in virtually every city agency and mayoral office.

Write to New York City Fellowship Programs at above address for complete information.

1091

PRESIDENT'S COMMISSION ON WHITE HOUSE FELLOWSHIPS
712 Jackson Place NW
Washington, D.C. 20503
202/395-4522; Fax 202/395-6179; E-mail: almanac@ace.esusda.gov

AMOUNT: Wage (up to GS-14 Step 3; approximately $65,000 in 1995)
DEADLINE(S): Dec 1
FIELD(S): Public Service; Government; Community Involvement; Leadership
Mid-career professionals spend one year as special assistants to senior executive branch officials in Washington. Highly competitive. Non-partisan; no age or educational requirements. Fellowship year runs September 1 through August 31.
1,200 candidates applying for 11 to 19 fellowships each year. Write for complete information.

1092

THE FUND FOR AMERICAN STUDIES (Institutes on Political Journalism, Business & Government Affairs, & Comparative Political & Economic Systems)
1526 18th Street NW
Washington, DC 20036
202/986-0384; 800/741-6964; Internet: www.dcinternships.com

AMOUNT: Up to $2,975
DEADLINE(S): Jan 31 (early decision); Mar 15 (general application deadline)
FIELD(S): Political Science; Economics; Journalism; Business Administration
The Fund for American Studies, in conjunction with Georgetown University, sponsors summer institutes that include internships, courses for credit, site briefings, and dialogues with policy leaders. Scholarships are available to sophomores and juniors to cover the cost of the program.

Approx. 100 awards per year. For Fund's programs only. Call, check website, or write for complete information.

1093

U.S. DEPT OF STATE (Internships)
P.O. Box 9317
Arlington, VA 22219
703/875-7165; Fax 703/875-7243

AMOUNT: Paid internships are at GS-4 to GS-6 levels; some are unpaid
DEADLINE(S): Nov 1 (for Summer); Mar 1 (for Fall); Jul 1 (for Spring)
FIELD(S): International Relations
Open to continuing college or university juniors, seniors or grad students who are U.S. citizens and have completed some academic studies in the type of work the student wishes to perform for the department.
Must be able to pass background investigation. Interns serve one semester or quarter during academic year or 10 weeks during summer. Most are in D.C. but some are abroad. Write for complete information.

1094

U.S. INSTITUTE OF PEACE (National Peace Essay Contest)
1550 M Street NW, Suite 700
Washington, D.C. 20005
202/429-3834; Fax 202/429-6063; Internet: essay_contest@usip.org

AMOUNT: $750-$5,000
DEADLINE(S): Varies (by year)
FIELD(S): American History; American Foreign Policy
1,500-word essay contest for college scholarships open to students in the 9th through 12th grades. U.S. citizenship required for students attending school overseas.
First-place state winners will receive an all-expense-paid trip to Washington for the 5-day awards program. 53 state winners; 3 national winners. Write for guidelines. Topic changes yearly.

1095

WASHINGTON CROSSING FOUNDATION (Annual National Washington Crossing Foundation Scholarship Award)

Eugene C. Fish, Esquire
Vice Chairman
P.O. Box 17
Washington Crossing, PA 18977-0017
215/493-6577

AMOUNT: $5,000-$10,000

DEADLINE(S): Jan 15

FIELD(S): Government Service; Public Service

For U.S. high school seniors planning a career in government service (local/state/federal). Each interested student is invited to write a typed, double-spaced, one-page essay stating why he or she plans a career in government service, including any inspiration derived from the leadership of George Washington in his famous crossing of the Delaware. Tenable at any accredited U.S. college or university. U.S. citizenship required.

Contact above location for complete information.

PSYCHOLOGY

1096

COMMITTEE ON INSTITUTIONAL COOPERATION (CIC Pre-doctoral Fellowships)

Kirkwood Hall 111, Indiana University
Bloomington, IN 47405
812/855-0823

AMOUNT: $11,000 + tuition (4 years)

DEADLINE(S): Dec 1

FIELD(S): Humanities; Social Sciences; Natural Sciences; Mathematics; Engineering

Pre-doctoral fellowships for U.S. citizens of African-American, American Indian, Mexican-American, or Puerto Rican her-

itage. Must hold or expect to receive bachelor's degree by late summer from a regionally accredited college or university.

Awards for specified universities in IL; IN; IA; MI; MN; OH; WI; PA. Write for details.

1097

EASTER SEAL SOCIETY OF IOWA, INC. (Scholarships & Awards)

P.O. Box 4002
Des Moines, IA 50333-4002
515/289-1933

AMOUNT: $400-$600

DEADLINE(S): Apr 15

FIELD(S): Physical Rehabilitation; Mental Rehabilitation; and related areas

Open only to Iowa residents who are full-time undergraduate sophomores, juniors, seniors, or graduate students at accredited institutions planning a career in the broad field of rehabilitation. Must indicate financial need and be in top 40% of their class.

6 scholarships per year. Must re-apply each year.

1098

EPILEPSY FOUNDATION OF AMERICA (Behavioral Sciences Student Fellowships)

4351 Garden City Drive
Landover, MD 20785
301/459-3700; 800/EFA-1000; Fax 301/577-2684; TDD: 800/332-2070; E-mail: postmaster@efa.org; Internet: www.efa.org

AMOUNT: $2,000

DEADLINE(S): Mar 3

FIELD(S): For the study of epilepsy in either research or practice settings in fields such as sociology, social work, psychology, anthropology, nursing, economics, vocational rehabilitation, counseling, political science, etc., relevant to epilepsy research

Applicants may propose a 3-month project to be undertaken in a clinical or laboratory setting where there are ongoing programs of research, service, or training in the field of epilepsy.

Project may be conducted during any free period of the student's year at a U.S. institution of the student's choice. Write for complete information.

1099

MISSISSIPPI OFFICE OF STATE STUDENT FINANCIAL AID (Psychology Apprenticeship Program)
3825 Ridgewood Road
Jackson, MS 39211-6453
601/982-6663; 800-327-2980

AMOUNT: Up to $1,000/mo. (grads); $500/mo. (undergrads)
DEADLINE(S): Apr 1
FIELD(S): Psychology

A stipend/apprenticeship and summer training program for Mississippi residents studying in the field of psychology. Students will be exposed to the professional practice of psychology in a Veterans Affairs Medical Center. Special consideration given to economically, educationally, and/or socially disadvantaged applicants.

Housing and board will be provided by Veterans Affairs Medical Center. Contact above location for details.

1100

NEW YORK STATE HIGHER EDUCATION SERVICES CORPORATION (N.Y. State Regents Professional/Health Care Opportunity Scholarships)
Cultural Education Center, Room 5C64
Albany, NY 12230
518/486-1319; Internet: www.hesc.com

AMOUNT: $1,000-$10,000/year
DEADLINE(S): Varies
FIELD(S): Medicine and Dentistry and related fields; Architecture; Nursing; Psychology; Audiology; Landscape Architecture; Social Work; Chiropractic; Law; Pharmacy; Accounting; Speech Language Pathology

For NY state residents who are economically disadvantaged and members of a minority group underrepresented in the chosen profession and attending school in NY state. Some programs carry a service obligation in New York for each year of support. For U.S. citizens or qualifying non-citizens.

Medical/dental scholarships require one year of professional work in NY.

1101

NEW YORK STATE HIGHER EDUCATION SERVICES CORPORATION
Cultural Education Center, Room 5C64
Albany, NY 12230
518/486-1319; Internet: www.hesc.com

AMOUNT: Varies
DEADLINE(S): Varies
FIELD(S): Medicine and Dentistry and related fields; Architecture; Nursing; Psychology; Audiology; Landscape Architecture; Social Work; Chiropractic; Law; Pharmacy; Accounting; Speech Language Pathology

For NY state residents who are economically disadvantaged and members of a minority group underrepresented in the chosen profession and attending school in NY state. Some programs carry a service obligation in New York for each year of support. For U.S. citizens or qualifying noncitizens.

Medical/dental scholarships require one year of professional work in NY.

1102

PARAPSYCHOLOGY FOUNDATION (Eileen J. Garrett Scholarship)
228 East 71st Street
New York, NY 10021
212/628-1550; Fax 212/628-1559

AMOUNT: $3,000
DEADLINE(S): Jul 15
FIELD(S): Parapsychology

Open to any undergrad or grad student wishing to pursue the academic study of the science of parapsychology. Funding is for study, research & experimentation only. Applicants must demonstrate previous academic interest in parapsychology.

Letters of reference are required from three individuals who are familiar with the applicant's work and/or studies in parapsychology. Write for complete information.

1103

PARAPSYCHOLOGY FOUNDATION, INC. (D. Scott Rogo Award for Parapsychological Award)
228 East 71st Street
New York, NY 10021
212/628-1550; Fax 212/628-1559

AMOUNT: $3,000
DEADLINE(S): Apr 15
FIELD(S): Parapsychology

Annual award given to an author working on a manuscript pertaining to the science of parapsychology. A brief synopsis of the proposed contents of the manuscript should be included in the initial application.

Awardee notified on or about May 1.

1104

SOCIETY FOR THE SCIENTIFIC STUDY OF SEXUALITY (Student Research Grant)
P.O. Box 208
Mount Vernon, IA 52314-0208
319/895-8407; Fax 319/895-6203; E-mail: TheSociety@worldnet.att.net; Internet: www.ssc.wisc.edu/ssss

AMOUNT: $750
DEADLINE(S): Feb 1; Sep 1
FIELD(S): Human Sexuality

Open to students doing research in the area of human sexuality. Must be enrolled in a degree-granting program at an accredited institution. Can be master's thesis or doctoral dissertation but this is not a requirement.

Write to Karen Polonko, Ph.D., at the above address for application & complete information. 3 awards annually.

1105

ZETA PHI BETA SORORITY, INC. NATIONAL EDUCATION FOUNDATION (Lullelia W. Harrison Scholarship in Counseling)
1734 New Hampshire Ave. NW
Washington, D.C. 20009
Written inquiry

AMOUNT: $500-$1,000
DEADLINE(S): Feb 1
FIELD(S): Counseling

For graduate or undergraduate students enrolled in a degree program in counseling. For full-time study for one academic year.

Send for application with SASE. Apply between Sept. 1 and Feb. 1 preceding the academic year. Process includes acquiring letter of recommendation, providing transcripts, and writing an essay.

SOCIOLOGY

1106

B'NAI B'RITH YOUTH ORGANIZATION (Scholarship Program)
1640 Rhode Island Ave. NW
Washington, D.C. 20036
202/857-6633

AMOUNT: $2,500 per year
DEADLINE(S): Varies (Each Spring)
FIELD(S): Social Work

Open to U.S. citizens of Jewish faith who are first- or second-year grad students attending accredited graduate schools of social work or who are college seniors planning to attend a graduate school of social work.

Must show evidence of good scholarship; interest in working for Jewish agencies & have knowledge of Jewish communal structure & institutions. Renewable. Write for complete information.

1107

EASTER SEAL SOCIETY OF IOWA, INC.
(Scholarships & Awards)
P.O. Box 4002
Des Moines, IA 50333-4002
515/289-1933

AMOUNT: $400-$600
DEADLINE(S): Apr 15
FIELD(S): Physical Rehabilitation; Mental Rehabilitation; and related areas

Open only to Iowa residents who are full-time undergraduate sophomores, juniors, seniors, or graduate students at accredited institutions planning a career in the broad field of rehabilitation. Must indicate financial need and be in top 40% of their class.

6 scholarships per year. Must re-apply each year.

1108

EPILEPSY FOUNDATION OF AMERICA
(Behavioral Sciences Student Fellowships)
4351 Garden City Drive
Landover, MD 20785
301/459-3700; 800/EFA-1000; Fax 301/577-2684; TDD 800/332-2070; E-mail: postmaster@efa.org; Internet: www.efa.org

AMOUNT: $2,000
DEADLINE(S): Mar 3
FIELD(S): For the study of epilepsy in either research or practice settings in fields such as sociology, social work, psychology, anthropology, nursing, economics, vocational rehabilitation, counseling, political science, etc., relevant to epilepsy research

Applicants may propose a 3-month project to be undertaken in a clinical or laboratory setting where there are ongoing programs of research, service, or training in the field of epilepsy.

Project may be conducted during any free period of the student's year at a U.S. institution of the student's choice. Write for complete information.

1109

JEWISH VOCATIONAL SERVICE (Marcus
& Theresa Levie Educational Fund
Scholarships)
1 S. Franklin Street
Chicago, IL 60606
312/357-4500 or 4521

AMOUNT: Up to $5000
DEADLINE(S): Mar 1
FIELD(S): Social Work; Medicine; Dentistry; Nursing & other related professions & vocations

Open to Cook County residents of the Jewish faith who plan careers in the helping professions. For undergraduate juniors and seniors and for graduate and vocational students. Applications available Dec. 1 from Scholarship Secretary.

Must show financial need. 85-100 awards per year. Renewal possible with reapplication. Write for complete information.

1110

NEW YORK CITY DEPT. CITYWIDE
ADMINISTRATIVE SERVICES (Urban
Fellows Program)
1 Centre Street, 24th Floor
New York, NY 10007
212/487-5600; Fax 212/487-5720

AMOUNT: $18,000 stipend
DEADLINE(S): Jan 20
FIELD(S): Public Administration; Urban Planning; Government; Public Service; Urban Affairs

Fellowship program provides one academic year (9 months) of full-time work experience in urban government. Open to graduating college seniors and recent college graduates. U.S. citizenship required.

Write for complete information.

1111

NEW YORK CITY DEPT. OF CITYWIDE ADMINISTRATIVE SERVICES
(Government Scholars Internship Program)
1 Centre Street, 24th Floor
New York, NY 10007
212/487-5600; Fax 212/487-5720

AMOUNT: $3,000 stipend
DEADLINE(S): Jan 13
FIELD(S): Public Administration; Urban
Planning; Government; Public Service;
Urban Affairs

10-week summer intern program open to
undergraduate sophomores, juniors, and
seniors. Program provides students with
unique opportunity to learn about NY City
government. Internships available in virtually every city agency and mayoral office.

Write to New York City Fellowship Programs
at above address for complete information.

1112

NEW YORK STATE HIGHER
EDUCATION SERVICES CORPORATION
(N.Y. State Regents Professional/Health Care
Opportunity Scholarships)
Cultural Education Center, Room 5C64
Albany, NY 12230
518/486-1319; Internet: www.hesc.com

AMOUNT: $1,000-$10,000/year
DEADLINE(S): Varies
FIELD(S): Medicine and Dentistry and
related fields; Architecture; Nursing;
Psychology; Audiology; Landscape
Architecture; Social Work; Chiropractic;
Law; Pharmacy; Accounting; Speech
Language Pathology

For NY state residents who are economically
disadvantaged and members of a minority
group underrepresented in the chosen profession and attending school in NY state.
Some programs carry a service obligation in
New York for each year of support. For U.S.
citizens or qualifying non-citizens.

Medical/dental scholarships require one year
of professional work in NY.

1113

NEW YORK STATE HIGHER
EDUCATION SERVICES CORPORATION
Cultural Education Center, Room 5C64
Albany, NY 12230
518/486-1319; Internet: www.hesc.com

AMOUNT: Varies
DEADLINE(S): Varies
FIELD(S): Medicine and Dentistry and
related fields; Architecture; Nursing;
Psychology; Audiology; Landscape
Architecture; Social Work; Chiropractic;
Law; Pharmacy; Accounting; Speech
Language Pathology

For NY state residents who are economically
disadvantaged and members of a minority
group underrepresented in the chosen profession and attending school in NY state.
Some programs carry a service obligation in
New York for each year of support. For U.S.
citizens or qualifying non-citizens.

Medical/dental scholarships require one year
of professional work in NY.

1114

PRESIDENT'S COMMISSION ON WHITE
HOUSE FELLOWSHIPS
712 Jackson Place NW
Washington, D.C. 20503
202/395-4522; Fax 202/395-6179; E-mail:
almanac@ace.esusda.gov

AMOUNT: Wage (up to GS-14 Step 3;
approximately $65,000 in 1995)
DEADLINE(S): Dec 1
FIELD(S): Public Service; Government;
Community Involvement; Leadership

Mid-career professionals spend one year as
special assistants to senior executive branch
officials in Washington. Highly competitive.
Non-partisan; no age or educational
requirements. Fellowship year runs
September 1 through August 31.

1,200 candidates applying for 11 to 19 fellowships each year. Write for complete information.

SCHOOL OF VOCATIONAL EDUCATION

1115

AMERICAN BOARD OF FUNERAL SERVICE EDUCATION (Scholarships)
13 Gurnet Road, #316
P.O. Box 1305
Brunswick, ME 04011
207/798-5801; Fax 207/798-5988

AMOUNT: $250; $500
DEADLINE(S): Mar 15; Sep 15
FIELD(S): Funeral Service
Open to students who have completed at least one term of study in an accredited program in funeral service. Applicants must submit IRS form 1040 to demonstrate need. Must be U.S. citizen.
Approximately 70 scholarships per year. Address inquiries to the scholarship chairman at address above.

1116

AMERICAN HEALTH AND BEAUTY AIDS INSTITUTE (Fred Luster, Sr. Education Foundation Cosmetology Scholarships)
401 North Michigan Ave.
Chicago, IL 60611-4267
312/644-6610

AMOUNT: Varies; Scholarships totaling $5,000 presented twice a year
DEADLINE(S): Mar 15
FIELD(S): Cosmetology
For students enrolled in beauty school and who have completed 300 classroom hours must have proven themselves scholastically.
Extracurricular activities, attendance, records, and previous competitions/awards are also taken into consideration.

1117

AMERICAN INSTITUTE OF BAKING (Scholarships)
1213 Bakers Way
Manhattan, KS 66502
800/633-5737; Fax 785/537-1493; E-mail: kembers@aibonline.org; Internet: www.aibonline.org

AMOUNT: $500-$4,000
DEADLINE(S): None
FIELD(S): Baking Industry (including electrical & electronic maintenance)
Award is for tuition for a 16- or 10-week course in baking science & technology or maintenance engineering at the Institute. Experience in baking or mechanics or an approved alternative is required. Must be U.S. citizen.
45 annual awards. Awards are intended for people who plan to seek new positions in the baking and maintenance engineering fields.

1118

AMERICAN SOCIETY FOR HOSPITAL FOOD SERVICE ADMINISTRATORS (Scholarships)
840 North Lake Shore Drive
Chicago, IL 60611
312/280-6416

AMOUNT: Up to $1,000
DEADLINE(S): Apr (late)
FIELD(S): Institutional Food Service Management
For full- or part-time undergraduate students of institutional food service management and also for current hospital food service managers furthering their education.
Contact above location for details.

1119

AMERICAN WELDING SOCIETY
(Scholarship Program)
550 NW Lejeune Road
Miami, FL 33126
305/443-9353; 800/443/9353

AMOUNT: Varies
DEADLINE(S): Apr 1
FIELD(S): Welding Technology

Open to students who reside in the U.S. and
are enrolled in an accredited welding and
joint material joining or similar program.
Awards are tenable at junior colleges, colleges, universities, and institutions in the
U.S.
Write for more information.

1120

AVIATION DISTRIBUTORS AND
MANUFACTURERS ASSOCIATION
INTERNATIONAL (ADMA International
Scholarship Fund)
1900 Arch Street
Philadelphia, PA 19103
215/564-3484

AMOUNT: Varies
DEADLINE(S): May 1
FIELD(S): Aviation Management;
Professional Pilot

Open to students seeking a career in aviation
management or as a professional pilot.
Emphasis may be in general aviation, airway science management, aviation maintenance, flight engineering or airway a/c systems management.

Applicants must be studying in the aviation
field in a four-year school having an aviation program and must have completed at
least two years of the program. Write for
complete information.

1121

AVIATION MAINTENANCE
EDUCATION FUND (AMEF Scholarship
Program)
P.O. Box 2826
Redmond, WA 98073
206/827-2295

AMOUNT: $250-$1,000
DEADLINE(S): None
FIELD(S): Aviation Maintenance Technology

AMEF scholarship program open to any worthy applicant who is enrolled in a Federal
Aviation Administration (FAA) certified
aviation maintenance technology program.
Write for complete information.

1122

BUSINESS & PROFESSIONAL WOMEN'S
FOUNDATION (Career Advancement
Scholarships)
2012 Massachusetts Ave. NW
Washington, D.C. 20036
202/293-1200

AMOUNT: $500-$1,000
DEADLINE(S): Apr 15 (postmark)
FIELD(S): Computer Science; Education;
Paralegal; Engineering; Science; Law;
Dentistry; Medicine

Open to women (30 or older) within 12-24
months of completing undergrad or grad
study in U.S. (including Puerto Rico &
Virgin Islands). Studies should lead to
entry/re-entry in work force or improve
career advancement chances.

Not for doctoral study. Must demonstrate
financial need. Send self-addressed stamped
($.64) #10 envelope for complete info.
Applications available Oct. 1 - April 1.

1123

CALIFORNIA STUDENT AID
COMMISSION (Cal. Grant "C" Program)
Grant Service Division
P.O. Box 419027
Rancho Cordova, CA 95741-9027

916/526-7590

AMOUNT: Up to $2,360 (tuition); up to $530 (training-related costs)

DEADLINE(S): Mar 2

FIELD(S): Vocational-Technical

Open to vocational-technical students enrolled in eligible 4-month to 2-year programs in California. Must be California resident and U.S. citizen/legal resident/eligible non-citizen.

Approximately 1,500 grants per year. Renewable. Contact your counselor, financial aid office, or address above for complete information.

1124

CDS INTERNATIONAL INC. (Congress-Bundestag Youth Exchange Program)
330 Seventh Ave., 19th Floor
New York, NY 10001
212/497-3500; Fax 212/497-3535; E-mail: cbyx@cdsintl.org; Internet: www.cdsintl.org

AMOUNT: Airfare, partial domestic travel, and host family payment

DEADLINE(S): Dec 15

FIELD(S): Business; Vocational/Technical Fields; Agricultural Fields

Year-long work/study programs in Germany for U.S. citizens aged 18-24. Program for Americans includes two-month language study, four-month tech or professional school study, and six-month internship. A cultural exchange designed to give participants an understanding and knowledge of everyday life in Germany.

60 awards per year. Contact Martin Black at above locations. Professional target and applicable work experience is required. Participants must provide their own spending money of $300-$350/month.

1125

CIVIL AIR PATROL (Vocational-Technical Grants)
CAP National Headquarters/ETTC
Maxwell Air Force Base, AL 36112
334/953-5315

AMOUNT: $750

DEADLINE(S): Jan 31

FIELD(S): Vocational-Technical Aerospace Studies

Open to CAP members who are qualified and interested in furthering their education in special aerospace courses at accredited vocational-technical institutions.

Write for complete information.

1126

EAA AVIATION FOUNDATION (Scholarship Program)
P.O. Box 3065
Oshkosh, WI 54903-3065
920/426-6815

AMOUNT: $200-$1,500

DEADLINE(S): May 1

FIELD(S): Aviation

Several different scholarship programs open to well-rounded individuals involved in school and community activities as well as aviation. Applicant's academic records should verify their ability to complete their educational program.

Financial need is a consideration.

1127

EMPIRE COLLEGE (Dean's Scholarship)
3033 Cleveland Ave.
Santa Rosa, CA 95403
707/546-4000

AMOUNT: $250-$1,500

DEADLINE(S): Apr 15

FIELD(S): Accounting; Secretarial; Legal; Medical (Clinical & Administrative); Travel & Tourism; General Business; Computer Assembly; Network Assembly

Open to high school seniors who meet admission requirements and want to attend Empire College in Santa Rosa, California. U.S. citizenship required.

10 scholarships per year. Contact Ms. Mary Farha at the above address for complete information.

1128

GEMOLOGICAL INSTITUTE OF AMERICA (Home Study and Resident Scholarships)
Financial Aid Office
1660 Stewart Street
Santa Monica, CA 90404
310/829-2991

AMOUNT: $500-$700
DEADLINE(S): Apr 1
FIELD(S): Gemology

A variety of scholarships offered to U.S. citizens or permanent residents who are at least 17 years of age and are employed in the jewelry industry or who plan to enter the field and enroll in a GIA educational course.

The Mary Abelson resident scholarship offers one full or partial tuition award for graduate jeweler programs every other year. Home-study scholarships are for undergrads. Write for complete information.

1129

HILGENFELD FOUNDATION FOR MORTUARY EDUCATION (Scholarship Grants)
P.O. Box 4311
Fullerton, CA 92634
Written inquiry

AMOUNT: Varies
DEADLINE(S): None
FIELD(S): Funeral Service and Education

Grants available to qualified individuals and organizations with interest in funeral service. Preference given to Southern California residents.

Grant funds available for individuals entering the funeral service profession and for individuals pursuing advanced degrees to advance in the teaching profession.

1130

INTERNATIONAL ASSN. OF ARSON INVESTIGATORS (John Charles Wilson Scholarship Fund)
300 S. Broadway, Suite #100
St. Louis, MO 63102
314/621-1966

AMOUNT: $1,000
DEADLINE(S): Feb 15
FIELD(S): Police Science; Fire Science & Affiliated Fields

Open to IAAI members, their immediate family & non-members who are recommended & sponsored by members in good standing. Awards are for undergraduate study in above areas at accredited 2-year & 4-year institutions.

Write for complete information.

1131

INTERNATIONAL FOOD SERVICE EXECUTIVES ASSOCIATION (Worthy Goal Scholarship)
1100 S. State Road, Suite 103
Margate, FL 33368
954/977-0767; Fax 954/977-0874; E-mail: hq@ifsea.org; Internet: ifsea.org/ifsea

AMOUNT: $500
DEADLINE(S): Feb 1
FIELD(S): Food Service Management

Scholarship for assisting deserving individuals to receive training in food service management. Additional scholarships are available through IFSEA branches.

Renewable by re-applying each year. Application available via "Fax on demand" from a phone attached to a fax machine at 954/977-0767 or send a #10 SASE to above address or check above website.

1132

INTERNATIONAL FOOD SERVICE EXECUTIVES ASSOCIATION (Scholarships)

1100 South State Road 7, Suite 103
Margate, FL 33068
305/977-0767

AMOUNT: $250-$500
DEADLINE(S): Feb 1
FIELD(S): Food Service

Scholarships for food-service-related majors. In addition to a bi-annual Statler Foundation scholarship, two scholarships are awarded in each of eight regions each year.
Send SASE for details.

1133

JAMES F. LINCOLN ARC WELDING FOUNDATION (Awards Program)

P.O. Box 17035
Cleveland, OH 44117
216/481-4300

AMOUNT: Up to $2,000
DEADLINE(S): Jun 15
FIELD(S): Arc Welding Technology

Open to undergraduate & graduate engineering & technology students who solve design engineering or fabrication problems involving the knowledge or application of arc welding.
Total of 29 awards; 17 for undergraduate and 12 for graduate students. Write for complete information.

1134

MARYLAND HIGHER EDUCATION COMMISSION (Reimbursement of Firefighter & Rescue Squad Members)

State Scholarship Administration
16 Francis Street
Annapolis, MD 21401
410/974-5370; TTY 800/735-2258; Internet: www.ubalt.edu/www.mhec

AMOUNT: $3,480
DEADLINE(S): Jul 1
FIELD(S): Firefighting or Emergency Medical Technology

For Maryland residents who are firefighters or rescue squad members. Reimbursement made one year after successful completion of course(s) in fire or EMT program.
Write for complete information.

1135

MARYLAND HIGHER EDUCATION COMMISSION (Tolbert Grants)

State Scholarship Administration
16 Francis Street
Annapolis, MD 21401-1781
410/974-5370; TTY 800/735-2258

AMOUNT: $200-$1,500
DEADLINE(S): Varies (FAFSA must be filed)
FIELD(S): Vocational-Technical (Private Career Schools)

Open to Maryland residents pursuing full-time study. Grants support training at Maryland private career (vocational-technical) schools. Must demonstrate financial need.
Renewable for one year. Applicants must be nominated by their schools. Write for complete information.

1136

MINNESOTA FEDERATION OF TEACHERS (Charlie Carpenter Vocational Scholarship)

168 Aurora Ave.
St. Paul, MN 55103
612/227-8583

AMOUNT: $1,000
DEADLINE(S): Mar
FIELD(S): Vocational-Technical

Candidate for this scholarship must be a current high school senior. He/she must be recommended by two senior high school instructors on the basis of financial need, academic achievement, promise of leadership ability, and character.

Tenable at any accredited vocational school. Write for complete information.

1137

NATIONAL ASSN. OF EXECUTIVE SECRETARIES AND ADMINISTRATIVE ASSISTANTS (Scholarship Award Program)
900 S. Washington Street, Suite G-13
Falls Church, VA 22046
Written inquiry

AMOUNT: $250
DEADLINE(S): May 31
FIELD(S): Secretarial

Open to post-secondary students working toward a college degree (Associate's; Bachelor's; Master's) who are NAESAA members or the spouse, child, or grandchild of a member.

Scholarship may be used for Certified Professional Secretary Exam or to buy required books. Write for complete information.

1138

NEW HAMPSHIRE ELECTRICAL CONTRACTORS ASSOC. (Phil Moran Scholarship Fund)
P.O. Box 1032
Concord, NH 03302-1032
603/224-3532; Fax 603/224-0369

AMOUNT: $1,000
DEADLINE(S): May 1
FIELD(S): Electricity (Industrial, Commercial, Residential)

Open to students who reside in New Hampshire and are (or will be) in the top 50% of their high school graduating class. Studies must relate to residential, commercial, or industrial electricity (NOT electronics or electrical engineering). For full-time or part-time study. Must be registered as an apprentice in NH. Must have high school diploma or GED.

Must re-apply each year to renew. Write for complete information.

1139

OGLE SCHOOL OF HAIR DESIGN (Scholarships)
2200 West Park Row
Arlington, TX 76013
817/461-2500

AMOUNT: Varies
DEADLINE(S): Varies
FIELD(S): Cosmetology

For high school seniors who begin training in the same calendar year they graduate from high school. For use at Ogle facilities in Arlington, Ft. Worth, Hurst, and Dallas, Texas.

Scholarships vary in number and amount based upon the number of applicants and scholarship pool size.

1140

PROFESSIONAL AVIATION MAINTENANCE ASSOCIATION (Careerquest Scholarships)
P.O. Box 410260
St. Louis, MO 63141
314/739-2580

AMOUNT: $1,000 per year
DEADLINE(S): Varies
FIELD(S): Aviation Maintenance

For students pursuing airframe and power-plant (A&P) technician certification through an FAA Part 147 aviation maintenance technician school. Must have completed 25% of required curriculum & have a 3.0 or better GPA.

6 awards per year—3 in spring, 3 in fall. Application must be submitted through student's school. Must demonstrate financial need. Write for complete information.

1141

**PROFESSIONAL AVIATION
MAINTENANCE ASSOCIATION (PAMA
Scholarship Fund)**
1200 18th Street NW, Suite 401
Washington, D.C. 20036-2598
202/296-0545

AMOUNT: Varies
DEADLINE(S): Jul 1; Nov 30
FIELD(S): Aviation Maintenance

Open to students enrolled in an institution to
obtain an airframe and powerplant (A&P)
license who have completed 25% of the
required curriculum. Must have 3.0 or better GPA, demonstrate financial need, and
be recommended by instructor.

Applications to be submitted through student's
school. Write for complete information.

1142

**PROFESSIONAL SECRETARIES
INTERNATIONAL—THE ASSOCIATION
FOR OFFICE PROFESSIONALS
(Scholarships)**
10502 NW Ambassador Drive
Kansas City, MO 64195-0404
816/891-6600; Fax 816/891-9118; E-mail:
info@psi.org; Internet: www.gvi.net/psi

AMOUNT: Varies (determined by each
chapter)
DEADLINE(S): Varies
FIELD(S): Secretarial; Administrative
Assistant; Office Management

A scholarship for persons interested in studying for a career as an office professional. No
citizenship restrictions.

Contact your local chapter or Susan Fenner,
Ph.D., at above address.

1143

**SPORTY'S PILOT SHOP (Aviation
Scholarship Program)**
P.O. Box 44327
Cincinnati, OH 45244

Written inquiry

AMOUNT: $15,000
DEADLINE(S): Jan 15
FIELD(S): Pilot Training

Open to full-time high school seniors or college students. The scholarship is to be used
over a two-year period for pilot training
programs. The funds may be used for flight
training expenses leading to a Recreational,
Private, Commercial, or Flight Instructor
Certificate. Students can be pursuing any
field of study.

Write to the above address for complete information.

1144

**U.S. DEPT. OF INTERIOR; BUREAU OF
INDIAN AFFAIRS (Adult Education
Grants)**
1849 C Street NW
MS-3512 MIB
Washington, D.C. 20240-0001
202/208-4871

AMOUNT: Varies
DEADLINE(S): Varies
FIELD(S): Vocational-Technical

Open to Native Americans for job training.
Grants for adult vocational training and job
placement services for individuals who are
unemployed or under-employed.

Applications are available through tribal contract office, area offices, or home agency.
Funds for vocational training and job placement only—not for formal degrees.

1145

**VERTICAL FLIGHT FOUNDATION
(Undergraduate/Graduate Scholarships)**
217 N. Washington Street
Alexandria, VA 22314
703/684-6777; Fax 703/739-9279

AMOUNT: Up to $2,000
DEADLINE(S): Feb 1
FIELD(S): Vertical Flight Engineering

Annual scholarships open to undergraduate &
graduate students in the above areas.
Academic excellence and proven interest in
pursuing careers in some aspect of helicopter
or vertical flight required. For full-time study
at accredited school of engineering.
Write for complete information.

1146

**WHIRLY-GIRLS INC. (International Women
Helicopter Pilots Scholarships)**
Executive Towers 10-D
207 West Clarendon Ave.
Phoenix, AZ 85013
602/263-0190; Fax 602/264-5812

AMOUNT: $4,500
DEADLINE(S): Nov 15
FIELD(S): Helicopter Flight Training

3 scholarships available to licensed women
pilots for flight training. Two are awarded
to Whirly-Girls who are helicopter pilots;
one is awarded to a licensed woman pilot
holding a private license (airplane, balloon
or glider).
Applications are available April 15. Write, call
or Fax for complete information.

GENERAL

1147

**1ST MARINE DIVISION ASSN.
(Scholarship Program)**
14325 Willard Road, Suite 107
Chantilly, VA 20151-2110
Phone: 703/803-3195; Fax 703/803-7114

AMOUNT: Varies
DEADLINE(S): Varies
FIELD(S): All fields of study

For dependents of persons who served in the
First Marine Division or in a unit attached
to or in support of the Division and are
deceased from any cause or permanently
100% disabled.
For undergraduate study only. Write for complete information.

1148

**37TH DIVISION VETERANS
ASSOCIATION (37th Infantry Division
Award)**
183 E. Mound Street, Suite 103
Columbus, OH 43215
614/228-3788

AMOUNT: Varies
DEADLINE(S): Apr 1
FIELD(S): All fields of study

Scholarship/grant open to high school seniors
or college students who are dependents of
children of the 37th Infantry Division
Veterans who served in World War I, II or
the Korean conflict.
Financial need is a consideration particularly if
the father is deceased. 2 scholarships per
year. Write for complete information.

1149

**ABBIE M. GRIFFIN EDUCATIONAL
FUND (Scholarships)**
c/o Winer & Bennett
111 Concord Street
Nashua, NH 03060
603/882-5157

AMOUNT: $300-$2,000
DEADLINE(S): May 1
FIELD(S): All areas of study

Open only to residents of Merrimack, NH.
Awards only to entering freshmen for full-
time undergraduate study at an accredited
college or university.
10-15 awards per year. Write for complete
information.

1150

**ABE AND ANNIE SEIBEL FOUNDATION
(Interest-free Educational Loan Fund)**
U.S. National Bank
P.O. Box 179
Galveston, TX 77553
409/763-1151

AMOUNT: Up to $3,000 a year

DEADLINE(S): Feb 28

FIELD(S): All fields of study

Open to Texas residents who will be or are enrolled (for at least 12 credit hours per semester) as undergraduate students at a Texas college or university. Must maintain 3.0 or better GPA. For study leading to first 4-year degree.

Write for complete information.

1151

AFS INTERCULTURAL PROGRAMS
(International Exchange Student Program)
220 E. 42nd Street, Third Floor
New York, NY 10017
212/949-4242; 800/AFS-INFO

AMOUNT: Varies

DEADLINE(S): Varies

FIELD(S): High school students involved with AFS

International exchange of high school students. Students live with host families and attend local secondary schools. Students go to and from 50 countries. Scholarship assistance for summer, school year, and semester.

Deadlines are in the Fall and Spring. 10,000 participants worldwide. Write for complete information. AFS participants only.

1152

AIR FORCE AID SOCIETY (General
Henry H. Arnold Education Grant Program)
1745 Jefferson Davis Hwy., #202
Arlington, VA 22202
800/429-9475

AMOUNT: $1,500 freshmen year of sons/daughters; $1,000/subsequent years

DEADLINE(S): Mar (Applications available then. Deadline is Apr)

FIELD(S): All fields of study

Open to undergrads who are dependent children of active duty, retired, or deceased members of the U.S. Air Force, spouses of active duty or retired members, or surviving spouses of members who died on active duty or in retired status residing in continental U.S. (lower 48 states) only. U.S. citizenship or legal residency required.

For full-time study at an accredited institution. Must maintain at least a 2.0 GPA. Must re-apply each year.

1153

AIR FORCE SERGEANTS'
ASSOCIATION (Scholarship Awards
Program)
P.O. Box 50
Temple Hills, MD 20748
301/899-3500

AMOUNT: $1,000-$2,500

DEADLINE(S): Apr 15

FIELD(S): All fields of study

Open to single dependent children (under 23) of AFSA members or its auxiliary. For undergraduate study at accredited institutions only. Awards are based on academic excellence.

For application and complete information send self-addressed stamped ($.75) business- size envelope to AFSA/AMF Scholarships Administrator; 5211 Auth Road, Suitland, MD 20746.

1154

AIRLINE PILOTS ASSOCIATION
(Scholarship Program)
1625 Massachusetts Ave. NW
Washington, D.C. 20036
202/797-4050

AMOUNT: $3,000 per year for up to 4 years

DEADLINE(S): Apr 1

FIELD(S): All fields of study

Open to undergraduate sons or daughters of medically retired or deceased pilot members of the Airline Pilots Association. Academic capability and financial need are considered. Renewable for up to 3 years.

Write for complete information only if above qualifications are met.

1155

AIRMEN MEMORIAL FOUNDATION
(AMF Scholarship Awards Program)
5211 Auth Road
Suitland, MD 20746
800/638-0594

AMOUNT: $500-$3,000

DEADLINE(S): Apr 15

FIELD(S): All fields of study

Open to unmarried dependent children (under 25) of Air Force enlisted personnel (active or retired) of all components, including Air National Guard & Reserves. For undergraduate study at any accredited academic or trade/technical school.

Send self-addressed stamped ($.75) business-size envelope to AFSA/AMF Scholarship Program, P.O. Box 50, Temple Hills, MD 20748 for application and complete information. Applications available November 1 through March 31.

1156

ALABAMA COMMISSION ON HIGHER EDUCATION (Scholarships; Grants; Loans; Work Study Programs)
P.O. Box 302000
Montgomery, AL 36130-2000
Written inquiry

AMOUNT: Varies

DEADLINE(S): Varies

FIELD(S): All fields of study

The commission administers a number of financial aid programs tenable at post-secondary institutions in Alabama. Some awards are need-based.

Write for the "Financial Aid Sources in Alabama" brochure or contact high school guidance counselor or college financial aid officer.

1157

ALABAMA DEPARTMENT OF VETERANS AFFAIRS (G.I. Dependents Scholarship Program)
P.O. Box 1509
Montgomery, AL 36102-1509
334/242-5077

AMOUNT: Varies

DEADLINE(S): Varies (Prior to 26th birthday)

FIELD(S): All fields of study

Open to dependent children (under age 26) of veterans who were permanent Alabama residents for at least 1 year prior to active duty and who died as a result of military service or were/are MIAs or POWs or became 20%-100% disabled.

Applicants must be Alabama residents. For attendance at state-supported Alabama institutions as well as vocational training schools. Totally disabled vets who are not original Alabama residents may qualify after 5 years of Alabama residency. Write for complete information.

1158

ALABAMA DEPARTMENT OF VETERANS AFFAIRS (G.I. Dependents Scholarship Program)
P.O. Box 1509
Montgomery, AL 36102-1509
334/242-5077

AMOUNT: Varies

DEADLINE(S): None

FIELD(S): All fields of study

Open to wife or widow (not remarried) of veteran who was an Alabama resident for at least 1 year prior to active duty and died as a result of military service, was/is MIA or a POW, or became 20%-100% disabled.

Vets who are not original Alabama residents but have a 100% service-connected disability may qualify after 5 years' residency in Alabama. Awards tenable at state-supported Alabama institutions. Contact Edward H. Minter III at above address for complete information.

1159

ALASKA COMMISSION ON POST-SECONDARY EDUCATION (Student Loan Program; Family Loan Program)

3030 Vintage Blvd.
Juneau, AK 99801-7109
907/465-2962

AMOUNT: $8,500 undergraduate; $9,500 graduate
DEADLINE(S): May 15
FIELD(S): All areas of study

Open to Alaska residents of at least 1 year. These low-interest loans (8% student; 5% family) support full-time and half-time study at any accredited vocational, undergraduate, or graduate institution.

Up to $8,500 available for vocational or undergraduate study and up to $9,500 for graduate study. Renewable. Write for complete information.

1160

ALASKA COMMISSION ON POST-SECONDARY EDUCATION (State Educational Incentive Grant Program)

3030 Vintage Blvd.
Juneau, AK 99801-7109
907/465-6741

AMOUNT: $100-$1,500
DEADLINE(S): May 31
FIELD(S): All fields of study

Open to Alaska residents of at least 1 year who are accepted to or enrolled in their first undergraduate degree or comparable certificate program at an accredited institution (in-state or out-of-state). Need must be demonstrated.

200 grants per year. Write for complete information.

1161

ALBERT BAKER FUND
(Student Loans)

5 Third Street, #717
San Francisco, CA 94103
415/543-7028

AMOUNT: $1,600-$2,500
DEADLINE(S): Jul 1
FIELD(S): All fields of study

Open to students who are members of the Mother Church—the First Church of Christ Scientist in Boston—and are active as Christian Scientists. Student must have other primary lender and be enrolled in an accredited college or university.

Foreign students must have cosigner who is a U.S. citizen. Average of 160 awards per year. Write or call for complete information. Applicant must be the one who calls.

1162

ALEXANDER GRAHAM BELL ASSOCIATION FOR THE DEAF (Elsie Bell Grosvenor Scholarship Awards)

3417 Volta Place NW
Washington, D.C. 20007-2778
202/337-5220

AMOUNT: $500-$1,000
DEADLINE(S): Apr 1 (all materials)
FIELD(S): All areas of study

Open to oral deaf students who were born with severe or profound hearing impairment or who suffered such impairment before acquiring language. Must be accepted into a full-time academic program for hearing students.

Must reside in or attend college in Washington, D.C. metropolitan area. Write for complete information.

1163

**ALEXANDER GRAHAM BELL
ASSOCIATION FOR THE DEAF (Lucille
A. Abt & Maude Winkler Scholarships)**
3417 Volta Place NW
Washington, D.C. 20007-2778
202/337-5220; E-mail: Agbell2@aol.com

AMOUNT: $1,000
DEADLINE(S): Apr 1 (all materials)
FIELD(S): All fields of study
Open to oral deaf students born with a severe
or profound hearing impairment or who
suffered such a loss before acquiring language. Must be accepted into a full-time
academic program for hearing students.
5 awards per year. Preference to North
American citizens. Write for complete
information.

1164

**ALEXANDER GRAHAM BELL
ASSOCIATION FOR THE DEAF (Herbert
P. Feibelman Jr. International Parents'
Organization Scholarship Awards)**
3417 Volta Place NW
Washington, D.C. 20007-2778
202/337-5220 (Voice or TDD); E-mail:
Agbell2@aol.com

AMOUNT: $1,000
DEADLINE(S): Apr 1 (all materials)
FIELD(S): All fields of study
Open to oral deaf students born with severe
or profound hearing impairment or who
suffered such loss before acquiring lan-
guage. Must be accepted into a full-time
academic program for hearing students.
Preference to North American citizens.
Write for complete information.

1165

**ALEXANDER GRAHAM BELL
ASSOCIATION FOR THE DEAF (Oral
Hearing-Impaired Section Scholarship Award)**
3417 Volta Place NW
Washington, D.C. 20007-2778

202/337-5220; E-mail: Agbell2@aol.com

AMOUNT: $1,000
DEADLINE(S): Apr 1 (all materials)
FIELD(S): All fields of study
Open to oral deaf undergraduate students
who were born with a severe or profound
hearing impairment or who have suffered
hearing loss before acquiring language.
Must be accepted into a full-time academic
program for hearing students.
Must be citizen of North America. Write for
complete information.

1166

**ALEXANDER GRAHAM BELL
ASSOCIATION FOR THE DEAF**
3417 Volta Place NW
Washington, D.C. 20007-2778
202/337-5220

AMOUNT: $250-$1,000
DEADLINE(S): Apr 1
FIELD(S): All areas of study
Open to students who are oral deaf or were
born with a profound hearing impairment
or suffered loss before acquiring language.
Must be accepted into a full-time academic
program for hearing students.
North American citizens given preference.
Write for complete information.

1167

**ALEXANDER GRAHAM BELL
ASSOCIATION FOR THE DEAF (School
Age Financial Aid Awards)**
3417 Volta Place
Washington, D.C. 20007-2778
202/337-5220; E-mail: Agbell2@aol.com

AMOUNT: Varies
DEADLINE(S): May 1 (request applications
between Mar 1 and Apr 1)
FIELD(S): All fields of study
For aural/oral students between the ages of 6
and 21 who have moderate to profound
hearing losses. Must use speech and residual
hearing and/or speechreading as primary

1177

AMERICAN RADIO RELAY LEAGUE FOUNDATION (New England FEMARA Scholarship)
225 Main Street
Newington, CT 06111
860/594-0200; Fax 860/594-0259; Internet: www.arrl.org/arrlf

AMOUNT: $600
DEADLINE(S): Feb 15
FIELD(S): All fields of study

Open to residents of the six New England states who are radio amateurs holding at least a technician's license.
Multiple scholarships per year for ham radio enthusiasts.

1178

AMERICAN RADIO RELAY LEAGUE FOUNDATION (Senator Barry Goldwater [#K7UGA] Scholarship Fund)
225 Main Street
Newington, CT 06111
860/594-0200; Fax 860/594-0259; Internet: www.arrl.org/arrlf

AMOUNT: $5,000+
DEADLINE(S): Feb 15
FIELD(S): All fields of study

Open to students who are licensed radio amateurs (at least novice level) & enrolled full-time as an undergraduate or graduate student at an accredited institution.
1 per year for ham radio enthusiasts.

1179

AMERICAN RADIO RELAY LEAGUE FOUNDATION ("You've Got a Friend in Pennsylvania" Scholarship Fund)
225 Main Street
Newington, CT 06111
860/594-0200; Fax 860/594-0259; Internet: www.arrl.org/arrlf

AMOUNT: $1,000
DEADLINE(S): Feb 15

FIELD(S): All fields of study
Open to ARRL members who hold a 'General' amateur radio license. Preference to PA residents.
Write for complete information.

1180

AMERICAN SAMOA GOVERNMENT (Financial Aid Program)
Dept. of Education
Office of Student Financial Program
Pago Pago, American Samoa 96799
684/633-4255

AMOUNT: $5,000
DEADLINE(S): Apr 30
FIELD(S): All fields of study

Scholarships open to residents of American Samoa. Awards support undergraduate & graduate study at all accredited colleges & universities. Applicants from off islands may be eligible if their parents are citizens of American Samoa.
Approximately 50 awards per year. Renewable. Write for complete information.

1181

ANITA H. RICHARD TRUST (David Carlyle III Scholarship)
353 Chicago Ave.
Savanna, IL 61074
815/273-2839

AMOUNT: $2,000 per semester for 4 years
DEADLINE(S): Apr 15 (every 4 years)
FIELD(S): All fields of study

Open to graduating seniors of Carrol County (IL) high schools. Awards tenable at accredited undergraduate colleges and universities. Must maintain at least a 2.0 GPA (4.0 scale), be a U.S. citizen and demonstrate financial need.
Award is given every 4 years and is advertised when it is available. Amount of award depends on interest rates. Write for complete information.

1182

APPALOOSA YOUTH FOUNDATION
(Youth Educational Scholarships)
P.O. Box 8403
Moscow, ID 83843
208/882-5578

AMOUNT: $1,000-$2,000
DEADLINE(S): Jun 10
FIELD(S): All fields of study

Open to members of the Appaloosa Youth
Association or the Appaloosa Horse Club,
children of Appaloosa Horse Club members, and individuals sponsored by a regional club or racing association.

9 scholarships per year—1 equine related; 8,
all areas of study. Renewable. Must demonstrate financial need, number of children,
and number of children in college. Contact
the Youth Coordinator at address above for
complete information.

1183

ARKANSAS DEPARTMENT OF HIGHER
EDUCATION (Student Assistance Grant
Program)
114 E. Capitol
Little Rock, AR 72201
501/342-9300

AMOUNT: $200-$624
DEADLINE(S): Apr 15
FIELD(S): All fields of study

Open to residents of Arkansas attending
undergraduate institutions in Arkansas.
Financial need and satisfactory academic
progress must be demonstrated. U.S. citizenship or legal residency required.

Awards are first-come-first-serve until funds
are exhausted. Approximately 9,500 grants
per year. Write for complete information.

1184

ARLINE P. PADELFORD SCHOLARSHIP
TRUST (Scholarships)
c/o State Street Bank & Trust Co.
P.O. Box 351
Boston, MA 02101
617/786-3000

AMOUNT: $600
DEADLINE(S): None specified
FIELD(S): All areas of study

Scholarships for worthy and deserving students at Taunton (MA) High School to pursue college or technical education.

12 scholarships per year. Contact Taunton
High guidance counselor for complete
information.

1185

ARMENIAN RELIEF SOCIETY OF
NORTH AMERICA INC. (Grants)
80 Bigelow Ave.
Watertown, MA 02172
617/926-3801

AMOUNT: $400-$1,000
DEADLINE(S): Apr 1
FIELD(S): All fields of study

Open to undergrad and grad students of
Armenian ancestry who are attending an
accredited 4-year college or university in
the U.S. and have completed at least one
semester. Awards based on need, merit &
involvement in Armenian community.

Write to scholarship committee (address
above) for complete information. Enclose
self-addressed stamped envelope and indicate whether undergrad or grad student.

1186

ARMENIAN STUDENTS' ASSOCIATION
OF AMERICA INC. (Scholarships;
Fellowships)
Scholarship Adm.
395 Concord Ave.
Belmont, MA 02178

Written inquiry

AMOUNT: $500-$2,500

DEADLINE(S): Jan 15 (Must request application by then. Not due till Mar 15)

FIELD(S): All fields of study

For full-time grads & undergrads attending a U.S. 4-year accredited college or university. Must have completed or be in process of completing 1st year of college or higher and have good academic performance.

Financial need must be demonstrated. Participation in extracurricular activities is required. Approximately 30 awards per year. Renewable. $10 application fee. Write for complete information.

1187

ARMY EMERGENCY RELIEF

Dept. of Scholarships
200 Stovall Street
Alexandria, VA 22332-0600
Written inquiry; Internet: www.aerhq.org

AMOUNT: Up to $1,500 per year

DEADLINE(S): Mar 1

FIELD(S): All fields of study

Open to unmarried dependent children of active, retired, or deceased members of the U.S. Army. Applicants may not have reached their 22nd birthday before June 1 of the school year that begins the following September. For undergraduate study.

Must submit financial aid form and official high school transcript. Write for complete information.

1188

ARTHUR C. & FLORENCE S. BOEHMER FUND (Scholarships)

c/o Rinn & Elliot
P.O. Box 1827
Lodi, CA 95241
209/369-2781

AMOUNT: Varies depending on yearly income

DEADLINE(S): Jun 15 (Applications available Mar 1 to Jun 15)

FIELD(S): Medical

Open to students who are graduates of a high school within the Lodi (San Joaquin County, CA) Unified School District. For undergraduate, graduate, or post-graduate study in the field of medicine at an accredited California institution.

Grade-point average of 2.9 or better required. Scholarships are renewable. Write for complete information.

1189

ASSOCIATION OF THE SONS OF POLAND (Scholarship Program)

333 Hackensack Street
Carlstadt, NJ 07072
201/935-2807

AMOUNT: $1,000 Scholarship; $100 Achievement Award

DEADLINE(S): May 14

FIELD(S): All fields of study

Open to high school students who have been members of the Association of the Sons of Poland for at least 2 years and are insured by the association. Must be entering an accredited college in September of the year of high school graduation.

Must be U.S. citizen. Write for complete information.

1190

ASTRAEA NATIONAL LESBIAN ACTION FOUNDATION (Margot Karle Scholarship)

116 E. 16th Street, 7th Floor
New York, NY 10003
212/529-8021

AMOUNT: $500

DEADLINE(S): Feb 15; Aug 15

FIELD(S): All fields of study

Must demonstrate financial need and a high degree of community involvement.

Available ONLY to undergrads enrolled in the City University of New York system.

1191

**AUTOMOTIVE HALL OF FAME INC.
(Scholarship Program)**
P.O. Box 1727
Midland, MI 48641-1727
517/631-5760; Fax 517-631-0524

AMOUNT: $250-$2,000
DEADLINE(S): Jun 30
FIELD(S): All fields of study

Open to full-time undergraduate college students who have a sincere interest in pursuing an automotive career upon graduation from college. Must be at least a sophomore when scholarship is granted, but freshmen may send in application.

16-24 awards per year. Renewable with reapplication. Write for complete information.

1192

**AYN RAND INSTITUTE (Fountainhead
Essay Contest)**
P.O. Box 6004, Dept. DB
Inglewood, CA 90312
310/306-9232; Fax 310/306-4925

AMOUNT: $5,000—1st prize; $1,000—2nd prize (5); $500—3rd prize (10)
DEADLINE(S): Apr 15
FIELD(S): All fields of study

Essay competition open to high school juniors & seniors. Contest is to encourage analytical thinking and writing excellence & to introduce students to the philosophic and psychological meaning of Ayn Rand's novel *The Fountainhead.*

16 awards per year. Write for complete information.

1193

BALSO FOUNDATION (Scholarships)
493 West Main Street
Cheshire, CT 06410
203/272-5381

AMOUNT: Varies
DEADLINE(S): Apr 15

FIELD(S): All fields of study

Open to residents of Cheshire CT. Scholarships are for full-time undergraduate study & are awarded based on academic & financial need. U.S. citizenship required.

10 to 15 awards per year. Renewable. Write for complete information.

1194

**BEATRICE AND FRANCIS THOMPSON
SCHOLARSHIP FUND (Scholarship)**
Ms. Diane Duffy
Co-trustee/Secretary
417 Summit Avenue
Oradell, NJ 07649
Written inquiry only

AMOUNT: $2,000-$4,000
DEADLINE(S): Nov 1 (for spring semester); Mar 1 (for fall semester)
FIELD(S): All areas of study

Open to undergraduate or voc-tech students whose parents are both deceased. Applicants should have a 2.5 or better GPA. Financial need is a consideration. Renewable.

Open to U.S. citizens who are Pennsylvania and New Jersey residents only.

1195

**BEMENT EDUCATIONAL GRANTS
COMMITTEE (Diocese of Western
Massachusetts Undergraduate Grants)**
37 Chestnut Street
Springfield, MA 01103
413/737-4786

AMOUNT: Up to $750
DEADLINE(S): Feb 15
FIELD(S): All fields of study

Undergraduate grants for unmarried students who are active Episcopalians in the Diocese of Western Massachusetts. High GPA. Financial need. Interview required as arranged.

60-70 awards per year. Renewable with reapplication. Write for complete information.

1196

**BETA THETA PI GENERAL
FRATERNITY (Scholarships & Fellowships)**
Administrative Office
208 East High Street
Oxford, OH 45056
513/523-7591

AMOUNT: $750-$1,500
DEADLINE(S): Apr
FIELD(S): All fields of study

Open to undergraduate and graduate students
who are Beta Theta Pi members in good
standing and have a competitive grade-
point average.
30 scholarships and 8 fellowships per year.
Non-renewable. Write for complete information.

1197

BLAINE HOUSE SCHOLARS PROGRAM
State House Station, #119
Augusta, ME 04333
207/287-2183 (800/228-3734 in state)

AMOUNT: $1,500 per year
DEADLINE(S): Apr 1
FIELD(S): All fields of study; preference to
Education majors

Maine residents. High school seniors, college
students & teachers are eligible to apply for
interest-free loans. Loans are competitive &
based on academic merit, relevance of field
of study, etc.
400 new awards per year. Renewable. Write
for complete information.

1198

**BLINDED VETERANS ASSOCIATION
(Kathern F. Gruber Scholarship Program)**
477 H Street NW
Washington, D.C. 20001-2694
800/669-7079; 202/371-8880; Fax 202/371-
8258

AMOUNT: $1,000-$2,000
DEADLINE(S): Apr 17

FIELD(S): All fields of study

Open to children and spouses of blinded veterans. The vet must be legally blind, either service or non-service connected. Must be
accepted or already enrolled full-time in a college or vocational school and be a U.S. citizen.
8 scholarships of $2,000 and 2 of $1,000. Write
for complete information.

1199

**BOETTCHER FOUNDATION
(Scholarships)**
600 17th Street, Suite 2210 South
Denver, CO 80202
303/534-1938

AMOUNT: Tuition + $2,800 stipend
DEADLINE(S): Feb 1
FIELD(S): All fields of study

Open to Colorado residents presently in the
top 7% of their high school class who have
been accepted as an incoming freshman at a
Colorado college or university. Minimum
ACT score 27; SAT 1100. U.S. citizen.
40 awards per year. Write for complete information or consult your high school counselor.

1200

**BOY SCOUTS OF AMERICA—
DR. HARRY BRITENSTOOL
SCHOLARSHIP COMMITTEE (Greater
New York City Councils Scholarship Fund)**
345 Hudson Street
New York, NY 10014-4588
212/242-1100 Ext. 271

AMOUNT: Varies
DEADLINE(S): Jun 1
FIELD(S): All fields of study

Undergraduate scholarships for students who
have been at one time registered with the
Greater New York councils, Boy Scouts of
America or employed by that organization.
Must show academic excellence, financial
need, and study at least 24 credit hours during the school year. U.S. citizens only.
Must submit essay on "What Scouting has
meant to me."

1201

BRITISH AMERICAN EDUCATIONAL FOUNDATION (Scholars' Program)
Box 2482
Providence, RI 02906
401/272-2438; Fax 401/273-6296

AMOUNT: Up to $10,000
DEADLINE(S): May 1
FIELD(S): Wide variety limited by British 'A' level offerings at each school

Open to American high school seniors who are 18 or younger and want to spend a year at an independent boarding school in the United Kingdom prior to entering college. Financial need is used to evaluate financial aid.

Write for complete information.

1202

BUCK INSTITUTE FOR EDUCATION (American Revolution Bicentennial Scholarships)
Marie Kanarr
18 Commercial Blvd.
Novato, CA 94949
415/883-0122

AMOUNT: $500-$2,000
DEADLINE(S): Mar 31
FIELD(S): All fields of study

For Marin County students who have been county residents since Sept. 1 of the year prior to submitting an application. Scholarships tenable at accredited colleges, universities, and vocational or trade programs.

Contact high school or college counselor or address above for complete information.

1203

BUCKNELL UNIVERSITY (Gertrude J. Deppen & Voris Auten Teetotaling Nonathlete Scholarship Fund)
Financial Aid Office
Lewisburg, PA 17837
717/524-1331

AMOUNT: Varies
DEADLINE(S): None
FIELD(S): All fields of study

Open to students who have lived in Mt. Carmel, PA for the last 10 years; graduated from Mt. Carmel High School and do not use alcohol, tobacco, narcotics or engage in strenuous athletic contests.

Award tenable at Bucknell University.

1204

BUFFALO FOUNDATION (Scholarships)
237 Main Street
Buffalo, NY 14203
716/852-2857

AMOUNT: Varies
DEADLINE(S): May 10
FIELD(S): All fields of study

Scholarships open to residents of Erie County, NY. Awards are limited to one member per family per year and are tenable at recognized undergraduate colleges and universities.

Approximately 400 awards per year. Write for complete information.

1205

C. BASCOM SLEMP FOUNDATION (Scholarships)
Star Bank NA
P.O. Box 5208
Cincinnati, OH 45201
513/762-8878

AMOUNT: $2,000
DEADLINE(S): Oct 1
FIELD(S): All fields of study

Open only to residents of Lee or Wise counties in Virginia. For undergraduate study.

30 awards per year. Write for complete information.

1206

CALIFORNIA CHICANO NEWS MEDIA ASSOCIATION (Joel Garcia Memorial Scholarship)
c/o USC School of Journalism
3716 S. Hope Street, Room 301
Los Angeles, CA 90007-4344
213/743-2440; Fax 213/744-1809; Internet:
www.ccnma.org

AMOUNT: Up to $2,000
DEADLINE(S): Apr 3
FIELD(S): All fields of study—however, must have a sincere desire for a career in the news media

Open to all Latino undergraduate students interested in pursuing careers in any facet of journalism. It is not necessary to be a journalism or communications major. For full-time students who are either California residents or attend an accredited college or university in California.

10-30 awards per year. Write for complete information.

1207

CALIFORNIA DEPARTMENT OF VETERANS AFFAIRS (College Fee Waiver Program)
1227 'O' Street
Sacramento, CA 95814
916/653-2573; 800/952-5626; Internet:
www.ns.net/cadva/

AMOUNT: Tuition and fee waiver
DEADLINE(S): None
FIELD(S): All fields of study

For spouses and children of military and California National Guard veterans who (as a result of military service) are disabled or died of service-related injuries. Awards are for study at California state universities, University of California campuses, and California community colleges.

Call, write, or visit website for information about this and other programs offered by the California Department of Veterans Affairs.

1208

CALIFORNIA GOVERNOR'S COMMITTEE FOR EMPLOYMENT OF DISABLED PERSONS (Hal Connolly Scholar-Athlete Award)
P.O. Box 826880, MIC 41
Sacramento, CA 94280-0001
916/654-8055; TDD 916/654-9820

AMOUNT: $1,000
DEADLINE(S): Feb 28
FIELD(S): All fields of study

Must have competed during high school in varsity-level or equivalent athletics and have a disability. Academic and athletic histories must demonstrate the qualities of leadership and accomplishment. Minimum 2.8 GPA. Age 19 or under.

Six awards—3 to females and 3 to males. Must be a California resident; write for more information.

1209

CALIFORNIA JUNIOR MISS PROGRAM (Scholarships & Awards)
P.O. Box 1863
Santa Rosa, CA 95402
707/576-7505

AMOUNT: $15,000
DEADLINE(S): Varies
FIELD(S): All fields of study

Competition open to girls in their junior year of high school who are U.S. citizens and California residents. Winner receives a $15,000 college scholarship; runners-up share up to $30,000 in awards. For undergraduate or graduate study.

Award can be used for books, fees, and tuition at any college in the world. Write to C. (Ting) Guggiana at above address for complete information.

1210

CALIFORNIA MASONIC FOUNDATION (General and Special Fund Scholarship Programs)

1111 California Street
San Francisco, CA 94108-2284
415/776-7000; Info. line: 415/292-9196; Fax 415/776-0483

AMOUNT: Varies
DEADLINE(S): Feb 28
FIELD(S): All fields of study

Undergraduate scholarships open to California residents accepted to or enrolled in accredited colleges or technical schools in the U.S. No religious or membership requirements. Must be U.S. citizen.

Special funds have been established with various restrictive conditions. Send self-addressed stamped envelope to Judy Liang at above address.

1211

CALIFORNIA STUDENT AID COMMISSION (Cal. Grant 'A' Program)

Grant Services Division
P.O. Box 419027
Rancho Cordova, CA 95741-9027
916/526-7590

AMOUNT: Varies
DEADLINE(S): Mar 2
FIELD(S): All fields of study

Open to low- and middle-income undergraduate California residents attending eligible schools in California. Grants support tuition and fee costs. Selection based on need & grades. U.S. citizenship or legal residency required.

Approximately 19,000 grants per year. Renewable. Contact your counselor, financial aid office, or address above for complete information.

1212

CALIFORNIA STUDENT AID COMMISSION (Cal. Grant 'B' Program)

Grant Services Division
P.O. Box 419027
Rancho Cordova, CA 95741-9027
916/526-7590

AMOUNT: $700 to $1,410 (living allowance); $1,584 (avg. state school tuition); $5,250 (avg. independent school tuition)
DEADLINE(S): Mar 2
FIELD(S): All fields of study

Open to very low-income undergrads with high potential attending eligible 2- & 4-year colleges in California. Grant supports living allowance and tuition/fee costs. Must be California resident and U.S. citizen/legal resident/eligible non-citizen.

Approximately 19,000 grants per year. Renewable. Contact your counselor, financial aid office, or address above for complete information.

1213

CALIFORNIA STUDENT AID COMMISSION (Law Enforcement Personnel Dependents Grant Program)

Grant Services Division
P.O. Box 419027
Rancho Cordova, CA 95741-9027
916/526-7590

AMOUNT: Up to $1,500 per year
DEADLINE(S): None given
FIELD(S): All fields of study

For the natural or adopted child of a California law enforcement officer, firefighter, correctional officer, or Calif. Youth Authority employee killed or 100% disabled in the performance of duty. For undergrad or grad study at eligible California schools. Must be resident of California and U.S. citizen.

Awards limited to a maximum of $6,000 over six years. May be used for tuition, fees, books, supplies, and living expenses. Contact Specialized Programs Branch at above location.

1214

CALIFORNIA TEACHERS ASSN. (CTA Scholarships)
P.O. Box 921
1705 Murchison Drive
Burlingame, CA 94011
415/697-1400

AMOUNT: $2,000
DEADLINE(S): Feb 15
FIELD(S): All fields of study

Open to active CTA members or their dependent children for undergraduate or graduate study. Applications available each October from CTA Human Rights Department, address above, or regional offices.

20 scholarships per year. Write for complete information.

1215

CAMP FOUNDATION (Scholarship Grants)
P.O. Box 813
Franklin, VA 23851
804/562-3439

AMOUNT: $4,000 (1); $2,500 (6)
DEADLINE(S): Mar 1
FIELD(S): All fields of study

Open to graduating high school seniors in the city of Franklin and the counties of Isle of Wight and Southampton, Virginia, or to residents of these areas who graduated from high school elsewhere. For undergraduate study.

These awards are made locally—NOT on a nationwide basis. Only those who meet residency requirements should write for complete information.

1216

CAPE CANAVERAL CHAPTER RETIRED OFFICERS ASSOC.
(Scholarships)
P.O. Box 254708
Patrick AFB, FL 32925-4708

Written inquiry

AMOUNT: $2,000/year
DEADLINE(S): Mar 31
FIELD(S): All fields of study

Open ONLY to Brevard County, Florida residents who have completed at least three semesters at any accredited four-year college in the U.S. and are descendants or dependents of active duty or retired military personnel. Must be U.S. citizen.

Awards renewable for one year. Send #10 SASE to the Scholarship Committee (address above) for complete information.

1217

CDR. WILLIAM S. STUHR SCHOLARSHIP FUND
1200 Fifth Ave., Apt. 9-D
New York, NY 10029
Written inquiry

AMOUNT: $1,125 per year for 4 years
DEADLINE(S): Varies (according to service—usually Feb 1)
FIELD(S): All fields of study

For high school seniors who are dependents of active duty or retired career members of one of five branches of the armed services. For study at an accredited 4-year college only.

Applicants should be in top 10% of their class and demonstrate leadership ability & financial need. Send self-addressed stamped envelope (business size) for information.

1218

CENTRAL SCHOLARSHIP BUREAU
(Interest-free Loans)
1700 Reisterstown Road, #220
Baltimore, MD 21208
410/415-5558

AMOUNT: $500-$8,000 (max. through grad school)
DEADLINE(S): Jun 1; Dec 1
FIELD(S): All fields of study

Interest-free loans for residents of metropolitan Baltimore area who have exhausted all other available avenues of funding. Aid is offered for study at any accredited undergrad or graduate institution.

Awards are made on a non-competitive basis to anyone with a sound educational plan. 125 loans per year. Must apply first through government and school. Write for complete information.

1219

CHATHAM COLLEGE (Merit Scholarship Program)
Woodland Road
Office of Admissions
Pittsburgh, PA 15232
412/365-1290

AMOUNT: Up to $10,000 per year
DEADLINE(S): None
FIELD(S): All fields of study

Women only. Awards open to entering first-year and transfer students accepted at Chatham College. Selection based on past academic performance.

Renewable for up to 4 years. Contact Office of Admissions for details.

1220

CHAUTAUQUA REGION COMMUNITY FOUNDATION INC. (Scholarships)
21 E. Third Street, Suite 301
Jamestown, NY 14701
716/661-3390

AMOUNT: $100-$2,000
DEADLINE(S): Jun 1 (college freshmen); Jul 15 (college students)
FIELD(S): All fields of study

Numerous scholarships with varying requirements open ONLY to students living in the vicinity of Jamestown, NY. Preference to students in 12 school districts in Southern Chautauqua County. For full-time study.

Write for complete information.

1221

CHEROKEE NATION (Higher Education Need-based Grant Program)
P.O. Box 948
Tahlequah, OK 74465
918/456-0671

AMOUNT: Varies
DEADLINE(S): Apr 1
FIELD(S): All fields of study

Grants available to members of the Cherokee Nation of Oklahoma. Awards are tenable at accredited undergraduate 2-year & 4-year colleges & universities in the U.S. U.S. citizenship required. Students must be eligible for Pell grants.

500 awards per year. Write for complete information.

1222

CHRISTIAN RECORD SERVICES INC. (Scholarships)
4444 South 52nd Street
Lincoln, NE 68516
402/488-0981

AMOUNT: $500-$1,000
DEADLINE(S): Apr 1
FIELD(S): All fields of study

Undergraduate scholarships available to legally blind students who are attending school in the U.S. Must demonstrate financial need. U.S. citizenship required.

10-15 awards per year. Write for complete information.

1223

CITIZEN'S SCHOLARSHIP FOUNDATION OF AMERICA, H&R BLOCK (Scholarships)
1505 Riverview Road
P.O. Box 297
St. Peter, MN 56082
507/931-1682

AMOUNT: Varies

DEADLINE(S): Apr 1

FIELD(S): All fields of study

For children of eligible employees of H&R Block Inc. or one of its owned subsidiaries. Based on academic capability and financial need. Must be enrolled full time.

35 awards per year. Contact address above for complete information.

1224

CLARK FOUNDATION (Scholarship Program)
P.O. Box 427
Cooperstown, NY 13326
607/547-9927

AMOUNT: $500-$5,000

DEADLINE(S): None

FIELD(S): All fields of study

Open to graduates of high schools in the districts of Cherry Valley, Cooperstown, Edmeston, Laurens, Milford, Richfield Springs, Scenevus, Springfield, Van Hornsville, West Winfield & Worcester. 700 scholarships per year. Renewable.

Must have high school diploma, rank in the upper one-third of graduating class and have a 3.0 or better GPA.

1225

COLLEGE FOUNDATION INC. (Federal PLUS Loans Under NC Federal Family Education Loan Program)
2100 Yonkers Road
P.O. Box 12100
Raleigh, NC 27605
919/821-4771; 888/234-6400; E-mail: info@cfi-nc.org; Internet: www.cfi-nc.org

AMOUNT: Difference between cost of attending and other financial aid received

DEADLINE(S): Varies

FIELD(S): All fields of study

For parent of student who is dependent (by federal definition) and enrolled in eligible U.S. college. If the student is at a college not in NC, borrower must be legal NC resi-

dent. Parent does not have to demonstrate need but must NOT have "adverse credit history." Must meet nationwide Federal Plus Loans requirements.

Approximately 2,600 loans per year. Must reapply each year. Write for complete information and an application.

1226

COLLEGE FOUNDATION INC. (North Carolina Federal Family Education Loan Program; Stafford Loans—Subsidized & Unsubsidized—and PLUS loans)
2100 Yonkers Road
P.O. Box 12100
Raleigh, NC 27605
919/821-4771; 1-888/CFI-6400; E-mail: info@cfi-nc.org; Internet: www.cfi-nc.org

AMOUNT: $2,625 and up

DEADLINE(S): Varies

FIELD(S): All fields of study

Open to U.S. citizens who are legal residents of NC enrolled in an eligible in-state or out-of-state college or an out-of-state student attending an eligible NC college. Must meet nationwide eligibility requirements of Stafford loans. Must complete and file the Free Application for Federal Student Aid (FAFSA).

Approximately 56,000 loans per year. Financial need must be established for subsidized loan. New loan application is required yearly. Write for complete information.

1227

COLLEGE FOUNDATION INC. (North Carolina Student Incentive Grant)
2100 Yonkers Road
P.O. Box 12100
Raleigh, NC 27605
919/821-4771; 888/234-6400; E-mail: info@cfi-nc.org; Internet: www.cfi-nc.org

AMOUNT: $200-$1,500

DEADLINE(S): Mar 15

FIELD(S): All fields of study

Undergraduate grants to students who are U.S. citizens, North Carolina residents, and attending or planning to attend college in North Carolina. Must demonstrate substantial financial need and maintain satisfactory academic progress. Must complete and file the Free Application for Federal Student Aid (FAFSA).

Approximately 4,300 grants per year. Renewable to a maximum of 5 years of undergraduate study.

1228

COLORADO MASONS BENEVOLENT FUND ASSOCIATION (Scholarship Program)
1130 Panorama Drive
Colorado Springs, CO 80904
719/471-9587

AMOUNT: Up to $20,000 over 4 years
DEADLINE(S): Mar 15
FIELD(S): All fields of study

Open to seniors in Colorado public high schools who plan to attend a Colorado college or university. Must be Colorado resident but Masonic affiliation is not required. Need is considered but is not paramount.

Applications are mailed early in November to all Colorado public schools. Contact Colorado schools. Do NOT write address above.

1229

COLORADO STATE UNIVERSITY (First Generation Award)
Financial Aid Office
Administration Annex
Fort Collins, CO 80523-8024
970/491-6321

AMOUNT: $3,100
DEADLINE(S): Apr 1
FIELD(S): All fields of study

Award is open to students whose parents have never received a bachelor's degree.

Students must be accepted for full-time study at CSU in a program leading to a bachelor's degree. Must demonstrate financial need.

Colorado residents ONLY. Write for complete information.

1230

COMMONWEALTH OF VIRGINIA DEPARTMENT OF VETERANS' AFFAIRS (War Orphans Education Program)
270 Franklin Road SW
Room 1012
Poff Federal Building
Roanoke, VA 24011-2215
703/857-7104

AMOUNT: Tuition + required fees
DEADLINE(S): None
FIELD(S): All fields of study

Open to surviving/dependent children (aged 16-25) of U.S. military personnel who were/are Virginia residents & as a result of war/armed conflict are deceased, disabled, a prisoner of war, or missing in action.

Must attend a state-supported secondary or post-secondary educational institution to pursue any vocational, technical, undergraduate, or graduate program. Write for complete information.

1231

COMMUNITY FOUNDATION OF GREATER LORAIN COUNTY (Various Scholarship Programs)
1865 N. Ridge Road E., Suite A
Lorain, OH 44055
216/277-0142 Fax: 216/277-6955

AMOUNT: Varies
DEADLINE(S): Varies
FIELD(S): All fields of study

For residents of Lorain County, Ohio. Various programs, ranging from opportunities for high school seniors through doctoral programs. Dollar amounts vary as do deadlines.

Contact the organization above for details.

1232

CONNECTICUT DEPT. OF HIGHER EDUCATION (State Scholastic Achievement Grant)
61 Woodland Street
Hartford, CT 06015-2391
860/566-2618; TDD 860/566-3910; Internet: www/lib.uconn.edu/ConnState/HigherEd/dhe.htm

AMOUNT: Up to $2,000
DEADLINE(S): Feb 15
FIELD(S): All fields of study

Open to Connecticut high school seniors and graduates who ranked in top 20% of their high school class or scored above 1200 on SAT. For undergraduate study at a Connecticut college or at colleges in states which have reciprocity agreements with Connecticut. U.S. citizenship or legal residency required.

3,000 awards per year. Write for complete information.

1233

CONNECTICUT DEPT. OF HIGHER EDUCATION (Student Financial Aid Programs)
61 Woodland Street
Hartford, CT 06105-2391
860/566-2618; TDD 860/566-3910

AMOUNT: Varies (programs differ)
DEADLINE(S): Varies (programs differ)
FIELD(S): All fields of study

Various state and federal programs providing financial aid to Connecticut students. Programs include tuition waivers for veterans and senior citizens, work-study programs, loans, scholarships, and grants.

Most programs emphasize financial need. Write for brochure listing programs and application information.

1234

CONRAIL-CONSOLIDATED RAIL CORPORATION (Women's Aid Scholarships for Men and Women)
Attn: Nancy Hoernig
2001 Market Street (18B)
P.O. Box 41418
Philadelphia, PA 19101-1418
215/209-1764

AMOUNT: $200-$1,500
DEADLINE(S): Apr 1
FIELD(S): All fields of study

Open to high school seniors who are children of ConRail, Penn Central or predecessor railroad company employees. Must demonstrate need & take SAT, TSWE & two achievement tests. For undergraduate study.

12 to 15 scholarships based on financial need and competitive exams. Renewable up to 4 years. Write for complete information.

1235

CYMDEITHAS GYMREIG/PHILADELPHIA (Scholarships)
Daniel Williams, Ysg., Hen Dy Hapus
367 S. River Street
Wilkes-Barre, PA 18702
Written inquiry only

AMOUNT: $500-$1,500
DEADLINE(S): Mar 1
FIELD(S): All fields of study

Open to undergrads of Welsh descent who live within 150 miles of Philadelphia or plan to enroll in a college within that area. Must prove Welsh descent and be active in a Welsh organization or church or participate in Welsh activities.

Must be U.S. citizen or legal resident. 5 to 6 awards per year. Renewable. Send SASE to Daniel E. Williams, Ysg., Cymdeithas Gymreig/Philadelphia (at the above address) for application and complete information.

1236

D. D. HACHAR CHARITABLE TRUST FUND (Undergraduate Scholarships)

Laredo National Bank
Trustee
P.O. Box 59
Laredo, TX 78042
512/723-1151 Ext. 670

AMOUNT: Varies

DEADLINE(S): Apr; Oct

FIELD(S): All fields of study

Open to residents of Laredo (Webb County), Texas. Scholarships available for undergraduate study. College freshmen and sophomores must maintain minimum 2.0 GPA; juniors and seniors at least 2.5 GPA. Must be enrolled full-time.

Annual family income cannot exceed $44,000. U.S. citizenship required. Write for complete information.

1237

DANISH SISTERHOOD OF AMERICA (Scholarship Program)

8004 Jasmine Blvd.
Port Richey, FL 34668-3224
Written inquiry only

AMOUNT: Varies

DEADLINE(S): Varies

FIELD(S): Continuing Education

Open to Danish Sisterhood of America members in good standing (and their children) who are attending approved schools. One-year or longer membership required. Awards are based on high academic achievement.

Write to National Vice President & Scholarship Chair Elizabeth K. Hunter at above address for complete information.

1238

DAUGHTERS OF PENELOPE (Undergraduate Scholarships)

1909 Q Street NW, Suite 500
Washington, D.C. 20009

202/234-9741; Fax 202/483-6983

AMOUNT: $500; $1,000; $1,500

DEADLINE(S): Jun 20

FIELD(S): All fields of study

Open to female undergraduates of Greek descent who are members of Daughters of Penelope or Maids of Athena or the daughter of a member of Daughters of Penelope or Order of AHEPA. Academic performance and need are main considerations.

Renewable. For membership information or an application, write to the above address.

1239

DAUGHTERS OF THE AMERICAN REVOLUTION (American Indians Scholarship)

Mrs. Lyle A. Ross
3738 South Mission Drive
Lake Havasu City, AZ 86406-4250
Written inquiry

AMOUNT: $500

DEADLINE(S): Jul 1; Nov 1

FIELD(S): All fields of study

Open to American Indians, both youth and adults, striving to get an education. Funds help students of any tribe in any state based on need, academic achievement, and ambition.

Send SASE to above address for complete information.

1240

DAUGHTERS OF THE AMERICAN REVOLUTION (Lillian and Arthur Dunn Scholarship)

Office of the Committee/Scholarships
National Society DAR
1776 D Street NW
Washington, D.C. 20006-5392
202/879-3292

AMOUNT: $1,000 per year for 4 years

DEADLINE(S): Feb 15

FIELD(S): All fields of study

Open to graduating high school seniors whose mothers are current DAR members (must be sponsored by mother's DAR chapter). Award is for undergrad study & can be renewed with annual transcript review & approval. U.S. citizenship required.

Write for complete information (include SASE).

1241

DAUGHTERS OF THE CINCINNATI (Scholarship Program)
122 East 58th Street
New York, NY 10022
212/319-6915

AMOUNT: Varies

DEADLINE(S): Mar 15

FIELD(S): All fields of study

Open to high school seniors who are daughters of commissioned officers (active, retired, or deceased) in the U.S. Army, Navy, Air Force, Marine Corps, or Coast Guard. For undergraduate study at any accredited four-year institution.

Awards based on need & merit. Include parent's rank and branch of service when writing for application or further information.

1242

DAUGHTERS OF UNION VETERANS OF THE CIVIL WAR (Grand Army of the Republic Living Memorial Scholarship)
503 South Walnut
Springfield, IL 62704
Written inquiry, postmarked by Feb 1 (MUST include SASE)

AMOUNT: $200

DEADLINE(S): Apr 30

FIELD(S): All fields of study

Open to lineal descendants of a union veteran of the Civil War. Must be a junior or senior in college, in good scholastic standing, of good moral character, and have a firm belief in the U.S. form of government.

For complete information send a self-addressed stamped envelope and proof of

direct lineage to a Civil War union veteran (military record). 3 to 4 awards per year.

1243

DAVID WASSERMAN SCHOLARSHIP FUND INC. (Award Program)
Adirondack Center
4722 State Hwy. 30
Amsterdam, NY 12010
Written inquiry

AMOUNT: $300 per year

DEADLINE(S): Apr 15

FIELD(S): All fields of study

Open to bona fide residents of Montgomery County, NY who are pursuing an undergraduate degree and are U.S. citizens.

20-25 awards per year. Renewable. Write for information and applications.

1244

DAVIS-ROBERTS SCHOLARSHIP FUND INC. (Scholarships to DeMolay & Job's Daughters)
P.O. Box 20645
Cheyenne, WY 82003
307/632-0491

AMOUNT: Varies

DEADLINE(S): Jun 15

FIELD(S): All fields of study

Open to Wyoming residents who are or have been a DeMolay or a Job's Daughter in the state of Wyoming. Scholarships for full-time undergraduate study. Financial need is a consideration. U.S. citizenship required.

12 to 14 awards annually. Renewable. Write for complete information.

1245

DEMOLAY FOUNDATION INC. (Scholarships)
10200 N. Executive Hills Blvd.
Kansas City, MO 64153
816/891-8333; Fax 816/891-9062; Internet: www.demolay.org

AMOUNT: $1,500

DEADLINE(S): Apr 1

FIELD(S): Dental; Medical

For undergraduate freshmen or sophomores with a 2.0 GPA or better. DeMolay membership is required. Considerations are leadership, academic achievement, and goals.

3 grants per year. Write for complete information.

1246

DEPARTMENT OF VETERANS AFFAIRS (Survivors and Dependents Educational Assistance Program)
810 Vermont Ave. NW
Washington, D.C. 20420
800/827-1000

AMOUNT: $404 per month for full-time study

DEADLINE(S): Varies

FIELD(S): All fields of study

Educational support for children (aged 18-26) and spouses/widows of veterans who are 100% disabled or deceased due to military service or are classified currently as prisoner of war or missing in action. Training in approved institution.

Spouses are eligible up to 10 years after determination of eligibility. Contact the nearest VA office for complete information.

1247

DESCENDANTS OF THE SIGNERS OF THE DECLARATION OF INDEPENDENCE (Scholarship Grant)
609 Irving Ave.
Deale, MD 20751
Written inquiry only

AMOUNT: Average $1,100

DEADLINE(S): Mar 15

FIELD(S): All fields of study

Undergrad and grad awards for students who are DSDI members (proof of direct descent of signer of Declaration of Independence necessary, STUDENT MUST BE A MEMBER OF DSDI before he/she can apply). Write to Scholarship Chairman at the above address for membership. Must be full-time student accepted or enrolled in a recognized U.S. four-year college or university.

Applicants for membership must provide proof of direct, lineal descendancy from a Signer. Enclose stamped self-addressed envelope.

1248

DISABLED AMERICAN VETERANS AUXILIARY (DAVA Student Loans)
3725 Alexandria Pike
Cold Spring, KY 41076
606/441-7300

AMOUNT: Up to $1,000 for 4 years

DEADLINE(S): Apr 25

FIELD(S): All fields of study

Open to citizens of U.S. who have been accepted by an institution of higher education & are children whose living mother is a life member of DAV Auxiliary or (if mother is deceased) father is a life member of at least 1 year. Must be a full-time student with a minimum of 12 credit hours and maintain at least a 2.0 GPA.

40-42 loans per year. Renewable. Write for complete information.

1249

DISTRICT OF COLUMBIA (State Student Incentive Grant Program)
2100 M. L. King, Jr. Ave. SE, Suite 401
Washington, D.C. 20020
202/727-3688

AMOUNT: $400-$1,500

DEADLINE(S): Jun

FIELD(S): All fields of study EXCEPT Law & Medicine

Open to U.S. citizens or legal residents who have lived in D.C. for at least 15 consecutive months, have at least a 2.0 GPA, can demonstrate financial need, and are enrolled in an eligible U.S. institution.

Renewable scholarships for undergraduate study. Must have high school diploma or equivalent. Write for complete information.

1250

DOG WRITERS' EDUCATIONAL TRUST
(Scholarships)

Mary Ellen Tarman
P.O. Box E
Hummelstown, PA 17036-0199
Written inquiries only

AMOUNT: Varies
DEADLINE(S): Dec 31
FIELD(S): All fields of study

For college students who have participated in organized activities with dogs or whose parents or other close relatives have done so.

Scholarships support undergraduate or graduate study. Send SASE to above location for complete information.

1251

DOLPHIN SCHOLARSHIP FOUNDATION (Scholarships)

1683 Dillingham Blvd.
Norfolk Naval Station
Norfolk, VA 23511
757/451-3660; Fax 757/489-8578

AMOUNT: $2,500/year
DEADLINE(S): Apr 15
FIELD(S): All fields of study

For high school or college dependent children of current or former members of the U.S. Navy Submarine Force who qualified in submarines and served in the force for at least 5 years or for Navy members who served at least 6 years in direct support of the Submarine Force or died in active duty.

25 awards/year. For students seeking BA or BS degree. Financial need is a consideration. Renewable for 4 years. Send SASE (business size) for complete information.

1252

DOYLE SCHOLARSHIP PROGRAM
(Scholarships)

1501 Mendocino Ave.
Santa Rosa, CA 95401
707/527-4740

AMOUNT: Varies
DEADLINE(S): Mar 1
FIELD(S): All fields of study

Applicants must be enrolled at Santa Rosa Junior College. Applications for the Doyle Scholarship program are made through the SRJC scholarship office. Awards are based on scholastic achievement and financial need. U.S. citizenship required.

Number of awards per year varies. Contact SRJC scholarship office for complete information.

1253

DURACELL/NATIONAL SCIENCE TEACHERS ASSOCIATION (Scholarship Competition)

1840 Wilson Blvd.
Arlington, VA 22201-3000
1-888/255-4242; E-mail: pbowers@nsta.org

AMOUNT: $200 to $20,000 in Savings Bonds
DEADLINE(S): Nov 1 (1st step papers); Jan 14 (entry deadline)
FIELD(S): All fields of study

Design competition open to all U.S. students in grades 7 through 12 who create & build an original working device powered by one or more Duracell batteries. 100 awards given. The teachers of the six top winners will each receive $2,000 in gift certificates for computers and accessories. All entrants will receive a gift and a certificate.

Official entry forms are available from science teachers or by writing to NSTA at the address above. Write for complete information.

1254

**EASTER SEAL SOCIETY OF IOWA, INC.
(James L. & Lavon Madden Mallory Annual
Disability Scholarship Program)**
P.O. Box 4002
Des Moines, IA 50333-4002
515/289-1933

AMOUNT: $1,000
DEADLINE(S): Apr 15
FIELD(S): All fields of study

Open ONLY to Iowa residents with a permanent disability who are graduating high school seniors. Award supports undergraduate study at a recognized college or university.
Write for complete information.

1255

**EBELL OF LOS ANGELES
SCHOLARSHIP PROGRAM (Scholarships)**
743 S. Lucerne Blvd.
Los Angeles, CA 90005-3707
213/931-1277

AMOUNT: $2,000 ($200/month for 10 months)
DEADLINE(S): May 1
FIELD(S): All fields of study

For Los Angeles County residents who are undergraduate sophomores, juniors, or seniors enrolled in a Los Angeles County college or university. Must be a U.S. citizen. GPA of 3.25 must be maintained for renewal.
50-60 awards per year. Financial need is a consideration. Write for complete information.

1256

**EDUCATION ASSISTANCE
CORPORATION FEDERAL FAMILY
EDUCATION LOAN PROGRAM (Loans)**
115 First Ave. SW
Aberdeen, SD 57401
605/225-6423

AMOUNT: Varies
DEADLINE(S): None
FIELD(S): All fields of study

South Dakota resident enrolled in an eligible school on at least a half-time basis. Must be a U.S. citizen, national or eligible non-resident.
Loans are renewable. Write to the above address for complete information.

1257

**EDUCATIONAL CREDIT
MANAGEMENT CORPORATION (Loan
Programs for Virginia Students)**
411 E. Franklin Street, Suite 300
Richmond, VA 23219-2243
804/644-6400; 888/775-ECMC; Fax 804/344-6743; E-mail: mellyson@ecmc.org

AMOUNT: Varies
DEADLINE(S): None
FIELD(S): All fields of study

Various loan programs open to students enrolled in approved institutions. Eligibility governed by ECMC and federal regulations.
Contact college financial aid office or write to address above for complete information.

1258

**EDUCATIONAL COMMUNICATIONS
SCHOLARSHIP FOUNDATION (High
School Scholarship Award)**
P.O. Box 5012
721 N. McKinley Road
Lake Forest, IL 60045-5012
847/295-6650; Fax 847/295-3972; E-mail: scholar@ecilf.com

AMOUNT: $1,000
DEADLINE(S): Mar 15 (Request application by then. Deadline is Jun 1)
FIELD(S): All fields of study

Open to current high school students who are U.S. citizens and have taken the SAT or ACT examination. Awards based on GPA, achievement test scores, leadership, work experience, essay, and financial need.

200 scholarships per year. For complete information, write, fax, or E-mail above location. Include name, home address, current year in high school, and approximate grade-point average.

1259

EDWARD RUTLEDGE CHARITY
(College Scholarships)
  Box 758
  Chippewa Falls, WI 54729
  715/723-6618

AMOUNT: $1,700
DEADLINE(S): Jul 1
FIELD(S): All fields of study

Scholarships open to residents of Chippewa County, Wisconsin. Awards are for full-time undergrad study at recognized colleges & universities. Grades and financial need are considerations. U.S. citizens only.

35 awards per year. Renewable. Contact address above for complete information.

1260

SCHOLARSHIP FUND (Undergraduate and Graduate Scholarships)
  10 Post Office Square So., Suite 1230
  Boston, MA 02109
  617/426-4434

AMOUNT: $250-$5,000
DEADLINE(S): Mar 1
FIELD(S): All fields of study

Open only to Boston residents under age 25 who can demonstrate financial need, scholastic ability, and good character. For undergraduate or graduate study but undergrads receive preference. Family home must be within Boston city limits.

Applicants must have lived in Boston from at least the beginning of their junior year in high school. Metropolitan Boston is NOT included.

1261

EISENHOWER MEMORIAL
SCHOLARSHIP FOUNDATION
(Undergraduate Scholarships)
  223 S. Pete Ellis Drive, Suite 27
  Bloomington, IN 47408
  812/332-2257

AMOUNT: $2,500-$10,000
DEADLINE(S): Nov
FIELD(S): All fields of study

Open to Indiana high school seniors in good standing who have never attended college; have faith in a divine being; and a firm belief in the free enterprise system and the American way of life. Financial need is not a consideration.

The awards are limited to certain Indiana colleges. Write for complete information.

1262

EMANUEL STERNBERGER
EDUCATIONAL FUND (Loan Program)
  P.O. Box 1735
  Greensboro, NC 27402
  910/275-6316

AMOUNT: $1,000 (1st year); $2,000 (subsequent years if funds are available); maximum $5,000
DEADLINE(S): Apr 30
FIELD(S): All fields of study

Open to North Carolina residents who are entering their junior or senior year of college or are graduate students. Considerations include grades, economic situation, references, and credit rating.

Personal interview is required. Can be used at any college or university. Write for complete information.

1263

ENGLISH-SPEAKING UNION (Lucy Dalbiac Luard Scholarship)
  16 E. 69th Street
  New York, NY 10021
  212/879-6800

AMOUNT: Full tuition and expenses

DEADLINE(S): Nov

FIELD(S): All fields of study

Open to students attending a United Negro College or Howard or Hampton University. Full scholarship to spend undergraduate junior year at a university in England. U.S. citizen.

Application must be made through student's college or university. Information and applications are sent each fall to the Academic Dean/VP for Academic Affairs at participating schools.

1264

ETHEL N. BOWEN FOUNDATION (Scholarships)
P.O. Box 1559
Bluefield , WV 24701
304/325-8181

AMOUNT: Varies

DEADLINE(S): Apr 30

FIELD(S): All fields of study

Undergraduate and occasional graduate scholarships open to residents of southwest Virginia.

20-25 awards per year. Write for complete information.

1265

FALCON FOUNDATION (Scholarships)
3116 Academy Drive, Suite 200
USF Academy, CO 80840-4480
719/333-4096

AMOUNT: $3,000

DEADLINE(S): Apr 30

FIELD(S): All fields of study

Scholarships to attend private preparatory schools for students who plan to seek admission to the U.S. Air Force Academy. Open to single students age 17-21 in excellent health and highly motivated to attend the Academy. Must be a U.S. citizen.

100 awards per year. Send a self-addressed stamped envelope for application.

1266

FEDERAL EMPLOYEE EDUCATION & ASSISTANCE FUND (FEEA Scholarship Program)
8441 W. Bowles Ave., Suite 200
Littleton, CO 80123
303/933-7580; 800/323-4140; Fax 303/933-7587

AMOUNT: $300-$1,500

DEADLINE(S): May 30 (applications available Jan through May)

FIELD(S): All fields of study

Open to current civilian federal & postal employees (with at least 3 years service) and dependent family members enrolled or planning to enroll in a 2-year, 4-year, or graduate-degree program. GPA of 3.0 or better.

Awards are merit based. Involvement in extra-curricular/community activities a factor. Send SASE (business size) for complete information. Student loans available directly through sponsor Signet Bank (800-955-0005).

1267

FEILD CO-OPERATIVE ASSOCIATION (Mississippi Resident Loans)
P.O. Box 5054
Jackson, MS 39296-5054
601/939-9295

AMOUNT: $2,000 per calendar year (12 months)

DEADLINE(S): May (Apply at any time)

FIELD(S): All fields of study

Open ONLY to Mississippi residents who are undergraduate juniors and seniors and graduate students with satisfactory academic standing. Demonstrate evidence of need & promise of financial responsibility. U.S. citizenship or legal residency required.

These are loans—NOT scholarships. Loans are renewable. Write for complete information.

1268

FIRST CAVALRY DIVISION ASSOCIATION (Scholarships)
302 N. Main
Copperas Cove, TX 76522
Written inquiry

AMOUNT: $600 per year up to 4 years max
DEADLINE(S): None specified
FIELD(S): All fields of study

Awards to children of soldiers who died or were declared 100% disabled from injuries while serving with the 1st Calvary Division during and since the Vietnam War or during Desert Storm.

If death occurred after 3/1/80 deceased parent must have been an Association member and serving with the division at the time of death. Send self-addressed stamped envelope for complete information.

1269

FIRST COMMERCIAL BANK (National Advisory Board Scholarship Program)
P.O. Box 1471
Little Rock, AR 72203
501/371-7012

AMOUNT: Varies
DEADLINE(S): Feb 1
FIELD(S): All fields of study

Open to Arkansas residents who are high school seniors and plan to attend an accredited Arkansas college or university that offers a bachelor's degree. Minimum ACT score of 28 to apply.

Renewable for up to 4 years. Write for complete information.

1270

FLEET RESERVE ASSOCIATION (Scholarships and Awards)
FRA Scholarship Administrator
125 N. West Street
Alexandria, VA 22314
708/683-1400; 800/424-1120

AMOUNT: Approximately $500
DEADLINE(S): Apr 15
FIELD(S): All fields of study

Open to children/spouses of Fleet Reserve Association members. Dependents of retired or deceased members also may apply. For undergraduate study. Awards based on financial need, scholastic standing, character & leadership qualities.

'Dependent child' is defined as unmarried; under 21; or under 23 if currently enrolled in college. Write for complete information.

1271

FLORENCE EVANS BUSHEE FOUNDATION (Scholarships)
One Beacon Street
Boston, MA 02108
617/573-0462

AMOUNT: Varies
DEADLINE(S): May 1
FIELD(S): All fields of undergraduate study

Open ONLY to undergraduate college students who reside in the Massachusetts towns of Byfield, Newbury, Newburyport, Rowley, or West Newbury.

Approx. 125 grants per year. Write for complete information.

1272

FLORIDA DEPT. OF EDUCATION (Florida Student Assistant Grants)
Office of Student Financial Assistance
1344 Florida Education Center
Tallahassee, FL 32399-0400
904/487-0049

AMOUNT: $200-$1,500
DEADLINE(S): Varies (with program)
FIELD(S): All fields of study

Three separate programs available to full-time degree-seeking undergrads who are enrolled at an eligible Florida institution. U.S. citizenship and Florida residency requirements apply. Priority to students with the lowest family resources.

Write for complete eligibility requirements and information.

1273

FOUNDATION FOR AMATEUR RADIO (Scholarships)

6903 Rhode Island Ave.
College Park, MD 20740
Written inquiry

AMOUNT: Varies each year
DEADLINE(S): Jun 1
FIELD(S): All fields of study

Program open to 'active licensed' radio amateurs ONLY. Since this specialized program changes so much each year the Foundation annually places announcements with complete eligibility requirements in the amateur radio magazines.

To determine your eligibility look for announcements in magazines such as *QST; CQ; 73; Worldradio*; etc. Write for complete information.

1274

FOUNDATION FOR EXCEPTIONAL CHILDREN (Scholarship Awards)

1920 Association Drive
Reston, VA 22091
703/264-3507

AMOUNT: $500
DEADLINE(S): Feb 1
FIELD(S): All fields of study

Undergraduate awards in 4 categories:
1. Students with disabilities. 2. Ethnic minority students with disabilities.
3. Gifted/talented students with disabilities.
4. Ethnic minority gifted/talented with disabilities.

Apply in one category only. Must be entering freshman. Write for complete information.

1275

FRANCIS OUIMET SCHOLARSHIP FUND

190 Park Road
Weston, MA 02193
617/891-6400

AMOUNT: $500-$4,500
DEADLINE(S): Dec 1
FIELD(S): All fields of study

Undergraduate needs-based scholarships for residents of Massachusetts who have worked as golf caddies, in pro shops, or as course superintendents of operations in Massachusetts for three years. Must work at a golf course.

263 awards. Renewable. Contact Bob Donovan at above address.

1276

FRED A. BRYAN COLLEGIATE STUDENTS FUND (Trust Fund Scholarships)

Norwest Bank Indiana NA
112 W. Jefferson Blvd.
South Bend, IN 46601
219/237-3314

AMOUNT: $1,400-$1,600
DEADLINE(S): Mar 1
FIELD(S): All fields of study

Open to male graduates of South Bend, Indiana high schools with preference to those who are or have been Boy Scouts. For undergraduate study at a recognized college or university. Financial need must be demonstrated. U.S. citizenship required.

Renewable for up to 4 years. Write for complete information.

1277

FRED B. & RUTH B. ZIGLER FOUNDATION (Scholarships)

P.O. Box 986
324 Broadway
Jennings, LA 70546

318/824-2413

AMOUNT: $1,250 per semester

DEADLINE(S): Mar 10

FIELD(S): All fields of study

Scholarships open to graduating seniors at Jefferson Davis Parish (LA) high schools. Awards are tenable at recognized colleges & universities.

10-18 scholarships per year. Renewable for up to 4 years. Write for complete information.

1278

FULLER E. CALLAWAY FOUNDATION (Hatton Lovejoy Scholarship)
209 Broome Street
La Grange, GA 30240
706/884-7348

AMOUNT: $3,300 per school year

DEADLINE(S): Feb 15

FIELD(S): All fields of study

Open to high school graduates who have lived in Troup County, GA for at least two years and rank in the upper 25% of their class.

10 scholarships per year. Write for complete information.

1279

GABRIEL J. BROWN TRUST (Trust Loan Fund)
112 Ave. E West
Bismarck, ND 58501
701/223-5916

AMOUNT: $1,000-4,000

DEADLINE(S): Jun 15

FIELD(S): All fields of study

Special low-interest loans (6%) open to residents of North Dakota who have completed at least 2 years of undergraduate study at a recognized college or university and have a 2.5 or better GPA. U.S. citizen.

Approximately 75 loans per year. Renewable. Write for complete information.

1280

GEORGE ABRAHAMIAN FOUNDATION (Scholarships for Local Armenians)
945 Admiral Street
Providence, RI 02904
401/831-2887

AMOUNT: Varies

DEADLINE(S): Sep 1

FIELD(S): All fields of study

Open to undergraduate and graduate students who are U.S. citizens of Armenian ancestry and live in Providence, RI, are of good character, have the ability to learn and can demonstrate financial need.

Renewable. Write for complete information.

1281

GEORGE E. ANDREWS TRUST (George E. Andrews Scholarship)
Trust Dept., Blackhawk State Bank
P.O. Box 719
Beloit, WI 53512-0179
608/364-8914

AMOUNT: $2,500 and up

DEADLINE(S): Feb 15

FIELD(S): All fields of study

Open to seniors at high schools in the City of Beloit, Town of Beloit, or Town of Turtle, Rock County, Wisconsin. Awards based on scholastic standing, financial need, moral character, industriousness and other factors.

To assist and encourage a worthy, needy, and industrious student by defraying the student's expense for the first year of college.

1282

GEORGE GROTEFEND SCHOLARSHIP FUND (Grotefend Scholarship)
1644 Magnolia Ave.
Redding, CA 96001
916/225-0227

AMOUNT: $150-$400

DEADLINE(S): Apr 20

FIELD(S): All fields of study

Scholarships open to applicants who completed all 4 years of high school in Shasta County, California. Awards support all levels of study at recognized colleges & universities.

300 awards per year. Write for complete information.

1283

GEORGE T. WELCH (Scholarships)
Baker Boyer Bank Trust Dept.
P.O. Box 1796
Walla Walla, WA 99362-0353
509/525-2000

AMOUNT: Up to $2,500 (amount varies)
DEADLINE(S): Mar 1
FIELD(S): All fields of study

Open ONLY to U.S. citizens who reside in Walla Walla County, Washington and have graduated from a Walla Walla high school.

Approximately 45 awards per year. Contact Holly T. Howard at address above for complete information.

1284

GLASS, MOLDERS, POTTERY, PLASTICS & ALLIED WORKERS INTERNATIONAL UNION (Scholarship Program)
P.O. Box 607
Media, PA 19063
610/565-5051

AMOUNT: $2,500 per year for 4 years
DEADLINE(S): Nov 1
FIELD(S): All fields of study

Open to dependent children of union members. Applicants must rank in the top 1/4 of high school senior class. Children of international union officers are NOT eligible. Awards tenable at accredited undergraduate colleges & universities.

Write for complete information.

1285

GRAHAM-FANCHER SCHOLARSHIP TRUST
149 Josephine Street, Suite A
Santa Cruz, CA 95060
408/423-3640

AMOUNT: Varies
DEADLINE(S): May 1
FIELD(S): All fields of study

Open to graduating seniors from high schools in Northern Santa Cruz County, CA. School and community activities and financial need are considerations.

20 awards per academic year. Write for complete information.

1286

GRAND LODGE OF ILLINOIS (Illinois Odd Fellow-Rebekah Scholarship Award)
P.O. Box 248
305 North Kickapoo Street
Lincoln, IL 62656
217/735-2561

AMOUNT: Varies
DEADLINE(S): Dec 1 (application request); Mar 1 (completed application)
FIELD(S): All fields of study

Illinois residents. Scholarships for undergraduate study. Applicants must use the official Odd Fellow-Rebekah scholarship form, submit official transcript of latest grades & demonstrate need. U.S. citizenship required.

Write to address above for complete information & application forms.

1287

GRAPHIC COMMUNICATIONS INTERNATIONAL UNION (GCIU—A. J. DeAndrade Scholarship Awards Program)
1900 L Street NW
Washington, D.C. 20036-5080
202/462-1400; Fax 202/331-9516

AMOUNT: $2,000 (payable $500 per year)

DEADLINE(S): Feb 15

FIELD(S): All fields of study

Open to citizens of U.S. or Canada who are high school seniors to be graduated in January or June of the current school year, and recent high school graduates who, by Sept. 1, will not have completed more than a half-year of college. Must be dependents of Graphic Communications International Union members.

10 awards per year. Write for complete information.

1288

GUIDEPOSTS MAGAZINE (Young Writers Contest)
16 E. 34th Street
New York, NY 10016
212/251-8100

AMOUNT: $1,000-$8,000 + electric typewriters

DEADLINE(S): Dec 1

FIELD(S): All fields of study

Open to any high school junior or senior (U.S. or foreign citizen) who writes an original 1,200-word personal experience story (in English) in which the writer's faith in God played a role. Stories should be true and written in the first person.

Scholarship prizes are not redeemable in cash, not transferable, and must be used within five years after high school graduation. Send SASE for details.

1289

H. T. EWALD FOUNDATION (Scholarship Awards)
15175 E. Jefferson Ave.
Grosse Pointe, MI 48230
313/821-1278

AMOUNT: $400-$2,500

DEADLINE(S): Apr 1

FIELD(S): All fields of study

Open to residents of the metropolitan Detroit (MI) area who will be entering college as freshmen. Awards are available for up to 4 years of undergraduate work. Based on financial need, academic achievement, and extracurricular activities.

10 to 18 awards per year. Write for complete information.

1290

HARNESS HORSEMEN INTERNATIONAL FOUNDATION (J. L. Hauck Memorial Scholarship Fund)
14 Main Street
Robbinsville, NJ 08691
609/259-3717

AMOUNT: $4,000

DEADLINE(S): Jun 1

FIELD(S): All fields of study

Open to sons & daughters of Harness Horsemen International Assn. members. Scholarship supports undergraduate study at any recognized college or university.

Renewable. Write for complete information.

1291

HARNESS TRACKS OF AMERICA (Scholarship)
4640 East Sunrise, Suite 200
Tucson, AZ 85718
520/529-2525; Fax 520/529-3235

AMOUNT: $3,000

DEADLINE(S): Jun 15

FIELD(S): All fields of study

Applicants MUST be children of licensed harness racing drivers, trainers, breeders, or caretakers (including retired or deceased) or young people actively engaged in harness racing. For study beyond the high school level.

5 scholarships per year for 1 year each awarded on the basis of merit & financial need. No student may be awarded more than 2 separate yearly scholarships. Write for complete information.

1292

HARRY E. & FLORENCE W. SNAYBERGER MEMORIAL FOUNDATION (Grant Award)
c/o Pennsylvania National Bank
& Trust Company
Trust Dept., Center & Norwegian
Pottsville, PA 17901-7150
717/622-4200

AMOUNT: Varies
DEADLINE(S): Feb
FIELD(S): All fields of study

Applicants must be residents of Schuylkill County, PA. Scholarships given based on college expense need.

Contact trust clerk Carolyn Bernatonis for complete information.

1293

HARVARD/RADCLIFFE OFFICE OF ADMISSIONS AND FINANCIAL AID (Scholarships, Grants, Loans & Work Study Programs)
Byerly Hall, 3rd floor
8 Garden Street
Cambridge, MA 02138
617/495-1581

AMOUNT: Varies
DEADLINE(S): None
FIELD(S): All fields of study

Needs-based funds available to all who are admitted and can show proof of need.

Applicants must be accepted for admission to Harvard before they will be considered for funding. Many factors other than family income are considered. Write for complete information.

1294

HATTIE M. STRONG FOUNDATION (No-interest Loans)
1620 Eye Street NW, Room 700
Washington, D.C. 20006
202/331-1619; Fax 202/466-2894

AMOUNT: Up to $3,000
DEADLINE(S): Mar 31 (Applications available Jan 1)
FIELD(S): All fields of study

Open to U.S. undergraduate and graduate students in their last year of study in the U.S. or abroad. Loans are made solely on the basis of individual merit. There is no interest and no collateral requirement. U.S. citizen or permanent resident. Repayment terms are based upon monthly income after graduation and arranged individually.

Financial need is a consideration. Approximately 240 awards per year. For complete information send SASE and include personal history, school attended, subject studied, date expected to complete studies, and amount of funds needed.

1295

HAUSS-HELMS FOUNDATION, INC. (Grant Program/Scholarships)
P.O. Box 25
Wapakoneta, OH 45895
419/738-4911

AMOUNT: Varies
DEADLINE(S): Apr 15
FIELD(S): All fields of study

Undergraduate scholarships open to residents of Auglaize or Allen county (Ohio) who are recommended by their high school principal, a responsible faculty member or their guidance counselor. U.S. citizen.

195 scholarships per year. Renewable with reapplication. Write for complete information.

1296

HAWAII EDUCATIONAL LOAN PROGRAM (PLUS/SLS)
1314 S. King Street, #861
Honolulu, HI 96814
808/536-3731

AMOUNT: Varies
DEADLINE(S): None

FIELD(S): All fields of study

This is a loan for parents of dependent students. The loan must be repaid. Variable interest rate changes annually.

Write for complete information.

1297

HERBERT LEHMAN EDUCATION FUND (Scholarships)
99 Hudson Street, #1600
New York, NY 10013
Written inquiry

AMOUNT: $1,200

DEADLINE(S): Apr 15

FIELD(S): All fields of study

Open to needy African-American high school students planning to begin undergraduate study at recently desegregated and publicly supported deep South institutions having a below-average enrollment of African-Americans.

U.S. citizenship required. 50-100 awards per year. Renewable. Requests for application forms must be in writing and requested by the applicant.

1298

HERSCHEL C. PRICE EDUCATIONAL FOUNDATION (Grants Program)
P.O. Box 412
Huntington, WV 25708
304/529-3852

AMOUNT: $250 to $2,500 per semester

DEADLINE(S): Oct 1; Apr 1

FIELD(S): All fields of study

Scholarships for students who are residents of West Virginia in attendance at WV institutions at the undergraduate level. Some graduate awards are available. U.S. citizen.

Write for complete information.

1299

HORACE SMITH FUND (Loans)
P.O. Box 3034
1441 Main Street
Springfield, MA 01101
413/739-4222

AMOUNT: Varies

DEADLINE(S): Jun 15 (college students); Jul 1 (high school)

FIELD(S): All fields of study

Open to graduates of Hampden County, MA secondary schools for undergraduate or graduate study. Financial need is of primary importance. Applications available after April 1. No interest if paid back within a year after the student completes his/her education.

Renewable. Write for complete information.

1300

HOWARD AND MAMIE NICHOLS SCHOLARSHIP TRUST (Scholarships)
Wells Fargo Bank Trust Dept.
5262 N. Blackstone
Fresno, CA 93710
Written inquiries only

AMOUNT: Varies

DEADLINE(S): Feb 28

FIELD(S): All fields of study

Open to graduates of Kern County, CA high schools for full-time undergraduate or graduate study at a post-secondary institution. Must demonstrate financial need and have a 2.0 or better GPA.

Approximately 100 awards per year. Renewable with reapplication. Write for complete information.

1301

HUALAPAI TRIBAL COUNCIL (Scholarship Program)
P.O. Box 179
Peach Springs, AZ 86434
520/769-2216

AMOUNT: Up to $2,500/semester

DEADLINE(S): Varies

FIELD(S): All fields of study

Scholarships are offered to American Indians only with priority given to members of the Hualapai Tribe. Must be enrolled as a student full-time and maintain passing grades. U.S. citizenship required.

Apply four weeks before each semester. Write to Sheri K. Yellowhawk at above address for complete information.

1302

IDAHO STATE BOARD OF EDUCATION (Paul Fowler Memorial Scholarship)
LBJ Building, Room 307
P.O. Box 83720
Boise, ID 83720-0037
208/334-2270

AMOUNT: $3,000

DEADLINE(S): Jan 31

FIELD(S): Academic fields of study

Open to Idaho residents who are graduating seniors from Idaho high schools and who are U.S. citizens. For undergraduate study at recognized colleges & universities. Must submit ACT score and class ranking.

2 scholarships awarded.

1303

ILLINOIS DEPARTMENT OF THE AMERICAN LEGION (Scholarships)
P.O. Box 2910
Bloomington, IL 61702-2910
309/663-0361

AMOUNT: $1,000

DEADLINE(S): Mar 15

FIELD(S): All fields of study

Scholarships for high school seniors who are sons and daughters of Illinois American Legion members. Awards are tenable at recognized undergraduate colleges, universities, and vocational or nursing schools.

U.S. citizenship required. Academic achievement and financial need considered.

20 scholarships per year. Write for complete information.

1304

ILLINOIS DEPARTMENT OF THE AMERICAN LEGION (Boy Scout Scholarships)
P.O. Box 2910
Bloomington, IL 61702-2910
309/663-0361

AMOUNT: $1,000; $200 runner-up awards (4)

DEADLINE(S): Apr 15

FIELD(S): All fields of study

Scholarships for high school seniors who are Boy Scouts or Explorer Scouts and are Illinois residents. Must write a 500-word essay on Legion's Americanism and Boy Scout programs. U.S. citizenship required. Academic achievement and financial need considered.

Contact local Boy Scout Office or Legion Boy Scout Chairman at the above address for complete application information.

1305

ILLINOIS STUDENT ASSISTANCE COMMISSION (State & Federal Scholarships, Grants, Loans)
1755 Lake Cook Road
Deerfield, IL 60015-5209
708/948-8550

AMOUNT: Varies with program

DEADLINE(S): Varies

FIELD(S): All fields of study

Commission administers a number of state and federal scholarship, grant and loan programs for Illinois residents.

Write for complete information.

1306

INDEPENDENCE FEDERAL SAVINGS BANK (Federal Family Education Loan Program)
1900 L Street NW, Suite 700
Washington, D.C. 20036
800/733-0473; 202/626-0473; Fax 202/775-4533

AMOUNT: Up to $5,500 undergrads; up to $10,000 graduates
DEADLINE(S): None
FIELD(S): All fields of study

Loans open to U.S. citizens or legal residents accepted for enrollment or enrolled in a school approved by the U.S. Dept. of Education and having a satisfactory academic record. A source of federal unsubsidized and subsidized Stafford loans and federal parent Plus loans.
Write for complete information.

1307

INTERNATIONAL ALLIANCE OF THEATRICAL STAGE EMPLOYEES AND MOVING PICTURE MACHINE OPERATORS (Richard F. Walsh Foundation)
1515 Broadway, Suite 601
New York, NY 10036
212/730-1770

AMOUNT: $1,750
DEADLINE(S): Dec 31
FIELD(S): All fields of study

Scholarship is offered to high school seniors who are children of members in good standing. Awards are based on transcripts, SAT scores and letter(s) of recommendation from clergy or teacher.
Award renewable for 4 years. Write for complete information.

1308

INTERNATIONAL ASSN. OF BRIDGE STRUCTURAL AND ORNAMENTAL IRON WORKERS (John H. Lyons Scholarship Program)
1750 New York Ave. NW, Suite 400
Washington, D.C. 20006
202/383-4800

AMOUNT: $2,500 per year maximum
DEADLINE(S): Mar 31
FIELD(S): All fields of study

Must be children of members or deceased members in good standing at the time of death. Applicants must rank in the upper half of high school graduating class. For undergraduate study in U.S. or Canada. Must be a senior in high school.
Scholarships will be awarded for one year and may be renewed for three academic years. Write for complete information.

1309

INTERNATIONAL BILL ONEXIOCA II (Founders Memorial Award)
911 Bartlett Place
Windsor, CA 95492
Written inquiry only

AMOUNT: $2,500
DEADLINE(S): Jan 31
FIELD(S): All fields of study

Annual award in memory of Hernesto K. Onexioca, founder. Anyone with the legal surname of Onexioca who is not a relative of Onexioca by blood or marriage and was born on Jan. 1 is eligible to apply.
All inquiries MUST include proof of name and birth date. Those without such proof will NOT be acknowledged.

1310

INTERNATIONAL BROTHERHOOD OF TEAMSTERS (Scholarship Fund)
25 Louisiana Ave. NW
Washington, D.C. 20001
202/624-8735

AMOUNT: $1,000-$1,500 per year

DEADLINE(S): Nov 30 (to local union)

FIELD(S): All fields of study

Open to high school seniors who are dependent children of Teamster members. For students in top 15% of their class with excellent SAT/ACT scores. U.S. or Canadian citizen. Must demonstrate financial need.

25 scholarships per year. Top 10 are for $1,500 & renewable up to 4 years. Remaining 15 are for $1,000 and for 1 year only. Write for complete information.

1311

INTERNATIONAL LADIES GARMENT WORKERS UNION (National College Award Program)
1710 Broadway
New York, NY 10019
212/265-7000

AMOUNT: $350 annually; renewable for up to four years

DEADLINE(S): Jan 31

FIELD(S): All fields of study

Open to sons or daughters of union members who have been members in good standing for at least 2 years. Applications accepted only from high school seniors.

10 schoiarships per year. Write for complete information.

1312

INTERNATIONAL SOCIETY FOR CLINICAL LABORATORY TECHNOLOGY (David Birenbaum Scholarship Fund)
917 Locust Street, Suite 1100
St. Louis, MO 63101-1413
314/241-1445

AMOUNT: Varies

DEADLINE(S): Jul 15

FIELD(S): All fields of study

Open to ISCLT members, and their spouses and dependent children. Requires graduation from an accredited high school or equivalent.

Write for complete information.

1313

INTERNATIONAL UNION OF BRICKLAYERS AND ALLIED CRAFTSMEN (Harry C. Bates Merit Scholarship Program)
815 15th Street NW
Washington, D.C. 20005
202/783-3788

AMOUNT: $500 to $2,000 per year up to 4 years

DEADLINE(S): Oct (PSAT tests)

FIELD(S): All fields of study

Open to natural or legally adopted children of current; retired or deceased BAC members. Competition is administered by National Merit Scholarship Corp. which conducts PSAT/NMSQT during October of student's junior year of high school.

Applicants must be national merit semifinalists. Award tenable at any accredited university or community college the student attends full-time. Write for complete information.

1314

INTERNATIONAL UNION OF ELECTRONIC, ELECTRICAL, SALARIES, MACHINE & FURNITURE WORKERS (J. B. Carey; D. J. Fitzmaurice & W. H. Bywater Scholarships)
1126 16th Street NW
Dept. of Social Action
Washington, D.C. 20036
202/296-1200

AMOUNT: $1,000—JBC (9 awards); $2,000—DJF (1); $3,000—WHB (1)

DEADLINE(S): Apr 15

FIELD(S): All fields of study

Programs open to dependents of union members. JBC scholarships support undergraduate study for 1 year in all fields of study. DJF scholarships support undergraduate study for 1 year in engineering only.

WHB scholarship available only to children of elected local union officials. Contact local union representative for complete information.

1315

IOWA COLLEGE STUDENT AID COMMISSION (Federal Stafford Loan Program; Federal PLUS Loans)
200 Tenth Street, 4th Floor
Des Moines, IA 50309-3609
515/281-3501

AMOUNT: $2,625-$4,000 undergraduate; $7,500 graduate
DEADLINE(S): None
FIELD(S): All fields of study

Loans open to Iowa residents enrolled in or attending approved institutions. Must be U.S. citizens or legal residents and demonstrate need.
Write for complete information.

1316

IOWA COLLEGE STUDENT AID COMMISSION (Iowa Tuition Grant Program)
200 Tenth Street, 4th Floor
Des Moines, IA 50309-3609
515/281-3501

AMOUNT: $3,400
DEADLINE(S): Jun 2
FIELD(S): All fields of study

Open to Iowa residents enrolled or planning to enroll as undergraduates at eligible privately supported colleges or universities, business schools, or hospital nursing programs in Iowa. Must demonstrate need.
U.S. citizen or legal resident. 10,140 grants per year. Renewable. Write for complete information.

1317

IOWA COLLEGE STUDENT AID COMMISSION (State of Iowa Scholarships)
200 Tenth Street, 4th Floor
Des Moines, IA 50309-3609
515/281-3501

AMOUNT: $400
DEADLINE(S): Nov 1
FIELD(S): All fields of study

Open to Iowa high school seniors who are in the top 15% of their class and plan to attend an eligible Iowa college or university. Considerations include ACT or SAT composite test scores, GPA & class rank. U.S. citizenship required.
3,000 scholarships per year. Contact your counselor or write to address above for complete information.

1318

IOWA COMMISSION OF VETERANS AFFAIRS (War Orphans Educational Scholarship Aid)
7700 NW Beaver Drive
Camp Dodge
Johnston, IA 50131
800/VET-IOWA; 515/242-5331; Fax 515/242-5659

AMOUNT: Up to $600 per year
DEADLINE(S): None specified
FIELD(S): All fields of study

Resident of Iowa for at least 2 years prior to application. Child of parent who died in or as a result of military service during wartime. Also eligible are orphans of National Guardsmen and other members of Reserve Components who died performing duties ordered by appropriate federal or state authorities. High school graduate or equivalent. Attend a post-secondary institution in Iowa.
Renewable. Write for complete information.

1319

IOWA FEDERATION OF LABOR AFL-CIO (Annual Scholarship Program)
2000 Walker Street, Suite A
Des Moines, IA 50317
515/262-9571

AMOUNT: $1,500
DEADLINE(S): Mar 28
FIELD(S): All fields of study

Competition based on essay. Open only to Iowa high school seniors.
Write for complete information.

1320

ITALIAN CATHOLIC FEDERATION INC. (College Scholarships for High School Seniors)
675 Hegenberger Road, #110
Oakland, CA 94621
888/ICF-1924

AMOUNT: $400-$1,000
DEADLINE(S): Mar 15
FIELD(S): All fields of study

Open to graduating high school seniors of Italian ancestry and Catholic faith. Winners may attend any accredited institution. Limited to students who live in states where the federation is located (California, Nevada, and Illinois) and be U.S. citizens.
Minimum GPA of 3.0 (4.0 scale). 200 scholarships per year. Send stamped self-addressed envelope to address above for further information.

1321

J. H. BAKER SCHOLARSHIP FUND (Student Loans)
c/o Tom Dechant, CPA
P.O. Box 280
La Crosse, KS 67548
913/222-2537

AMOUNT: $1,850 per year
DEADLINE(S): Jul 15

FIELD(S): All undergrad fields of study
For graduates of high schools in the Kansas counties of Rush, Barton, Ellis, Ness, and Pawnee. Must be under 25 years of age. Selection is based on academic performance, character, ability, and need.
Contact address above for complete information.

1322

J. WOOD PLATT CADDIE SCHOLARSHIP TRUST (Scholarships)
Drawer 808
Southeastern, PA 19399
215/687-2340

AMOUNT: Up to $9,000
DEADLINE(S): May 1
FIELD(S): All fields of study

Open to high school seniors & undergraduate students who have served as a caddie at a Golf Association of Philadelphia member club, have financial need, and have capability to successfully complete their undergraduate degree.
Renewable. Write for complete information.

1323

JACKSONVILLE UNIVERSITY (Scholarships & Grants Programs)
Director of Student Financial Assistance
Jacksonville, FL 32211
904/745-7060

AMOUNT: Varies
DEADLINE(S): Jan 1
FIELD(S): All fields of study

Jacksonville University offers numerous scholarships, grants-in-aid, service awards and campus employment. Financial need is not necessarily a consideration. Early applications are advised.
Candidates must apply for admission and for financial aid. 100 awards per year for study at Jacksonville University. Write for complete information.

1324

JAMES G. K. MCCLURE EDUCATIONAL AND DEVELOPMENT FUND (Western North Carolina Scholarships)
11 Sugar Hollow Road
Fairview, NC 28730
704/628-2114

AMOUNT: $300-$1,500
DEADLINE(S): May 15
FIELD(S): All fields of study

Open to students residing in western North Carolina who are entering the freshman class of a North Carolina college or university. Financial need is a consideration.
Write for complete information.

1325

JAMES M. HOFFMAN SCHOLARSHIP (Undergraduate Scholarship)
Southtrust Bank Asset Management Co.
P.O. Box 1000
Anniston, AL 36202
205/238-1000 Ext. 338

AMOUNT: Varies
DEADLINE(S): Mar 1
FIELD(S): All fields of study

For high school seniors attending schools in Calhoun County, Alabama. For undergraduate study at accredited colleges and universities. Must submit copies of parents' W-2 forms.
Write to attention of William K. Priddy for complete information.

1326

JAMES W. COLGAN LOAN FUND (Undergraduate Loans)
P.O. Box 900 3-MASPM21TRU
Springfield, MA 01101
413/787-8524

AMOUNT: Varies
DEADLINE(S): Apr 15
FIELD(S): All fields of study

Educational loans available to Massachusetts residents who are enrolled as an undergraduate college student in or outside of Massachusetts. Financial need and grades are considerations.
Must have been a Massachusetts resident for 5 years before applying. Loans are not renewable. Send SASE to Thea E. Katsounakis, Trust Officer, Fleet National Bank, at above address for complete information.

1327

JAMES Z. NAURISON SCHOLARSHIP FUND
P.O. Box 15769
1500 Main Street
Springfield, MA 01115
413/732-2858

AMOUNT: $400-$2,000
DEADLINE(S): Mar 15
FIELD(S): All fields of study

Open to undergraduate and graduate students who are residents of the Massachusetts counties of Berkshire, Franklin, Hampden, or Hampshire or of the cities of Suffield or Enfield, CT. Awards based on financial need and academic record. Must fill out FAFSA and send a copy with your application, along with transcript(s).
Renewable up to four years. Approximately 300 awards per year. Self-addressed stamped envelope must accompany request for application.

1328

JAPANESE AMERICAN CITIZENS LEAGUE (Abe and Esther Hagiwara Student Aid Award)
1765 Sutter Street
San Francisco, CA 94115
415/921-5225; E-mail: jacl@jacl.org

AMOUNT: Varies
DEADLINE(S): Apr 1
FIELD(S): All fields of study

Open to JACL members or their children only. MUST demonstrate severe financial need. The purpose of this award is to provide financial assistance to a student who otherwise would have to delay or terminate his/her education due to a lack of financing.

For membership information or an application, send a self-addressed stamped envelope to the above address.

1329

JAPANESE AMERICAN CITIZENS LEAGUE (Entering Freshmen Awards)
1765 Sutter Street
San Francisco, CA 94115
415/921-5225; E-mail: jacl@jacl.org

AMOUNT: Varies

DEADLINE(S): Mar 1

FIELD(S): All fields of study

Open to JACL members or their children only. For entering freshmen planning to enroll in a college, university, trade school, business school, or any institution of higher learning.

Various scholarships. For membership information or an application, send a self-addressed stamped envelope to the above address, stating your level of study.

1330

JAPANESE AMERICAN CITIZENS LEAGUE (Undergraduate Awards)
1765 Sutter Street
San Francisco, CA 94115
415/921-5225; E-mail: jacl@jacl.org

AMOUNT: Varies

DEADLINE(S): Apr 1

FIELD(S): All fields of study

Open to JACL members or their children only. For undergraduate students enrolled in, or planning to enroll in, a college, university, trade school, business school, or any institution of higher learning.

Various scholarships. For membership information or an application, send a self-

addressed stamped envelope to the above address, stating your level of study.

1331

JAYCEE WAR MEMORIAL SCHOLARSHIP PROGRAM (Scholarships)
P.O. Box 7
Tulsa, OK 74102
Written inquiry

AMOUNT: $1,000

DEADLINE(S): Mar 1

FIELD(S): All fields of study

Open to U.S. citizens who are enrolled in or accepted for admission to a college or university. Must possess academic potential and leadership traits. Financial need must be demonstrated.

Applications available ONLY between July 1 and February 1. Send self-addressed stamped business-size envelope & $5 application fee to JWMF, Dept. 94922, Tulsa, OK 74194-0001.

1332

JEANNETTE RANKIN FOUNDATION (Competitive Awards)
P.O. Box 6653
Athens, GA 30604
Written inquiry

AMOUNT: $1,000

DEADLINE(S): Jan 15; Mar 1 (Application request & deadline)

FIELD(S): All fields of study (undergraduate & voc-tech)

Open to women aged 35 or older accepted or enrolled in a certified program of voc-tech training or an undergrad program (NOT for grad study or 2nd undergrad degree). U.S. citizenship is required. Financial need is major factor in selection.

Request application between September 1-January 15; include business-size SASE labeled 'JRF 1998' in the lower left-hand corner; state sex, age, and level of study or training.

1333

JEWISH FAMILY AND CHILDREN'S SERVICES (Anna and Charles Stockwitz Children and Youth Fund)
1600 Scott Street
San Francisco, CA 94115
415/561-1226

AMOUNT: $5,000 per year (student loans)
DEADLINE(S): None
FIELD(S): All fields of study

Loans and grants open to undergrads who are U.S. permanent residents or citizens. Must be of the Jewish faith and age 25 or less. Must reside in San Francisco, San Mateo, Santa Clara, Marin, or Sonoma counties. Loan repayment is flexible; interest is approx. 80% of current prime.

Grant applicants must demonstrate financial need. Loan applicants must show ability to repay. Contact local JFCS office for complete information.

1334

JEWISH FAMILY AND CHILDREN'S SERVICES (College Loan Fund)
1600 Scott Street
San Francisco, CA 94115
415/561-1226

AMOUNT: $5,000 maximum (student loan)
DEADLINE(S): None
FIELD(S): All fields of study

Open to worthy college students of the Jewish faith with limited resources but with a demonstrated ability to repay. Must be U.S. permanent resident and living in San Francisco, San Mateo, Santa Clara, Marin, or Sonoma counties, California.

Guarantors or co-makers are required but not collateral. Repayment terms flexible; interest usually set at 80% of current prime rate. Contact local JFCS office for forms and complete information.

1335

JEWISH FAMILY AND CHILDREN'S SERVICES (Fogel Loan Fund)
1600 Scott Street
San Francisco, CA 94115
415/561-1226

AMOUNT: Varies
DEADLINE(S): None
FIELD(S): All fields of study

Loans to help individuals of all ages for college or vocational studies and for personal, business, or professional purposes. Applicant must be a U.S. permanent resident of Jewish faith and have a sound plan for repayment.

Must be a resident of San Francisco, San Mateo, Santa Clara, Marin, or Sonoma counties, California. Guarantor or co-makers required but no collateral is needed. Contact JFCS office for complete information.

1336

JEWISH FAMILY AND CHILDREN'S SERVICES (Jacob Rassen Memorial Scholarship Fund)
1600 Scott Street
San Francisco, CA 94115
415/561-1226

AMOUNT: Up to $2,000
DEADLINE(S): None
FIELD(S): Study trip to Israel

Open to Jewish students under age 22 who demonstrate academic achievement and financial need and the desire to enhance Jewish identity and increase knowledge of & connection to Israel. Must be U.S. permanent resident.

The opportunity to travel and study in Israel. Must reside in San Francisco, San Mateo, Santa Clara, Marin, or Sonoma counties in California. Contact local JFCS office for forms and complete information.

1337

JEWISH FAMILY AND CHILDREN'S SERVICES (Stanley Olson Youth Scholarship Fund)
1600 Scott Street
San Francisco, CA 94115
415/561-1226

AMOUNT: Up to $2,500
DEADLINE(S): None
FIELD(S): All fields of study (preference to liberal arts majors)

Open to undergrad or grad students of Jewish faith who are 25 or younger; have demonstrated academic achievement and financial need and have been accepted for enrollment in a college or university. Must be U.S. permanent resident.

Must reside in San Francisco, San Mateo, Santa Clara, Marin, or Sonoma counties. Contact local JFCS office for applications and complete information.

1338

JEWISH FAMILY AND CHILDREN'S SERVICES (Vivienne Camp College Scholarship Fund)
1600 Scott Street
San Francisco, CA 94115
415/561-1226

AMOUNT: $3,500 per year
DEADLINE(S): None
FIELD(S): All fields of study

Open to students of Jewish faith for undergrad or vocational study. Must be U.S. permanent resident and have demonstrated academic achievement, financial need. Must be broad-based in extracurricular activities and community involvement.

Must have been accepted to a California college or vocational school and reside in San Francisco, San Mateo, Santa Clara, Marin, or Sonoma counties in California. Contact local JFCS office for forms and complete information.

1339

JEWISH SOCIAL SERVICE AGENCY OF METROPOLITAN WASHINGTON (Loan Fund)
6123 Montrose Road
Rockville, MD 20852
301/881-3700

AMOUNT: Up to $2,000
DEADLINE(S): Ongoing
FIELD(S): All fields of study

Open to Jewish applicants 18 or older who are within eighteen months of completing an undergraduate or graduate degree or a vocational training program and are residents of the Washington metropolitan area. No-interest loan based on financial need.

A one-time award. U.S. citizen or permanent resident who will seek citizenship. Recipient must agree to a stipulation to pay $50 per month within three months after graduation. Write for complete information.

1340

JEWISH SOCIAL SERVICE AGENCY OF METROPOLITAN WASHINGTON (Max and Emmy Dreyfuss Undergraduate Scholarship)
6123 Montrose Road
Rockville, MD 20852
301/881-3700

AMOUNT: Up to $3,500/year
DEADLINE(S): Jun 1
FIELD(S): All fields of study

Open to Jewish undergraduates no older than 30 who are enrolled in an accredited undergraduate four-year degree program and are from the Washington metropolitan area. Special consideration is given to refugees.

Renewable upon reapplication for four years. Awards based on financial need. Call Scholarship and Loan Coordinator at above number to request application.

1341

**JOHN C. CHAFFIN EDUCATIONAL
FUND (Scholarships and Loans Programs)**
100 Walnut Street
Newtonville, MA 02160
617/552-7652

AMOUNT: Scholarships: $500/semester;
Loans: $600/semester
DEADLINE(S): None given
FIELD(S): All fields of study

Open only to graduates of Newton North and
Newton South High Schools in Newton,
Massachusetts. Preference to students
enrolling in four-year accredited undergraduate programs; trustees may also support
those attending less than four-year degree
and non-degree granting school provided
they are accredited schools.

Approximately 30 awards per year.
Renewable to a maximum of $2,000 for
scholarships and $4,800 for loans. Loans
begin to accrue 6% interest rate six months
after graduation. Write for complete information.

1342

**JOHNSON AND WALES UNIVERSITY
(Gaebe Eagle Scout Scholarships)**
8 Abbott Place
Providence, RI 02903
401/598-1000

AMOUNT: $300
DEADLINE(S): Apr 30
FIELD(S): All fields of study

Open to undergraduate freshmen who have
been accepted at Johnson and Wales
University. Must be Eagle Scout who has
received a religious award of his faith.

All eligible freshmen receive award of $300.
Write for complete information.

1343

**JOHNSON CONTROLS FOUNDATION
(Scholarship Program)**
5757 N. Green Bay Ave., X-34
Milwaukee, WI 53201
414/228-2296

AMOUNT: $1,750 per year ($7,000 over 4
years)
DEADLINE(S): Feb 1
FIELD(S): All fields of study

Eligibility for scholarships limited to children
of employees of Johnson Controls Inc. Must
be in upper 30% of high school graduating
class and must maintain standards in college
for renewal. Scholarships for full-time study
only.

U.S. citizenship required. Write for complete
information.

1344

**JUNIATA COLLEGE (Frederick & Mary F.
Beckley Scholarship Fund for Needy 'Left-
handed' Upper Classmen)**
Financial Aid Office
Huntingdon, PA 16652
814/643-4310

AMOUNT: $700-$1,000
DEADLINE(S): None
FIELD(S): All fields of study

Awards are open to needy left-handed students who have junior or senior standing at
Juniata College.

Write for complete information.

1345

**JUNIOR LEAGUE OF NORTHERN
VIRGINIA (Scholarships)**
7921 Jones Branch Drive, #320
McLean, VA 22102
703/893-0258

AMOUNT: $500-$2,000
DEADLINE(S): Dec 1

FIELD(S): All fields of study

Open to women who are 23 years old or more and accepted to or enrolled in an accredited college or university as an undergraduate or graduate student. Must be resident of Northern Virginia, a U.S. citizen, and demonstrate financial need.

8-10 awards per year. Write for complete information.

1346

KANSAS AMERICAN LEGION
(Scholarships)
    1314 SW Topeka Blvd.
    Topeka, KS 66612
    Written inquiry

AMOUNT: $150-$1,000
DEADLINE(S): Feb 15; Jul 15
FIELD(S): All fields of study

Variety of scholarships and awards for Kansas residents to attend Kansas colleges, universities, or trade schools. Some are limited to Legion members and/or designated fields of study.

Write for complete information.

1347

KANSAS BOARD OF REGENTS (Kansas State Scholarship)
    700 SW Harrison, Suite 1410
    Topeka, KS 66603
    913/296-3517

AMOUNT: Up to $1,000
DEADLINE(S): Mar 15
FIELD(S): All fields of study

For Kansas residents who are high school seniors and will be full-time undergraduate students at eligible Kansas independent colleges and universities. U.S. citizenship required. Financial need and academic standing are considered.

Renewable for up to five years but students must re-apply and maintain a 3.0 GPA. Write for complete information.

1348

KANSAS COMMISSION ON VETERANS' AFFAIRS (Scholarships)
    700 SW Jackson Street, #701
    Topeka, KS 66603
    913/296-3976

AMOUNT: Free tuition and fees in state-supported institutions
DEADLINE(S): Varies
FIELD(S): All fields of study

Open to dependent child of person who entered U.S. military service as a resident of Kansas & was prisoner of war, missing, or killed in action or died as a result of service-connected disabilities incurred during service in Vietnam.

Application must be made prior to enrollment. Renewable to maximum of 12 semesters. Write for complete information.

1349

KENTUCKY CENTER FOR VETERANS AFFAIRS (Benefits for Veterans & Their Dependents)
    545 S. 3rd Street, Room 123
    Louisville, KY 40202
    501/595-4447

AMOUNT: Varies
DEADLINE(S): None
FIELD(S): All fields of study

Kentucky residents. Open to dependent children, spouses & non-remarried widows of permanently & totally disabled war veterans who served during periods of federally recognized hostilities or who were MIA or a POW.

Veteran must be a resident of KY or—if deceased—a resident at time of death.

1350

KENTUCKY HIGHER EDUCATION ASSISTANCE AUTHORITY (College Access Program [CAP] Grant)
    1050 U.S. 127 South
    Frankfort, KY 40601

502/564-7990

AMOUNT: $246 to $490 per semester
DEADLINE(S): Mar 15 (priority date)
FIELD(S): All fields of study

Open to Kentucky residents who are U.S. citizens or legal residents enrolled or planning to enroll at least half-time in a 2- or 4-year undergrad (or voc-tech) program at an eligible Kentucky institution.
Renewable with reapplication. Write for complete information.

1351

KENTUCKY HIGHER EDUCATION ASSISTANCE AUTHORITY (Student Loan Program)
1050 U.S. 127 South, Suite 102
Frankfort, KY 40601-4323
502/564-7990; 800/928-8926

AMOUNT: $2,625-$18,500 (amount varies according to academic standing and whether student is dependent or independent)
DEADLINE(S): Varies
FIELD(S): All fields of study

Open to U.S. citizens or legal residents enrolled or accepted for enrollment (on at least a half-time basis) at an eligible post-secondary educational institution.
Write for complete information.

1352

KNIGHTS OF COLUMBUS (Fourth Degree Pro Deo & Pro Patria Scholarships)
P.O. Box 1670
New Haven, CT 06507-0901
203/772-2130 Ext. 332; Fax 203/773-3000

AMOUNT: $1,500
DEADLINE(S): Mar 1
FIELD(S): All fields of study

Open to students enrolling in the freshman class in a Catholic college who can show evidence of satisfactory academic performance. Must be a member or dependent of a Knights of Columbus member or dependent of a Columbian Squires member in good standing or of a deceased member.
62 scholarships per year; 50 at any Catholic college and 12 at the Catholic University of America in Washington, D.C. Renewable up to 4 years.

1353

KNIGHTS OF COLUMBUS (Francis P. Matthews and John E. Swift Educational Trust Scholarship)
P.O. Drawer 1670
New Haven, CT 06507
203/772-2130 Ext. 332; Fax 203/773-3000

AMOUNT: Varies
DEADLINE(S): None specified
FIELD(S): All fields of study

Open to children of Knights of Columbus members who died in military service or became totally and permanently disabled from causes directly connected with a period of conflict or from duties as a policeman or fireman.
For undergraduate studies at a Catholic college. Unspecified number of awards per year. Write for complete information.

1354

KNIGHTS OF COLUMBUS (Squires Scholarship Program)
P.O. Drawer 1670
New Haven, CT 06507
203/772-2130 Ext. 332

AMOUNT: $1,500
DEADLINE(S): Mar 1
FIELD(S): All fields of study

Open to students entering their freshman year at a Catholic college who are members in good standing of the Columbian Squires and have demonstrated academic excellence.
Renewable up to four years. Write for complete information.

1355

KNIGHTS TEMPLAR EDUCATIONAL FOUNDATION (Special Low-Interest Loans)
5097 N. Elston, Suite 101
Chicago, IL 60630-2460
312/777-3300

AMOUNT: $6,000 maximum per student
DEADLINE(S): Varies
FIELD(S): All fields of study

Special low-interest loans (5% fixed rate). No payments while in school. Interest and repayments start after graduation or when you leave school. Open to voc-tech students or junior/senior undergraduate students or graduate students.

U.S. citizen or legal resident. Request information from Charles R. Neumann (Grand Recorder-Secretary). Call or write to your state's grand commandery for proper application.

1356

LEAGUE OF UNITED LATIN AMERICAN CITIZENS (LULAC National Scholarship Fund)
2100 M Street NW, Suite 602
Washington, D.C. 20037
Internet: www.lulac.org/

AMOUNT: Varies
DEADLINE(S): None specified
FIELD(S): All fields of study

Open to high school graduates of Hispanic origin who are enrolled in an undergraduate college or university. Open to students residing in states in which LULAC councils exist.

See high school counselor or send self-addressed stamped envelope for complete information.

1357

LEONARD H. BULKELEY SCHOLARSHIP FUND (Scholarship Grants)
c/o R. N. Woodworth, Treasurer
17 Crocker Street
New London, CT 06320

860/447-1461

AMOUNT: $1,000 (approximately)
DEADLINE(S): Apr 1
FIELD(S): All fields of study

Open ONLY to residents of New London, CT for undergraduate study in an accredited college or university. Must demonstrate financial need.

Write for complete information.

1358

LEOPOLD SCHEPP FOUNDATION (Undergraduate Awards)
551 Fifth Ave., Suite 3000
New York, NY 10176-2597
212/986-3078

AMOUNT: Up to $7,500
DEADLINE(S): Not given
FIELD(S): All fields of study

Undergraduates should write detailing their education to date, year in school, length of course of study, vocational goal, financial need, age, citizenship, and availability for interview in New York City.

Approximately 200 new awards per year. Recipients may re-apply for subsequent years. Applicants should already be in college and not older than 30. High school seniors may NOT apply. Print or type name and address. Send SASE with above information for application.

1359

LLOYD D. SWEET SCHOLARSHIP FOUNDATION (Scholarships)
Box 638 (Attn: Academic year)
Chinook, MT 59523
406/357-2236

AMOUNT: Varies
DEADLINE(S): Mar 2
FIELD(S): All fields of study

Scholarships open to graduates of Chinook (MT) High School. Awards are for full-time undergraduate or graduate study at accredited colleges and universities in the U.S.

Approximately 75 awards per year. Write for complete information.

1360

LOUISIANA DEPT. OF VETERANS AFFAIRS (Awards Program)

P.O. Box 94095
Capitol Station
Baton Rouge, LA 70804
504/922-0500; Fax 504/922-0511

AMOUNT: Varies

DEADLINE(S): Varies

FIELD(S): All fields of study

Louisiana resident. Open to children (aged 16-25) & widows/spouses of deceased/disabled (100%) war veterans who were Louisiana residents for at least 1 year prior to service. For undergraduate study at state-supported schools in Louisiana.

Approximately 200 awards per year. Renewable up to 4 years. Write for complete information.

1361

LOUISIANA OFFICE OF STUDENT FINANCIAL ASSISTANCE (Tuition Opportunity Program for Students— Opportunity Award)

P.O. Box 91202
Baton Rouge, LA 70821-9202
800/259-5626 Ext. 1012; Fax 504/922-0790;
Internet: www.osfa.state.la.us

AMOUNT: Tuition waver at a LA public school or average public school tuition at an LAICU private school

DEADLINE(S): Jun 1

FIELD(S): All fields of study

Must apply as a first-time freshman within 4 semesters of graduation from an approved LA high school. Must have 2.5 GPA, the prior year's state average on the ACT (min. 19), and completion of 16.5 units of the core curriculum. For use at Louisiana public colleges, universities, or technical schools and member schools of the Louisiana

Association of Independent Colleges and Universities.

Apply by completing the Free Application for Federal Student Aid (FAFSA).

1362

LUTHERAN BROTHERHOOD (Scholarships)

625 Fourth Ave. South
Minneapolis, MN 55415
800/328-7168

AMOUNT: $800-$1,500

DEADLINE(S): Feb 12

FIELD(S): All fields of study

Undergraduate scholarships open to Lutheran Brotherhood members. Recipients are chosen by an independent panel of judges on basis of scholastic achievement (minimum high school GPA of 3.5), school & community involvement & future plans.

$500 award for public school; $1,000 award for private non-Lutheran school; $2,000 award for Lutheran school. Renewable. Write for complete information.

1363

LUTHERAN BROTHERHOOD (Stafford Student Loans)

625 Fourth Ave. South
Minneapolis, MN 55415
800/328-7168

AMOUNT: $2,650-$7,500

DEADLINE(S): None

FIELD(S): All fields of study

Loans open to Lutheran students on a first-come first-served basis who have been accepted for admission by an eligible higher education institution and are making satisfactory progress. Must meet federal requirements.

Contact address above for complete information.

1364

MAINE EDUCATION ASSISTANCE DIVISION—FINANCE AUTHORITY OF MAINE (Scholarships)
State House Station, #119
Augusta, ME 04333
207/289-2183

AMOUNT: $500 (public institutions); $1,000 (private)
DEADLINE(S): May 1
FIELD(S): All fields of study

Open to Maine residents attending regionally accredited colleges in AK; CT; DC; DE; MA; MD; NH; PA; RI; VT. Awards are for full-time undergraduate study.

8,000 awards per year. Application is the Maine Financial Aid form available in college financial aid office.

1365

MAINE VETERAN'S SERVICES (Grants for Dependents)
State House Station, #117
Augusta, ME 04333-0117
207/626-4464; 800/345-0116

AMOUNT: Free tuition at state-supported Maine schools
DEADLINE(S): None
FIELD(S): All fields of study

For Maine residents who are children or step-children (ages 16-21 and high school graduates) or spouses (or widows) of military veterans who are totally disabled due to service or who died in service or as a result of service. Tenable at all branches of the University of Maine System, all State of Maine Vocational Technical Colleges, and Maine Maritime Academy at Castine.

Veteran must have lived in Maine at time of entering service or for 5 years prior to application. Write for complete information.

1366

MAKARIOS SCHOLARSHIP FUND INC. (Scholarships)
13 East 40th Street
New York, NY 10016
212/696-4590

AMOUNT: $1,000 flexible
DEADLINE(S): May 31
FIELD(S): All fields of study

Open to students of Cypriot. Awards support full-time undergraduate or graduate study at accredited colleges or universities in the U.S. Must demonstrate financial need. Must be resident of Cyprus with a student visa & study full-time.

Number of awards flexible; write for complete information.

1367

MARIN EDUCATIONAL FUND (Undergraduate Scholarship Program)
1010 'B' Street, Suite 300
San Rafael, CA 94901
415/459-4240

AMOUNT: $800-$2,000
DEADLINE(S): Mar 2
FIELD(S): All fields of study

Open to Marin County (CA) residents only for undergraduate study in 2- or 4-year colleges and for fifth-year teaching credentials. Must be enrolled at least half-time and demonstrate financial need.

Write for complete information.

1368

MARQUETTE UNIVERSITY (South African Scholarship Program)
Alumni Memorial Union 425
Milwaukee, WI 53233
414/288-7289

AMOUNT: Tuition + lab fees & special course fees
DEADLINE(S): Mar 15

FIELD(S): All fields of undergraduate study

One award to non-white South African citizens who can meet the admission requirements for academic, personal & English language abilities. Must have financial sponsor for living expenses.

The maximum duration of any scholarship is normally four calendar years with the duration reduced proportionately for students who receive transfer credit.

1369

MARTIN LUTHER KING, JR. SCHOLARSHIP FOUNDATION (Scholarships)

P.O. Box 751
Portland, OR 97207
503/229-3000

AMOUNT: Full tuition

DEADLINE(S): Jul 31 (Fall); Dec 2 (Winter); Mar 3 (Spring)

FIELD(S): All fields of study

Open to students at all levels of study who reside in Oregon and plan to attend or already attend an Oregon school. A GPA of 3.0 or better and proof of admission to a post-secondary institution required.

Write for complete information.

1370

MARY M. AARON MEMORIAL TRUST

1190 Civic Center Blvd.
Yuba City, CA 95997
Written inquiry

AMOUNT: Approximately $375 to $750

DEADLINE(S): Mar 15

FIELD(S): All fields of study

Open to any needy student from Sutter County, CA attending an accredited 2-year (approx. $375) or 4-year (approx. $750) California college or university. Grants based on financial need. Grades & activities are not considered.

Write for complete information.

1371

MARYLAND HIGHER EDUCATION COMMISSION (Delegate Scholarships)

State Scholarship Administration
16 Francis Street
Annapolis, MD 21401-1781
410/974-5370; TTY: 800/735-2258

AMOUNT: Varies; $200 minimum

DEADLINE(S): Varies

FIELD(S): All fields of study

For Maryland residents who are undergraduate or graduate students in Maryland (or out-of-state with a unique major). Must be U.S. citizen.

Duration is up to 4 years; 2-4 scholarships per district. Also for full- or part-time study at certain private career schools and diploma schools of nursing. Write to your delegate for complete information.

1372

MARYLAND HIGHER EDUCATION COMMISSION (Educational Assistance Grant)

State Scholarship Administration
16 Francis Street
Annapolis, MD 21401-1781
410/974-5370; TTY: 800/735-2258

AMOUNT: $200-$3,000

DEADLINE(S): Mar 1 (via FAFSA)

FIELD(S): All fields of study

Open to Maryland residents for full-time undergraduate study at a Maryland degree-granting institution or hospital school of nursing. Financial need must be demonstrated.

Renewable with reapplication for up to 3 years. Write for complete information.

1373

MARYLAND HIGHER EDUCATION COMMISSION (Edward T. Conroy Memorial Scholarships)
State Scholarship Administration
16 Francis Street
Annapolis, MD 21401-1781
410/974-5370; TTY: 800/735-2258

AMOUNT: Up to $3,800 for tuition and mandatory fees
DEADLINE(S): Jul 15
FIELD(S): All fields of study

For sons and daughters of persons 100% disabled or killed in the line of military duty who were Maryland residents at the time of disability or death, to sons and daughters of MIAs or POWs, and to sons, daughters, and un-remarried spouses of public safety employees disabled or killed in the line of duty. Also for 100%-disabled public safety employees.

For undergraduate or graduate study, full- or part-time, in a MD institution. Write for complete information.

1374

MARYLAND HIGHER EDUCATION COMMISSION (Senatorial Scholarship Program)
State Scholarship Administration
16 Francis Street
Annapolis, MD 21401-1781
410/974-5370; TTY: 800/735-2258

AMOUNT: $400-$2,000
DEADLINE(S): Mar 1 (via FAFSA)
FIELD(S): All fields of study

Open to Maryland residents for undergrad or grad study at MD degree-granting institutions, certain private career schools, nursing diploma schools in Maryland. For full- or part-time study. SAT or ACT required for some applicants.

Students with unique majors or with impaired hearing may attend out of state. Duration is 1-4 years with automatic renewal until

degree is granted. Senator selects recipients. Write for complete information.

1375

MASSACHUSETTS BOARD OF HIGHER EDUCATION (Public Service Grant)
Office of Student Financial Assistance
330 Stuart Street, 3rd Floor
Boston, MA 02116
617/727-9420

AMOUNT: Varies with school (covers tuition, not fees)
DEADLINE(S): May 1
FIELD(S): All fields of study

Open to permanent Massachusetts residents who are the child of deceased police/fire/corrections officer killed in line of duty or child of deceased veteran whose death was service-related.
Write for complete information.

1376

MASSACHUSETTS BOARD OF HIGHER EDUCATION (Veterans Tuition Exemption Program)
330 Stuart Street, 3rd Floor
Boston, MA 02116
617/727-9420

AMOUNT: Tuition exemption
DEADLINE(S): None
FIELD(S): All fields of study

Open to military veterans who are permanent residents of Massachusetts. Awards are tenable at Massachusetts post-secondary institutions.

Contact veterans agent at college or address above for complete information.

1377

MASSACHUSETTS COMPANY (The M. Geneva Gray Scholarship Fund)
Trust Dept.
125 High Street
Boston, MA 02110
617/556-2335

AMOUNT: Up to $1,000

DEADLINE(S): Mar 1

FIELD(S): All fields of study

Open to undergraduate students who are MA residents and are unable to qualify for financial aid due to high parental income. Family must have more than one child to educate. Income between $25,000 and $50,000.

There are no academic requirements other than enrollment and good standing. Send a self-addressed stamped envelope for an application and list of instructions.

1378

MASSACHUSETTS HIGHER EDUCATION COORDINATING COUNCIL (General Scholarship Program)
330 Stuart Street, 3rd Floor
Boston, MA 02116
617/727-9420

AMOUNT: $250-$2,500

DEADLINE(S): May 1

FIELD(S): All fields of study

Open to permanent residents of Massachusetts. Awards are for undergraduate study at accredited colleges and universities in Massachusetts.

40,000-50,000 awards per year. Write for complete information.

1379

MASSACHUSETTS OFFICE OF STUDENT FINANCIAL ASSISTANCE (National Guard Educational Assistance Scholarship Program)
330 Stuart Street, 3rd Floor
Boston, MA 02116
617/727-9420

AMOUNT: Tuition waiver

DEADLINE(S): None

FIELD(S): All fields of study

Program open to undergraduate students who are enrolled at a Massachusetts public college or university & are active members of

the Massachusetts National Guard or the Massachusetts Air National Guard.

Contact the veterans office at your college or address above for complete information.

1380

MCCURDY MEMORIAL SCHOLARSHIP FOUNDATION (Emily Scofield Scholarship Fund)
134 West Van Buren Street
Battle Creek, MI 49017
616/962-9591

AMOUNT: $100-$1,000

DEADLINE(S): Mar 31

FIELD(S): All fields of study

Scholarships for residents of Calhoun County, Michigan. Must be undergraduate.

4-5 scholarships per year. Renewable with reapplication and satisfactory grades. Write for complete information.

1381

MCCURDY MEMORIAL SCHOLARSHIP FOUNDATION (McCurdy Scholarship)
134 West Van Buren Street
Battle Creek, MI 49017
616/962-9591

AMOUNT: $1,000

DEADLINE(S): Mar 31

FIELD(S): All fields of study

Must be a resident of Calhoun County, Michigan. Program is for undergraduate students.

7 scholarships per year. Renewable with reapplication and satisfactory grades. Write for complete information.

1382

MERCANTILE BANK OF TOPEKA (Claude & Ina Brey Memorial Endowment Fund)
c/o Trust Dept.
P.O. Box 192
Topeka, KS 66601
913/291-1118

AMOUNT: $500

DEADLINE(S): Apr 15

FIELD(S): All fields of study

Scholarships open to fourth-degree Kansas Grange members. Awards tenable at recognized undergraduate colleges & universities. U.S. citizen.

8 awards per year. Renewable. For complete information write to Marlene Bush, P.O. Box 186, Melvern, KS 66510.

1383

MEXICAN AMERICAN BUSINESS AND PROFESSIONAL SCHOLARSHIP ASSOCIATION (Scholarship Program)
P.O. Box 22292
Los Angeles, CA 90022
Written inquiry only

AMOUNT: $100-$1,000

DEADLINE(S): May 1 (postmark)

FIELD(S): All fields of study

Open to Los Angeles County residents who are of Mexican-American descent and are enrolled full-time in an undergraduate program. Awards are based on financial need and past academic performance.

Write for complete information.

1384

MICHIGAN COMMISSION ON INDIAN AFFAIRS; MICHIGAN DEPT. OF CIVIL RIGHTS (Tuition Waiver Program)
201 N. Washington Square, Suite 700
Lansing, MI 48933
517/373-0654

AMOUNT: Tuition (only) waiver

DEADLINE(S): Varies (8 weeks prior to class registration)

FIELD(S): All fields of study

Open to any Michigan resident who is at least 1/4 North American Indian (certified by their tribal nation) & willing to attend any public Michigan community college, college or university.

Award is for all levels of study and is renewable. Must be Michigan resident for at least 12 months before class registration. Write for complete information.

1385

MICHIGAN GUARANTY AGENCY (Stafford and PLUS Loans)
P.O. Box 30047
Lansing, MI 48909
800/642-5626; Fax 517/335-6703

AMOUNT: Varies

DEADLINE(S): None

FIELD(S): All fields of study

Guaranteed student loans available to students or parents of students who are Michigan residents enrolled in an eligible institution.

Write for complete information.

1386

MICHIGAN HIGHER EDUCATION ASSISTANCE AUTHORITY (Michigan Competitive Scholarships)
Office of Scholarships and Grants
P.O. Box 30462
Lansing, MI 48909
517/373-3394

AMOUNT: $100-$1,200

DEADLINE(S): Feb 21 (for freshmen)

FIELD(S): All fields of study (except BRE degree)

Open to U.S. citizens who have lived in Michigan at least a year and are enrolled at least half time in an eligible Michigan college. Must demonstrate financial need and submit ACT scores.

Scholarships renewable. Applicants must file the FAFSA form. Fact sheets are available from high school counselors. Write for complete information.

1387

MICHIGAN HIGHER EDUCATION ASSISTANCE AUTHORITY (Michigan Tuition Grants)
Office of Scholarships and Grants
P.O. Box 30462
Lansing, MI 48909
517/373-3394

AMOUNT: $100-$2,450
DEADLINE(S): Varies
FIELD(S): All fields of study (except BRE degree)

Open to Michigan residents enrolled at least half time at independent nonprofit Michigan institutions (list available from above address). Both undergraduate and graduate students who can demonstrate financial need are eligible.

Grants renewable. Applicants must file the FAFSA form. Write for complete information.

1388

MICHIGAN VETERANS TRUST FUND (Tuition Grants Program)
611 West Ottawa, 3rd Floor
Lansing, MI 48913
517/335-1629

AMOUNT: Tuition
DEADLINE(S): None
FIELD(S): All fields of study

Open to Michigan residents of at least 12 months preceding enrollment who are aged 16-22 and are the child of a Michigan veteran killed in action or who later died or was totally disabled due to a service-connected cause.

Grants are for undergraduate study at Michigan tax-supported schools. Write for complete information.

1389

MILITARY ORDER OF THE PURPLE HEART (Sons, Daughters, and Grandchildren Scholarship Program)
National Headquarters
5413-B Backlick Road
Springfield, VA 22151
703/642-5360; Fax 703/642-2054

AMOUNT: $1,000 per year (4 years maximum)
DEADLINE(S): Mar 15
FIELD(S): All fields of study

Open to children and grandchildren of Military Order of Purple Heart Members or Purple Heart Recipients. For full-time study at any level by U.S. citizen or legal resident. Must demonstrate academic achievement and financial need.

Renewable for up to 4 years provided a 3.5 GPA is maintained. $5 processing fee. Write for complete information.

1390

MINNESOTA HIGHER EDUCATION SERVICES OFFICE (Scholarships, Grants, Loans, and Work-Study Programs)
Capitol Square Bldg., Suite 400
550 Cedar Street
St. Paul, MN 55101
612/296-3974; Fax 612/297-8880; E-mail: info@heso.state.mn.us; Internet: www.heso.state.mn.us/

AMOUNT: Varies
DEADLINE(S): None specified
FIELD(S): All fields of study

Grants, scholarships, and loans for Minnesota residents to attend colleges and universities. Includes summer programs at college campuses for grades 7-12. Most programs require attendance at Minnesota institutions. High school juniors and seniors should begin planning ahead. Special programs for minorities, health fields, veterans and their dependents, and reciprocity for out-of-state tuition in certain other states.

Send for booklet "Focus on Financial Aid" at above address and/or check website.

1391

MINNESOTA STATE DEPARTMENT OF VETERANS AFFAIRS (Deceased Veterans' Dependents Scholarships)
Veterans Service Bldg.
Benefits Div.
St. Paul, MN 55155-2079
612/296-2562

AMOUNT: Tuition + $350
DEADLINE(S): None
FIELD(S): All fields of study

Open to 2-year (or more) residents of MN who are sons/daughters of veterans killed or who died as a result of a service-caused condition. Parent must have been a resident of MN at time of entry into service. U.S. citizens or legal residents.

Awards tenable at MN undergraduate colleges & universities. Scholarships are renewable up to a bachelor's degree. Write for complete information.

1392

MINNESOTA STATE DEPARTMENT OF VETERANS AFFAIRS (Veterans Grants)
Veterans Service Bldg.
Benefits Div.
St. Paul, MN 55155-2079
612/296-2562

AMOUNT: $350
DEADLINE(S): None
FIELD(S): All fields of study

Open to veterans who were residents of MN at the time of their entry into the armed forces of the U.S. & were honorably discharged after having served on active duty for at least 181 consecutive days. Must be U.S. citizen or legal resident.

Must attend accredited institution in Minnesota & have time remaining on federal education period. Must have exhausted through use any federal educational entitle-

ment. Financial need must be demonstrated. Write for complete information.

1393

MINNIE PEARL SCHOLARSHIP PROGRAM
1817 Patterson Street
Nashville, TN 37203
Voice/TDD 800/545-HEAR

AMOUNT: $2,000 (or amount of tuition; whichever is less)
DEADLINE(S): Feb 15
FIELD(S): All fields of study

Open to mainstream high school seniors with a significant bi-lateral hearing loss, a 3.0 or better GPA, and who are enrolled in or have been accepted by an accredited college, university, or tech school. For full-time study. U.S. citizens only.

Number of awards varies each year. Renewable throughout college career. Write for complete information.

1394

MISSISSIPPI OFFICE OF STATE STUDENT FINANCIAL AID (Law Enforcement Officers and Firemen Scholarship Program)
3825 Ridgewood Road
Jackson, MS 39211-6453
601/982-6570; 800/327-2980

AMOUNT: Tuition; room; required fees
DEADLINE(S): None specified
FIELD(S): All fields of study

Open to children, stepchildren, or spouse of Mississippi law enforcement officers or full-time firemen who were fatally injured or were totally disabled while on duty. Children must be under age 23.

Tuition-free scholarships for 8 semesters at any state-supported college or university in Mississippi. Write for complete information.

1395

MISSISSIPPI OFFICE OF STATE STUDENT FINANCIAL AID (Southeast Asia POW/MIA Scholarship Program)
3825 Ridgewood Road
Jackson, MS 39211-6453
601/982-6570; 800/982-6663

AMOUNT: Tuition; room; required fees
DEADLINE(S): None specified
FIELD(S): All fields of study

Open to dependent children of military veterans formerly or currently listed as missing in action in Southeast Asia or as prisoners of war as a result of military action against the U.S. Naval Vessel Pueblo.

Tuition-free scholarships for 8 semesters at any state-supported Mississippi college or university. Write for complete information.

1396

MISSOURI COORDINATING BOARD FOR HIGHER EDUCATION (Missouri Student Grant Program)
3515 Amazonas Drive
Jefferson City, MO 65109-5717
573/751-3940

AMOUNT: $100-$1,500
DEADLINE(S): Apr 30
FIELD(S): All fields of study (except Theology & Divinity)

Undergraduate grants open to Missouri residents who are U.S. citizens attending a Missouri school full time. Missouri FFS or FAF required.

Submit free application for Federal Student Aid (FAFSA) to the Central Processor. Missouri residents must check that they want information released to the state. Write for complete information.

1397

MISSOURI COORDINATING BOARD FOR HIGHER EDUCATION (Missouri Student Loan Program—Federal Stafford Loans)
3515 Amazonas Drive
Jefferson City, MO 65109-5717
573/751-3940

AMOUNT: Up to $23,000 (total) for undergraduate study; $8,500 per year for graduate students to a maximum of $65,000 (both undergrad & grad)
DEADLINE(S): Varies
FIELD(S): All fields of study

Open to Missouri students attending a Missouri school at least half time and making satisfactory academic progress. U.S. citizenship or legal residency required.

Apply before the end of academic period. Renewable by reapplying each year. Write for complete information.

1398

MISSOURI COORDINATING BOARD FOR HIGHER EDUCATION (Higher Education Academic Scholarship Program "Bright Flight")
3515 Amazonas Drive
Jefferson City, MO 65109-5717
573/751-3940

AMOUNT: $2,000
DEADLINE(S): Jul 31
FIELD(S): All fields of study (except Theology & Divinity)

Undergraduate scholarships for Missouri residents who are U.S. citizens. Must be high school graduate accepted or enrolled full-time as an undergraduate & have a composite ACT or SAT score in top 3% for Missouri schools. Apply for fall term immediately following graduation from high school or obtaining GED.

Renewable yearly as an undergraduate. Write for complete information.

1399

MOBIL CORPORATION (Desert Storm Scholarship Program)
3225 Gallows Road
Fairfax, VA 22037-0001
Written inquiry only

AMOUNT: Varies
DEADLINE(S): Varies (with institution)
FIELD(S): All fields of study

Open to veterans of Operation Desert Shield/Desert Storm, their spouses, and their children. The spouses and children of those who died in the operations receive highest priority. For full-time undergraduate study leading to a bachelor's degree.
Scholarships are renewable and available at 20 U.S. colleges and universities. Financial need is a consideration. Write for list of participating schools and complete information.

1400

MODERN WOODMEN OF AMERICA (Fraternal College Scholarship Program)
1701 First Avenue
Rock Island, IL 61201
Written inquiry only

AMOUNT: $500-$2,000
DEADLINE(S): Jan 1
FIELD(S): All fields of study

Open to high school seniors who have been beneficial members of Modern Woodmen for at least two years and are in the upper half of their graduating class. For use at any accredited four-year college in the U.S.
36 awards per year renewable for four years. Write for complete information.

1401

MONGOLIA SOCIETY (Dr. Gombojab Hangin Memorial Scholarship)
322 Goodbody Hall
Indiana Univ.
Bloomington, IN 47405
812/855-4078; Fax 812/855-7500; E-mail: MONSOC@Indiana.edu

AMOUNT: $2,500
DEADLINE(S): Jan 1
FIELD(S): All fields of study

Open to students of Mongolian heritage (defined as an individual of Mongolian ethnic origins who is a citizen of Mongolia, the People's Republic of China, or the former Soviet Union) to pursue studies in the U.S. Award does not include transportation from recipient's country to U.S. nor does it include room and board at university. Upon conclusion of the award year, recipient must write a report of his/her activities which resulted from receipt of the scholarship.
Recipient will receive scholarship monies in one lump sum after enrollment in the scholarship holder's institution in the U.S. Write for complete information.

1402

MONTANA UNIVERSITY SYSTEM (Indian Fees Waiver Program)
2500 Broadway
P.O. Box 203101
Helena, MT 59620-3101
406/444-6594

AMOUNT: Waiver of registration and incidental fees
DEADLINE(S): None
FIELD(S): All fields of study

One-fourth or more Indian blood & Montana residency for at least 1 year before enrolling in Montana University System required. Financial need must be demonstrated.
Each unit of the Montana University System makes its own rules governing selection. 500 waivers per year. Write for complete information.

1403

MONTANA UNIVERSITY SYSTEM (Montana Guaranteed Student Loan Program)
2500 Broadway
P.O. Box 203101
Helena, MT 59620-3101

406/444-6594

AMOUNT: $2,625-$7,500 per year
undergrads; $18,500 per year grads
DEADLINE(S): None
FIELD(S): All fields of study

The MGSLP is not a lender—it does not make loans to students. Rather it guarantees loans which are made by regular lending institutions such as banks and savings and loan associations. Must demonstrate financial need.

Open to all U.S. residents. Write for complete information.

1404

MONTANA UNIVERSITY SYSTEM (Montana State Student Incentive Grants)
2500 Broadway
P.O. Box 203101
Helena, MT 59620-3101
406/444-6594

AMOUNT: Up to $600
DEADLINE(S): None
FIELD(S): All fields of study

Open to Montana residents who are full-time undergraduate students attending accredited schools in Montana. Must demonstrate need.

1,150 awards per year. Contact financial aid office of the school you plan to attend as these grants are decentralized.

1405

MOTHER JOSEPH ROGAN MARYMOUNT FOUNDATION (Grant Program & Loan Program)
c/o Boatmen's Trust Company
P.O. Box 14737
St. Louis, MO 63101
314/391-6248

AMOUNT: $400-$750
DEADLINE(S): May 1
FIELD(S): All fields of study

Grants and loans for students who are U.S. citizens; live in the metropolitan St. Louis area, and are entering or enrolled in a high school, vocational/technical school, college or university.
Write for complete information.

1406

NAACP NATIONAL OFFICE (Agnes Jones Jackson Scholarship)
4805 Mt. Hope Drive
Baltimore, MD 21215
401/358-8900

AMOUNT: $1,500 undergrads; $2,500 grads
DEADLINE(S): Apr 30
FIELD(S): All fields of study

Undergraduates must have GPA of 2.5+; graduates must possess 3.0 GPA. Applicants must be NAACP members and must be under the age of 25 by Apr 30.

Send legal-size self-addressed stamped envelope to address above for application and complete information.

1407

NATIONAL AMPUTATION FOUNDATION (Scholarships)
38-40 Church Street
Malverne, NY 11565
516/887-3600

AMOUNT: $125 per year
DEADLINE(S): None
FIELD(S): All fields of study

Open to high school seniors with major limb amputations. Awards support undergraduate full-time study at any recognized college or university.

24 awards per year. Write for complete information.

1408

**NATIONAL ASSOCIATION OF
SECONDARY SCHOOL PRINCIPALS
(National Honor Society Scholarships)**
1904 Association Drive
Reston, VA 22091
800/253-7746

AMOUNT: $1,000
DEADLINE(S): Feb 1
FIELD(S): All fields of study

Open to National Honor Society Members.
Each chapter nominates two seniors to
compete for scholarships at the national
level.

250 scholarships per year. Contact your NHS
chapter, high school principal or guidance
counselor for complete information.

1409

**NATIONAL COUNCIL OF JEWISH
WOMEN—GREATER BOSTON SECTION
(Amelia Greenbaum/Rabbi Marshall Lifson
Scholarship Program)**
831 Beacon Street, #138
Newton Centre, MA 02159
617/783-9660

AMOUNT: $400 maximum
DEADLINE(S): Apr 30
FIELD(S): All fields of study

Open to Jewish women who are residents of
Boston (or vicinity) & attend a
Massachusetts college or university as an
undergraduate. Must demonstrate financial
need.

Write for complete information.

1410

**NATIONAL FEDERATION OF THE
BLIND (Hermione Grant Calhoun
Scholarships)**
805 Fifth Ave.
Grinnell, IA 50112
515/236-3366

AMOUNT: $3,000
DEADLINE(S): Mar 31
FIELD(S): All fields of study

Scholarship open to legally blind female
undergraduate or graduate student. Awards
based on academic excellence, service to the
community, and financial need.

Awards are given at the organization's annual
convention.

1411

**NATIONAL FEDERATION OF THE
BLIND (Melva T. Owen Memorial
Scholarship)**
805 Fifth Ave.
Grinnell, IA 50112
515/236-3366

AMOUNT: $4,000
DEADLINE(S): Mar 31
FIELD(S): All fields of study

Open to legally blind students for all post-secondary areas of study directed toward
attaining financial independence. Excludes
religion and those seeking only to further
their general and cultural education.

Awards based on academic excellence, service
to the community and financial need. Write
for complete information.

1412

**NATIONAL FEDERATION OF THE
BLIND (Scholarships)**
805 Fifth Ave.
Grinnell, IA 50112
515/236-3366

AMOUNT: $3,000-$10,000
DEADLINE(S): Mar 31
FIELD(S): All fields of study

26 scholarships (22 for $3,000 ea; 3 for $4,000
ea; 1 for $10,000 ea) will be given.
Applicants must be legally blind and studying (or planning to study) full time at the
post-secondary level.

Awards are on the basis of academic excellence, community service and financial need. Write for complete information.

1413

NATIONAL HISPANIC SCHOLARSHIP FUND (Scholarships)

One Sansome Street, Suite 1000
San Francisco, CA 94104
415/445-9930; Fax 415/445-9942; E-mail:
info@nhsf.org; Internet: www.nhsf.org

AMOUNT: $500-$2,000
DEADLINE(S): Aug 15 (Applications available then. Deadline is Oct 1)
FIELD(S): All fields of study

For U.S. citizens or permanent residents of Hispanic parentage enrolled full-time as undergraduate or graduate student in a U.S. or Puerto Rican college or university. Applicants must have completed at least 15 units/credits prior to fall registration. Academic achievement, personal strengths, leadership, and financial need are the selection criteria.

Community college units must be transferable to a 4-year institution. Send business-sized self-addressed stamped envelope for complete information.

1414

NATIONAL MAKE IT WITH WOOL COMPETITION (Scholarship/Awards)

1323 Elkhorn
Belle Fourche, SD 57717
605/892-2332

AMOUNT: Various awards including $2,000 scholarship
DEADLINE(S): Varies (with state)
FIELD(S): All fields of study

Sewing, knitting, and crocheting competition open to students who make a wool garment from a current pattern. Fabric must contain at least 60% wool. Awards tenable at any recognized college or university.

Teenagers and older pay an entry fee of $5; pre-teens pay $2. State winners advance to national competition. Write for complete information.

1415

NATIONAL MERIT SCHOLARSHIP PROGRAM

1560 Sherman Ave., Suite 200
Evanston, IL 60201
847/866-5100

AMOUNT: Varies
DEADLINE(S): Varies
FIELD(S): All fields of study

Open to students who enter the competition for scholarships by taking the PSAT/NMSQT in October of their junior year in high school. U.S. citizenship required.

See PSAT/NMSQT student bulletin for deadlines. Scholarship winners are chosen on the basis of abilities, skills, and accomplishments without regard to gender, race, ethnic origin, or religion.

1416

NATIONAL SOCIETY OF THE SONS OF THE AMERICAN REVOLUTION (Eagle Scout Scholarship)

1000 S. Fourth Street
Louisville, KY 40203
502/589-1776

AMOUNT: $5,000 (1st); $1,000 (2nd)
DEADLINE(S): Dec 31
FIELD(S): All fields of study

Open to the current class of Eagle Scouts who passed their board of review between July 1 & the following June 30 of each year. College plans DO NOT have to be complete in order to receive the cash scholarships.

An essay of 500 words or less on a patriotic theme is required. Contact your local SAR Eagle Scout Chairman for complete information.

1417

NATIONAL TWENTY AND FOUR
(Memorial Scholarships)
c/o Ethel M. Matuschka
6000 Lucerne Ct., #2
Mequon, WI 53092
Written inquiry

AMOUNT: Maximum of $500
DEADLINE(S): May 1
FIELD(S): All fields of study

Open to members & dependents of members
between the ages of 16 and 25. Selection is
based on financial need, scholastic standing
& school activities.

Write for complete information ONLY if
above qualifications are met.

1418

NATIVE SONS OF THE GOLDEN WEST
(Annual High School Public Speaking
Contest)
160 Everglade Drive
San Francisco, CA 94132
415/566-4117

AMOUNT: $600-$2,000
DEADLINE(S): Dec 1
FIELD(S): California History

Public speaking competition open to
California high school students under age
20. Speeches should be 7-9 minutes in
length and may be on any subject related to
California's past or present.

District eliminations take place in February
and March; finals are in May. Write for
complete information.

1419

NAVY SUPPLY CORPS FOUNDATION
(Scholarships)
1425 Prince Ave.
Athens, GA 30606-2205
706/354-4111

AMOUNT: $2,000

DEADLINE(S): Feb 15
FIELD(S): All fields of study

For dependent sons/daughters of Navy Supply
Corps Officers (including Warrant & Supply
Corps) associated enlisted ratings on active
duty, in reserve status, retired-with-pay, or
deceased. For undergraduate study at
accredited 2-yr/4-yr colleges. 3.0 GPA for
high school/college required.

Approx. 50 awards per year. Send SASE for
complete information.

1420

NEGRO EDUCATIONAL EMERGENCY
DRIVE (NEED Scholarship Program)
643 Liberty Ave., 17th Floor
Pittsburgh, PA 15222
412/566-2760

AMOUNT: $100-$1,000
DEADLINE(S): Apr 30
FIELD(S): All fields of study

Pennsylvania residency & U.S. citizenship
required. Open to Black students with a
high school diploma or GED who reside in
Allegheny, Armstrong, Beaver, Butler,
Washington or Westmoreland counties.

400 scholarships per year. Renewable. Write
for complete information.

1421

NELLIE MAE (Student Loans)
50 Braintree Hill Park, Suite 300
Braintree, MA 02184-1763
617/849-1325; 800/634-9308

AMOUNT: Up to cost of education less
financial aid
DEADLINE(S): None specified
FIELD(S): All fields of study

Variety of loans available for undergraduate
and graduate study at accredited degree-
granting colleges or universities. Varied
repayment and interest rate options.
Savings programs for on-time repayments.

Write for complete information.

1422

NEVADA DEPT. OF EDUCATION
(Student Incentive Grant Program)
700 E. Fifth Street
Carson City, NV 89701
702/687-9228

AMOUNT: Varies

DEADLINE(S): Varies

FIELD(S): All fields of study

Student incentive grants available to Nevada residents enrolled in eligible Nevada institutions. For both graduate and undergraduate study.

Application must be made through the financial aid office of eligible participating institutions.

1423

NEW BEDFORD PORT SOCIETY-
LADIES BRANCH (Limited Scholarship
Grant)
15 Johnny Cake Hill
New Bedford, MA 02740
Written inquiry only

AMOUNT: $300-$400

DEADLINE(S): May 1

FIELD(S): All fields of study

Open to residents of greater New Bedford who are descended from seafarers such as whaling masters and other fishermen. For undergrad and marine biology studies.

Renewable. Write for complete information.

1424

NEW BRITAIN LABOR COUNCIL AFL-
CIO (Beyer-Ropiak Scholarship)
1 Grove Street, #315B
New Britain, CT 06051
Written inquiry

AMOUNT: $500

DEADLINE(S): Jun 1

FIELD(S): All fields of study

Son/daughter/ward of AFL-CIO member whose local is affiliated with New Britain Central Labor Council eligible to apply. For full-time undergraduate study only.

Write for complete information.

1425

NEW ENGLAND BOARD OF HIGHER
EDUCATION (New England Regional
Student Program)
45 Temple Place
Boston, MA 02111
617/357-9620

AMOUNT: Tuition reduction (varies)

DEADLINE(S): Varies

FIELD(S): All fields of study

Under this program New England residents may attend public colleges and universities in other New England states at a reduced tuition rate for certain majors which are not available in their own state's public institutions.

Write to the above address for complete information.

1426

NEW HAMPSHIRE AMERICAN LEGION
(Scholarships)
Department Adjutant
State House Annex
Concord, NH 03301
Written inquiry only

AMOUNT: $1,000

DEADLINE(S): May 1

FIELD(S): All fields of study

Various scholarships and awards open to New Hampshire residents for college or vocational/technical school studies. Some are limited to children of Legion members.

Write for complete information.

1427

NEW HAMPSHIRE CHARITABLE FOUNDATION (Student Aid Scholarship Funds)

37 Pleasant Street
Concord, NH 03301
603/225-6641

AMOUNT: $100-$2,500
DEADLINE(S): Apr 22
FIELD(S): All fields of study

More than 90 separate scholarship and loan programs for New Hampshire residents are administered by the NHCF. Student must be enrolled in an accredited 2-year or 4-year college or university. Must be legal resident of New Hampshire.
Write for complete information.

1428

NEW HAMPSHIRE HIGHER EDUCATION ASSISTANCE FOUNDATION (Federal Family Education Loan Program)

P.O. Box 877
Concord, NH 03302-0877
603/225-6612; 800/525-2577

AMOUNT: Varies with program
DEADLINE(S): None
FIELD(S): All fields of study

Open to New Hampshire residents pursuing a college education in or out of state and to non-residents who attend a New Hampshire college or university. The foundation administers a variety of student and parent loan programs. U.S. citizen.
Write for complete information.

1429

NEW JERSEY DEPT. OF HIGHER EDUCATION (Educational Opportunity Fund Grants)

Office of Student Assistance
CN 540
Trenton, NJ 08625

609/588-3230; 800/792-8670 in NJ; TDD 609/588-2526

AMOUNT: $200-$2,100 undergrads; $200-$4,150 graduate students
DEADLINE(S): Varies
FIELD(S): All fields of study

Must be New Jersey resident for at least 12 months prior to application. Grants for economically and educationally disadvantaged students. For undergraduate or graduate study in New Jersey. Must demonstrate need and be U.S. citizen or legal resident.
Grants renewable. Write for complete information.

1430

NEW JERSEY DEPT. OF HIGHER EDUCATION (Public Tuition Benefits Program)

Office of Student Assistance
CN 540
Trenton, NJ 08625
609/588-3230; 800/792-8670 in NJ

AMOUNT: Actual cost of tuition
DEADLINE(S): Oct 1; Mar 1
FIELD(S): All fields of study

Open to New Jersey residents who are dependents of emergency service personnel and law officers killed in the line of duty in NJ For undergraduate study in NJ. U.S. citizenship or legal residency required.
Renewable. Write for complete information.

1431

NEW JERSEY DEPT. OF MILITARY & VETERANS AFFAIRS (Veterans Tuition Credit Program)

Eggert Crossing Road
CN #340
Attn. DVL6S
Trenton, NJ 08625-0340
609/530-6961; 800/624-0508 in NJ

AMOUNT: $400 (full-time); $200 (half-time)
DEADLINE(S): Oct 1; Mar 1

FIELD(S): All fields of study

Open to U.S. military veterans who served between Dec. 31, 1960 & May 7, 1975 and were residents of New Jersey for one year prior to application or were NJ residents at time of induction or discharge. Proof of residency is required.

Applies to all levels of study. Write for complete information.

1432

NEW JERSEY DEPT. OF MILITARY & VETERANS AFFAIRS (POW/MIA Dependents Grants)
Eggert Crossing Road
CN 340
Attn: DCUA-FO
Trenton, NJ 08625-0340
609/530-6961; 800/624-0508 in NJ

AMOUNT: Full tuition
DEADLINE(S): Oct 1; Mar 1
FIELD(S): All fields of study

For New Jersey residents who are dependent children of U.S. military personnel who were officially declared POW or MIA after Jan 1, 1960. Grants will pay undergraduate tuition at any accredited public or independent college/university in NJ.

Write for complete information.

1433

NEW JERSEY STATE GOLF ASSOC. (Caddie Scholarships)
P.O. Box 6947
Freehold, NJ 07728
973/338-8334

AMOUNT: $800-$2,500
DEADLINE(S): May 1
FIELD(S): All fields of study

Open to students who have served as a caddie at a New Jersey golf club which is a member of the NJ state golf association. For full-time undergraduate study at an accredited college or university.

Awards are based on scholastic achievement, financial need, SAT scores, character, and length of service as a caddie. 40+ new awards per year. Renewable for 3 additional years. Write for complete information.

1434

NEW MEXICO COMMISSION ON HIGHER EDUCATION (Student Incentive Grant)
P.O. Box 15910
Santa Fe, NM 87506-5910
505/827-7383; Fax 505/827-7393; E-mail: highered@che.state.nm.us; Internet: www.nmche.org

AMOUNT: $600 average
DEADLINE(S): Varies
FIELD(S): All fields of study

Open to New Mexico residents who are undergraduates attending public and selected private nonprofit post-secondary institutions in New Mexico. Must be enrolled at least half-time.

Renewable. Approximately 12,000 grants per year. Contact college financial aid office for deadlines and other information.

1435

NEW MEXICO VETERANS' SERVICE COMMISSION (Scholarship Program)
P.O. Box 2324
Santa Fe, NM 87503
505/827-6300

AMOUNT: Full tuition + $300
DEADLINE(S): None
FIELD(S): All fields of study

Open to New Mexico residents (aged 16-26) who are son or daughter of person who was killed in action or died as a result of military service in the U.S. Armed Forces during a period of armed conflict.

Veteran must have been NM resident at time of entry into service and must have served during a period of armed conflict. Approx. 13 full tuition scholarships for undergrads per year. Write for complete information.

1436

NEW YORK STATE EDUCATION DEPT.
(Awards, Scholarships, and Fellowships)
Bureau of NEOP/UATEA/Scholarships
Room 1076 EB
Albany, NY 12234
518/486-1319; Fax 518/486-5346

AMOUNT: Varies
DEADLINE(S): Varies
FIELD(S): All fields of study

Various state and federal programs administered by the NY State Education
Department open to residents of New York
state. One year's NY residency immediately
preceding effective date of award is
required.
Write for complete information.

1437

NEW YORK STATE SENATE
(Undergraduate Session Assistants Program)
NYS Student Programs Office
90 South Swan, Room 401
Albany, NY 12247
518/455-2611; Fax 518/432-5470; E-mail:
students@senate.state.ny.us

AMOUNT: $2,800 stipend
DEADLINE(S): Oct 31
FIELD(S): All fields of study

Open to talented undergraduates (except
freshmen) who want first-hand experience
at the New York state legislature. Need a
good academic record. All majors may
apply. Must be enrolled in a college or university in New York state. U.S. citizenship.
3.0 GPA required. Must demonstrate keen
writing skills and have the recommendation
and support of on-campus faculty.
Contact Dr. Russell J. Williams at above location for complete information.

1438

NON-COMMISSIONED OFFICERS
ASSOCIATION (Scholarships)
P.O. Box 33610
San Antonio, TX 78265-3610
512/653-6161

AMOUNT: $900-$1,000
DEADLINE(S): Mar 31
FIELD(S): All fields of study

Undergraduate and vocational training scholarships open to children and spouses of members of the Non-Commissioned Officers
Association. Children of members must be
under age 25 to receive initial grants.
35 awards per year. Full-time students who
maintain at least a 3.0 GPA may reapply
each year for scholarship renewal. Write for
complete information.

1439

NORTH CAROLINA DIVISION OF
SERVICES FOR THE BLIND
(Rehabilitation Assistance for Visually
Impaired)
309 Ashe Ave.
Raleigh, NC 27606
919/733-9700

AMOUNT: Tuition + fees, books & supplies
DEADLINE(S): None
FIELD(S): All fields of study

Open to North Carolina residents who are
legally blind or have a progressive eye condition which may result in blindness (there-
by creating an impediment for the individual) and who are undergrad or grad students at a NC school.
Write for complete information.

1440

NORTH CAROLINA DIVISION OF
VETERANS AFFAIRS (Dependents
Scholarship Program)
325 N. Salisbury Street, Suite 1065
Raleigh, NC 27603

919/733-3851

AMOUNT: $1,500 to $3,000 (private college); tuition & fees + room & board (public college)

DEADLINE(S): May 31

FIELD(S): All fields of study

Undergraduate scholarships open to children of veterans who died as a result of wartime service or were disabled, POW, MIA or received pension from the VA. Veteran entered service as NC resident or applicant NC resident since birth.

Awards tenable at private & public colleges in North Carolina. 350-400 awards per year. Renewable up to 4 years. Write for complete information.

1441

NORTH CAROLINA STATE EDUCATION ASSISTANCE AUTHORITY (Student Financial Aid for North Carolinians)
P.O. Box 2688
Chapel Hill, NC 27515
919/549-8614

AMOUNT: Varies

DEADLINE(S): Varies

FIELD(S): All fields of study

The state of NC, private NC organizations & the federal government fund numerous scholarships, grants, work-study, and loan programs for North Carolina residents at all levels of study.

The NC State Education Assistance Authority annually publishes a financial aid booklet describing in detail various programs for North Carolina residents. A copy is available free to undergrads who plan to attend a school in NC.

1442

NORTH CAROLINA STATE UNIVERSITY (John Gatling Scholarship Program)
2119 Pullen Hall, Box 7342
Raleigh, NC 27695

919/515-3671

AMOUNT: $8,000 per year

DEADLINE(S): Feb 1

FIELD(S): All fields of study

If born with surname of 'Gatlin' or 'Gatling' this program will provide $8,000 toward the cost of attending NC state university as an undergraduate provided you meet NC state university entrance and transfer requirements. U.S. citizen.

Award is renewable each year if full time (24 or more credits per year) & maintain at least 2.0 GPA. Contact the NCSU merit awards program coordinator at address above for complete information.

1443

NORTH DAKOTA INDIAN SCHOLARSHIP PROGRAM (Scholarships)
State Capitol Building, 10th Floor
Bismarck, ND 58505
701/328-2960

AMOUNT: Up to $2,000

DEADLINE(S): Jul 15

FIELD(S): All fields of study

Open to North Dakota residents who have at least 1/4 Indian blood or are enrolled members of a North Dakota tribe. Awards are tenable at recognized undergraduate colleges & universities in North Dakota. U.S. citizenship required.

100 150 scholarships per year. Renewable. Write for complete information.

1444

NORTH DAKOTA STUDENT FINANCIAL ASSISTANCE AGENCY (Grants)
State Capitol, 10th Floor
600 East Blvd.
Bismarck, ND 58505
701/328-4114

AMOUNT: Up to $600

DEADLINE(S): Apr 15

FIELD(S): All fields of study

General

Open to residents of North Dakota for undergraduate study at colleges & universities in North Dakota. Must be citizen or legal resident of U.S.

2,400 awards per year. Renewable. Write for complete information.

1445

OHIO BOARD OF REGENTS (Ohio Academic Scholarship Program)
State Grants & Scholarships Dept.
P.O. Box 182452
Columbus, OH 43218-2452
888/833-1133; 614/752-9536; Fax 614/752-5903

AMOUNT: $2,000/year for up to 4 years
DEADLINE(S): Feb 23
FIELD(S): All fields of study

Open to seniors at chartered Ohio high schools who are Ohio residents and intend to be enrolled as full-time undergraduate students in eligible Ohio institutions of higher education.

1,000 awards per year. Scholarships are automatically renewable for up to four years of undergraduate study provided satisfactory progress is made. Apply through high school guidance office.

1446

OHIO BOARD OF REGENTS (Ohio Instructional Grant Program)
State Grants/Scholarship Dept.
P.O. Box 182452
Columbus, OH 43218-2452
888/833-1133; 614/466-7420; Fax 614-752-5903

AMOUNT: $288-$4,296
DEADLINE(S): Oct 1
FIELD(S): All fields of study

For Ohio residents enrolled full-time in an eligible Ohio or Pennsylvania institution of higher education. Must be in a good academic standing and demonstrate financial need. Based on family income and number of dependents in the family.

90,000 renewable grants per year. Benefits are restricted to the student's instructional and general fee charges. Apply by completing the FAFSA form.

1447

OHIO BOARD OF REGENTS (Ohio Student Choice Grant)
State Grants/Scholarships Dept.
P.O. Box 182452
Columbus, OH 43218-2452
888/833-1133; 614/644-7420; Fax 614-752-5903

AMOUNT: Varies
DEADLINE(S): Ongoing
FIELD(S): All fields of study

For Ohio residents enrolled as full-time undergraduate students at an eligible private nonprofit Ohio college or university. Assists in narrowing the tuition gap between the state's public and private nonprofit colleges and universities.

23,000 awards per year renewable for a maximum of 5 years. Write for complete information.

1448

OHIO BOARD OF REGENTS (War Orphans Scholarship Program)
State Grants/Scholarship Dept.
P.O. Box 182452
Columbus, OH 43218-2452
888/833-1133; 614/466-7420; Fax 614/752-5903

AMOUNT: Full tuition at public schools; equivalent amount at private schools
DEADLINE(S): Jul 1
FIELD(S): All fields of study

For Ohio residents who are dependents of veterans who served during war and as a result is now severely disabled or deceased. Must be enrolled for full-time undergraduate study at an Ohio institution.

Varies per year. Contact above address, high school guidance offices, veterans service offices, and college financial aid offices for complete information.

1449

OHIO UNIVERSITY (Charles Kilburger Scholarship)
Asst. Dir. Student Services
1570 Granville Pike
Lancaster, OH 43130
614/654-6711

AMOUNT: Tuition
DEADLINE(S): Feb 1
FIELD(S): All fields of study

Scholarship open to seniors graduating from a Fairfield County (Ohio) high school who will enroll at Ohio University–Lancaster for at least two years. For undergraduate study only. U.S. citizenship required.

Applications available ONLY from Fairfield County, OH high school counselors. Must demonstrate financial need.

1450

OPERATING ENGINEERS LOCAL UNION NO. 3 (IUOE Scholarship Program)
1620 South Loop Road
Alameda, CA 94502
510/748-7400

AMOUNT: Up to $3,000
DEADLINE(S): Mar 1
FIELD(S): All fields of study

Open to dependent children of members of IUOE Local No. 3 who are high school seniors with at least a 3.0 GPA. Awards tenable at recognized undergraduate colleges & universities. U.S. citizenship required.
Write for complete information.

1451

ORDER OF THE EASTERN STAR (Grand Chapter of California Scholarships)
870 Market Street, Suite 722
San Francisco, CA 94102-2996

Written inquiry

AMOUNT: $250-$500 (2-year college); $500-$1,000 (4-year college)
DEADLINE(S): May 1
FIELD(S): All fields of study, including vocational/technical

Open to California members of Eastern Star who are accepted to or enrolled in a California college, university, or trade school and have at least a 3.5 GPA (4.0 scale). Must demonstrate financial need and be U.S. citizen.

Write to Mrs. Shirley Orth Grand Secretary, address above, for complete information.

1452

OREGON DEPARTMENT OF VETERANS' AFFAIRS (Educational Aid for Oregon Veterans)
700 Summer Street NE, Suite 150
Salem, OR 97310-1270
800/692-9666; 503/373-2085

AMOUNT: $35 to $50 per month
DEADLINE(S): None
FIELD(S): All fields of study

For veterans on active duty during the Korean War, Jun 25, 1950 to Jan 31, 1955 or who received a campaign or expeditionary medal or ribbon awarded by the Armed Forces of the United States for services after Jun 30, 1958. Must be resident of Oregon and U.S. citizen with a qualifying military service record at time of application. For study in an accredited Oregon school.
Write for complete information.

1453

OREGON STATE SCHOLARSHIP COMMISSION (Federal Family Education Loan Program)
1500 Valley River Drive, #100
Eugene, OR 97401
800/452-8807; 541/687-7400; Internet: www.teleport.com~ossc

AMOUNT: $2,625-$6,635 undergrad; $8,500-$18,500 graduate (annual maximum)

DEADLINE(S): None specified

FIELD(S): All fields of study

Open to U.S. citizens or permanent residents who are attending an eligible Oregon institution and to Oregon residents attending any eligible institution outside of Oregon at least half-time.

Write or visit website for complete information.

1454

OREGON STATE SCHOLARSHIP COMMISSION (Oregon Need Grants)

1500 Valley River Drive, #100
Eugene, OR 97401
503/687-7400

AMOUNT: $906-$1,584

DEADLINE(S): Apr 1

FIELD(S): All fields of study

Open to Oregon residents enrolled full-time in any 2- or 4-year nonprofit college or university in Oregon. Must be U.S. citizen or legal resident and demonstrate financial need.

It is not necessary to take SAT/ACT for need grants. 22,000 awards and grants per year. Renewable. Write for complete information.

1455

OREGON STATE SCHOLARSHIP COMMISSION (Private Scholarship Programs Administered by the Commission)

1500 Valley River Drive, #100
Eugene,OR 97401
503/687-7395

AMOUNT: $250-$3,000

DEADLINE(S): Mar 1

FIELD(S): All fields of study

100 different private scholarship programs are administered by the Commission and are for Oregon residents only. Some are tied to a specific field and/or level of study but in general they are available to all levels and fields of study.

Dependent students must have parents residing in Oregon. Independent students must live in Oregon for 12 months prior to Sept 1 of the academic year for which the application is made. For complete information send a 55-cent, stamped self-addressed #10 business-sized envelope to the above address.

1456

ORPHAN FOUNDATION OF AMERICA (Scholarship Program)

380 Maple Ave. West, Suite LL5
Vienna, VA 22180
Written inquiries only

AMOUNT: $800-$2,500

DEADLINE(S): May 1

FIELD(S): All fields of study

Program open to 'orphans' or youth in foster care at the age of 18 who have not been adopted. Awards tenable at any recognized undergraduate or vocational school in the U.S. Must be U.S. citizen or legal resident.

50+ scholarships per year. Renewable with reapplication. Send self-addressed stamped envelope for application and information.

1457

PARENTS WITHOUT PARTNERS (International Scholarship)

401 N. Michigan Ave.
Chicago, IL 60611-4267
312/644-6610

AMOUNT: Varies

DEADLINE(S): Mar 15

FIELD(S): All fields of study

Open to dependent children (up to 25 years of age) of Parents Without Partners members. Can be a graduating high school senior or college student. For undergraduate study at trade or vocational school, college or university.

Write for complete information (send postage-paid envelope).

1458

PAUL AND MARY HAAS FOUNDATION (Scholarship Grants)
P.O. Box 2928
Corpus Christi, TX 78403
512/887-6955

AMOUNT: $1,000 per semester

DEADLINE(S): Varies (Initially fall of high school senior year)

FIELD(S): All fields of study

Program open to high school seniors who are Corpus Christi, TX residents. Awards support full-time pursuit of first undergraduate degree.

Approximately 50 awards per year. Must prove financial need. Write for complete information.

1459

PENNSYLVANIA DEPARTMENT OF MILITARY AFFAIRS—BUREAU OF VETERANS AFFAIRS (Scholarships)
Fort Indiantown Gap
Annville, PA 17003-5002
717/861-8904; 717/861-8910

AMOUNT: Up to $500/term ($4,000 for 4 years)

DEADLINE(S): None

FIELD(S): All fields of study

Open to children of military veterans who died or were totally disabled as a result of war, armed conflict or terrorist attack. Must have lived in Pennsylvania for 5 years prior to application, be age 16-23 & demonstrate financial need.

70 awards per year. Renewable. For study at Pennsylvania schools. Must be U.S. citizen. Write for complete information.

1460

PENNSYLVANIA HIGHER EDUCATION ASSISTANCE AGENCY (Robert C. Byrd Honors Scholarship Program)
P.O. Box 8114
Harrisburg, PA 17105-8114
717/720-2850

AMOUNT: Determined yearly by the federal government

DEADLINE(S): May 1

FIELD(S): All fields of study

Open to Penn. high school seniors in the top 5 percent of their graduating class with a 3.5 or better GPA & an SAT score of 1200 or higher. Must be U.S. citizen and have been accepted for enrollment in an institution of higher education.

Renewable to a maximum of four years. Write for complete information.

1461

PERRY & STELLA TRACY SCHOLARSHIP FUND (Scholarships)
Wells Fargo Private Banking Group
P.O. Box 2511
Sacramento, CA 95812
916/440-4449

AMOUNT: $350-$750

DEADLINE(S): None given

FIELD(S): All fields of study

Open to applicants who are graduates of El Dorado County high schools and have resided in El Dorado County, CA for at least 2 years. Awards are tenable at recognized undergraduate colleges & universities.

Approximately 125 awards per year. Renewable. Contact high school counselor for complete information. Do NOT contact Wells Fargo.

1462

PHI KAPPA THETA NATIONAL FOUNDATION (Scholarship Program)

c/o Scott Bova
3901 W. 86th Street, Suite 425
Indianapolis, IN 46265
317/872-9934

AMOUNT: $1,500 maximum
DEADLINE(S): Apr 30
FIELD(S): All fields of study

Undergraduate scholarships for members of Phi Kappa Theta, a men's social fraternity. Applications are sent to all chapters; extras are available at national office. Not available to high school or graduate students.

Renewable. 5 scholarships annually. Financial need is a consideration but is relative to the other applicants. Write for complete information.

1463

PHILIPS NORTH AMERICA CORPORATION (Scholarship Program)

100 East 42nd Street
New York, NY 10017
212/850-5000

AMOUNT: $2,500; $500-$1,500
DEADLINE(S): Jan (Apply in Jan. Deadline is Mar 1)
FIELD(S): All fields of study

Open to dependent children of Philips North America employees. Applicants must be high school seniors who expect to graduate during the current year. Considerations include academic record, SAT or ACT scores & biographical questionnaire.

52 awards per year. Financial need is considered except for two $3,500 awards which are merit-based only. Participation in extracurricular activities and sports are considered. Write for complete information.

1464

PICKETT & HATCHER EDUCATIONAL FUND INC. (Loans)

P.O. Box 8169
Columbus, GA 31908-8169
706/327-6586

AMOUNT: $16,000 max
DEADLINE(S): Varies
FIELD(S): All fields of study EXCEPT Law, Medicine, and Ministry

Open to U.S. citizens who are legal residents of and attend colleges located in the southeastern portion of the U.S. Must enroll in four-year program of study in four-year college. Loans are not made for graduate or voc-tech studies.

Write for applications and complete information in January preceding academic year in which loan is needed. May not have other educational loans.

1465

PORTUGUESE CONTINENTAL UNION (Scholarships)

899 Boylston Street
Boston, MA 02115
617/536-2916

AMOUNT: Varies
DEADLINE(S): Mar 31
FIELD(S): All fields of study

Open to members of the Portuguese Continental Union of the U.S. with at least one-year membership in good standing and who plan to enroll or are enrolled in any accredited college or university.

Financial need is a consideration. Write for complete information.

1466

PRESBYTERIAN CHURCH (U.S.A.) (Native American Education Grant)

Financial Aid for Studies
100 Witherspoon Street
Louisville, KY 40202-1396

502/569-5760

AMOUNT: $200-$1,500
DEADLINE(S): Jun 1
FIELD(S): All fields of study

For Native Americans and Alaska Natives who are Presbyterian and who have completed at least one semester of work at an accredited institution of higher education. Preference to students at the undergraduate level.

U.S. citizenship or permanent residency required. Renewal is based on continued financial need and satisfactory academic progress. Write for complete information.

1467

PRESBYTERIAN CHURCH (U.S.A.)
(National Presbyterian College Scholarship)
100 Witherspoon Street
Louisville, KY 40202-1396
502/569-5776; Fax 502/569-8766

AMOUNT: $500-$1,400
DEADLINE(S): Dec 1
FIELD(S): All fields of study

Scholarships for incoming freshmen at one of the participating colleges related to the Presbyterian Church (U.S.A.). Applicants must be superior high school seniors and members of the Presbyterian Church. Must be U.S. citizen or legal resident and demonstrate financial need.

Application and brochure available after September 1. Contact Financial Aid for Studies at above location. Financial need is a consideration. Write for complete information.

1468

PRESBYTERIAN CHURCH (U.S.A.)
(Samuel Robinson Award)
100 Witherspoon Street
Louisville, KY 40202-1396
502/569-5745

AMOUNT: $1,000

DEADLINE(S): Apr 1
FIELD(S): All fields of study

Open to undergraduate students enrolled in one of the 69 colleges related to the Presbyterian Church. Applicants must successfully recite the answers to the Westminster Shorter Catechism and write a 2,000-word original essay on a related assigned topic.

20-30 awards per year. Write to Financial Aid for Studies at above location for complete information.

1469

PRESBYTERIAN CHURCH (U.S.A.)
(Undergraduate/Graduate Student Loans)
100 Witherspoon Street
Louisville, KY 40202-1396
502/569-5776; Fax 502/569-8766

AMOUNT: $200-$1,500 per year
DEADLINE(S): Apr 1
FIELD(S): All fields of study

Loans open to members of the Presbyterian Church (U.S.A.) who are U.S. citizens or permanent residents. For full-time undergraduate or graduate study. No interest while in school. Repayment begins six months after graduation or discontinuation of studies. No more than $4,000 may be borrowed during a student's entire education program.

Must be in academic good standing. An additional feature is a Service Loan, allowing student to work 300 hours in campus-related, church-related project. Must be recommended by the campus pastor or chaplin of the campus university. Write to Financial Aid for Studies at above location for complete information.

1470

PRINCE GEORGE'S CHAMBER OF COMMERCE FOUNDATION (Scholarship)
4601 Presidents Drive, Suite 230
Lanham, MD 20706
301/731-5000

AMOUNT: Full tuition at Maryland schools; partial tuition at out-of-state schools

DEADLINE(S): May 15

FIELD(S): All fields of study

Open to residents of Prince George's County, MD for undergraduate study. Must be U.S. citizen. Financial need is a consideration. Write for complete information.

1471

PROFESSIONAL BOWLERS ASSOCIATION (Billy Welu Memorial Scholarship)
Young American Bowling Alliance
5301 S. 76th Street
Greendale, WI 53129
216/836-5568

AMOUNT: $1,000

DEADLINE(S): May 15

FIELD(S): All fields of study

The scholarship is designed to assist undergraduate students who are enrolled in college and are current members of a college ABS, WIBC, or YABA league.

The aim of the PBA is to support and promote the sport of bowling. Send self-addressed stamped #10 envelope to above address.

1472

PROFESSIONAL HORSEMEN'S SCHOLARSHIP FUND, INC.
c/o Mrs. Ann Grenci
204 Old Sleepy Hollow Road
Pleasantville, NY 10570
561/694-6893 (Nov.-Apr.);
914/769-1493 (May-Oct. 15)

AMOUNT: Up to $1,000

DEADLINE(S): May 1

FIELD(S): All fields of study

For members or dependents of members of the Professional Horsemen's Association. Awards can be used for college or trade school.

Up to 10 awards annually. Write to Mrs. Ann Grenci at above address for complete information.

1473

PUBLIC EMPLOYEES ROUNDTABLE (Public Service Scholarships)
P.O. Box 14270
Washington, D.C. 20044
202/927-5000; Fax 202/927-5001

AMOUNT: $500-$1,000

DEADLINE(S): May 15

FIELD(S): All fields of study

Open to graduate students & undergraduate sophomores, juniors, seniors who are planning a career in government. Minimum of 3.5 cumulative GPA. Preference to applicants with some public service work experience (paid or unpaid).

10 to 15 awards per year. Applications available as of February 1. Send self-addressed stamped envelope for application.

1474

RECORDING FOR THE BLIND (Mary P. Oenslager Scholastic Achievement Awards)
20 Roszel Road
Princeton, NJ 08540
609/452-0606; Fax 609/520-7990

AMOUNT: $1,000; $2,000; $6,000

DEADLINE(S): Feb 1

FIELD(S): All fields of study

Open to legally or totally blind college students registered with RFB&D for at least one year prior to the filing deadline, who have received or will receive a bachelor's degree from a 4-year college or university in the United States or its territories, and who have a 3.0 GPA or better.

Bachelor's degree must be received between July 1 of year preceding application deadline date and June 30 of year of application deadline date. Write for complete information.

1475

RHODE ISLAND HIGHER EDUCATION ASSISTANCE AUTHORITY (Loan Program; PLUS Loans)
560 Jefferson Blvd.
Warwick, RI 02886
401/736-1100

AMOUNT: Up to $5,500 for undergrads & up to $8,500 for graduates (subsidized); up to $5,000 for undergrads & up to $10,000 for graduates (unsubsidized)
DEADLINE(S): None specified
FIELD(S): All fields of study

Open to Rhode Island residents or non-residents attending an eligible school. Must be U.S. citizen or legal resident and be enrolled at least half-time. Rhode Island residents may attend schools outside the state.

Must demonstrate financial need. Write for current interest rates and complete information.

1476

RHODE ISLAND HIGHER EDUCATION ASSISTANCE AUTHORITY (Undergraduate Grant & Scholarship Program)
560 Jefferson Blvd.
Warwick, RI 02886
401/736-1100

AMOUNT: $250-$2,000
DEADLINE(S): Mar 1
FIELD(S): All fields of study

Open to Rhode Island residents who are enrolled or planning to enroll at least 1/2 time in a program that leads to a degree or certificate at the post-secondary, undergraduate level. Grant is limited to eligible schools in U.S., Canada, and Mexico.

Must demonstrate financial need, cost of education minus estimated Pell Grant minus expected family contribution equal need (must have at least $1,000 in financial need). Write for complete information.

1477

RICHARD E. MERWIN INTERNATIONAL AWARD
P.O. Box 6694
Coddingtown, CA 95406-0694
Written inquiry only

AMOUNT: $1,000
DEADLINE(S): Aug 18
FIELD(S): All fields of study

Must have been born Jun 5. Must reside in the U.S., and attend a school in Europe. Scholarships based on a 400-word essay on how to expand inter-cultural activity for study. Must have been born in Europe and desire to study there after living in the U.S.

For undergraduate or graduate study. Write for complete information.

1478

RIPON COLLEGE (Various Academic Scholarships; Pickard Scholarship)
Admissions Office
P.O. Box 248
300 Seward Street
Ripon, WI 54971
414/748-8102; 800/94RIPON

AMOUNT: Up to $9,000 (DHS); $12,500 and full tuition (Pickard)
DEADLINE(S): Mar 1
FIELD(S): All fields of study

For entering first-year students. Scholarships and distinguished honor scholarships will be awarded on basis of total high school record, recommendations, and interview.

There are 7 $12,500 Pickard scholarships and one full tuition. Must apply and be accepted for admission at Ripon College. Write for more information.

1479

ROTARY FOUNDATION OF ROTARY INTERNATIONAL (Ambassadorial Scholarships)
1 Rotary Center
1560 Sherman Ave.
Evanston, IL 60201-3698
847/866-3000; Fax 847/328-8554; E-mail: sheynina@riorc.mhs.compuserve.com; Internet: www.rotary.org

AMOUNT: Varies—up to $23,000/year
DEADLINE(S): Varies (with local Rotary Club)
FIELD(S): All fields of study

International travel/study opportunity for individuals of all ages who are citizens of a country in which there is a Rotary Club; must have completed at least two years of university coursework or equivalent professional experience. For as short a time as three months to three years.

1,300 annual awards. Contact local Rotary Club for deadlines and application submissions. Deadlines can be as early as March and as late as July 15. Check website above for details.

1480

ROUCH FOUNDATION (A. P. Rouch & Louise Rouch Scholarship Grant)
c/o Trust Dept.
Twin Falls Bank & Trust Co.
Twin Falls, ID 83303
208/733-1722 Ext. 221

AMOUNT: Varies
DEADLINE(S): May 1
FIELD(S): All fields of study

Open to orphaned or underprivileged students who live in Twin Falls, Idaho or the immediate vicinity. Awards can be used at Idaho schools. Must demonstrate financial need.

Number of awards per year varies. Renewable. Contact Assistant Trust Officer Janice Stover at above address for complete information.

1481

ROYAL A. & MILDRED D. EDDY STUDENT LOAN TRUST FUND; LOUISE I. LATSHAW STUDENT LOAN TRUST FUND (Student Loans)
NBD Bank Trust Dept.
8585 Broadway, Suite 396
Merriville, IN 46410
Written inquiry

AMOUNT: $2,000/year
DEADLINE(S): Ongoing
FIELD(S): All fields of study

Loan fund available to undergraduate juniors & seniors who are U.S. citizens. Two credit-worthy co-signers are required. Interest rate is 10%, and payments must begin five months after graduation. For study in the U.S. only.

Write to above address for complete information.

1482

ROYAL NEIGHBORS OF AMERICA (Fraternal Scholarships)
230 16th Street
Rock Island, IL 61201
309/788-4561

AMOUNT: $500 to $2,000 a year for 4 years
DEADLINE(S): Dec 1
FIELD(S): All fields of study

Open to high school seniors who are RNA members of at least 2 years & in the upper quarter of their class. Awards tenable by U.S. citizens at recognized undergrad colleges & universities.

22 nonrenewable $500 scholarships for freshman year only and 10 national scholarships that are renewable for 4 years. Write for complete information.

1483

SACHS FOUNDATION (Scholarship Program)
90 S. Cascade Ave., Suite 1410
Colorado Springs, CO 80903

719/633-2353

AMOUNT: $3,000 (undergrad); $4,000 (graduate)

DEADLINE(S): Feb 15

FIELD(S): All fields of study

Open to Black residents of Colorado who are high school graduates, U.S. citizens, have a 3.4 or better GPA & can demonstrate financial need. For undergrad study at any accredited college or university. Very few graduate grants are awarded.

Approximately 50 scholarships per year. Renewable if 2.5 or better GPA is maintained. Grants are for up to 4 years in duration. Write for complete information.

1484

SACRAMENTO SCOTTISH RITE OF FREEMASONRY (Charles M. Goethe Memorial Scholarship)
P.O. Box 19497
Sacramento, CA 95819-0497
916/452-5881

AMOUNT: Varies

DEADLINE(S): Jun 10

FIELD(S): All fields of study

For any field of study but preference is to students majoring in eugenics or biological sciences. Grants are limited to students who are members or senior members of the Order of Demolay. Also open to children of members or deceased members of a California Masonic Lodge.

Write for complete information.

1485

SAMUEL LEMBERG SCHOLARSHIP LOAN FUND INC. (Scholarship-Loans)
60 East 42nd Street, Suite 1814
New York, NY 10165
Written inquiry

AMOUNT: Up to $5,000 per academic year

DEADLINE(S): Apr 1

FIELD(S): All fields of study

Special no-interest scholarship-loans open to Jewish men and women pursuing any undergraduate, graduate or professional degree. Recipients assume an obligation to repay their loans within 10 years after the completion of their studies.

Write for complete information.

1486

SAN FRANCISCO STATE UNIVERSITY (Over-60 Program)
Admissions Office
1600 Holloway Ave.
San Francisco, CA 94132
415/338-2037

AMOUNT: Admissions & registration fees waiver

DEADLINE(S): None

FIELD(S): All fields of study

Open to California residents over 60 years of age who have lived in the state for at least one year by September 20. Must meet the university's regular admissions standards. Total cost is $3.50 per semester.

Write Admissions Office for complete information.

1487

SAN JOSE STATE UNIVERSITY (Scholarships)
Financial Aid Office SJSU
One Washington Square
San Jose, CA 95192-0036
408/924-6063

AMOUNT: $100-$2,000

DEADLINE(S): Mar 15

FIELD(S): All fields of study

Scholarships are awarded competitively to students enrolled at San Jose State on the basis of grade-point average. Most require a demonstration of financial need.

Students interested in graduate fellowships and assistantships should apply directly to their department Dean's office. 450 scholarships per year. Write for complete information.

1488

SAN RAFAEL INDOOR SPORTS CLUB INC. (Scholarships for Disabled Students)

c/o College of Marin
Financial Aid Office
Kentfield, CA 94904
415/924-3549

AMOUNT: $300 per year
DEADLINE(S): May 1
FIELD(S): All fields of study

Open to students enrolled in or planning to enroll in the disabled students program at the College of Marin. Must have a course load of six units or more and maintain a 3.0 or better GPA.

Write for complete information.

1489

SANTA BARBARA FOUNDATION (Student Loan Program)

15 E. Carrillo Street
Santa Barbara, CA 93101-2780
805/963-1873; Fax 805/966-2345; E-mail:
dano@SBFoundation.org

AMOUNT: Varies
DEADLINE(S): Jan 30
FIELD(S): All fields of study

Open to graduates of Santa Barbara County high schools who have attended schools in the county since 7th grade. For 3 years of undergraduate study. Applicants must be U.S. citizens or permanent residents. Financial need is a consideration. When 50% of the undergraduate loan has been repaid in a timely manner, the loan is considered paid in full.

Up to 550 awards per year. Applications available October 1 to January 26. Contact above address for complete information.

1490

SCHOLARSHIP FOUNDATION OF ST. LOUIS (Interest-free Loan Program)

8215 Clayton Road
St. Louis, MO 63117
314/725-7990

AMOUNT: Up to $3,000
DEADLINE(S): Apr 15
FIELD(S): All areas except ministry

Residents of the St. Louis area who are high school graduates and who can demonstrate financial need. Loans are interest-free. Six years to repay following graduation.

Loans are renewable up to a maximum of $15,000 per person provided student is in good academic standing and continues to show need. Write for complete information.

1491

SCREEN ACTORS GUILD FOUNDATION (John L. Dales Scholarship Fund)

5757 Wilshire Blvd.
Los Angeles, CA 90036-3600
213/549-6610

AMOUNT: Varies—Determined annually
DEADLINE(S): Apr 30
FIELD(S): All fields of study

Scholarships open to SAG members with at least five years' membership or dependent children of members with at least eight years' membership. Awards are for any level of undergraduate, graduate, or post-graduate study at an accredited institution.

Financial need is a consideration. Renewable yearly with reapplication. Write for complete information.

1492

SEAFARERS' WELFARE PLAN (Charlie Logan Scholarship Program for Seamen)

5201 Auth Way
Camp Springs, MD 20746
301/899-0675

AMOUNT: $6,000-$15,000

DEADLINE(S): Apr 15

FIELD(S): All fields of study

Open to seamen who has no less than 2 years of actual employment on vessels of companies signatory to the seafarers' welfare plan. Must have had 125 days' employment in previous calendar year.

Renewable up to 2 years. Write for complete information.

1493

SEAFARERS' WELFARE PLAN (Charlie Logan Scholarship Program for Dependents)
5201 Auth Way
Camp Springs, MD 20746
301/899-0675

AMOUNT: $15,000

DEADLINE(S): Apr 15

FIELD(S): All fields of study

Open to dependent children of seaman who have been employed for at least 3 years by a contributor to seafarer's welfare plan. Student must be H.S. (or equiv) grad in upper 1/3 of class, unmarried, and under 19 years of age.

Write for complete information and restrictions.

1494

SELBY FOUNDATION (Direct Scholarship Program)
1800 Second Street, Suite 905
Sarasota, FL 34236
941/957-0442

AMOUNT: $500-$2,000

DEADLINE(S): Mar 1

FIELD(S): All fields of study

For undergraduate study by residents of Sarasota County, FL who are attending an accredited college full-time and have a GPA of 3.0 or better. Must demonstrate financial need and be U.S. citizen.

Write for complete information.

1495

SEMINOLE TRIBE OF FLORIDA (Higher Education Awards)
6073 Stirling Road
Hollywood, FL 33024
305/584-0400 Ext. 154

AMOUNT: None specified

DEADLINE(S): Apr 15; Jul 15; Nov 15

FIELD(S): All fields of study

Open to enrolled members of the Seminole Tribe of Florida or to those eligible to become a member. For undergraduate or graduate study at an accredited college or university.

Awards renewable. Write for complete information.

1496

SENECA NATION HIGHER EDUCATION (Education Grants)
Box 231
Salamanca, NY 14779
716/945-1790

AMOUNT: Up to $5,000

DEADLINE(S): Jul 15; Dec 31; May 20

FIELD(S): All fields of study

Open to enrolled members of the Seneca Nation of Indians who are in need of funding for post-secondary education and are accepted in an accredited program of study. May be used toward associate's, bachelor's, master's or doctor's degree.

Award is based on financial need. Write for complete information.

1497

SERVICE EMPLOYEES INTERNATIONAL UNION (Scholarship Program)
1313 L Street NW
Washington, D.C. 20005
800/448-7348

AMOUNT: $1,000

DEADLINE(S): Mar 12

FIELD(S): All fields of study

Scholarships open to Service Employees International Union members (in good standing) and their dependent children. Awards can be used at a community college or trade/tech school or to continue education at a 4-year college or university.

There are 20 awards per year; 9 are non-renewable. Write for complete information.

1498

SICO FOUNDATION (Scholarships)
Scholarships Coordinator
Mount Joy, PA 17552
Written inquiry

AMOUNT: $1,000 per year

DEADLINE(S): Feb 15

FIELD(S): All fields of study

Open to high school seniors residing in the state of Delaware or the Pennsylvania counties of Adams, Berks, Chester, Cumberland, Dauphin, Delaware, Lancaster, Lebanon, or York.

Also available to residents of New Jersey counties of Atlantic, Cape May, Cumberland, Gloucester, and Salem and to residents of Cecil County, Maryland. Write for complete information.

1499

SOCIETY OF DAUGHTERS OF THE U.S. ARMY (Scholarships)
7717 Rock Ledge Ct.
Springfield, VA 22152
Written inquiry

AMOUNT: $1,000

DEADLINE(S): Mar 1 (to receive application); Mar 31 (completed application)

FIELD(S): All fields of study

Open to daughters, step-, and granddaughters of commissioned officers of the U.S. Army who are on active duty, are retired, or who died on active duty, or after eligible retire-ment. Must demonstrate financial need and merit.

Approximately 8 scholarships per year. Renewable. Include qualifying parent's name, rank, Social Security number, and dates of service. Send self-addressed stamped envelope between November 1 and March 1.

1500

SONS OF ITALY FOUNDATION (National Leadership Grants)
219 E Street NE
Washington, D.C. 20002
202/547-2900

AMOUNT: $2,000-$5,000

DEADLINE(S): Feb 28

FIELD(S): All fields of study

National leadership grant competition is open to any full-time student of Italian heritage studying at an accredited college or university. For undergraduate or graduate study.

Write for complete information. Also contact local and state lodges for information regarding scholarships offered to members and their children.

1501

SONS OF NORWAY FOUNDATION (Astrid G. Cates Scholarship Fund)
1455 West Lake Street
Minneapolis, MN 55408
Written inquiry

AMOUNT: $250-$750

DEADLINE(S): Mar 1

FIELD(S): All fields of study

Applicants must be between the ages of 17-22 and be current members of Sons of Norway or children or grandchildren of current Sons of Norway members. Must demonstrate financial need.

Write for complete information.

1502

SONS OF THE AMERICAN REVOLUTION (Joseph S. Rumbaugh Historical Oration Contest)

1000 South 4th Street
Louisville, KY 40203
Written inquiry

AMOUNT: $2,000 (1st prize); $1,000 (2nd prize); $500 (3rd prize)
DEADLINE(S): Feb 1
FIELD(S): All fields of study

Oratory competition for high school sophomores, juniors, and seniors who submit an original 5- to 6-minute oration on a personality, event, or document of the American Revolutionary War and how it relates to the U.S. today.

Oration must be delivered from memory without props or charts. Applicants must be U.S. citizens. Write for complete information.

1503

SOROPTIMIST FOUNDATIONS (Soroptimist International of the Americas—Women's Opportunity Awards)

Two Penn Center Plaza, Suite 1000
Philadelphia, PA 19102-1883
215/557-9300; Fax 568-5200; E-mail: siahq@omni.voicenet.com

AMOUNT: $3,000-$5,000 (54 awards); $10,000 (1 award)
DEADLINE(S): Dec 15
FIELD(S): All fields of study

Open to mature women heads of households furthering their skills/training to upgrade employment status. Preference to voc-tech training or undergrad degree completion. Not available for grad work. Must document financial need.

54 regional U.S. awards; 17 in other countries/territories within the territorial limits of Soroptimist International of the Americas. Contact local club or send SASE to SIA (Attn: Women's Opportunity

Award) at above address for complete information.

1504

SOUTH CAROLINA GOVERNOR'S OFFICE; DIVISION OF VETERANS AFFAIRS (Tuition Assistance for Children of Certain War Veterans)

1205 Pendleton Street
Columbia, SC 29201
803/255-4317; Fax 803/255-4257

AMOUNT: Tuition waiver
DEADLINE(S): None
FIELD(S): All fields of study

For children of veterans who were legal residents of South Carolina at time of entry into military service & who (during service) were MIA, POW, killed in action, totally disabled, or died of disease, as rated by the Veterans Administration, and/or who is a recipient of the Medal of Honor.

South Carolina residency & U.S. citizenship required. For undergraduate study at South Carolina state-supported schools. Write for complete information.

1505

SOUTH CAROLINA STUDENT LOAN CORPORATION (Loans)

P.O. Box 21487
Columbia, SC 29221
803/798-0916; Internet: www.slc.sc.edu

AMOUNT: Varies
DEADLINE(S): Varies
FIELD(S): All fields of study

Open to South Carolina residents who are U.S. citizens or eligible non-citizens. Must be enrolled or accepted for enrollment at an eligible post-secondary school. Amount of loan determined by cost of school and financial need.

Interest is variable not to exceed at 8.25%. Loan must be renewed annually. Write or visit website for complete information.

1506

SOUTH CAROLINA TUITION GRANTS COMMITTEE (Higher Education Tuition Grants Program)

P.O. Box 12159
Keenan Bldg., 1st Floor
Columbia, SC 29211-2159
803/734-1200

AMOUNT: Up to $3,260
DEADLINE(S): None specified
FIELD(S): All fields of study

Open to residents of South Carolina who are accepted to or enrolled in eligible private post-secondary institutions in South Carolina. Must demonstrate financial need & academic merit. U.S. citizenship or legal residency required.

Approximately 8,000 grants per year. Renewable. Contact financial aid office or write to address above for complete information.

1507

SOUTH DAKOTA DIVISION OF VETERANS AFFAIRS (Aid to Dependents of Deceased Veterans)

500 E. Capitol Ave.
Pierre, SD 57501-5070
605/773-3269; Fax 605/773-5380

AMOUNT: Free tuition in state-supported schools
DEADLINE(S): None specified
FIELD(S): All fields of study

Open to residents of SD under 25 years of age who are children of veterans who were residents of SD at least 6 months immediately prior to entry into active service & who died from any cause while in the service of the U.S. armed forces.

Must attend a state-supported college or university in SD. Write for complete information.

1508

STATE COLLEGE AND UNIVERSITY SYSTEMS OF WEST VIRGINIA— CENTRAL OFFICE (WV Higher Education Grant Program)

1018 Kanawha Blvd. E, Suite 700
Charleston, WV 25301-2827
304/558-4614; Fax 304/558-4622; E-mail: long@scusco.WVnet.edu; Internet: www.scusco.WVNET.edu

AMOUNT: $350-$2,348
DEADLINE(S): Jan 1; Mar 1
FIELD(S): All fields of study

Open to high school grads who have lived in WV for one year prior to application and are enrolled full-time as an undergrad in an approved WV or PA educational institution. Must be U.S. citizen and demonstrate financial need.

Approximately 8,000 grants per year. Renewable up to 8 semesters. Write for complete information.

1509

STATE OF NEW JERSEY OFFICE OF STUDENT ASSISTANCE (Edward J. Bloustein Distinguished Scholars Program)

CN 540
Trenton, NJ 08625
609/588-3230; 800/792-8670 in NJ; TDD: 609/588-2526

AMOUNT: $1,000 per year for 4 years
DEADLINE(S): Oct 1
FIELD(S): All fields of study

Open to New Jersey residents who are academically outstanding high school students planning to attend a NJ college or university. U.S. citizenship or legal residency required.

Students may not apply directly to the program. Applications must be made through the high school. Contact guidance counselor or address above for complete scholarship information.

1510

STATE OF NEW JERSEY OFFICE OF STUDENT ASSISTANCE (Tuition Aid Grants)
> CN 540
> Trenton, NJ 08625
> 609/588-3230; 800/792-8670 in NJ; TDD: 609/588-2526

AMOUNT: $760-$5,570
DEADLINE(S): Varies
FIELD(S): All fields of study

For students who have been New Jersey residents for at least 12 months and who are or intend to be enrolled as full-time undergraduate in any college, university or degree-granting post-secondary institution in NJ. U.S. citizen or legal resident.

Grants renewable. Write to Office of Student Assistance for complete information.

1511

STATE OF NEW JERSEY OFFICE OF STUDENT ASSISTANCE (Garden State Scholarships)
> CN 540
> Trenton, NJ 08625
> 609/588-3230; 800/792-8670 in NJ; TDD: 609/588-2526

AMOUNT: $500 per year for 4 years
DEADLINE(S): Oct 1
FIELD(S): All fields of study

Must be a resident of New Jersey for at least 12 months prior to receiving award. For undergraduate study in NJ. Demonstrate scholastic achievement & need. U.S. citizen or legal resident.

Renewable. Students may not apply directly to the program. Contact high school guidance counselor or address above for complete information.

1512

STATE OF NEW JERSEY OFFICE OF STUDENT ASSISTANCE (NJ Class Loan Program)
> CN 540
> Trenton, NJ 08625
> 609/588-3200; 800/35-NJ-LOAN; TDD: 609/588-2526

AMOUNT: May not exceed cost of attendance minus other financial assistance
DEADLINE(S): None specified
FIELD(S): All fields of study

For U.S. citizens or legal residents who are NJ residents. Must be enrolled at least half-time at an approved school making satisfactory academic progress toward a degree. Repayment is 15 years from date of first disbursement. Various options available.

Apply at least two months prior to need. Write for complete information.

1513

STATE STUDENT ASSISTANCE COMMISSION OF INDIANA (Higher Education & Freedom of Choice Grants)
> 150 W. Market Street, Suite 500
> Indianapolis, IN 46204
> 317/232-2350

AMOUNT: $500-$7,412
DEADLINE(S): Mar 2
FIELD(S): All fields of study

Open to Indiana residents who are accepted to or enrolled in eligible Indiana institutions as full-time undergraduate students. U.S. citizen or legal resident.

Approx. 56,000 grants per year. Grants are based on financial need. Students must complete the Free Application for Federal Student Aid (FAFSA). No other application is required. Write for complete information.

1514

STATE STUDENT ASSISTANCE COMMISSION OF INDIANA (Robert C. Byrd Honors Scholarships)
150 W. Market Street, 5th Floor
Indianapolis, IN 46204
317/232-2350; Fax 317/232-3260; E-mail:
grants@ssaci.in.us; Internet:
www.ai.org/ssaci/

AMOUNT: $1,110
DEADLINE(S): Apr 24
FIELD(S): All fields of study
For Indiana high school seniors with GPA of
3.0 or better for use at a not-for-profit private or public institution in the U.S. U.S. citizenship required.
144 annual awards. Score of 1300 on SAT or
65 on ACT required.

1515

STEVEN KNEZEVICH TRUST (Grants)
100 E. Wisconsin Ave., Suite 1020
Milwaukee, WI 53202
414/271-6364

AMOUNT: $100-$800
DEADLINE(S): Nov 1
FIELD(S): All fields of study
Undergraduate & graduate grants for students
of Serbian descent. Must establish evidence
of ancestral heritage. It is common practice
for students to be interviewed in Milwaukee
prior to granting the award.
Address inquiries to Stanley Hack. Include
self-addressed stamped envelope.

1516

STUDENT AID FOUNDATION (Loans)
2520 E. Piedmont Road, Suite F-180
Marietta, GA 30062
770/973-7077; Fax 770/973-2220

AMOUNT: Undergraduates, $2,500/year;
graduate students, $3,000/year
DEADLINE(S): Apr 15
FIELD(S): All fields of study
Low-interest loans for women who are residents of Georgia or are attending schools in
Georgia. Grades, financial need, personal
integrity, and sense of responsibility are
considerations.
70 loans per year. Renewable with reapplication.

1517

STUDENT LOAN GUARANTEE FOUNDATION OF ARKANSAS (Loan Dept.)
219 South Victory
Little Rock, AR 72201
800/622-3446

AMOUNT: $2,625 (1st year); $3,500 (2nd);
$5,500 (3rd & 4th); $8,500 (graduate)
DEADLINE(S): Varies
FIELD(S): All fields of study leading to a
degree or certificate
Loans open to eligible borrowers using a
SL67A participating lender.
Write for complete information.

1518

SUNKIST GROWERS INC (A. W. Bodine-Sunkist Memorial Scholarship)
P.O. Box 7888
Van Nuys, CA 91409
818/379-7510

AMOUNT: $2,000-$3,000
DEADLINE(S): Apr 30
FIELD(S): All fields of study
Open to California and Arizona undergradu-
ates who come from an agricultural back-
ground and are in need of financial assis-
tance. Must have a 3.0 GPA.
Write for complete information.

1519

SWISS BENEVOLENT SOCIETY OF CHICAGO (Scholarship Fund)
6440 N. Bosworth Ave.
Chicago, IL 60626

Written inquiry

AMOUNT: $750-$2,500

DEADLINE(S): Nov 15 (Request application then. Deadline is Feb 28)

FIELD(S): All fields of study

Undergraduate scholarships open to Swiss nationals or those of proven Swiss descent who are permanent residents of Illinois or Southern Wisconsin & accepted to or enrolled in accredited colleges or universities. Minimum 3.5 GPA required.

Swiss students studying in the U.S. on a student or visitors visa are NOT eligible. Write for complete information.

1520

SWISS BENEVOLENT SOCIETY OF SAN FRANCISCO (Clement & Frieda Amstutz Fund Scholarship)
c/o Swiss Consulate General
456 Montgomery Street, Suite 1500
San Francisco, CA 94104-1233
415/788-2272

AMOUNT: Varies

DEADLINE(S): May 15

FIELD(S): All fields of study

Undergrad scholarships at U.S. colleges open to Swiss nationals who have lived within a 150-mile radius of the San Francisco City Hall for 3 years prior to application date. Applicant must have applied for admission to any institution of higher learning in the U.S. (community colleges and trade schools excluded).

Number of awards varies each year. Write for complete information.

1521

TEXAS A&M UNIVERSITY (Academic Excellence Awards)
Student Financial Aid Office
College Station, TX 77843-1252
409/845-3236 or 3987

AMOUNT: $500-$1,500

DEADLINE(S): Mar 1

FIELD(S): All fields of study

Open to full-time undergraduate and graduate students at Texas A&M University. Awards are intended to recognize and assist students who are making excellent scholastic progress, campus and community activities, leadership positions, and work experience.

Approximately 600 awards per year. Awards granted for one year. Applications are available at the student financial aid office during January & February.

1522

TEXAS A&M UNIVERSITY (Opportunity Award Scholarship)
Student Financial Aid Office
Texas A&M University
College Station, TX 77843-1252
409/845-3236 or 3987

AMOUNT: $500- $2,500

DEADLINE(S): Jan 15

FIELD(S): All fields of study

Scholarships to Texas A&M University for college freshmen with outstanding high school records. Selection based on leadership ability, character, SAT scores, activities, and high school record. U.S. citizen or permanent resident.

Recipients from outside Texas receive a waiver on no-resident tuition. Contact financial aid office for complete information.

1523

TEXAS A&M UNIVERSITY (President's Achievement Award Scholarship and Aggie Spirit Award Scholarship)
Office of Honors Programs & Academic Scholarships
College Station, TX 77843-1252
409/845-1957

AMOUNT: President's: $3,000/year; Aggies: $1,000/year

DEADLINE(S): Jan 8

FIELD(S): All fields of study

This competitive academic scholarship program provides 4-year scholarships for African-American and Hispanic high school seniors who will be attending Texas A&M University. For U.S. citizens or permanent residents. Must maintain 2.5 GPA to remain in good scholarship standing.

Recipients from outside Texas receive a waiver of non-resident tuition.

1524

TEXAS A&M UNIVERSITY (President's Endowed Scholarship; Lechner Scholarship; McFadden Scholarship)

Office of Honors Programs & Academic Scholarships
College Station, TX 77843-1252
409/845-1957

AMOUNT: $2,000-$3,000 per year over 4 years
DEADLINE(S): Jan 8
FIELD(S): All fields of study

For high school seniors who will be attending Texas A&M. Must score 1300 or higher on SAT (or equivalent of 30 on ACT) and rank in the top 10% of high school graduating class or are National Merit Scholarship semi-finalists.

U.S. citizenship or legal residency required. Non-Texans qualify for a waiver on non-resident tuition.

1525

TEXAS ELECTRIC COOPERATIVES INC. (Ann Lane Homemaker Scholarship)

P.O. Box 9589
Austin, TX 78766-9589
512/454-0311

AMOUNT: $1,000
DEADLINE(S): Mar 1
FIELD(S): Home Economics

Open to Texas residents who are graduating high school seniors and active members of a local Future Homemakers of America chapter. Award tenable at accredited under-

graduate colleges or universities. Must be U.S. citizen.

Write for complete information.

1526

TEXAS HIGHER EDUCATION COORDINATING BOARD (Scholarships, Grants, and Loans)

P.O. Box 12788
Capitol Station
Austin, TX 78711-2788
512/427-6340; 800/242-3062; TDD 800/735-2988

AMOUNT: Varies
DEADLINE(S): Varies (with program)
FIELD(S): All fields of study

Open to students attending Texas institutions. Numerous state-administered student financial aid programs (including scholarships, grants, and loans) are offered.

Contact your school's financial aid office or write to the address above for the booklet "Financial Aid for Texas Students" which describes all programs in detail.

1527

THE BUSINESS PRODUCTS INDUSTRY ASSOCIATION

301 North Fairfax Street
Alexandria, VA 22314
703/549-9040

AMOUNT: $2,000
DEADLINE(S): Mar 15
FIELD(S): All fields of study

Open to applicants who are employed by (or related to an employee of) a member company of the Business Products Industry Association. Membership status will be verified.

80 scholarships per year. Write for complete information.

1528

THE KNOTT SCHOLARSHIP FUNDS (Scholarships)

St. Mary's Seminary & University
5400 Roland Ave.
Baltimore, MD 21210-1929
410/323-4300

AMOUNT: Full tuition

DEADLINE(S): None specified

FIELD(S): All fields of study

Open to Catholic students to attend Catholic parish elementary or Catholic secondary school in Baltimore (city) or the counties of Baltimore, Carroll, Frederick, Harford, Anne Arundel, or Howard, or one of the 3 Catholic colleges in Maryland. Residency in the Archdiocese of Baltimore is required. Scholarships based primarily on outstanding academic achievement.

Student involvement in church, school and community taken into account. Send business-sized self-addressed stamped envelope for information, stating level of education.

1529

THE WASIE FOUNDATION (Scholarship Program)

First Bank Place, Suite 4700
601 2nd Ave. South
Minneapolis, MN 55402
612/332-3883

AMOUNT: $1,000-$7,500

DEADLINE(S): Apr 15

FIELD(S): All fields of study

Undergraduate and graduate scholarships open to qualified students of Polish descent who are of the Christian faith. Awards tenable only in Minnesota at 10 specified institutions of higher education. Approx. 30 awards per year.

Applicants must be full-time students and may not be a member of the Communist party. Applications are available in January and must be returned by April 15.

1530

THETA DELTA CHI EDUCATIONAL FOUNDATION (Scholarship)

135 Bay State Road
Boston, MA 02215
Written inquiry

AMOUNT: $1,000

DEADLINE(S): Apr 30

FIELD(S): All fields of study

Scholarships open to active members of Theta Delta Chi. Considerations include past service to the fraternity, scholastic achievements and promise, and financial need. Preference to undergrads, but graduate students will be considered.

Write for complete information.

1531

THIRD MARINE DIVISION ASSOCIATION (Scholarships)

P.O. Box 634
Inverness, FL 34451
Written inquiry

AMOUNT: $500-$2,400

DEADLINE(S): Apr 15

FIELD(S): All fields of study

Undergrad scholarships for dependent children of USMC & USN personnel who died as a result of service in Vietnam or the Southeast Asia Operations Desert Shield and Desert Storm as a result of service with the 3rd Marine Division.

Also open to children of Association members (living or dead) who held membership 2 years or more. Must demonstrate financial need. Awards renewable. Write for complete information.

1532

THOMAS J. WATSON FOUNDATION (The Thomas J. Watson Fellowship Program)

217 Angell Street
Providence, RI 02906-2120
401/274-1952

AMOUNT: $18,000 single; $25,000 with accompanying financial & legal dependent

DEADLINE(S): Nov 1

FIELD(S): All fields of study

Open to graduating seniors at the 48 U.S. colleges on the foundation's roster. Fellowship provides for one year of independent study and travel abroad immediately following graduation.

Candidates must be nominated by their college. Up to 60 awards per year. Write for list of participating institutions and complete information.

1533

TOWSON STATE UNIVERSITY
(Scholarship & Award Programs)
Scholarship Office
Towson, MD 21252
410/830-2654

AMOUNT: Varies

DEADLINE(S): Varies

FIELD(S): All fields of study

Numerous scholarship and award programs available to entering freshmen and to graduate and transfer students attending Towson State University.

Write for scholarships and awards booklet which describes each program in detail. Awards are for Towson State University students only.

1534

TRANSPORT WORKERS UNION OF AMERICA (Michael J. Quill Scholarship Fund)
80 West End Ave.
New York, NY 10023
212/873-6000

AMOUNT: $1,200

DEADLINE(S): May 1

FIELD(S): All fields of study

Open to high school seniors (under 21) who are dependents of TWU members in good standing or of a deceased member who was in good standing at time of death. Dependent brothers or sisters of members in good standing also may apply.

15 scholarships per year. Renewable up to 4 years. Write for complete information.

1535

TUITION GRANT PROGRAM—
ADJUTANT GENERAL'S DEPARTMENT
(Ohio National Guard Tuition Grant Program)
Adj. Gen. Dept.
Attn: AGOH-TG
2825 W. Granville Road
Columbus, OH 43235
614/889-7143

AMOUNT: Public schools: 60% of tuition; private schools: 60% of avg. state school fees

DEADLINE(S): Nov 1; Feb 1; Apr 1

FIELD(S): All fields of study

Open to undergraduate residents of Ohio with an enlisted obligation of six years in the Ohio National Guard. Provides 12 quarter or 8 semester hours.

Write to the tuition grant office at above address for complete information.

1536

TULANE UNIVERSITY (Scholarships & Fellowships)
Admissions Office
New Orleans, LA 70118
504/865-5731; Internet: www.tulane.edu

AMOUNT: Varies

DEADLINE(S): Varies

FIELD(S): All fields of study

Numerous need-based and merit-based scholarship & fellowship programs for undergraduate and graduate study at Tulane University. There is also an honors program for outstanding students accepted for enrollment at Tulane.

Write for complete information.

1537

TWO/TEN INTERNATIONAL FOOTWEAR FOUNDATION (Scholarship Program)
56 Main Street
Watertown, MA 02172
617/923-4500; 800/346-3210

AMOUNT: $200-$2,000
DEADLINE(S): Jan 15
FIELD(S): All fields of study

Open to children of footwear, leather, and allied industry workers (employed a minimum of 1 year) or to students employed a minimum of 500 hours in one of the above industries. Must be high school senior or within 4 years of graduation.

200-250 awards annually. For full-time undergrad study at 2- or 4-year college, voc-tech, or nursing school. Financial need & superlative academic achievement must be demonstrated. Renewable if criteria continue to be met. Write for complete information.

1538

TY COBB EDUCATIONAL FOUNDATION (Undergraduate Scholarship Program)
P.O. Box 725
Forest Park, GA 30051
Written inquiry

AMOUNT: Varies
DEADLINE(S): May
FIELD(S): All fields of study

For Georgia residents who have completed at least one academic year in an accredited college with a 'B' grade average. Must demonstrate financial need.

Renewable with reapplication and completion of 45 quarter or 30 semester credit hours. Write for complete information.

1539

UNITE (Philadelphia-South Jersey District Council Scholarship Awards)
Education Director
35 S. 4th Street
Philadelphia, PA 19106
215/351-0750

AMOUNT: $1,000 per year
DEADLINE(S): Apr 15 (to return application)
FIELD(S): All fields of study

Open to high school students or graduates within 2 years who are children of Philadelphia-South Jersey District Council members of UNITE, International Ladies Garment Workers Union (for at least 2 years) or to children of members who have died within the last 2 years.

Students currently enrolled in college are NOT eligible to apply.

1540

U.S. AIR FORCE ACADEMY (Academy Appointment)
HQ USAF/RRS (Admissions Office)
2304 Cadet Drive, Suite 200
USF Academy, CO 80840-5025
719/472-2520; Fax 719/333-3012; Internet: www.usafa.af.mil

AMOUNT: Full tuition & all costs + salary
DEADLINE(S): Jan 31
FIELD(S): Engineering; Social Sciences; Math; Physical Sciences; Interdisciplinary Studies

Appointment is for a 4-year undergraduate degree followed by a commission as a second lieutenant in the USAF. Recipients are obligated to six years of active duty. Must be U.S. citizen between the ages of 17 and 22, unmarried, and with no dependents.

Nomination is required for appointment. Essay, interview, and SAT/ACT scores required. Write for information on obtaining nomination and for detailed admission requirements.

1541

U.S. DEPT OF INTERIOR; BUREAU OF INDIAN AFFAIRS (Higher Education Grant Programs)
1849 C Street NW, MS-3512 MIB
Washington, D.C. 20240-0001
202/208-4871; Internet: www.doi.giv/bia

AMOUNT: Varies—depending on need
DEADLINE(S): Varies
FIELD(S): All fields of study

Open to enrolled members of Indian tribes or Alaskan native descendants eligible to receive services from the Secretary of the Interior. For study leading to associate's, bachelor's, or graduate degree.

Must demonstrate financial need. Contact home agency, area office, tribe, BIA office, or financial aid office at chosen college. Check website for details, including address and phone numbers of area offices nationwide.

1542

U.S. DEPT OF INTERIOR; BUREAU OF INDIAN AFFAIRS (Higher Education Grant Programs—Northern Calif. & Nevada)
Western Nevada Agency
1677 Hot Springs Road
Carson City, NV 89707
702/887-3515; Fax 702/887-0496; Internet: www.doi.giv/bia

AMOUNT: Varies, depending on need
DEADLINE(S): Jul 15; Dec 15
FIELD(S): All fields of study

Open to enrolled members of Indian tribes or Alaskan native descendants eligible to receive services from the Secretary of the Interior and who reside in Northern California or Nevada. For study leading to associate's, bachelor's, graduate degrees, or adult education.

Must demonstrate financial need. Contact home agency, area office, tribe, or BIA office. Check website for details, including address and phone numbers of area offices nationwide.

1543

UNITE! (Duchessi-Sallee Scholarship)
1710 Broadway
New York, NY 10019
212/265-7000

AMOUNT: $1,000
DEADLINE(S): Mar 15
FIELD(S): All fields of study

Three winners are selected each year for scholarships to any 2-year or 4-year degree-granting college. Awards are made ONLY to incoming freshmen who are the daughter or son of a union member in good standing for 2 years or more.

Scholarship is renewable for one additional year. Write for complete information.

1544

UNITED DAUGHTERS OF THE CONFEDERACY (Scholarships)
Business Office
Memorial Bldg.
328 North Blvd.
Richmond, VA 23220-4057
804/355-1636

AMOUNT: $800-$1,000
DEADLINE(S): Feb 15
FIELD(S): All fields of study

Open to descendants of worthy confederate veterans. Applicants who are collateral descendants must be active members of the United Daughters of the Confederacy or of the Children of the Confederacy & MUST be sponsored by a UDC chapter.

Most awards for undergraduate study. For complete information, send self-addressed stamped #10 envelope to address above or contact the education director in the division where you reside.

1545

UNITED FEDERATION OF TEACHERS (Albert Shanker College Scholarship Fund)
260 Park Ave. South
New York, NY 10010

212/529-2110; Fax 212/533-2704

AMOUNT: $1,000/year

DEADLINE(S): Dec 15

FIELD(S): All fields of study

Open to New York City residents who attend New York City public high schools. Scholarships support undergraduate study at recognized colleges and universities. Financial need and academic standing are considerations.

Students are eligible in the year they graduate. Approximately 250 awards per year. Renewable. Write for complete information.

1546

UNITED FOOD & COMMERCIAL WORKERS INTERNATIONAL UNION
(UFCW Scholarship Program)
1775 K Street NW
Washington, D.C. 20006
201/223-3111

AMOUNT: $1,000 per year for 4 years

DEADLINE(S): Dec 31

FIELD(S): All fields of study

Open to UFCW members or high school seniors who are children of members. Applicants must meet certain eligibility requirements. Awards for full-time study only.

7 awards per year. Contact Douglas H. Dority, president, address above, for complete information.

1547

UNITED FOOD & COMMERCIAL WORKERS UNION—LOCAL 555
(Scholarship Program)
P.O. Box 23555
Tigard, OR 97223
503/684-2822

AMOUNT: $1,000

DEADLINE(S): May 9

FIELD(S): All fields of study

Program open ONLY to Local 555 members (in good standing for at least 1 year) and their children and spouses. Scholarships may be used at any accredited university, college, technical-vocational school, junior college, or community college.

Write for complete information ONLY if you are a UFCW Local 555 member or relative of a member.

1548

UNITED NEGRO COLLEGE FUND
(Scholarships)
8260 Willow Oaks Corporate Drive
Fairfax, VA 22031
703/205-3400; 800/331-2244

AMOUNT: $500 to $7,500 per year

DEADLINE(S): Varies

FIELD(S): All fields of study

Scholarships available to students who enroll in one of the 41 United Negro College Fund member institutions. Financial need must be established through the financial aid office at a UNCF college.

For information and a list of the UNCF campuses, write to the address above.

1549

UNITED PAPERWORKERS INTERNATIONAL UNION (Scholarship Program)
P.O. Box 1475
Nashville, TN 37202
615/834-8590

AMOUNT: $1,000

DEADLINE(S): Mar 15

FIELD(S): All fields of study

Scholarships open to high school seniors who are sons or daughters of paid-up union members of at least one year. Awards tenable at accredited undergraduate colleges & universities. Must be U.S. or Canadian citizen.

22 awards per year. Recipients are asked to take at least one labor course during their

college career. Financial need is a consideration. Write for complete information.

1550

UNITED STEELWORKERS OF AMERICA—DISTRICT 7 (Hugh Carcella Scholarship Program)
1017 W. 9th Ave., A & B
King of Prussia, PA 19406
215/265-7577

AMOUNT: $750-$3000
DEADLINE(S): Mar 15
FIELD(S): All fields of study

Must be a member in good standing or son or daughter or legal ward of member of United Steelworkers of America—District 7 Local Union to participate in the scholarship program. Must be entering freshman pursuing a BS degree.

8 scholarships per year. Renewable. Write for complete information.

1551

UNITED STUDENT AID FUNDS INC. (Guaranteed Student Loan Program; PLUS Loans)
1912 Capital Ave., #320
Cheyenne, WY 82001
307/635-3259

AMOUNT: $2,625 to $5,500 (undergrads); $8,500 (grads)
DEADLINE(S): None
FIELD(S): All fields of study

Low-interest loans are available to Wyoming residents who are citizens or permanent residents of the U.S. and enrolled at least 1/2 time in school. Must demonstrate financial need.

Write for complete information.

1552

UNITED TRANSPORTATION UNION (Scholarship Program)
14600 Detroit Ave.
Cleveland, OH 44107

216/228-9400

AMOUNT: $500
DEADLINE(S): Mar 31
FIELD(S): All fields of study

Open to U.S. or Canadian citizens who are high school graduates under age 25 and are either UTU members or the children or grandchildren of UTU members. Must maintain satisfactory academic record.

50 scholarships per year. Renewable up to 4 years. Awarded on lottery system. Write for complete information.

1553

UNIVERSITY OF NEBRASKA AT LINCOLN (Regents; David; Davis; National Merit & Departmental Scholarships)
16 Administration Bldg.
Lincoln, NE 68588-0411
401/472-2030

AMOUNT: Varies
DEADLINE(S): Dec 15 (preceding Fall semester)
FIELD(S): All fields of study

Open to Nebraska high school graduates who have taken the ACT or SAT and sent scores to UNL. Variety of scholarships available—some for minorities; some based on financial need; and various other requirements.

By submitting application for freshman scholarship, student is competing for approximately 1,500 other individual scholarship programs at UNL. Write for complete information.

1554

UNIVERSITY OF NEW MEXICO (Scholarships)
Mesa Hall North
Albuquerque, NM 87131-2081
505/277-6090

AMOUNT: Varying amounts to $2,000
DEADLINE(S): Feb 1
FIELD(S): All fields of study

The University of New Mexico awards to eligible first-time freshmen more than 1,000 scholarships from six major scholarship programs. Considerations include extracurricular activities and personal statement. Must be U.S. citizen.

Contact Department of Student Financial Aid and Scholarships (address above) for complete information.

1555

**UNIVERSITY OF OXFORD—
SOMERVILLE COLLEGE (Janet Watson Bursary)**
College Secretary
Somerville College
Oxford OX2 6HD United Kingdom
1865-270629/19; Fax 1865-270620

AMOUNT: 3,500 pounds sterling for each of 2 years
DEADLINE(S): Mar 2
FIELD(S): All fields of study

Bursary is offered for U.S. citizens who are graduate students wishing to read for a further degree at the University of Oxford in England. Renewable for a second year.
Write for complete information.

1556

**UNIVERSITY OF WINDSOR
(Undergraduate Scholarships)**
Student Awards Office
Windsor Ontario N9B 3P4 Canada
519/253-4232

AMOUNT: Approximately $600
DEADLINE(S): May 31; Dec 31
FIELD(S): All fields of study

Open to students who are graduates of a U.S. high school, have superior grades, and wish to study at Windsor University in Ontario, Canada. In-course awards are available to those who are already enrolled. Students must complete all admissions requirements.

Renewable for three years if qualifying average is maintained. Write for complete information and a catalog of available undergraduate scholarships.

1557

URANN FOUNDATION (Scholarship Program)
Robert C. LeBoeuf, Administrator
P.O. Box 1788
Brockton, MA 02403
617/588-7744

AMOUNT: Varies
DEADLINE(S): Apr 15
FIELD(S): All fields of study

Scholarship program open to children of cranberry growers & their employees (in the state of Massachusetts ONLY). Awards are tenable at eligible 2-year & 4-year undergraduate colleges & universities.
Write for complete information.

1558

U.S. COAST GUARD MUTUAL ASSISTANCE (Adm. Roland Student Loan Program)
2100 2nd Street SW
Washington, D.C. 20593-0001
202/267-1683

AMOUNT: Up to $2,700 per year (undergrads); $7,500 (grads)
DEADLINE(S): None specified
FIELD(S): All fields of study

For members & dependents of Coast Guard Mutual Assistance members who are enrolled at least half-time in an approved post-secondary school.
Loans renewable for up to four years. Must reapply annually. Write for complete information.

1559

U.S. DEPT OF VETERANS AFFAIRS (Vocational Rehabilitation)

810 Vermont Ave. NW (28)
Washington, D.C. 20420
VA regional office in each state or 800/827-1000

AMOUNT: Tuition; books; fees; equipment; subsistence allowance

DEADLINE(S): Varies (Within 12 years from date of notification of entitlement to VA comp)

FIELD(S): All fields of study

Open to U.S. military veterans disabled during active duty, honorably discharged & in need of rehab services to overcome an employment handicap. At least a 20% disability comp rating (or 10% with a serious employment handicap) required.

Program will provide college, trade, technical, on-job or on-farm training (at home or in a special rehab facility if vet's disability requires). Contact nearest VA office for complete information.

1560

U.S. DEPT. OF EDUCATION (Robert C. Byrd Honors Scholarship Program)

600 Independence Ave. SW
Portals Bldg., Room C-80
Washington, D.C. 20202-5329
202/260-3394

AMOUNT: $1,500/year

DEADLINE(S): Varies (by state)

FIELD(S): All fields of study

Open to outstanding high school seniors who graduate in the same academic year the award is being made & who have been accepted for enrollment at an institution of higher education. Must be U.S. citizen or permanent resident.

Available for up to 4 years of study. State educational agencies receive funding from the U.S. Dept. of Education. Apply through state educational agency or contact school counselor for complete information.

1561

U.S. MARINE CORPS SCHOLARSHIP FOUNDATION INC (Scholarships)

P.O. Box 3008
Princeton, NJ 08543
800/292-7777

AMOUNT: $500-$2,500

DEADLINE(S): Apr 1 (applications available Jan 1)

FIELD(S): All fields of study

Open to children of U.S. Marine Corps members or the dependent children of former Marines for undergraduate or vocational study. Applicant's gross family income should not exceed $41,000.

Renewable with written reapplication each year. Write for complete information.

1562

U.S. SUBMARINE VETERANS OF WWII (Scholarship Program)

1683 Dillingham Blvd.
Norfolk Naval Station
Norfolk, VA 23511
757/451-3660; Fax 757/489-8578

AMOUNT: $1,750/year

DEADLINE(S): Apr 15

FIELD(S): All fields of study

For children of paid-up regular members of U.S. submarine veterans of WWII. Applicant must be an unmarried high school senior or have graduated from high school no more than 4 years prior to applying and be under the age of 24.

List those submarines in which your sponsor served during WWII and include sponsor's membership card number when requesting application.

1563

UTILITY WORKERS UNION OF AMERICA (Private Utility Workers Union of America Scholarship Program Award)
815 16th Street NW
Washington, D.C. 20006
202/347-8105

AMOUNT: $500-$2,000 per year
DEADLINE(S): Jan 1 (of junior year in high school)
FIELD(S): All fields of study

Scholarships are for sons and daughters of utility workers union members in good standing. Winners are selected from the group of high school juniors who take the national merit scholarship exams.

2 four-year scholarships awarded annually. Write for complete information.

1564

VERMONT STUDENT ASSISTANCE CORPORATION (Incentive Grants for Undergraduates)
Champlain Mill
P.O. Box 2000
Winooski, VT 05404
802/655-9602

AMOUNT: $500-$5,200
DEADLINE(S): Mar 1
FIELD(S): All fields of study

Open to Vermont residents enrolled as full-time undergraduate students in approved degree programs. Must demonstrate financial need and be U.S. citizen or legal resident.

Write for complete information.

1565

VETERANS OF FOREIGN WARS OF THE UNITED STATES (Voice of Democracy Audio-Essay Scholarship Contest)
VFW Bldg.
406 W. 34th Street
Kansas City, MO 64111

816/968-1117; Fax 816/968-1157; E-mail: harmer@vfw.org; Internet: www.vfw.org

AMOUNT: $1,000-$20,000
DEADLINE(S): Nov 1
FIELD(S): Scholarship awards for all fields of study

Open to 10th, 11th, and 12th graders in public, private, and parochial high schools. Contestants will be judged on their treatment of an annual theme. They may not refer to themselves, their schools, states, or cities, etc., as a means of identification.

55 national awards per year. Foreign exchange students not eligible. Contact local VFW post or high school for details.

1566

VIKKI CARR SCHOLARSHIP FOUNDATION (Scholarships)
P.O. Box 5126
Beverly Hills, CA 90210
Written inquiry

AMOUNT: Up to $3,000
DEADLINE(S): Apr 15
FIELD(S): All fields of study

Open to Latino residents of California and Texas between the ages of 17 and 22. Awards are for undergrad study at accredited colleges and universities. No U.S. citizenship requirement.

5-10 awards per year. Applications available Jan 1. Send SASE for complete information at California address above or Texas address: P.O. Box 780968, San Antonio, TX 78278.

1567

VIRGIN ISLANDS BOARD OF EDUCATION (Exceptional Children Scholarship)
P.O. Box 11900
St. Thomas, VI 00801
809/774-4546

AMOUNT: $2,000

DEADLINE(S): Mar 31

FIELD(S): All fields of study

Open to bona fide residents of the Virgin Islands who suffer from physical, mental or emotional impairment & have demonstrated exceptional abilities & the need of educational training not available in Virgin Islands schools.

NOT for study at the college level. Write for complete information.

1568

VIRGIN ISLANDS BOARD OF EDUCATION (Territorial Scholarship Grants)
P.O. Box 11900
St. Thomas, VI 00801
809/774-4546

AMOUNT: $1,000-$3,000

DEADLINE(S): Mar 31

FIELD(S): All fields of study

Grants open to bona fide residents of the Virgin Islands who have a cumulative GPA of at least 'C' & are enrolled in an accredited institution of higher learning.

300-400 loans & grants per year. Renewable provided recipient maintains an average of 'C' or better. Loans are also available. Write for complete information.

1569

VIRGINIA STATE COUNCIL OF HIGHER EDUCATION (Tuition Assistance Grant Program)
James Monroe Bldg.
101 N. 14th Street
Richmond, VA 23219
804/786-1690; E-mail: fainfo@schev.edu

AMOUNT: Up to $2,000

DEADLINE(S): Jul 31

FIELD(S): All fields of study except theology

Open to Virginia residents who are full-time undergraduate, graduate, or professional students at eligible private colleges and universities in Virginia. Must be working on

first degree. Late applications may be considered if funds are available.

Contact the financial aid office at the college you plan to attend.

1570

VIRGINIA STATE COUNCIL OF HIGHER EDUCATION (College Scholarship Assistance Program)
James Monroe Bldg.
101 N. 14th Street
Richmond, VA 23219
804/786-1690; E-mail: fainfo@schev.edu

AMOUNT: $400-$5,000

DEADLINE(S): Varies

FIELD(S): All fields of study except religion

Open to Virginia residents who are undergraduate students with at least 6 credit hours at eligible Virginia colleges and universities. May not be used for religious training or theological education.

Write for complete information or contact your institution's financial aid office.

1571

VIRGINIA STATE COUNCIL OF HIGHER EDUCATION (Undergraduate Student Financial Assistance "Last Dollar" Program)
James Monroe Bldg.
101 N. 14th Street
Richmond, VA 23219
804/786-1690; E-mail: fainfo@schev.edu

AMOUNT: Ranges from $400 to the cost of full-time tuition and fees

DEADLINE(S): Varies (with each school)

FIELD(S): All fields of study

"Last dollar" is a need-based program designed to assist minority Virginia students to attend Virginia public colleges or universities. Minorities include Black, American Indian, Asian/Pacific Islander, and Hispanic. Must be a Virginia resident.

Contact the financial aid office at your college or university.

1572

VIRGINIA STATE COUNCIL OF HIGHER EDUCATION (Virginia Transfer Grant Program)
James Monroe Bldg
101 N. 14th Street
Richmond, VA 23219
804/786-1690; E-mail: fainfo@schev.edu

AMOUNT: Up to full tuition and fees
DEADLINE(S): Varies (check with financial aid office)
FIELD(S): All fields of study

For minority students who enroll in one of the Commonwealth's 13 historically white college or universities and all transfer students at Norfolk State and Virginia State Universities. Applicants must qualify for entry as first-time transfer students.

Contact college financial aid office for complete information.

1573

WASHINGTON HIGHER EDUCATION COORDINATING BOARD (Washington State Educational Opportunity Grant)
P.O. Box 43430
917 Lakeridge Way
Olympia, WA 98504-3430
360/753-7850

AMOUNT: $2,500
DEADLINE(S): Jun 1
FIELD(S): All fields of study

Open to financially needy, placebound residents of Washington state residing in one of 14 certain counties. Awards tenable at eligible Washington colleges & universities. For upper division (juniors and seniors) students.

In 1996-67, 400 such grants were awarded. Applications available after January 1. For details, write to above address.

1574

WASHINGTON POST (Thomas Ewing Memorial Educational Grants for Newspaper Carriers)
1150 15th Street NW
Washington, D.C. 20079
202/334-5799

AMOUNT: $1,000-$2,000
DEADLINE(S): Jan
FIELD(S): All fields of study

Open to current post carriers who have been on-route the past 18 months. Award is intended to assist & encourage pursuit of higher education at any level.

25-35 awards per year. Write for complete information.

1575

WASHINGTON STATE PTA (Financial Grant Foundation Program)
2003 65th Ave. West
Tacoma, WA 98466-6215
206/565-2153

AMOUNT: $1,000
DEADLINE(S): Mar 3
FIELD(S): All fields of study

Open to Washington state residents. Grant program is designed to assist Washington state high school seniors & graduates who will be entering freshmen at an accredited college or university. Financial need is primary consideration.

Write for complete information.

1576

WELLESLEY COLLEGE (Alice Freeman Palmer Fellowships)
Career Center
Secretary, Graduate Fellowships
Wellesley, MA 02181-8200
617/283-3525

AMOUNT: Up to $4,000 stipend
DEADLINE(S): Dec

FIELD(S): All fields of study

Open to unmarried women under 27 years of age who are Wellesley College graduates. Fellowships are for graduate study or research at institutions in the U.S. or abroad. Should remain unmarried throughout tenure.

Write for complete information.

1577

WELLESLEY COLLEGE (Fellowships for Wellesley Graduates)
Career Center
Secretary, Graduate Fellowships
Wellesley, MA 02181-8200
617/283-3525

AMOUNT: $1,000 to $14,000 stipend
DEADLINE(S): Dec
FIELD(S): All fields of study

Numerous fellowship programs open to Wellesley College graduating seniors and Wellesley College graduates. For graduate study or research at institutions in the U.S. or abroad.

Applications available starting September 1. Write for complete information.

1578

WEST VIRGINIA DIVISION OF VETERANS' AFFAIRS (War Orphans Education Program)
1321 Plaza East, Suite 101
Charleston, WV 25301
304/558-3661

AMOUNT: $400 to $500/year; Waiver of tuition
DEADLINE(S): Jul 15; Dec 1
FIELD(S): All fields of study

Open to surviving children (aged 16-23) of deceased veterans whose active duty service in armed forces of the U.S. involved hostile action. Student must have been a resident of West Virginia for one year prior to initial application. Death of parent must have occurred on active duty *or* if subsequent to

discharge, death must have been the result of a disability incurred during such wartime service.

Awards tenable at any state-supported high school, college, or university. Write for complete information.

1579

WESTERN GOLF ASSOCIATION/EVANS SCHOLARS FOUNDATION (Caddie Scholarships)
1 Briar Road
Golf, IL 60029
847/724-4600

AMOUNT: Full tuition & housing
DEADLINE(S): Nov 1
FIELD(S): All fields of study

Open to U.S. high school seniors in the top 25% of their class who have served as a caddie at a WGA member club for at least 2 years. Outstanding personal character & financial need are considerations.

Applications are accepted after completion of junior year in high school (between July 1 and November 1). 200 awards per year; renewable for 4 years. Contact your local country club or write to address above for complete information.

1580

WILLIAM BRADLEY SCHOLARSHIP FOUNDATION INC. (William Bradley Scholarship)
125 Ozark Drive
Crystal City, MO 63019-1703
314/937-2570

AMOUNT: $400
DEADLINE(S): Apr 1
FIELD(S): All fields of study

Open to graduating seniors of Crystal City High School, Festus High School or St. Pius X High School in Jefferson County, Missouri. Must rank in the top 10% of class.

Write for complete information.

1581

**WILLIAM H. CHAPMAN FOUNDATION
(Scholarships)**
P.O. Box 1321
New London, CT 06320
203/443-8010

AMOUNT: $200-$1,150
DEADLINE(S): Apr 1
FIELD(S): All fields of study

Open ONLY to residents of New London County, CT. Awards support full-time undergraduate study at accredited colleges and universities. U.S. citizenship or legal residency required. Must demonstrate financial need.

Approximately 100 awards per year. Renewable with reapplication. Write for complete information.

1582

**WINDHAM FOUNDATION INC.
(Scholarships)**
P.O. Box 70
Grafton, VT 05146
802/843-2211

AMOUNT: $500-$1,500
DEADLINE(S): Apr 1
FIELD(S): All fields of study

Program is open ONLY to students who are residents of Windham County Vermont. Scholarships are tenable at recognized undergraduate colleges & universities.

Approximately 400 awards per year. Renewable up to 4 years. Write for complete information.

1583

**WISCONSIN DEPARTMENT OF
VETERANS AFFAIRS (Deceased Veterans'
Survivors Economic Assistance
Loan/Education Grants)**
P.O. Box 7843
Madison, WI 53707
608/266-1311

AMOUNT: $5,000 maximum
DEADLINE(S): None specified
FIELD(S): All fields of study

Open to surviving spouses (who have not remarried) of deceased eligible veterans and to the minor dependent children of the deceased veterans. Must be residents of Wisconsin at the time of application.

Approximately 5,700 grants & loans per year. Contact a Wisconsin veterans' service officer in your county of residence for complete information.

1584

**WISCONSIN HIGHER EDUCATION AIDS
BOARD (Student Financial Aid Program)**
P.O. Box 7885
Madison, WI 53707
608/267-2206; Fax 608/267-2808

AMOUNT: Varies
DEADLINE(S): None specified
FIELD(S): All fields of study

Board administers a variety of state and federal programs that are available to Wisconsin residents who are enrolled at least half time and maintain satisfactory academic record. Most require demonstration of financial need.

Write for complete information.

1585

**WOMEN'S SPORTS FOUNDATION (Travel
& Training Grants)**
Eisenhower Park
East Meadow, NY 11554
516/542-4700

AMOUNT: Up to $1,500 (individual); up to $3,000 (team)
DEADLINE(S): Mar 15; Jul 15; Nov 15
FIELD(S): All fields of study

This fund was established to provide assistance to aspiring female athletes & female teams to achieve higher performance levels & ranking within their sport. U.S. citizen.

Grants are available for training, coaching, equipment & travel to scheduled competitive events. Write for complete information.

1586

YAKIMA INDIAN NATION (Scholarship Program)
P.O. Box 151
Toppenish, WA 98948
509/865-5121

AMOUNT: $1,000 per year

DEADLINE(S): Jul 1

FIELD(S): All fields of study

Program open to enrolled members of the Yakima Indian Nation. Awards tenable at recognized undergraduate & graduate institutions. U.S. citizenship required.

Approximately 200 awards per year. Write for complete information.

1587

YOUTH FOR UNDERSTANDING INTERNATIONAL EXCHANGE (Scholarship Programs)
3501 Newark Street NW
Washington, D.C. 20016-3199
800/TEENAGE; Internet: www.yfu.org

AMOUNT: Program expenses

DEADLINE(S): Oct (Applications available then. Deadline is Jan)

FIELD(S): All fields of study

Scholarships for high school students who wish to go overseas for a summer or for a school year. Some are corporate-sponsored and for dependents of employees of 60+ corporations, some are for specific countries only, and some are for students from specific states or cities/counties.

Parents of interested students should check with their personnel office at work to see if their firm is a participant. Call above number for brochure.

Helpful Publications

1588

10 STEPS IN WRITING THE RESEARCH PAPER
Roberta Markman, Peter Markman, and
   Marie Waddell; ISBN 08120-1868-10
   Barron's Educational Series Inc.
   250 Wireless Blvd.
   Hauppauge, NY 11788

COST-$9.95

Arranged to lead the student step-by-step
   through the writing of a research paper—
   from finding a suitable subject to checking
   the final copy. Easy enough for the begin-
   ner, complete enough for the graduate student. 177 pages.

1589

250 WAYS TO PUT YOUR TALENT TO WORK IN THE HEALTH FIELD
   National Health Council, Inc.
   1730 M Street NW, Suite 500
   Washington, D.C. 20036

COST-$6.00

A resource book containing career information on various health fields.

1590

ABCS OF FINANCIAL AID (MONTANA FINANCIAL AID HANDBOOK)
Montana Guaranteed Student Loan Program
   Montana Guaranteed Student Loan
     Program
   2500 Broadway
   Helena, MT 59620-3101

COST-Free

Describes educational costs and financial aid
   available in Montana for Montana residents
   or those attending school in Montana only.
   It covers application and award procedures
   and financial aid programs.

1591

ACADEMIC YEAR ABROAD
Sara J. Steen, Editor
   Institute of International Education
   IIE Books
   809 United Nations Plaza
   New York, NY 10017-3580

COST-$44.95 + $5 handling

Provides information on more than 2,350 post-
   secondary study programs outside the U.S.

1592

AFL-CIO GUIDE TO UNION-SPONSORED SCHOLARSHIPS
AFL-CIO Department of Education
   AFL-CIO
   815 16th Street NW
   Washington, D.C. 20006

COST-Free to union members; $3.00 non-
   union

Comprehensive guide for union members and
   their dependent children. Describes local,
   national and international union-spon-
   sored scholarship programs. Includes a
   bibliography of other financial aid sources.

1593

AMERICAN INSTITUTE OF ARCHITECTS INFORMATION POSTER AND BOOKLET
AIA
   American Institute of Architects
   1735 New York Ave. NW
   Washington, D.C. 20006

COST-Free

Provides list of accredited professional programs and scholarship information.

1594

ANNUAL REGISTER OF GRANT SUPPORT
Reed Reference Publishing
>Reed Reference Publishing Company
>121 Chanlon Rd.
>New Providence, NJ 07974

COST-$165.00 + $11.55 shipping/handling

Annual reference book found in most major libraries. Details thousands of grants for research that are available to individuals and organizations.

1595

ART CALENDAR
Carolyn Blakeslee, Editor in Chief
>Art Calendar
>P.O. Box 199
>Upper Fairmount, MD 21867

COST-$32.00/one year

Monthly publication contains articles of interest to artists including listings of grants; fellowships; exhibits; etc. Annual edition lists opportunities without deadlines. Sample copy of monthly is available for $5.

1596

BARRON'S GUIDE TO LAW SCHOOLS (12TH EDITION)
Barron's College Division;
>ISBN 0-8120-9558-8
>Barron's Educational Series Inc.
>250 Wireless Blvd.
>Hauppauge, NY 11788

COST-$14.95

Comprehensive guide covering more than 200 ABA-approved American law schools. Advice on attending law school.

1597

BASIC FACTS ON STUDY ABROAD
IIE
>Institute of International Education
>IIE Books
>809 United Nations Plaza
>New York, NY 10017

COST-Free

Brochure offering essential information on planning for undergraduate and graduate study outside the U.S.

1598

BIG BOOK OF MINORITY OPPORTUNITIES (6TH EDITION)
Willis L. Johnson, Editor;
>ISBN 0-912048-89-1
>Garrett Park Press
>P.O. Box 190
>Garrett Park, MD 20896

COST-$39.00; $35.00 prepaid

This directory of special programs for minority group members boasts over 4,000 listings of scholarships, fellowships, loans, grants, assistantships, internships, occupational information, career guidance, fee waivers, and more. 449 pages.

1599

CFKR CAREER MATERIALS CATALOG
CFKR
>CFKR Career Materials Inc.
>11860 Kemper Rd., Unit 7
>Auburn, CA 95603

COST-Free

A catalog of printed materials, software and videotapes covering career planning, college financing and college test preparation. Includes materials applicable to all ages—from the primary grades through graduate school.

1600

CHALLENGE IN AGRICULTURE
American Farm Bureau Federation
225 Touhy Ave.
Park Ridge, IL 60068

COST-Free
Scholarship listings, career opportunities, and web page directory regarding careers and research in various agricultural fields.

1601

CHRONICLE CAREER INDEX
CGP; ISBN#1-55631-243-1
Chronicle Guidance Publications
P.O. Box 1190
66 Aurora Street
Moravia, NY 13118

COST-$14.25 + $1.43 shipping/handling (Order No. 502CI)
Listings of career and vocational materials for students and counselors. Describes over 500 sources of publications and audio-visual materials. 90 pages. Revised annually.

1602

CHRONICLE FINANCIAL AID GUIDE
CGP; ISBN 1-55631-269-5
Chronicle Guidance Publications
P.O. Box 1190
66 Aurora Street
Moravia, NY 13118-1190

COST-$22.47 + $2.25 shipping (Order #502A)
Annual guide containing information on financial aid programs offered nationally and regionally by public and private organizations. Programs support study for high school seniors, college undergraduates, graduates, and adult learners. 322 pages.

1603

CHRONICLE FOUR-YEAR COLLEGE DATABOOK
CGP; ISBN 1-55631-267-9
Chronicle Guidance Publications
P.O. Box 1190
66 Aurora Street
Moravia, NY 13118-1190

COST-$22.49 + $2.25 shipping/handling (Order No. 502CM4)
Reference book in two sections. "Majors" section lists 2,175 institutions offering 788 4-year graduate and professional majors. "Charts" section contains information and statistics on each of the schools. 474 pages.

1604

CHRONICLE TWO-YEAR COLLEGE DATABOOK
CGP; ISBN 1-55631-268-7
Chronicle Guidance Publications
P.O. Box 1190
66 Aurora Street
Moravia, NY 13118-1190

COST-$22.46 plus $2.25 shipping/handling (Order No. 502CM2)
Reference book in two sections. "Majors" section lists 2,432 institutions offering 738 certificate/diploma, associate, and transfer programs. "Charts" section contains comprehensive information and statistics on each institution. 372 pages.

1605

COLLEGE DEGREES BY MAIL
John Bear, Ph.D; ISBN 0-89815-379-4
Ten Speed Press
Box 7123
Berkeley, CA 94707

COST-$12.95 + $2.50 shipping/handling
Listing of 100 colleges that offer bachelor's, master's, doctoral, and law degrees through home study. Book is the successor to Bear's

Guide to Earning Non-Traditional College Degrees. Updated annually. 216 pages.

1606

COLLEGE FINANCIAL AID EMERGENCY KIT

Joyce Lain Kennedy and Dr. Herm Davis

Sun Features Inc.
Box 368-K
Cardiff, CA 92007

COST-$6.95 (includes postage and handling)

40-page booklet filled with tips on how to meet tuition and room and board costs. It tells what is available, whom to ask, and how to ask.

1607

COLLEGE HANDBOOK (THE)

CBP; ISBN 0-87447-479-5

College Board Publications
P.O. Box 886
New York, NY 10101

COST-$20.00 + $3.95 shipping/handling; CA and PA residents add sales tax

Describes in detail over 3,200 two- and four-year undergraduate institutions in the USA. Includes information on admission requirements; costs; financial aid; majors; activities; enrollment; campus life and more. 1,600 pages.

1608

COLLEGE SMARTS—THE OFFICIAL FRESHMAN HANDBOOK

Joyce Slayton Mitchell; ISBN 0-912048-92-1

Garrett Park Press
P.O. Box 190F
Garrett Park, MD 20896

COST-$10.95

Cogent advice for the college freshman. Covers such practical subjects as what things to take; coping with dorm life and your roommate; registration; fraternity/sorority rush; even your laundry. Advice is practical and to the point.

1609

COOPERATIVE EDUCATION COLLEGE ROSTER

NCCE

National Commission for Cooperative Education
360 Huntington Ave., 384CP
Boston, MA 02115-5096

COST-Free

Explains what co-op education is, details its advantages, and lists colleges and universities that offer co-op education programs.

1610

CAREERS BOOKLET; WHERE TO STUDY

Public Relations Society of America
33 Irving Place
New York, NY 10003

COST-$3.50 (booklet); $5.00

1611

DIRECTORY OF ACCREDITED INSTITUTIONS

ACICS

Accrediting Council for Independent Colleges and Schools
750 1st Street NE, Suite 980
Washington, D.C. 20002

COST-Free

Annual directory containing information on more than 650 institutions offering business or business-related career programs and accredited by ACICS.

1612

DIRECTORY OF ATHLETIC SCHOLARSHIPS

Alan Green; ISBN 0-8169-2892-3

Facts on File Inc.
460 Park Ave. South
New York, NY 10016

COST-$24.95

Discusses the ins and outs of the recruiting process; school-by-school index; sport-by-sport index; and state-by-state index.

1613

DIRECTORY OF FINANCIAL AIDS FOR MINORITIES (1995-1997)

Gail A. Schlachter & R. David Weber; ISBN 0-918276-28-4

Reference Service Press
5000 Windplay Drive, Suite 4
El Dorado Hills, CA 95762

COST-$47.50 + $4.00 shipping

Describes over 2,000 scholarships; fellowships; grants; loans; awards and internships set aside for American minorities and minority organizations. Covers all levels of study. 666 pages. Cloth.

1614

DIRECTORY OF FINANCIAL AID FOR STUDENTS OF ARMENIAN DESCENT

Armenian Assembly of America

Armenian Assembly of America
122 C Street NW, Suite 350
Washington, D.C. 20001

COST-Free

The Armenian Assembly prepares this annual booklet that describes numerous scholarship, loan & grant programs available from sources in the Armenian community.

1615

DIRECTORY OF FINANCIAL AIDS FOR WOMEN (1995-1997)

Gail A. Schlachter; ISBN 0-918276-27-6

Reference Service Press
5000 Windplay Drive, Suite 4
El Dorado Hills, CA 95762

COST-$45.00 + $4.00 shipping

Contains over 1,500 descriptions of scholarships; fellowships; grants; loans; awards and internships set aside for women and women's organizations. Covers all levels of study. 498 pages. Cloth.

1616

DIRECTORY OF NATIONAL INFORMATION SOURCES ON DISABILITIES (6TH EDITION 1994-95)

National Rehabilitation Information Research Center

National Rehabilitation Information Research Center
8455 Colesville Road, Suite 935
Silver Spring, MD 20910-3319

COST-$5.00

Two-volume directory inventories public/federal/private resources at the national level that offer information and/or direct services to people with disabilities & people involved in educating, training, or helping people with disabilities.

1617

DIRECTORY OF POSTSECONDARY EDUCATIONAL RESOURCES IN ALASKA

ACPE

Alaska Commission on Postsecondary Education
3030 Vintage Blvd.
Juneau, AK 99801

COST-Free

Comprehensive directory of post-secondary institutions and programs in Alaska plus information on state and federal grants, loans, and scholarships for Alaska residents (those who have lived in Alaska for two years).

1618

DIRECTORY OF RESEARCH GRANTS

Oryx

Oryx Press
4041 N. Central Ave., #700
Phoenix, AZ 85012

COST-$135.00

Annual reference book found in most major libraries. Excellent tool for any person or organization looking for research funding. Organized by grant title and contains extensive indexes.

1619

DIRECTORY OF TECHNICAL SCHOOLS, COLLEGES AND UNIVERSITIES OFFERING COURSES IN GRAPHIC COMMUNICATIONS

National Scholarship Trust Fund of the Graphic Arts

National Scholarship Trust Fund
of the Graphic Arts
200 Deer Run Rd.
Sewickley, PA 15153-2600

COST-Free

A listing of accredited institutions which offer degrees in graphic arts and related fields.

1620

DIRECTORY OF UNDERGRADUATE POLITICAL SCIENCE FACULTY

Patricia Spellman

American Political Science Association
1527 New Hampshire Ave. NW
Washington, D.C. 20036

COST-$35.00 (non-members); $20.00 (APSA members) + $4.00 postage

Directory listing nearly 600 separate political science departments. It includes department names, addresses, telephone numbers, names & specializations of faculty members.

1621

DOLLARS FOR COLLEGE (QUICK GUIDES TO FINANCIAL AID IN SEVERAL SUBJECT AREAS)

Write for complete listing.

Garrett Park Press
P.O. Box 190
Garrett Park, MD 20896

COST-$7.95 each; $60.00 for set of all twelve. Add $1.50 for shipping regardless of order amount.

A series of 12 booklets on specific subject areas. 300-400+ programs listed for each subject area.

1622

EDITOR & PUBLISHER JOURNALISM AWARDS AND FELLOWSHIPS DIRECTORY

Editor & Publisher
11 West 19th Street
New York, NY 10011

COST-$8.00

A source of information for awards, fellowships, grants, and scholarships for journalism students and professionals. Also available as a pullout section of the December issues of *Editor & Publisher* magazine. Both national and international awards.

1623

EEO BIMONTHLY

Timothy M. Clancy, Executive Editor

CASS Recruitment Publications Inc.
1800 Sherman Place, Suite 300
Evanston, IL 60201

COST-$42.00/year

Bimonthly publication containing detailed career opportunity profiles on American companies, geographic employer listings and occupational index.

1624

ENCYCLOPEDIA OF ASSOCIATIONS— VOL. 1

ISBN 0-8103-7945-7

Gale Research Inc.
835 Penobscot Bldg.
Detroit, MI 48226

COST-$415.00

An outstanding research tool. 3-part set of reference books found in most major libraries. Contains detailed information on over 22,000 associations; organizations; unions; etc. Includes name and key word index.

1625

EXPLORING CAREERS IN MUSIC-1990
Paul Bjorneberg; ISBN 0-940796-86-4

Music Educators National Conference
1806 Robert Fulton Drive
Reston, VA 20191

COST-$13.25/$10.60 for MENC members

Informative booklet geared toward young people which discusses careers in the performing arts, music education, the music business, recording industry, and allied fields.

1626

EDUCATION AND TRAINING PROGRAMS IN OCEANOGRAPHY AND RELATED FIELDS
Marine Technology Society

Marine Technology Society
1828 L Street NW, Suite 906
Washington, D.C. 20036

COST-$6 shipping/handling

A guide to current marine degree programs and vocational instruction available in the marine field. Consolidates and highlights data needed by high school students as well as college students seeking advanced degrees.

1627

FEDERAL BENEFITS FOR VETERANS & DEPENDENTS (S/N 051-000-00212-1)
Veterans Administration

Superintendent of Documents
U.S. Government Printing Office
Washington, D.C. 20402

COST-$5.50

94-page booklet containing details of all Federal benefit programs available to veterans and their dependents.

1628

FELLOWSHIP GUIDE TO WESTERN EUROPE
Gina Bria Vescori, Editor

Council for European Studies
c/o Columbia University
808-809 International Affairs Bldg.
New York, NY 10027

COST-$8.00 (prepaid—check to Columbia Univ.)

This booklet is intended to assist U.S. students in finding funds for European travel and study in the social sciences and humanities.

1629

FINANCIAL AID FOR MINORITIES IN BUSINESS AND LAW
ISBN 0-912048-88-3

Garrett Park Press
P.O. Box 190F
Garrett Park, MD 20896

COST-$5.95

This booklet lists 380 sources of financial aid and clarifies application procedures. Includes a bibliography of other sources of funding information.

1630

FINANCIAL AID FOR MINORITIES IN EDUCATION
ISBN 0-912048-99-9

Garrett Park Press
P.O. Box 190F
Garrett Park, MD 20896

COST-$5.95

This booklet lists financial aid opportunities for minorities interested in elementary, secondary, and administrative programs in such fields as counseling, special education, and speech pathology.

1631

FINANCIAL AID FOR MINORITIES IN ENGINEERING AND SCIENCE
ISBN 0-912048-98-0

Garrett Park Press
P.O. Box 190F
Garrett Park, MD 20896

COST-$5.95

Describes 310 individual awards and general programs offered for undergraduate and graduate study by private organizations, foundations, federal and state governments, colleges, and universities.

1632

FINANCIAL AID FOR MINORITIES IN HEALTH FIELDS
ISBN 0-912048-96-4

Garrett Park Press
P.O. Box 190F
Garrett Park, MD 20896

COST-$5.95

Includes 320 individual awards and general programs offered for graduate or professional study by private organizations, foundations, federal and state governments, colleges, and universities.

1633

FINANCIAL AID FOR MINORITIES IN JOURNALISM AND MASS COMMUNICATIONS
ISBN 0-912048-84-0

Garrett Park Press
P.O. Box 190F
Garrett Park, MD 20896

COST-$5.95

This booklet lists 350 specific sources of financial aid for minority students and tells how to apply for it.

1634

FINANCIAL AID FOR MINORITIES— AWARDS OPEN TO STUDENTS WITH ANY MAJOR
ISBN 0-912048-93-1

Garrett Park Press
P.O. Box 190F
Garrett Park, MD 20896

COST-$5.95

This booklet lists 380 sources of financial aid and clarifies application procedures. Includes a bibliography of other sources of funding information.

1635

FINANCIAL AID FOR THE DISABLED AND THEIR FAMILIES
Gail Ann Schlachter and R. David Weber

Reference Service Press
5000 Windplay Drive, Suite 4
El Dorado Hills, CA 95762

COST-$38.50 + $4.00 shipping

Contains descriptions of 900 scholarships, fellowships, grants, loans, awards and internships set aside for the disabled and their families. Covers all levels of study. 310 pages.

1636

FINANCIAL AID FOR VETERANS; MILITARY PERSONNEL & THEIR FAMILIES
Gail Ann Schlachter and R. David Weber

Reference Service Press
5000 Windplay Drive, Suite 4
El Dorado Hills, CA 95762

COST-$38.50 + $4 shipping

Contains over 950 descriptions of scholarships, fellowships, grants, loans, awards and internships set aside for veterans, military personnel and their families. Covers all levels of study. 300 pages.

1637

FINANCIAL AID INFORMATION FOR PHYSICIAN ASSISTANT STUDENTS

American Academy of Physician Assistants
950 North Washington Street
Alexandria, VA 22314

COST-Free

A comprehensive listing of scholarships, traineeships, grants, loans, and related publications related to the physician assistant field of study.

1638

FINANCIAL AID RESOURCE GUIDE-#17.97

National Clearinghouse for Professions in Special Education
The Council for Exceptional Children
1920 Association Drive
Reston, VA 20191-1589

COST-Free

General information on finding financial assistance for students preparing for careers in special education and related services.

1639

FINANCIAL ASSISTANCE FOR LIBRARY & INFORMATION STUDIES
ALA

American Library Association
Office for Library Personnel Resources
50 E. Huron Street
Chicago, IL 60611

COST-$1.00 for postage/handling

An excellent summary of fellowships, scholarships, grants-in-aid, loan funds and other financial assistance for library education. Published each fall for the following year.

1640

FINDING MONEY FOR COLLEGE
John Bear, Ph.D.
Ten Speed Press

P.O. Box 7123
Berkeley, CA 94707

COST-$8.95 + $3.50 shipping and handling

In this book Dr. Bear builds on the extensive research he has done in education searching out unconventional, overlooked, ordinary, but not well-understood sources of assistance and tells how to pursue them. Updated every two years. 168 pages.

1641

FISKE GUIDE TO COLLEGES—1996 EDITION
New York Times Books; ISBN 812-92534-1
Times Books
400 Hahn Rd.
Westminster, MD 21157

COST-$18.00

Describes the top-rated 265 out of 2,000 possible four-year schools in the U.S. They are rated for academics, social life, and quality of life.

1642

FLORIDA STUDENT FINANCIAL AID—FACT SHEETS
Department of Education
Florida Dept. of Education
1344 Florida Education Center
Tallahassee, FL 32399

COST-Free

Booklet containing information on Florida grants, scholarships and teacher programs.

1643

FUNDING A COLLEGE EDUCATION
Alice Drum and Richard Kneedler
Harvard Business School Publishing
Attn: Customer Service
60 Harvard Way
Boston, MA 02163

COST-$14.95 + shipping/handling

An insider's guide, written by two college administrators and college students, to the essentials of college financial aid. It will help you sort through facts and forms to secure financial aid for your child's college education, at the right school for him/her.

1644

GED...THE KEY TO YOUR FUTURE
American Council on Education
GED Testing Service of the American Council on Education
One Dupont Circle NW
Washington, D.C. 20036

COST-Free
If you or someone you know left high school before graduation, this free brochure will explain what the GED tests are and how they provide the opportunity to earn a high school equivalency diploma.

1645

GET SMART FAST
Sondra Geoffrion
Access Success Associates
P.O. Box 1686
Goleta, CA 93116

COST-$6.95 each + $2.50 postage USA; $4.00 foreign; California residents add sales tax
Your grades will improve dramatically with this 61-page handbook for academic success which explains how to master the art of studying, discovering what will be tested, preparing for and taking tests strategically, etc.

1646

GOVERNMENT ASSISTANCE ALMANAC (9TH EDITION)
J. Robert Dumouchel; ISBN 0-7808-0061-3
OmniGraphics Inc.
2500 Penobscot Bldg.
Detroit, MI 48226

COST-$135.00
Comprehensive guide to more than $834 billion worth of federal programs available to the American public. Contains 825 pages and 1,370 entries detailing programs of benefit to students, educators, researchers and consumers.

1647

GUIDE TO SOURCES OF INFORMATION ON PARAPSYCHOLOGY
Eileen J. Garrett Library
Parapsychology Foundation
228 E. 71st Street
New York, NY 10021

COST-$3.00
An annual listing of sources of information on major parapsychology organizations, journals, books and research.

1648

GUIDELINES FOR THE PREPARATION OF SCHOOL ADMINISTRATORS
AASA
American Association of School Administrators
1801 N. Moore Street
Arlington, VA 22209

COST-$7.00 prepaid
People who are planning a career in school administration will find this book helpful in explaining the demands and expectations of schools as well as those who play key roles in recommending or establishing certification requirements.

1649

HANDBOOK OF PRIVATE SCHOOLS
ISBN 0-87558-135-8
Porter Sargent Publishers Inc.
11 Beacon Street, Suite 1400
Boston, MA 02108

COST-$85.00 + $2.74 postage and handling

Annual reference book found in most major libraries. Describes in detail 1,700 American elementary and secondary private schools. 1,396 pages.

1650

HIGH SCHOOL STUDENT'S APPLICATION WORKBOOK
Ken and Pat Voak

> Ken & Pat Voak Publications
> 230 Old Graham Hill Rd.
> Santa Cruz, CA 95060

COST-$5.00

Complete workbook designed to help students record and evaluate their high school years. Includes standardized forms that give the student an idea of what information will be asked on applications for colleges, jobs, scholarships, etc.

1651

HOW TO FIND OUT ABOUT FINANCIAL AID
Gail Ann Schlachter

> Reference Service Press
> 5000 Windplay Drive, Suite 4
> El Dorado Hills, CA 95762

COST-$37.50 + $4.00 shipping

A comprehensive guide to more than 700 print and online directories that identify over $21 billion in financial aid available to undergraduates, graduate students and researchers.

1652

INDEX OF MAJORS & GRADUATE DEGREES
CBP; ISBN 0-87447-480-9

> College Board Publications
> P.O. Box 886
> New York, NY 10101

COST-$17.00 + $3.95 shipping/handling; CA and PA residents add sales tax

Describes over 580 major programs of study at 2,900 undergraduate and graduate schools. Also lists schools that have religious affiliations, special academic programs and special admissions procedures. 700 pages.

1653

INTERNATIONAL JOBS
Eric Kocher

> Addison-Wesley Publishing Co.
> 1 Jacob Way
> Reading, MA 01867

COST-$14.95

A handbook listing more than 500 career opportunities around the world.

1654

INTERNSHIPS
Peterson's; ISBN 1-56079-286-8

> Peterson's Guides
> P.O. Box 2123
> 202 Carnegie Center
> Princeton, NJ 08543-2123

COST-$29.95 + $6.75 shipping/handling

Lists on-the-job training opportunities in today's job market. Listings are arranged by career field and indexed geographically.

1655

INTERNATIONAL FORESTRY AND NATURAL RESOURCES
Hard copies no longer available; feel free to download and print your own copy

> United States Department of Agriculture (A Guide to Grants, Fellowships, and Scholarships in International Forestry and Natural Resources)
> P.O. Box 96090
> Washington, D.C. 20090-6090

COST-

An online guide to grants, fellowships, and scholarships in international forestry and natural resources.

1656

JOB OPPORTUNITIES FOR THE BLIND (JOB)

JOB offers the only recorded (audio cassette) job magazine in the U.S., along with over 40 other publications (most on cassette; some in print for employer education)

National Federation of the Blind
1800 Johnson Street
Baltimore, MD 21230

COST-Free

JOB is operated by the NFB in partnership with the U.S. Dept. of Labor. It offers a free recorded job magazine, other publications, and a national reference service to blind job seekers on all aspects of looking for work, to employers and to those assisting blind persons.

1657

JOURNALISM AND MASS COMMUNICATION DIRECTORY

AEJMC

Association for Education in Journalism & Mass Communications
University of South Carolina
1621 College Street
Columbia, SC 29208

COST-$25.00 USA; $35.00 foreign

Annual directory listing over 350 schools and departments of journalism and mass communication; information on national funds, fellowships and foundations; collegiate and scholastic services. Over 3,000 individual members.

1658

JOURNALIST'S ROAD TO SUCCESS—A CAREER AND SCHOLARSHIP GUIDE

DJNF

Dow Jones Newspaper Fund Inc.
P.O. Box 300
Princeton, NJ 08543

COST-Send $3.00 check or money order.

Highly recommended for print or broadcast communications students or journalists. Comprehensive booklet describing what and where to study; how to pay for it; where the jobs are and how to find them. For informtion call 1-800-DOWFUND or http://www.dowjones.com/newsfund

1659

MAKING A DIFFERENCE—CAREER OPPORTUNITIES IN DISABILITY-RELATED FIELDS

The Arc

The Arc, National Headquarters
P.O. Box 1047
Arlington, TX 76004

COST-$10.00 (includes shipping/handling)

A handbook of over 50 professions that serve people who have disabilities. Includes career overview; employment settings; populations served; salary/educational/certification requirements.

1660

MAKING IT THROUGH COLLEGE

PSC

Professional Staff Congress
25 W. 43rd Street, 5th Floor
New York, NY 10036

COST-$1.00

Handy booklet containing information on coping with competition, getting organized, study techniques, solving work overloads, and more. 14 pages.

1661

MAKING THE MOST OF YOUR COLLEGE EDUCATION

Marianne N. Ragins; Also see website: http://members.aol.com/mnragins/workshop.htm.

The Scholarship Workshop
P.O. Box 6845
Macon, GA 31208

COST-$13.95 (includes shipping and handling)

By the author of *Winning Scholarships for College: An Insider's Guide,* this book shows you how to pack your college years with career-building experiences that can lead to graduate and professional schools clamoring to admit you and how to gain multiple job offers.

1662

MEDICAL SCHOOL ADMISSION REQUIREMENTS

Cynthia T. Bennett

Association of American Medical Colleges
2450 N Street NW
Washington, D.C. 20037

COST-$15.00 + shipping (1998-99 edition will be $25 + $5 shipping)

Contains admission requirements of accredited medical schools in the U.S. and Canada.

1663

MEDICINE—A CHANCE TO MAKE A DIFFERENCE

AMA

American Medical Association
Order Processing
515 N. State Street
Chicago, IL 60610

COST-$5.00 + $4.95 shipping/handling (pkg. of 10 brochures)

For college students considering a career in medicine. Answers questions about the profession and medical education including prerequisites, admission requirements and choosing a medical school.

1664

MITCHELL EXPRESS—THE FAST TRACK TO THE TOP COLLEGES

Joyce Slayton Mitchell; ISBN 1-880774-03-8

Garrett Park Press
P.O. Box 190F
Garrett Park, MD 20896

COST-$15.00

A college catalog-sized directory describing 270 of America's most popular colleges. It profiles the colleges and provides information on admissions and financial aid and campus life. 269 pages.

1665

MUSIC SCHOLARSHIP GUIDE (3RD EDITION)

Sandra V. Fridy; ISBN 1-56545-050-7

Music Educators National Conference
1806 Robert Fulton Drive
Reston, VA 20191

COST-$30.25 ($24.20 MENC members)

Lists over 2,000 undergraduate music scholarships in more than 600 public and private edcuational institutions (colleges & universities) in the United States and Canada including eligibility requirements, application deadlines, contact information.

1666

NATIONAL DIRECTORY OF CORPORATE GIVING

TFC; ISBN 0-87954-400-7

Foundation Center (The)
79 Fifth Ave./16th Street
New York, NY 10003

COST-$199.50 (Including shipping/handling)

Book profilcs 2,000 programs making contributions to nonprofit organizations. A valuable tool to assist grant seekers in finding potential support.

1667

NEED A LIFT? (47TH EDITION)

Pre-paid only. Send check or money order to address below

The American Legion
Attn: National Emblem Sales
P.O. Box 1050
Indianapolis, IN 46206

COST-$3.00

Outstanding guide to federal and state government-related financial aid as well as private sector programs. Contains information on the financial aid process (how, when, and where to start) and addresses for scholarship, loan, and career information. 150 pages.

1668

NEWSPAPERS, DIVERSITY & YOU
DJNF

Dow Jones Newspaper Fund, Inc.
P.O. Box 300
Princeton, NJ 08543-0300

COST-Free

Information on grants, scholarships, and internships specifically for students of color studying for print journalism careers. Write or visit website to order:
www.dowjones.com/newsfund

1669

OCCUPATIONAL OUTLOOK HANDBOOK
U.S. Bureau of Labor Statistics; 1996-97; ISBN: 0-934783-72-1 (soft cover) and 0-934783-73-X (hard cover)

CFKR Career Materials
11860 Kemper Road, Unit 7
Auburn, CA 95603

COST-$17.95

Annual publication designed to assist individuals in selecting appropriate careers. Describes approximately 250 occupations in great detail and includes current and projected job prospects for each. 508 pages.

1670

OFF TO COLLEGE
Guidance Research Group
Order Fulfillment Dept-98-RSCH
P.O. Box 931
Montgomery, AL 36101

COST-$3.00

An excellent annual booklet in magazine form that helps incoming freshmen prepare for success in college living through personal essays concerning a variety of campus experiences.

1671

OFFICIAL HANDBOOK FOR THE CLEP EXAMINATIONS
CBP; ISBN 0-87447-455-8

College Board Publications
P.O. Box 886
New York, NY 10101

COST-$15.00

Official guide to College Level Examination Program (CLEP) tests from the actual sponsors of the tests. Contains sample questions and answers; advice on how to prepare for tests; which colleges grant credit for CLEP and more. 500 pages.

1672

ORDER FORM FOR BOOK LIST ON THEATRE\WRITING CAREERS
Theatre Directories
P.O. Box 510
Dorset, VT 05251-0510

COST-Free pamphlet/directory of books

A pamphlet listing books on training programs for careers in theatre and playwriting.

1673

PETERSON'S COLLEGES WITH PROGRAMS FOR STUDENTS WITH LEARNING DISABILITIES AND A.D.D. (5TH EDITION)
Peterson's; ISBN 1-56079-400-3

Peterson's Guides
P.O. Box 2123
Princeton, NJ 08543-2123

COST-$32.95

Comprehensive guide to over 1,000 two-year and four-year colleges and universities offering special academic programs for students with dyslexia and other learning disabilities.

1674

PETERSON'S GUIDE TO FOUR-YEAR COLLEGES 1998
Peterson's; ISBN 1-56079-783-5

Peterson's Guides
P.O. Box 2123
Princeton, NJ 08543-2123

COST-$24.95
Detailed profiles of over 1,900 accredited 4-year colleges in the U.S. and Canada. Also includes entrance difficulty directory, majors directory, and college cost directory.

1675

PHARMACY SCHOOL ADMISSION REQUIREMENTS
AACP

American Association of Colleges of Pharmacy
Office of Student Affairs
1426 Prince Street
Alexandria, VA 22314

COST-$25.00 prepaid plus $3.00 shipping and handling
100-page booklet containing comparative information charts along with the general history of accredited pharmacy programs and current admission requirements.

1676

PLANNING FOR A DENTAL EDUCATION
AADS

American Association of Dental Schools
1625 Massachusetts Ave. NW
Washington, D.C. 20036-2212

COST-Free

Brochure discusses dentistry as a career and offers advice on planning for a dental education.

1677

POWER STUDY TO UP YOUR GRADES AND GPA
Sondra Geoffrion

Access Success Associates
P.O. Box 1686
Goleta, CA 93116

COST-$4.95 + $2.50 U.S.; $4.00 foreign; California residents add sales tax
One of five excellent booklets explaining techniques to discover what will be tested, cut study time in half, prepare thoroughly, write essays, and take tests. Other titles cover math, English, social studies, and science.

1678

POWER STUDY TO UP YOUR GRADES IN MATH
Sondra Geoffrion

Access Success Associates
P.O. Box 1686
Goleta, CA 93116

COST-$4.95 + $2.50 U.S.; $4.00 foreign; California residents add sales tax
One of five excellent booklets explaining correct procedures to solve problems with speed, accuracy, and correctness. Also how to prepare for and take tests.

1679

POWER STUDY TO UP YOUR GRADES IN ENGLISH
Sondra Geoffrion

Access Success Associates
P.O. Box 1686
Goleta, CA 93116

COST-$4.95 + $2.50 U.S.; $4.00 foreign; California residents add sales tax

One of five excellent booklets explaining techniques to discover what will be tested, cut study time in half, prepare thoroughly, write essays, and take tests. Other titles cover math, social studies, science, and improving grade point average.

1680

POWER STUDY TO UP YOUR GRADES IN SOCIAL STUDIES

Sondra Geoffrion

Access Success Associates
P.O. Box 1686
Goleta, CA 93116

COST-$4.95 + $2.50 U.S.; $4.00 foreign; California residents add sales tax

One of five excellent booklets explaining techniques to discover what will be tested, cut study time in half, prepare thoroughly, write essays, take tests. Other titles cover math, English, science and improving grade point average.

1681

POWER STUDY TO UP YOUR GRADES IN SCIENCE

Sondra Geoffrion

Access Success Associates
P.O. Box 1686
Goleta, CA 93116

COST-$4.95 + $2.50 U.S.; $4.00 foreign; California residents add sales tax

One of five excellent booklets explaining how to discover what will be tested, cut study time in half, prepare thoroughly, write essays, and take tests. Other titles cover math, English, social studies, and improving grade point average.

1682

PRINCETON REVIEW—COLLEGE ADMISSIONS—CRACKING THE SYSTEM

Adam Robinson and John Katzman, Editors

Villard Books
201 E. 50th Street
New York, NY 10022

COST-$7.95

Offers high school students bold strategies for getting into the college of their choice. 153 pages.

1683

PROCEEDINGS AND ADDRESSES OF THE AMERICAN PHILOSOPHICAL ASSN.

APA

American Philosophical Association
University of Delaware
Newark, DE 19716

COST-$10

Annual issue contains lists of grants and fellowships of interest to philosophers.

1684

PHYSICIAN ASSISTANT PROGRAMS DIRECTORY

SpecWorks
810 South Bond Street
Baltimore, MD 21231

COST-$35.00

A catalog of of physician assistant educational programs, including addresses, admissions procedures and requirements, course outlines, length of program, university and institutional affiliations, tuition, and sources of financial assistance.

1685

RESOURCE GUIDE
Oak Ridge Institute for Science and
Education
P.O. Box 117
Oak Ridge, TN 37831-0117

COST-Free

This booklet is a valuable resource of scholarship, fellowship, and grant opportunities developed under the auspices of the U.S. Dept. of Energy. Most entries, but not all, are in the sciences. For high school students through post-doctorate.

1686

SAVE A FORTUNE
Phillip Godwin; ISBN 0-945332-05-X

Agora Books
842 E. Baltimore Street
Baltimore, MD 21202

COST-$14.95

A common sense plan for building wealth through saving rather than earning. Includes information on how to save on taxes, education, housing, travel, health, etc. 209 pages.

1687

**SCHOLARSHIPS & LOANS FOR
NURSING EDUCATION**
NLN Press; ISBN 0-88737-730-0

National League for Nursing
350 Hudson Street
New York, NY 10014-4584

COST-$16.95 + $3.95 postage/handling

Guide to financial aid for nursing and health care professions. Lists scholarships, fellowships, grants, traineeships, loans, and special awards. 125 pages.

1688

**SELECTED FINANCIAL AID
REFERENCES FOR STUDENTS WITH
DISABILITIES-#107.96**
National Clearinghouse for Professions in
Special Education
The Council for Exceptional Children
1920 Association Drive
Reston, VA 20191-1589

COST-Free

A list of specific sources of financial assistance for students with disabilities preparing for careers in special education and related services, such as physical therapy, occupational therapy, speech-language pathology, and others.

1689

**SELECTED FINANCIAL AID
RESOURCES FOR INDIVIDUALS FROM
CULTURALLY/ETHNICALLY DIVERSE
BACKGROUNDS-#104.96**
National Clearinghouse for Professions in
Special Education
The Council for Exceptional Children
1920 Association Drive
Reston, VA 20191-1589

COST-Free

A list of specific sources of financial assistance for minority students preparing for careers in special education and related services, such as physical therapy, occupational therapy, speech-language pathology, and others.

1690

**SELECTED FINANCIAL AID
RESOURCES FOR RELATED SERVICES-
#103.97**
National Clearinghouse for Professions in
Special Education
The Council for Exceptional Children
1920 Association Drive
Reston, VA 20191-1589

COST-Free

A list of specific sources of financial assistance for students preparing for careers in services related to special education, such as physical therapy, occupational therapy, speech-language pathology, and others.

1691

SELECTED FINANCIAL AID RESOURCES FOR SPECIAL EDUCATION-#102.97

National Clearinghouse for Professions in Special Education
The Council for Exceptional Children
1920 Association Drive
Reston, VA 20191-1589

COST-Free

A list of specific sources of financial assistance for students preparing for careers in special education and related services.

1692

STATE RESOURCE SHEETS

National Clearinghouse for Professions in Special Education
The Council for Exceptional Children
1920 Association Drive
Reston, VA 20191-1589

COST-Free

A list of sources of financial assistance in specific states for students preparing for careers in special education and related services, such as physical therapy, occupational therapy, speech-language pathology, and others. When ordering, specify the state or states in which you attend or may attend college.

1693

STUDENT FINANCIAL AID AND SCHOLARSHIPS AT WYOMING COLLEGES

University of Wyoming
University of Wyoming Office of Student Financial Aid
P.O. Box 3335
Laramie, WY 82071-3335

COST-Free

Describes post-secondary student aid and scholarship programs that are available to Wyoming students. Booklets can be obtained at all Wyoming high schools and colleges.

1694

STUDENT GUIDE—FINANCIAL AID FROM THE U.S. DEPARTMENT OF EDUCATION

U.S. Department of Education
Federal Student Aid Information Center
P.O. Box 84
Washington, D.C. 20044

COST-Free

Lists qualifications and sources of information for federal grants, loans and work-study programs.

1695

STUDY ABROAD (VOLUME 30; 1998-1999)

UNESCO
United Nations Educational, Scientific and Cultural Organization
Bernan Associates, UNESCO Agent
4611-F Assembly Drive
Lanham, MD 20706

COST-$29.95 + postage/handling

Printed in English, French & Spanish, this volume lists 3,700 international study programs in all academic and professional fields in more than 124 countries. Also available on CD-ROM.

1696

TAFT CORPORATE GIVING DIRECTORY (1996 EDITION)
ISBN 0-914756-79-6

Taft Group
12300 Twinbrook Pkwy., Suite 520
Rockville, MD 20852-1607

COST-$375.00

This reference book is found in most major libraries. It contains comprehensive information on over 500 foundations sponsored by top corporations. 859 pages.

1697

THE BIG BOOK OF OPPORTUNITIES FOR WOMEN
ISBN 0-89434-183-9

Garrett Park Press
P.O. Box 190F
Garrett Park, MD 20896

COST-$39.00; $35.00 prepaid

A director of sources of financial aid, career guidance, internships, and occupations—more than 4,000 sources. 455 pages.

1698

THE FOUNDATION DIRECTORY
ISBN 0-87954-449-6 (soft cover);
0-87954-484-8 (hard cover)

The Foundation Center
79 Fifth Ave.
New York, NY 10003

COST-$160.00 soft cover; $185.00 hard cover; + $4.50 shipping by UPS

Authoritative annual reference book found in most major libraries. Contains detailed information on over 6,300 of America's largest foundations. Indexes allow

grantseekers, researchers, etc., to quickly locate foundations of interest.

1699

THE SCHOLARSHIP WATCH
National Academy of American Scholars
1249 S. Diamond Bar Blvd., #325
Diamond Bar, CA 91765-4122

COST-$25/yr.

A newsletter printed biannually containing extensive information about scholarship sources and techniques for acquiring financial aid.

1700

THEIR WORLD
NCLD

National Center for Learning Disabilities
381 Park Ave. South, Suite 1420
New York, NY 10016

COST-$10.00

Annual magazine devoted to helping parents of learning disabled children as well as professionals in the learning disabled field and increasing public awareness of learning disabilities.

1701

UAA COLLEGIATE AVIATION SCHOLARSHIP LISTING
Gary W. Kiteley, Executive Director
University Aviation Assn.
3410 Skyway Drive
Auburn, AL 36830

COST-$4.95 members; $9.95 non-members + $3 shipping/handling

Listing of financial aid sources, methods of applying for general purpose aid, and a listing of aviation scholarships arranged by broad classification.

1702

VACATION STUDY ABROAD
Sara J. Steen, Editor

Institute of International Education
IIE Books
809 United Nations Plaza
New York, NY 10017-3580

COST-$39.95 + $5 shipping and handling

Guide to some 1,800 summer or short-term study-abroad programs sponsored by U.S. colleges, universities, private institutions, and foreign institutions. 400 pages.

1703

WHAT COLOR IS YOUR PARACHUTE?
Richard N. Bolles; ISBN 0-89815-492-8

Ten Speed Press
P.O. Box 7123
Berkeley, CA 94707

COST-$14.95 + $3.50 postage

Step-by-step career-planning guide. Highly recommended for anyone who is job hunting or changing careers. Valuable tips on assessing your skills, writing résumés, and handling job interviews. 464 pages.

1704

WINNING SCHOLARSHIPS FOR COLLEGE—AN INSIDER'S GUIDE
Marianne N. Ragins

The Scholarship Workshop
P.O. Box 6845
Macon, GA 31208

COST-$13.95 (includes shipping and handling)

As a high school senior the author was offered college scholarships totalling over $400,000. This 158-page book describes the application process, reveals strategies for finding scholarships, and offers advice on presenting credentials.

1705

WORK, STUDY, TRAVEL ABROAD—THE WHOLE WORLD HANDBOOK
Council on International Educational Exchange

Council on International Educational Exchange
Publications Dept.
205 E. 42nd Street
New York, NY 10017

COST-$6.95 + $1.50 shipping (prepaid only)

Excellent book on the basics of traveling, working, and studying abroad. How to find out about study-abroad opportunities, grants, scholarships, exchange programs, and teaching opportunities. Also information on the cheapest ways to travel.

1706

WORLD DIRECTORY OF MEDICAL SCHOOLS
WHO

World Health Organization
(1211 Geneva 27; Switzerland)

WHO Publication Center
49 Sheridan Ave.
Albany, NY 12210

COST-$35 (includes shipping/handling)

Comprehensive book that describes the medical education programs and schools in each country. Arranged in order by country or area.

Career Information

1707

AGRONOMY
(career information)

AMERICAN SOCIETY OF
AGRONOMY
677 S. Segoe Road
Madison, WI 53711

1708

ALTERNATIVE MEDICINE
(career information)

HOMEOPATHIC EDUCATIONAL
SERVICES
2124B Kittredge Street
Berkeley, CA 94704

1709

MANAGEMENT
(career information)

AMERICAN MANAGEMENT ASSN.
135 W. 50th Street
New York, NY 10020

1710

MANAGEMENT
A pamphlet describing the profession of physican assistant—what to study and where to go to school, the salaries, and the specialties.

AMERICAN ACADEMY OF
PHYSICIAN ASSISTANTS
950 North Washington Street
Alexandria, VA 22314-1552

1711

AIR, INC.
(career information)

AVIATION INFORMATION
RESOURCES (AIR, Inc.)
1001 Riverdale Court
Atlanta, GA 30337-6005

1712

ACCOUNTING
(career Information)

INSTITUTE OF MANAGEMENT
ACCOUNTANTS
10 Paragon Drive
Montvale, NJ 07645

1713

ACCOUNTING
(career information)

AMERICAN INSTITUTE OF
CERTIFIED PUBLIC ACCOUNTANTS
1211 Avenue of the Americas
New York, NY 10036

1714

ACCOUNTING
(career information)

NATIONAL SOCIETY OF PUBLIC
ACCOUNTANTS
1010 N. Fairfax Street
Alexandria, VA 22314

1715

ACTUARIAL SCIENCE
(career information)

SOCIETY OF ACTUARIES
475 N. Martingale Road, Suite 800
Schaumburg, IL 60173-2226

1716

ACUPUNCTURE/ORIENTAL MEDICINE
(career information)

NATIONAL ACUPUNCTURE AND
ORIENTAL MEDICINE ALLIANCE
14637 Starr Road SE
Olalla, WA 98359

1717

ACUPUNCTURE/ORIENTAL MEDICINE
(career information)

> CALIFORNIA SOCIETY FOR
> ORIENTAL MEDICINE (CSOM)
> 12926 Riverside Drive, #B
> Sherman Oaks, CA 91423

1718

ACUPUNCTURE/ORIENTAL MEDICINE IN RELATION TO DRUG/ALCOHOLISM RECOVERY
(career information)

> NATIONAL ACUPUNCTURE
> DETOXIFICATION ASSOCIATION
> 3220 N Street NW, Suite 275
> Washington, D.C. 20007

1719

ADVERTISING
(career information)

> AMERICAN ADVERTISING
> FEDERATION
> Education Services
> 1101 Vermont Ave. NW, Suite 500
> Washington, D.C. 20005-6306

1720

AERONAUTICS
(career Information)

> AMERICAN INSTITUTE OF
> AERONAUTICS AND ASTRONAUTICS
> (Student Programs Department)
> 1801 Alexander Bell Drive, Suite 500
> Reston, VA 20191-4344

1721

AEROSPACE EDUCATION
(career information)

> AEROSPACE EDUCATION
> FOUNDATION
> 1501 Lee Highway
> Arlington, VA 22209

1722

AGRICULTURAL AND BIOLOGICAL ENGINEERING
(career information)

> ASAE SOCIETY FOR ENGINEERING
> IN AGRICULTURAL FOOD AND
> BIOLOGICAL SYSTEMS
> 2950 Niles Road
> St. Joseph, MI 49085

1723

AGRICULTURE
(career Information)

> AMERICAN FARM BUREAU
> FEDERATION
> 225 Touhy Ave.
> Park Ridge, IL 60068

1724

AIR FORCE
(career information)

> AIR FORCE OPPORTUNITY CENTER
> P.O. Box 3505
> Capitol Heights, MD 20791

1725

AIR FORCE ACADEMY/AFROTC
(career information)

> DIRECTOR OF SELECTIONS
> HQ USAFA/RRS
> 2304 Cadet Drive, Suite 200
> USAF Academy, CO 80840-5025

1726

AIRLINE
(career information)

> AIR TRANSPORT ASSOCIATION OF
> AMERICA
> 1301 Pennsylvania Ave. NW, Suite 1100
> Washington, D.C. 20004-1707

1727

ANIMAL SCIENCE
(career information)
NATIONAL ASSN. OF ANIMAL
BREEDERS INC.
401 Bernadette Drive
P.O. Box 1033
Columbia, MO 65205

1728

ANTHROPOLOGY
(career information)
AMERICAN ANTHROPOLOGICAL
ASSOCIATION
4350 North Fairfax Drive, Suite 640
Arlington, VA 22203-1620

1729

APPRAISER—REAL ESTATE;
GEMOLOGY; MACHINERY &
EQUIPMENT; PERSONAL PROPERTY
(career information)
AMERICAN SOCIETY OF
APPRAISERS
P.O. Box 17265
Washington, D.C. 20041

1730

APPRENTICESHIP
(career information)
U.S. DEPT. OF LABOR; BUREAU OF
APPRENTICESHIP AND TRAINING
200 Constitution Ave. NW
Room N-4649
Washington, D.C. 20210

1731

ARCHAEOLOGY
(career information)
ARCHAEOLOGICAL INSTITUTE OF
AMERICA
656 Beacon Street
Boston, MA 02215-2010

1732

ARCHITECTURE
(career information)
THE AMERICAN ARCHITECTURAL
FOUNDATION
(AIA/AAF Scholarship Program)
1735 New York Ave. NW
Washington, D.C. 20006-5292

1733

ASTRONOMY
(career Information)
AMERICAN ASTRONOMICAL
SOCIETY
Education Office, Adler Planetarium
1300 S. Lake Shore Drive
Chicago, IL 60605

1734

AUDIOLOGY; SPEECH PATHOLOGY
(career information)
AMERICAN SPEECH-LANGUAGE-
HEARING ASSOCIATION
10801 Rockville Pike
Rockville, MD 20852

1735

AUTHOR/WRITER
(career information)
PEN AMERICAN CENTER
568 Broadway, Suite 401
New York, NY 10012

1736

AUTOMOTIVE ENGINEERING
(career information)
SOCIETY OF AUTOMOTIVE
ENGINEERS, INC.
400 Commonwealth Drive
Warrendale, PA 15096-0001

1737

BANKING
(career information)

AMERICAN BANKERS ASSOCIATION
Library & Information Systems
1120 Connecticut Ave. NW
Washington, D.C. 20036

1738

BIOLOGIST
(career information)

AMERICAN INSTITUTE OF
BIOLOGICAL SCIENCES
1444 Eye Street NW, Suite 200
Washington, D.C. 20005

1739

BIOTECHNOLOGY
(career information)

BIOTECHNOLOGY INDUSTRY
ORGANIZATION
1625 K Street NW, Suite 1100
Washington, D.C. 20006

1740

BLACK FILMMAKERS
(career information)

BLACK AMERICAN CINEMA
SOCIETY
6922 Hollywood Blvd., Suite 923
Hollywood, CA 90028

1741

BROADCAST NEWS
(career information)

RADIO AND TELEVISION NEWS
DIRECTORS ASSN.
1000 Connecticut Ave. NW, Suite 615
Washington, D.C. 20036-5302

1742

BROADCASTING
(career information)

AMERICAN WOMEN IN RADIO &
TELEVISION
1650 Tysons Boulevard, Suite 200
McLean, VA 22102

1743

CAREERS IN THE MATHEMATICAL SCIENCES AND MORE CAREERS IN THE MATHEMATICAL SCIENCES
(career information)

MATHEMATICAL ASSOCIATION OF
AMERICA
P.O. Box 90973
Washington, D.C. 20090

1744

CARTOONING
(career information)

NEWSPAPER FEATURES COUNCIL
37 Arch Street
Greenwich, CT 06830

1745

CHEMICAL ENGINEERING
(career information)

AMERICAN INSTITUTE OF
CHEMICAL ENGINEERS
Communications Dept.
345 E. 47th Street
New York, NY 10017

1746

CHIROPRACTIC
(career and school information)

INTERNATIONAL CHIROPRACTORS
ASSOCIATION
1110 N. Glebe Road, Suite 1000
Arlington, VA 22201

1747

CHIROPRACTIC
(career information)
> AMERICAN CHIROPRACTIC ASSN.
> 1701 Clarendon Blvd.
> Arlington, VA 22209

1748

CIVIL ENGINEERING
(career information)
> AMERICAN SOCIETY OF CIVIL
> ENGINEERS
> 1801 Alexander Bell Drive
> Reston, VA 20191-4400

1749

CLINICAL CHEMIST
(career information)
> AMERICAN ASSOCIATION FOR
> CLINICAL CHEMISTRY
> 2101 L Street NW, Suite 202
> Washington, D.C. 20037-1526

1750

COMMUNICATIONS
(career/accredited schools information);
Internet: www.ukans.edu/~acejmc
> ACCREDITING COUNCIL ON
> EDUCATION IN JOURNALISM &
> MASS COMMUNICATIONS
> Stauffer-Flint Hall
> University of Kansas School of Journalism
> Lawrence, KS 66045

1751

COMPUTER SCIENCE
(career information)
> IEEE COMPUTER SOCIETY
> 1730 Massachusetts Ave. NW
> Washington, D.C. 20036-1992

1752

CONSTRUCTION
(career information)
> ASSOCIATED GENERAL
> CONTRACTORS OF AMERICA
> 1957 E Street NW
> Washington, D.C. 20006

1753

COSMETOLOGY
(career information)
> AMERICAN ASSOCIATION OF
> COSMETOLOGY SCHOOLS
> 901 N. Washington Street, Suite 206
> Alexandria, VA 22314

1754

CRAFTS
(career information)
> AMERICAN CRAFT COUNCIL
> LIBRARY
> 72 Spring Street
> New York, NY 10012

1755

CREATIVE WRITING
(career information)
> NATIONAL WRITERS ASSOCIATION
> 1450 S. Havana, Suite 424
> Aurora, CO 80012

1756

DANCE
(career information)
> NATIONAL DANCE
> ASSOCIATION/AAHPERD
> 1900 Association Drive
> Reston, VA 20291-1599

1757

DATA PROCESSING MANAGEMENT
(career information)

DATA PROCESSING MANAGEMENT
ASSN.
505 Busse Highway
Park Ridge, IL 60068

1758

DENTAL ASSISTANT
(career information)

AMERICAN DENTAL ASSISTANTS
ASSN.
203 N. LaSalle Street, Suite 1320
Chicago, IL 60601

1759

DENTAL HYGIENIST
(career information)

AMERICAN DENTAL HYGIENISTS
ASSN. INSTITUTE FOR ORAL
HEALTH
444 N. Michigan Ave., Suite 3400
Chicago, IL 60611

1760

DENTAL LABORATORY TECHNOLOGY
(career information)

NATIONAL ASSN. OF DENTAL
LABORATORIES
555 E. Braddock Road
Alexandria, VA 22314-2199

1761

DENTAL PROFESSION
(career information)

ADA ENDOWMENT AND
ASSISTANCE FUND, INC.
211 E. Chicago Ave.
Chicago, IL 60611

1762

DIETITIAN
(career information)

AMERICAN DIETETIC ASSN.
Attn: Membership Department
216 W. Jackson Blvd., Suite 800
Chicago, IL 60606

1763

DISABLED
(career information)

THE ARC
P.O. Box 1047
Arlington, TX 76004

1764

DRAMA/ACTING
(career information)

SCREEN ACTORS GUILD
5757 Wilshire Blvd.
Los Angeles, CA 90036-3600

1765

EDUCATION
(career information)

AMERICAN FEDERATION OF
TEACHERS
Public Affairs Department
555 New Jersey Ave. NW
Washington, D.C. 20001

1766

ELECTRICAL ENGINEERING
(career information)

INSTITUTE OF ELECTRICAL &
ELECTRONICS ENGINEERS
United States Activities
1828 L Street NW, Suite 1202
Washington, D.C. 20036-5104

1767

ENGINEERING (PROGRAMS & CAREER INFORMATION)

JUNIOR ENGINEERING TECHNICAL
SOCIETY, INC. (JETS)
1420 King Street, Suite 405
Alexandria, VA 22314

1768

ENGINEERING
(career information)

NATIONAL SOCIETY OF
PROFESSIONAL ENGINEERS
1420 King Street
Alexandria, VA 22314

1769

ENTOMOLOGY
(career information)

ENTOMOLOGICAL SOCIETY OF
AMERICA
9301 Annapolis Road
Lanham, MD 20706

1770

ENVIRONMENTAL
(studies and career information)

U.S. ENVIRONMENTAL PROTECTION
AGENCY
Office of Communications, Education, and
    Public Affairs Envionmental Education
    Division
401 M Street SW
Washington, D.C. 20460

1771

FBI
(career information)

FEDERAL BUREAU OF
INVESTIGATION
Department of Justice
Washington, D.C. 20535

1772

FASHION DESIGN
(educational information)

FASHION INSTITUTE OF
TECHNOLOGY
Seventh Ave. at 27th Street
New York, NY 10001-5992

1773

FIRE SERVICE
(career information)

NATIONAL FIRE PROTECTION ASSN.
(Public Fire Protection)
1 Batterymarch Park
P.O. Box 9101
Quincy, MA 02269-9101

1774

FISHERIES
(career and university information)

AMERICAN FISHERIES SOCIETY
5410 Grovesnor Lane, Suite 110
Bethesda, MD 20814-2199

1775

FLORISTRY
(career information)

SOCIETY OF AMERICAN FLORISTS
1601 Duke Street
Alexandria, VA 22314

1776

FOOD SERVICE
(career information)

EDUCATIONAL FOUNDATION OF
THE NATIONAL RESTAURANT
ASSOCIATION
250 S. Wacker Drive, Suite 1400
Chicago, IL 60606

1777

FOOD TECHNOLOGY/SCIENCE
(career information)

INSTITUTE OF FOOD
TECHNOLOGISTS
221 N. LaSalle Street
Chicago, IL 60601

1778

FOOD AND NUTRITION SERVICE
(career information)

U.S. DEPT. OF AGRICULTURE, FOOD
AND NUTRITION SERVICE
Personnel Division
Room 620
1301 Park Center Drive
Alexandria, VA 22302

1779

FOREIGN LANGUAGES
(career information)

MODERN LANGUAGE ASSN. OF
AMERICA
10 Astor Place
New York, NY 10003

1780

FOREIGN SERVICE OFFICER
(career information)

U.S. DEPT. OF HEALTH
RECRUITMENT DIVISION
P.O. Box 9317
Rosslyn Station
Arlington, VA 22219

1781

FOREST SERVICE
(career information)

U.S. DEPT. OF AGRICULTURE
14th & Independence Ave.
Room 801 RPE
Washington, D.C. 20250

1782

FORESTRY
(career information)

SOCIETY OF AMERICAN FORESTERS
5400 Grovesnor Lane
Bethesda, MD 20814

1783

FUNERAL DIRECTOR
(career information)

NATIONAL FUNERAL DIRECTORS
ASSN.
P.O. Box 27641
Milwaukee, WI 53227-0641

1784

GEOGRAPHY
(career information)

ASSOCIATION OF AMERICAN
GEOGRAPHERS
1710 16th Street NW
Washington, D.C. 20009-3198

1785

GEOLOGICAL SCIENCES
(career information)

AMERICAN GEOLOGICAL
INSTITUTE
4220 King Street
Alexandria, VA 22302

1786

GEOPHYSICS
(career information)

AMERICAN GEOPHYSICAL UNION
2000 Florida Ave. NW
Washington, D.C. 20009

1787

GRAPHIC ARTS
(career information)

NATIONAL SCHOLARSHIP TRUST
FUND OF THE GRAPHIC ARTS
200 Deer Run Road
Sewickley, PA 15153-2600

1788

GRAPHIC ARTS
(career information)

AMERICAN INSTITUTE OF GRAPHIC
ARTS
164 Fifth Ave.
New York, NY 10010

1789

GRAPHIC COMMUNICATIONS
(career, education, and scholarship information)

EDUCATION COUNCIL OF THE
GRAPHIC ARTS INDUSTRY
1899 Preston White Drive
Reston, VA 20191

1790

**HEALTH PROFESSIONAL STUDENT
OPPORTUNITIES**

U.S. DEPT. OF HEALTH & HUMAN
SERVICES—NATIONAL HEALTH
SERVICE CORPS
2070 Chain Bridge Road, Suite 450
Vienna, VA 22182

1791

**HEATING AND AIR CONDITIONING
ENGINEER**
(career information)

REFRIGERATION SERVICE
ENGINEERS SOCIETY
1666 Rand Road
Des Plaines, IL 60016

1792

HOME ECONOMICS
(career information)

AMERICAN ASSOCIATION OF
FAMILY & CONSUMER SCIENCES
1555 King Street
Alexandria, VA 22314

1793

HOMEOPATHIC MEDICINE
(career information)

NATIONAL CENTER FOR
HOMEOPATHY
801 North Fairfax Street, Suite 306
Alexandria, VA 22314

1794

HORTICULTURE
(career information)

AMERICAN ASSOCIATION OF
NURSERYMEN
1250 I Street NW
Washington, D.C. 20005

1795

HOSPITAL ADMINISTRATION
(career information)

AMERICAN COLLEGE OF HEALTH
CARE EXECUTIVES
One N. Franklin Street, Suite 1700
Chicago, IL 60606-3491

1796

HOTEL MANAGEMENT
(career information)

AMERICAN HOTEL FOUNDATION
1201 New York Ave. NW, Suite 600
Washington, D.C. 20005

1797

ILLUMINATING ENGINEERING
(career information)

ILLUMINATING ENGINEERING
SOCIETY OF NORTH AMERICA
120 Wall Street, 17th Floor
New York, NY 10005

1798

INSURANCE
(career information)

INSURANCE INFORMATION
INSTITUTE
110 William Street
New York, NY 10038

1799

INSURANCE
(career information)

ALLIANCE OF AMERICAN INSURERS
1501 Woodfield Road, Suite 400W
Schaumburg, IL 60173

1800

JOURNALISM
(career Information); http://www.asne.org

AMERICAN SOCIETY OF
NEWSPAPER EDITORS
11690B Sunrise Valley Drive
Reston, VA 20191-1409

1801

LANDSCAPE ARCHITECTURE
(career information)

AMERICAN SOCIETY OF
LANDSCAPE ARCHITECTS
4401 Connecticut Ave. NW, 5th Floor
Washington, D.C. 20008

1802

LAW
(career information)

AMERICAN BAR ASSOCIATION
750 N. Lake Shore Drive
Chicago, IL 60611

1803

LAW LIBRARIANSHIP
(career information)

AMERICAN ASSOCIATION OF LAW
LIBRARIES
53 W. Jackson Blvd., Suite 940
Chicago, IL 60604

1804

LEARNING DISABLED
(education and career information)

LEARNING DISABILITIES ASSN. OF
AMERICA
4156 Library Road
Pittsburgh, PA 15234

1805

LIBRARY SCIENCE
(career information)

AMERICAN LIBRARY ASSN.
Office for Library Personnel Resources
50 E. Huron Street
Chicago, IL 60611

1806

MANAGEMENT
(career information)

CLUB MANAGERS ASSOCIATION OF
AMERICA
1733 King Street
Alexandria, VA 22314

1807

MATHEMATICS TEACHER
(career information)

NATIONAL COUNCIL OF TEACHERS
OF MATHEMATICS
1906 Association Drive
Reston, VA 22091-1593

1808

MECHANICAL ENGINEERING
(career information)

AMERICAN SOCIETY OF
MECHANICAL ENGINEERS
United Engineering Center
345 E. 47th Street
New York, NY 10017

1809

**MEDICAL LABORATORY
TECHNOLOGY**
(career information)

AMERICAN SOCIETY OF CLINICAL
PATHOLOGISTS
Careers
2100 W. Harrison
Chicago, IL 60612

1810

MEDICAL RECORDS
(career information)

AMERICAN HEALTH INFORMATION
MANAGEMENT ASSOCIATION
919 N. Michigan Ave., Suite 1400
Chicago, IL 60611

1811

MEDICAL TECHNOLOGY
(career information)

AMERICAN MEDICAL
TECHNOLOGISTS
710 Higgins Road
Park Ridge, IL 60068

1812

MEDICINE
(career information)

AMERICAN MEDICAL ASSOCIATION
515 N. State Street
Chicago, IL 60610

1813

**METALLURGY AND MATERIALS
SCIENCE**
(career information)

ASM FOUNDATION FOR EDUCATION
& RESEARCH
Student Outreach Program
Materials Park, OH 44073

1814

MICROBIOLOGY
(career information)

AMERICAN SOCIETY FOR
MICROBIOLOGY
Office of Education & Training
1325 Massachusetts Ave. NW
Washington, D.C. 20005

1815

MOTION PICTURE
(career information)

SOCIETY OF MOTION PICTURE AND
TELEVISION ENGINEERS
595 W. Hartsdale Ave.
White Plains, NY 10607

1816

MUSIC
(career information)

MUSIC EDUCATORS NATIONAL
CONFERENCE
1806 Robert Fulton Drive
Reston, VA 20191

1817

MUSIC THERAPY
(career information)
> NATIONAL ASSN. FOR MUSIC
> THERAPY
> 8455 Colesville Road, Suite 1000
> Silver Spring, MD 20910

1818

NATUROPATHIC MEDICINE
(career information)
> AMERICAN ASSOCIATION OF
> NATUROPATHIC PHYSICIANS
> 601 Valley Street, Suite #105
> Seattle, WA 98109

1819

NAVAL ARCHITECTURE
(career information)
> SOCIETY OF NAVAL ARCHITECTS &
> MARINE ENGINEERS
> 601 Pavonia Ave.
> Jersey City, NJ 07306

1820

NAVAL/MARINE ENGINEERING
(career information)
> SOCIETY OF NAVAL ARCHITECTS &
> MARINE ENGINEERS
> 601 Pavonia Ave.
> Jersey City, NJ 07306

1821

NEWSPAPER INDUSTRY
(career information)
> NEWSPAPER ASSN. OF AMERICA
> The Newspaper Center
> 11600 Sunrise Valley Drive
> Reston, VA 22091

1822

NURSE ANESTHETIST
(career information)
> AMERICAN ASSOCIATION OF NURSE
> ANESTHETISTS
> 222 S. Prospect Ave.
> Park Ridge, IL 60068-4001

1823

NURSING
(career information)
> NATIONAL LEAGUE FOR NURSING
> INC.
> 350 Hudson Street
> New York, NY 10014

1824

NURSING
(graduate research grants)
> AMERICAN NURSES FOUNDATION
> 600 Maryland Ave. SW, Suite 100 West
> Washington, D.C. 20024

1825

**OCEANOGRAPHY AND MARINE
SCIENCE**
(career information)
> MARINE TECHNOLOGY SOCIETY
> 1828 L Street NW, Suite 906
> Washington, D.C. 20036

1826

OPTOMETRIC ASSISTANT/TECHNICIAN
(career information)
> AMERICAN OPTOMETRIC ASSN.
> Paraoptometric Section
> 243 N. Lindbergh Blvd.
> St. Louis, MO 63141-7881

1827

OPTOMETRY
(career information)
NATIONAL OPTOMETRIC ASSN.
P.O. Box F
E. Chicago, IN 46312

1828

OPTOMETRY
(career information)
AMERICAN OPTOMETRIC ASSN.
243 N. Lindbergh Blvd.
St. Louis, MO 63141-7881

1829

OSTEOPATHIC MEDICINE
(career information)
AMERICAN OSTEOPATHIC
ASSOCIATION
Dept. of Predoctoral Education
142 East Ontario
Chicago, IL 60611

1830

PALEONTOLOGY
(career information)
PALEONTOLOGICAL SOCIETY
P.O. Box 1897
Lawrence, KS 66044-8897

1831

PATHOLOGY AS A CAREER IN MEDICINE
(career information)
INTERSOCIETY COMMITTEE ON
PATHOLOGY INFORMATION
4733 Bethesda Ave., Suite 700
Bethesda, MD 20814

1832

PEDIATRICS
(career information)
AMERICAN ACADEMY OF
PEDIATRICS
141 NW Point Blvd.
P.O. Box 927
Elk Grove Village, IL 60009

1833

PETROLEUM ENGINEERING
(career information)
SOCIETY OF PETROLEUM
ENGINEERS
P.O. Box 833836
Richardson, TX 75083

1834

PHARMACOLOGY
(career information)
AMERICAN SOCIETY FOR PHARMA-
COLOGY & EXPERIMENTAL
THERAPEUTICS, INC.
9650 Rockville Pike
Bethesda, MD 20814-3995

1835

PHARMACY
(career information)
AMERICAN ASSOCIATION OF
COLLEGES OF PHARMACY
Office of Student Affairs
1426 Prince Street
Alexandria, VA 22314

1836

PHARMACY
(career information)
AMERICAN FOUNDATION FOR
PHARMACEUTICAL EDUCATION
One Church Street, Suite 202
Rockville, MD 20850

1837

PHARMACY
(school information booklet)
> AMERICAN COUNCIL ON
> PHARMACEUTICAL EDUCATION
> 311 W. Superior, #512
> Chicago, IL 60610

1838

PHOTOJOURNALISM
(career information for university-level photo-journalism students)
> NATIONAL PRESS PHOTOGRAPHERS
> ASSN.
> 3200 Croasdaile Drive, #306
> Durham, NC 27705

1839

PHYSICAL THERAPY
(career information)
> AMERICAN PHYSICAL THERAPY
> ASSN.
> 1111 N. Fairfax Street
> Alexandria, VA 22314

1840

PHYSICS
(career information)
> AMERICAN INSTITUTE OF PHYSICS
> One Physics Ellipse
> College Park, MD 20740

1841

PILOT
(career information)
> INTERNATIONAL ORGANIZATION
> OF WOMEN PILOTS
> P.O. BOX 59965
> Will Rogers World Airport
> Oklahoma City, OK 73159

1842

PODIATRY
(career information)
> AMERICAN PODIATRIC MEDICAL
> ASSN.
> 9312 Old Georgetown Road
> Bethesda, MD 20814

1843

POLITICAL SCIENCE
(career information)
> AMERICAN POLITICAL SCIENCE
> ASSN.
> 1527 New Hampshire Ave. NW
> Washington, D.C. 20036

1844

**PRECISION MACHINING
TECHNOLOGY**
(career information)
> NATIONAL TOOLING AND
> MACHINING ASSN.
> 9300 Livingston Road
> Ft. Washington, MD 20744

1845

PSYCHIATRY
(career information)
> AMERICAN PSYCHIATRIC ASSN.,
> DIVISION OF PUBLIC AFFAIRS
> 1400 K Street NW
> Washington, D.C. 20005

1846

PSYCHOLOGY
(career information)
> AMERICAN PSYCHOLOGICAL ASSN.
> 750 First Street NE
> Washington, D.C. 20002

1847

PUBLIC RELATIONS
(career information)

PUBLIC RELATIONS SOCIETY OF
AMERICA
33 Irving Place
New York, NY 10003

1848

RADIOLOGIC TECHNOLOGY
(career information)

AMERICAN SOCIETY OF
RADIOLOGIC TECHNOLOGISTS
15000 Central Ave. SE
Albuquerque, NM 87123

1849

RANGE MANAGEMENT
(career information)

SOCIETY FOR RANGE
MANAGEMENT
1839 York Street
Denver, CO 80206

1850

REHABILITATION COUNSELING
(career information)

NATIONAL REHABILITATION
COUNSELING ASSN.
8807 Sudley Road, #102
Manassas, VA 22110-4719

1851

RESPIRATORY THERAPY
(career information)

AMERICAN RESPIRATORY CARE
FOUNDATION
11030 Ables Lane
Dallas, TX 75229

1852

RURAL ELECTRIFICATION
(career information)

U.S. DEPT. OF AGRICULTURE; RURAL
ELECTRIFICATION ADMINISTRATION
14th and Independence Ave. SW
Room 4032
Washington, D.C. 20250

1853

SCHOOL ADMINISTRATION
(career information)

AMERICAN ASSOCIATION OF
SCHOOL ADMINISTRATORS
1801 N. Moore Street
Arlington, VA 22209

1854

SCIENCE TEACHER
(career information)

NATIONAL SCIENCE TEACHERS
ASSN.
Attn: Office of Public Information
1840 Wilson Blvd.
Arlington, VA 22201

1855

SECRETARY
(career information)

PROFESSIONAL SECRETARIES
INTERNATIONAL—THE
ASSOCIATION FOR OFFICE
PROFESSIONALS
Attn: Ms. Bobbi Burton
10502 NW Ambassador Drive
Kansas City, MO 64195-0404

1856

SOCIAL WORK
(career information)

NATIONAL ASSN. OF SOCIAL
WORKERS
750 First Street NE, Suite 700
Washington, D.C. 20002

1857

SOCIOLOGY
(career information)
 AMERICAN SOCIOLOGICAL ASSN.
 1722 N Street NW
 Washington, D.C. 20036

1858

SOIL CONSERVATION
(career information)
 SOIL & WATER CONSERVATION
 SOCIETY
 7515 NE Ankeny Road
 Ankeny, IA 50021-9764

1859

SPECIAL EDUCATION TEACHING
(career information)
 NATIONAL CLEARINGHOUSE FOR
 PROFESSIONS IN SPECIAL
 EDUCATION
 The Council for Exceptional Children
 1920 Association Drive
 Reston, VA 20191-1589

1860

SPEECH & HEARING THERAPY
(career information—send self-addressed 8-1/2
x 11 envelope + $1.25 postage/handling)
 ALEXANDER GRAHAM BELL
 ASSOCIATION FOR THE DEAF
 3417 Volta Place NW
 Washington, D.C. 20007-2778

1861

U.S. NAVY OFFICER
(career information)
 U.S. NAVAL ACADEMY
 Candidate Guidance Office
 117 Decatur Road
 Annapolis, MD 21402-5018

1862

UNITED STATES ARMY
(career information)
 U.S. MILITARY ACADEMY
 Director of Admissions
 606 Thayer Road
 West Point, NY 10996

1863

UNITED STATES COAST GUARD
(career information)
 U.S. COAST GUARD ACADEMY
 Director of Admissions
 15 Mohegan Ave.
 New London, CT 06320

1864

**UNITED STATES MARINE CORPS
OFFICER**
(Marine Corps Reserve Officers Training Corps
and U.S. Naval Academy career opportunities)
 MARINE CORPS COMMANDANT
 Headquarters, U.S. Marine Corps
 2 Navy Annex
 Washington, D.C. 20380

1865

**UNITED STATES NAVY OR MARINE
CORPS**
(career information)
 U.S. NAVAL ACADEMY
 Candidate Guidance Office
 117 Decatur Road
 Annapolis, MD 21402-5018

1866

**UNITED STATES NAVY OR MARINE
CORPS**
(career information)
 NAVY AND MARINE CORPS ROTC
 COLLEGE SCHOLARSHIPS BULLETIN
 Navy Recruiting Command Code 314
 801 N. Randolph Street
 Arlington, VA 22203-9933

1867

URBAN PLANNER
(career information)
AMERICAN PLANNING ASSN.
1776 Massachusetts Ave. NW
Washington, D.C. 20036

1868

VETERINARIAN
(career information)
AMERICAN VETERINARY MEDICAL
ASSN.
1931 N. Meacham Road, Suite 100
Schaumburg, IL 60173

1869

WATER POLLUTION CONTROL
(career information)
WATER POLLUTION CONTROL
FEDERATION
Education Dept.
601 Wythe Street
Alexandria, VA 22314

1870

WELDING TECHNOLOGY
(career information)
HOBART INSTITUTE OF WELDING
TECHNOLOGY
Trade Square East
Troy, OH 45373

1871

WOMEN PILOTS
(career information)
NINETY-NINES (International
Organization of Women Pilots)
P.O. Box 59965
Oklahoma City, OK 73159

1872

YOUTH LEADERSHIP
(career information)
BOYS & GIRLS CLUBS OF AMERICA
1230 W. Peachtree Street NW
Atlanta, GA 30309

1873

YOUTH LEADERSHIP
(career information)
BOY SCOUTS OF AMERICA
National Eagle Scout Association, S220
1325 W. Walnut Hill Lane
P.O. Box 152079
Irving, TX 75015

Alphabetical Index